THIRD WORLD 94/95

Fifth Edition

Editor

Robert J. Griffiths

University of North Carolina at Greensboro

Robert J. Griffiths is assistant professor of political science at the University of North Carolina at Greensboro. He received his Ph.D. from the University of Connecticut in 1987. His teaching and research interests include comparative and international politics, and he teaches courses in African politics, the politics of development, international law and organization, and U.S. national security policy. His publications include articles on the Third World and global commons negotiations and South African civil-military relations.

Annual Editions

A Library of Information from the Public Press

Cover illustration by Mike Eagle

The Dushkin Publishing Group, Inc.
Sluice Dock, Guilford, Connecticut 06437

The Annual Editions Series

Annual Editions is a series of over 60 volumes designed to provide the reader with convenient, low-cost access to a wide range of current, carefully selected articles from some of the most important magazines, newspapers, and journals published today. Annual Editions are updated on an annual basis through a continuous monitoring of over 300 periodical sources. All Annual Editions have a number of features designed to make them particularly useful, including topic guides, annotated tables of contents, unit overviews, and indexes. For the teacher using Annual Editions in the classroom, an Instructor's Resource Guide with test questions is available for each volume.

VOLUMES AVAILABLE

Africa
Aging
American Foreign Policy
American Government
American History, Pre-Civil War
American History, Post-Civil War
Anthropology
Biology
Business Ethics
Canadian Politics
Child Growth and Development
China
Comparative Politics
Computers in Education
Computers in Business
Computers in Society
Criminal Justice
Drugs, Society, and Behavior
Dying, Death, and Bereavement
Early Childhood Education
Economics
Educating Exceptional Children
Education
Educational Psychology
Environment
Geography
Global Issues
Health
Human Development
Human Resources
Human Sexuality
India and South Asia
International Business
Japan and the Pacific Rim
Latin America
Life Management
Macroeconomics
Management
Marketing
Marriage and Family
Mass Media
Microeconomics
Middle East and the Islamic World
Money and Banking
Multicultural Education
Nutrition
Personal Growth and Behavior
Physical Anthropology
Psychology
Public Administration
Race and Ethnic Relations
Russia, Eurasia, and Central/Eastern Europe
Social Problems
Sociology
State and Local Government
Third World
Urban Society
Violence and Terrorism
Western Civilization, Pre-Reformation
Western Civilization, Post-Reformation
Western Europe
World History, Pre-Modern
World History, Modern
World Politics

Library of Congress Cataloging in Publication Data
Main entry under title: Annual editions: Third World. 1994/95.
1. Underdeveloped areas—Periodicals. I. Griffiths, Robert J., *comp.* II. Title: The Third World.
ISBN 1-56134-257-2 303.4′4

Fifth Edition

Printed in the United States of America

Printed on Recycled Paper

Editors/ Advisory Board

Members of the Advisory Board are instrumental in the final selection of articles for each edition of Annual Editions. Their review of articles for content, level, currentness, and appropriateness provides critical direction to the editor and staff. We think you'll find their careful consideration well reflected in this volume.

To the Reader

In publishing ANNUAL EDITIONS we recognize the enormous role played by the magazines, newspapers, and journals of the *public press* in providing current, first-rate educational information in a broad spectrum of interest areas. Within the articles, the best scientists, practitioners, researchers, and commentators draw issues into new perspective as accepted theories and viewpoints are called into account by new events, recent discoveries change old facts, and fresh debate breaks out over important controversies.

Many of the articles resulting from this enormous editorial effort are appropriate for students, researchers, and professionals seeking accurate, current material to help bridge the gap between principles and theories and the real world. These articles, however, become more useful for study when those of lasting value are carefully *collected, organized, indexed,* and *reproduced* in a *low-cost format*, which provides easy and permanent access when the material is needed. That is the role played by *Annual Editions*. Under the direction of each volume's *Editor*, who is an expert in the subject area, and with the guidance of an *Advisory Board*, we seek each year to provide in each *ANNUAL EDITION* a current, well-balanced, carefully selected collection of the best of the public press for your study and enjoyment. We think you'll find this volume useful, and we hope you'll take a moment to let us know what you think.

The end of the cold war has brought about major changes in international affairs. What this means for the Third World is still uncertain. Although the superpower confrontation no longer distorts our understanding nor diverts our attention to the issues and problems that confront the developing countries, there is also the danger that many of these nations will become further marginalized. On the other hand, the emerging world order may offer the international community the opportunity to concentrate on seeking solutions to the dilemmas of Third World modernization and development.

The Third World comprises the vast majority of the Earth's population. It is incredibly diverse and defies easy generalizations. The problems of developing countries are complex, urgent, and not easily resolved. Peace and security, international trade, the debt crisis, and the environment illustrate growing interdependence and the need for a cooperative approach to addressing these issues. Clearly, however, Third World problems are contentious and there are differing points of view regarding viable solutions. Moreover, Third World issues compete for attention on an agenda that is often dominated by relations between the industrialized nations, the problems of eastern Europe and the former USSR, and states' domestic concerns.

The fifth edition of *Annual Editions: Third World* seeks to give students an understanding of the complexity of the Third World and to acquaint them with the challenges that these nations confront. I feel very strongly that there is a need for greater awareness of, and attention to, the Third World, and I hope that this volume contributes to these goals.

The articles for this edition are completely new and the book has been reorganized with new units on weapons proliferation and arms control, efforts at transition from authoritarian rule, population and environment, and women and development. I have chosen articles that I hope are interesting and informative, and that can serve as a basis for further investigation and discussion. In addition to choosing articles that deal with the major issues in the study of the Third World, I have attempted to suggest the similarities and differences between Third World countries and the connections between the Third World's problems and those of the industrialized nations.

I would particularly like to thank Ian Nielsen, publisher of *Annual Editions,* for the opportunity to put together a reader on a subject that is the focus of my teaching and research. As a first-time editor of this volume, his comments and suggestions were a valuable contribution to me.

No book on a topic as broad as the Third World can be comprehensive, and there are certainly additional and alternative readings that might be included. As always, suggestions for improvement are welcome. Please use the form at the end of the book for your comments.

Robert J. Griffiths
Editor

Contents

Unit 1

Understanding the Third World

Four selections examine how the developing world's problems are interrelated with world order.

Unit 2

Trade, Aid, and Debt

Nine articles discuss the impact of the debt crisis on the developing world and how politics have compounded some of the problems.

The concepts in bold italics are developed in the article. For further expansion please refer to the Topic Guide and the Index.

Unit 3

Conflict and Instability

Ten articles discuss the current state of ethnic conflicts throughout the developing world.

Unit 4

Weapons Proliferation and Arms Control

Eight selections discuss the extent of the global arms trade and the danger of the increasing availability of weapons in the developing world.

The concepts in bold italics are developed in the article. For further expansion please refer to the Topic Guide and the Index.

Unit 5

Transitions

Ten selections discuss the problems faced by developing countries as they evolve politically and economically.

The concepts in bold italics are developed in the article. For further expansion please refer to the Topic Guide and the Index.

Unit 6

Population, Poverty, and Environment

Nine articles examine some of the effects the Third World's population growth has on the Earth's sustainability.

The concepts in bold italics are developed in the article. For further expansion please refer to the Topic Guide and the Index.

Unit 7

Women and Development

Seven articles discuss the role of women in the developing world.

The concepts in bold italics are developed in the article. For further expansion please refer to the Topic Guide and the Index.

Topic Guide

This topic guide suggests how the selections in this book relate to topics of traditional concern to students and professionals involved with the study of the Third World. It is useful for locating articles that relate to each other for reading and research. The guide is arranged alphabetically according to topic. Articles may, of course, treat topics that do not appear in the topic guide. In turn, entries in the topic guide do not necessarily constitute a comprehensive listing of all the contents of each selection.

TOPIC AREA	TREATED IN:
Agriculture	55. Women's Work 56. Extending Help to Women Farmers
Apartheid	35. Finding Common Ground 36. Birth of a Nation
Arms Control	26. Proliferation Primer 27. Tactical Missiles 28. IAEA: Neutralizing Iraq's Nuclear Weapons Potential 29. Atomic Shock Waves 30. Levers for Plowshares
Cold War Legacy	15. We Must Hear the Third World 22. Familiar Face of Battle
Collective Security	2. South Looks North
Colonialism	1. Third World and New World Order 8. Rethinking Development 21. Sudan's Human and Political Crisis 32. Collapse of Socialist Development 33. Crisis of Legitimacy in Africa
Debt Crisis	1. Third World and New World Order 2. South Looks North 8. Rethinking Development 9. Still in the Missionary Position 10. Third World: Living With Debt? 11. African Debt: Borrowed Time 12. Disaster That Didn't Happen
Democracy	2. South Looks North 21. Sudan's Human and Political Crisis 22. Familiar Face of Battle 23. Gulf Between the Rulers and the Ruled 34. Algeria 35. Finding Common Ground 36. Birth of a Nation 37. In Test With Democracy 38. Difficult Birth 41. Peru's Fujimori
Dependency	8. Rethinking Development 32. Collapse of Socialist Development
Development	3. Economist's Blind Eye 8. Rethinking Development 13. Why Is Africa Eating Asia's Dust? 30. Levers for Plowshares 45. Urban Explosion 55. Women's Work
Economic Assistance	1. Third World and New World Order 2. South Looks North 8. Rethinking Development 9. Still in the Missionary Position 15. We Must Hear the Third World
Economic Reform	1. Third World and New World Order 5. Developing Countries and the World Trade System 8. Rethinking Development 9. Still in the Missionary Position 40. Out of the Ditch
Education	51. Burden of Womanhood 52. Educating Girls 54. Female Empowerment
Environment	15. We Must Hear the Third World 42. World Population 44. Poverty, Population, Pollution 47. North vs. South on Pollution 48. Stop Dumping on the South 49. Greener Bank 55. Women's Work
Ethnic Conflict	14. Ethnic Conflicts Worldwide 15. We Must Hear the Third World 20. Asia's Bosnia 21. Sudan's Human and Political Crisis 22. Familiar Face of Battle
Gender Discrimination	51. Burden of Womanhood 52. Educating Girls 53. Women in the Workplace 55. Women's Work 56. Extending Help to Women Farmers 57. Women's Health
Globalization of Economy	2. South Looks North 15. We Must Hear the Third World
Gulf War	1. Third World and New World Order 2. South Looks North 15. We Must Hear the Third World 23. Gulf Between the Rulers and the Ruled 28. IAEA: Neutralizing Iraq's Nuclear Weapons Potential
Hindu Militancy	18. India: Crisis of Secularism
Human Rights	20. Asia's Bosnia 40. Out of the Ditch 41. Peru's Fujimori
International Institutions	2. South Looks North 5. Developing Countries and the World Trade System 10. Third World: Living With Debt? 28. IAEA: Neutralizing Iraq's Nuclear Weapons Potential 29. Atomic Shock Waves 30. Levers for Plowshares 38. Difficult Birth

TOPIC AREA	TREATED IN:	TOPIC AREA	TREATED IN:
International Institutions (cont.)	41. Peru's Fujimori 44. Poverty, Population, Pollution 49. Greener Bank 50. Growing Influence of NGOs	Poverty	1. Third World and New World Order 8. Rethinking Development 44. Poverty, Population, Pollution 45. Urban Explosion 49. Greener Bank
International Trade	2. South Looks North 5. Developing Countries and the World Trade System 6. Benefits and Beggars 7. In Mexico, NAFTA Isn't Just About Trade 8. Rethinking Development	Secularism	18. India: Crisis of Secularism
		Socialism	32. Collapse of Socialist Development
		State Intervention	8. Rethinking Development 32. Collapse of Socialist Development 43. Demographic Dimension
Islam	16. Islam Resumes Its March 17. Islamic Threat 19. Trouble in the South 21. Sudan's Human and Political Crisis 23. Gulf Between the Rulers and the Ruled 34. Algeria	Structural Adjustment	1. Third World and New World Order 8. Rethinking Development 10. Third World: Living With Debt?
		Terrorism	20. Asia's Bosnia 34. Algeria 41. Peru's Fujimori
Middle East	16. Islam Resumes Its March 23. Gulf Between the Rulers and the Ruled 28. IAEA: Neutralizing Iraq's Nuclear Weapons Potential	USSR, Breakup of	2. South Looks North 24. World's Top Arms Merchant 25. Third World Militaries 26. Proliferation Primer 27. Tactical Missiles 32. Collapse of Socialist Development
Military and Politics	20. Asia's Bosnia 34. Algeria 41. Peru's Fujimori	Weapons Proliferation	15. We Must Hear the Third World 24. World's Top Arms Merchant 25. Third World Militaries 26. Proliferation Primer 27. Tactical Missiles 29. Atomic Shock Waves
NIEO	1. Third World and New World Order 2. South Looks North		
Population	15. We Must Hear the Third World 42. World Population 43. Demographic Dimension 44. Poverty, Population, Pollution 45. Urban Explosion 46. Family Planning 54. Female Empowerment		

Understanding the Third World

Our understanding of the Third World has been partially obscured by the term itself. Third World was never a term of much precision or explanatory power. Further clouding its meaning is that it is a holdover from cold war terminology when the First World referred to the industrialized West and Japan, the Second World encompassed the socialist states, and the Third World was a catchall term for the remaining states of the world. Lumping together the over 100-plus nations that comprise this Third World category disguised the wide diversity among these coun-

Unit 1

tries. Disparities in size, population, resources, form of government, industrialization, distribution of wealth, ethnic diversity, and a host of other indicators have always characterized the Third World and made understanding this large, diverse group of countries difficult.

Despite this diversity, most of the nations of the Third World share some characteristics. With very few exceptions, these nations share a colonial past that has affected them politically and economically. Many Third World countries have large populations and almost all are experiencing rapid population growth with annual growth rates between two to four percent. Poverty is widespread in both rural and urban areas with the latter often containing the poorest of the poor. While the majority of the Third World's inhabitants continue to live in the countryside, there is a massive rural-to-urban migration underway, and cities are growing very rapidly. Wealth is unevenly distributed; education, employment opportunities, and access to health care are luxuries that few enjoy. Corruption and mismanagement are also common.

Although there have been some success stories in the Third World, especially in East Asia, most developing countries continue to lag behind in most indications of economic and political development. Many of the poorest countries in the Third World finished the 1980s in worse shape than they started the decade. The reasons for this economic performance are complex with internal, as well as external, factors playing a role. Among the causes are the colonial legacy, fluctuating prices for Third World exports, increasingly expensive imports, donor fatigue among foreign aid contributors, the debt crisis, and the aforementioned domestic problems.

As the Third World continues to struggle to improve living standards, the 1990s represent both change and continuity. The demise of the cold war ended the use of the Third World as an ideological battlefield. The emerging world order offers both benefits and challenges to Third World countries, however. While it is no longer the site of proxy conflicts between the superpowers, the Third World now faces the prospect of becoming even more marginalized as attention and resources are focused on the transition in the former USSR and Eastern Europe. On the other hand, the end of the cold war offers a greater opportunity to direct the world's attention to the plight of the Third World without the overriding concerns of ideology. Whether this will happen remains to be seen. In short, the Third World faces a very uncertain future as the post–cold war world emerges, and as some of the articles in this section emphasize, there are reasons to be skeptical about the prospects for many of these countries.

In the meantime, the gap between rich and poor nations persists. There are some optimistic signs, however. The Third World's share of output is increasing, and if growth continues and stability can be reasonably assured, the attractiveness of Third World investment and markets will also increase. At the same time, it is important not to focus exclusively on economic factors, as this may obscure other features of the development process such as dignity, empowerment, and other social values.

The post–cold war era has profound implications for the Third World. Indeed, the end of the cold war has renewed questions regarding the suitability of retaining the term "Third World." Uncertainty about the usefulness of the term is indicative of the uncertainty that faces the Third World, and it emphasizes the importance of better understanding the issues and dilemmas that face the majority of the Earth's inhabitants.

Looking Ahead: Challenge Questions

What conditions tend to characterize Third World nations?

What potential role does the Third World play in any emerging world order? How might this role differ from its role in the past?

What challenges face the Third World in the post–cold war era?

Are there disadvantages to viewing the Third World from a Western perspective? How might this ethnocentrism be overcome?

Why are there reasons to be skeptical about the prospects for many Third World countries in the post–cold war era?

Are there reasons to be optimistic concerning the Third World's ability to make progress toward solving its many problems?

Why is the term "Third World" so imprecise? Can you think of a more suitable term?

THE THIRD WORLD AND THE NEW WORLD ORDER IN THE 1990s

Julius O. Ihonvbere

Julius O. Ihonvbere is in the Department of Government, The University of Texas at Austin, 536 Burdine Hall, Austin, TX 78712-1087, USA (Tel: + 1 (512) 471-5121; fax: + 1 (512) 471-1061).

This article examines how well the developing countries fared at the end of the 1980s; identifies contemporary constraints on growth and development in developing formations; and makes projections on the future of Third World economies in view of the developments discussed.

> We can not forget that while the iron curtain has been brought down, the poverty curtain still separates two parts of the world community.
>
> *Javier Perez de Cuellar*[1]

> . . . the decision-making process that govern the international flows of trade, capital and technology are controlled by the major developed countries of the North and by the international institutions they dominate. The countries of the South are unfavourably placed in the world economic system; they are individually powerless to influence these processes and institutions; and hence the global economic environment . . .
>
> The South Commission[2]

> The developing world continued to experience protracted problems of indebtedness, adverse terms of trade, great poverty and deteriorating social conditions. Low-income and least developed countries had been particularly vulnerable.
>
> Commonwealth Heads of Government[3]

The beginning of the 1990s is an appropriate time to assess how well the Third World fared in the 1980s. It is also an opportune moment to make projections into the future based on developments in the global system towards the end of the 1980s. Without doubt, the break down of old ideological orthodoxies, the crumbling of the Berlin Wall, the end of the Cold War, the upsurge of pro-democracy movements the world over and the emergence of the USA as the only superpower in the global system call for a review and analysis of the place of weaker countries in the international division of labour. As well, the unprecedented spate of changes in Southern Africa; the release of Nelson Mandela; the prospects for a United European economy in 1992; negotiations for free trade arrangements in North America; and the triumph of market forces all over the world, except perhaps in Cuba, equally dictate a need to examine how these would affect relations between the developed and developing nations of the world.

In this article, our goals are first to examine how well the developing countries fared at the end of the 1980s; second, to identify contemporary constraints on growth and development in developing formations; and third, to make projections on the future of Third World economies in view of the developments highlighted above.

THE DEVELOPING WORLD AT THE END OF THE 1980S: FROM CRISIS TO CRISIS

It is not possible adequately to study and appreciate the predicaments of developing countries without understanding the historical experiences of the respective social formations. By and large, the contact between these formations and the forces of Western imperialism culminated in the distortion, disarticulation and underdevelopment of these societies. The state structures were severely deformed; the dominant classes were underdeveloped and marginalized in the processes of production and exchange; science and technology policies were relegated to the background; cultural forms were perverted; the local economies were subjected to foreign domination and manipulation and the dominated economies were structurally incorporated into an unequal, exploitative and hostile international division of labour.[4]

At the time these societies won *political* independence, it was obvious that they had not just been relegated to the periphery of global power and production relations but

From *Futures*, December 1992, pp. 987-1002. Reprinted by permission.

also that they lacked the internal structures to mobilize their peoples, generate capital, promote productivity and participate in international trade on the basis on interdependence. Hence, they were all dependent on the metropolitan countries for technology, foreign aid, military supplies, markets for the sale of their raw materials and other forms of assistance.

The Third World is certainly not a homogenous formation. The contact with the forces of Western imperialism did not have similar effects. The impact and implications of this contact was not uniform. As well, the geostrategic importance of these societies to the metropolitan countries differs significantly, and their resource endowments, populations and vulnerability to external penetration, manipulation, domination and exploitation equally differ. Furthermore, the conditions under which they achieved political independence were not uniform while post-colonial alignment and realignment of class forces within these societies have differed. It is important that we take due cognizance of these critical issues if we are to understand contradictions and coalitions within the ranks of developing countries—why development has been uneven and why they have been unable to take advantage of some concessions in the global system or pressure the developed countries sufficiently to force major concessions. When data on the predicaments of developing countries are provided at the aggregate levels therefore, it is critical that we note the disparities and specificities within and between these societies.

The 1980s were particularly bad for the majority of developing countries. True, a few achievements were made in a handful of African and Latin American countries and perhaps mostly in East Asia in the areas of agriculture and industrialization.[5] However, for the majority of countries, the decade was more or less a disaster. As the World Bank has aptly noted, the 'World economy in the 1980s was dominated first by sharp recession, then by steady and prolonged growth in the industrial countries, high real interest rates, declining real commodity prices, massive movements in exchange rates, and the collapse of voluntary private lending to many developing countries'.[6] Even those countries that had made some concrete economic gains in the 1970s and managed to recover somewhat from the oil shocks were severely affected by massive 'external shocks'. Higher real interest rates, reduced international capital flows, and lower commodity prices[7] contributed to economic dislocation, inflation, unemployment and higher foreign debt profiles.

The 1982 recession caused serious economic dislocations all over the world but affected the developing world the most. The newly industrializing countries (NICs) of East Asia that depended heavily on manufactured exports were badly hit by the recession, although they were to recover by the mid-1980s. Real interest rates in the 1980s 'have been higher than at any time since the great depression'; the price of oil more than doubled and by 1981 it was six times its 1973 price and the majority of developing countries began to rely on 'external borrowing and too little on domestic sources'.[8] All this encouraged increased protectionism in the developed economies, declining foreign assistance, and resistance to trade concessions to developing countries. The net result was general social, economic and political crisis in the Third World.[9]

In a recent address to the Board of Directors of the World Bank, Barbar Conable, the Bank's President noted that despite the 'impressive advances' in many Third World countries, 'poverty has proven a stubborn foe. For instance, three of the world's most populous nations—India, China and Indonesia—have made great progress toward reducing poverty. Even so, more than 1 billion, half of them in South Asia, still live on less than a dollar a day. During the next ten years, the population of the developing world is likely to increase by at least 850 million people, many of whom will be born into absolute poverty.'[10] Conable further noted that some Third World regions 'have regressed economically' while 'living standards in Latin America have fallen below those of the 1970s'. In the case of sub-Saharan Africa, Conable noted that parts of the region 'have suffered a veritable collapse of living standards, institutions, and infrastructure', and in a rather pessimistic tone the World Bank boss concluded that in view of 'Africa's rapidly rising population, the number of poor people will continue to increase, even if economic growth accelerates. There poverty faces its greatest challenge'.[11] Of course, these problems have now been joined in dangerous proportions by environmental degradation, the rapid spread of the AIDS virus and other natural disasters which underdeveloped countries have been unable to control.

Therese P. Sevigny, the Under-Secretary-General for Public Information at the UN revealed recently that though the organization's second mandate is 'supporting economic and social development in the developing countries', it could not boast of any credible achievement in this area. In fact, according to Sevigny, 'National and international efforts to reduce poverty and narrow the gap between the rich, industrialized North and the poor, developing regions of the South failed abysmally in the last decade'.[12] In terms of actual statistics and data, this 'abysmal failure' can be seen in the fact that of the 84 countries whose economic conditions were examined by the UN Department of International Economic and Social Affairs at the end of the 1980s, 54 of them had 'falling per capita income'. In 14 countries, per capita income fell by over 35%. In 13 years, the debt of Third World countries increased from \$170 billion in 1975 to \$1200 billion in 1988; and development assistance to the developing countries from the developed countries declined from 0.37% of GNP in 1980 to 0.33% in 1989.

In addition, for at least a billion people in the developing countries, one-fifth of humanity, 'obtaining the most essential elements of social sustenance—food, health care, shelter, jobs, education—continues to be an everyday struggle'.[13] Three million children are still dying every year because they are not immunized; half a million women—99% of them in the developing world—die in childbirth; although the developing world has 80% of the world's population, less than 5% of global spending on health is directed at their health problems and requirements; 900 million adults are illiterate; about 100 million are without shelter, radios, televisions and other basic necessities taken for granted in the developing world; and by the year 2000, 'around 1 billion people in developing countries (will) be living in absolute poverty'.[14] Sevigny summarized the dismal conditions of the developing world at the beginning of the 1990s:

> The statistics of the global divide are striking. Some 70 per cent of world income is produced and consumed by 15 per cent of the world's population. In the 41 least developed countries, average per capita income is well under $300, in sharp contrast to the $14,500 average of developed market economies. In Latin America, living standards are lower today than they were in the 1970s. The situation is even worse in Africa where living standards have fallen to the level of the 1960s. Each year in the developing world, 14 million children die before their fifth birthday, and another 1250 million children under five are malnourished.[15]

The UN now admits that the 'world's poorest, in fact, got poorer in the 1980s' and that there is a direct correlation between poverty and '. . . mounting instability . . . widespread unrest, turmoil and violence which is now afflicting an unprecedented number of countries' in the developing world.[16]

For at least a billion people in the developing countries, obtaining food, health care, shelter, jobs, and education continues to be an everyday struggle.

The South Commission, in its 1990 report equally draws attention to conditions of mass poverty, economic dislocation, deindustrialization, declining foreign aid, mass net transfer of resources of about $40 billion a year from the Third World to the developed world, decaying institutions, political tensions and instability and the general inability of poverty-stricken and debt-ridden countries to provide for the basic human needs of the majority. These conditions, coupled with increasing debt-servicing ratios, declining commodity prices, declining investor and donor interest in the Third World; an increasing brain drain, capital flight and deteriorating social conditions led to repressions, riots, coups and counter-coups, political tensions and instability and increasing pressures on the state, its agents and agencies.[17]

Reflecting on the powerlessness of the developing countries, the South Commission wrote that the 'fate of the South is increasingly dictated by the perceptions and policies of governments in the North, of the multilateral institutions which a few of these governments control, and of the network of private institutions that are increasingly prominent. Domination has been reinforced where partnership was needed and hoped for by the South.'[18] Noting that several rounds of multilateral trade negotiations have made little impact towards removing the numerous discriminatory barriers to the exports of the South to the North, the Commission also notes that 'the international financial system has failed to provide the positive flows of capital to the developing countries' and the result has been 'stagnation and retrogression in most countries of the South'.[19] Thus at the end of the 1980s, the developing countries were hardly better-off than they were at the beginning of the 1960s and the global environment was no more hospitable than it was three decades earlier.[20]

THE THIRD WORLD AND THE NEW WORLD ORDER: ISSUES AND FEARS

Following persistent demands and debates, especially at the level of the UN, the developed countries reluctantly agreed to the need to establish a global basis for a New International Economic Order (NIEO) in 1975. Thus in September 1975, the Seventh Special Session of the General Assembly adopted the Declaration and Programme of Action on the Establishment of a New International Economic Order. This declaration 'formally acknowledged for the first time that economic injustice was as much a threat to world security and peace as were military and political tensions and conflicts'.[21] The broad implications of this Declaration were: (1) that 'the existing system discriminated against the weakest members of the international community through trade barriers, limited access to technology and capital, and inadequate monetary and financial arrangements'; (2) that the developing nations 'deserve at least an equal opportunity to participate in the world economic system without losing control of their natural resources or their freedom to follow their own priorities or policies'; and (3) that the constraints and contradictions in existing political and economic arrangements in the world order can only be resolved through the gradual, rather than violent 'restructuring of international institutions and a reorientation of policies governing relations between the developed and developing countries'.[22]

This Declaration was followed by hundreds of conferences, meetings, negotiations, establishment of institutions and so on, all aimed at restructuring the global flows of resources and capital;[23] the redistribution of power and resources; and the narrowing of the gap between the rich and the poor countries. For instance at UNCTAD IV in Nairobi in 1976, the Integrated Programme for Commodities which made provisions for international intervention to stabilize commodity markets was established. This Programme was to be backed by a Common Fund.

As well, the Charter on Economic Rights and Duties of States; the Convention on Multimodal Transport; the Agreement on Restrictive Business Practices and several policies aimed at addressing deteriorating economic and social conditions in the developing world were some of the achievements of the North-South Dialogue which followed the Declaration of the NIEO.

While these and other developments addressed some of the problems facing the poorer countries, in broad terms, they achieved little in terms of democratizing global political institutions, increasing access to the markets of the developed nations for technology, influencing a redistribution of global resources, increasing assistance to developing countries beyond the consideration of ideology and geopolitics and empowering the poorer countries to confront their own economic and social problems.[24] To be sure, many developed countries were plagued with severe economic problems as 'growing unemployment and relatively high rates of inflation which . . . in turn led to serious social and political strains, forcing many governments to plead for inward looking policies in an effort to solve domestic problems in preference for international problems'.[25] These internal pressures provided sufficient excuses for the developed countries to renege on earlier arrangements and agreements on the NIEO.

As the South Commission has argued, most of the gains of the NIEO have had 'little substance beyond declaratory value' because when it came to discussing 'specific aspects of the New International Economic Order . . . the developed countries won the major advantage from the beginning; they ensured that the negotiations would take place in different forums, thus fragmenting them, straining negotiating capabilities of the South, and allowing procrastination in the adoption of agreements capable of being implemented'.[26] Thus, in so 'long as the threat was perceived as possible, the North kept the dialogue going; when it subsided, the North withdrew'.[27] In fact, as soon as the developed countries succeeded in containing the pressures which the OPEC oil price increases had created in the early 1970s, they practically lost interest in any discussions about restructuring the global economy and by June 1977, the expectations for a NIEO 'had disappeared into thin air. The developed countries, having successfully recycled the surpluses of petro-dollars, were no longer interested in a new deal for the Third World. They were in fact, seeking assurance of oil supply and stable oil prices for themselves.'[26]

The final blow to the North-South dialogue came in 1981 at the Cancun Summit of 22 Heads of State and Government. The ideological shifts in the USA—Ronald Reagan; in the UK—Margaret Thatcher; and in West Germany—Helmut Kohl—reflecting an unrepentant belief in market forces and little sympathy for poorer countries resulted in an inability to reach agreement on the need for concessions to the developing world. According to the South Commission, by 1981, the developed countries had become preoccupied with internal problems, and at Cancun they 'gave no priority to agreeing on a new basis for North-South economic relations or to defining the nature, scope, and prospects of interdependence links in the world economy'.[29] In fact at UNCTAD VI in Belgrade in 1983, attempts to revive the North-South dialogue through the efforts of the Group of 77 failed as the developed countries turned down all pleas and arguments taking the position that they, the developed nations, were already recovering from the global economic crisis; that the benefits of their recovery will ultimately spill over to the developing countries; and that debt-distressed and crisis-ridden Third World nations should approach the IMF and the World Bank to adopt monetarist policies in order to structurally adjust their economies.[30]

By the mid-1980s, several developments in the global system provided some indicators of possibilities for changes in the relations between developed and developing countries. The majority of Third World nations adopted structural adjustment programmes to respond to their deepening economic problems.[31] Policies of deregulation, desubsidization, devaluation, export drive, liberalization and tight fiscal control, in the context of poverty, political instability, corruption, declining foreign assistance and investments, appeared, in the majority of cases, to have deepened the crisis of the developing countries. Beyond this, however, was the diversion of interest, aid and investments away from the developing world to Eastern Europe. Part of the reason for this shift was to prop up the Soviet regime and encourage it on the track of market reforms. Investors argued that the new enthusiasm for the market in Eastern Europe as well as the existence of required infrastructures put it far ahead of most developing regions in terms of investments, political risks and returns. It is true that the West has denied that it was supporting this trend, yet there are sufficient indicators to support the claim.

In any case, the stringent requirements prescribed for further assistance to developing nations have not been extended to the countries of Eastern Europe. When the Soviet Union claimed in late 1990 that it was experiencing problems with moving food from rural to urban centres, the governments in the West rushed to provide it with billions of dollars worth of credit and food aid. For instance, as Edward Greenspan noted, the EC 'agreed to send the equivalent of $1 billion (US) in emergency food aid to the Soviet Union in an undisguised effort to prop up President Mikhail Gorbachev . . . In addition to the Soviet food aid, EC leaders were also discussing a package of emergency food and energy assistance worth the equivalent of about $350 million for Romania and Bulgaria'.[32] A third of this package was to be in the form of a grant while the balance was to be in the form of export subsidies. Canada also opened a $100 million line of credit to the Soviet Union. Other forms of assistance to East

European nations included a $970 million assistance to help Czechoslovakia 'make its currency convertible' and a $55 million assistance to Poland in 1989.

Since the collapse of the Soviet Union, aid to the Commonwealth of Independent States has been staggering: Germany gave $34.88 billion; Italy, $5.85 billion; the USA, $4.08 billion; the EC, $3.88 billion; Japan, $2.72 billion; Spain, $1.36 billion; France, $1.22 billion; the UK, $0.07 billion and others, $14.01 billion.[33] The Group of Seven has also promised aid totalling $24 billion to help Russia stabilize its currency and with debt rescheduling.[34] In April 1992, the USA announced a Special Marshall Plan totalling $150 billion to assist the restructuring process in Eastern Europe.

Reflecting on this development in the case of Africa, the Economic Commission for Africa noted in its *1990 Economic Report on Africa* that 'resource flows to Africa will dwindle as and when resources are diverted for the development of depressed areas within the European Economic Community. This prospect is all the more evident with the emerging closer ties between Eastern and Western Europe. These factors . . . can only lead to the further marginalization of Africa in the 1990s and beyond.'[35] Adebayo Adedeji, the Executive-Secretary of the ECA has also noted that the problems of resource mobilization in Africa have been aggravated by the 'declining resource flows to Africa under complaints of aid fatigue, (and) the diverting of such flows to Eastern Europe . . .'.[36] The South Commission, arguing on behalf of the developing countries in general has also noted that with improving relations between Eastern and Western European nations, the East European nations now give 'priority to improving economic relations with the West rather than to negotiations in favour of greater justice for the South'. As well, the Commission argued that 'both attention and technical and financial resources are being diverted from development in the South to economic reconstruction in Eastern Europe'.[37]

As developing countries are unable to service their debts, credit lines are closed by suppliers and the scarcity of essential goods has led to riots, conflicts, coups, and political turnover.

To make matters worse, the developing countries lost the Soviet Union as a relatively more reliable ally in the global struggle against exploitation, injustice and foreign domination.[38] In fact, Gorbachev, in trying to reduce the 'over-extension' of the Soviet Union's global responsibilities and generate foreign exchange issued decrees requiring all military and commercial deals with Third World countries to be in hard currencies; and the immediate repayment of all debts owed to the Soviet Union.[39]

Donors have added another conditionality to the stringent conditions for providing further assistance even loans to developing countries—'political conditionality'. To this end, it was demanded that developing countries must show evidence of increasing democratization, political pluralism and respect for human rights before they could be considered for assistance. The World Bank's 1989 report on sub-Saharan Africa was very clear on this conditionality when it made prescriptions on the urgent need to attack corruption, mismanagement, promote the autonomy of the judiciary and create an 'enabling environment' for mobilization, democracy and participatory politics.[40] The UK Foreign Secretary, Douglas Hurd, gave support to this conditionality when he stated recently that 'Aid must go where it can clearly do good' and those who wished to receive UK aid must show evidence of 'pluralism, public accountability, respect for the rule of law, human rights and market principles'.[41]

Of course, it has been argued that the West has adopted this position to complicate the recovery process in the developing world because, in the first place, it continues to directly and/or indirectly support repressive regimes all over the Third World, and it has resisted all efforts to improve commodity prices and democratize the international system, especially the international financial system.[42] The whole idea of adjustment with a human face which the World Bank started to advocate only in 1989, was an afterthought following the numerous disasters and deteriorations caused by the orthodox adjustment packages imposed on developing countries in the past. The harsh monetarist prescriptions have been politically resisted by the poor. The acts of resistance have been met with increasing repression and political containment. Taken together it remains one major contradiction in the recovery process.[43]

Issues of declining exports and declining foreign exchange earnings in the context of rising costs of imports have added to the rising foreign debt profile of developing countries. As real interest rates continue to increase, the debt-servicing ratios have also gone up averaging between 30% and 135%. This has reduced resources available for developmental purposes and severely constrained the possibilities for recovery. As the South Commission has argued, prospects for recovery and increasing productivity in the South are limited because these debt-distressed countries 'need a substantial reduction of their burden of debt-servicing in order that they may be left with sufficient resources to achieve a level of growth that would enable them to service their debt soundly in the future'.[44] As the regimes are unable to service their debts, credit lines are closed by suppliers and the scarcity of essential goods have led to riots, conflicts, coups and regime turnover.

Sevigny gives the interesting case of Zambia which she describes as 'a simple example of the havoc developing country debt plays with people's lives'.[45] The victory of the Movement for Multi-Party Democracy (MMD) led by Fred Chiluba did nothing to result in increased sympathies for Zambia from the Bank and Fund or from creditors. In the 1960s and until the mid-1970s, Zambia enjoyed an economic boom largely as a result of the high prices of copper, the country's major export. Then copper prices fell precipitously. Zambia, as a result of declining foreign exchange earnings and thinking that the fall in price was only temporary, borrowed heavily from the international community. Unfortunately, the massive decline in the price of copper continued and the country's foreign debts increased from 40% of GDP in 1975 to 400% of GDP in 1986. As Sevigny notes, by 1986, 'Zambia's annual scheduled debt service payment had gone up to $900 million—equivalent to 95 per cent of all its export earnings. That meant that if it paid its obligations, it would have no money at all for its vital imports, which are the basis of much of its economy, and which also includes essentials like food, fertilizer, and medicines.'[46] Like many other developing countries, this situation meant an inability to service foreign debts effectively, keep credit lines open, retain the country's credit worthiness, and provide for the basic needs of the people. Zambia was forced to increase prices of essential items like food, and in line with IMF and World Bank as well as creditor requirements, it embarked on an adjustment programme. The result was political instability, an attempted military coup, several riots and increased repression and human rights abuses.

Debt servicing has now become a new avenue for draining the resources of poorer countries to the developed countries especially by the IMF. Again, the South Commission is clear on the implications of these developments for the survival of developing countries: 'The upshot is that debt has become a form of bondage, and the indebted economies have become indentured economies—a clear manifestation of neo-colonialism. This state of affairs cannot go on. The debt and its service must be reduced to a level that allows growth to proceed at an acceptable pace.'[47] As the maturity dates for loans to developing countries grew shorter by 35% from 6.7 years in 1970 to 4.0 years in 1987, 'interest rates of all creditors increased 172% from 3.7% in 1970 to 10% in 1987'.[48]

These developments have thus encouraged the net flow of resources from the developing to the developed world. With declining investments and declining foreign exchange earnings from exports, most developing economies have become 'collateral for refinancing already existing debt. Refinancing in this way also becomes more a nursing measure to prolong life rather than permit total collapse. Both creditors and debtors find themselves in an almost vicious circle in which the former must give to receive and the latter must receive to give.'[49] But the political implication for poor countries externally is that it mortgages their foreign policies and suffocates their room for manoeuvre in the global system. Internally, it redirects all efforts to satisfying the creditors and leaves very limited resources for meeting the basic needs of the people. The net result is deepening alienation, contradictions and conflicts. Either way, it is the poorer country that loses.

In spite of the apparent changes in the international system, especially in the area of East-West relations, the international economic system was actually moving in the opposite direction. Rather than show evidence of democratization to accommodate the demands of the developing countries, it moved towards the creation of protectionist regional economic blocs. The prospects for a united European market at the end of 1992 set in motion through the 1987 Single European Act, and the December 1987 Canada–US Free Trade Agreement which is now going to include Mexico are not pointers to the democratization of the world economy. The Overseas Development Institute (ODI) made it clear that Europe 1992 is designed in the first instance for the European economy, not for the developing world. As it put it, 'the net effect on ldcs as a whole is likely to be slightly positive. This is not to say that all developing countries will gain. The poorest economies in the least buoyant shape will not clearly benefit—unless they gain from exporting presently dutiable tropical beverages (commodities which are currently severely depressed).'[50]

What this implies is that only those developing countries that are relevant in supplying required raw materials to the European market will reap some benefits. This will of course increase their dependence on the European market as producers of raw materials. In spite of the Lomé Convention, which through STABEX provides some new arrangements for preferential treatment to African, Caribbean and Pacific states and in spite of Generalized System of Preferences (GSP), the developing countries are certainly going to face increasing marginalization in the emerging international divisions of power and labour. The South Commission has noted that 'the establishment of regional trading blocs raises important issues for the future of the international system' and that the South 'should be alert to the danger that these developments could result in narrowed access to developed country markets for its exports'.[51] The Commission went on to accuse the developed countries of direct and deliberate discrimination against developing countries:

> EC trade policies involve a high level of discrimination against imports from the South . . . the coverage of the GSP and the relief it offers are limited, and furthermore subject to unilateral termination by the EC on grounds of 'graduation' ie the withdrawal of concessional treatment with respect to a developing country that 'graduates' from lower to a higher level of economic development. The Lome Convention, in turn, offers limited concessions on commodities that come within the scope of the EC's Common Agricultural policy . . . In consequence of the recent intensification of protectionism in the developed countries, developing countries' exports have been subjected to discriminatory restrictions precisely in those sectors where they have a clear comparative advantage. . . .[52]

The establishment of a united European market in 1992 will not change the continuing use of tariff and non-tariff barriers, even direct political considerations, to discriminate against the developing countries.

To make matters even worse, the Uruguay Round of multilateral trade negotiation has achieved little. The 13 developing and industrial countries which came together to form the Cairns Group ostensibly to promote common interests as agricultural producers, achieved little as the negotiation broke down over disagreements on the issue of subsidies to farmers. The World Bank had predicted that the 'failure of the Uruguay Round would not only hamper the growth of world trade but also represent a rejection of the development strategy that has been promoted by the international community and multilateral organizations, at the very time the developing countries are coming to accept it'.[53] The developed countries did not go into the negotiations with a view to ensuring its workability given their current interests in regional blocs, hence the irreconcilable conflicts between the USA and the EC. The net losers are the developing nations which had hoped that new agreements would open up new opportunities for their exports to the developed country markets.

It was in the context of the problems above that the Gulf war broke out following the Iraqi invasion of Kuwait in August 1990. The war, which culminated in the US declaration of a new world order on 2 March 1991, revealed in very grim dimensions the marginal role of developing countries in the global system, the real meaning of the new world order as conceived by the USA; the implications of having the USA as the only superpower in the global system and the implications of the disintegration of the Soviet Union.[54] It also revealed clearly how the UN is likely to function under US hegemony and the implications of this for developing countries. We do not go into details on these issues here. We highlight only a few of them as they relate to our overall discussion.

The Gulf war saw in the first place the relegation of the UN to the background by the USA and its manipulation to give global legitimacy to a purely US agenda in the Middle East. That the USA was able to get the support of all the great powers, the Soviet Union and several debt-ridden, dependent and vulnerable developing countries equally provided it with a justification to push for the resolution of the crisis through war. The USA rejected the French and Soviet peace initiatives and proceeded to mount the largest military assault against a debt-ridden Third World country with a largely peasant-based army. The over $55 billion spent on the war is sufficient to eliminate virtually all the economic and social problems plaguing most developing countries if properly managed and invested. In any case, the war did not resolve the crisis in the Middle East and has in fact created new tensions and conflicts in and beyond the Middle East.[55] Since the end of the war, the USA has spent well over $40 million in trying to overthrow the Iraqi regime. What is more, political leaders in the West now openly campaign for the overthrow of legitimate, even if unpopular, governments. The implications of this development go far beyond the character of the Iraqi regime to reflect the open desire to set not just global economic and political programmes but also to determine the internal programmes of certain nations.

Yet, for the developing world, it was a shock to see how powerless the UN became, accepting and supporting through the Security Council all proposals submitted to it by the USA. It was also a shock to see the Soviet Union under Gorbachev, in return for US non-interference in the developments in the Baltic as well as to guarantee continuing US economic assistance in its reform programme, was unable to prevent war between a superpower and its allies and a developing nation. At the Security Council, it either made weak amendments to the US initiatives or simply supported US proposals. The Chinese 'abstained' from supporting US positions, but such abstentions made little difference and could, in the context of US positions, be regarded as support for the USA. The UK was at times even more enthusiastic for war than the USA and France, after initial efforts at the dying minutes to prevent war, did not use its veto power, but gave full support for the war. That France allowed the USA to infest computers ordered by the Iraqi air force for its defence systems before the outbreak of war, reveals the vulnerability of developing nations in a global system dominated and manipulated by the developed nations.

For the Third World, the Middle East crisis showed the preparedness of the West to defend countries that had direct relevance to their geostrategic and economic interests; after all, in spite of the numerous provocative activities of South Africa, the USA never considered a military threat, even less an invasion. Second, it showed that the West was capable of finding the money and resources, and the 'will' to pursue its own interests in spite of the frequent complaint of 'aid fatigue', 'compassion fatigue', and dwindling resources to aid developing countries. Third, the developing countries saw that they had lost the UN, at least for now, as a forum to pursue interests that were not necessarily congruent with the interests of the USA. After all, the USA could get all members of the Security Council to do its bidding even when it was obvious to all that Iraq, with a peasant-based army, stood no chance whatsoever against all the superpowers and great powers. Finally, the developing countries saw the loss of the only real check they had on the USA—the Soviet Union. Long before the war, Al Mazrui had reflected on this issue when he noted that 'We have lost something now that the moral competition is no longer operative. No longer is the Soviet Union acting as the conscience of the US and vice versa. We are also losing other things. There will be diversion of resources from the Third World . . . toward Eastern Europe. There will be diversion of investment, aid and trade. There will be less interest in markets that are regarded as less promising and less likely to maximize returns'.[56]

The new world order contains few programmes for recovery, growth, and development for the Third World.

Since the end of the war, the USA and its allies have been preoccupied with resolving the numerous problems that have become accentuated or were created in the region such as the problems of the Kurds; extinguishing the over 500 burning oil wells in Kuwait; containing political tensions and pressures in many of the countries in the region; trying to redefine power relations especially between Iran, Iraq, Lebanon, Israel and Syria in the region; resolving the Palestinian question without dialogue with Yassar Arafat as the PLO leader; and solving the severe environmental problems caused by the destruction of chemical plants, the pollution of rivers and the impact of heavy weapons employed by the allies against Iraq.

Following the defeat of Iraq, George Bush, declared the dawn of a new world order. The main element of this new order was the USA's absolute and unchallengeable power and dominance of the world system. It involves the ability to get other states to follow its leadership in containing Iraq; the use (even testing) of US weapons in the war and the domination of the UN. The 'American Century' for the USA came from the triumph of the market, the disintegration of the Soviet Union, the heavy reliance of the developing even developed countries on US leadership, and the containment of Iraq (and more recently Libya) as a demonstration of what the USA could do to nations which threatened its interests. As George Bush himself put it, there is 'nothing the American people can't handle . . . The first test of the new world order has been passed'.[57] For Martin Anderson, the new world order means that the 'United States has risen to be the biggest power in the world' and the 'Persian Gulf war has shown, clearly and unequivocably, that we're the number one military power . . . The United States has achieved moral, economic and military supremacy—probably for the first time in history. It is the first time since World War II that the leadership of the United States is undisputed.'[58] What is instructive, however, is that for the USA this 'supremacy' and 'leadership' as well as the 'new world order' which has followed the defeat of Iraq, contains no *economic* programme whatsoever. It is purely a military issue; the economic fall-out from the Gulf war has been to reward some of its allies like Kenya, Turkey, Israel and Egypt.

The new order does not contain any visible programme to redefine the economic relations between the developed and developing nations; calling an international conference on the debt crisis as demanded by the OAU and the South Commission to harmonize responses to the debt crisis; resolving the arms trade as well as the massive net transfer of resources from developing to developed nations; and reorganizing the global flow of resources, aid and investment to favour the developing nations. More important, the new world order contains no programme to deal with growing world poverty which has continued to mediate reform and recovery policies in the developing world as well as generating deep contradictions which culminate in violence, political instability, civil and inter-state conflicts as well as inability to protect the basic rights of people. There is no new approach to the AIDS crisis and the environment. In fact, at the 1992 Earth Summit in Brazil, the USA stood alone in opposition to all other nations on taking decisive steps to protect the environment because of economic considerations. What these show is that the developing nations do not feature seriously in the USA's conception of the new world order.

THE NEW WORLD ORDER AND THE THIRD WORLD: IMPLICATIONS FOR THE 1990S

The UN has projected that 'the lot of the world's poorest, overburdened as it was in the 1980s, is projected . . . to deteriorate even more in the 1990s, just as the already unconscionable gap between the industrialized and developing countries is also projected to widen'.[59] The Economic Commission for Africa, in reviewing the prospects for the region in the 1990s, has also projected that 'given the current world political and economic situation, Africa is becoming further marginalized in world affairs, both geo-politically and economically'[60] and only an alternative set of development policies can generate a basis for recovery. The South Commission in its recent report noted that resource flows to the developing countries have declined; several rounds of multilateral trade negotiations have not removed the discriminatory barriers against exports from the developing world; and in virtually all areas of economic and political relations, the developing countries have been the more vulnerable and exploited. The Commission concluded that 'in the absence of an effective remedial action, stagnation and retrogression in most countries of the South will persist in the 1990s. The "lost decade" may thus be extended'.[61] Pursuing this line a bit further, the Commission argued that 'hundreds of millions of the people living in the South suffer from hunger, malnutrition, and preventable diseases, and are illiterate or lack education and modern skills. The 1990s threaten even more hardship for the people of the South and even greater instability for their countries.'[62] These are not particularly bright projections for the 1990s.

It can be safely argued that not all developing countries are going to slide down the path of economic, social and political decay at the same pace. But, the projections from virtually all international bodies at the end of the 1980s show clearly that the new world order contains few programmes for recovery, growth and development for the Third World. It would seem therefore that a combination of *internal* and *external* policies are urgently required to stem the steady slide towards disaster in the majority of developing nations. In the context of ongoing changes in the world, there is no alternative to empowering popular organizations, rural communities and diverting resources away from flamboyant foreign policies and prestige projects towards rural development, food and cash crop production, industrialization, skills development and the provision of basic needs for the majority. Democratic spaces must be opened up to allow for accountability, respect for human rights, popular participation and a serious check on corruption, waste and mismanagement. Structural adjustment programmes are required in all developing nations, although such programmes must pay serious attention to the survival of vulnerable groups. The new emphasis at the level of policy must be on *productivity* as against mere distribution and consumption. These policies will inevitably lead to a new *national economic order* which is a prerequisite for winning concessions from the global economy.

At the regional level, developing countries must move away from the traditional attitude to regional cooperation. The politicization and proliferation of regional integration schemes as well as the lack of political will, disrespect for protocols and charters, and a general inability to withstand the initial and inevitable costs of harmonization of policies have in the past led to disintegration and decay. Europe 1992, the North American Free Trade Area and developments in the Pacific Rim show very clearly that this is the way to go in the 1990s. A more serious approach than what the OAU is contemplating in the African Economic Community scheduled to come into operation in AD 2025 is required to respond to the rapid creation of trade blocs in the global economy.[63] This would facilitate specialization, the rational utilization of scarce resources, the ability to regulate and perhaps control foreign investments, and reduce unhealthy competition for foreign aid, technology, technical assistance and other supports. Also, regionalism will, if properly organized and taken seriously, have far-reaching implications for resolving political conflicts. The role of the EC in the crisis and conflicts in Eastern Europe is a pointer in this direction.

In spite of the limited concessions currently available in the global system, there is still some room for hope about the future. A new reality will soon dawn on the USA which will compel it to divert attention to its deepening internal crisis, concede the responsibility for maintaining global peace to the UN and to work with other trade blocs on how best to organize the global economy. Before this happens however, the redirection of aid, investment and support for development efforts; the failure of structural adjustment programmes; the addition of 'political conditionality' to the list of conditionalities required by the West to aid developing countries; the implications of US hegemony in the global economy given its poor record of support for development in the past; and the blowing wind of change all over the world, all hold strong possibilities for the required change that will move the Third World out of its present predicaments.

These developments are bound to compel leaders, communities, popular organizations and institutions to ask new questions, plan new models of development, abandon old and discredited orthodoxies and recognize the need to involve the people and their organizations in the new agenda for change and development. The end of the Cold War and the disintegration of the Soviet Union effectively eliminates the tradition of playing the East against the West. It also makes unnecessary the need to support corrupt and repressive regimes in the Third World in the name of containing communism. What becomes possible is a new agenda for mobilizing the people for a struggle for democracy, democratization, empowerment, development and self-reliance. This will undoubtedly be the path for the 1990s. Third World leaders must recognize that the days of political posturing, defensive radicalism, propaganda and rhetoric are over; that new opportunities and markets have opened up in Eastern Europe; and that conditions of political conflicts, instability, deteriorating quality of life, and general uncertainty are bound to scare investors and reduce global compassion and support.

It is instructive to note that all over the Third World dictatorial and repressive regimes are crumbling, popular forces are organizing across ethnic, religious, regional and gender lines for justice, participation, equality, accountability, empowerment and mobilization. The struggle for *democracy* which had been on since the euphoria of political independence evaporated all over the developing world, had received added enthusiasm from the monumental changes in Eastern Europe. As well, issues of the *environment*, gender, popular participation, accountability of the leadership to the people and genuine grassroot democratization have become topical issues for political debates and contests all over the Third World.

It would appear, therefore, that one major hope for recovery and development in the Third World lies in their abandonment of previous structures, institutions and relations of exploitation, repression and mismanagement which have contributed in no small way to the current crisis. This degree of internal restructuring will empower the Third World to wage a new form of struggle for the reform of global power relations on a fairly interdependent basis as against the current grounds of inequality, dependence and marginalization. It is increasingly being recognized that poverty is inimical to peace and that 'deepening poverty is already leading to mounting instability' and that the 'world is currently moving at two wildly divergent speeds that threaten to tear apart the "new world order" that super-powers and regional political agreements are ushering in'.[64] Until the new world order is seriously built around the deepening problems of the developing countries, it is currently unlikely to benefit in any way from the changing conditions in the global system.

NOTES AND REFERENCES

1. Javier Perez de Cuellar, UN Secretary-General, UN Day Message, October 1990.
2. The South Commission, *The Challenge to the South: The Report of the South Commission* (London, Oxford University Press, 1990), page 2.
3. Commonwealth Heads of Government, *The Kuala Lumpur Communique October 1989* (London, Commonwealth Secretariat, 1989), page 27.
4. See the contributions to Toivo Miljan (editor), *The Political Economy of North-South Relations* (Peterborough, Canada, Broadview Press, 1987).
5. See Brandt Commission, *Common Crisis, North-South: Cooperation for World Recovery* (London, Pan Books, 1983); David Goldsbrough, 'Foreign direct investment in developing countries: trends, policy issues and prospects', *Finance and Development, 22*(1), 1986.
6. World Bank, *World Development Report 1989* (New York, Oxford University Press for the World Bank, 1989), page 6.
7. *Ibid.*
8. *Ibid*, page 23.
9. See Thomas M. Magstadt, *Nations and Governments: Comparative Politics in Regional Perspective* (New York, St Martins Press, 1991), Parts IV-VII.
10. Barber B. Conable, *Address to the Board of Governors* (Washington, DC, The World Bank Group, 25 September 1990), page 6.
11. *Ibid*, pages 6–7.
12. Therese P. Sevigny, 'From crisis to consensus: The United Nations and the challenge of development', Keynote Speech at the Inaugural Conference of the Institute for International Cooperation, University of Ottawa, Canada, 14 November 1990, page 2.
13. *Ibid*, page 3.
14. *Ibid*, page 4.
15. *Ibid*, page 4.
16. *Ibid*, pages 3 and 4.
17. See Claude Ake, *Revolutionary Pressures in Africa* (London, Zed Press, 1978); and the South Commission, *op cit*, reference 2.
18. *Ibid*, page 3.
19. *Ibid*, page 19.
20. See Organization of African Unity, *Lagos Plan of Action for the Economic Development of Africa, 1980–2000* (Geneva, Institute for Labour Studies, 1981); Brandt Commission, *North-South: A Programme for Survival. Report of the Independent Commission on International Development Issues* (London, Pan Books, 1980).
21. South Commission, *op cit* reference 2, page 216.
22. Sartaj Aziz, 'The search for a common ground', in Anthony J. Dolman and Jan van Ettinger (editors), *Partners in Tomorrow: Strategies for a New International Order* (New York, E. P. Dutton, 1978), page 14.
23. See Stephen D. Krasner, 'Third World vulnerabilities and global negotiations', *Review of International Studies, 9(4)*, October 1983; P. T. Bauer and B. S. Yamey, 'Against the New International Economic Order', *Commentary* (63), April 1977; and the contributions to Jagdish N. Bhagwati (editor), *The New International Economic Order: The North-South Debate* (Cambridge, MA, MIT Press, 1977).
24. See Frances Stewart, Brandt II—the mirage of collective action in a self-serving world', *Third World Quarterly, 5(3)*, July 1983; R. Cassen, R. Jolly and R. Wood, *Rich Country Interests and Third World Development* (London, Croom Helm, 1982); and Jimoh Omo-Fadaka, 'The mirage of NIEO: reflections on a Third World dystopia', *Alternatives, 10*(2), Fall 1984.
25. *Ibid*, page 15.
26. South Commission, *op cit*, reference 2, page 217.
27. *Ibid*, page 216.
28. Aziz, *op cit* reference 22, page 15.
29. South Commission, *op cit* reference 2, page 217.
30. See *ibid.*
31. See World Bank, *World Development Report 1989* (Washington, DC, The World Bank, 1989); G. K. Helleiner, 'Lessons for sub-Saharan Africa from Latin American experience?', *The African Development Review 1*(1), 1989; and Albert Fishlow, 'The state of Latin American economies' in *Economic and Social Progress in Latin America, External Debt: Crisis and Adjustment* (Washington, DC, Inter-American Development Bank, 1985).
32. Edward Greenspan, 'Soviets to get $1-billion in EC food aid—European leaders hope to shore up Gorbachev', *The Globe and Mail* (Toronto, Canada), 15 December 1990.
33. *Newsweek*, 30 March 1992, page 9.
34. *Newsweek*, 13 April 1992, page 44.
35. Economic Commission for Africa, *Economic Report on Africa 1990* (Addis Ababa, ECA, 1990), page viii.
36. Adebayo Adedeji, *The African Alternative: Putting the People First* (Addis Ababa, ECA, 1990), page 40.
37. South Commission, *op cit*, reference 2, pages 20–21.
38. This is not to say some aspects of Soviet relations with Third World countries were not exploitative or guided by purely ideological considerations. Yet, on a comparative basis, in the struggle against colonialism, racism, global exploitation and so on, the Soviet Union was a more reliable ally than any Western country. See Noam Chomsky, 'The struggle for democracy in a changed world', and Igor Belikov, 'Perestroika, the Soviet Union and the Third World', *Review of African Political Economy*, (50), March 1991.
39. See Julius O. Ihonvbere, 'The dynamics of change in Eastern Europe and their implications for Africa', *Coexistence—A Journal of East-West Relations, 29*(3), September 1992; Charles Adade, 'Soviets abandon Africa', *West Africa*, 8 October 1990; and Carol Saivetz, 'New thinking and Soviet Third World policy', *Current History, 88*(540), October 1989.
40. See World Bank, *op cit*, reference 31, chapters 1-3.
41. 'The prospects for Africa in the 1990s', *West Africa*, 25 June–1 July 1990.
42. See Salim Lone, 'Africa: drifting off the map of the world's concerns', *International Herald Tribune*, 24 August 1990; 'Donors demand political reforms', *Africa Recovery*, July-September 1990; and 'Link national, international democratization', *Africa Recovery*, July-September 1990.
43. See Julius O. Ihonvbere, 'Making structural adjustment programs work in Africa: towards a policy and research agenda', mimeo, University of Texas at Austin, 1991; and 'The crisis of structural adjustment programs in Africa: issues and explanations', *Philosophy and Social Action*, 1992.
44. South Commission *op cit*, reference 2, page 226.
45. Sevigny *op cit*, reference 12, page 6.
46. *Ibid.*
47. The South Commission, *op cit*, reference 2, page 227.
48. Karamo N. M. Sonko, 'Debt in the eye of a storm: the African crisis in a global context', *Africa Today, 37(4)*, 1990, page 21.
49. *Ibid*, page 22.
50. Overseas Development Institute, 'The developing countries and 1992', Briefing Paper, November 1989, page 4.
51. South Commission, *op cit*, reference 2, page 244.

52. *Ibid,* pages 243 and 244.
53. World Bank, *op cit,* reference 31, page 16.
54. See Richard Barnet, Ian Buruma and Owen Harries, 'Defining the new world order, What is it? Whose is it?', *Harper's,* May 1991; Adel Safty, 'Stranglehold on UN no way to a new order', *The Globe and Mail* (Toronto), 5 April 1991; Salim Mansur, 'The United Nations and the Gulf War', *Perspectives* (Canadian Institute of International Affairs), 5(2), March 1991; Kim Richard Nossal, 'The Gulf war and the future of the UN', in *ibid;* and Jeremy Seabrook, 'Gulf war—view from the South', *New Statesman and Society,* 15 February 1991.
55. See David Vick, 'Africa bites the bullet in Gulf war aftermath', *African Business,* May 1991; and Julius O. Ihonvbere, 'The Persian Gulf crisis and Africa: implications for the 1990s', *International Studies,* 1992.
56. Ali A. Mazrui, 'Eastern European revolutions: African origins?', *TransAfrica Forum,* 7(2), Summer 1990, page 8.
57. Quoted in Linda Diebel, 'US hails 'new world order': but many fear era of intolerance', *The Toronto Star,* 3 March 1991.
58. Martin Anderson quoted in *ibid.*
59. Sevigny, *op cit* reference 12, page 4.
60. Economic Commission for Africa, *African Charter for Popular Participation in Development* (Addis Ababa, ECA, 1990), page 18.
61. South Commission, *op cit,* reference 2, page 19.
62. *Ibid,* page 23.
63. See Julius O. Ihonvbere, 'Towards an African common market in AD 2025?: the African Crisis, regionalism and prospects for recovery', paper presented at the International Workshop on 'Eastern Europe and Africa: parallels and lessons', Queen's University, Kingston, Ontario, Canada, April 1992.
64. Sevigny, *op cit,* reference 12, page 4.

"The collapse of international communism has led not only to the Western presumption of 'marketplace magic' but also to the spread around the globe of. . .what has been termed liberal triumphalism. [T]he third world has never found market-led development to be the panacea its newly converted adherents hope for, [and while] the notion of democracy holds much greater appeal" its aura may mask a multitude of deeper problems.

The South Looks North: The Third World in the New World Order

DEEPA OLLAPALLY

DEEPA OLLAPALLY, *an assistant professor of political science at Swarthmore College, is the author of* Confronting Conflict: Domestic Factors and U.S. Foreign Policy in the Third World *(Westport, Conn.: Greenwood Press, 1993).*

The end of the cold war has produced an anomalous situation for the world's developing countries. Although superpower competition was played out most often and most virulently in the developing world, the West's euphoria over the collapse of Soviet power has not been matched in third world nations.[1] While the implications of the new international system clearly are not uniform among the developing countries, there is reason to be skeptical about third world prospects generally.

Such skepticism is found among third world leaders as diverse as Robert Mugabe of socialist Zimbabwe and Malaysia's Mohamad Mahathir, who has steered his country's economy with capitalist strategies for growth. What these two had to say at the meeting of the nonaligned nations in Caracas on November 27, 1991, is instructive. Mahathir declared, "Lamentably these changes do not augur well for the countries of the developing South. . . . Indeed, the new unipolar world is fraught with dangers of a return to the old dominance of the powerful over the weak. . . . A new world order is propounded seemingly to legitimize interference in the affairs of independent nations. . . ."

At the same meeting, Mugabe charged—as his colleagues have long been contending in one form or another, especially since the 1974 United Nations–based demand for a New International Economic Order—"The current. . .order continues to accentuate poverty in the developing countries. . . . Developed countries are continually manipulating international systems to their benefit yet purporting to be democratic." These comments raise the question whether the former axis of conflict between the United States and the Soviet Union is being replaced by the North-South divide between rich and poor countries.

The thinking in the North—particularly the United States—increasingly locates security threats in the third world. The United States Joint Chiefs of Staff noted in a 1991 report that "major portions of the world lag in the continuing struggle to improve the human condition. This lag, coupled with heightened expectations born of the ever-widening span of knowledge of progress in other areas of the world, are giving rise to insurgencies, terrorism, drug trafficking, and nationalist fervor." This reorientation in the developed world's perception of where danger might lie is bound to cause concern in third world capitals, since the players involved are so unequal.

The Joint Chiefs of Staff report alludes to the link between instability and dire economic conditions—a connection third world analysts are accustomed to treating as a foregone conclusion. Thus an important issue for this era after the cold war will be whether the conditions of underdevelopment can be overcome.

INTO THE FIRE?

From the South's perspective, the new international environment does not necessarily portend more favorable prospects for their primary concern: improving material conditions at home. Now as during the cold war, the third world is in a generally weak position in the international political economy; change at that level has been lacking, amid the other momentous shifts of a world in transition.

One key problem is that the developing countries' growing need for aid is being met with "aid fatigue" in the North. Without superpower competition, what was

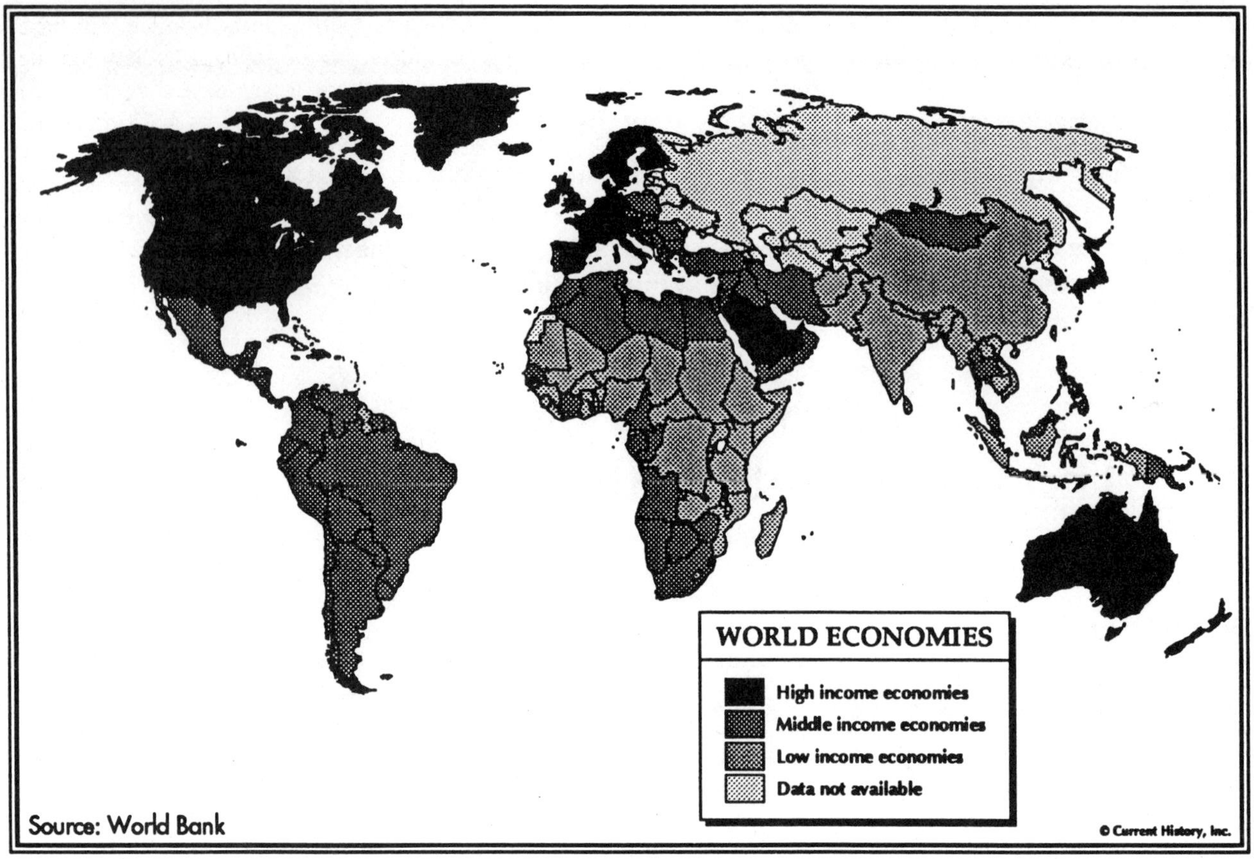

under cold war logic the most compelling reason for the advanced industrial nations to assist developing countries has evaporated. Indeed, in its place has arisen a plethora of new demands from the erstwhile second world for aid and investment capital. Given the political importance of keeping these former Communist states on the path toward liberalization and preventing backsliding, the West has pledged financial help and will almost certainly provide more, diverting resources that might have gone to the South. So after remaining essentially stagnant during the 1980s, official development assistance to the third world dropped 2 percent in 1989 from the year before, according to the Organization for Economic Cooperation and Development, and continued to decline in 1990.

Simultaneously, the political economies of the developed countries appear to be turning inward, which at the very least leads to benign neglect of international needs and at worst could spell economic nationalism. The trend emerged in the late 1970s, when Northern countries, having decided that fighting inflation was their number one economic priority, proceeded to introduce recessionary macroeconomic policy that relied heavily on monetary instruments. This resulted in a significant slowdown in the North and a downturn in demand for Southern commodities—a downturn not seen since the 1930s; at the same time, interest rates rose to unprecedented heights, with the untenable consequence that developing countries paid more and more to service their foreign debt while receiving less and less for their exports. In effect, the third world has ended up absorbing a good part of the costs of the North's attempt to curb inflation.

Although the recovery in the developed economies began in 1983, compared to past recoveries this one has been singularly unimpressive. The critical point for the South is that there has been no noticeable improvement in external economic conditions for most of the developing countries. The debt crises that began with Mexico in 1982 triggered a sharp reduction in international lending by commercial banks so that repayments of principal and interest charges exceeded loans from 1983 onward; thus the usual North-to-South debt-related financial flows were reversed. Direct foreign investment also fell dramatically in real terms in the early 1980s, and while it picked up by 1986, most of the benefits were concentrated in the newly industrializing countries of Asia. Indeed, the 1980s has come to be regarded as a "lost decade" for development. While internal factors contributed to the development crises in many third world countries, it is impossible to discount the impact of the inhospitable broader economic environment.

The situation has persisted into the 1990s. With the failure of the Communist experiment in the Soviet Union and eastern Europe, the virtues of the market model have been accepted as fact with renewed vigor in Western policy circles, as well as at the World Bank and the International Monetary Fund (IMF). Whether the lessons drawn from what was the second world may be extrapolated is not at all clear; as opposed to eastern Europe's experience, for most developing countries it has been their association with capitalism that has failed to produce growth and development.

The newly industrializing nations of Asia, whose economic success is by now legendary, are the one group in the third world exempt from the generally dismal picture. But in practically all cases, government intervention in the economy in one form or other was pervasive; pure market principles were not adhered to. Almost all the countries were under authoritarian regimes with repressive social policies, especially when it came to labor. And these Asian states were lucky because at the critical stage of their export-led strategy the international economic climate was highly receptive, unlike at present.

THE NEW PROTECTIONISM

From the point of view of aspiring industrializers, post–cold war conditions have, if anything, worsened their prospects. The growing protectionism in the West has tended to be directed against items of special importance to the South, such as textiles, petrochemicals, steel, processed agricultural products, automotive parts, and electronics. The so-called "new protectionism" based on nontariff barriers such as voluntary export restraints and "orderly marketing arrangements" has had the pernicious effect of blocking entry to the market for even the most efficient producers.

There is no evidence that this trend will be reversed. The United States is confronted by an increasing number of domestic constituencies demanding protection from international competition, and this is clearly eroding earlier government commitment to global integration and free trade. As the cold war recedes, critics from across the political spectrum argue against keeping markets open for erstwhile allies and partners practicing protectionism in the name of a defunct pact against communism. Taiwan and South Korea reaped enormous benefits thanks to their strategic importance, with the United States tolerating their restrictive market practices, but developing countries today cannot count on anything similar.

The high point for the third world's ability to get the developed countries to move toward concessions, symbolized by the New International Economic Order, is not likely to be reached again. The much touted Global Negotiations at the UN, which were supposed to have done so much for North-South relations in the 1980s, were derailed by the debt crisis and the domestic economic climate in the North. The ongoing Uruguay Round of trade talks under General Agreement on Tariffs and Trade (GATT) auspices that began in 1986 would have been an appropriate venue for a revival of the flagging North-South dialogue, but have served only to underscore the differences between the two sides on trade matters; if anything, the North, led by the United States, has hardened its position as the round has progressed.

One fundamental area of disagreement is intellectual property rights, which has brought what may be termed the most "assertive industrializers," including Brazil and India, into the fray. Third world countries tend to have much less restrictive patent protection than the developed countries, and sometimes none at all; significantly, patents are granted for processes rather than products. This more permissive approach is geared toward encouraging technological gains and adaptations that developing countries believe essential if they are to overcome their technology deficit. The South sees the North's efforts to construct a more restrictive system as simply increasing the monopolistic power of the multinationals.

Another emerging point of contention is America's insistence on including services such as banking, insurance, and telecommunications in GATT negotiations. Doing this would open these sectors in the developing world to highly competitive American corporations, with huge benefits for them. Again, the developing world, led by the assertive industrializers, is resisting, since this is certain to stymie growth in nascent service sectors as well as invite foreign control over key parts of the national economy.

Responding to its deteriorating global position, the United States has designed new mechanisms to shore up its economy. Provisions of the 1988 Omnibus Trade and Competitiveness Act specifically empower the executive to retaliate against countries deemed to have "unfairly" discouraged American exports. By 1990 more than half the 32 cases being investigated under the provisions involved developing countries. Two of those singled out as the "worst violators" were Brazil and India—as coincidence would have it, the leading spokesmen for the third world at the Uruguay Round.

The drive by the advanced industrial nations to maintain and even improve their economic status relative to the developing world is crystallizing in the formation of regional trade blocs, exemplified by moves in the European Community, by the North American Free Trade Agreement, and in Japan's evolving ties with the Association of Southeast Asian Nations. As cold war alliance politics disappears and economic competition among the first world countries gives rise to the tactics of bloc politics, the impact on the developing world is mixed. African, Middle Eastern, and South Asian countries will have a more difficult time insinuating themselves into these schemes. And as for those third world nations in the blocs, one wonders whether they will continue to serve as the weak periphery—providing, for example, cheap labor and a poorly protected environment that richer countries can pollute. On the whole, the economic sovereignty of developing countries may be more fragile now than under the "old world order."

EXPORTING DEMOCRACY

The collapse of international communism has led not only to the Western presumption of "marketplace magic" but also to the spread around the globe of its liberal democratic ideology, or what has been termed liberal triumphalism. While the third world has never found market-led development to be the panacea its newly converted adherents hope for, the notion of democracy holds much greater appeal. The example of eastern Europe clearly reveals the importance of participation and the likelihood of political decay if public confidence is not maintained. But United States actions in the developing world after the cold war suggest that a wide gap looms between the reality and the rhetoric. Selective support of the drive toward democracy still seems to be the norm.

Haiti is a good case in point. The military overthrow of President Jean-Bertrand Aristide—the charismatic priest elected in 1990 in the country's first fully free democratic elections after 29 years of despotic rule by the Duvalier family—has been met with tentative countermeasures such as a poorly enforced embargo by the Organization of American States and half-hearted moves to put together a multinational monitoring mission. The United States, which wields tremendous clout in the OAS and Haiti, bears special responsibility for the ineffective response. Pressured by American investors with holdings in Haiti, the administration of President George Bush failed to invoke the full range of sanctions available to it, and then diluted the sanctions it did put in place; for example, less than three months after the coup it exempted American corporations with Haitian assembly plants from the embargo. The reluctance to take more forceful action to restore democracy in Haiti stems in large part from an antipathy to Aristide's controversial populist and left-leaning politics.[2] United States policies after the cold war have changed far less than one might have imagined and suggests that the trade-off between narrow interests and the broader objective of spreading democracy will be settled in favor of the former. Even the more liberal Clinton administration took a hard line on refugees fleeing Haiti, although many of these people rightly feared political persecution at home.

Just how committed are the United States and other Western powers to democracy in the developing world? As it stands, even when democracy is promoted, the West tends to equate it with parliamentary elections and multiparty politics. But the formal mechanisms of democracy can easily mask the social and economic inequalities that are characteristic of most third world societies and that thwart genuine popular representation. What these developing countries require is the creation of preconditions for genuine democracy, such as more equal income distribution, improved literacy rates, land reform, and access to information. These, however, are precisely the measures likely to trigger opposition from elites, which in turn could lead to popular revolt. Thus the path to true democracy in the South is likely to be tumultuous at best and tortuous at worst because of the threat democratization represents for entrenched elites who, during the cold war years, rested secure in the knowledge that their respective foreign patrons would stand by them. While the former Soviet Union has shed its third world associates wholesale, leaving them to their own devices, the United States has not shown similar dispatch in reversing its policies toward authoritarian regimes.

What the United States, along with the IMF, *has* been pushing developing countries toward with renewed vigor is liberalization and privatization schemes. Liberalization, which is often part of an overall IMF "austerity" program, invariably exacts painful social costs in poor countries. In a freewheeling democracy, such costs cannot be expected to go unchallenged, and the challenges would imperil American and other Western interests; indeed, from the West's point of view, greater and not less social control would then be necessary. But this would contradict declared policy on democracy. Thus for the North the choice is between fostering forces of genuine democracy and supporting peaceful transitions in the third world, or facing violent social upheavals that would be politically embarrassing and potentially dangerous for Northern interests, as well as disastrous for the countries involved.

Insistence on replicating Western liberal democratic conceptions of political economy and ideology in the developing world is likely to be counterproductive. It is becoming increasingly clear that exported Western ideology, whether of the socialist or capitalist variety, has not provided definitive answers for the South. Indeed, the 1979 Iranian revolution and the Algerian upheavals of 1991 stand as vivid testimony to the perception that both capitalism and socialism failed in their mission to deliver material goods. The turn toward Islamic revivalism, in this context, may best be interpreted as a search for a more domestically authentic vision that transcends the twin ideologies of the cold war.

Thus, along with its ongoing crisis of development, the South is also now experiencing what may be called a crisis of vision. And the vision of a new world order as put into practice thus far by the United States does not appear decisively different from a unilateral project to secure American interests in a more complex and variegated international environment.

How collective is collective security?

A key aspect of the new world order is collective security and respect for international law. This is clearly welcome by the weaker countries, since they stand to gain most when rules rather than force govern international relations. Collective security also implies more democratic decision making in the management of conflicts, with a shift away from the capitals of powerful countries and toward multilateral institutions such as the UN.

But if the first post–cold war conflict is any guide to the shape of the new order, serious questions must be raised regarding the UN's ability to go beyond the interests of its dominant members. Even the organization's generally cautious former secretary general, Javier Pérez de Cuéllar, has suggested the UN was misused by the United States in its prosecution of the Persian Gulf War.[3] What became apparent in the shaping of the response to Iraq's invasion of Kuwait was the UN's general willingness to accommodate United States objectives without any real debate. Under American pressure and shrewd carrot-and-stick diplomacy, more independent-minded countries such as China and France, succumbed. Belying the more peaceful vision for the world after the cold war put forward by President Bush, the United States wasted a tremendous opportunity to use creative diplomacy and economic sanctions prescribed by the UN charter rather than resorting to war. Another casualty of the war has been the brief hopes of developing countries that a "global peace dividend" resulting from the ending of the cold war might be used for development purposes.

The Gulf War also underscored the ineffectiveness of the nonaligned movement, which had already been sapped by the collapse of the second world. The group was an inconsequential player in the Persian Gulf crisis, making only feeble attempts to resolve hostilities short of war. The traditional pillars of nonalignment found themselves hardly up to the task, what with India and Yugoslavia immersed in their internal problems and Egypt and Iraq on opposite sides. Thus nonalignment's political import as a "third force" in the bipolar world is unlikely to be reproduced in the new order—and an important means for expressing the interests of developing countries will be eroded.

The new era promised improvement in the resolution of regional conflicts that had been stoked by superpower competition. It was expected that the United States and the former Soviet Union would jointly hammer out compromise solutions that warring parties could abide by. In actuality, the Russians have opted out of these third world conflicts entirely, leaving a single peace broker. And historical loyalties or enmities toward local actors place limits on United States–sponsored conflict resolution. In Angola, where internal conflict was exacerbated by superpower rivalry for 16 years, the post–cold war settlement found the United States continuing to aid the National Union for the Total Independence of Angola (UNITA), its favored faction in the three-way nationalist struggle, right up to the May 1991 peace agreement between the government and UNITA. The United States also has shown little interest in ensuring that peace processes, once started, go forward. Again in Angola, the Bush administration agreed to a meager $14.5 million in aid for the transition to democracy, including the demobilization of government and UNITA military forces, even though it had managed to allocate an estimated $75 million annually to UNITA in the final years before the cease-fire. In Afghanistan, another casualty of the cold war, the United States and the Soviet Union were eager to disengage, without leaving behind any stable political structure. The central message for countries that, wittingly or unwittingly, served as proxies for superpower conflict seems to be that the remaining superpower has little if any obligation toward them.

Unlike the Western world, the developing world would seem to have little to celebrate with the ending of the cold war. Whether in the areas of political economy, security, or ideology, the space on the global agenda for third world concerns has shrunk. The developing countries' bargaining power and leverage, never great, have steadily eroded since the onset of the debt crises in the early 1980s. With the cold war over, developing countries matter even less for the North.

But with three-quarters of humankind living in the third world and the gap between rich countries and poor continuing to widen, the potential for instability in the international system—ranging from the movement of refugees to the North to social upheavals in the South—is high. Unless the West is fully cognizant of such pressures and the need to address them, the benefits that were expected to come from the more beneficent climate of the post–cold war period are likely to be short-lived for all.

---

[1]Although the term "third world" may be questioned, it retains conceptual meaning and is used interchangeably with "developing countries" in this article.

[2]A good discussion can be found in Pamela Constable, "Dateline Haiti: Caribbean Stalemate," *Foreign Policy*, vol. 89 (Winter 1992–1993).

[3]Clovis Maksoud, former ambassador from the Arab League to the UN, provides an insider's account in "The Arab World's Quandary," *World Policy Journal*, vol. 8, no. 3 (Summer 1991).

The economist's blind eye

The vital argument between Gandhi and Nehru... The invention of the market... Challenging the economic way of looking at life.

'SHOULD India ever resolve to imitate England, it will be the ruin of the nation.' In 1909, while still in South Africa, Mohandas Gandhi formulated the conviction upon which he then, over a period of 40 years, fought for the independence of India. Although he won the fight, the cause was lost; no sooner was independence achieved than his principle fell into oblivion.

Gandhi wanted to drive the British out of the country in order to allow India to become more Indian; Nehru, on the other hand, saw independence as the opportunity to make India more Western. An assassin's bullet prevented the controversy between the two heroes of the nation from coming into the open, but the decade-long correspondence between them clearly demonstrates the issues.

Gandhi was not won over to technical civilization with its machines, engines and factories, because he saw in it a culture which knew no more sublime end than that of minimizing bodily effort and maximizing physical well-being. He could only shrug his shoulders at such an obsession with gaining comfort; as if a good life could be built on that! Didn't India's tradition, undisturbed for thousands of years, have more substantial things to offer?

Although far from being a traditionalist on many issues, Gandhi insisted on a society which, in accordance with Hindu tradition, gave priority to a spiritual way of life. An English style of industrialism is out of place wherever *swaraj*, the calm freedom to follow personal truth, is to rule; Gandhi pleaded for a renewal of the countless villages of India and for a form of progress to be judged accordingly. In his eyes, India was committed to an idea of the good and proper life that contradicted the ideals prevalent in England during the age of automation. For this reason, a wholesale imitation of the West was simply out of the question. Individual elements should, in his mind, be adopted only insofar as they could help give better expression to India's aspirations.

Nehru disagreed. He saw no alternative but to introduce the young nation to the achievements of the West as soon as possible and take the road towards an economic civilization. Even in the early days, and in spite of his great admiration for the man, he found Gandhi 'completely unreal' in his vision. Though he intended to avoid the excesses of capitalism, he still viewed Indian society primarily as an economy, that is, as a society defining itself in terms of its performance in providing goods.

From an economic viewpoint, however, the nature of humanity, the function of politics and the character of social reform all assume a particular meaning. People are seen as living in a permanent situation of scarcity, since they always have less than they desire. The most noble task of politics is therefore to create the conditions for material wealth; and this in turn requires the reorganization of society from a host of locally-based subsistence communities into a nationwide economy.

Nehru thus fostered precisely that Western self-delusion which was also at the core of the development idea: that the essential reality of a society consists in nothing else than its functional achievements; the rest is just folklore or private affairs. From this viewpoint the economy overshadows every other reality; the laws of economy dominate society and not the rules of society the economy. This is why, whenever development strategists set their sights on a country, they do not see a society that *has* an economy, but a society that *is* an economy.

When production is not god

Observing a group of Maya Indians who work their fields in the mountains around Quiche in Guatemala, and seeing the barren ground, the primitive tools and the scanty yield, one might easily come to the conclusion that nothing in the world is more important to them than increasing productivity. Remedies could swiftly be found: better crop rotation, improved seeds, small machines, privatization, and anything else the cookbook of business management might recommend.

All this is not necessarily wrong but the economic viewpoint is notoriously colour blind: it recognises the cost-yield relation with extreme clarity, but is hardly able to perceive other dimensions of reality. For example, economists have difficulty in recognizing that the land bestows identity upon the Indios since it represents the bridge to their ancestors. Likewise economists often fail to note the central importance of collective forms of labour, in which the village community finds visible expression. The outlook of the Maya is incompatible with that of the economists.

To put this in the form of a paradox: not everything that looks like an economic activity is necessarily a part of economics. Indeed, economics offers only one of many ways of looking at goods-oriented activities and putting them in a larger context. In every society things are produced, distributed and consumed; but only in modern Westernized societies are prices and products, conditions of ownership and work, predominantly shaped by the laws of economic efficiency. Elsewhere different rules are valid, other models prevail.

The Bemba in Zambia, for example, see a good harvest or a successful hunting expedition as a gift from their ancestors – they court the ancestors' favour in the hope of higher production. Then there are the cycles of cultivation practised by farmers in Maharashtra, which neatly fit into the yearly round of weddings, festivals and pilgrimages. New methods of cultivation can soon disrupt this social calendar.

In societies that are not built on the compulsion to amass material wealth, economic activity is also not geared to slick, zippy output. Rather, economic activities like choosing an occupation, cultivating the land, or exchanging goods, are understood as ways of enacting that particular social drama in which the members of the community happen to see themselves as the actors. That drama's story largely defines what belongs to whom, who produces what and how it is exchanged. The 'economy' is closely bound up with life but it does not stamp its rules and rhythms on the rest of society. Only in the West does the economy dictate the drama and everyone's role in it.

An invention of the West

As late as 1744, Zedler's Universal Encyclopaedia unwittingly gave a naive definition of the term 'market': '...that spacious public place, surrounded by ornate buildings or enclosed by stands, where, at certain times, all kinds of victuals and other wares are offered for sale; hence the same place is also called market-place'.

The market, heralded both as blessing and as bane over the last two centuries, this powerful idea – nothing more than a location! The author of the encyclopaedia seemed only to be thinking of crowds,

'Only in the West does the economy dictate the drama and everyone's role in it.'

stands and baskets; there is no mention of 'market shares', 'price fluctuations' or 'equilibrium'. Between his time and ours a far-reaching change has taken place in the self-image of society.

Adam Smith was the first thinker who, when using the term 'market', no longer envisaged a locally determinable outlet for goods, but that society-wide space throughout which all prices intercommunicate. This innovation was no accident, but mirrored a new social reality: an economy of national scope. Before then, a domestic market was not something to be taken for granted; even in Europe at the end of the seventeenth century, one could hardly find trade between different regions of the same country!

Of course from time immemorial there has been trade – one need only think of the North German Hanseatic League or the splendour of Venice – but this was trade with distant countries, which remained limited to a few cities as bridgeheads. History knows markets in all shapes and sizes, but they were local and temporary places of exchange between towns and the surrounding countryside.

In Adam Smith's century, however, the nation-state drew a web of the trade relations over the whole of society and established the domestic market. Like today's developing countries, the young states of that time pushed hard to make economic principles prevail everywhere, be it only to finance their own existence. That was the birth of the national economy, even on a lexical level: while the term 'economy' had formerly been applied to the 'domestic economy' of the prince, now the whole nation was transformed into a 'political economy'. And Smith became the theoretician of a society governed by the rules of the market.

Alternatives to the economy?

The transformation of society into a political economy was, of course, only achieved after a prolonged struggle demanding many sacrifices. After all, people were not shaped by a commercial ethos—it did not influence how they regarded work or property, their idea of good conduct or their sense of time. The merchant was not yet an entrepreneur, land was not saleable, competition was frowned upon, usury disreputable, and those who worked for wages lived on the fringes of society. As a result, the progress of capitalism was punctutated by bitter disputes about whether and to what extent land and forest, grain and money, and workers themselves, could be treated as commodities.

In the last decades, similar radical changes have taken place in large parts of the Third World as economic ideology has tightened its grip. Traditions of sufficiency have been pushed aside, local exchange relations dissolved, collective forms of ownership broken up, and subsistence economies wiped out. For a long time the guiding light of international development policy was to create societies of paid workers and consumers everywhere. Experts scrutinized countries to identify 'obstacles to development' which were hampering the free mobility of 'production factors'. No cost was too high and few sacrifices were too great in the quest to turn societies into smoothly-running political economies.

Without any doubt, miracles were thus wrought, and a great tide swept through the countries of the Southern hemisphere; history had taken an enormous leap. However, it is becoming ever clearer that a disaster is in the offing. At the very moment the economy has finally achieved worldwide dominion, social disruptions and environmental destruction have become rampant.

The domination of the economy is showing its menacing side. Societies find themselves cornered: they cannot afford to surrender to this monster, but they cannot escape from it either. In fact the economy, during its rise to the top, has stamped out alternatives to itself which are not so hazardous for both humans and nature.

How is it possible to reinvent economic institutions that allow people to live gracefully without making them prisoners of the pernicious drive to accumulate? Maybe there will be more creative power in the Third World to meet this historical challenge. Simply because, in spite of everything, many people there still remember a way of life in which economic performance was not paramount.

LET'S ABOLISH THE THIRD WORLD

It never made much sense, and it doesn't exist in practice. So why not get rid of it in theory?

Sometimes language lags history. Take the Third World. Did we ever have another name for the poor, unstable nations of the south? In fact, the Third World is a 1950s coinage, invented in Paris by French intellectuals looking for a way to lump together the newly independent former European colonies in Asia and Africa. They defined *le tiers monde* by what it wasn't: neither the First World (the West) nor the Second (the Soviet bloc). But now the cold war is over, and we are learning a new political lexicon, free of old standbys like "Soviet Union" that no longer refer to anything. It's a good time to get rid of the Third World, too.

The Third World should have been abolished long ago. From the very beginning, the concept swept vast differences of culture, religion and ethnicity under the rug. How much did El Salvador and Senegal really have in common? And what did either share with Bangladesh? One of the bloodiest wars since Vietnam took place between two Third World brothers, Iran and Iraq. Many former colonies remained closer to erstwhile European metropoles than to their fellow "new nations."

Nevertheless, the Third World grew. Intellectuals and politicians added a socioeconomic connotation to its original geopolitical meaning. It came to include all those exploited countries that could meet the unhappy standard set by Prime Minister Lee Kuan Yew of Singapore in 1969: "poor, strife-ridden, chaotic." (That was how Latin America got into the club.) There's a tendency now to repackage the Third World as the "South" in a global North-South, rich-poor division. To be sure, in this sense the Third World does refer to something real: vast social problems—disease, hunger, bad housing—matched by a chronic inability to solve them. And relative deprivation does give poor nations some common interests: freer access to Western markets, for example.

But there are moral hazards in defining people by what they cannot do or what they do not have. If being Third World meant being poor, and if being poor meant being a perennial victim of the First and Second Worlds, why take responsibility for your own fate? From Cuba to Burma, Third Worldism became the refuge of scoundrels, the "progressive" finery in which despots draped their repression and economic mismanagement. Remember "African socialism" in Julius Nyerere's Tanzania? It left the country's economy a shambles. A good many Western intellectuals hailed it as a "homegrown" Third World ideology.

Paternalism is one characteristic Western response to a "victimized" Third World. Racism is another. To nativists such as France's Jean-Marie Le Pen or Patrick Buchanan, "Third World" is a code phrase for what they see as the inherent inferiority of tropical societies made up of dark-skinned people. Either way, the phrase Third World, so suggestive of some alien plant, abets stereotyping. "The Third World is a form of bloodless universality that robs individuals and societies of their particularity," wrote the late Trinidad-born novelist Shiva Naipaul. "To blandly subsume, say, Ethiopia, India, and Brazil under the one banner of Third Worldhood is as absurd and as denigrating as the old assertion that all Chinese look alike."

Today, two new forces are finishing off the tattered Third World idea. The first is the West's victory in the cold war. There are no longer two competing "worlds" with which to contrast a "third." Leaders can't play one superpower off the other, or advertise their misguided policies as alternative to "equally inappropriate" communism and capitalism. The second is rapid growth in many once poor countries. The World Bank says developing countries will grow twice as fast in the '90s as the industrialized G-7. So much for the alleged immutability of "Third World" poverty—and for the notion that development must await a massive transfer of resources from north to south. No one would call the Singapore of Lee Kuan Yew poor, strife-ridden or chaotic: per capita GNP is more than $10,000, and its 1990 growth rate was 8 percent. South Korea, Taiwan and Hong Kong also have robust economies, and Thailand and Malaysia are moving up fast.

American steelmakers have recently lodged "dumping" complaints against half a dozen Asian and Latin American countries. Cheap wages explains much of these foreign steelmakers' success, but the U.S. industry's cry is still a backhanded compliment. "A nation without a manufacturing base is a nation heading toward Third World status," wrote presidential candidate Paul Tsongas. But Tsongas was using obsolete imagery to make his point: soon, bustling basic industries may be the *hallmark* of a "Third World" nation.

Patina of modernity: Nor can the Third World idea withstand revelations about what life was really like in the former "Second World." It was assumed that, whatever the U.S.S.R.'s political deformities, that country was at least modern enough to give the West a run for its money in science and technology. In fact, below a patina of modernity lay gross industrial inefficiency, environmental decay and ethnic strife. Nowadays, it's more common to hear conditions in the former Soviet Union itself described as "Third World," and Russia seeks aid from South Korea. Elsewhere in Europe, Yugoslavia's inter-ethnic war is as bad as anything in Asia or Africa. The United States itself is pocked with "Third World" enclaves: groups with Bangladeshi life expectancies and Latin American infant-mortality rates.

A concept invoked to explain so many things probably can't explain very much at all. The ills that have come to be associated with the Third World are not confined to the southern half of this planet. Nor are democracy and prosperity the exclusive prerogatives of the North. Unfair as international relations may be, over time, economic development and political stability come to countries that work, save and organize to achieve them. Decline and political disorder come to those who neglect education, public health—and freedom. The rules apply regardless of race, ethnicity, religion or climate. There's only one world.

CHARLES LANE

Trade, Aid, and Debt

Economic issues are among the most pressing concerns that face Third World countries. Progress on the variety of problems that developing countries confront requires economic growth and stabilization. A combination of internal and external factors complicate this quest for growth and stabilization.

The position of the Third World in the international trading system contributes to the difficulty of achieving consistent economic growth. From the incorporation of these countries into the international economic system during colonialism to the present, their role has been primarily as suppliers of raw materials and agricultural products. Third World dependence on commodity exports has meant that these countries have had to deal with fluctuating and frequently declining prices for their exports. At the same time, prices for imports have increased. At best, this has made development planning difficult; at worst, it has led to economic stagnation and decline.

Most Third World nations have had limited success in breaking out of this dilemma by diversifying their economies. Third World industrialization and the export of light manufactures has led to competition with less efficient industries in the industrialized world. The response of industrialized countries has often been protectionism and demands for trade reciprocity, which can overwhelm Third World markets. Efforts to avoid the consequences of protectionism include the Generalized System of Preferences, which emerged in the 1970s to reduce tariff barriers on Third World manufactured goods. This system has enjoyed limited success due in part to the reluctance of the industrialized countries to expand the system and the complications of participating. The politics that underlie trade policy is evident in the negotiation of the North American Free Trade Agreement (NAFTA) and demonstrate the potential political and economic consequences to both developed and developing countries of pursuing such a policy.

The economic situation in the Third World is not entirely attributable to colonial legacy and protectionism on the part of industrialized countries. Trade and industrialization schemes involving heavy government direction were often ill-conceived or resulted in corruption and mismanagement. Industrialized countries frequently point to these inefficiencies in calling for market-oriented reforms, but market solutions can only be effective in conjunction with reductions in trade barriers that will allow the Third World greater export opportunities.

Third World countries have received substantial amounts of foreign aid over the years. This effort, however, has been a disappointment for both donors and recipients. The need for development aid exceeds the ability or willingness of donors to provide it. Critics from developing countries complain not only about the amount of aid available, but also about tying aid to political objectives, decisions about whom to aid, and equity in distribution. Donors are dismayed at the lack of development progress, corruption and mismanagement, and a thankless attitude on the part of some recipients. This has resulted in donor fatigue that has been exacerbated by domestic problems within donor countries that makes aid even less politically popular. Clearly foreign aid is less than satisfying or productive from the standpoint of both donors and recipients.

The debt crisis has further compounded economic problems in the Third World. During the 1970s, Third World economic performance and the availability of petrodollars led to extensive commercial lending to fill the gap between export earnings and foreign aid and increasing development expenditures. The second oil price hike in the late 1970s, declining export earnings, and worldwide recession in the early 1980s left many Third World countries unable to meet their debt obligations. By the mid-1980s this debt crisis threatened commercial banks that had extended loans to developing countries. The debt plans formulated by U.S. Treasury secretaries James Baker and Nicholas Brady advocated debt rescheduling and continued lending in return for growth-oriented economic reforms. Access to the World Bank and the International Monetary Fund financing became conditional on the adoption of structural adjustment programs that involved steps such as reduced public expenditures, devaluation of currencies, and export promotion, all geared to debt reduction. The consequences of these programs have been painful for Third World countries. Less public services, higher prices, and greater exploitation of resources that have resulted from these programs have caused some countries to abandon the plans, jeopardizing their credit worthiness and continued access to additional funds. The commercial banks have weathered the crisis, with some actually profiting. Third World countries, however, continue to struggle with their debt burdens.

Despite the generally bleak economic picture in much of the Third World, there have been some success stories. The success of the newly industrialized countries in East Asia has led analysts to question why some countries

Unit 2

have prospered while others have lagged behind. Potential reasons advanced for this discrepancy include resources, economic management, the colonial legacy, and corruption. Whatever the basis for these differences, these discrepancies further underscore the diversity of the Third World as well as its continuing differentiation.

Looking Ahead: Challenge Questions

What is the position of the Third World in the international trading system?

What steps have Third World countries recently taken to try to improve their position in the international trading system?

What is the purpose of the Generalized System of Preferences? Why has this scheme been of questionable value to Third World participants?

In what ways have state-centered trade and industrial policies harmed Third World economies? What do developing countries have to do to improve their economies?

What is the "fundamentalism" of the West? How does it compare to religious fundamentalism? What are the consequences of this view?

What circumstances led to the Third World's debt crisis?

Why has Africa been particularly affected by the debt crisis?

What solutions have been offered to the Third World's debt crisis? What have been the results of these programs?

How would you contrast the perspectives on the effects of the debt crisis from the standpoint of both the Third World and the industrialized countries?

How do the development experiences of Asia and Africa differ? What may account for these differences?

The Developing Countries and the World Trading System

Since the beginning of the Uruguay Round, in September 1986, a steadily increasing number of developing countries have taken substantial steps to liberalise their trade regimes and to boost their participation within the processes of the GATT and thus in the world economy. This movement highlights a marked shift from protectionism, and offers hope for a lasting and equitable expansion of trade.[1]

Anne Richards

Anne Richards is a senior economist in the OECD Trade Directorate.

For the first time in the history of the General Agreement on Tariffs and Trade—it was founded in 1947—large numbers of developing countries (LDCs) are liberalising their trade policies within the GATT system. The striking diversity of these countries merits attention. Countries whose trade regimes had been highly inward-oriented are joining those already engaged in market-opening reforms. Countries whose involvement in the GATT had been marginal joined those already participating actively. And countries that are among the poorest and least developed joined those with higher per capita incomes. This trend is now affecting the majority of GATT members (or about 80 of the more than 108 sovereign states that are Contracting Parties to the GATT) and may be one of the most important developments alongside the Uruguay Round.

1. **Integration of Developing Countries into the International Trading System,** OECD Publications, Paris, 1992.

The rate of new LDC accessions (on average, almost four countries per year since 1986) indicates a growing reliance on the GATT: it is more than twice the corresponding rate observed for the entire history of the GATT before then. And the new accessions—11 developing countries have since formally acceded since September 1986 and eight others are in various phases of negotiating their accession—involve even farther-reaching commitments than in earlier accessions to abide by GATT rules and disciplines. These commitments, which are binding under international law, cover, for example, the application of tariffs and non-tariff measures; notification and consultation requirements; and compliance with GATT rules on anti-dumping, subsidies, and regional or bilateral trade arrangements.

This process of integration into the international trading system allows developing countries to have a much bigger say in shaping the rules governing world trade and to incorporate these rules in their own domestic policies. It comprises three types of steps (not necessarily distinct in time). First, the rationalisation and simplification of import regimes turns cumbersome and obscure import restraints into a simple structure of tariffs and other price based measures. Second, it means fuller participation in the institutional GATT framework, especially adhering to the various Tokyo Round Codes and Agreements that are the principal GATT instruments for promoting more liberal and uniform practices in special areas such as government procurement. Third, it liberalises trade regimes, lowering import tariffs to internationally acceptable rates and removing export taxes.

The benefits associated with fuller integration—such as trade growth and a much wider variety of goods and services available, and to more people—are spread to all participants in world trade, but accrue mainly and fastest to the integrating LDCs themselves.There are six types of trade policies and practices which most clearly indicate progress towards fuller integration:

- new accessions to the GATT, whereby countries agree to abide by GATT rules and disciplines

Reprinted from *The OECD Observer,* No. 177, August/September 1992, pp. 23-25.

• the reduction and binding of tariffs, whereby they are lowered and ceilings set on maximum rates
• the liberalisation of quantitative restrictions (QRs), eliminating export-constricting and, in particular, complex import-licensing schemes
• more disciplined recourse to GATT Article XVIII:B—a set of special rules that permit developing countries to apply temporary import protection in the event of severe balance-of-payments difficulties
• increased participation in the Tokyo Round Codes and Agreements, which requires adherence to internationally agreed practices on dumping, subsidies, and government procurement, for example
• voluntary reviews under the GATT's new Trade Policy Review Mechanism (TPRM).

Steps to Freer Trade

What were the trade regimes against which these developments can be judged? Most developing countries have tended to use high and wide-ranging tariffs, without setting limits on the highest permissible rates (known as 'tariff bindings'), and without complying adequately with basic GATT requirements on the notification of tariff practices. As a result, heavy effective rates of protection have held back the buoyancy of their trade sectors.

Over the last five years, no fewer than 31 developing countries have notified the GATT of comprehensive tariff reforms; and about one-third of them made commitments to bind at least some portion of their tariffs. This highly diversified group includes not only well-recognised liberalising countries such as Chile, Korea, and Mexico but also countries that had previously maintained complex, inward-oriented trade regimes and whose participation in the GATT had been minimal, such as Bangladesh, Ghana and The Gambia.

In addition to tariffs, QRs have been used heavily by the large majority of developing countries to control imports. These measures have hurt exporters and consumers especially and have locked in the transfer of rents from trade controls into inefficient sectors that are frequently the preserve of a few privileged companies. Since such restrictions in most LDCs have been overlapping and non-transparent (making transactions in those countries much more costly than world prices would call for), increased compliance with GATT requirements on notification (which makes import barriers explicit and thus exposes them to international pressure), as well as the continuing liberalisation of QRs, are an important sign of progress.

Of the 28 countries freeing QRs, nearly half have abolished their import-licensing systems, which prohibited imports unless special, often costly, permits were acquired. These systems, a pervasive form of QR in LDCs, curtailed both imports and exports, worsened inflation, and expanded the scope for corruption.

One of the Articles of the GATT constitution—Article XVIII:B—permits developing countries, if they respect certain conditions, to use QRs when they are experiencing balance-of-payments difficulties. In a turn-around from previous attitudes, many LDCs are now agreeing to set time-limits on the duration of the restrictions imposed and to transform remaining QRs into price-based measures (such as tariffs that reflect changes in world prices). They are also better disposed towards GATT rules that call for increased reliance on macroeconomic and structural-adjustment policies—in place of import restrictions—to address balance-of-payments difficulties.

Over the past five years 14 countries have informed the GATT of reforms to eliminate QRs that were previously imposed to help their balance of payments. Of these, six—Argentina, Brazil, Colombia, Ghana, South Korea and Peru—have agreed entirely to give up their right to use Article XVIII:B. Since only one LDC had ever renounced this privilege before the Uruguay Round, this trend marks an unprecedented development.

Agreements on Openness

Another feature which enhances and broadens the participation of the LDCs in the GATT institutional framework is their increased adherence to its various Codes and Agreements (such as the Code on Anti-dumping and the Agreement on Government Procurement). These date from the Tokyo Round (1973–79) and are the only GATT vehicles for regulating and reducing non-tariff barriers in certain areas.

Before the Uruguay Round, very few developing countries had signed even one of the Codes and Agreements, most preferring to remain as observers in these GATT bodies but unable to influence the rules and decisions being made there. Now, nine countries have taken steps to increase their participation in the Codes and Agreements.

In the case of the Code on Anti-dumping, for example, more active participation from LDCs brings their own domestic rules against dumping in line with internationally agreed legislation. All international trading partners thus gain from the stimulus to world trade that the wider application of consistent and liberal trading rules provides.

The Trade Policy Review Mechanism, one of the results of the Uruguay Round in the first half of 1989, has established a regular process whereby the full range of a country's trade policies and practices is evaluated for its impact on the multilateral trading system. After a first review, which is voluntary, a country agrees to undergo a cycle of regular reviews—every two years for the four largest trading entities (the EC counting as one); every four years for the next 16 largest trading entities; and every six years for all others except the least developed countries, which may apply a more flexible cycle. Since the TPRM began to function eleven LDCs have held a first review, and another eight countries are scheduled for examination shortly. Influential at home and abroad, these reviews have revealed the extent to which all these countries' policies and practices have been moving towards more open markets.

Most developing countries entered the 1980s with a legacy of heavily protectionist trade regimes that constrained their trade and growth. The extent to which they have turned to the GATT system to anchor their trade reforms is one of the most important developments alongside results of the Uruguay Round negociations. The liberalisation process is a long one, and the risks of a setback are ever-present. But if this new trend can be sustained, the engagement of all the trading partners of the globe offers an enormous opportunity for the improvement of living standards throughout the world.

OECD Bibliography

• **Regional Integration and Developing Countries,** forthcoming 1992
• **Integration of Developing Countries into the International Trading System,** 1992
• **Trade in Services and Developing Countries,** 1989.

Benefits and beggars

Dick Wilson

Dick Wilson is a London-based journalist and author specialising in Asian affairs.

The virtual collapse or indefinite postponement of the Uruguay Round of the Gatt may arouse new interest in the generalised system of preferences (GSP). Enthusiasm for the GSP has steadily waned since it was hailed in the 1970s as a vital reform of world trading to help developing countries earn more foreign exchange. As such, it gave a useful boost to the Asian NICs.

Delegates at the eighth UN Conference on Trade and Development (Unctad) in Cartagena de Indias, Colombia, in February went through the motions of calling for improvements in the GSP. But the special committee on preferences is not expected to make much headway at its annual meeting in Geneva on 18 May.

Unctad puts the annual trade now covered by the GSP scheme at more than US$60 billion. But a new OECD [Organization for Economic Cooperation and Development] report estimates additional trade attributable to the GSP at less than 0.5% of total OECD imports, or only 1.5% of total exports from developing countries.

OECD countries import US$370 billion a year from the GSP beneficiaries. But a substantial part of that amount has never been subject to duty, even before the GSP, and another part is excluded for policy reasons. A third part could have benefited theoretically, but did not qualify for technical reasons. The result is that only about US$70 billion worth of goods actually enjoys the benefit of the GSP. That is equivalent to only US$20 a year of extra imports per head of population in the developing countries. Hardly a revolution in trade.

The utilisation by developing countries of what is on offer under the GSP has not increased. In 1988, the latest year for which the calculation is available, the utilisation rate was the lowest ever.

The GSP is complicated, unpredictable and controlled essentially by importers.

East Asian countries have been the principal beneficiaries of the GSP. The most successful—the so-called "tiger" economies of Singapore, Hongkong, South Korea and Taiwan—are now being "graduated" from the scheme. The US has already removed the four Asian NICs, and Australia will do the same in July.

The EC will wait until the Uruguay Round is settled, meanwhile extending its scheme on a yearly basis. It wants to graduate the NICs from the scheme, but to sweeten the move by withdrawing GSP quotas.

In a 1986 report for Unctad, Prof. Craig MacPhee concluded that small companies in the NICs would suffer from being excluded from GSP benefits, while big ones would be able to relocate by investment in Southeast Asia and China. And that, in fact, is what has happened. The GSP is one of the motives for Northeast Asian manufacturing investment in Southeast Asia, especially in Malaysia, Thailand and Indonesia.

But is the GSP so crucial to corporate success? When the scheme was born in 1971, average tariff rates on manufactures in the major Western markets were as high as 15%. Gatt rounds have lowered that level to around 3–4%, and to enjoy a preferential nil-entry over that kind of wall is not nearly so attractive.

It is true that the manufactures in which developing countries tend to specialise are usually protected at a somewhat higher level, some of them in the 10–12% range. But the rate of take-up is still so low that it may be questioned whether these arrangements are really worth the enormous administrative effort they involve.

Certainly Taiwan, which has been the Cinderella of the NICs in terms of qualifying for GSP privileges, does not seem to have suffered from their denial: its economy is overflowing with foreign exchange. Hongkong officials say that only about 2% of the colony's textile and garments exports to the EC qualify for GSP, and yet the volume of earnings has been maintained.

The GSP was meant to bridge the trade gaps of poorer countries, but when that appeared too ambitious a goal, the new rationalisation was to encourage investment in their industries, and strengthen business ties to help their development.

But the scheme is complicated, hedged about with exceptions, exclusions and cutoffs, too unpredictable for inexperienced exporters to cope with, and controlled essentially by importers.

By accepting charity, the developing countries found themselves in the beggar's role in the Gatt when they could have aimed at the status of equal negotiating partners. The new OECD

Reprinted by permission from *Far Eastern Economic Review,* March 19, 1992, p. 44.

report reads like a premature obituary, regretting that the developing world invested so much effort in a scheme which "produced less promising results than initially expected," with trade flows concentrated on "a handful of less developed countries that had already become successful exporters."

Unfortunately, there is no international machinery by which a fair and orderly review of "graduation" can be carried out. Few would deny that the NICs received more than they deserved or needed, at least by comparison with the rest of the developing world.

Now the Southeast Asian countries and China will be the next group of significant beneficiaries, but with the value of the GSP seriously eroded. Even if the Uruguay Round continues to be stalled, the extension of free trade areas in North America and Europe, and the application of the GSP to Eastern Europe, even to countries which used to give preferences, will further weaken the benefit.

The late Harry Johnson, that guru of development, said 25 years ago that the GSP would be useless without drastic reform of currency overvaluation and of protectionist import substitution, which were making poorer countries uncompetitive in the first place. He has now been proved right, and Southeast Asia is following his advice, as international pressure builds up for developing economies to become more competitive through their own efforts rather than by relying on artificial and demeaning preferential treatment.

Trade liberalisation, carefully accompanied by ordered economic deregulation, is now the recipe for progress. Funeral notices for the GSP may be premature, but its future as a major prop for economic development is highly doubtful.

In Mexico, Nafta Isn't Just About Trade

The pro-American Government has risked its future with a skeptical public.

Tim Golden

Mexico City

If any more evidence were needed of his huge stake in the North American Free Trade Agreement, President Carlos Salinas de Gortari offered it generously as negotiations finally came to an end.

After insisting that they would never accept trade sanctions to enforce their environmental and labor laws, Mexican officials agreed to American demands for such penalties in the supplemental accords announced Aug. 13. When that wasn't enough for some congressmen in Washington, Mr. Salinas promised to give millions of Mexican workers a pay raise by linking the minimum wage to productivity.

No one ever said the trade agreement—which has been approved by the Canadian Parliament and is expected to be approved in Mexico soon—would be a partnership of equals. But as the prospects have seemed to darken for its approval in the United States Congress this fall, some supporters of the pact have begun to argue its importance for Mexico in almost apocalpytic terms: The future of a stable, responsible, pro-American government here now hangs in the balance, they say.

As it became evident that the side accords had failed to win over skeptical House Democrats, Mexico's trade envoy in Washington suggested bluntly that the United States might as well choose between the agreement and political uncertainty in Mexico. The official, Hermann von Bertrab, said that after 64 years of uninterrupted rule by Mr. Salinas's Institutional Revolutionary Party, so much as a delay in the trade pact could spell defeat for his chosen successor (Mexican presidents cannot be re-elected).

Gov. Ann Richards of Texas was less coy. A rejection of the agreement would so enrage Mexicans, she said, that "some very serious disturbances" could be expected in Mexico and along the border.

Few people in Mexico dispute that a defeat on Capitol Hill this fall would bring Mr. Salinas's most important initiative crashing down at a singularly bad time. Yet the strength and scope of the expected anti-American backlash are hard to predict.

NO TURNING BACK

To some analysts here, the same economic and political forces that have moved Mexico toward the trade pact make serious upheaval almost unthinkable. Chances of an abrupt reversal of the economic course Mr. Salinas has followed since taking office in 1988 are considered equally remote. Even if his party loses the election, the analysts say, it seems unlikely that its leftist or rightist opposition could re-nationalize the state companies that have been privatized, resume the wild, deficit spending of the past, or turn sharply away from the United States.

"The end of his presidency would be a failure—that's the essential problem," said Federico Estevez, a political scientist at the Autonomous Technological Institute of Mexico. "But I'm not sure that you can push back the reforms regardless of who comes to power next year." Mr. Estevez, a supporter of the agreement, added: "I would like to argue that we'll fall apart, but we won't fall apart."

The trade agreement began as a great gamble for Mr. Salinas in a country of legendary nationalism, and he has raised his bet considerably over the last year. Though his aides have sometimes sought to downplay the pact's importance, calling it just one of many steps in Mexico's transformation, Mr. Salinas has sold it assiduously to wary countrymen, promising that only more jobs and better pay can come of it. He has endured the humiliation

Basics of the Accord

What's in It

The Nafta agreement, initialed by President Bush last year and blessed by the Clinton Administration last week, would bring Mexico into a free-trade area with the United States and Canada.

Mexican tariffs against American products currently average about 13 percent, while American tariffs against Mexican goods average 6 percent. But they are complemented by a host of non-tariff restrictions on everything from blue jeans to frozen orange juice concentrate.

Not all barriers would fall on Jan. 1, 1994. Some of the most sensitive—for example, Mexico's restrictions on imported auto parts—would be phased out over a decade. And "import surge" protocols would allow breathing spells for domestic industries devastated by foreign competition. But according to the Administration, half of all American exports would have open access to Mexico on Day One.

Winner and Losers

The rapidly modernizing Mexican economy is a big importer of machines and commodities—what Americans produce best. Since Mexico is already relatively open to these goods, the agreement itself would probably only have a modest impact on American sales. But locking into place President Carlos Salinas de Gortari's commitment to free markets, internal and external, would assure a long-term boost to American industries ranging from aircraft to grain to telephone equipment. And by keeping Mexico's growth on track, it would probably serve many other American industries that would be slaking Mexican consumers' thirst for the material life.

The pact is striking because it marries economies with vastly different levels of wages and productivity. Jobs and profits would undoubtedly be lost in labor-intensive, low-wage American industries including apparel, shoes and household glassware. But Ross Perot's "giant sucking sound" of jobs and investments flowing south is likely to be muffled because the Mexican economy is tiny compared to the U.S. one. Even in the most optimistic scenarios for Mexican growth, it will remain a minor player in most American markets for decades.

In any case, Mexican industry already has relatively easy access to American consumers, as do producers in low-wage countries from Thailand to Turkey. So, for that matter, do illegal Mexican immigrants, who by consensus constitute greater competition for low-wage American jobs than do legal Mexican imports.

Gary Hufbauer, an economist at the Institute for International Economics, estimates that the job growth in American high-wage industries will initially exceed job losses in low-wage industries because exports to Mexico are growing so rapidly. And if the past is a good measure, there will be little or no net impact on jobs as markets redeploy redundant workers to more competitive American industries.

Other Sticking Points

Environmentalists worry that Mexican industrial pollution will poison the American side of the border, as well as fouling Mexico's air and water. American unions have jumped on the regulatory bandwagon, pointing to Mexico's malign neglect of working conditions.

It is not clear, though, why the accord would undermine the environment or labor standards; indeed, trade and investment liberalization would probably reduce cross-border pollution since it would end the artificial concentration of industry in free-trade border zones. Still, the Clinton Administration has worked to defuse the issues, writing side agreements providing for watchdog groups to monitor compliance with national laws.

Another challenge—one with no political teeth—comes from economists who are troubled by the rise of regional trade blocs. They fear that an open border with Mexico would divert more cost-reducing trade with Asia and Eastern Europe. And they wonder whether the North American economic alliance will spur Japan to form a competing bloc on the other side of the Pacific.

The Bumpy Road to Approval

Canada's Parliament has already approved the treaty and Mexico's soon will. Current betting is that Nafta will have a relatively easy time in the United States Senate but will face sharp elbows in the House.

Ross Perot is rallying the opposition, tarring the treaty as a symbol of Washington's indifference to Joe Sixpack. Some environmental groups also remain opposed to it. And the House majority leader, Richard Gephardt, has expressed dissatisfaction with the final package. The contest may turn on the ability of the White House to limit defections among Democrats who have ties to organized labor or to business constituents threatened by Mexican competition.

But the White House's promised lobbying blitz could still be stalled before it has a chance to be tested. A Federal judge ruled last month that treaty approval required an environmental impact statement. If the Justice Department loses the appeal, movement on Nafta could be frozen for months or years.

PETER PASSELL

of a series of policy reversals that have followed fast on criticism from the United States. And to a Mexican audience that understands little about separation of powers, rogue legislators or other ways of Washington, he has explained little, insisting that the agreement's passage is inevitable.

The starkest risk, though, remains economic. Last year, in trying to overhaul its oil-centered export base and opening its borders to a flood of foreign goods at the same time, Mexico ran up a deficit of $22.8 billion in its current account, the broadest measure of trade. Even with the Government budget running a surplus, the country counts heavily on foreign investment to cover the shortfall; it counts on the promise of a trade pact to draw and hold the investment.

The consequences of the agreement's failure would depend on how it failed. But whether the pact was flatly rejected by Congress or merely delayed beyond Jan. 1, when it is supposed to take effect, many economists say the disruption could spook foreign investors, especially those with relatively liquid assets like stocks and treasury bills. Because imports cannot be stanched as quickly as those funds can flow back abroad, the current-account deficit would probably rise. Most economists think the Mexican peso is overvalued already. A more serious trade imbalance would raise the pressure for a politically costly devaluation in order to make Mexican exports cheaper and foreign imports more expensive.

"I think the failure of Nafta would lead to a devaluation," said Sidney Weintraub, a political economist at the University of Texas. "But that wouldn't have an immediate effect in containing imports." He and others expect the Salinas Administration would therefore have to restrict imports as well in order to hold down the trade imbalance.

Given the likelihood that some Mexicans would demand retaliation if American legislators rejected the agreement, imports from the United States would be an obvious target. But several Mexican officials said a more serious reversal in the country's relationship with the partner that accounts for more than two-thirds of its trade would be disastrous. Without an agreement, Mexico would need foreign investors more than ever, they noted, and would probably have to open the economy further to attract them.

Aides to Mr. Salinas say that with Mexicans still divided over the trade accord, he is anxious that the Presidential election not turn into a referendum on the issue. Some analysts say the agreement's failure could also shape his crucial decision on which of the quietly rivalrous aides he will nominate to succeed him. And although no governing party candidate has ever lost, the moment has traditionally been one of gathering political tensions, one when presidencies that once seemed glorious begin to grow lame and collapse.

In theory, an opposition candidate like Cuauhtémoc Cárdenas, the leftist who nearly beat Mr. Salinas in 1988, might seize such a moment. In practice, however, Mr. Cárdenas's party has lost so much support that many political analysts doubt that even a failed trade agreement could lift it to the threshold of power again. Then there is another point militating against the sort of disaster that supporters of the trade agreement have begun to foresee: Privately, at least, aides to Mr. Cárdenas say he has no interest in becoming the new champion of anti-Americanism, or even necessarily the new slayer of free trade.

Rethinking development: A market-friendly strategy for the poor

Amy L. Sherman

Amy L. Sherman *is editor of* Stewardship Journal. *This article is adapted from her recent book,* Preferential Option: A Christian and Neoliberal Strategy for Latin America's Poor *(Eerdmans).*

WITH THE FALL of the Berlin Wall, worldwide attention has focused on the democratic revolution in world politics. But another revolution, an economic one, is also altering once-familiar territory. Under its influence, other walls—those erected against free markets and free trade in the name of socialist and statist forms of development—are gradually being torn down. Throughout the underdeveloped world and especially in Latin America, governments are trying to convert their state-centered economies into capitalist ones. And just as the political revolution has stimulated much rethinking about East-West issues, so the market revolution requires reassessments of international development and the North-South debate.

Though in some Third World (and formerly Second World) countries economic reforms are more talk than reality, most of the developing world is rethinking economic strategies. The trend is away from state-centered models of development and toward an appreciation of free-market principles. The phrase "structural adjustment," ubiquitous in the late '80s and early '90s, has been coined to capture this transformation. Some less-developed countries (LDCs) have achieved important successes; others are struggling to swallow the bitter medicine of economic austerity. Average citizens in countries undergoing adjustment feel it—some quite keenly. Traveling in Poland and Guatemala last summer, I heard plenty of complaints about spiraling food prices and unemployment.

Obvious suffering and hardship in underdeveloped countries struggling to implement market-friendly reforms has some people in the U.S. religious community questioning whether the transition is a good idea at all. With the popular and decisive rejection of socialism throughout Eastern Europe, observers can hardly champion Marxist-oriented strategies that allegedly benefit the poor. But few are willing to embrace the market either. Longed for instead is that attractive but all-too-elusive "third way" between capitalism and socialism that somehow would be both humane and efficient.

Unfortunately, no such third way exists. Attempts to create one in many LDCs resulted mostly in the establishment of various forms of "statism"—less brutal and usually less ideological versions of a government-controlled economy than their cousin, communism. Statist models, like their relative, have gone bankrupt; indeed, many of the Third World's economic woes today can be traced to their misguided policies. Frustration within the LDCs and among the international development institutions (World Bank, International Monetary Fund) over the failures of statism have fueled the reform movement. To understand why the statist model proved so detrimental to the poor and why market reforms are necessary, it is important to clarify statism and the motives behind it. After all, economic strategies do not emerge in a vacuum but depend on interpretations of economic situations. Economic strategies are implemented in response to these interpretations.

The "statist consensus" grew out of two primary assumptions about the nature of Third World poverty. First, according to this consensus, blame for economic stagnation in the LDCs was assigned largely to exploitive North-South relationships in the global economy. Neocolonial and dependency theory analysis declared that Western colonial powers had first oppressed and pillaged parts of the underdeveloped world and then, after the independence period, continued with such expropriation through unfair trading practices. Development in industrialized countries actually "created" underdevelopment in the LDCs. In other words, the rich countries were rich *because* the poor countries were poor. Moreover, they were kept poor because the industrialized countries controlled the rules and institutions of the global economic order and manipulated them to their advantage. Trading relations between the North and South were beneficial to the former only at the expense of the latter. The South exported cheap raw materials with steadily deteriorating prices but at the same time had to import ever more expensive manufactured goods from the North.

Second, this consensus interpretation maintained that if an LDC's poverty was attributable to problems within its own domestic economy, the chief systemic distortion could quickly be identified as the internal "capitalist" economic structure that benefited wealthy oligarchs at the expense of the masses. Inequitable income distribution was seen as the clearest reflection of this deformation, and unemployment, rural poverty and worker exploitation were counted as its common side-effects.

These assumptions contained half-truths but missed much of the story. Colonialism brought with it multiple woes but several economic benefits as well—including the development of an infrastructure, the seeds of an education and health system, and new technologies. If colonial policies had produced unmitigated disaster for the colonies, we would expect that the countries with the greatest sustained contact with the Western powers would today be the least well-off. In fact, the poorest LDCs are those that have had the least contact.

Similarly, if trade relations between the North and South were exclusively beneficial to the North, we would expect that those developing countries with the greatest export orientation and extensive trade relations would be most exploited by the global economy. Instead, the economic miracles of the developing world—the countries that, like the East Asian "tigers" of Taiwan, Hong Kong, Singapore and South Korea, have graduated out of underdeveloped status, or the countries like Chile, Malaysia and Thailand that are on the way toward doing so—are those countries that most aggressively traded in the international market.

Nonetheless, the glaring contradiction between the opulence of the industrialized nations and the economic despair of the LDCs inevitably produced a sense that the two are somehow casually related. When idealistic leaders in Africa and Asia came to power in the '50s and '60s they—like those in Latin America a few decades earlier—surveyed the social ills around them and pushed for an activist response.

ON THE BASIS of such diagnoses of their socioeconomic woes, these governments developed a two-part, state-centered response. First, they advocated that LDCs withdraw as much as possible from what they had determined was an exploitive world economy, pursue "self-sufficiency" and emphasize import-substituting industrialization. Agriculture and an export-oriented economy was to be avoided in favor of significant government involvement in the economy, especially in heavy industry. The idea was to produce necessary goods domestically in order to avoid dependence on trade with the rich countries. This meant, second, that market forces could not be left alone to drive investment and production decisions. Rather, central planning and state-led industrialization through public firms would be necessary. Centralization would bring an added benefit, many believed: the government as employer would, unlike greedy private capitalists, see to it that workers would be protected with adequate salaries, safe working conditions and good benefits. The state, perceived as a neutral entity acting in the public interest, would automatically ensure that national development would benefit all of society's members rather than only the economic elites.

This development strategy was attractive to many observers outside the LDCs, especially those in religious communities. It appeared more humane than free-market strategies because it seemed to put the poor at the center of the development equation, and it forthrightly embraced the state's responsibility to intervene in the economy whenever basic human needs were at stake, and also to prevent exploitation by private capitalists. Such a strategy was also deemed just because it called for more equitable international economic relations, argued for massive resource transfers from the rich countries to the poor ones, and promised to initiate policies within the domestic economy that would affect a redistribution from the wealthy few to the impoverished many. No wonder governments like Julius Nyerere's of Tanzania that proffered a Catholic-inspired "African socialist" development strategy won the applause of many religious Americans. In particular, much of the religious left accepted dependency theory analysis. They blamed the North for the South's poverty and accepted state controls over the economy as a necessary measure to prevent abuses of the poor by capitalists, former oligarchs and foreign multinational corporations.

Tragically, the policies implemented under statist regimes actually worsened the suffering of the poor and brought about the Third World's current severe economic crisis. Statist regimes of varying stripes (populist and mercantilist) undertook several policy initiatives that at first glance seemed compassionate or favorable to the poor. When the actual consequences of such policies are examined, however, it is clear that whatever the good intentions, many people were killed with kindness.

Statist regimes often enforced numerous regulations on economic activity to protect the poor from potential abuses in the private sector. Governments also tried to shield people from exploitation by multinational companies by strictly regulating foreign investment. These regimes in many cases provided publicly sponsored employment for citizens, taxed the rich heavily to produce funds for social spending on health, education and welfare, and instituted minimum-wage laws to protect lower-income workers.

Peruvian author Hernando de Soto was among the first to document systematically the actual effects of such ostensibly "pro-poor" policies. His watershed book *The Other Path* (1989) argued that the government's very efforts to help the poor often did them the most harm. Laws and regulations originally intended to assist the poor and effect wealth redistribution in the society instead lead over time to a concentration of economic power in the hands of government bureaucrats. These officials, controlling all sorts of business permits, licenses, registration documents and titling procedures, could trade these economic goodies for bribes or political favors from wealthy and politically connected businessmen. This regulatory system created innumerable opportunities for collusion between corrupt officials and businessmen. Together they could corner markets, establish monopolies and shut out the poor from access to the formal (the legal or above-ground) economy.

These tactics had the effect of pushing lower-class "micro-entrepreneurs" into the underground or informal economy where they lacked the security of property, access to credit, ability to enforce contracts and opportunities for expansion.

To specify how these 20th-century mercantilist economic structures hurt the poor, De Soto devised a number of experiments in which he proposed different avenues that poor families might take to improve their economic situation. In one experiment De Soto's researchers found that a poor family aspiring to legally establish a small garment business would need 289 days to fulfill all the prescribed bureaucratic steps and $1,231 (32 times the average monthly wage) to pay the required fees and bribes. In his analysis, poor families stayed poor because most of them had neither this kind of time nor money.

Researchers found that a poor family aspiring to legally establish a small garment business would need 289 days to fulfill all the bureaucratic requirements.

MOREOVER, WHEN the social spending of populist regimes in LDCs is carefully analyzed, a picture emerges of state expenditures that benefit the urban middle and upper classes, not the poorest of the poor. The World Bank's Guy Pfeffermann has done extensive analysis of social welfare spending in Latin America and found that much spending that outside observers considered "compassionate" actually benefited the richer citizens at the expense of the poor (*Public Expenditure in Latin America*, 1987).

Some common policies implemented by statist regimes included overvaluing the exchange rate to make imports more affordable, enforcing price ceilings on various products, subsidizing public transportation and curative health care, and investing in higher education. Such policies disproportionately benefit the urban middle and upper classes—they are the only ones with both purchasing power and access to imported goods; they are the ones who make greatest use of public transport; and it is their children who gain from curative health care programs and government-subsidized secondary education. Had populist regimes been more interested in spending public monies in primary education, literacy programs and preventative health care efforts in impoverished rural areas, their pro-poor rhetoric would have been more credible. As it was, the social spending that did occur led to bloated public deficits that in turn fueled an inflation that hurt the poorest the hardest. Government manipulation of exchange rates may have protected domestic firms, but these were owned by middle- and upper-class citizens and provided employment to the best-off workers in the society—unionized white, pink and blue collar. Meanwhile, such policies hurt the two economic sectors in which the poor are most highly represented: the labor-intensive export sector and agriculture.

Additionally, overregulation of the economy by state bureaucrats produced innumerable inefficiencies that blocked economic growth. A major source of inefficiency was precisely the government's clout in the economic realm: economic decisions were most often made on the basis of political considerations. Management positions in state-owned enterprises were given not to the most competent individuals but to those who were owed a political favor. Even when the detrimental effects of excessive social spending on public budgets was clear, populist government leaders dependent on the urban, middle-class vote did not dare to cut back and live within the government's means. Meanwhile, legal companies without privileged political access wasted hundreds of hours and dollars bogged down in red-tape procedures that provided make-work for innumerable and unnecessary civil servants. Money that these firms could have used to find new jobs or make better, more competitive products was simply wasted.

Other allegedly compassionate policies common to nonmarket economies oppressed the poor with similar force. On the premise that the capitalist world economy exploited Third World farmers, populist LDC governments instituted state marketing boards as the sole legal purchasers of domestic crops. This was supposed to provide a sure and steady market for poor farmers. In reality it impoverished them, since they were inevitably offered below-market prices for their goods and were forbidden from selling them in markets where they could obtain a better price. This discouraged agricultural production, encouraged urban migration, and in some instances created food shortages. Under the influence of statist policies, some LDCs that had been net food exporters became net food importers. On the premise that the poor must be protected from exploitation by employers, many governments instituted minimum-wage laws and various other regulations restricting a firm's ability to fire employees. These benefits were a boon to the few employees who could actually get jobs, but exacerbated the problems of the unemployed. Under such regulations firms could not afford to hire as many people as they might have, and inefficient workers had to be kept in order to avoid state-imposed penalties for discharging them. This continued the cycle of business incompetence, economic stagnation and high unemployment.

LDC governments also imposed price controls on basic necessities such as bread and milk in order to keep their cost affordable to society's more needy members. Again, this seemingly compassionate policy created a nightmare for the underclass. Since price controls were set below market-clearing prices, producers of the goods lacked incentive to increase production, some went bankrupt, and others gave up and moved to the cities. Shortages ensued which in turn offered windfall opportunities for unscrupulous government officials and black-marketeers. In situations of scarcity it was rarely the poor and politically voiceless who gained access to needed goods; rather this was the privilege of the rich and powerful. They consumed what they needed and sold what they didn't to the poor and the black market, where prices were far higher than they would have been without price controls.

The failures of the statist approach have become so obvious in the last several years that even before the fall of the Berlin Wall which signaled the death of socialism, various LDCs were beginning to implement market-oriented reform. Since 1989 this trend has accelerated.

NO ONE DOUBTS that the transition from statist to market-friendly economies will take years and will produce social dislocations and hardships. Structural adjustments designed to achieve the transition such as pruning government bureaucracies, privatizing inefficient state-owned companies, rationalizing the exchange rate, decontrolling prices, cutting social spending, are bitter medicines. But they may not be as bitter for the poor as is often assumed. Social services and social spending that are being cut back typically benefited the middle and upper classes, not the poor, and it is these relatively better-off citizens who feel their absence the most. This is not to say, of course, that the poor too do not experience the pains of structural adjustment. Yet accompanying the question of who suffers is a further important question about the causes of such suffering. Some observers of the anguish in LDCs now undergoing austerity programs have failed to distinguish between suffering caused by the adjustment measures themselves, suffering caused by the misguided statist policies that made adjustment necessary in the first place, and suffering caused by the delay or abandonment of the reform measures.

Further, agreement on solutions to the economic problems of LDCs is hampered to a significant degree by a tendency to mislabel failed options. Mercantilist policies can be considered, loosely, as the right-wing version of statism; populist policies as the left-wing version. Stripped of the different rhetoric used by their implementors, both sets of policies are largely the same in form and consequence. Unfortunately, mercantilist regimes such as Marcos's in the Philippines and Somoza's in Nicaragua were often mislabeled as "capitalist." Their economic systems were undeniably unfair, exploitive and discriminatory—but they weren't capitalist. This mislabeling has produced a tragic and unwarranted suspicion of free-market policies. In contrast to what many in the religious left believe, the problem in the impoverished LDCs is not too much capitalism, but too little.

A better way to help the poor would be to affirm what the empirical record suggests, that market-friendly systems offer the best long-term prospects for development, and to encourage initiatives designed to temper the pains of adjustment and protect the poorest members of society during the difficult transition years. When a woman is diagnosed with cancer, her friends may lament the suffering she must endure in chemotherapy treatments, but they are unlikely to discourage her from undergoing the very activity that may cure her. Instead they busy themselves babysitting the children, bringing in meals, cleaning the house and helping pay the doctor's bills. Third World governments, First World governments, the international development institutions and private development agencies can do analogous things. Governments in the LDCs need not adopt a radically laissez-faire attitude during the transition to the market. The point is to remove government's involvement from the economic activities it does poorly and at the expense of private actors, and to shift its energies into the tasks which government must perform if market reforms are to work. These include rebuilding infrastructure, clearly defining and defending property and contract rights, and funding preventative health care and primary education.

The industrialized countries can help too. First, they can bring the Uruguay Round of GATT talks to a successful close and begin the process of reducing tariff barriers and dismantling protectionist arrangements such as the Multi-Fibre Agreement and the European Community's coordinated agricultural policy. These policies discriminate against exports of food and textiles from the underdeveloped countries, hurting the poor and making it difficult for LDCs to shift toward an export-oriented development strategy.

Second, the rich countries can offer debt relief to the LDC governments most tenaciously implementing structural adjustment measures. Debt relief should be used as a reward for those countries making the most progress in moving toward the market. Progress can be measured, for example, by a country's success in reducing the public deficit, privatizing para-state enterprises, opening up to foreign investment, rationalizing the exchange rate, decreasing military spending and legalizing informal enterprise.

Third, the North can significantly increase foreign aid specifically earmarked for support of quasigovernmental or nongovernmental institutions established to mitigate the social costs of adjustment. As a result of Bolivia's successful Emergency Social Fund, social-adjustment funds are becoming more common in LDCs undertaking the transition to the market. These funds in essence function as philanthropic foundations. They make grants to local governments and community associations, NGOs, church groups and other private actors who design and implement projects aimed at

Third World governments must redirect public funds toward the mediating structures: community groups and church-led development projects.

meeting the special circumstances attending structural adjustment. With such economic adjustment, societies need to increase private health care services in light of government cutbacks, to retrain workers, to provide credit and training to microentrepreneurs, and to make allowances for low-wage emergency employment, most likely in construction projects, to the poorest of the poor. When Western aid money is channeled directly to funds that provide for such circumstances, less is wasted on administrative overhead, less is siphoned off by corrupt government officials, and more gets into the hands of local associations in touch with real needs.

IN SHORT, Third World governments must reconceive their social responsibilities and redesign their policies to show a healthy respect for the energies of the private sector. They must also redirect public funds to provide aid—without stifling bureaucracy and regulation—to the mediating structures of civil society: local nongovernmental organizations, community groups, church-led development projects and so on. Less government is needed in many areas of public life; more, better and more efficient government is needed in other areas. It is imperative that governments shift from their urban bias and carefully target their social welfare support to the poorest members of society, who usually are rural residents. Only in this way can the twin goals of poverty alleviation and structural adjustment (trimming public budgets) be served. Chile has led the way in such efforts and demonstrated that "marketization" of the economy and poverty alleviation can proceed simultaneously.

While General Pinochet's policies of political repression were condemnable, his economic policies did bring about what Chileans call their economic miracle. Chile has adopted a comprehensive surveying and targeting strategy which carefuly directs social welfare expenditure to the poorest 30 percent of the population. Consequently, absolute poverty has been reduced—from 21 percent of the population so classified in 1973 to 14 percent in 1988. Chile's inflation rate and unemployment rate (5 percent) are among the lowest in Latin America. Chile also boasts the best or second-best performance in a variety of social welfare indicators. Life expectancy there is 71 years, infant mortality is 22 per thousand, and over 90 percent of Chilean children are immunized against the typical childhood diseases. Almost the entire urban population (97 percent) and 82 percent of the rural population has access to safe drinking water. Most impressively, Chile has accomplished this in the midst of radical and long-term restructuring of its economy and with a far smaller expenditure than its neighbors. With an eye on Chile's success, other LDC governments are now signaling they want to imitate its economic policies (while shunning Pinochet's politics). But governments willing to shift their expenditures from traditional urban constituencies to the poorest third of their populations need financial help and encouragement from the West. The poorest people are typically politically weak, while the urban middle and upper classes are well organized and vocal, making life uncomfortable for democratically elected reformers. The international development community and the West must show their solidarity with those leaders willing to pursue fiscally prudent and socially responsible policies that are unpopular with urban elites who are used to preferential treatment.

The choice by LDCs to implement such a two-pronged strategy of market reforms and highly targeted poverty alleviation will be much easier to achieve in the context of a growing world economy and decreasing protectionism on the part of the industrialized countries. It will also be encouraged by timely, carefully targeted and generous Western aid aimed at underwriting social adjustment funds that work to mitigate the worst woes of austerity and help sustain public support for the painful but necessary reforms. The economic lessons learned from the past 40-some years of development experience are clear. What remains to be seen is whether the LDCs have the political will to implement those lessons, and whether the West has the will to adopt the complementary policies that can make the capitalist revolution of the late 20th century one that produces economic growth which benefits the world's poor.

A response to 'Rethinking development'

Michael J. Francis

Michael J. Francis *is a professor of government and international studies at the University of Notre Dame and the author of a number of works on U.S. policy toward Latin America, including* The Limits of Hegemony *and* The Victory of Allende.

Amy Sherman's "Rethinking Development" strikes me as a particularly enlightened and lucid statement of the neoliberal economic prescription for Third World development. I agree with her that a strong private sector is necessary for economic growth, that "statist" policies have been unsuccessful in the Third World, that populist governments tended to benefit the middle and upper classes rather than the poor, and that the poor need protection against the rigors of developing the kind of private sector necessary to compete in the world economy. On the other hand, troublesome aspects of her analysis, and of neoliberal economic solutions generally, raise pointed issues about social justice in the Third World.

It is well that we begin by noting that the idea of free markets as the path to economic development is far from new. In the 1920s and '30s Washington was encouraging missions to Latin America to set up commercial systems that would stimulate trade-driven growth. The Eisenhower administration consistently preached free enterprise to the Third World, and John F. Kennedy's Alliance for Progress was heavily dependent on private investment.

We are now back in one of those historical cycles in which free market (neoliberal) solutions have become the dominant ideology. This ideology's ascendancy is due in part to a widely held interpretation of the U.S.S.R.'s disintegration: it fell apart, many believe, because of the inherent weaknesses of central planning. But this interpretation is reinforced by pressure from international lending and assistance agencies which, not incidentally, largely represent the First World's vision of the future and the First World's interests.

We need to remind ourselves that victories such as the West's in the cold war may solve some problems, but they inevitably create others. Unless history has suddenly "ended," it is probable that the popularity of dictatorial politics will eventually return (perhaps linked to the failure of democracy), and what are now seen as bankrupt statist economic solutions will re-emerge perhaps out of frustrations that inevitably confront capitalist development. The popularity of political and economic ideas ebbs and flows like the tides, and right now it is high tide for democracy (at least in terms of public pronouncements) and capitalism (again, in terms of rhetoric). My nightmare is that the present euphoria of victory may lead us to make human sacrifices—the poor of the Third World—to a god of neoliberalism that won't deliver the goods.

We should not, therefore, stand aside and ignore the debate over economic development in the Third World. Important issues of morality and self-interest cannot be shrugged off by those of us in the developed world. Because the stakes are so high, then, I'd like to raise five issues or questions that bear on Sherman's perspective.

First, we should remind ourselves that the link between democracy and capitalism is not a direct one. There is such a thing as democratic socialism—Sweden, for example. Unfortunately, in their effort to make debating points, zealots of laissez-faire economics (a group in which I would *not* place Sherman) have tried to argue that democracy naturally equates with free enterprise and that virtually all state economic regulation is communism. Sherman does come quite close to making that claim when she talks about the fall of the Soviet empire.

Second, the flat statement that no third way exists between capitalism and socialism, implying that we must be one or the other, strikes me as much too dogmatic. In the real world a wide variety of capitalisms have taken root in various countries, as have a wide range of socialisms. At some point these overlap. Apparently Sherman's definition of a third or middle way demands that it be an economic system completely different from socialism or capitalism. If that is what she means, then perhaps (although I can't be sure) there is no third way. If we are merely talking about some mixture of the two, however, then the world is full of such alternatives.

Third, much of the recent literature glorifying the effectiveness of the market implies that governments necessarily make poor economic decisions. Sherman's discussion is littered with examples of inept governments and failed statist developmental schemes. I would be the last person to defend the efficiency, honesty or representative nature of many Third World governments, but the problem of effective governance cannot be ignored by giving the market a free rein. Efforts to help these governments improve themselves are at least as important as nurturing a healthy private sector. You cannot solve economic problems without first solving some political problems, despite what neoliberal economists imply. Furthermore, before we accept the idea that governments necessarily make irrational or ill-advised decisions, it should be pointed out that some governments have shown good economic judgment. The Japanese and the Germans—to name today's high-flying examples—have made some sound economic decisions over the past four decades. So to proceed on the assumption, implicit or explicit, that governments can't by their very nature make reasonable economic choices strikes me as an exaggeration. One confuses inept governments (one kind of problem) with the difficulties of socialism (a different kind of problem).

Fourth, Sherman cites the success stories of capitalist development: Taiwan, Hong Kong, Singapore, South Korea, Chile, Malaysia, Thailand. However, even when one looks at the specifics in each of these cases, the reality often doesn't resemble the neoliberal stereotype of a government that merely stands aside and lets the market reign. In fact, these governments were often quite actively setting conditions for investment, keeping unions in check, developing educational systems that trained appropriate workers, building infrastructure, selecting some investments over others, providing state-financed inducements for investment and so on. These are not supine states letting the market rule.

My last objection is the most serious. An attractive aspect of Sherman's presentation is that she sees and feels the poor's suffering during the period of an expanding private sector. Unlike some neoliberal commentators, she recognizes that institutions have to be formulated to protect the lower classes. At this point, however, her humane instincts fall victim to her neoliberal economics: she wants the responsibility for social welfare laid substantially on nongovernmental or quasigovernmental institutions, apparently on the grounds that governments can't provide this service. This variation of George Bush's "thousand points of light" goes in the wrong direction: depending on private charity is not the way to build effective safety nets for the poor. We need to see social welfare as an appropriate function of government and assist in constructing and supporting effective welfare systems.

Sherman perceives the need for such governmental activity, but she then lapses into a privatization framework for social welfare that is inappropriate even if her basic point is sound—governments have social responsibilities. As she indicates, many research projects are now looking at what government policies have worked and which have not worked in providing effective protection for the lower classes. This is an admirable direction for research in both political science and economics—certainly far more useful than building abstract mathematical models, which is often the case. The idea that governments do poorly in providing welfare services and that private agencies can do better is not persuasive to me. It is, nevertheless, a topic that needs to be discussed extensively.

I also have a number of small squabbles with Sherman's argument. Is the infamously bureaucratically regulated government of Peru an example of anything other than Peru? Can a minimum wage not be set in such a manner that protects at least a few from exploitation while not pricing potential employees out of the market? Given the fact that Chile's social welfare statistics were excellent by Third World standards prior to Pinochet, does the post-1973 governmental process deserve much credit for these figures today? Furthermore, applying the mercantilist label to Somoza and Marcos strikes me as discrediting a policy that quite fairly applies to the approach of a number of successful capitalist countries, such as Japan.

Sherman's key insight lies in her observation that "governments in the LDCs need not adopt a radically laissez-faire attitude during the transition to the market." One hopes that further discussions will suggest ways of utilizing, and at the same time tempering, the market. We've had quite enough demands for ideologically pure economic models.

Amy L. Sherman replies:

MICHAEL FRANCIS raises some important points about my argument that may be best addressed by clarifying the "neo" in the neoliberal strategy of development. When discussing the cases of the Four East Asian tigers and the newest Newly Industrialized Countries (Chile, Malaysia, Thailand), Francis asserts that they do not "resemble the neoliberal stereotype of a government that merely stands aside and lets the market reign." He is correct in saying that these governments did not stand aside and adopt a laissez-faire policy; he is incorrect in suggesting that the "neoliberal stereotype" is of a government that does. It is precisely the "neo" in the neoliberal philosophy that motivates my statement that "less government is needed in many areas of public life; more, better, and more efficient government is needed in other areas." Francis seems to have missed this.

The "liberal" in neoliberal strategy asserts the imperative of embracing the market mechanism as the most efficient one for ordering production and distribution of resources (a position that Francis acknowledges). The "neo" refers to the imperative for government action. But government action must be reconceived and redirected away from the path followed so often by statist Third World regimes with such disastrous results for the poor. A neoliberal strategy means government investment in infrastructure, "human capital" and nongovernmental provision of social welfare services.

Francis criticizes me for thinking that governments necessarily make irrational decisions, but that is not my position. When governments have control over economic decisions (about supply, price, production and distribution), I maintain that they usually make those decisions on the basis of political calculations rather than market-sensitive economic ones. The problem with statist regimes is that they typically take actions that are economically nonsensical because those actions are politically attractive. This tendency explains the dynamics of urban bias in underdeveloped countries, as Robert Bates argued in his 1981 work, *Markets and States in Tropical Africa: The Political Basis of Agricultural Policies.* Bates explained that "reasonable" government leaders could pursue economic policies obviously harmful to their countries' economies because (a) bureaucrats could personally benefit from some of the decisions (such as increasing their own responsibilities over economic matters and thus controlling economic "goodies" that businessmen are willing to "buy" from them in bribes), and (b) politicians could use economic decisions to win political support, thereby coopting certain public sectors while squeezing others.

Of course, this phenomenon is not limited to the Third World. Some of the policies of the industrialized countries I criticized in my article fall into the same category. New Zealand cheese is cheaper than French cheese, and it makes no economic sense that French people cannot purchase it for less; but the French government has determined that it is politically attractive to subsidize French dairy farmers through protectionist policies against New Zealand cheese. The key point is that this kind of economic irrationality is usually exacerbated whenever political agencies (the state) rather than economic agents (individuals and businesses in the private sector, acting according to market signals) are given increasing responsibility over economic decisions.

Some governments (such as the East Asian NICs) have been capable of making economic decisions that are, on the whole, rational. The interesting question is how they were able to avoid the mistakes of others. One important answer seems to be that these governments utilized competitive exchange rates that kept their economies in touch with the international economy. This measure acted as a disciplining mechanism as well as a source of critical information. But there may be other reasons as well: Did the neo-Confucianist culture and background of these societies predispose them to create better public servants? Did their authoritarian political structure shield them from the problem that populist regimes experience—having to dispense economic benefits to those whose political support is critical? Further reflection along these lines would be most instructive.

FRANCIS IS DISMAYED that I argue for a strong nongovernmental role in mitigating the social dislocations created by transitions to the market. On this point we may have both a theological and a strategic difference of opinion. I think Christians should be reluctant to turn over to the state the task of loving and serving our neighbors, because the state is incapable of treating them as anything other than a faceless mass. If we contend that the government has to be involved because the Christian community has fundamentally failed to meet its responsibilities, we should say this with a sense of regret and a feeling that we are adopting the second-best solution. I do not hear this tone in Francis's statement that "we need to see social welfare as an appropriate function of government and assist in constructing and supporting effective welfare systems." As I read scripture, social welfare appears first as a function of individuals, families and churches, not of government. To the degree that I'm willing to accede to Francis's statement, it is with a heavy heart, not enthusiasm.

Francis seems concerned also that a nongovernmental response will be inadequate strategically. But large-scale help is feasible if we consider the Bolivian Emergency Social Fund model. This program accepted public responsibility for creating a social safety net but limited that responsibility to funding, technical support and regulation. The actual programs for helping people were, for the most part, designed and implemented by private organizations, and over 3 million Bolivians benefited.

WHEN WE AGREE as a society that "something ought to be done about it!"—the "it" being anything from teenage pregnancy to homelessness to underemployment—we need not also agree that the government ought to be the one doing the "something." The successful Chilean outreach to the poorest third of the population suggests the potential of nongovernmental programs. And contrary to Francis's assertion, the success I refer to came *after* 1973. Chile's pre-1973 social welfare statistics were hardly "excellent." According to UNICEF data, in 1973, compared to seven other Latin American countries (Argentina, Brazil, Costa Rica, Colombia, Guatemala, Mexico, Venezuela), Chile ranked near the bottom—sixth place in terms of infant mortality, last in terms of the child death rate, and seventh in terms of access to safe water. In 1987 Chile tied for second place in all these categories. Chile reduced diarrhea mortality from 7.1/1000 live births in 1975 to 0.7/1000 in 1986; it increased potable water services in urban areas from 78 percent of the population served in 1976 to 98 percent served in 1987; and it increased spending on education for the poorest third of the population from 28.6 percent of expenditures in 1974 to 37.5 percent in 1986. (See Tarcicio Castaneda, *Combatting Poverty*, 1992.) Throughout the '80s Chile consistently redirected public expenditure away from university education toward primary education. In short, Chile's neoliberal policies targeted the most needy citizens, reconceived the government's social welfare role by cutting back on direct provision of services and frequently "subcontracting" them to private entities, and simultaneously increased the quality and quantity of such services. The results of these measures show that Chile has reduced absolute poverty in dramatic ways since 1973.

The neoliberal strategy would win more friends if it called itself a "third way." But "third ways" have been either euphemisms for essentially socialist schemes or code names for utopian strategies that propose an economic system (that exists nowhere in the real world) capable, allegedly, of combining the best elements of capitalism and socialism. Sweden is neither a third way, nor neoliberal, nor an example of democratic socialism. It is a capitalist economy with a large government-run welfare state. (It is also a country that is becoming acutely aware that its welfare interventions have eroded some of the positive benefits of its capitalist system.) Francis is right to say that no true capitalism or true socialism exists; what we have is economies that are either "more socialist" or "more capitalist." The neoliberal strategy is emphatically more capitalist, and if more LDCs adopt both its "neo" and "liberal" components, the poor will be the winners.

Still in the missionary position

The fundamentalist west is still preaching to the rest—having swapped its guns and Bibles for the dictates and mantras of the free market, says Jeremy Seabrook

Events . . . in Rio [June 1992] have shown that the most persistent obstacle to any significant agreement at the Earth Summit is coming, not from third world intransigence, not from the unwillingness of some countries to curb population growth, but from the inability of the rich countries to transcend what increasingly looks like a form of western fundamentalism.

Western fundamentalism? Surely there is no such thing. Tolerance, liberty, pluralism, freedom of thought and speech—these are the complete opposite of the values of theocratic tyrannies and totalitarian ideologies. Indeed, the freedoms we enjoy have evolved through a long process of liberation from the controlling revelations of religion, scriptures and absolute truths.

The problem is to recognise the forms of our own fundamentalism. It has deserted Bibles, holy writ and tabernacles, and found more subtle conduits for its truths. The west may have ceased for the most part to impose its superior strength by military conquest on the recalcitrant peoples of the globe, but this does not mean its universalising mission is over. It is simply that the agency of its missionary zeal has changed. Its model of economic development is now a vehicle for fervour; a model that has yielded such wealth in the west that it has now become a source of hope and emulation worldwide.

It was the imposition of apparently irresistible western patterns of development on Iran that drew the fateful response from Islam. Indeed, Islam has been the only force in the world that has resisted modernisation, progress and the western way of wealth; all other societies appear to have gone down without a struggle. Not even communism, that great rival faith, has been able to withstand its superior power. One consequence of this success is that the superintendence of the economic affairs of a growing number of countries in the south has been passed to western financial institutions, Gatt negotiators, experts, specialists and creators of wealth. By this apparently voluntary surrender, older patterns of domination and control have been replicated.

Because we understand "fundamentalism" to be a purely religious phenomenon, it is easy to misperceive the same processes in seemingly secular institutions. The west's economistic ideology has become more rigid, even as the inflexibilities of communism have yielded. The west, once inhibited by the communist threat, now feels free to disseminate its truths across the world. This is International Monetary Fundamentalism: the imposition of identical prescriptions on all countries that come under its tutelage no matter what conditions prevail locally. Whether it is Peru, Poland, the Philippines, Nigeria, Ghana, Venezuela, Algeria, the advice, exhortations and orders are always the same; and the consequences, for the poorest, identical.

Nor should we exaggerate the distance between western economistic ideology and its religious roots. Early apologists of political economy were at pains to liberate their doctrines from the constraints of religious ethics. But once economics was freed from religious or moral considerations, it still sought to assimilate its necessities to universal laws. No society can exist without a belief system. The desire to accumulate and the pursuit of individual self-interest, it was argued, were a reflection of the workings of human nature, and so were divinely decreed. There was no right of appeal.

But there was hope. Redemption was possible: the market's hidden hand would ensure that the pursuit of selfish ends would result, miraculously, in the public good. And whose was that concealed extremity, if not God's?

The secular creed has far fewer secular antecedents than we like to think; but the act of faith has somehow been swallowed by the economic machine, which then proclaims itself driven by reason, common sense and pragmatism.

So the western economic system is now the vehicle of the west's universalising mission; just as it was once the destiny of the west to civilise the whole world, which it duly did, brutalising large sections of humanity in the process, eradicating others. The underlying racist thrust of this project, having destroyed the indigenous cultures of the Americas and Australia, was brought home to Europe in the 1930s, in the doctrines of fascism.

This dealt a severe blow to the civilising pretensions of the west. Instead, after 1945, what we saw was a furious, expiatory process of economic reconstruction in Europe, Germany in particular, as well as Japan. It is no accident that we spoke in the sixties of economic miracles, the economy being the only area of experience capable of making the knowing and disabused people of the west suspend disbelief in the supernatural.

What could be more natural than that the creation of such spectacular wealth as we have seen should now become the basis for our expansionist, conquering mission in the world? The west can readily discard its archaic holy texts, and rely on the apparently pragmatic revelations of those who have delivered the goods to so many happy people. This is how the promise of "development" became a pledge to the rest of the world that they could follow in our footsteps, if only they would do as we bid.

But here is a problem. The amassing of the west's wealth depended for centuries on the occupation of other people's lands, and the tribute exacted by their conquerors. These conditions are simply not available to those now being urged to follow the western path. It is becoming ever clearer to people in the third world that western promises are disingenuous and unrealisable; are, in fact, prescriptions for subordination, the maintenance of western privilege, and have little to do with lifting the mass of suffering humanity out of hunger and despair. Since 1945, western prosperity continued to be founded on the flow of wealth from poor to rich, by means of adverse terms of trade, the import of third-world raw materials to feed their industrial economies. The rawest material of all was human—the large numbers of Turks, Indians, Afro-Caribbeans and Indonesians brought in to keep wages down. Latterly, the south's enormous debts have become another means of transferring wealth to the rich, to such a degree that it has been estimated that the net flow from south to north—if we include the effects of debt servicing, brain drain, resource transfers—is up to US$200 billion a year.

It is clear to many people in the developing world that they are in the presence of a faith no less rigid for being unnamed, unrecognised by the west, than that which animates the supporters of any other fundamentalism. The missionaries of the west—the negotiators of IMF, World Bank project makers, Gatt negotiators, representatives of transnational corporations—constitute a formidable army of fanatical soldiery in pursuit of an undeclared *jihad,* which has pretensions to supervise what is now openly referred to as "the global economy".

Algeria is an interesting example: the US$24 billion debt to the west, the vast army of young unemployed, are part of the tribute demanded by the western system. The rise of the Islamic Salvation Front (FIS) is a direct response to those who have so faithfully sought to implement the impoverishing policies ordered by the west.

Nor should we imagine the west is so blinded by its "success" in its heartland that it is unaware of the consequences for those places where its preachings must be practised. The recent World Development Report of the World Bank admits that the percentage of "inflation episodes" that ended in stabilisation was 67 for "authoritarian" systems, but only 29 for democracies. More than 10 per cent of "adjustment programmes" in democratic systems led to "breakdown of the system 12 months or less after the programme started".

The report contains statistics about what it euphemistically calls "irregular executive transfers", explained as "changes in the office of the national executive from one leader to another, outside conventional legal or customary procedures for transferring powers". In an excess of candour, it goes on to list the number of coups, and shows that there has been at least one coup attempt per developing country every five years. The most recent of these was in Venezuela in February 1992. "The foiled coup capped mounting social discontent in Venezuela which had been undergoing strong economic reforms prescribed by the IMF. While these reforms are expected to correct the economy in the long run, there is much hardship . . ." (*Times of India,* 5 February 1992).

There are other layers of seductive virtue expounded by the west. Western aid, they say, must be dependent on something called "good governance". The market economy is indivisible from democratic freedoms. Britain, as the pioneer of industrial society, was scarcely recognisable at the time as the democracy that it now recommends to the rest of the world during the time of violent, driven change and upheaval that industrialisation demands; as people were evicted from an impoverished countryside and forced to migrate to city slums. Quite the reverse: the early 19th century with its Combination Acts, its illiberal and draconian penal code, makes many tyrannical regimes supervising IMF structural adjustment programmes of today look almost benign.

The west does not issue *fatwas* against individuals. We prefer sentences of mass death, to be executed by the impersonal forces of "economic necessity". Human agency is thus eliminated from the workings of economic forces, which have become a force of nature. Capitalism has become cosmos, its laws as immutable as those of birth and death. Economic dissidents do, of course, exist in the west; and they exercise their precious freedoms by sleeping under bridges and in doorways, protected from the cold by the consolations of cardboard and cheap alcohol.

It is clear that the west has become sole proprietor of forms of secular salvation, which it promotes with the inflexible certitudes normally associated with gospels of transcendence. The 40,000 children who die from avoidable disease and malnutrition, indigenous peoples evicted for the sake of the forest or mineral resources on which the global economy has prior claim, generations of young people in Thailand and the Philippines driven into the tourist sex industry, human rights abuses against those resisting "development" (see Amnesty International's report on the Philippines, February 1992), the vast slum settlements fringing the megacities of the south, developmental refugees, militarisation and destruction of the resource-base to service debt—here are a few of those whose lives are laid waste by a fundamentalism that cannot recognise itself for what it is, but continues to promote itself as the highest freedom.

The west does not issue fatwas against individuals. We prefer sentences of mass death

But no absolute creed can be totally consistent in its application. The west proffers its cruel orders freely to the world, but forbears to apply them at home, where this becomes inconvenient or runs counter to vested interests. The coercive policies are for export only. They preach opening up economies, free trade, culling subsidies, "liberalisation", even while they protect their own markets, subsidise European and US agriculture, Japanese rice farmers, close their doors against third-world textiles, order India to modify its patent law, infringe sovereignty and manipulate elites under their tutelage.

It is an ideology of dominance. What is more, it replicates in a broad sense the older ideology of racial superiority, officially abandoned, but that still manages to create a world in which the vast majority of the world's rich are white (or Japanese), and the poor non-white.

The outcome of the workings of "impersonal" economic forces is not so different from that of the earlier mission to teach and instruct the backward, superstitious and child-like peoples of the world in the civilising ways of the west. That so happy an arrangement depends on the workings of universal laws surely stretches credibility to the limits. But this has become the object of an evangelising fervour and indiscriminate application to all those countries whose affairs fall under the enlightened control of the IMF and World Bank, with what results for the happiness, prosperity and social justice for the people we now see, in Kenya, Nigeria, Venezuela, the Philippines, Brazil, and which we can now expect in India, surely the biggest prize to date.

If we want to understand the "rise of fundamentalism" in the world, we ought to begin by looking at our own far from insignificant role in the generation of this destructive phenomenon.

The Third World: Living With Debt?

Mark Cook

Mark Cook is Head of Economics at Nene College, Northampton.

With the Gulf war, the break-up of the Soviet Union, the democratisation of Eastern Europe, the Single European Market and this year's elections in the US and the UK, one area of concern has taken a back seat, that is Third World debt. Ignoring the problem, however, will not make it go away; external debt problems are here to stay imposing restructuring costs, lower standards of living and development problems for many Less Developed Countries (LDCs).

Why this more low key approach to the debt crisis and can there be any painless way of resolving LDCs' debt problems? To answer these and other questions requires us to examine, briefly, how the debt crisis arose and the methods by which the developed countries, the international banking system and the IMF have attempted to come to terms with the problems.

History points to the oil price hikes of 1973/74 and 1979 as a major step in the growing indebtedness of LDCs. The industrialised West and the non-oil LDCs ran up huge balance of payments deficits as their economies could not adapt quick enough. At first the international banks were eager lenders to the Less Developed Countries (LDCs), since the LDCs appeared to be reasonable credit risks. The prices of their export commodities were high, they had high growth rates and so could reasonably be expected to pay back the loans at some future date. Furthermore, the international banks believed that the existence of 'lender of the last resort' arrangements with their central banks meant that this facility would be on offer to them if the LDCs were unable to pay off their debts, thus some commercial banks took on riskier portfolios in return for higher returns.

By 1976 debts by the LDCs totalled $228 billion with bank debts at $49 billion. For the LDCs creditworthiness had become a problem. Commercial banks may well have wished to reduce their lending, but for US banks, a loan which serviced for 90 days must be declared as 'non-performing' and may no longer be 'booked' as an asset. So it was imperative for them to keep earlier loans 'alive'. Some LDCs which were oil producers received larger export earnings but also sought even more ambitious growth programmes, financed by foreign bank debt. In the US after the 1979 oil price rise, the tightening of money supply growth and a loose fiscal stance served to raise interest rates both in nominal and real terms. Since the majority of LDC debt was denominated in dollars the impact on these countries of high interest rates was enormous. In addition, the recession in industrialised countries and the adverse terms of trade effects all boded ill for the LDCs. External debts became unmanageable and by August 1982, Mexico unilaterally announced that it could no longer meet the interest and capital repayments on its $80 billion overseas bank debt. Within months, dozens of other LDCs followed suit.

The problem with the debt crisis was a two-fold one; commercial bank exposure to debt and the difficulties in servicing debt repayments. Solutions concentrated on these two areas with a bias towards the former in the early 1980s. Initial policies, therefore, were aimed at keeping the pressure on debtor nations so that the debt could be serviced whilst at the same time looking for ways to relieve the pressure on the banks. Five major proposals have been tried and tested:

1. Debt rescheduling: this is renegotiation of the terms of the loan, that is postponing and extending the repayment of principal and interest.
2. Debt/Equity Swaps: developing countries debts are exchanged for equity in commercial projects in the debtor country. The existence of these debt/equity swaps has stimulated growth of a 'secondary' market where creditor commercial banks may sell their developing country debt. The buyers in this market can then trade this debt for an equity position in the debtor country. The LDC can benefit from the debt/equity swap if they are able to 'capture this discount' in the secondary market. The size of the secondary market is small, however,

and it would take many years of such action to reduce substantially LDC debt. A further problem is that if the direct re-purchase of the debt by the debtor nation occurs by exchanging this for local currency, there is the likelihood that this will lead to an increase in the money supply, thereby inducing inflation. If the debtor nation tries to reduce the money supply by selling bonds then in essence, the debtor country is ridding itself of external debt and replacing it with domestic debt.

3. Debt cancellation: some of LDC debt is cancelled, thus increasing the ability to service the remainder of their debts. The credit-worthy middle income countries who were planning to borrow more funds in the future disavowed themselves from such a proposal since they felt that they would then be considered as very risky investments and therefore face higher interest charges. Before long, therefore, it was fairly obvious that the request for debt relief was confined to official loans to low income countries. There are problems with such an approach, firstly relief is distributed unequally and mainly to those LDCs which had borrowed more in the past, secondly, if debt relief is expected in the future, it might encourage LDCs to borrow far more than they can really afford in the current time period, and thirdly, if debt relief does happen in the future then it will destroy lenders' incentive to give loans.
4. Debt conversion: here some of the existing debt is converted into a new asset. For example, a country might convert some of its existing debt, which carries a floating market interest rate, into a new debt which carries a fixed interest rate below the market interest rate with some, if not all, future interest payments guaranteed.
5. Debt-for-debt swaps: a bank not wishing to take a loss on a loan to an LDC sells it to an investor keeping the original amount on the books but changes the terms to make it considerably more favourable to the debtor country.

There are many other types of instruments that have also been suggested to reduce the debts faced by LDCs. These would include buybacks, re-lending, on-lending, co-financing, exit bonds, bridge finance, securitisation, and interest rate capping. On the whole all these methods fall between two categories, that is debt forgiveness on the one hand to 'muddling through' on the other.

It should not be thought that the way to solve the debt crisis was left only to the international banking sector, the International Monetary Fund (IMF) has been an important source of funding for debtor nations though the IMF requires borrowers to 'adjust' their economies. Such structural reform policies involve targets for macroeconomic variables such as the money supply or the reduction in government borrowing, the abolition or liberalisation of foreign exchange and import controls, etc. Some LDCs perceive the IMF as being an arm of the rich capitalist nations using policies to retain the status quo between developing and developed nations. Furthermore, it should be noted that the Fund's resources are limited and that direct financial assistance is restricted to the smaller LDCs and aid to the larger LDCs is more symbolic in nature. For example, the size of Brazil's debt was approximately the same size as the subscriptions to the Fund made by all its members. Therefore, for the IMF to help solve the debt crisis it has relied heavily on involving the international banking sector to deal with the problem through some of the schemes outlined earlier. This approach appears to have succeeded since wide-scale default and consequent bank collapse has been averted. The problems are that the banks wished to reduce their exposure to LDC debt and this partnership with the IMF actually did not allow them to do this, and secondly it forced the burden of adjustment onto some of the poorest countries of the world.

In addition, the IMF policy to reduce LDCs' indebtedness by targeting their imports has meant that reductions in these are normally in the form of capital and industrial goods which are easier to sacrifice rather than essential imports such as fuel and food. This has an adverse effect on future LDC export performance sacrificing growth in order that they can export capital. The growth rate of the 15 major debtors was 1.6% between 1983–1989 with population growth rates of 2.3% per annum, implying that living standards have been declining during this period. Nor have the developed countries escaped. S. George (1988) has estimated that up to 700,000 jobs may have been lost in the US and the UK between 1982–89 due to reduced demand for their exports to LDCs. Also by encouraging exports of primary commodities over-supply has resulted. The price reductions that followed coupled with the inelastic demands for these commodities only served to reduce the revenue for the LDCs. Concentrating on export goods rather than goods for home consumption also had its problems; some countries now feel that such policies are socially unacceptable and unworkable. In the latter part of the 1980s, 25 of the LDCs who had sought assistance from the IMF, experienced serious civil disorder or public hostility towards the IMF imposed measures.

Both the IMF, commercial banks and the debtor governments perhaps have realised that the process of tackling the debt crisis must be through a mechanism of economic growth rather than through a process of economic restraint. Instead of simply making transfers to the LDCs so that they can keep the debt alive there is a need to return once more to a situation where there are positive net capital flows into LDCs. Once this fact was recognised it spawned a number of initiatives built on these premises such as the Baker Plan (1985), and the Brady Plan (1989).

The Baker Plan's main goal was the reduction in the net outflow of money from the highly indebted, middle income debtor countries (15 countries, 10 of which were in South America), thereby improving economic growth. The Plan required the commercial banks to re-lend $20 billion and the IMF $9 billion over three years to these countries, through country-by-country negotiations. In 1985 these countries owed $80 billion in interest to the international banking sector. The $20 billion of new loans, however, never really materialised, banks really wanted to reduce lending to debtor countries, raise new capital, and reduce their overall exposure, which is what appeared to happen so that by the end of 1988 the exposure of the banks had fallen to under 100% of capital.

The Baker Plan also highlighted a number of difficulties:

1. Although debt reduction would help the debtor countries to return to creditworthiness, banks were unwilling or were unable to lend to countries that had failed to repay their debts.
2. Stretching-out debt repayments although laudable, was deemed to be insufficient to restore prosperity.
3. Most of the money which was lent by the commercial banks went straight back to them as interest payments for earlier loans.
4. The IMF's stand-by agreements were only intended to overcome short term problems, and appeared of little use in financing a long-term programme of development. As time progressed these indebted countries began paying back their stand-bys. Thus from 1986, the IMF was receiving more in debt service from the heavily indebted LDCs than it was extending to them in new loans, a position the commercial banks had found themselves in since 1983.

Given the present state of debts by LDCs some form of 'debt forgiveness' appeared to be one of the best possible methods for overcoming the debt crisis. This was one of the elements of the Brady Plan. The commercial banks were called upon to accept an orderly process of debt reduction and were encouraged by the IMF and the World Bank with funds of $10 billion and with a similar sum to come from the Japanese government. The Plan implicitly recognised that many debtor countries would be unable to repay their commercial banks debts in full, even if the repayment period was extended. The focus on cutting the debt on a case-by-case basis contrasted with the Baker Plan which held that eventually all the commercial bank debt should be repaid on market terms. Although the Brady Plan was not hard on specifics its general mechanism for debt reduction was for creditor banks to agree voluntarily to reduce the value of their claims (either by reducing interest rates or principal) in return for guarantees on the remaining portion of the debt. The banks could still hold onto the existing debt in the belief that they would eventually get paid. The IMF and World Bank helped finance the guarantees either by providing collateral on the reduced value of the debt or by giving debtor governments financial support to repurchase their debt for cash at the secondary market rate. There were certain constraints to face if a country was to benefit from the Brady Plan, that was, to apply for debt reduction the debtor countries should be undertaking sound economic policies aimed at encouraging domestic savings and foreign investments and promoting the return of 'flight capital'. Perhaps the most important feature of the Plan was the view that the debt problem was seen as a development problem rather than a problem of liquidity.

The Brady Plan, therefore, relied on the 'voluntary' action of creditors to bring about the debt reduction, but there were reasons to doubt whether this 'voluntary' approach could deliver an adequate amount of debt reduction. Moreover, there was debate as to who would determine the allocation of burdens among the lenders. In addition we have the 'free rider' problem. Each individual bank could openly support the Brady Plan hoping that other banks, the IMF, Japan etc. would bear the losses. In such a voluntary arrangement all may well fail to participate. Moreover, Western European governments were not eager to support such a plan when it was mainly geared to help the US banks. Finally, if the Brady Plan tackled commercial bank claims, surely, the argument goes, it should also tackle money owed to official creditors. Debts owed to official sources were the major worry for some countries and as the Brady Plan stands these countries would still face huge debts.

It would appear that the initiatives by the international community have yielded limited, but positive, results. Between 1981 and 1987 the current account deficit of the Latin American countries was reduced by $30 billion and that of the African countries by $15 billion. The Baker Plan reduced the current account deficits of the favoured 15 countries by 1985/87 to one tenth the 1980–82 level and in addition reduced the growth in total debt.

Nevertheless, the African countries appear to be in dire straits. A number of them are heavily indebted, they have very little export cover and interest payments [make] up an uncomfortable proportion of exports. Primary product prices are relatively low and their exports, particularly food, face difficulties in highly protected export markets.

Many creditor nations and the commercial banks saw the debt crisis in the beginning as a short term liquidity crisis rather than a long-term development crisis. The commercial banks, too were desperate in the early years to keep all their loans alive without this fact they would have been over-exposed and many of them would have gone bankrupt. The situation had changed somewhat by the late 1980s and early 1990s as the commercial banks have put sufficient funds aside as bad debt provision helped to some extent by flexible tax regimes. It is surprising that the commercial banks still appear to want full payment for their initial loans since the value of these debts on the secondary market are worth, at the most, 70% of their face value. What is required is for the commercial banks to acknowledge this fact, as well as writing-off some of the outstanding debt. In other words they should follow the agreements proposed at the Toronto Summit in 1987. On an official level John Major has led the way when he wrote off some £550 million of external debt in October 1991, followed by a number of other Commonwealth leaders. But even this may not be enough; the developed countries, along with their commercial banks, the IMF and the World Bank need to produce a blueprint for sustained growth in the developing countries. Without this the developing countries' economies may never improve and remain always, debt ridden societies.

REFERENCE:

George, S. (1988). *A Fate Worse Than Debt,* Penguin, London.

African debt

Borrowed time

Last month President Bill Clinton announced a package of $43 billion of aid to Russia, including substantial forgiveness of its foreign debt. Last week his treasury under-secretary, Lawrence Summers, said that America would write off half the debts of 18 of the poorest countries in Africa. If you assume—as the Treasury does—that little of the original $228m debt owed to America by these countries would have been recovered anyway, this will cost the Treasury, over three years, the princely sum of $21m.

Though the sum is small, it is a significant change of heart. America and Japan are the only members of the Paris club of rich-country creditors that have not reduced Africa's debts. The Bush administration was reluctant to forgive Africa's debt, even though it had pushed commercial banks towards solving part of the debt problem in Latin America. As a means of helping Africa's debt burden, however, it barely scratches the surface of the problem.

The Americans say their proposal will allow them to forgive $228m-worth of African debts owed on non-concessional (ie, market-rate) loans. Compared with the total debts of the 18 poorest African countries (about $50 billion), the American offering is tiny. Compared with the total debt of sub-Saharan Africa ($183 billion), it is minuscule. Africa's debt may appear manageable next to the $447 billion Latin American countries owe. But relative to Africa's puny economies, it dwarfs the Latin problem (see chart). And it is growing.

Africa's debt has more than tripled since 1980. This is partly because Africans are borrowing more, but chiefly a result of the build-up of unpaid interest over the past decade. Africa as a whole now meets only half its debt-servicing obligations. Five countries—Nigeria, Côte d'Ivoire, Kenya, Zambia and Zimbabwe—contribute two-thirds of all interest payments by Africans. Mozambique, emerging shakily from civil war, meets only 12% of its interest payments.

Even this meagre effort is a struggle. Africa as a whole spends four times more on the interest on its debts than on health. Burundi, a wretchedly poor country, manages to service almost all its debt, but doing so gobbles up 30% of its budget each year.

Moreover, in order to keep up payments on their debts, governments use up scarce foreign exchange. Uganda spends two-thirds of all the foreign currency it earns from exports on servicing its debts. The average share for sub-Saharan Africa is about a fifth. The price of these outflows of foreign exchange to the West is billions of dollars-worth of unsurfaced roads, unpurified water and untreated illnesses.

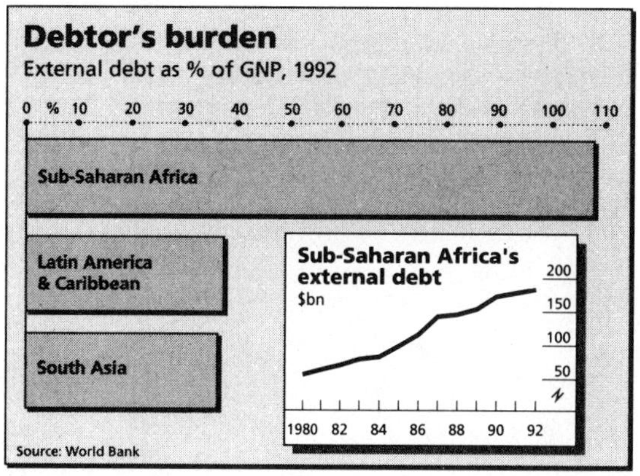

Creditors concerned about Africa's debt burden have generally opted for rescheduling rather than outright cancellation. This simply postpones the pain. True, the Paris club, a group of rich-country creditors, has cancelled some African debt outright. Between 1989 and 1991, its chief members wrote off $10 billion of sub-Saharan Africa's concessional (ie, low-interest) debt. But, according to a recent report by Oxfam, a British charity with much African experience, most of this was on loans that were not being repaid anyway, so barely dented the servicing problem. To date, creditor governments have cancelled 11% of Africa's concessional bilateral debts.

A succession of rescheduling deals, known by the places—Toronto, Trinidad—in which creditors dreamt them up, have been proposed in recent years. None has done much to ease Africa's long-term debt burden. The "Trinidad terms", proposed in 1990 by John Major when he was Britain's chancellor, write off two-thirds of a poor country's debt incurred before a certain date, and reschedule the rest over 25 years. Britain has offered this deal to 15 of its poor African debtors. Most Paris-club countries prefer the less generous "enhanced Toronto terms", which cancel only half a poor country's debts contracted before a certain date. That is what America is now offering 18 African countries—on the condition that they implement IMF-approved reforms.

Yet for a country like Uganda, which was offered an "enhanced Toronto" deal last year, the impact is minimal: only half its $2.8 billion debt is eligible for relief because the rest was incurred after the agreed date. Even a Trinidad deal does little more than bring the amount of interest that Africans owe closer to what they are managing to pay anyway. The World Bank reckons that a Trinidad deal would still be unsustainable for weak economies like those of Somalia, Mozambique and Sudan.

This is why organisations like Oxfam argue that virtually all non-concessional debt should be written off by creditors, not just a smaller share of debt taken on before a certain date. Ishrat Husain, the World Bank's chief economist for Africa, argues that the debt overhang is now a serious turn-off to private investors. He would prefer to see Africa's debt obligation reduced to no more than the $10 billion it is managing to pay each year.This would need the co-operation of non-Paris-club creditors, like Russia, to whom large sums are owed by former Soviet protegés, such as Ethiopia and Mozambique. It would also need to embrace countries like Nigeria, which are still unrealistically classed as middle-income and therefore not eligible for Paris-club relief.

There is a further problem. A growing share of all Africa's debt is lodged not with governments, which can choose to write off loans if they so wish, but with multilateral institutions like the IMF. From 1980 to 1992, the multilaterals' share of African debt grew from 19% to 28%. Loans from these institutions cannot be rescheduled or written off if countries are to go on borrowing.

If the West could be confident that full debt forgiveness would automatically be matched by a growth in spending on things like schools and clinics, then the zeal with which it pursued debt-forgiveness might be greater. But the conviction too often remains that any extra money in the government pot will somehow find its way into the pockets of the country's leaders.

The disaster that didn't happen

Ten years ago Mexico announced to the world that it could no longer service its external debt. Similar news from Brazil and Argentina came soon afterwards. The Latin American debt crisis had begun. William R. Rhodes, vice chairman of Citibank, is the commercial banker most closely identified with managing the crisis. He looks back at the evolution of events and the lessons to be learned

THE philosopher William James once said that "great emergencies and crises show us how much greater our vital resources are than we had supposed". As we now look back on the events of the past ten years, I would point to three aspects of the third-world debt crisis that bear that out.

First, despite all the gloom and doom that surrounded the early stages of the crisis, the international financial system did not collapse. I don't think I have ever been in a more collectively pessimistic setting than the IMF/World Bank meetings of September 1982 in Toronto. The standing joke was that the efforts to contain the crisis amounted to no more than "rearranging the deck chairs on the Titanic".

Such gallows humour was not unfounded. Among the money-centre banks in New York, for example, the exposure to troubled debtor countries exceeded their capital. The real threat was the possibility that a major bank would encounter funding problems in the markets, which in turn could have set off a chain reaction that would have severely shaken the international financial system. It did not happen. The banks were given the time to raise capital and increase reserves, and the debtor countries began reforming their economies.

Second, in the early years, all the major parties—the commercial banks, the debtor countries, the creditor countries and the international financial institutions—temporarily put aside their own interests and worked for a collective purpose. If greed drives people apart, fear brings them together. That was certainly the case then. It was perhaps best exemplified by the then leader of Mexico's economic team, Jesus Silva Herzog, and his chief debt negotiator, Angel Gurria. Both believed that the best interests of all could be achieved by co-operation, rather than confrontation.

Third, the long-term response to the crisis did more than just allow the major countries of Latin America to cope with their debt. It also provided time to put in place the structural adjustments such as trade liberalisation, privatisation, deregulation and tax reform that have now brought both growth and investment to several countries in the region. Success was due in large part to political leaders who rose to the occasion, as in the reform programme implemented by the economic team in Mexico, under presidents Miguel de la Madrid and Carlos Salinas, and the programme for opening the economy enacted by two successive Chilean governments. Chile's reform has succeeded to the point where one of the leading American credit-rating agencies recently gave the country an investment-grade rating, much improving its standing in international capital markets. Argentina, under the leadership of President Carlos Menem and his finance minister, Domingo Cavallo, is containing inflation, returning to growth and recovering access to capital markets.

A vacation cut short

I was on holiday in 1982 when I was called back to New York with the ominous warning that "the Mexicans are in trouble". At a meeting on August 20th at the New York Federal Reserve Bank, the commercial banks learned that Mexico could no longer service its debt. I was struck by two overriding thoughts. First, we had to assume that the crisis could be managed, and, to contain any panic, we had to convince the world's financial community that we could manage it. Second, we were entering entirely uncharted waters. True, there had been earlier debt crises, and several countries were in various stages of restructuring their debt. But with the announcement by Mexico and expectations of more bad news from Argentina and Brazil, we had no formula for dealing with a crisis of this size.

With hindsight, that may have been a blessing in disguise. Not being bound by any conventional wisdom, we were able to respond to the crisis in a much more flexible and focused manner.

One of the principles that came to the fore in the early days is still very applicable: the need for a case-by-case approach. While that is today taken for granted, some bankers and academics at the time were pressing for "global solutions"—a kind of "one-size-fits-all" answer to the debt problem. A look at the distinctive varieties of the Brady plan employed over the past three years in Mexico, Venezuela, Argentina, Brazil, the Philippines and Uruguay shows how ill-suited a generic response would have been.

The steps to safety

The crisis passed through several phases. In the first, commercial banks assembled short-term emergency financing packages whereby debt due to mature over the next two years or so was stretched out over five to seven years. In addition, new money was committed to meet borrowers' immediate cash needs, as in the 1982-83 restructurings of Mexico, Argentina and Brazil.

The second phase was aimed at buying time; time for the countries to implement reforms and for the banks to build capital and reserves. At the heart of this was the agreement that the IMF would monitor a country's economic performance over periods substantially longer than it normally does under stand-by arrangements, and that the resultant information would be made available to the commercial banks.

During this phase, in 1984, Mexico and its creditor banks agreed on the first multi-year restructuring agreement. The Mexican restructuring also featured the first use of debt/equity swaps, a concept that the Chileans took even greater advantage of in a deal negotiated the following year.

The third phase began in October 1985, at the IMF/World Bank meeting in Seoul, when America's Treasury secretary, James Baker, announced his plan for world debt. It emphasised growth-oriented structural economic reforms in debtor countries. In return for these reforms, commercial banks were asked to continue to make new loans available—Mr Baker suggested $20 billion over three years. At the same time, the World Bank was brought into the fray; until then, the debt strategy had been dominated principally by the IMF. This phase also saw Mexico and Chile begin to emphasise structural adjustments in the areas of trade and privatisation.

Though the Baker plan is often attacked for not having raised sufficient new money, a study by the Institute for International Economics showed that banks disbursed over $13 billion in net new loans to the Baker countries over the three-year period envisaged. That the $20 billion mark was not reached says as much about the inability of some countries to make the necessary structural adjustments as it does about the banks' occasional unwillingness to lend.

With the Argentinian agreement in 1987, the role of the market increased, as the list of restructuring options was substantially expanded. The longer menu included co-financings with the World Bank, trade financing facilities and new-money bonds. This was the first time that an exit bond with a fixed, below-market interest rate was offered in an attempt to stimulate debt-reduction. Though this Argentinian bond was a failure, it helped set the stage for the next phase, voluntary debt-reduction.

In the same year Citibank, motivated by Brazil's moratorium on its medium- and long-term commercial-bank debt, raised its reserves (provisions) against doubtful third-world debts. Many American, British and Canadian banks followed suit. These higher reserves gave banks greater flexibility to manage their loan portfolios, through such debt-reduction options as exchanges of debt for equity and cash buy-backs of debt.

1987 also saw the deal between J.P. Morgan and Mexico, which attempted debt-reduction by offering banks the chance to exchange loans for bonds, at a discount, with the principal collateralised by United States Treasury zero-coupon bonds. This did not produce the results that some had hoped for, but it did become one of the bases of the Brady plan, named after Nicholas Brady, who succeeded Mr Baker at the Treasury.

In September 1988 Brazil signed a medium-term financing package to bring it out of its moratorium. Although the Brazilians never fully implemented this agreement, it demonstrated for the first time that new money and voluntary reduction of existing debt were not mutually exclusive. Both the banks and the debtor countries were now looking to voluntary debt-reduction as a big part of these financial packages. The package itself contained $5.2 billion of new money. As with Argentina, the original debt was exchanged at par for fixed-rate bonds paying below-market rates. Unlike the comparable Argentinian bonds, these ones succeeded; they were the forerunner of the par bonds in the Brady-plan agreements. Some 100 banks subscribed a total of $1.1 billion. If the Brazilian government had not initially restricted participation, we probably could have obtained two or three times as much. It is notable that, although Brazil later suspended interest payments on its medium-term debt to commercial banks, it never stopped paying interest on its bonds.

Enter the Brady plan

In a speech to the Bretton Woods Committee in March 1989, Mr Brady proposed voluntary debt-reduction by commercial banks, and—though this was largely overlooked—urged further flows of new money. As part of the Brady plan, the IMF and the World Bank agreed to offer resources to back debt-reduction programmes for countries with viable economic programmes.

All this set the stage for the Mexican debt package that was signed in February 1990. It included most of the debt-reduction techniques used earlier, such as debt/equity conversions, interest-rate reductions and principal-reduction bonds. It also incorporated many of the new-money techniques, including bonds, trade finance and on-lending facilities. In addition, the package introduced two new techniques: collateralised interest for debt-reduction bonds, and value-recovery, which allowed the banks to receive additional payments if the price of Mexico's oil exceeded an agreed level. At the same time as the Salinas administration was negotiating this agreement with the commercial banks, it was also accelerating the pace of structural reform.

Since the Mexican agreement, the Brady plan has been used to restructure the commercial bank debt of Venezuela, Uruguay, the Philippines, Costa Rica and Nigeria. It also forms the basis of the debt agreements with Brazil and Argentina.

Back to normal?

Some people have been suggesting that the debt crisis in Latin America will be wrapped up almost exactly ten years after it started. Certainly there has been a fair amount of progress. Signing of the Argentinian package is expected some time in October, and, despite the political volatility in Brazil, the Brazilian senate is still expected to approve that country's restructuring by the end of September, after which it can be sent to its creditor banks. The completion of these two agreements will signal the phase-out of the debt saga among the major economies of Latin America. Although it is outside the region, the signing of a Brady-style agreement by the Philippines this July was another very positive sign.

There are still Latin American countries, however, that have yet to put the problem behind them, notably Peru and Ecuador (though Ecuador's new government has already announced a new economic-reform plan and initiated discussions with individual members of the bank steering committee). And, beyond Latin America, several countries in Africa and in Central and Eastern Europe need to address both their debt problems and the issue of structural reform.

Compelling motivation

In any circumstances there are good reasons for a country to regularise relations with its international creditors. Foremost is the need for access to capital markets, access that is severely limited for countries not meeting their external obligations.

In today's world there are still more compelling reasons. A rough estimate of the amount of capital needed for privatisations in Latin America, South-East Asia and Central and Eastern Europe is $500 billion, and as much again for the former Soviet Union. The resulting $1 trillion is all the more striking when one considers that privatisations in the developing world are financed, in large part, through just one type of capital, risk capital. At the same time, both developed and developing economies also have a broad range of other capital needs, adding to the overall demand. Meanwhile, two of the largest providers of risk capital in the past decade, Japan and Germany, have their hands full in their own backyards.

Given the strong demand for capital around the world, the countries best positioned to get it are those that have become genuinely competitive and creditworthy. It was no coincidence that the pace of the Mexican privatisation programme was accelerated after President Salinas spent a state visit to Europe listening to senior officials there talk about the direct-investment opportunities in Central and Eastern Europe. That same motivation also accounted, in part, for his decision to initiate discussions on the inclusion of Mexico in the North American Free Trade Agreement.

Lessons for reformers

Just as great crises reveal the full extent of our resources, they also hold important lessons. A close look at the experiences of Mexico, Chile and, to a great extent, Argentina shows that all three met the following criteria in successfully implementing their respective economic-reform programmes.

- A head of state who demonstrates political will and strong leadership.
- A viable, coherent and comprehensive economic plan that is implemented in a proper sequence.
- A motivated and competent economic team, working together, not in rivalry.
- Belief in the plan from the head of government, his cabinet and other senior officials involved, who must have the conviction to stay the course.
- An integrated programme to sell the plan to all levels of society through the media. The plan is often difficult to implement, but people will accept it, if they see that there is light at the end of the tunnel.
- Continuity in implementation of reform from one administration to the next.

These criteria are notable for two reasons. They are drawn from the actual experiences of the countries involved. Second, they are applicable not only to the countries of Latin America, but elsewhere in the developing world as well. Adherence to them will help greatly, in any country, in implementing economic reform.

Only time, though, will tell if the trend toward reform in Latin America is permanent. I am confident that much of the progress made so far will stick, in most countries. But reform can be fragile. The cost of economic adjustment should never be underestimated, and there is still a great need to convince all levels of society that opening up the economy will bring with it the long-term benefits of sustained growth.

Why Is Africa Eating Asia's Dust?

While one scrambles toward development, the other slips into despair

Keith B. Richburg

Washington Post Foreign Service

NAIROBI—Ugandan President Yoweri Museveni is a thoughtful, analytical man who often takes on a professorial tone when discussing Africa's myriad problems. So he seemed uncharacteristically at a loss when asked at a recent news conference: Why has African development lagged so far behind that of East Asia, a region that suffered from a somewhat similar set of obstacles?

After offering several well-explored explanations, he paused and admitted some hesitancy to go further. Finally, he said what seemed most on his mind: "The discipline of Asians compared to Africans." People from East Asian countries with scarce resources and large populations "may tend to be more disciplined than people who take life for granted," he said. Some Africans, he intoned, "have so much land that they don't know what to do with it."

It is an explanation heard time and again to a question that fascinates and perplexes anyone who has spent time in both Africa and East Asia. Why has East Asia over the past two decades become a model of economic success, while Africa, since independence, has seen largely failure—increasing poverty, hunger and economies propped up by foreign aid? Is it largely a matter of discipline, as Museveni suggests, or are other factors at work?

There was nothing innate in the peoples of East Asia and Africa that made this outcome inevitable. In 1957, Ghana—one of the bright hopes of black Africa—had a higher gross national product than South Korea, then emerging from a devastating war. Now South Korea is a newly industrialized country—one of the "four dragons" of Southeast Asia. Ghana, meanwhile, has actually slid backwards; its gross national product is lower than it was at independence. It is fair to ask, what happened?

For four years, from 1986 until late 1990, I traveled throughout Southeast Asia as a Washington Post correspondent, seeing firsthand the economic dynamism of a region that has been largely defined by its successful growth and development. Some countries—Singapore, Malaysia and Indonesia—emerged just as Africa did from under colonial tutelage. Singapore became independent as a tiny city-state, with no natural resources. Indonesia and Malaysia at independence were as divided, along ethnic, religious and linguistic lines, as many African countries are today. Thailand, which was never colonized, was a front-line state for the Indochina wars of the late 1960s and was beset by its own Communist insurgency.

Yet from these uncertain beginnings, Southeast Asian nations have prospered. Their average growth rates for the 1980s measured between 8 percent and 10 percent. They avoided the pitfall of heavy external debt through deft management of their economies. And they have successfully diversified away from reliance on single commodity exports, making them less vulnerable to world market price shocks.

There are, of course, examples in East Asia of non-prospering countries, such as Cambodia, Vietnam and Laos—all of which opted for a Communist path and were wracked by lengthy wars. And the Philippines—once the most prosperous country in East Asia—was ravaged by 20 years of authoritarian rule by Ferdinand Marcos.

Moving last year to sub-Saharan Africa, I found a continent in a dismal state of disrepair. From the statistics and the background briefings, one expects to find Africa underdeveloped; the surprise is discovering just how underdeveloped it is. Africa has most of the world's poorest nations. Its children are most likely to die before the age of 5. Its adults are least likely to live beyond the age 50. Africans are, on the whole, more malnourished, less educated and more likely to be afflicted by fatal diseases than any other people on earth.

Any Asia-Africa comparison must allow for many important differences. Although the two continents became independent at roughly the same time, they didn't begin the economic race at the same starting point. East Asian

ECONOMIC DISPARITY

A generation ago, Nigeria's gross national product and exports topped those of South Korea, Malaysia and Thailand. Today, however, Nigeria lags behind its Asian counterparts.

Nigeria is not atypical. In Ghana, Kenya, Tanzania and Zaire as well, per capita gross national product has declined over the past decade even as it has increased steadily in Asia's Little Dragons.

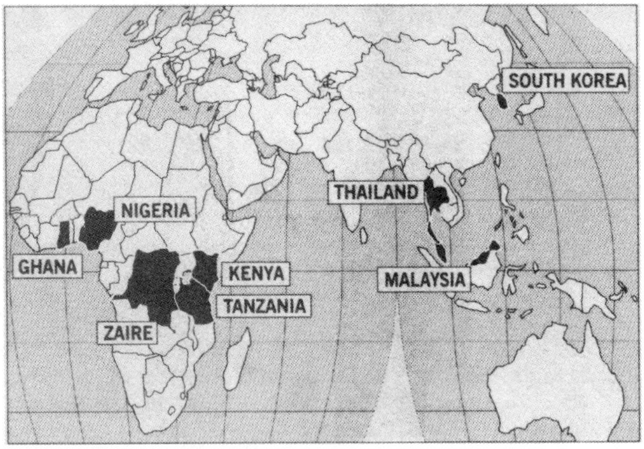

PER CAPITA GROSS NATIONAL PRODUCT
IN THOUSANDS OF U.S. DOLLARS

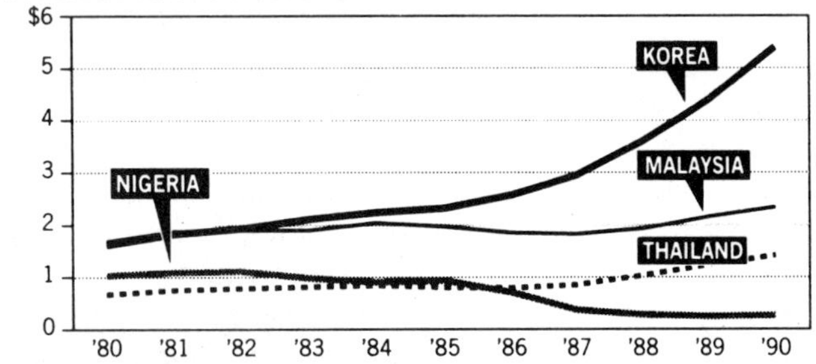

GROSS NATIONAL PRODUCT
IN BILLIONS OF U.S. DOLLARS

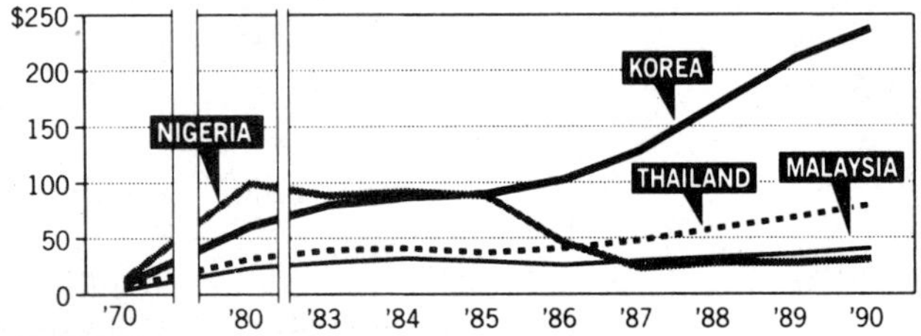

EXPORTS
IN BILLIONS OF U.S. DOLLARS

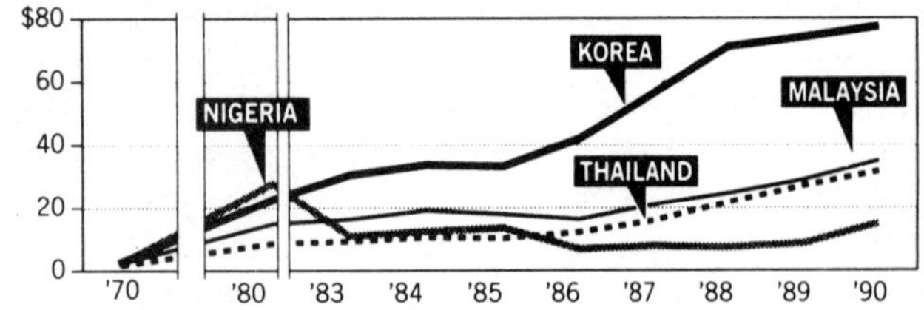

SOURCE: World Bank

economies had a substantial head start; they had developed elaborate patterns of trade and development long before the European colonists arrived. The East Asians, in addition to starting out ahead, also have had a stronger push from the West. In the years since independence, they have received far more Western and Japanese investment. And East Asia, unlike Africa, did not have to spend its early post-colonial years recovering from the physical and psychological trauma associated with three centuries of slavery.

What follows is not a detailed statistical comparison; it is rather a set of interviews and impressions gathered by a reporter who has lived in both places. For the past seven months, I have lived in Kenya and traveled to seven other countries of this troubled continent. One, Somalia, has in fact ceased to be a functioning country, divided as it is between armed warring clans and now in a state of anarchy. Zaire and Malawi are reeling under repressive dictatorships—and in Zaire, years of corruption and neglect have brought the official economy to collapse. Ethiopia and Uganda are struggling to emerge from the shadow of decades of ethnic conflict and dictatorial repression that have driven the economies of both those countries into the ground.

Tanzania in many ways is the saddest, because it has enjoyed 30 years of peace and considerable foreign assistance, but its economy has been ravaged by years of socialist mismanagement. Dar es Salaam, its capital, is in a worse state of disrepair than Hanoi; the road system has collapsed, telephones do not work, electricity is sporadic, its store shelves are bare. Tanzania remains, by many estimates, the third-poorest place on earth.

Kenya and Nigeria, along with Ghana, represented hope in sub-Saharan Africa. But neither has realized its potential. Both have seen their economic advances canceled out by debilitating corruption. Nigeria has often been compared to Indonesia—big, diverse and oil-rich. But where Indonesia managed the oil boom of the 1970s successfully, and has begun to diversify away from its dependence on oil, Nigeria used the boom years to borrow heavily, creating a debt burden that today constrains government action. And Nigeria, unlike Indonesia, remains dependent on oil for 95 percent of its export earnings and 80 percent of its budget receipts.

These resource-rich African countries need not have emerged as basket cases. And Tanzania and Malawi have had ample opportunities to develop through foreign assistance.

Foreign reporters often are criticized for not reporting more "good news" from Africa. There seems a simple reason for that: So much of what happens here is so bad. In East Asia, the stories are largely about economic growth. But in Africa, the issues are more basic. Thirty years after independence, Africans are still trying to learn how to live together in civil societies and how to forge a sense of national identity inside the artificial boundaries of their nation-states.

The continent today is on the economic sidelines. It accounts for a mere pittance of the world's trade. Its share of world markets has fallen by half since the 1970s.

African trade accounts for less than 0.1 percent of North American imports.

How did Africa reach this current predicament? And what lessons, if any, does the East Asian success hold for this troubled region?

Africans themselves, when asked the questions, often point to a familiar list of reasons: the legacy of colonialism; the problem of having diverse ethnic groups within national boundaries; the long-running East–West conflict that constrained Africa's independent decision-making; small countries with fragmented markets; widespread corruption of Africa's ruling elite; and now, more recently, the lack of popular participation in governance. "There is absolutely no way you can achieve economic development without democracy," said Museveni.

Yet many of the East Asian nations also have had to contend with these problems. East Asia, more than Africa, became a playing field for the East–West rivalry. Some of East Asia's most economically successful countries—Thailand, Malaysia and Indonesia, for example—are notoriously corrupt. And precious few East Asian countries can be called democratic, as evidenced by the recent protests in Thailand against the military's continued domination of politics.

An answer, then, would seem to lie deeper. It may be found in the respective patterns of colonialism, in the economic choices pursued and in the differences in the post-independence leadership that emerged in East Asia and Africa. And, as Museveni suggests, it may also be a question of differing cultural traditions.

At a restaurant in Washington last year, a diplomat from the Embassy of Cameroon was explaining to a reporter the problem of Africa's black elite. Go to the cafes and the bistros, he said. See them in their European suits, reading the latest editions of European newspapers. The problem of African development, he said, is that the educated elite have never developed indigenous models, but instead have tried to transplant Europe to Africa.

It doesn't take long in Africa to see what the diplomat was talking about. Basil Davidson, a renowned British scholar on Africa, writes in his new book "The Black Man's Burden" how European colonialism in Africa set out to deny and eventually eliminate the continent's pre-colonial history. And in that, the Europeans found willing accomplices among Africa's European-oriented elite, the "modernizers," who were in constant conflict with Africa's "traditionalists," including the acknowledged tribal chiefs.

These modernizing Africans clung to the notion that anything traditional was by definition primitive. And it was this elite that came to the forefront of the independence movements and proceeded to impose European models on their new African states. Rather than seek to build on tradition, as the Confucianist societies of East Asia tried to do even in their revolutionary phases, the new Africans often sought to purge what was deepest and most authentic in their cultures.

That influence can still be seen today. Judges in Kenyan courts wear white wigs and speak in a flowery, archaic English that might be considered "quaint." Governmental institutions in the former British colonies—from parliaments to the "special branch" internal security forces—are near-duplicates of their counterparts at Westminster and Whitehall. Colonial governments in Africa were dictatorships backed up by a top-heavy bureaucracy. Independence seems to have substituted black autocrats for the old white colonial governors, with little thought of Africa's traditions.

The suppression of indigenous culture has been especially pronounced in the former French colonies of West Africa, which were treated as an overseas department of France, notes Pauline Baker, an Africa specialist with the Aspen Institute. "The French tried to have black Frenchmen," she says.

After traveling through East Africa, the late Shiva Naipaul concluded in his book "North of South" that the black man's contact with the European had only succeeded in destroying African culture. "Black Africa, with its gimcrack tyrannies, its field marshals and emperors, its false philosophies, its fabricated statehoods, returns to Europe its own features," he wrote, "but grotesquely caricatured—as they might be seen in one of those distorting funhouse mirrors."

Black African leaders also point to the deleterious effects on their continent's development, heritage and traditions caused by slavery. They note that slavery robbed the continent of its brightest and most able-bodied men and women for more than 300 years, and some leaders today are going so far as to demand "reparations" from the West.

Contrast that to East Asia. A common feature of Western colonialism was that it never managed to supplant historic traditions—be it the emphasis on education, the hierarchical respect for elders, or the religious traditions of Confucianism, Buddhism and, in Indonesia and Malaysia, Islam, which had come later. Only in the Philippines did the Spanish friars succeed in converting most of the population to Roman Catholicism.

Today, a common theme of East Asian leaders is how to modernize without Westernizing, how to pick and choose the most relevant of Western technology without losing sight of their traditions. A fear commonly voiced around Asia is that encroaching Westernization threatens to erode East Asian culture. Four years ago, Singapore's deputy prime minister, Lee Hsien Loong, summed up the challenge in an interview. "If we reach the point where we all become Americanized," he said, "then that's the end of Singapore."

After independence, many of the African countries became swayed by socialism, the ideology in vogue throughout Europe at the time. Theirs became an African variety, whether dubbed "humanism" as in Zambia, or *ujamaa* in Tanzania. But even in avowedly capitalist countries such as Kenya, the result became the same: government ownership of most enterprises, and a distrust of private-sector initiative and foreign investment.

Asia found another way. Theirs was a brand of state-centered capitalism that was neither completely free enterprise nor dogmatically Marxist. The state intervened in the economy, but in a positive way, supporting "winning" corporations and settling wage disputes. East Asia also had three wars fought on its soil—World War II, Korea and Vietnam—leading the United States to offer benign trading relations to secure stable partners in its fight against Communist expansion.

In a paper examining East Asian and African responses to the global debt crisis, World Bank economist Ishrat Husain detailed how from the mid-1970s, East Asian countries adopted "outward" development policies—meaning liberal trade with low tariff barriers to imports, and realistic exchange rates that enhanced exports. This outward orientation allowed the East Asians to diversify their imports while the international competition improved the efficiency of its producers.

Africa, on the other hand, pursued "inward" economic policies, throwing up trade restrictions and maintaining overvalued currencies.

Herman Cohen, the U.S. assistant secretary for African affairs, sees another reason East Asia has largely prospered. "They did all the right things—plus land reform," he says. By privatizing land holdings, East Asian countries saw agricultural production increase, Cohen says. In Africa, land was communally owned in traditional society and expropriated by the state after independence; prices for farm products typically have been set by state marketing boards.

In comparing East Asia and Africa, it has become fashionable among those who know both regions to say the key difference is that Africa has not produced a Lee Kuan Yew. As long-time prime minister of tiny Singapore, Lee has come to personify the idea of benevolent authoritarianism, a paternalistic ruler who brooked no dissent but nonetheless guided his city-state into the ranks of East Asia's "little dragons."

Africa has had its share of towering figures. But by contrast, some of the best known—such as Tanzania's Julius Nyerere and Zambia's Kenneth Kaunda—ran their countries' economies into the ground. Africa also has produced more than its share of dictators, tyrants and buffoons—such as Uganda's Idi Amin and Jean Bedel Bokassa, who declared himself emperor and his impoverished country the Central African Empire. Zaire's Mobutu Sese Seko and Malawi's H. Kamuzu Banda cling to power through repression. In between are a host of corrupt dictators and military men who seem more intent on padding their European bank accounts than improving the lot of their impoverished peoples.

To be sure, Asia is not without its corruption. In Thailand, corrupt military officers and unscrupulous politicians are involved in a host of illegal activities. But there is a difference between corruption Asian-style and its African equivalent. In Asia, the corruption has not been as debilitating to economic growth. In fact, corruption and growth seem to run parallel.

A Western economist in Nigeria, who lived previously in Indonesia, puts it this way: "In Indonesia, the president's daughter might get the contract to build the toll roads, but the roads do get built and they do facilitate traffic flow. . . . That sort of corruption is productive corruption as opposed to malignant corruption."

In Addis Ababa, an official of the Organization of African Unity, Mamadon Bah, was explaining to a visiting reporter the problem of bringing more democracy to the continent. "What we need in Africa these days is mainly discipline," he said, "but discipline from the top."

Any discussion of cultural differences between Asians and Africans by definition treads on explosive ground, since it feeds on past racist stereotypes of Asians as hard-working and Africans as lazy.

"People work like dogs in Kenya," says Makau wa Mutua, a Kenyan exile at the Harvard University law school's human rights program. "Nobody sits around waiting for mangos to drop from trees." Referring to Museveni's comments about discipline, Mutua recalls how Kenyan President Daniel arap Moi once visited Asia and similarly came back urging Kenyans to emulate the Asian example. "As a leader, one has to talk about discipline to get people to work harder," Mutua says. "That is the stereotype of the Asian machine, that people work so hard. But I think that's pure garbage."

Still, many other Africans agree with Museveni and the OAU official that cultural factors do play a role in development. They argue that lack of discipline among African leaders is a particular problem. For even the hardest-working African has difficulty building a solid life if his country's political leadership is corrupt and undisciplined.

Pauline Baker speaks of the "five bads" that she says help explain Africa's poor record of economic development: "bad luck, bad environment, bad policy, bad government and bad faith [by Western governments that failed to deliver on expected aid and investment]." Baker says that although cultural analysis has gone out of fashion among academics, it may be appropriate to add a sixth factor—"bad outlook."

As examples of the cultural factors that enrich African life but may limit economic development, Baker cites "the role of the extended family" and "the role of tradition." In Africa, she notes, "the real obligations are blood ties to the family or tribe, rather than national ties." The extended family provides a private welfare system that helps take care of people, but it also limits the development of a middle class. The lucky entrepreneur who makes a little money finds he is expected to house, feed and educate his cousins, nieces and nephews. He is pulled back, toward family and village. It is typical, says Baker, that the first thing a newly wealthy city dweller will do with his money is build a big house back in his village.

In most of the Southeast Asian countries, discipline has been imposed from the top. Singapore's People's Action Party under Lee Kuan Yew has been highly authoritarian, micro-managing people's lives to the point of prohibiting chewing gum, using financial incentives to encourage better-educated couples to have more children and launching nationwide campaigns to encourage people to smile more. Governments in Malaysia and Indonesia, trying to forge cohesion out of diverse populations, have force-fed their people a common language policy. In all the Southeast Asian countries except the Philippines, civil liberties are sacrificed as a necessary price of stability—something Asians call the "social contract" between rulers and the ruled.

These Asian regimes draw support from cultural traditions that foster order, hierarchy and stability. The Confucian tradition, for example, is widespread throughout East Asia. It encourages a disciplined work ethic and a stable, stratified political system; it also reinforces the Asian emphasis on education, which is prized in disciplined, authoritarian societies such as Korea and China almost as a secular religion.

Africa has had its share of authoritarian regimes. But far from fostering discipline, most of them have led to chaos. Dictators who tried to enforce unity and discipline—Ethiopia's Mengistu Haile Mariam and Somalia's Mohamed Siad Barre are just two examples—were overthrown last year in bloody revolutions; other African autocrats are teetering. The single feature of African autocracies seems to be their inability to impose their will on their populations.

Even when the military tries to impose political discipline from the top down, as in Nigeria, moral discipline remains lax among the top leaders—and corruption is widespread.

On the individual level, the question of discipline is more difficult to address. No one, for example, would say that the average farmer in Tanzania or Malawi works less than his Asian counterpart. People in hard-pressed Kinshasa, Zaire, survive only by their endurance—working several jobs, selling goods on the streets. In Uganda, government offices are largely empty during the daytime, because low-paid bureaucrats are out running private businesses. In Kenya, even when no milk was available on store shelves because of government price controls, farmers with cows were busy building their own networks of urban buyers. Together, this private sector activity accounts for a disciplined economic sector often overlooked in official statistics.

Lawrence Harrison, a retired Foreign Service officer who has written two books exploring cultural values in the developing world, says he has found Confucianism to be the key ingredient in East Asian development.

"Confucius imparts to his followers a strong sense of future, the importance of education, the importance of merit, the importance of saving for future generations," he says. "All of those things in an economic sense are things that you don't associate with the African culture."

But some African leaders are beginning to express similar themes in their own terms. As Museveni put it recently in Kampala, Uganda, this is the time "for the people of Africa to take their destiny in their own hands."

Conflict and Instability

Conflict and instability are frequently regarded as synonymous with the Third World. During the cold war many observers traced Third World conflict and instability to the ideological struggle between East and West. Despite the end of the cold war, however, these twin problems persist throughout the Third World. The persistence of these problems drives home a point that those who viewed international politics from a purely ideological perspective often overlooked: that the sources of Third World conflict and instability were deeper, more varied, and much more complicated than simply a struggle between communism and capitalism. While the thinking regarding the causes may have changed, what has not changed is that Third World conflict and instability remains a major threat to global peace and security.

Third World conflict and instability stems from a combination of sources. Among these are ethnic and religious diversity, nationalism, struggle for state control, and cold war legacy. In many cases boundaries that date from the colonial era encompass many distinct groups providing the diversity that characterizes most Third World nations. This diversity can increase tension among groups competing for scarce resources and opportunities. Where some groups benefit or are perceived as enjoying privileges at the expense of others, ethnicity can offer a convenient vehicle around which to organize and mobilize. Moreover, ethnic politics lends itself to manipulation by both regimes seeking to protect privileges, maintain order, or retain power and those challenging existing governments. In such a politically and ethnically charged atmosphere, conflict and instability frequently result as groups seek to gain control of a state apparatus that can extract resources and allocate benefits. Even ethnic homogeneity is no guarantee against disorder, however, as the situation in Somalia illustrates. The fighting that led to the breakdown of civic order and international intervention is based on clan affiliations among ethnically homogeneous Somali.

Early literature on modernization and development postulated that as Third World societies progressed from traditional to modern, primary attachments such as ethnicity and religious affiliation would fade and be replaced by new forms of organization. Clearly, ethnicity remains a potent force, as does religion. Ethnic politics and the resurgence of religious fundamentalism demonstrate that such attachments have survived the drive toward modernization.

Islamic fundamentalists are active throughout the Middle East, Africa, and Asia. Rejecting secularism and vehemently anti-Western, these fundamentalists seek to install governments based on Islamic law. Inspired and encouraged by the theocratic regime in Iran, fundamentalists are challenging governments, particularly in the Middle East. In Sudan, the regime has proclaimed the rule of Islamic law and has prosecuted the war against the non-Muslim southern provinces with renewed vigor. In the Philippines the secessionist movement in Mindanao, traditionally based on Moro nationalism, has recently come to be influenced more heavily by Islamic fundamentalism. For many in the West, this resurgence of Islam, perceived as anti-Western and intolerant, looms as possible successor to the communist threat. The 1993 World Trade Center bombing and the plot to bomb other targets in New York City by Islamic radicals elevated the threat from regional to international.

India is currently experiencing a resurgence of Hindu nationalism. Violence erupted between Hindus and Muslims after a Hindu mob destroyed a mosque in Ayodhya in December 1992. This violence demonstrates the strengthened position of groups that advocate Hindu rights and oppose what they consider preferential treatment of minorities. Separatist movements in Punjab and Kashmir have contributed to this resurgent Hindu nationalism, resulting in a serious challenge to India's secularism. Moreover, this Hindu nationalism could increase tensions between India and Pakistan with important regional implications.

Some conflicts continue as a legacy of the cold war. In Angola, Union for Total Independence of Angola (UNITA) rebels refused to accept defeat in the 1992 elections and renewed the civil war that raged as a proxy conflict during the 1970s and 1980s. The ideological component has receded since the MPLA (Popular Movement for the Liberation of Angola) government abandoned Marxism and the conflict has now reverted to a power struggle with ethnic overtones. Exacerbated by cold war rivalries, this conflict continues while the United States and the former USSR turn their attention to other concerns.

In the Middle East many of the contributing factors to Third World conflict and instability come together making the region incredibly complex and tense. In September 1993 Israel and the Palestine Liberation Organization (PLO) reached an agreement to grant limited autonomy to Palestinians in the Gaza Strip and the West Bank town of

Unit 3

Jericho. It was expected that the strength of the radical Hammas movement and the opposition of hard-line elements within the PLO would continue to complicate any agreement. Even as the Israeli-Palestinian agreement was concluded and peace agreements between Israel and its Arab neighbors were to follow, there remain many potentially conflicting issues. Instability resulting from Islamic fundamentalism and intra-Arab struggles is a distinct possibility. The gap between rich and poor Arabs was emphasized during the Persian Gulf War as the haves and have-nots lined up on different sides. Differences between Arab countries on a response to Iraq's invasion of Kuwait also emerged. With progress on the Palestinian issue, these and other potential conflicts, such as water rights, will become more prominent. Indeed, there seem to be more areas of disagreement than agreement throughout the region.

The end of the cold war has eliminated a simplistic approach to the problems of conflict and instability in the Third World. The current, less ideological climate has forced the international community to recognize that these threats are far more complicated, yet no less dangerous.

Looking Ahead: Challenge Questions

What are the sources of conflict in the Third World? What factors contribute to the intensity of these conflicts?

What do you believe accounts for the resurgence of Islamic fundamentalism?

Why does Islamic fundamentalism pose a threat to governments, particularly in the Middle East? What are fundamentalists' political prospects in these countries?

How does the resurgence of Hindu nationalism affect India's secularism? What is the basis for this resurgence?

Why has tension between the Philippine government and rebels in Mindanao recently increased? How has the nature of this rebellion changed?

What are the parallels between the circumstances in Myanmar (Burma) and Bosnia?

What are the causes of the current crisis in Sudan? What potential solutions exist?

How did the cold war affect the civil war in Angola? Why has this conflict continued despite the end of the cold war and international efforts to promote democratization?

Why is there potential for political instability in the Persian Gulf monarchies?

Ethnic Conflicts Worldwide

Europe

SPAIN Nationalists saying they represent 3 million Basques seek an independent state on the border with France. Since 1968, 717 people have been killed in the country and 49 in France.

GERMANY Right-wing and neo-Nazi groups carried out more than 2,000 attacks last year on some of the 650,000 foreigners seeking asylum, resulting in 17 deaths and nearly 600 injuries.

CROATIA Serb separatists control about a third of the territory. An estimated 25,000 people have been killed since Croatia declared independence in 1991.

BOSNIA AND HERZEGOVINA Serb forces have captured about 70 percent of the country and carried out an "ethnic cleansing" campaign that has expelled and killed Muslims and Croats and brought widespread condemnation. Tens of thousands of people are thought to have been killed.

MOLDOVA The mainly Romanian population seeks ties with Romania. The Dniester region in the east, where most of the population is of Russian and Ukrainian origin, declared independence in 1990, fearing the country would unite with Romania. About 800 people have been killed.

GEORGIA Abkhazia, a region dominated by Muslims, seeks independence or union with Russia. From 700 to 1,500 people are estimated to have been killed and 80,000 displaced in the fighting. South Ossetia, a region also dominated by Muslims, seeks union with the republic of North Ossetia in Russia. About 1,500 people are estimated to have died in the fighting.

RUSSIA Chechenya and Ingushetia seek greater autonomy within the country. Ingushetia and North Ossetia are fighting over territory in clashes that have killed more than 300 people.

CYPRUS About 150,000 ethnic Greeks were forced to leave the northern half of the country when it was invaded by Turkey in 1974. The UN has stationed peacekeeping troops and brokers talks between the Greeks and ethnic Turks.

Middle East

SUDAN The government, dominated by Arab Muslims from the north, is fighting a longstanding insurgency by black Christians and animists in the south.

EGYPT More than 70 people have been killed in clashes between Islamic militants and government security forces and in attacks by militants on foreigners and Coptic Christians.

ISRAEL About 1,000 Palestinians have been killed by Israeli soldiers, 500 have been killed by fellow Palestinians, and about 100 Israelis have been killed in Palestinian attacks since the intifada erupted in 1987.

AZERBAIJAN Troops from Muslim-dominated Azerbaijan, aided by Russian forces, are fighting to end a rebellion by Nagorno-Karabakh, an enclave within the country populated largely by Christian Armenians, who favor independence or affiliation with Armenia. An estimated 3,000 people on both sides have been killed since 1989.

TURKEY The Marxist Kurdish Workers party has sought a Kurdish state in fighting that has killed 2,500 since 1984.

IRAQ In the north, two major Kurdish parties rule in an enclave protected militarily by the United States and its allies. Several hundred have died in clashes with Iraqi forces since the 1991 Persian Gulf War. In the south, leaders of a rebellion by Shiite Muslims say that tens of thousands of Shiites have been killed by forces of the Sunni-dominated government since the end of the war.

AFGHANISTAN After the withdrawal of Soviet troops and the overthrow of the Soviet-installed leader, Najibullah, last year, the country has collapsed into a civil war involving competing ethnic factions. The Hazars control central and western areas near Iran, the Pathans are largely in control in the east, and the Tajiks largely control the north. Thousands of people are estimated to have been killed recently.

TAJIKISTAN Tens of thousands of Tajik Muslims have been driven from their land by resurgent Communist armies seeking to suppress Islamic political power. More than 25,000 people have been killed and 500,000 displaced since 1991.

KYRGYZSTAN Continuing tensions between the Kyrgyz and minority Uzbeks have resulted in the recent call by the latter for assimilation with Uzbekistan. About 200 people were killed in the town of Osh in ethnic riots in 1990.

Africa South of the Sahara

MAURITANIA Security forces under the Arab-dominated military government have clashed with opposition groups angry over expulsions and oppression of the black minority population.

SENEGAL In Casamance, a coastal region mostly populated by the Diola ethnic group, there is opposition to Muslim domination in the government. Hundreds of people have been killed and thousands have been displaced in clashes with government forces.

LIBERIA At least 20,000 have been killed and hundreds of thousands have been uprooted in a civil war. Drawing support from the Gio and Mano ethnic groups, the guerrilla leader Charles Taylor controls most of the country. President Samuel Doe, from the Krahn group, was killed in 1990, and Monrovia is held by an interim government installed by an organization of West African nations.

MALI A demand for sovereignty by ethnic Tuaregs, who also live in neighboring Niger, has led to fighting in Mali and Niger.

TOGO Scores of people were killed last year as government forces loyal to leader General Gnassingbé Eyadéma of the Kabiye ethnic group battled opposition forces, including those from the rival Ewe.

NIGERIA The country has many ethnic conflicts, but violence has been the sharpest in fighting between the Hausa, a predominantly Muslim group in the north, and the mostly Christian Yoruba in the south.

CHAD President Idriss Déby, who ousted President Hissen Habré in 1990, has faced sporadic rebellions in the west and south. Some have reportedly involved clashes between Déby's Zakawa ethnic group and Habré's Gourane ethnic group.

DJIBOUTI Demanding a more prominent role in the government and a muliparty democracy, members of the Afar ethnic group have clashed with the ruling Issa.

SOMALIA Clan fighting escalated into full-scale civil war in 1991 and 1992 in which 300,000 people died and 1 million were made homeless from war or starvation. An American-led military force has intervened to establish stability.

UGANDA The army, composed principally of members of the Baganda and Banyarwanda ethnic groups, continues to wage sporadic warfare with northern rebels, mainly from the Acholi and Langi.

RWANDA Fighting is continuing between the government, dominated by the Hutu people, and a rebel force led by the minority Tutsi, despite a peace agreement in July 1992. Tens of thousands of people have died in ethnic fighting in the last 30 years.

BURUNDI Ethnic clashes between the majority ethnic group, the Hutu, and the minority Tutsi, who govern the country, have led to thousands of deaths.

KENYA Clashes among various ethnic groups in 1991 and 1992 have reportedly killed 1,000 people and uprooted 50,000 and led to charges that the government of President Daniel arap Moi was fomenting such conflict to discredit moves toward democracy.

ZAIRE Thousands of people have died in the last year in a civil war between forces opposing and loyal to President Mobutu Sese Seko; various forces are from competing ethnic groups.

ANGOLA Renewed fighting between the government and guerrilla forces led by Jonas Savimbi of the National Union for the Total Independence of Angola, or UNITA, has left thousands dead. There is also a violent secessionist movement in the enclave of Cabinda.

SOUTH AFRICA Since 1984, about 15,000 people have been killed in political violence related to a black insurrection against the white South African government. About 3,000 were killed in 1992, many in clashes between Zulus and rival black groups.

Asia

PAKISTAN Thousands of people have died in conflicts between government forces and groups of secessionists and dissidents in Sindh province and the Northwest Frontier province.

INDIA Tensions between Hindus and Muslims exploded in December when Hindu militants razed a mosque in the northern state of Uttar Pradesh. Rioting that followed in many places across India led to 2,000 killings by official count, and many more by unofficial estimates. Killings by Muslims and Hindus continue. In Kashmir, 5,000 militants, civilians, and Indian troops have been killed since a rebellion by the largely Muslim population began in 1990. An estimated 120,000 people, mostly Hindus, have fled Kashmir for other parts of India. In Punjab state, about 20,000 Hindus and Sikhs are estimated to have been killed since a rebellion by Sikh militants erupted in 1982. In Assam state, more than 200 have been reported killed as an insurgency by secessionists erupted in 1990. In Nagaland, insurgent Bodos have been fighting for a separate state; about 300 people have been killed.

BHUTAN A revolt by ethnic Nepalese against the government and reprisals by government forces have led to thousands of Nepalese fleeing the country in the last 2 years.

SRI LANKA An insurgency by mostly Hindu Tamils in the north and east has been carried out against the government, which is dominated by the mostly Buddhist Sinhalese. Since 1983, an estimated 28,000 people have been killed in the Tamil rebellion, and another 50,000 in the government's crackdown on Sinhalese militants.

BANGLADESH A migration by members of the country's Muslim majority into the thinly populated Chittagong Hill Tracts region in the south has led to an insurgency by the area's Chakmas, a mainly Buddhist people, leaving hundreds of people dead and tens of thousands displaced.

MYANMAR In the last 2 years, more than 250,000 Muslims, charging harassment, have fled across the western border to Bangladesh. Hundreds are also believed to have died in clashes between Burmese soldiers and separatist Karen and other rebels along the Thai-Burmese border in the last 2 years.

CHINA Tibetans rebelled against Chinese rule in 1959, with an estimated 87,000 Tibetans killed. After an easing of Chinese rule, Beijing cracked down in 1987. Several dozen people are believed to have been killed in various incidents. In Xinjiang province, the Chinese government suppressed a rebellion among Muslims of Turkic descent in 1990 in which an estimated 50 people died.

CAMBODIA Rebel factions signed a peace accord ending a 13-year civil war. A Supreme National Council made up of the rebel factions and the Cambodian government is to advise the UN, which administers the country's affairs until a new government can be formed after elections this year. Khmer Rouge soldiers, who blame Vietnam for many of the country's problems, have carried out attacks on the 100,000 Vietnamese who live in the country.

PHILIPPINES Tens of thousands of people have been killed in fighting between the government and Muslim separatists on the island of Mindanao.

INDONESIA A civil war broke out in East Timor in 1975 after Portugal withdrew, and the government crushed the pro-independence rebellion. Human rights groups charge that 100,000 to 200,000 of the 600,000 mostly Roman Catholic East Timorese have died of starvation, disease, or execution since the area was annexed. A separatist movement also exists in northern Sumatra, where Indonesian forces are said by Amnesty International to have killed 2,000 people.

Latin America

GUATEMALA An essentially political conflict between the government and leftist guerrillas has had ethnic overtones because of the long history of repression of Indians. At least 43,000 refugees fled to Mexico, but some are beginning to return.

COLOMBIA A group representing rights of Indians, Quintin Lamee, suspended an armed rebellion in 1991, but other Marxist groups claiming to represent peasants are continuing guerrilla attacks on the government.

PERU Since 1980, a Maoist guerrilla group known as the Shining Path has waged war and won control of about a third of Peru, drawing support from largely Indian or mixed-race populations. About 26,000 people have been killed in the war and an estimated 600,000 have fled their homes to other parts of the country.

BRAZIL Indian tribes in the Amazon region are pressing the government to recognize their traditional homelands. In the northern Amazon state of Roraima, the federal government is campaigning to expel gold miners from the lands of the Yanomami tribes.

Source: Portions of this survey are adapted with permission from *The New York Times*, February 7, 1993. Copyright © 1993 The New York Times Company. Additional information is from Morton Halperin and David Scheffer, *Self-Determination in the New World Order* (Washington, D.C.: Carnegie Endowment for International Peace, 1992).

We must hear the Third World

MICHAEL T. KLARE

Michael T. Klare is Five College Associate Professor of Peace and World Security Studies at Hampshire College in Amherst, Massachusetts.

The end of the Cold War has produced or revealed global changes that have enormous significance for the U.S. peace movement. It is vitally important that the peace movement attempt to analyze these changes and reconstruct its strategy accordingly. While the threats associated with the Cold War have largely disappeared, the world still faces many threats to peace and security. Some of these threats arise from the legacy of the Cold War, a legacy that will imperil the world for generations to come. This legacy includes the large stockpiles of nuclear warheads that we must somehow locate, monitor, safeguard, and destroy. This may not prove an easy task, given the disintegration of the Soviet Union and the unrest in Eastern Europe. Indeed, controlling and eliminating all of these weapons—and preventing their accidental use—may prove the most important and difficult task facing the world community in the months and years ahead.

There are also large stockpiles of chemical weapons that we must safely dispose of, and large quantities of conventional weapons that we must destroy or place in safe storage, lest they flow into the international arms market. The poisonous nuclear wastes produced by forty-five years of bomb production must be disposed of in a safe manner. And we must convert the immense military-industrial infrastructures of the Cold War to productive use without causing great social and economic hardship.

That is the legacy of the Cold War. But a host of other threats to international peace and stability command our attention. Most of these threats arise from social, political, and economic stresses and strains in the Third World, and in parts of what used to be called the Second World—that is, the Sino-Soviet bloc.

As the divide grows between North and South, rich and poor, haves and have-nots, frustrations and resentments among the less fortunate tend to increase and often find expression through the reassertion of traditional ethnic, national, religious, and tribal identities. This reassertion intensifies the hostility toward those of differing identities. Such a clash is occurring on a global basis, and it represents the greatest source of conflict in the current, post-Cold War environment.

Most of the stresses we now see in the Third World and Eastern Europe have been developing over a long period—going back in many cases to the onset of the colonial era. But they appear to have gained increased urgency and vigor with the end of the Cold War. I say "appear" because in some cases we simply didn't *see* these stresses before because of our preoccupation with East-West security concerns. Had we been watching more closely over the past decade or so, we would have been able to detect these developments.

The end of the Cold war and the erosion of central Soviet power (and central Yugoslav power) allowed the ethnic antagonisms that have simmered beneath the surface to erupt with extra vigor. It is a mistake, however, to view these explosions as a result of the Cold War's end; rather, they should be seen as a consequence of the central authorities' failure to address existing ethnic and national aspirations in an honest and constructive way.

The turbulence in the Third World and in Eastern Europe affects world peace and security at three levels. It is increasing tension between North and South; it is fueling interstate rivalries in the Third World; and it is exacerbating ethnic, tribal, religious, and caste antagonisms within Third World countries.

Many of the existing conflicts operate at all three levels. The "Arab-Israeli dispute," for instance, entails ethnic conflict between Jews and Palestinians, regional conflict between Israel and its Arab neighbors, and a welter of stressful relations between these countries and the major Northern powers. The same was true of the Persian Gulf conflict, which entailed ethnic fighting within Iraq, regional conflict between Iraq and its neighbors (especially Kuwait, Saudi Arabia, and Israel), and North-South conflict between Iraq and those Northern powers that feared its growing military potential. This interplay of internal, regional, and global hostilities is likely to be more and more common in the conflicts of the future.

Among the major threats to global peace and security in the post-Cold War era are these:

1. Efforts by nations of the South to enhance their military power vis-à-vis the North (through the acquisition of nuclear, chemical, and conventional weapons).

2. Efforts by nations of the North, especially the United States, to assert dominance throughout the Third World by direct military action, as in Operation Desert Storm.

3. Arms races and hostilities between competing regional powers of the South, as in the Iran-Iraq war, the Arab-Israeli conflicts, the India-Pakistan conflict, and the conflict between the Koreas. An especially dangerous aspect of such rivalries is the tendency of nations on one side of

From *The Progressive*, April 1992, pp. 19-21. Reprinted by permission of *The Progressive*, 409 East Main Street, Madison, WI 53703.

such disputes to foment or support internal ethnic or tribal disorders within the territory of their rivals.

4. Conflicts over borders or territorial dispositions originally constructed by the colonial powers and now considered illegitimate by the current leaders of the countries involved (e.g., Ethiopia/Somalia, Iraq/Kuwait, and the conflict over the Falklands/Malvinas).

5. Efforts by ethno-nationalist groups within multi-ethnic states to secede and establish their own nation-states, along with efforts by central government authorities to suppress such drives (as, for instance, in Croatia, Eritrea, Kashmir, Iraqi Kurdistan, the southern Sudan, and the Tamil-populated parts of Sri Lanka).

6. The channeling of socio-economic antagonisms into armed violence, as in Lebanon, Burundi, Guatemala, and the Punjab region of India. Similarly, the intensification of conflict between settler (ex-colonial) societies and indigenous peoples, as in South Africa, Israel and the West Bank, and much of the Western Hemisphere.

7. Violent struggles between authoritarian governments and popular forces seeking social and political change, as in Algeria, Burma, El Salvador, and Haiti.

8. The persistence of revolutionary movements employing a guerrilla strategy, as in Colombia, Peru, and the Philippines.

Three developments are intensifying these long-simmering conflicts: the globalization of the economy, environmental degradation and population growth, and the growing availability of modern arms.

With capital moving rapidly from one location to another around the world, some states and peoples find it easier to integrate themselves into the global economy; others do not. And within states, new pockets of wealth appear alongside stretches of desperate poverty.

The legacy of colonialism often has a hand in this uneven pattern, since those Third World peoples who were given at least minimal educational and employment opportunities are now better positioned to adapt to the needs of the world economy, while those excluded from educational opportunities often find themselves at a distinct disadvantage.

As some peoples prosper while others stagnate, there is a natural tendency for the less fortunate to emphasize the ethnic, religious, and tribal identities that separate themselves from the more fortunate, and to express these differences in violent forms.

There is also a natural tendency for some groups within a multi-ethnic system to break out of their existing state structure and seek economic alliances with more affluent centers. Hence, the desire of the Baltic republics and Slovenia and Croatia to remove themselves from the economically depressed Soviet Union and Yugoslavia and to forge links with the European Community.

Uneven economic development brings additional destabilizing pressures—particularly the migration of huge numbers of people. Two migratory patterns can be discerned:

First, there is a growing migration of impoverished peoples to the megalopolises of the South—Mexico City, São Paulo, Lima, Cairo, Bombay, Bangkok, Manila. This intensifies ethnic and class warfare and results in growing unemployment, criminality, and the deterioration of the urban infrastructure.

Second, there is a growing migration of Southern (and Eastern) peoples into the affluent areas of the North (and West), sparking anti-immigrant sentiment in the Northern countries, along with increased ethnic and racial conflict within the immigrant communities of the North. This tension has recently flared up, for instance, in ethnically based gang warfare in Los Angeles and rioting in Brooklyn and Washington, D.C.

As global industrialization proceeds and the pace of economic activity accelerates, more and more stress is being placed on the global ecosphere. This process of environmental decay tends to affect some peoples more than others, and it usually exacerbates the existing conflicts and tensions.

The uneven impact of environmental degradation is most evident in the so-called marginal lands—the highlands, jungles, swamps, and deserts where indigenous peoples have scratched out a sustainable existence. But as a result of environmental and climatic changes, they are losing their capacity to do so. As a result, many of these peoples have been forced to join the vast migratory streams described above.

What's more, the untapped resources of lands once considered too remote or too inhospitable for successful economic exploitation—such as the Amazonian rain forest, the forests of Borneo and New Guinea, the oil-rich areas of Alaska's North Slope, and the rivers of northern Quebec—are now falling prey to resource companies seeking new areas for exploitation. These intrusions inevitably threaten indigenous peoples, in some cases resulting in the virtual extermination of tribes and cultures.

Adding to environmental stress is uncontrolled population growth, which increases demands on limited water, forest, and land resources and heightens frictions along ethnic and tribal lines. In areas where one major river system empties through several countries and is the source of drinking and irrigation water for many

If the Third World continues to be shut out of political and economic decisions that affect it, a paralyzing new Cold War could break out.

peoples (e.g., the Nile, the Jordan, or the Euphrates), there is a growing risk of conflict and violence.

Finally, the growing availability of modern arms—including nuclear, chemical, and high-tech conventional weapons—raises the stakes in all of the conflict types described above. As we move into the 1990s, more and more countries will acquire the skills and technology to produce modern weapons on their own. Even more widespread is the ability to manufacture conventional weapons, especially the sort that are employed in local, internal, and insurgent conflicts.

As these capabilities grow, it becomes easier for belligerents (whether states, guerrillas, terrorists, or sectarian militias) to conduct wars of great violence and duration. This became particularly evident in the Iran-Iraq war, which lasted eight bloody years and took the lives of one million people, and in such long-lasting guerrilla and sectarian conflicts as those in Afghanistan, Angola, El Salvador, Ethiopia, Lebanon, and the Sudan.

Even as some of these conflicts are brought to a conclusion, the weapons employed in them have found new use in emerging conflicts. For instance, a shipment of weapons no longer needed by Lebanon's warring factions was reportedly sent to the newly constituted armed forces of Croatia.

How should the peace movement repond to these daunting challenges? It is obviously difficult to spell out a blueprint for successful peace action in all of these areas, but it is nevertheless essential that we begin to develop an agenda to deal with the problems that loom ahead of us.

Here, then, is my list of major peace-movement priorities for the 1990s:

First, we must confront and overcome the legacies of the Cold War. This means continuing our campaigns for nuclear and chemical disarmament, the dissolution of the nuclear-weapons production complex, the dissolution of NATO, and the conversion of military industries into productive civilian enterprises.

Second, we must oppose the tendency of the U.S. Government to act as the world's policeman. For the Pentagon, Iraq was prologue. American military officials fully expect that Operation Desert Storm will be succeeded by a continuing series of armed confrontations between the emerging military powers of the Third World. "The Gulf War presaged very much the type of conflict we are likely to confront again in this era," Secretary of Defense Dick Cheney told Congress last spring. The Pentagon insists that U.S. forces maintain a substantial capacity for military intervention abroad, and the peace movement needs to recognize this and resist it.

Third, we need to campaign for the adoption of rigorous multilateral controls on the export of nuclear, chemical, and conventional weapons. To encourage Third World states to cooperate in nonproliferation efforts, we should insist that increased economic and technical assistance be provided to countries which agree to reduce their military spending. At the same time, we must oppose the use of military action as a substitute for effective nonproliferation.

Fourth, we need to redesign the major international institutions so as to give real power and authority to Third World countries. Two institutions in particular demand a more democratic structure: the Security Council of the United Nations and the International Monetary Fund. If the Third World continues to be shut out of the major political and economic decisions that affect it, a paralyzing new Cold War could break out between North and South.

Fifth, we need to place more emphasis on international peacekeeping, mediation, and conflict resolution. We need to work through the United Nations and regional peacekeeping efforts, such as the Arias plan for Central America, the Treaty of Tlatelolco, and the South Pacific Nuclear Free Zone.

Sixth, we need to support increased economic assistance to the poorest Third World countries, with this aid provided in such a fashion as to benefit needy communities directly. Likewise, we should support U.S. assistance (whether through governmental or nongovernmental channels) for environmentally sound self-help development projects in poor Third World countries.

And lastly, we need to encourage dialogue and cultural understanding across ethnic, religious, tribal, racial, and national boundaries—the front lines of the post-Cold War period. This is by no means a complete or comprehensive list, but I offer it as a starting point for thinking about the peace movement's strategy in the crucial years to come.

Islam resumes its march

One anti-western ism is growing stronger. Three reports: on the evolution of Islamic fundamentalism among Arabs, on the Islamic revival in Central Asia and on the merits of Islamic banking

SUDANESE groups declare a *jihad* (holy war) against the non-Muslim south, Algerian Islamic radicals are turned into outlaws, Saudi Arabia's king and Egypt's president separately denounce fundamentalism. Islamic militancy is again sending an agitated wave through the Middle East.

Is it right to be scared? The reassuring answer is that this movement will, like earlier waves of Islamic assertiveness, dissolve in ripples. Against this it is argued that the populism of the current breed of revivalists, and the fact that the public is fed up with, and humiliated by, the failure of nationalist leaders, make the new men more threatening than the ones who went before. They are dedicated to purging their societies of the culture that has drifted in from the West; several also want political power for themselves as leaders of states governed exclusively by Islamic law.

"Fundamentalism" is Christian shorthand that evokes born-again Protestants who insist on the literal truth of the Bible; since neither the word nor the concept exists in Arabic, a translation had to be invented. Yet, in a sense, Islam is *per se* fundamentalist. The guide to every condition and circumstance of life is supposedly contained within the mystifications of the Koran, the *sunna* (the sayings and doings of the Prophet Muhammad), and the *sharia*, a

Islam's heartland*

1 West Bank and Gaza The fundamentalist group Hamas, which rejects co-existence with Israel, is gaining ground from the Palestine Liberation Organisation and winning the support of Palestinians fighting Israeli occupation

2 Turkey The Welfare Party, seeking closer ties with the Islamic world, fought the October 1991 election in alliance with two nationalist parties; the alliance won 17% of votes, but no seats. Several small fundamentalist groups engage in terrorism

3 Syria The Muslim Brotherhood has been outlawed and brutally repressed since the early 1980s, but is believed to have residual support

4 Lebanon Two Shia Muslim groups, Hezbollah and Amal, are supported by Iran and Syria respectively. Hezbollah is winning the competition between them

5 Iraq Underground Shia fundamentalist groups have strong support in southern Iraq, and played a big part in the rebellion after the Gulf war. The largest, Dawa, founded in 1968, has been severely repressed, with many leaders and militants executed

6 Iran An Islamic republic since 1979. The government is dominated by a political elite of Shia clerics and allied laymen. Their hold on power is reinforced by arrests, executions and the suppression of free speech. Islamic law introduced in 1983, but its implementaion is half-hearted thanks to differences within the leadership. More than 100 offences carry the death penalty

17 Morocco Islamic groups were prominent in anti-government protests in 1990 and 1991. The biggest, Justice and Welfare, never legalised, was ordered to disband in 1990. Its leader is under house arrest and some members are in prison. The party has gone underground with other clandestine, more radical groups, such as Islamic Youth

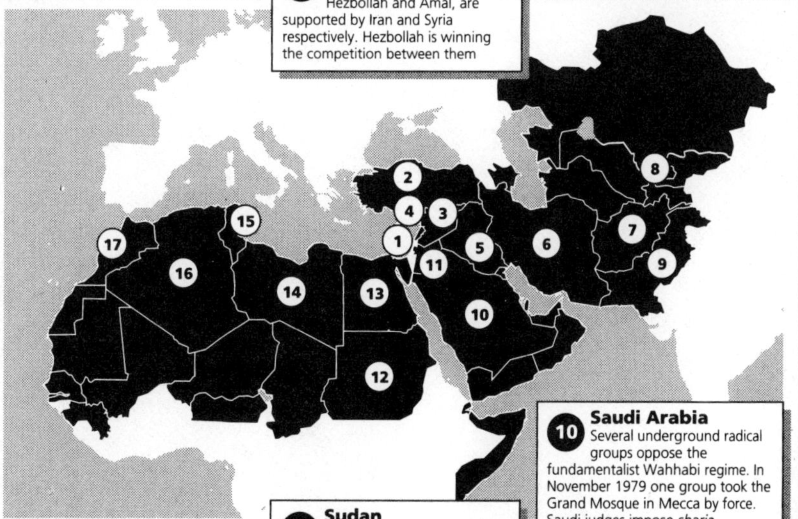

7 Afghanistan Four Sunni fundamentalist parties—Hizb-i-Islami, Hizb-i-Islami-Khalis, Jamiat-i-Islami, Ittihad-i-Islami—and several smaller Shia groups oppose President Najibullah. Their call for a strict Islamic republic is supported by a minority of Afghans

16 Algeria The Islamic Salvation Front (FIS), legalised in 1989, won 55% of the vote in the June 1989 regional election, and 49% in the first round of the general election in December 1991. The government cancelled the second round. Most FIS leaders were jailed. The party was banned formally in March 1992 and local councils under the control of the FIS dissolved

8 Central Asia Independent Azerbaijan, Kazakhstan, Turkmenistan, Uzbekistan, Kirgizstan and Tajikistan are going through an Islamic revival, with much mosque-building and religious observance. Iran and Saudi Arabia compete for influence. Some want an Islamic state like Iran; others prefer a secular state like Turkey. The fundamentalist Islamic Renaissance Party has failed to create a single Islamic movement across Central Asia

10 Saudi Arabia Several underground radical groups oppose the fundamentalist Wahhabi regime. In November 1979 one group took the Grand Mosque in Mecca by force. Saudi judges impose *sharia* punishments: public beheadings and hands amputated for theft

15 Tunisia Members of the Ennahdha (Renaissance) party competed in the April 1989 election as independents. Since early 1990 the party, never legal, has been repressed, its newspaper closed and militants arrested after clashes with police and the discovery of alleged plans for "Islamic revolution". The leadership split in 1991

13 Egypt The Muslim Brotherhood, founded in 1928, has come through periods of militancy and persecution. It is still barred from operating as a political party, but fought the 1987 election in alliance with two secular parties, winning 37 seats. Radical groups, such as Jihad (which assassinated Sadat), operate underground. There are frequent clashes with the police; hundreds of militants were arrested this year

12 Sudan A military junta under Lieut-General Omar Bashir came to power in 1989 and is increasingly dominated by the fundamentalist National Islamic Front led by Hassan Turabi. The junta has links with Iran, which has sent 2,000 Revolutionary Guards to Sudan. A new penal code based on *sharia* law was introduced in 1990, except in three Christian southern provinces, and came into full force this year. Radical groups collect money in Saudi Arabia for *jihad* against the south

11 Jordan The Muslim Brotherhood is the largest single block in parliament with 22 seats. It was given five cabinet seats in January 1991, as the Gulf war approached, but lost them in June, as King Hussein planned peace talks with Israel, which the Brotherhood opposes

9 Pakistan The Islamic Democratic Alliance (IDA), which links several Islamic and right-wing parties advocating more Islamisation, formed the government after winning 105 seats in the 217-seat parliament in the October 1990 election. The IDA includes the fundamentalist Jamaat-i-Islami, which seeks an Islamic state. Islamic law has operated since 1979, but Islamic punishments, apart from occasional floggings, are rarely carried out

14 Libya Unstructured Islamic groups are the greatest internal threat to the regime, clashing frequently with security forces. Several hundred militants are in prison

*Countries and areas shaded have a Muslim majority. Apologies to Bangladesh, Indonesia and Malaysia

codification of the rules and principles in the Koran and the *sunna*. In Islam, mosque and state are not to be separated.

Islam's glory years are long past. The men of God put the decline down to the degeneration of their faith, and to the pollution that blows in from the outside world; they say that things began to go wrong for Muslims when they ceased to be good Muslims. From the middle of the 19th century on, revivalists began preaching a dual message. Since the word of God had been corrupted over the centuries by lip-serving rulers, they called for the recreation of a society that followed the pristine seventh-century principles of the Prophet and his four immediate successors. But, argued these reformists, the baby should not be thrown out with the bath water. If Islam was to win back its old ascendancy it would have to compete in the modern world and absorb the more admirable innovations of foreigners.

The tenor of the message began changing in the second half of this century, first in Egypt and then, with a thump, in Iran. The new revivalists are more radical than their predecessors. They still call for a return to that primitive (and idealised) society but many now speak as demagogues seeking power rather than as scholars sermonising from the pulpit. Some call for *jihad* to rescue the *umma* (the Islamic community of nations) from the secular policies of nationalist leaders and their foreign patrons. Foreigners are seen, at best, as the purveyors of corrupt standards; at worst as the enemies of God.

These new men are clerics, religious laymen and politicians who hitch themselves for opportunist reasons to the Islamic wagon. Many of the dictatorial Muslim rulers—Nasser, Hafez Assad, Saddam Hussein—who allowed no secular opposition hesitated, though not for long, to persecute the men who challenged them from the mosques. While the hesitation prevailed, Islamic militancy was the only reasonably safe route for dissent.

The religious message found a receptive audience, among a wide cross-section of people, from doctors and lawyers to the very rich and, above all, to the very poor. The listeners include the faithful who dream of a pure Islamic state, who are distressed by the loss of old certainties and angered by the cynicism or cruelty of their rulers; it also includes people who see their livelihoods being swept away by imported changes, and the growing number of urban unemployed.

Yet political success has been limited. Since the new brand of radicalism surfaced in the 1950s, the militants have had a revolutionary triumph, a military coup, and an electoral near-miss. First came the 1979 Iranian revolution, inspiring joy and fear but not, as many had prophesied, followed by a series of smaller repeat performances in Arab countries. The fundamentalists' thwarted victory in Algeria's parliamentary election in 1991-92 sent fresh tremors through the region. In between, Sudan was turned, by army coup, into an Islamic state that has now adopted *sharia* criminal as well as civil law.

Most Middle Eastern governments fight their fundamentalists, with guns and the occasional pot of cream. All governments pay at least lip service to Islam, but all are afraid of being pushed by militants into radical Islamic ways and several have reacted savagely. Syria's President Assad, who slaughtered several thousand militants and their families and neighbours in Hama in 1982, leads the brutality stakes. Egypt plays a double-handed game: fundamentalists are treated harshly—imprisoned and sometimes tortured—when they are not being coopted into the political system.

Saudi Arabia is the one Muslim country that has never been anything but a classic fundamentalist Islamic state, with the Koran as its constitution and the *sharia* its criminal and civil law. "Our Islamic faith", said King Fahd last weekend, "includes an integrated system and complete creed." Western-style democracy, he said, was inappropriate.

The Islamic threat

Main target: fellow Muslims. Best answer: democracy

IT IS the mightiest power in the Levant and North Africa. Governments tremble before it. Arabs everywhere turn to it for salvation from their various miseries. This power is not Egypt, Iraq or indeed any nation, but the humble mosque. Over the past year or so, for the first time in a decade, Islamic fundamentalism has become the principal threat to the survival of regimes throughout the Arab world. Because this is an argument about how people think and live, not merely about lines on maps, its outcome may do much more than either the old conflict with Israel or the new one between Iraq and its neighbours to shape the Arab future.

Like most big social movements, the expanding power of the mosque is a complicated affair. It takes different forms in different countries and its consequences are graver in some places than in others. But the threat is real enough. In Algeria about 600 people have been killed since the army stopped the Islamic opposition from winning last year's parliamentary election. Egypt this winter has seemed in danger of slipping the same way: President Husni Mubarak called this week for a "global alliance" against the menace. Given that Egypt and Algeria are the most populous countries of the Arab world, Muslim commentators who dismiss the fundamentalist threat as a bogey conjured up by Islam's slanderers in Israel and the West could not be more wrong.

A real threat; but one too often distorted. The caricature of the moment is that two radical Islamic states, Iran and Sudan, are intent on fostering religious revolutions among their neighbours. Iran insinuates its poison northward into the ex-Soviet Muslim republics of Central Asia and westward into the decaying body politic of Iraq; Sudan does a similar job on Egypt and the Maghreb. Credulous Muslims inside the target countries are recruited into an Islamic Murder Incorporated. Their hearts filled with hatred, they are urged to overthrow their secular governments, reinstate a set of laws (the *sharia*) formulated centuries ago, and draw the world ineluctably towards an apocalyptic war of religions.

There is something in this: caricatures do not work unless they capture some sort of likeness. But it is caricature nonetheless. It exaggerates, first, the degree to which fundamentalism is a single phenomenon, planned and controlled by rogue states and pushed deliberately across national boundaries. Though the priests who rule Iran may indeed wish that Islam could be used that way, the plain fact is that after 14 years of trying they have signally failed to export their revolution (except, perhaps, to Lebanon). It is laughable to suppose that the shambolic Sudanese will succeed where the Iranians failed.

The caricature's second distortion has to do with that apocalyptic war of religions. It is true that the old cultural jostling between Islam and its rivals has not yet stopped. It is prolonged by the unresolved fight over Palestine and renewed by the Christian slaughter of Muslims in Bosnia and Hindu revivalism in India. In much of the Muslim world, and specially in the Arab part of it, these things add to a sense of grievance and isolation. But the principal challenge to Arab regimes is home-grown, authentic, and has far more to do with local economic failure than with the fate of the *umma*, the overall world community of Muslim believers. It is Arab rulers, not western ones, who are most at risk from Islamic fundamentalism, and it is they who need to answer it. The question is how.

Algeria's example, and how to learn from it

A problem with local causes requires local answers. Recent events suggest only one safe generalisation: the appeal of the mosque grows when that of the government shrinks. In Algeria 16 months ago, when the authority of the socialist clique that had ruled unopposed for 30 years had shrivelled to nothing, it was only natural that victory in the first round of the country's first free election should go to the mosque-based party, the Islamic Salvation Front (FIS). During the years of repression, the mosques were the only institutions that had remained vibrant, and whose leaders seemed untainted by corruption.

A lot of FIS voters wanted to boot out a rotten government, not to live under *sharia* or launch a holy war. Because of that, a parliament under the party's control would probably have been a more liberal affair than outsiders imagined. Once made responsible for running the economy, the Islamists could no longer have fed off economic failure. But because the election's second round was cancelled, nobody will ever know. The only certainty is that the military clampdown of the past year has done nothing to increase the appeal of the government at the expense of the mosque. Only the readiness of the ruling party to see through an election—and, if necessary, to go uncertainly into opposition—could have done that.

Must Egypt follow in Algeria's dismal path? Its tactics used to be shrewder. Mr Mubarak gave the venerable Muslim Brotherhood a limited voice in politics, while fighting remorselessly against the violent underground. Lately he has shown signs of letting a handful of terrorist attacks against tourists provoke him into a general onslaught on the mosque. Repression can work for a while. But in the long run this is a battle no Arab government can win—unless it has the courage to arm itself first with a mandate from the people.

India: the crisis of secularism

James Chiriyankandath

The destruction of the Babri Masjid in Ayodhya by Hindus committed to constructing a temple at the alleged birthplace of the god Ram has stoked up the fires of communal conflict in India. The violence that convulsed Bombay and Ahmedabad in January added 700 lives to the 1,300 who had died in the turmoil immediately following the demolition of the disused mosque on 6 December 1992.

This bloodiest and most widespread outbreak of Hindu-Moslem violence since the partition of the subcontinent in 1947 underlines the depth of the crisis now engulfing India. The crisis has been compounded by the Congress government's flawed tactics, especially its combination of prevarication, accommodation of Hindu demands and half-hearted punitive action. But its roots lie far deeper. First, in the political fragility of the secularism espoused by the leaders of modern India; and second, in the passions aroused by the attempt of the Bharatiya Janata Party (BJP) to tap the political potential of Hindu identity.

Though a 1976 constitutional amendment introduced the word 'secular' to describe the Republic, the basic law of the state contains ambiguous elements. It grants the state the authority to provide for the right of all Hindus, irrespective of caste, to enter temples and other Hindu public institutions; and it allows the government to fund educational institutions run by religious minorities (as well as oversee the communally established Aligarh Moslem and Benares Hindu universities). Such provisions express a fuzzy conception of secularism which, rather than making the state independent of religion, ostensibly seeks to accord equal respect to all religions. This has facilitated the state's inconsistent – and thereby often discriminatory – involvement in religious affairs. It has also helped, implicitly, to legitimise the communal and caste-based strategies, and ostentatious public religiosity, that form an integral part of the repertoire of Indian politicians. The fact that no national political party has felt able consistently to shun such tactics has provided the BJP with powerful ammunition with which to attack what it refers to as 'pseudo-secularism'.

The BJP's recent success – from winning 2 seats and 7 per cent of the vote in the 1984 parliamentary poll to 119 seats and 20 per cent in 1991 – has to be viewed in the context of a decade of unprecedented change. The rapid spread of modern consumerism, with the television revolution no longer limited to affluent urbanites, has contributed to aggravating a pervasive sense of social and cultural insecurity. The growth of a powerful nexus between politicians and the criminal underworld in many parts of the country – together with the emergence of potent separatist movements and a contingent rise in terrorism and state repression – has also helped fuel disillusionment with the political system.

The BJP has proved well placed to exploit the opportunities afforded by this state of flux. Having effectively become the political arm of the Rashtriya Swayamsevak Sangh (RSS – National Volunteer Organisation), a movement launched in 1925 with the regeneration of Hindu India as its objective, it is linked to the family of RSS organisations known collectively as the *sangh parivar*. They range from the Vishwa Hindu Parishad (World Council of Hindus) and its youth wing, the Bajrang Dal (at the forefront of the Ayodhya agitation) to bodies active in such diverse fields as education, labour, culture, the media and organising Hindus overseas. The RSS alone, with around 30,000 *shakhas* (branches that meet daily), has about 3m active members, some 3,000 of whom are *pracharaks* (celibate full-time workers).

While the BJP is thus the best organised national political force, the progress it has achieved owes much to the counterproductive strategies pursued by its centrist rivals – Congress and the Janata Dal. The Congress Party, which regained power in 1980, had been transformed under Mrs Gandhi into a precarious personality-based, vote-gathering machine. As such, it increasingly began to rely upon ill-disguised invocations of a majority Hindu identity. Significant in Rajiv Gandhi's sweeping election triumph in 1984, this trend showed itself again in the officially inspired 1986 court decision to overturn a 36-year-old judicial order and allow Hindus to perform devotions before the idol of Ram that had been installed within the Babri Masjid in 1949.

Congress might have hoped that this concession to the VHP's campaign to 'liberate Ram's birthplace' would neutralise any effort by the BJP to capitalise on the issue. However, the almost simultaneous decision to introduce a bill that overturned a Supreme Court judgment on a Moslem divorcee's right to maintenance highlighted the failure of successive governments to do away with separate Moslem personal law and establish the constitutional objective of a uniform civil code. It meant that Congress was seen as pandering to communal demands at every turn.

Meanwhile, guided by the party president, L.K. Advani, an RSS veteran, the BJP had fully endorsed the Ram Janmabhoomi campaign. The party's unprecedented success in winning 85 seats in the 1989 general election was facilitated not only by Rajiv Gandhi's vain attempt to appropriate the garb of Hindu nationalism, but also by the tacit anti-Congress alliance with the new Janata Dal combine of V.P. Singh. The latter's miscalculation soon became apparent. In November 1990 the Singh government fell when the BJP withdrew parliamentary support after the arrest of Advani as he conducted a tumultuous *rath yatra* (chariot journey) to Ayodhya.

Subsequently, Advani confirmed what both Congress and Janata leaders appear to have signally failed to grasp – that the Ayodhya movement was not about the reclamation of a religious heritage but the assertion of a distinct national identity. He

From *The World Today*, Vol. 49, No. 3, March 1993, pp. 54-56.

declared: 'What happened in Ayodhya ... was the start of the foundation of the Hindu *Rashtra* [nation].'[1] The most authoritative exposition of Hindu *Rashtra* is found in *Bunch of Thoughts*, a collection by the last *Sarsanghchalak* (philosopher-guide of the RSS), M.S. Golwalkar. Emphasising throughout the uniqueness of Hindus and their identity with the motherland, he refers to Indian Moslems, Christians and Communists as alien threats and says:

> 'All that is expected of our Moslem and Christian co-citizens is the shedding of...their foreign mental complexion and merging themselves in the common national stream.'[2]

The denouement of the Ayodhya dispute must be seen against this background. The Prime Minister, Narasimha Rao, took office in June 1991 committed to the late Rajiv Gandhi's equivocal stance: the Congress(I) was committed to constructing the temple without dismantling the mosque. In September 1991 Parliament passed a bill protecting the status of all places of worship (excluding Ayodhya) as they stood at Indian independence. Intended to reassure Moslem opinion, it was opposed by the BJP (the VHP has listed 3,000 mosques to be reclaimed) and failed to contribute to a resolution of the controversy.

In July 1992 a looming confrontation over the Uttar Pradesh BJP state government's reluctance to enforce a court stay on temple construction activity was only averted by a personal assurance from the Prime Minister to the Hindu religious leaders involved that the government would seek to resolve the problem in a time-bound manner. In response work on the site was suspended for three months. However, tripartite talks involving the government, the VHP and the Moslem All-India Babri Masjid Action Committee broke down in November owing to the VHP's inflexibility.

The government's behaviour leading up to 6 December and since then has held echoes of Congress' failed strategy in the 1980s: an attempt to appropriate the Ram plank while still seeking to reassure the country's 110m Moslems. It refused to act on warnings from several quarters, including its own Intelligence Bureau, that the UP government was unlikely to abide by any undertakings to prosecute legal orders safeguarding the mosque.

Adhering to an unusually restrictive interpretation, the Prime Minister did not use constitutional provisions that would have allowed the dismissal of the state government and the use of central forces to protect the mosque. Instead, Rao opted for action after the event: the imposition of President's rule in Uttar Pradesh; the detention of six prominent figures, including Advani, on charges of incitement to communal hatred and riot; a ban on five communal organisations – the RSS, the VHP, the Bajrang Dal and two small Moslem groups (less than 4000 members of the banned organisations have been detained and the activities of the *sangh parivar* have been scarcely affected); and, under pressure from within the Cabinet, the dismissal of the three remaining BJP state governments.

These actions smacked of panic and did little to dispel the impression of ineptitude and weakness. The bans and dismissals and the temporary imprisonment of Advani provided valuable propaganda for the BJP and only served to undermine the few BJP leaders urging restraint (the religious figures at the forefront of the Ayodhya campaign have gone to the length of demanding a thorough revision of the 'anti-Hindu' Constitution).

In Ayodhya the government has acquired the disputed site in the face of opposition from the leadership of the principal Moslem bodies, most of whom had previously been surprisingly restrained in reacting to the crisis. It has also asked the Supreme Court for its opinion on whether a Hindu structure existed prior to the Babri Masjid, declaring that the situation of a mosque and a temple, to be built by two yet to be established trusts, will depend on this. Meanwhile, a makeshift temple has been erected at the site to house the Hindu idols, and thousands of pilgrims have been permitted to pay their respects.

Given its predicament, the minority government is fortunate that it has three-and-a-half years of its term to run. The Congress(I) can rely on at least the tacit parliamentary support of the communist parties and the splintered Janata Dal, none of which want to risk an election in the current climate. (Opinion surveys taken after 6 December suggest that while the BJP is still well short of gaining an electoral majority, it is enjoying a surge in support, especially in north India.)

There is little indication that Congress or the parties of the centre-left are capable of making use of any electoral respite to counter the BJP's Hindu nationalist agenda. In terms of responding to the politics of identity that have become salient over the past decade, they have not discovered a clear, credible alternative to the kind of secularism that the BJP has so effectively challenged.

Narasimha Rao's bid to accommodate popular Hindu sentiment is likely to alienate Moslems without seriously undermining the BJP, since by its very nature the issue of a religio-national identity does not lend itself to half-measures. But the beleaguered 71-year-old Prime Minister's Congress rivals, such as the Human Resources Minister, Arjun Singh, who has favoured a stronger anti-BJP line, have yet to propose a coherent alternative strategy. While the Communists remain confined to regional pockets, the policy followed by V.P. Singh's rump of the Janata Dal, of vociferously championing more positive discrimination for lower caste Hindus, has also failed to neutralise the overarching, if primarily upper caste, appeal of Hindu *Rashtra*.

The international repercussions of a drift to a Hindu India are considerable. The cancellation of the South Asian Association for Regional Cooperation summit in Dhaka in January reflected India's worsening relations with Pakistan and Bangladesh. That situation will certainly be exacerbated by intensifying the Hindu-Moslem conflict. Such unrest will also make it more difficult for India to attract foreign investment, essential if the present economic liberalisation programme is not to run aground. Finally, an assertive, Hindu nationalist India (the BJP is committed to a nuclear weapons programme) riven by internal conflict presents a disquieting prospect for a 'New World Order' already having to wrestle with the serious problems thrown up by aggressive nationalisms in the erstwhile Soviet Union and the former Yugoslavia.

NOTES

1. *India Today*, 15 December 1990.
2. M.S. Golwalkar, *Bunch of Thoughts* (Bangalore: Jagarana Prakashana, 2nd ed., 1980). p. 208.

PHILIPPINES

Trouble in the South

A Wave of Violence in Muslim Mindanao Raises Fears of War

Just last August a beaming President Fidel Ramos promised the people of Mindanao he would turn their resource-rich islands into the Philippines' "economic growth centre." They had given Ramos their votes and with them the election. He responded with millions of dollars for new roads, airports and telephone lines. "Mindanao—Now or Never" became the rallying cry at trade fairs and investment forums.

But as January rolled around it became increasingly difficult to ignore an alarming number of bombings, kidnappings and killings in the southern archipelago. Last week it became almost impossible, as Ramos ordered military security for foreign-funded projects worth billions of dollars. In one of the great understatements of his presidency, Ramos admitted of the region: "Peace and order remains a problem."

The cold truth is that western Mindanao may be on the verge of a renewed separatist war after years of uneasy peace. At a recent National Security Council meeting, Defence Secretary Renato de Villa said the region's two main rebel groups—the Moro National Liberation Front (MNLF) and its smaller spin-off, the Moro Islamic Liberation Front (MILF)—were rearming and recruiting for an undetermined purpose. The two groups have almost tripled in size since 1987. They now have more than 21,000 fighters—double the strength of Sri Lanka's separatist Tamil Tigers.

The eye of the brewing storm is the mountainous island province of Basilan. On Feb. 9 a "Lost Command," a 160-man renegade unit that had broken away from the MNLF, allegedly massacred 21 marines and four militiamen there. That was followed by a Feb. 28 bombing at Zamboanga's international airport that injured 20 people, the March 2 bombing of two marine speedboats that killed a regional assemblyman and wounded a provincial governor, and the March 23 bombing of an administration-party rally, killing four and wounding 42. They were among a spate of attacks leading up to the March 25 elections in the four provinces in the Autonomous Region for Muslim Mindanao (ARMM). In response the military by last week had deployed half its 80 infantry battalions in Mindanao. Says Sen. Blas Ople, chairman of the Senate Foreign Relations Committee, who attended the Security Council briefing: "The foremost threat to national security now is in Mindanao."

It's a threat with a familiar face. The MNLF became active in 1972 after President Ferdinand Marcos declared martial law. Later joined by the MILF, it fought a bloody struggle for a separate Muslim state that left some 100,000 people dead. Their fight ended, or so it was hoped, when the two sides consented to the 1976 Tripoli Agreement. It called for a ceasefire and autonomy for thirteen southern provinces with large Muslim populations. The pact was never fully implemented.

In September 1986 MNLF chief Nur Misuari and President Corazon Aquino agreed to an informal ceasefire. Ratification in 1986 of the new Constitution led to a 1989 referendum that gave autonomy to four provinces. The other nine declined to join. Just as they had boycotted the referendum, the rebels refused to participate in last month's ARMM election. They say the autonomy package fell short of the Tripoli Agreement. Last week the rebels appeared ready to break the 79-month-old truce. Declared MNLF spokesman Sharif Sain Jali in an interview with Asiaweek: "The ceasefire is over."

Even more alarming this time around is the sudden parallel rise of the armed radical group Abu Sayaff (*see* "New Recruits in a 'Holy War' "). Led by a young Islamic preacher, the militants are "using Islam as their vanguard to establish an independent Islamic state," says Interior & Local Government Secretary Rafael Alunan. Abu Sayaff has warned government troops that every time they "inflict suffering to

---

PRICES REPORTED IN ASIAWEEK ARE IN U.S. DOLLARS UNLESS OTHERWISE SPECIFIED.

INTERVIEW/SANTANINA RASUL

'Victims of Exploitation'

As the highest-ranking Muslim official in the Philippines, Sen. Santanina Rasul specialises in the problems of her people. The Senate's only Muslim member spoke to Senior Correspondent Antonio Lopez last week in the wake of the elections in the Autonomous Region for Muslim Mindanao in the country's anxious south. Excerpts:

Now that the administration candidate has been installed as governor, what is the outlook for the region?

Gov. Lininding Pangandaman's landslide victory is an indication that the government has the support of the people in the region. He can now ask for financial support. In Manila you have an executive [President Fidel Ramos] who knows the problems of Mindanao and can provide solutions.

What about the Moro National Liberation Front?

The government stands to benefit from talking with the MNLF. They can be an instrument of peace. But they can also be an instrument for destabilisation. As long as there is reason for Muslims to be discontented, the separatist movement will always be there. The government speaks of security in military terms. For the Muslims security is a collective feeling that their way of life, culture, religion and rights will not be trampled.

And the Islamic fundamentalists?

There's nothing wrong with fundamentalism. What's wrong is when it becomes radical and uses Islam to suit political objectives.

Why is the situation in Mindanao so fragile?

People have been victims of exploitation and neglect for a long time. The Muslim areas have no infrastructure, no communications, no school buildings, no teachers. The government must make the Muslims feel they are part of the nation. There were two or three Muslims in the cabinets [of the past three administrations]. Now there's not a single one. Muslim leaders feel alienated.

innocent Muslims," Christians will also suffer "by Allah's grace."

For now, though, the MNLF still poses the greatest threat. Its defence chief, Abou Amri Taddik, says the MNLF believes "in Mao Zedong's Long March" rather than Abu Sayaff's jihad. The first sign that the separatist guerillas were moving again came with reports that 6,000 high-powered rifles were smuggled into Mindanao last year.

Violence escalated in January, shortly after the government backed out of secret peace talks. The meeting was to have taken place in Jakarta under the auspices of the Organisation of the Islamic Conference. The guerillas are demanding a transitional separate government for ten of Mindanao's 22 provinces. They also want to scrap the law that created the ARMM. "The MNLF and the OIC were embarrassed by the postponement," says MNLF spokesman Sain Jali. He speaks of springing an "April surprise." That could be anything from raising the MNLF flag over Jolo to launching an all-out assault. Warned Misuari in a radio interview: "If the peace process fails, I'm sure there will be war. Some of the younger people are getting impatient."

The March 25 election further angered the MNLF. Over 80% of the ARMM's 1 million voters ignored a guerilla call to boycott the election of a governor, vice-governor and 21 assembly members. Voters overwhelmingly rejected incumbent Governor Zacaria Candao in favor of Ramos's choice, Lininding Pangandaman. The Ramos forces had characterised Candao's three-year administration as corrupt and inefficient. A disgruntled Candao blamed his defeat on "massive electoral fraud and cheating." On leaving office, Candao, a former MILF leader who still commands loyalty from armed followers, vowed to continue "the struggle for autonomy."

Pangandaman, 66, blames four main groups for the lawlessness in Muslim Mindanao: the MNLF and MILF secessionists, feuding political warlords, wanted criminals, and civilians who have armed themselves against the first three groups. Basilan Governor and former guerilla leader Gerry Salapuddin points to years of poverty and government neglect. "In many municipalities the people don't have water, electricity, roads and schools," he says. "People go to Sabah to seek greener pastures, or send their sons and daughters to the Gulf for employment." Pangandaman, a former envoy to Saudi Arabia, vows to ensure that remittances keep pouring in from West Asia. He also hopes to put people to work by tapping the region's agricultural potential. But corn doesn't grow overnight.

Even before the election, the focus was shifting to Basilan. Though 71% Muslim, the province's 250,000 people rejected autonomy in 1989. With its rugged terrain and surrounding sea, Basilan, twice the size of Singapore, has become a favourite hideout for guerillas and bandits.

When the "Lost Command" attacked the marines Feb. 9, the army decided to flush out the Basilan bandits and rebels. After the ambush—

MOVEMENTS

New Recruits in a 'Holy War'

With the Mindanao insurgency into its third decade, the sons of the first guerillas are joining the cause. But some are less concerned with Moro nationalism than with fighting an Islamic "holy war."

The Basilan-based Abu Sayaff group was established two years ago by 28-year-old Libyan-educated preacher Abubakar Abdurajak Janjalani. Followers fashion themselves as "mujahideen commando freedom-fighters" and are well armed with mortars and anti-tank and anti-aircraft weapons. They are believed to be behind a spate of bombings and killings before last month's Muslim Mindanao election. They are also suspected in the February kidnapping of businessman Luis Biel and his five-year-old grandson, and in last month's abduction of priest Bernardo Blanco. "They are a security problem," says Brig.-Gen. Guillermo Ruiz, Mindanao's marine commander and chief of the Basilan Island Command. "They go beyond the teachings of Islam."

Born under martial law, many Abu Sayaff recruits are said to be poor, well-versed in the Koran and open to calls for a separate Islamic state. "They were sons and orphans of Moro National Liberation Front rebels," says Mashur Jundam of the University of the Philippines' Islamic Studies Institute. "These children went to Sabah, where they studied and from where they were sent on scholarships to study Islam in [West Asian] countries. It's alarming. These Moro fighters have their own flag and pledge of allegiance."

Estimates of the group's strength range from 100 to 400 men under arms and growing. "Based on their strict and literal translation of the Holy Koran, they have declared a jihad or holy war," says Interior & Local Government Secretary Rafael Alunan, who considers the group part of a global phenomenon. "They feel a lot of people have strayed from the path of the Holy Koran."

Abu Sayaff "accuses Nur Misuari's MNLF of not waging the real jihad," says Basilan Governor and former MNLF commander Gerry Salapuddin. "Only theirs is the real jihad." Indeed, Abu Sayaff has drawn many followers from the MNLF and the Moro Islamic Liberation Front. Leader Janjalani is wanted for allegedly ordering the shooting of Asad Asid, a former rebel who refused to join Abu Sayaff. "If this group becomes more assertive," warns Sen. Blas Ople, "you have the MNLF and MILF as ready-made mujahideen armies."

MUSLIM ELDERS HAVE DISTANCED THEMselves from the organisation. Says Ustadz Kasim Ismael, president of the Arabic & Islamic School of Basilan: "There is no reason for a holy war."

which many say followed the arrest and disappearance of a village imam—troop deployment was increased from two to six battalions. "This is a police action," asserts Brig.-Gen. Guillermo Ruiz, 52, of the operation. Ruiz commands the 5,300-strong marine corps in Mindanao and the 3,000-man Basilan Island Command. Says he: "We're going after more than 1,000 criminal elements, 300 of whom have arrest warrants."

So far he hasn't had much luck. Two months of daily search-and-destroy operations have yielded only sixteen of the 300 suspects. But he has managed to outrage the island population. His troubles began after the Feb. 9 ambush, when troops allegedly went on a rampage in the village of Tuburan. Residents say soldiers burned down 300 houses and three school buildings. More than

FIGHTING FILIPINOS

Organisation	Forces	Firearms
Armed Forces of the Philippines	122,177	122,177
Philippine National Police	97,527	90,000
Citizen Armed Force Geographical Units	74,587	50,000
Moro National Liberation Front and Moro Islamic Liberation Front	21,320	13,360
New People's Army (Communist Party of the Philippines)	11,920	8,730
Criminal syndicates	6,125	1,975

Source: Philippine government. Most of the figures are estimates

Asiaweek Chart

12,000 people were displaced. "We all fled our village because we were afraid of being caught in the crossfire," says farmer Asala Samma. "And then it was torched. I lost more than 100 chickens and several goats."

"The marines did not do the burning," insists Ruiz, citing a Manila fact-finding mission. "The Lost Command did it." Still, the island's religious elders wrote to President Ramos last week demanding that the military coordinate its activities with them. "The rights of civilians should be respected," said the eleven imams. "Their homes should not be burned and their properties should not be seized. We cannot stand this situation any more. If nothing happens, we're going to the hills." The radical Abu Sayaff sent a more ominous warning. If the army did not withdraw from Basilan, the group said, it would kill Bernardo Blanco, the 65-year-old Spanish priest it kidnapped in March.

Ruiz says the island "is tense in some isolated hinterland areas, but the situation in seven municipalities of Basilan is peaceful." Sen. Santanina Rasul draws a different picture. "There are checkpoints all over the island," she says. "Children cannot go to school. The local government is not functioning any more. The situation in Basilan could engulf the rest of Mindanao."

If hostilities break out elsewhere, the most likely battlegrounds are the mainly Muslim city of Marawi and Christian-majority Cotabato City, seat of the ARMM government. Marawi was the scene of fierce fighting in 1972 when the MNLF captured the city. Cotabato has lately rivalled Metro-Manila as the kidnapping centre of the nation. It also harbours heavily armed rebels loyal to defeated governor Candao.

A new war in the south would cost the country plenty. For starters, the government had planned to demobilise six army divisions, or 5,000 men. That seems unlikely now. More important, increased hostilities in Mindanao could set back the government's development plans by years. With 15 million people and an area a quarter the size of Japan, Mindanao is the Philippines' last frontier. The region's exports exceeded $1 billion last year and contributed one-fifth of the nation's gross domestic product. It contains one of the world's richest nickel deposits and accounts for three-quarters of the Philippines' iron reserves and nearly a third of its coal. Multinationals Dole, Del Monte, United Fruit and Nestle are just a few of the foreign investors Ramos hopes the military will protect.

Our vision of the Philippines 2000," said Ramos last week, "cannot be achieved without achieving Mindanao 2000." If that's the case, Ramos's plan to turn his country into a newly industrialised nation within seven years faces a stiff challenge in the south.

ASIA'S BOSNIA

Susan Blaustein

SUSAN BLAUSTEIN is a Washington-based free-lance writer who recently returned from Rangoon.

As masters in the art of ethnic cleansing, Bosnian Serbs have rivals. Further away, sealed off from the international media and protected by a phalanx of regional appeasers, Burma's ruling junta has been conducting ethnic warfare—replete with mass murders, relocations and rapes—that provides a steely Eastern counterpart to Milosevic's rampage. For years the West has known this. But startling new documentation came in late February in a fifty-page report from the United Nations Commission on Human Rights. It details the activities of the ruling State Law and Order Restoration Council (SLORC), which came to power in 1988 after slaughtering thousands of pro-democracy demonstrators.

With the help of a billion dollars' worth of Chinese arms and fighter aircraft, the Rangoon regime has been waging a vicious campaign to subdue the Karen, Mon, Karenni, Kayah, Kachin, Shan, Wa, Kokong, Naga and Muslim minorities in outlying areas bordering Thailand, China, India and Bangladesh. These various ethnic groups, composed mostly of upland peasant farmers, have merged their ragtag rebel armies into a scrappy, tenacious guerrilla force that is outnumbered ten-to-one by SLORC's 400,000-man army.

Like the Serbian regime, SLORC has used terror to get its way. Burmese army troops have looted, razed and burned some 850 up-country villages, raped several thousand women, forced more than a million people from their homes and "eliminated" those "bandit-insurgents" who refused to relocate. The human rights commission states that "many women provided testimony that women in villages relocated by the army were rounded up and taken to military barracks where they were continually raped.... Often the 'pretty' or young ones were raped immediately in front of family members and then taken away." In the report, prisoners recount being forced to watch soldiers rape Muslim women from Arakan state who "were allegedly brought to army barracks and kept there for raping.... Women who had returned to their villages stated that some of the women among them had died as a result of the continual rapes. Two female health workers ... reported that in their clinic, women with rape wounds ... had died from bleeding or subsequent infection."

Pressing village women and men into slave labor, portering and mine-sweeping is another well-documented SLORC war game. The U.N. report cites credible testimony that "hundreds of young boys" have been carted off in trucks from Shan state while collecting water near barracks. One man "reportedly witnessed boys being put on the front line carrying military equipment and huge rice bags. When they were caught in the crossfire, many of the boys were killed." Villagers forced to build roads and railways along the Thai border told the U.N. team that "hundreds of persons were killed by the military" when they could not keep up with the work, and that "the laborers died most frequently as a result of constant beatings, unsanitary conditions, lack of food and medical treatment."

The report details eleven cases of death from torture in custody, though it asserts the true number of deaths is far greater. Torture victims report techniques "including severe beatings with metal rods and chains covered with rubber; the 'iron road' which consisted of a metal rod being rubbed up and down the shins; being burned with cigarettes; being made to maintain certain positions such as the 'motorcycle' for hours; near suffocation or drownings; water torture; sleep deprivation; being made to dig 'one's own grave'; and being forced to watch others detainees being tortured." Students detained in Rangoon's infamous Insein Prison said they had been "kept in a special block" where they "were beaten daily" and subjected to "'beating parties' to which one of the prison authorities would invite his friends."

A year ago SLORC announced the release of all political prisoners. Although some 1,700 are known to have been released, many of these are believed to have been common criminals. In any case, thousands remain in jail and hundreds more, including high school students and their parents, have been arrested or "disappeared."

The U.N. commission devotes two of the most haunting paragraphs in its report to a group of HIV-positive prostitutes from upland ethnic villages. They had worked in Thailand, were deported when the Thais tested them for AIDS and were allegedly "killed with cyanide capsules by Myanmar authorities." For the last year or two, since increased AIDS awareness has made Thai prostitutes less desirable to Thai men, Burmese village girls as young as 13 have been sold by desperate parents to Thai scouts or, as the commission reports, "lured into prostitution in Thailand by men promising jobs with high pay." Forced repatriation of the infected prostitutes stopped, a top Thai law enforcement official told the commission, when it became clear the women's lives were endangered by returning them to Burma.

Hundreds of Burmese students who fled when SLORC took over are also believed by their families to have been killed, detained or "disappeared" once Thailand sent them back to Rangoon, prompting the Thais to stop repatriating and instead to accommodate them temporarily in hastily built student "camps" inside Thailand. According to the report, witnesses claim that the bodies of hundreds of students were buried in mass graves in a military site near the Rangoon airport and in Hlaing Thaya New Township. Witnesses told the commission of having observed "the military transporting bodies in trucks" to this SLORC-built satellite town: "In one truckload, most of the bodies had bullet wounds, but ... in another, the heads and faces of most of the students had been beaten and crushed."

Ethnic hatred in Burma, as in the Balkans, comes with the territory. Since independence from Britain in 1948, successive Rangoon governments have carried out periodic, violent pogroms designed to exterminate or expel many of Burma's 134 ethnic minorities. As in Yugoslavia, Burma's nationhood was an imperialist invention; for six decades British rule smothered ancient ethnic enmities. These erupted, however, on the eve of independence in the assassination of Aung San, Burma's national hero and father of Aung San Suu Kyi, modern Burma's democratic opposition leader, now under house arrest. Aung San is generally believed to have been murdered by outraged members of his own ethnic Burmese stock when he promised all minority regions autonomy and the ultimate right to secede from a new federal union. When the British pulled out, the Karen and other minorities immediately took on the ethnic Burmese, who quickly assumed all high-ranking posts in the military, expelled all members of other minorities from the ranks and by the early 1950s had become Burma's de facto rulers. Since 1962, when General Ne Win seized power in a coup, the Burmese armed forces have pursued a "Burmanization" policy, rationalized as essential to "preserving the Union."

In 1988 Burmese students and the urban middle class, buoyed by the wave of democratization in Asia, revolted against the repressive military regime, only to suffer a severe and deadly crackdown. When the military foolishly allowed elections in 1990, Aung San Suu Kyi led her opposition party to an overwhelming victory, prompting SLORC to arrest thousands of democratic party members and continue its murderous rule. Now SLORC has intensified the terror, declaring "the first main National Cause" to be "the non-disintegration of the Union," a talismanic phrase used to justify its iron hand in ethnically cleansing its population.

SLORC's Burma, like Milosevic's Serbia, is buttressed by neighbors whose avaricious self-interests preclude intervention in a domestic dispute. SLORC has been patronized by its largest trading partner, China, and quietly tolerated by the Thais, whose long-standing policy of constructive engagement has been a thin disguise for appropriating much of Burma's teak, fish, rubber, rubies and jade. Under President Bush, the U.S. Embassy in Rangoon condemned SLORC atrocities, but Bush himself did little to counteract them. As in the Balkans, Bush was far more concerned with avoiding entanglement and appeasing allies: in the Balkans, Russia, Britain and France; in Burma's case, China. So far the Clinton administration has backed the new, civilian-led Thai government, which has subtly begun to assume a more assertive diplomatic role. In late February, despite shrill opposition from China and the Thai military, the Thai foreign ministry assisted the Dalai Lama and seven other Nobel laureates in making a pilgrimage to the Thai-Burma border, where they called for the release from detention of fellow laureate Aung San Suu Kyi and the imposition of an international economic and arms embargo.

In December the Thai government privately told SLORC it was willing to broker a peace conference among Burma's warring factions, as Indonesia did for Cambodia. SLORC privately told the Thais, according to one U.S. State Department official, to "butt out." The United States should heartily support such Thai initiatives and work with Thailand to persuade Japan, the region's most powerful player, to co-sponsor such talks before plunging back into Burma with aid and trade, as it is now poised to do. All three countries might bring Indonesia, Malaysia, Bangladesh and other Islamic nations on board by appealing to their outrage at the atrocities perpetrated against their Muslim brethren. The broad agenda for such a forum would be to seek an end to Burma's civil war, the release of all political prisoners, the transfer of power to the democratically elected, civilian government and the final end of ethnic cleansing.

The Clinton administration might balance its inaction in the Balkans with a more aggressive moral stance in this other brutal, ethnic war. Condemning SLORC and working with allies for the junta's collapse would herald a dramatic shift in foreign policy priorities after four years of reading Bush's lips on human rights concerns. But so far, Burma's horrors seem to have moved this administration no more than the last. "We have no Burma policy," one frustrated senior State Department official told me. "We're drifting."

The unpopular military government of Omar Bashir is engaged in a campaign "designed to methodically transform the very fabric of Sudanese society, molding it into an increasingly militarized and ideological police state in the Iranian style." Meanwhile, an estimated 500,000 Sudanese have died as a result of war and drought, and 1.5 million more may be on the brink of starvation.

Sudan's Human and Political Crisis

KHALID MEDANI

KHALID MEDANI *has worked as a free-lance journalist in Sudan and Egypt; he is currently a research assistant at the Brookings Institution's Africa Project.*

A prominent Sudanese scholar once wrote that "there are no religious differences in Africa and. . .any conflicts that. . .arise are purely secular in nature"—a controversial declaration, but one that provokes a relatively uncharted course allowing for discovery. Nowhere is such an exploration more needed than in attempts to understand the tragedy that has befallen Sudan.

In Sudan as in Somalia, war rather than any natural catastrophe is the chief culprit behind the humanitarian crisis. Sudanese history over the last four decades has been characterized by systematic human rights abuses, particularly in the south, stemming from an intermittent civil war. Successive governments, including the civilian precursor to the present regime, have brutalized civilians in the south suspected of sympathizing with the guerrillas of the Sudanese Peoples Liberation Army (SPLA). But under strongman Omar Bashir this policy has been followed with a zeal and ferocity that warrant international condemnation.

Together with drought, desertification, and other ecological calamities, Bashir's military campaigns in the south and fighting between insurgent groups there have resulted in a war-induced famine. Over the last decade these factors have been responsible for the deaths of an estimated 500,000 Sudanese (250,000 in 1988 alone). More than 4 million have been displaced—one-third the entire population of the south. Among these, the United States Agency for International Development estimates that almost 3 million people require emergency food assistance and more than half of these may be on the brink of starvation. In some areas all the children under the age of five have died. Throughout the south, thousands are afflicted by epidemics of a host of diseases. Acute food shortages have aggravated traditional ethnic enmities, which—combined with the influx of automatic weapons—has led to wholesale massacres.

The humanitarian crisis has been further compounded by spiraling factionalism in the southern insurgency, which in recent years has wrought as much havoc on the civilian population in the south as the war waged by the government (which has encouraged the factionalism). On August 28, 1989, a faction of the Sudanese Peoples Liberation Army led by Commanders Riek Mashar and Lam Akol (known as the Nasir faction) split from the mainstream rebel movement headed by John Garang's Torit faction—ostensibly over allegations of human rights violations and the latter's reluctance to consider the issue of separation for the south, but also over control of relief supplies. That leaders of the Nasir faction seemed to derive the bulk of their support from the Nuer ethnic group, whereas Garang commands the allegiance of his own Dinka tribe, indicates the injection of an ethnic factor into the dispute.

Within this context of a fractured southern opposition and a south increasingly plagued by internecine strife, Sudanese armed forces launched what proved to be a relatively successful dry-season offensive in March 1992. They were aided by the SPLA's loss of its strategic bases in Ethiopia following the fall of the Mengistu regime in May 1990, but most of all by an inflow to the Bashir regime of Iranian-financed Chinese arms worth an estimated $300 million. By the end of last year Garang's fortunes, already badly damaged, took a turn for the worse as Khartoum managed to lift the siege of the southern capital of Juba and also to capture the key southern towns of Bor, Kapoeta, and Garang's home base of Torit near the Ugandan border. Contributing to rebel woes, in September the already divided SPLA fractured further, when Garang's deputy and longtime ally, Commander William Nuyon Bany, defected and formed another rebel group.

The offensive achieved for Khartoum the additional objective of obstructing relief supplies to those civilians it considered sympathetic to the rebels. The UN's much beleaguered Operation Lifeline Sudan finally came to a halt as the security situation deteriorated. In August government forces summarily executed two Sudanese employees of the Agency for International Development in Juba for "collaborating" with the SPLA. By the end of November the majority of international organizations in the country had evacuated their personnel following the murder of a Norwegian journalist and three relief workers, allegedly by forces loyal to Garang. Recently, after a tentative agreement between the government and representatives of the major insurgencies, UN and other relief agencies have trickled back to the south, but they continue to be hampered by the conflict.

AN INEQUITABLE HISTORY

Western analysts and journalists have more often than not portrayed the war in Sudan as stemming from a cleavage between a monolithic Muslim Arab north increasingly energized by the ideology of Islamic revivalism and a southern Sudanese population distinguished only generally as "black" African, Christian or animist, and of a secular political outlook. This view is actively encouraged by apologists of the Islamic fundamentalist regime in Khartoum, whose interests lie in subverting the diversity of the various communities in Sudan (most notably within the Muslim community itself). In thinly disguised schemes, the apologists manufacture the illusion that the people of the predominantly Muslim north are unequivocally committed to the local fundamentalists' particular version of political Islam.

The reality is that Islamic fundamentalism is a relatively modern phenomenon in Sudan, and the roots of the present conflict are not only more structural in nature but date to the colonial era. Far from being a benign occupation, British rule in Sudan between 1899 and 1956 was formative in establishing the obstacles that were to eventually render north-south reconciliation a truly arduous task. Under the British, development efforts were almost exclusively concentrated in the northern portion of the country—primarily in the fertile lands between the Blue Nile and the White Nile south of Khartoum, but also in central Kordofan to the west and Kassala province in the east.

Colonial authorities advanced what they called their "separate development" policy by promulgating legislation in the south that effectively prevented any economic, political or cultural ties with the north. No doubt conscious that they could not possibly control all Sudan's vast territory and a population comprising as many as 500 ethnic groups, the British pursued a divide-and-rule policy. Only a year after the conquest of Sudan, Lord Kitchener, the first governor-general, carefully instructed his regional governors in the proper running of Sudanese political affairs: the "task before us all," he told them, "is [to be] thoroughly in touch with the better class of native, through whom we may hope gradually to influence the whole population."

This "better class of native" eventually emerged along traditional sectarian lines and under the banner of the most powerful of the Muslim sects that had dominated the political, social, and economic life of northern Sudan since the fourteenth century. Considerable British patronage, combined with the manner in which Britain negotiated the independence bargain with northern elites, boosted the political fortunes of two parties that were to determine much of the civilian politics of Sudan after independence: the Umma party, affiliated with the Ansar sect, and what is now the Democratic Unionist party, linked to the Khatmiyya sect. This facilitated the consolidation of an Arabic and Islamic identity in the north, as distinct from a south influenced by Christian missionaries who under British sponsorship provided educational and social as well as religious services to the population. These contrasting political identities, in combination with uneven economic development, have driven the Sudanese conflict since it first erupted in 1955, following a short-lived mutiny by a group of southern officers that was put down by the British. Yet in the words of John Garang, it was the latter—"the differential development between northern and southern Sudan"—that played the more important role in triggering the first phase of the civil war, which was to last 17 years.[1]

In Khartoum sectarian factionalism helped produce a procession of impotent coalition governments unable or unwilling to act on the nation's problems—a pattern to be repeated with every democratically elected government to come. Eventually the leadership of the Umma party took the unusual step of inviting General Ibrahim Abboud to topple its own government in a military coup. In 1958, a mere two years after independence, Abboud took power, and immediately proceeded to carry out a brutal policy of forced Arabization and Islamization in the south that exaggerated the deep cleavages between the country's two halves. Trumpeting the cause of independence for the south, the Anya Nya guerrilla movement (the military affiliate of the Southern Sudanese Liberation Movement) coalesced in the early 1960s to wage war against the regime.

The government voted into power following Abboud's ouster in a 1964 popular uprising was once again dominated by the political parties affiliated with the Khatmiyya and Ansar sects, with the Communist party and the Islamic Charter Front acting as influential spoilers. Predictably no genuine progress was made during this period in relations with the south.

---

[1]John Garang, "Identifying, Selecting, and Implementing Rural Development Strategies in Southern Region, Sudan" (Ph.D. diss., Iowa State University, 1981), pp.42–43.

This changed in May 1969, when Gaafar Nimeiri assumed power in a bloodless military coup. Nimeiri's initial popularity aided a process that led to the March 1972 Addis Ababa accords, which created an autonomous southern regional government within a national unity government; Nimeiri was thus able to promise the south protection of its distinct political and cultural identity. The accords secured a degree of peace between north and south; paradoxically, they also opened a Pandora's box of interethnic disputes in the south as elites there, effectively deprived of full participation in the central government, vied for power, thereby weakening their bargaining position with Khartoum. Without a common enemy in the north, many groups of southerners began to perceive other southern groups as threats. While many saw the Addis Ababa agreement as a miracle of negotiation, it was clear from the outset that despite its many positive elements, the pact was not a permanent solution, but had only laid the groundwork for one.

THE ECONOMIC CATALYST

OPEC's oil price hikes—one year after the Addis Ababa peace accords—played an important role not only in the ultimate resumption of civil conflict in the 1980s but also in the ascent of the Sudanese Islamic fundamentalists. As the Arab oil-producing states accumulated enormous profits, they became extremely interested in overcoming their reliance on the outside world for food, and targeted Sudan as the potential breadbasket of the Arab world.

Far from improving Sudan's economy, however, the flurry of development in the mid- and late 1970s led to deepening woes and exacerbated regional disparities and grievances. Deficient planning, a rising import bill resulting from escalating fuel costs, and pervasive government corruption trapped Sudan in a vicious circle of increasing debt and declining production. Between 1978 and 1982 foreign debt rose from $3 billion to $5.2 billion, and was almost double that three years later when Nimeiri was ousted. Even more ominously, regional inequalities were now dangerously exacerbated. Between 1971 and 1980, more than 80 percent of all government expenditure was centered in Khartoum and Blue Nile and Kassala provinces, with little distributed in other northern regions and almost none going to the south.

With the formal economy in shambles, productive activity came to be concentrated almost exclusively in the "hidden economy," fed by remittances from the hundreds of thousands of Sudanese who, beginning in the mid-1970s, had for economic reasons migrated to the Arab Gulf countries. In 1985 formal remittances represented more than 70 percent of the value of Sudan's exports and 35 percent of all imports. Most of these assets, estimated at close to $3 billion, were channeled through black market transactions that quickly came to be monopolized by the Islamic fundamentalists.

Another development in the late 1970s that significantly promoted the fundamentalists' political clout was Nimeiri's encouragement of Islamic banks in hopes of attracting ever more capital from the Gulf while simultaneously cultivating the allegiance of the Muslim Brothers. The financial power of the Brothers gave them economic leverage that they first used in cultivating a well-organized, albeit numerically small, constituency among the urban middle class, students, and elements of the military establishment. Later, they pressed for the full application of Islamic law (Sharia).

The active support of the Muslim Brothers helped turn Nimeiri into a ruthless dictator who would pitch the country back into civil war. By the early 1980s he had become desperate, with the economy crippled by an $8-billion debt and his political base ever narrower. In June 1983, under the pretext of granting more power to the marginalized groups in the south but primarily to secure revenues after the discovery of oil in the southern town of Bentiu, Nimeiri unilaterally decreed the south's division into three regions—effectively abrogating the Addis Ababa agreement and the peace between north and south it had brought. In September Nimeiri imposed the Sharia, with a view to undermining sectarian parties and appeasing fundamentalists. The September Laws, as they came to be known, introduced archaic and inhuman criminal penalties that included flogging and the amputation of limbs for offenses such as petty theft and the consumption of alcohol. More ominously, they made religion one of the leading divisive factors in the Sudanese conflict.

Garang's formation of the Sudanese Peoples Liberation Movement in July 1983, a full three months before Nimeiri's implementation of Sharia, was in response to a central government not only increasingly set against the south, but one that had become extremely unpopular in the north as well. Garang rejected secessionism, calling instead for a "national revolution" that would restructure the country's economy to correct its regional and social inequities and fashion a new, united Sudan that transcended all barriers of religion, race, culture, and even gender.

It was less clear, however, whether many of his movement's rank and file shared Garang's vision of a united Sudan, or whether they fought for the more limited objective of liberating their homelands from a government they considered alien. Garang's success on the battlefield throughout the 1980s, however, meant that he was able to effectively silence those southern voices calling for separation. His was an ambitious goal, but one whose realization seemed possible following Nimeiri's ouster by an intifada (popular uprising) on April 5, 1985, triggered by a government attempt to implement an International Monetary Fund (IMF) austerity program.

A FLEETING VICTORY FOR THE DEMOCRATS

While the history of Sudan after independence has been dominated by two military regimes, both were brought down not by military might but by a coalition of "Modern Forces" (*al-quwah al-haditha*) consisting of federations of professionals, civil servants, tenant unions, and artisans sharing a markedly secular political orientation. Without precedent in Africa, these forces took to the streets in mainly peaceful protests, and were largely responsible for the fall of the two military governments. On each occasion the call for a lasting resolution of the civil war was at the top of the agenda; after Nimeiri's departure in 1985 the Modern Forces diligently pressed the democratically elected government to realize this objective.

Reminiscent of previous bouts of parliamentary government, Sudan's most recent experiment with democracy saw as many as five different coalition governments in three years before the last was overthrown by a military coup in 1989. Yet in the midst of these crises, significant efforts were made toward negotiating a viable settlement to the southern conflict. This time peace seemed imminent precisely because a cross-section of Sudanese, comprising intellectuals and members of the professional and trade unions, took to the streets in December 1988. In a strongly worded memorandum supported by a broad segment of the military, these opponents of the regime effectively presented Prime Minister Sadiq al-Mahdi with an ultimatum: resolve the civil war and repeal the September Laws. A reluctant Mahdi was forced to move toward implementing a 1988 agreement between Garang and the Democratic Unionist party leader, Sayed Mohamed Osman al-Mirghani, involving an immediate cease-fire, a freeze on the September Laws until a constitutional conference could be convened to deliberate on them, and abrogation of defense pacts with countries the SPLA viewed as hostile to its interests. For its part, the Islamic Front found these terms so threatening to its Islamist political agenda that it withdrew from the governing coalition. The front's leadership was particularly distressed by Mahdi's decision to incorporate into the new government members of the professional and trade unions whose secular outlook and democratic inclinations were well known.

On June 30, 1989, only 24 hours before representatives of the SPLA and the major political parties were to meet to review the final draft of the peace agreement, a coup led by Omar Bashir ousted the Mahdi government, aborting the fragile—but nonetheless promising—democratic experiment. The timing of the coup and the regime's actions that followed made it abundantly clear that Bashir and the other members of the Revolutionary Command Council were linked to the Islamists.

Following the council's dissolution of all political parties, trade unions, and civil associations and the repeal of all freedoms of speech and assembly, extrajudicial detentions, torture, and summary executions were carried out across the country. The group with the greatest number of victims among its members was the Modern Forces. Any doubts as to the close link between the regime and the Islamic Front were quickly dispelled as the instigators of the June coup forcibly retired hundreds of military officers and replaced hundreds of civil servants with front members. This ongoing campaign is designed to transform the very fabric of Sudanese society, molding it into an increasingly militarized and ideological police state in the Iranian style. It soon became evident, however, that the Islamic Front's unpopularity in Sudan, and the bankrupt economy, would make this task difficult, particularly as the front become increasingly isolated internationally.

IRAN: SPREADING FUNDAMENTALISM?

Khartoum's abysmal human rights record and its fateful decision to support Saddam Hussein during the 1991 Persian Gulf war cemented its regional and international isolation, and left the regime little choice but to turn to the Islamic Republic of Iran for political and economic salvation. The alliance between Iran and Sudan, closely nurtured in the period following President Ali Hashimi Rafsanjani's visit to Khartoum in December 1992, sent shudders through the Arab world and beyond, sparking concern that Iran might attempt to use Sudan as a springboard to promote political Islam in Egypt and across North Africa.[2]

In reality the Khartoum-Teheran venture was induced by pragmatism rather than ideological affinity. Denied financial assistance from their old benefactors in the Gulf and repeatedly spurned by the IMF on requests for fresh loans, the Sudanese fundamentalists hoped to gain commercial and military support by consolidating relations with Iran. Teheran, on the other hand, wanted to use Sudan not so much to encourage Islamic governments in sub-Saharan Africa but to pursue its well-known regional ambitions and politically outmaneuver its key adversaries in the region, Egypt and Saudi Arabia.

So far, however, Iran's chief contribution has been to assist in establishing a ubiquitous security apparatus in Sudan, made up of the Popular Defense Forces, the security police, and the clandestine Security of the Front (which is linked to the National Islamic Front), whose operations have led to the worsening humanitarian crisis in the country. Iranian military assistance and technical training have enabled the government to purchase the Chinese weaponry that it has used to

[2]Indeed, by March 1993 Egyptian President Hosni Mubarak, troubled by the increasing Islamist threat within his own borders, warned Sudan that Egypt would attack any Iranian naval ships allowed access to Sudan's Red Sea coast.

devastating effect against the south, as well as in violent suppressions of rebellions in northern urban areas sparked by an inflation rate of 120 percent and in the "pacification" of the western province of Darfur. In the central portion of the country, it has enabled Khartoum to carry out against the Muslims of the Nuba Mountains what Amnesty International has termed an "ethnic cleansing," involving widespread arrests, killings, and the forced relocation of hundreds of thousands from their fertile—and much coveted—ancestral lands.

The spreading of Islamic fundamentalism has been hampered by the relatively limited financial transfers from Iran (approximating $86 million). Recent overtures by the Bashir regime to Teheran for more credit transfers have not gained more than an agreement to expand air and sea transportation routes between the two nations. Nevertheless, millions of dollars derived from Iran and from fundamentalist supporters elsewhere have been diverted to fundamentalist groups in Egypt and North Africa through the Popular Arab and Islamic Conference (PAIC), headed by National Islamic Front leader Hassan Turabi. An umbrella group for several Islamic fundamentalist organizations, the PAIC is ostensibly concerned with no more than "sending forth [the Islamic] idea."

Democracy as Conflict Resolution

Any efforts at finding a lasting resolution to the Sudanese crisis should take full account of the country's history, looking beyond reductive notions of the north-south dichotomy. Khartoum's links with the wider world of political Islam, and the factionalism in the southern rebel groups, require a more ambitious agenda.

Alleviating the humanitarian crisis in the south must be the first priority. In this respect it is difficult to see a peace agreement resolving the civil conflict, particularly when one considers the factors contributing to the ascendancy of the Sudanese fundamentalists and their calculated abortion of the democratic experiment. A series of negotiations between the Bashir regime and the SPLA culminating in the Sudanese Peace Conference convened in Abuja, Nigeria, last May yielded little progress beyond a nebulous agreement on a federal structure for the nation. Moreover, Iranian military support of Khartoum and divisions in the SPLA make an agreement unlikely.

The international community must contemplate restoring some semblance of well-being to the affected populations in Sudan. The appointment of a special human rights observer and the establishment of "safe havens" to allow for the secure delivery of relief supplies, while urgently needed, must be augmented with a larger observer mission under UN auspices consisting of hundreds of local human rights observers not only in the south, but in the north, in Darfur province, and in the Nuba Mountains region. Their security should be guaranteed pending an agreement with the Sudanese government and the SPLA factions as well as the exiled democratic opposition.

Such an experiment, like the one now under way in Haiti, has a number of advantages. It establishes a permanent monitoring presence and promotes local participation and strengthens independent civil institutions, providing a viable alternative to the slew of government and rebel organizations that habitually have redirected or obstructed relief supplies to further their own political ends. In combination with intense diplomatic pressure and regional coordination, it could also set the stage for national reconciliation and the restoration of democracy.

Several developments indicate that there is some room—albeit still limited—to maneuver. Khartoum's isolation, particularly in the international financial arena, should be an important factor in policy considerations. In April 1992 the government instituted reforms that went beyond the IMF's policy recommendations, ending subsidies on goods from bread to gasoline and embarking on an ambitious privatization program. This scheme, whose chief contribution has been to impoverish large segments of the nation while benefiting Islamic Front supporters, is clearly designed to garner desperately needed funds from multilateral and bilateral donors.

A close review of Sudanese history shows no peaceful resolution to the conflict can be managed without including the country's resilient, secular, Modern Forces. Almost immediately after the Bashir coup, the Modern Forces, in conjunction with the old political parties and the SPLA, organized under the umbrella of the National Democratic Alliance. This group, while still fractured, should be given a hearing by the United States and the international community, and its work toward reestablishing democracy vigorously encouraged. Moreover, the Democratic Alliance's present lack of coherent policy on the central issues of peace, power sharing, and Islamic law could potentially be resolved with international prodding.

Insistence on democracy as the ultimate tool of conflict resolution should not be viewed as an attempt to subvert Sudan's sovereignty, but rather as a demonstration of confidence in the genuine democratic aspirations of the Sudanese people, unencumbered by dreams of conquest or rallying gestures at fortress walls.

The familiar face of battle

In Angola, an old American ally chooses civil war over democracy

Bernadette de Conceicao remembers the mothers' screams. It was night when she and 200 other refugees fleeing the city of Huambo reached the banks of the rain-swollen Catumbela River in Angola's central highlands. Government soldiers on the opposite bank began pulling people across with a rope. But for many of the refugees, weakened from walking for days without food, the current was too strong. Throughout the night, women in the group sobbed and cried while at least 70 people–many of them children–were swept away and drowned.

De Conceicao buried one of her own children near the river, an 8-month-old girl who starved to death during the flight from Huambo, a city of 400,000 people. "She died because I didn't have milk," says de Conceicao, a 33-year-old Portuguese national who fled the city when rebels of the Uniao Nacional para a Independencia Total de Angola–UNITA–captured Huambo after a 56-day siege that left as many as 15,000 dead. According to de Conceicao, the provincial capital has been annihilated, its buildings flattened by artillery fire, homes and businesses ransacked and the city's wells stuffed with corpses.

War and peace. Like Huambo, Angola's hopes for peace have been devastated by the fighting that has raged since UNITA leader Jonas Savimbi rejected the results of the country's first democratic elections late last year. Though peace talks have reopened in Ivory Coast between UNITA and MPLA, the Movimento Popular de Libertacao de Angola government of President José Eduardo dos Santos, the agreements reached so far are constantly being undermined by the renewed civil war.

Last year's elections were supposed to end a 16-year civil war in which the United States and South Africa supported UNITA while the Soviet Union and Cuba backed the MPLA. American diplomats were confident that Savimbi, whom Ronald Reagan once compared to America's Founding Fathers and whom the CIA backed during the cold war with $250 million worth of arms and training, would accept the results of the United Nations-supervised elections, in which he received 40.1 percent of the vote to dos Santos's 49.6 percent.

But Savimbi balked, and one-party rule has given way to civil war and ethnic cleansing rather than to democracy. Now, democrats in other African countries fear that the so-called Savimbi Option has set a dangerous precedent. Despite promises to support democracy, the Clinton administration has been reluctant to recognize the elected dos Santos government and has resisted British- and Portuguese-backed U.N. Security Council resolutions to lift an arms embargo against the MPLA. Washington's explanations, which many in Africa and in the U.S. Congress find unconvincing at best, are that dos Santos did not win a majority in the election and his government does not control all of the country.

There no longer is any ideological reason for Washington to stick with Savimbi: The Angolan conflict was stripped of any ideological content it may have had when dos Santos abandoned Marxism in 1990 and is now largely an ethnic battle between the eight groups that inhabit the mineral-rich north and the majority of Ovimbundu people in the south, who support Savimbi's UNITA. Like the Serbs in the former Yugoslavia, the Ovimbundu, who under Portuguese colonization toiled as plantation hands while northerners were accepted into an *assimilado* class of civil servants, think history has wronged them.

Any hope of burying Angola's unequal past has been destroyed by the fighting that erupted in January. In cities throughout the north, thousands of Ovimbundu have been dragged from their homes and murdered by civilians armed by the police. Thousands of northerners living in pro-UNITA towns have met a similar fate.

Although the CIA and South Africa are no longer backing Savimbi, Belgian officials say the well-armed rebel leader is able to buy ammunition through the South African homeland of Bophuthatswana and from former officers in the South African security services–without the approval of the South African government. In addition, Belgian sources charge, China is supplying arms to Savimbi through the Zairian port of Matadi. These sources also say that Zaire's president, Mobutu Sésé Séko, allows UNITA to ship weapons through a former CIA supply base at Kamina in exchange for a share of the revenues from Angolan diamond mines. In Lunda Norte province, the heart of Angola's $200 million-a-year diamond industry, gems are mined by illegal diggers working in a loose partnership with UNITA.

The government has cobbled together its own war effort using a number of antiquated cargo planes, most of them leased from the likes of Aeroflot and Uzbekistan Airways. Despite the government's effort, Savimbi controls more territory than he did during the 16-year civil war, an estimated 70 percent of the country and three provincial capitals. Critics charge that during last year's United Nations-supervised troop demobilization, the government allowed most of its forces to be shrunk to about 10,000 soldiers but UNITA used the breather to position 30,000 to 35,000 troops throughout the country.

As a result, UNITA was able to seize key areas in the country's mineral-rich north when fighting erupted last year, and the government's main concern now is its northern oil fields. The 555,000-barrel-a-day industry, which operates through partnerships with Texaco, Chevron, France's Elf Aquitaine Angola and other European oil companies, accounts for more than 90 percent of Angola's export earnings and is the cornerstone of the country's international credit rating–one of the highest in Africa. If the international arms embargo against Luanda were lifted, the MPLA could use its oil-backed credit lines to obtain new loans for weapons.

A government offensive launched last month is regaining some lost territory in the north. A few days after MPLA government troops recaptured the oil town of Soyo at the mouth of the Congo River, Angolan soldiers sat atop a Soviet-made T-54 tank drinking captured South African beer and guarding a fuel dump owned by Chevron, Elf and the Angolan state oil company, Sonangol. On the banks of the river, emaciated dogs chewed on the bloated corpses of three people killed in the crossfire. "In this war nobody is interested in taking prisoners," says Gen. Eusebio Brito Texeira, command-

From *U.S. News & World Report,* May 3, 1993, pp. 56-57, 59.

er of the MPLA forces that retook Soyo. "There's no room for it."

It is Angola's civilians, however, who are bearing the brunt of the conflict. At a children's hospital in Luanda, 30 youngsters are admitted each day suffering from a cholera epidemic that has swept through the city's barrios. Inflation is now running at 500 percent, and outside the capital, consumer goods have all but disappeared from store shelves. In Dondo, a small city in Lunda Norte, residents reportedly are willing to trade diamonds for a pair of bluejeans.

According to Philippe Borel, director of operations for Angola at the World Food Program, which is feeding 475,000 Angolans, at least 1.7 million people are now at risk of famine. Their numbers will grow as more people flee their farms and homesteads for the relative safety of the cities. In Luena, one of the many government-held towns encircled by UNITA, the WFP estimates that 90,000 *deslocados* (displaced people) are crowded into 15 square blocks.

UNITA's pressure on the provincial cities has left many Angolan towns utterly dependent upon WFP airlifts for food. In Malange, an MPLA stronghold set amid the old Portuguese coffee plantations, food arrives on a WFP-chartered Antonov An-32. Arguments break out on the tarmac between the local WFP official and MPLA commanders, who want to put civilians on the plane in violation of the WFP's mandate. In the airport terminal, hundreds wait in hopes of boarding the daily government flight that delivers weapons to the besieged city.

Ghost town. Beyond the airport is a ghost town of empty streets, boarded-up shops and fading wall murals bearing the likenesses of Lenin, Marx and Engels. The Escola Ché Guevara is empty, its students having fled with the women and children of the town or having been forced into the Army. "They all want to leave Malange," says Deputy Gov. Pedro Sebastian.

In the city's only hospital, it is apparent why people are so desperate to flee. In the emergency room an old farmer who tripped a land mine in his fields quietly moans as blood pours out of the bandages encasing his shattered leg. In the next room his companion, a young woman, screams in pain. In the children's wards, tiny amputees sitting forlornly on their beds bear mute testament to a war in which success is measured in the lost limbs of the enemy.

The New York-based human-rights organization Africa Watch estimates that there could be as many as 12 million land mines in Angolan soil. An estimated 330,000 mines are believed to have been laid around the southern town of Cuito Cuanavale, for example, and only 80,000 have been accounted for. Seven of the 37 types of land mines identified by Africa Watch are made in the United States.

In Luanda, the heady, carnival-like atmosphere that prevailed during the run-up to elections has been replaced by the anger of a people who have had peace snatched away from them. In bars and restaurants, the hardened, take-no-prisoners attitude is evident as residents speak of having to kill Savimbi or annihilate the Ovimbundu before this war will end. In an ironic throwback to Angola's Marxist past, freshly painted graffiti on a downtown wall sums up the mood. It says: *"A Luta Continua"*—The Struggle Continues.

Eric Ransdell in Angola
with Louise Lief in Brussels

The Gulf between the rulers and the ruled

The Gulf war ended two years ago. . . . Yet still, says Dilip Hiro, the reigning oligarchies, in particular the Saudis, refuse to countenance promised reforms

The two major problems facing the Middle East are: self-determination for the Palestinians, and the grossly unequal ownership of petroleum among Arab countries. While continued denial of national rights to Palestinians is widely recognised as a major barrier to stability in the region, there is scant awareness of the destabilising effect of the perilously wide gap between the oil haves and have-nots in the Arab world.

Facts are stark enough. While six Gulf monarchies, with a mere million inhabitants, possess 46 per cent of the proven global petroleum reserves, the remaining 15 members of the Arab League, with an aggregate population of 170 million, have only a third of the Gulf states' share. With world reserves at 1,012 billion barrels, the per capita figure in the Gulf monarchies is 25,700 barrels as opposed to 870 elsewhere in the Arab League. That is, the disproportion in oil wealth is 30:1.

The wealth accruing from the extraction of petroleum in the oil sheikhdoms, accomplished by tens of thousands of local and expatriate workers, ends up as the private property of the ruling oligarchies. Since the aggregate oil reserves of Bahrain, Kuwait, Oman, Qatar, Saudi Arabia and the United Arab Emirates (more specifically, three of its seven principalities) amount to 462.6 billion barrels, and since all these countries are run as feudal autocracies, eight ruling families now possess oil reserves which, priced at $20 a barrel, are worth $9,252 billion.

Such outrageously skewed ownership of property in the world's most heavily armed region, with a long history of volatility and violence, is an ongoing recipe for destabilisation and violent upheavals.

After the quadrupling of the petroleum price in 1973–74 had inflated their riches to unimagined heights, the oil sheikhs became the target of Ayatollah Ruhollah Khomeini, the leader of the 1979 Islamic revolution in Iran. He attacked them for perpetuating hereditary power which, he argued, was not sanctioned by Islam. He condemned them for refusing to share power with their subjects as enjoined by the Koran; being morally and materially corrupt; selling oil cheaply to the west, particularly America, the Great Satan; and having failed to liberate Palestine, including Jerusalem—which contains Islam's third holiest shrine—from the Zionists.

Khomeini's condemnation was a source of great worry to the oil sheikhs, who claimed to derive their political legitimacy from Islam and Islamic precepts. So acute was their fear that the Saudi rulers, the single most important group in the Arabian peninsula, encouraged the Iraqi president, Saddam Hussein, to attack Iran in September 1980.

Saddam Hussein accomplished what he set out to do even though it took him eight years: he contained the tide of revolutionary Islam, and made the future of the Gulf monarchies safe. But two years after the end of the Iran-Iraq war in August 1988, he adopted, consciously or subconsciously, the two-point programme for the Gulf that Khomeini had conceived but failed to implement: raising oil prices and overthrowing the Gulf monarchs.

In his speech on 10 August 1990, Saddam Hussein articulated his viewpoint. "Through its partitioning of the [Arab] lands, western imperialism founded weak mini-states and installed the families who rendered it services that facilitated its [exploitative] mission," he said. "Thus it prevented the majority of the sons of the people and the [Arab] nation from benefiting from their own wealth. As a result of the new wealth passing into the hands of the minority of the [Arab] nation to be exploited for the benefit of the foreigner and the few new rulers, financial and social corruption spread in these mini-states . . . [and from there to] many quarters of the majority of the Arab countries." It is a viewpoint shared by an increasing number of Arab intellectuals and religious leaders.

The onus is thus on the Gulf sheikhs to redress the situation by following just external and domestic policies. Following Islamic edicts, they should show concern for those Arabs who live in countries with large populations but little or no oil wealth, and share their wealth with them. The best way to do so would be through a multilateral aid agency funded by them on the basis of an equitable formula. This would end the use of oil money on a bilateral basis as a tool to impose the will of the donor on the receiver, a strategy used most blatantly by the Saudi royals.

External security is best achieved through regional pact(s), and not by relying on western powers, however friendly and willing. Having backed the Damascus Declaration in early March 1991 on the posting of a joint Arab peacekeeping force, consisting of 35,000 Egyptian and 20,000 Syrian troops, in the region, Kuwait reneged.

Reproduced with permission of *New Statesman & Society,* February 26, 1993, pp. 18-20.

Six months later, it signed a 10-year defence cooperation agreement with America, allowing it to stockpile military supplies, conduct training exercises, and have access to Kuwaiti ports and airfields. It thus upset such Arab stalwarts as Egypt and Syria, and provided ammunition to those Arab nationalists who depict the Gulf sheikhs as avaricious ogres more ready to buy western protection through monetary inducements of arms purchases, and a sustained strategy of keeping oil prices low to subsidise western economies, than serving the interests of fellow Arabs.

Kuwait has a problem in motivating even its own nationals to fight for its territorial integrity. The rate at which Kuwait's 20,000-strong armed forces melted in the face of the Iraqi invasion on 2 August 1990 was scandalous. A similar situation prevails in other Gulf monarchies, whose armed forces rely to a very substantial degree on foreign nationals—or mercenaries, to put it bluntly.

The primary reason for the lack of loyalty among the subjects of the Gulf monarchies is that they have no stake in the social system, which is best secured through representative government, public accountability, and civil and human rights for all.

Such a scenario is nowhere in sight, given the vehement resistance to electoral politics, based on adult franchise, in the Gulf monarchies, especially in Saudi Arabia. "The democratic system prevailing in the world does not suit us in the region," King Fahd declared on 29 March 1992. "Islam is our social and political law. It is a complete constitution of social and economic laws and a system of government and justice."

King Fahd seemed oblivious of the fact that, just across the Gulf, the Iranian regime, also claiming legitimacy from Islam, had held four parliamentary and four presidential elections since the revolution in 1979. Iran's electoral system, based on universal suffrage, rests on the Koranic verses that read: "Consult them on affairs" (3:159), and "Their affairs are by consultation among them" (42:38). The Iranians interpret "them" to mean citizens of a realm, not hand-picked advisers, as the Saudi monarch would have it.

The Iranian elections are conducted within the context of a written constitution—something Saudi Arabia, founded 61 years ago, still lacks. When a draft constitution, prepared under his order, was presented to King Saud in 1960 for approval, he rejected it, saying: "The Koran is the oldest and the most efficient of the world's constitutions."

After the seizure of the Grand Mosque in Mecca on 20 November 1979 by 300 militant Islamists in protest at the autocracy and corruption of the Saudi royal family, and the subsequent bloodshed, King Khalid (1975–82) appointed a committee to draft a constitution, followed by an announcement by Crown Prince Fahd that a Consultative Council of 60 to 70 nominated members would be established "in the near future".

Nothing happened for 13 years.

Then, on 1 March 1992, a year after the cataclysmic Gulf war, King Fahd referred to "the momentous events in the recent past" as the (implied) reason for the political reform he announced. His decrees promised a Consultative Council of 60 commoners to be nominated by him within six months, adherence to the rule of law, and an enlarged body of princes to select a new monarch.

Actually, the demand for a Consultative Council to "debate and decide on all domestic and foreign affairs" was the first of ten demands made by more than 100 leading religious scholars, judges and academics, and submitted to King Fahd by Sheikh Abdul Aziz ibn Baz, the head of the country's 17-member Supreme Religious Council (SRC) in May 1991. Since Saudi Arabia was created by Abdul Aziz, the present king's father, in 1932 by an alliance between his family and the leader of the puritanical Wahhabi sect in central Arabia, the SRC is one of the two main pillars on which the kingdom rests.

Other demands of the SRC included reforming the military and arms suppliers with a view to creating "modern, strong and independent Islamic armed forces" backed by a sophisticated arms industry; preserving the interests, purity and unity of the country by "keeping it out of non-Islamic pacts and treaties"; comprehensive social justice based on "equality for all citizens" within the framework of Islamic laws; and, equally important, punishment of all who enriched themselves by illegal means "whoever they are, wherever they are, without any exception of rank".

As before, there was no follow-up on the establishment of the promised Consultative Council. But, in August, about 100 Islamic luminaries submitted to King Fahd a 45-page memorandum, widening and deepening the scope of the ten-point petition of May 1991.

The monarch was not amused. Nor was the head of the SRC. In September, the SRC issued a denunication of the latest memorandum. This statement was signed by only ten of the 17 SRC members, giving rise to rumours that the remaining seven (implicitly) backed the document—a disturbing development for the Saudi monarch. Early in October, he had another piece of bad news. Elections to the revived parliament of Kuwait (which had been dissolved in June 1986 by the emir of Kuwait, under Saudi pressure) were held as promised, and—horror of horrors—the opposition had triumphed.

Only 15 of the 50 elected parliamentary seats went to the pro-government candidates. Of the 35 seats won by the opposition, 16 went to those who belonged to one of the three Islamist parties or had Islamist endorsement. This despite the fact that voting was limited to only 81,400 men out of a total of 410,000 adult citizens who would be eligible to vote under the universal suffrage that exists in such Muslim countries as Iran and Pakistan. And the Kuwaiti government had spent $10 billion to bribe the voters by raising salaries by 25 per cent, writing off the personal debts of all Kuwaiti citizens, and paying seven months' salary to those who had stayed on during the Iraqi occupation.

Due to the traumatic experience of foreign occupation and war, the Kuwaiti voters had become politically more conscious. Instead of enquiring about public services during the election campaign, as they did before, they focused on Kuwait's investments abroad, and the country's security and defence.

Not surprisingly, the new parliament has busied itself with these issues. It passed a law that authorised it to scrutinise all state investments. Its select committees have decided to investigate *inter alia* the depletion of the Reserve Fund for Future Generations by about $55 billion; the government decision in October to buy up all of Kuwaiti banks' debts; and the virtual disappearance of $5 billion of public money invested in a Spanish chemical company, the scandal involving two important members of the ruling al Sabah family.

Established in 1976, the Reserve Fund for Future Generations was built up by injecting 10 per cent of oil revenues into it each year. This brought the total to $85 billion in 1989, seven-eighths of it invested abroad, and managed mostly by the Kuwait Investment Authority, a department of the finance ministry. It is now believed to be worth only $30 billion. Allowing for the $23 billion that Kuwait contributed towards the Gulf war fund, $32 billion remain to be accounted for.

As for the government wiping out Kuwaiti banks' debts, 9,300 debtors are involved. About one-sixth of these are reportedly responsible for 90 per cent of the total debt of $22 billion. They include some of the richest merchants and members of the ruling family. To protect their foreign assets, they have refused to declare them to their creditors' banks.

Financial scandals in Kuwait are nothing new. When the informal stock exchange, Suq al Manakh, collapsed in September 1982, the government stepped in to save the situation, and found itself lumbered with $97 billion in paper debt. When the parliament of the day attempted to discover which al Sabahs owed money and how much, it was dissolved.

As then, so now, the real target of the parliamentary investigators is believed to be Sheikh Ali Khalifa al Sabah, former oil and finance minister, and a powerful member of the ruling family. The opposition see him as arrogant and authoritarian. Though the parliamentary committees lack judicial powers, MPs maintain that if they uncover any wrongdoing, they reserve the right to prosecute.

The moral for the Gulf's ruling dynasties is plain. Representative government can put in jeopardy the future of even the most powerful oligarchs. Thanks to the limited parliamentary democracy in Kuwait, it has been possible to pinpoint instances of major scandals of corruption and mismanagement of public funds. But in the absence of any representative chamber in Saudi Arabia, rumours and innuendos abound.

Since a free press does not exist in the Saudi kingdom, the task of circulating the stories of corruption and other misdemeanours by the ruling elite has fallen on clandestine audio-tapes carrying the sermons of several prominent dissident clerics. Among many such tapes, the one nicknamed "The Supergun" is particularly noteworthy. It denounces royal princes, ministers, high-ranking officials and army officers for corruption, drug-taking, alcoholism and other deviations from the path of Islam. It accuses the royal family of embezzlement and squandering the country's oil wealth which, it claims, ends up in the pockets of the leading princes. The speaker is Abu al Bara al Najidi, *nom de plume* of a former Islamic judge in Saudi Arabia, now reportedly based in Pakistan/Afghanistan.

The government's response has been to offer large rewards for identifying the author(s) of such tapes and banning 40 clerics from delivering sermons in mosques. In mid-December, King Fahd warned Islamic preachers against using the mosque for political purposes, and replaced those SRC members who three months earlier had failed to sign the condemnation of the demand for comprehensive reform along Islamic lines.

But, unlike in the past, the signatories were not cowed by this. In late December, following the shooting down of an Iraqi warplane by the US aircraft in southern Iraq's no-fly zone, they warned the Saudi government against siding with "the infidels" in their battle with "our Muslim brethren in Iraq". That explained why, following the western air strikes against Iraqi targets in mid-January, Riyadh maintained official silence about the use of Saudi airbases by US warplanes.

Undoubtedly, the House of Saud faces rising opposition—primarily from the traditional religious leaders who see Islam undermined by the waywardness of the ruling family at home and western pressures abroad, and secondarily from foreign-educated intellectuals who desire democratic liberties.

For both groups, the reform package offered by the monarch last March was too little too late. Eleven months later, all they had was the name of the chairman of the promised consultative council: Sheikh Abdullah ibn Jubair, a member of the SRC.

A striking feature of this phenomenon has been America's total silence. Washington knows well that the rigorous censorship that blocked news of Iraq's invasion of Kuwait for three days is very much in place. It knows too that there are at least 100 political prisoners, that torture of detainees is routine, that detention without trial can last years and that there is no appeal against wrongful arrest.

America, the foremost upholder of civil and human rights and democracy, has so far refrained from cajoling the Saudi royals towards political pluralism. Why? First, it is much simpler to manipulate a few ruling families—to secure fat orders for arms and ensure that oil price remains low—than a wide variety of personalities and policies bound to be thrown up by a democratic system. Second, elected governments in the Arabian peninsula would reflect the ideologies of Arab nationalism and Islamic fundamentalism prevalent among large sections of the population, and veer away from the west, stressing self-reliance and Islamic fellowship.

The free and fair poll in Jordan in November 1988 resulted in the election of 32 Islamic fundamentalists or their sympathisers in a house of 80, and about half as many Arab nationalists. The distance that the Jordanian government and King Hussein put between themselves and the west during the Gulf crisis of 1990–91 reflected this reality.

More seriously, if the status quo continues undisturbed, it is only a matter of time before another Saddam or Khomeini moves against the avaricious oil sheiks. And next time, the "infidel" west would not find it so easy to intervene militarily, albeit under the umbrella of the United Nations, as it did in 1991.

The current western policy of overarming these monarchies with sophisticated weapons without any pressure for political liberalisation is a rerun of what was done in the case of Iran under the Shah in the mid- and late-seventies. The consequences of that disastrous policy—manifested in the emergence of a revolutionary Islamic Iran—are still with us. Will the west ever learn from the past?

Weapons Proliferation and Arms Control

Arms transfers to the Third World constitute a threat to regional, as well as international, peace and security. The potential for Third World conflict and instability has generated a strong demand among consumers in the developing world for weapons and has resulted in a large market for international arms traders. Arms sales to the Third World during the 1980s totaled over $300 billion, providing many Third World countries with formidable arsenals of conventional weapons for use against both internal and external security threats. The largest portion of these arms sales went to the Middle East and the Indian subcontinent—two regions where tensions have always been high. There is ultimately a limit to the Third World arms market and financial constraints may slow spending. But the availability of increasingly sophisticated weapons provides consumers with the incentive to upgrade their arsenals, especially if their adversaries do so. The demonstrated capability of the Exocet missile in the Falklands/Malvinas crisis illustrated the allure of weapons technology and its escalating cost.

Arms producers have their own incentive to increase their market shares in order to improve economies of scale, contribute favorably to their balance of payments, and perhaps increase their influence in the Third World. Although cold war rivalry is no longer a contributing factor to arms sales, regional conflict continues to provide markets for conventional weaponry.

Another contributing factor to the international arms trade is the entry of Third World arms producers into the market. A number of Third World countries have developed the capacity to produce arms and are actively seeking to promote exports. While these weapons may not rival the technical sophistication of those produced by industrialized countries, their cost makes them an attractive alternative. Third World arms production increases the availability of weapons, stiffens competition within the market, and offers diversity of supply. These factors complicate efforts to control conventional weapons transfers.

Even more disturbing than the spread of sophisticated conventional weapons is the potential for proliferation of nuclear weapons. The Nuclear Non-Proliferation Treaty (NPT) came into force in 1970 and requires signatories that possess nuclear weapons to refrain from transferring this technology to nonnuclear weapons states. The treaty also obliges nonweapons states that have signed not to attempt to acquire nuclear weapons. Although over 150 nations are party to the agreement (including all five countries that have declared their possession of nuclear weapons), India, Pakistan, and Israel (all assumed to either have the weapons or the ability to manufacture them) remain outside the treaty. Argentina and Brazil also remain outside the treaty, but they are cooperating with other Latin American countries to establish a nuclear-free zone in the region. South Africa disclosed that it had built six nuclear weapons, but subsequently dismantled them. Pretoria joined the Non-Proliferation Treaty as a non-weapons state in 1991, but questions have arisen regarding its compliance with IAEA inspections. A number of NPT signatories appear to be working toward developing nuclear weapons. These countries include North Korea (which never fully complied with the treaty's inspection terms and recently threatened to withdraw from the treaty), Iran, Libya, and Iraq. Iraq's capability to manufacture nuclear weapons has been curtailed in the aftermath of the Persian Gulf war.

Many consider the spread of nuclear weapons to be a major threat to international peace and security, generating regional arms races and increasing the likelihood that such weapons will be used. Others regard the proliferation of nuclear weapons with less alarm, claiming that deterrence will work at the regional level in much the same fashion as it worked between the superpowers during the cold war. Whatever the perspective, the proliferation of nuclear weapons remains a controversial issue. The controversy is likely to become more prominent as the 1995 date for renewing the Non-Proliferation Treaty approaches.

Ballistic missile technology to deliver nuclear weapons is increasingly available too. Perhaps even more dangerous, however, this missile technology can be adapted to deliver chemical and biological weapons, the so-called "poor man's nuclear weapons," which are easier to obtain and produce. The concerns about chemical weapons capability were evident during the Gulf War when the coalition forces feared that their troops might face Iraqi chemical weapons on the battlefield. Iraq's SCUD missile attacks against Israel also raised fears that these inaccurate and unpredictable weapons might be equipped with chemical weapons. Although these fears never materialized, it raised awareness regarding the combination of these threats.

The 1987 Missile Technology Control Regime (MTCR), adopted by Western countries to try to halt the flow of this technology, has not proven particularly successful in limiting the spread of ballistic missiles with a range of 100–1000 kilometers. These missiles represent the great-

Unit 4

est threat in the Third World. Adherence to the MTCR is voluntary and some countries with ballistic missile technology remain outside the regime. China's recent shipment of missiles to Iran clearly illustrates the difficulties of controlling this technology transfer.

Weapons proliferation and militarization in the Third World not only increase the potential for conflict and instability, but it also drains resources away from development efforts. The more spent on the military, the less available for education, health care, family planning, etc. How to encourage a reduction in military spending and the channeling of resources toward more productive purposes remains a dilemma.

Looking Ahead: Challenge Questions

What are the trends in arms sales to the Third World? How would you explain these trends?

What are the implications of increasing Third World arms production?

Why is nuclear weapons proliferation difficult to control?

What are the implications of the spread of ballistic missile technology throughout the Third World?

What role has the International Atomic Energy Agency played in eliminating Iraq's nuclear weapons program? What lessons has the agency learned?

Why is North Korea's nuclear weapons program considered such a threat?

How might industrialized countries encourage reduced military spending by Third World countries?

What are the consequences of high levels of military spending by Third World countries?

In what ways might Third World military spending be considered a reasonable investment?

THE WORLD'S TOP ARMS MERCHANT

The U.S. grabs more of a shrinking market

Third World Network
FEATURES

In the 1980s, global arms-spending rocketed to nearly $1 trillion yearly—or about $2 million a minute. The magnitudes have tapered off slightly since 1991, and what augurs a qualitative reduction has been the exit of the former Soviet Union, one of the paramount international death merchants. But its place will be taken by others, with the U.S. being the grand trafficker leading the pack. Of the almost $1 trillion spent on arms annually in the 1980s, around $860 billion was spent by the advanced capitalist countries and the command economies and $140 billion by the Third World. Hitherto dominated by the two superpowers, which grabbed two thirds of arms exports to the Third World between 1983 and 1990, the arms bazaar is a concentrated market. Sales to the Third World during that time were worth more than $301 billion, with the Middle East accounting for more than 50 percent of the traffic. Saudi Arabia, which spent $57.3 billion, and Iraq, which spent $30.4 billion, were recipients of almost one third of Third World purchases. U.S. policy has contributed massively (and not only in Israel, where there are 300 nuclear warheads) to the militarization of the Middle East.

Ten countries have accounted for 85-90 percent of worldwide exports: the U.S.S.R., the U.S., France, Britain, Germany, China, Czechoslovakia, Poland, Italy, and Switzerland. Conversely, seven countries in the Middle East and three in the Indian subcontinent (India, Afghanistan, and Pakistan) have absorbed the bulk of arms imports. In the arms traffic, the two leading arms merchants were running neck and neck in 1983, when the U.S.S.R. spurted ahead, a trend that has been drastically reversed. The enhancement of U.S. market share in the Third World and the Middle East was discernible prior to the collapse of the Soviet Union. There was nothing fortuitous in this. It had become an explicit marketing objective of the Pentagon.

It appears highly improbable that President Boris Yeltsin's Russia will ever be able to recoup anything near the lost market share of the former U.S.S.R. The collapse of the former U.S.S.R.—and its implications for international arms traffic—transpired precisely when the world business cycle was dropping and the resources to buy arms in the Third World and elsewhere had diminished. This deceleration of global capitalism is matched by yet other factors: the drive to Third World self-sufficiency, of which Iran, India, and Pakistan are prime examples, and the shift of many leading Third World countries from conventional to non-conventional arms: biological, nuclear, and chemical.

Undoubtedly, the U.S. and other arms sellers will continue to push arms sales. But one perceives, nonetheless, an upper limit. For most Third World countries, debt-servicing and military outlays take up 50-70 percent of central government revenues. Moreover, there is the escalating cost of arms. Since World War II, prices of U.S. high-tech weapons have climbed 200-fold. Given the cumulative impact of these factors, the prospects for the Third World's being a sustained dumping ground for the arms are not so sanguine.

The international arms trade is a mere 2.6 percent of global trade. There is an upper limit to the number of laser-guided and television-guided bombs, computerized radar systems, Patriot missiles, and so forth that the Third World and the Middle East can absorb. There is, of course, another palpable element at work, and that is the mounting hostility of world opinion against militarization.

U.S. President George Bush's foreign-policy obsession distracted public opinion from the abysmal failings of the U.S. economy, but the public mood has drastically shifted. The continued pathology of U.S. arms-spending can only further intensify the problems in America. Not only did U.S. productivity decelerate in the 1970s and 1980s, but real

Frederick Clairmonte; from the Third World Network Features agency of Penang, Malaysia. Clairmonte was formerly with the United Nations Conference on Trade and Development.

From *World Press Review*, September 1992, pp. 13-18. Reprinted by permission.

hourly wages declined, as well. The crescendo of poverty in the U.S. has attained deafening proportions.

This is the entrenched affliction that President Dwight Eisenhower bravely sought to correct—unsuccessfully. "Every gun that is made, every warship launched, every rocket fired signifies in the final sense a theft from those who are cold and are not fed. This world in arms is not spending money alone. It is spending the sweat of its workers, the genius of its scientists, the hopes of its children." This was his warning against the menace of frantic proliferation that he branded "the military-industrial complex," a Frankenstein monstrosity whose growth in the decades to come Eisenhower could only dimly have conceived. In every year from 1951 to 1991, military outlays exceeded the combined net profits of all U.S. corporations.

There is ample reason to celebrate the exit of the Evil Empire from the first circle of death merchants. But, distressingly, the lessons to be drawn from the tragedy of the U.S. military-industrial complex and its connections with the Third World have yet to be understood by the U.S. political caste. But even in Bush's America, populist, anti-militarist, and other pressures are inexorably climbing. This is a movement that will gather momentum in the years ahead.

'Supermarket' In the Pacific

Asia Is on a Buying Spree

Asia MAGAZINE

John Dikkenberg

In 1983, Western intelligence agents made a shocking discovery. It appeared that China had sold Pakistan the plans for a nuclear bomb, plus enough weapons-grade uranium to make two soccer-ball-shaped warheads. As far as Western arms-watchers were aware, this was the first time that one developing country had given the complete design of a tested nuclear weapon to another. The U.S. made a working model of the bomb, triggered it, and watched the global balance of power blow up in a big puff of smoke. The watchers now believe that one Pakistani nuclear complex can mass-produce more doomsday devices. Not only that: Pakistan has the missiles to fire these payloads deep into India, Afghanistan, or central China. Ironically—in a perfect example of the dog-eat-dog world of global arms-dealing, in which there are no scruples, ethics, or borders—China sold these missiles to Pakistan in the first place.

Asia is on an arms-buying spree. The British publication *Jane's Defence Weekly* says that there is a military buildup of "unprecedented proportions," although the rest of the world is scaling down in the new spring of the thawing East-West cold war. Much of Asia's supermarket splurge can be put down to "forced modernization," an Australian government spokesman says.

Arm in arm with the regional binge comes an Asian arms race, which has heated up in the wake of the Soviet Union's withdrawal from Vietnam and the closure of the U.S. Subic and Clark military bases in the Philippines. The resulting power vacuum has prompted many Asian countries to reconsider their internal and external security ties, according to sources that include the International Institute of Strategic Studies in London.

Asia has five big military players, each with a solid gravitational field: China, India, Japan, North Korea, and South Korea. Taiwan and the Association of Southeast Asian Nations are nipping closely at their heels. Four of the big five are substantial arms dealers whose networks span the globe. China is the region's largest arms exporter, with expansive inroads into the Third World, while India has been the largest local importer, buying about $5 billion worth of overseas arms in 1987 alone—more than war-locked Iran and Iraq combined. To pay for this huge arms bill, India is preparing to enter the world arms supermarket as a large-scale exporter. The U.S. is selling about $3 billion worth of arms to Asia and the Pacific countries every year. This mega-sum puts the U.S. only marginally ahead of China.

The Asian arms race has caught international attention, especially since some Asian defense quirks are legendary. For instance, South Korea, fearing a North-South Armageddon, has many state-of-the-art fighter aircraft in mothballs. The North has amassed 40 special forces midget submarines for sneaky operations and a "suicide" river-crossing regiment. Taiwan has a "Star-Trek"-like, underground anti-nuclear air-force base. Seoul, Beijing, Pyongyang, and Singapore all have dual underground railway-station-air-raid shelters.

There are also fears of a nuclear arms race in Asia. If North Korea gets the "bomb," South Korea, Japan, and Taiwan will attempt to follow suit, says Paul Godwin, of the U.S. National Defense University. Beyond the "bomb" is another Asian threat. This is the much-feared biological-chemical weapon of the kind used by Iraq's Saddam Hussein against the rival Kurds.

Apart from the legitimate arms market, there is a shadowy area of gray arms, a huge under-the-table labyrinth run by arms peddlers who have earned themselves the title "merchants of death." A few of them will sell arms to anyone, including to the most heinous terrorist groups. Some arms deals, such as China's recent and controversial $1-billion weapons sale to Burma, are suspected to have been paid for by drug money—a "rampant and formidable problem," according to Godwin. Drugs are also believed to have been a bargaining chip in the U.S.-led arms trade through Pakistan to the anti-Soviet rebels during the Afghan war.

The arms race is never far from the dark side. Asia has some of the most volatile borders in the world, plus some of mankind's longest-running wars. North and South Korea have been officially at war since 1953. Japan and Russia refuse to sign a peace treaty to end World War II because of a tug of war over the northern Kuril islands, while India and Pakistan have clashed three times since independence.

From the weekly "Asia Magazine" of Hong Kong.

Meanwhile, China, Vietnam, Malaysia, Brunei, the Philippines, and Taiwan dispute the 433 Spratly islands in the South China sea, while Vietnam and Indonesia are haggling over the Natuna islands. Brunei disputes maritime borders with Malaysia, and there is a Sino-Vietnamese conflict over the Gulf of Tonkin border.

China has also switched its military planning from the possibility of an early, major nuclear war to "limited local wars," particularly on its southern and maritime borders, and is arming accordingly. However, China is seen by the world as a rogue nation that is trying to buy high technology while trying to sell missiles and nuclear weapons overseas to make up for a slump in the arms market.

To monitor arms exports, the Central Military Commission of the Chinese Communist Party has set up a Special Weapons Sales Review Board. However, Asian and Western countries would like to see China's arms sales come under the direction of the Foreign Ministry, which is seen as less compromising.

Who peddles most of the legitimate arms in Asia? Usually the military. In many Asian countries, the military has a solid stake in the honey pots of the private sector. Like everywhere else, it is not what you know that gets you places but who you know, especially in the secret corners of the arms world.

The U.S. Looks To Latin America

Sales There Raise Big Questions

EL MERCURIO

For the first time in 25 years, said the *Washington Post* recently, the government of the United States is encouraging sales of American weapons to nations in the Third World. It added that the White House, after the Persian Gulf war, had subsidized exhibitions of American-made arms at trade shows around the world. Obviously, U.S. President George Bush wants to make sure that the crisis in the arms industry—given the collapse of the cold war—does not mean a disaster for the states, such as California, where major arms makers are based.

An announcement by the United States that it will sell arms to Chile and Argentina has aroused considerable notice. According to official Argentine sources, Buenos Aires has asked for 50 F-16 fighter bombers, and Washington has made a counter-offer of 40 A-4M Skyhawks, which are effective planes but less powerful and older than those the Argentines requested. Chile seems to have been offered a similar deal to replace its aging fleet of Hawker Hunters, which have been in service for more than 30 years. The Americans reportedly have also offered to give two C-130 transport planes and two A-37s to the Chilean air force and a tanker, a P-3 reconnaissance plane, and an oceanographic vessel to its navy.

For the past year, the United States has been evaluating what it can sell to Argentina and Chile. This is part of an American policy of improving relations with these nations' armed forces, which have been very poor since the U.S. imposed an arms embargo in 1978. It is likely that Chile will turn to the U.S. to replace its Hawker Hunters, because, unlike the army and the navy, the Chilean air force has kept close ties to the United States. Most of its active fleet is American-made. The army, on the other hand, has bought most of its new weapons from Europe, Israel, and South Africa, while the navy has stuck to British suppliers.

The weapons that the United States is selling to developing nations such as Argentina and Chile, at "nominal prices," are its surplus equipment. This permits it to kill two birds with one stone: First, it impedes these nations' efforts to develop their domestic arms industries, and second, it helps the United States recover military leadership in the region.

What is interesting is that the United States has set itself up as the guardian of the peaceful new world order yet, at the same time, is willing to sell conventional weapons, as it did after World War II and the Korean war. It is selling these weapons, but only to its friends and only after making sure not to upset regional balances of power.

The United States' role as sole superpower is based on its fundamental control of the nuclear, chemical, and conventional weapons industries. The new world order—proclaimed by Bush at the end of the Gulf war—includes constantly increasing control by the U.S. over arms traffic. The U.S. will seek to stop the sale of any strategic weapons that could upset a regional equilibrium.

But the United States is certainly selling arms. In May, 1991, Bush asked the nations of the Middle East to get rid of their chemical weapons, stop the proliferation of nuclear weapons, and freeze arms sales. Two weeks later, however, the United States was the first to violate this pledge when it sold Apache attack helicopters to Bahrain and the United Arab Emirates and 10 F-5 fighter planes to Israel. U.S. Secretary of Defense Dick Cheney defended these acts with very much the same words that the State Department spokesman used when describing the sale of arms to Chile and Argentina: "The United States will satisfy the legitimate defense needs of our friends."

The superpower has taken on the job of protecting the global balance. Bush says that, in this new era, regional conflicts will be settled by peaceful means. So Chile's military worries that the armed forces will no longer be necessary except for such problems as drug-smuggling. The armed forces would be transformed into police forces, which is why the Americans are now concentrating their military aid—sophisticated helicopters, machine guns, and rifles—on Bolivia, Peru, and Colombia.

From the conservative "El Mercurio" of Santiago.

Repeating Mistakes In the Middle East

THE FLOOD OF ARMS CONTINUES

THE TIMES

MICHAEL EVANS

For $25 million you can buy a Russian MiG-29 Fulcrum fighter aircraft. Two million dollars will be sufficient to pick up a T-72 tank straight off the production line, or just $200,000 for one from the surplus stockpile. Truckloads of ammunition, artillery shells, machine guns, automatic pistols, and assault rifles can be purchased for a few dollars more from eager Russian arms manufacturers desperate for hard currency. As a senior civil servant at Britain's Defense Ministry put it recently, "The Russians are declaring open house on arms exports."

There has already been widespread alarm over the risk of Russian tactical nuclear warheads' being smuggled out of the country into the hands of would-be nuclear-power players such as the Iranians, the Iraqis, and the Libyans. The sale of sophisticated conventional weapons to the wrong people is also viewed with concern.

The West, however, can hardly bleat about the surge of Russian arms-for-currency sales. Since the defeat of Iraq's Saddam Hussein early last year, the principal Western members of the Operation Desert Storm coalition have been competing with one another to get in first with their bids for one of the largest arms-modernization programs in the Middle East. Every Persian Gulf state living in the shadow of the defeated but surviving Iraqi leader is in the market for sophisticated, combat-proven equipment. Britain, France, and the United States will benefit from the billion-dollar arms bonanza.

At the heart of the Middle East arms buildup lies Al-Yamama, or Dove of Peace, the name given to the massive defense program agreed to by Saudi Arabia and Britain. The memoranda of understanding laying the groundwork for Al-Yamama were signed in 1985 and 1988, but the success of the British equipment in the Gulf war has given the huge contract a new impetus and emphasis. The deal, which effectively will provide the Saudis with a new air force as well as one of the biggest air bases in the region, is in two parts. Al-Yamama 1 could eventually be worth $28.5 billion. Al-Yamama 2 is still only an agreement in principle, but could be worth another $28.5 billion–$38 billion.

Al-Yamama is a classic case of arms-selling to the "good guys." The theory of government-to-government arms-dealing is that you sell to friends and boycott potential enemies, or at least those countries that are deemed to represent a threat to their neighbors and, by implication, to their Western supporters. In practice, however, friends can sometimes become enemies. Iraq is only the most recent example.

Today, arms-selling, in particular the trade in sophisticated, potentially offensive weapons such as combat aircraft, guided missiles, tanks, and heavy artillery, is supposed to be influenced by a new post-Gulf-war philosophy shared by

From the conservative "Times" of London.

The Allure of Money

A huge number of Russian individuals and associations are trying to engage in the selling of arms, according to data received by Russia's Ministry of Foreign Economic Relations (MFER). The MFER itself is currently preparing several major contracts for the sale of naval, aeronautical, and armored equipment. Negotiations are being completed on a major deal with Malaysia for the sale of airplanes. Incidentally, various Russian intermediaries, including a well-known pop singer, tried to meddle in the Malaysian contract.

"Official" arms merchants generally refuse to discuss illegal arms sales. But unofficial exports through third countries (the former Soviet republics) are quite real, and there is indirect evidence that some shipments have already reached the "final" foreign client through Central Asia.

The frequent promises of "freedom and autonomy" that Russian President Boris Yeltsin gives to arms manufacturers have led many Russian dealers to establish fairly close contacts with foreign go-betweens to prepare contracts. Now, even if the sales are not approved, the contacts will obviously continue.

Meanwhile, when Russia tries to solve the problems of converting its defense plants to civilian production, Azerbaijan and especially Armenia do everything possible to develop their military-industrial potential.

According to Russian Lieutenant-General Anatoly Funtikov, first deputy chief of armaments, the Defense Ministry has gigantic stockpiles of armaments and will sell them. "Funds are needed for the social protection of officers and to build housing for those without apartments," he says. "If this money is not found, social tensions in the army and in society will inevitably rise. The sale of armaments can, without question, provide substantial funds—maybe not immediately but over several years."

The Foreign Ministry obviously would like there to be no arms sales whatsoever—they get nothing but trouble from them and no benefit. Everyone else would like to sell weapons, but the foreign market is narrow. If the army dumps even a portion of its stockpiles of modern weapons in the world market, many defense plants will be doomed. That may finally prod the obstinate directors of the military-industrial complex toward true conversion to civilian production.

—Pavel Felgengauer, "Nezavisimaya Gazeta" (liberal), Moscow.

the "big five" national arms dealers—the U.S., Russia, China, Britain, and France. Let us learn from the Iraqi experience, they said, and never again allow a country to build up such an enormous offensive capability under our very noses. The United Nations has set up an arms register, in which member states are supposed to log sales of heavy equipment to countries in regions such as the Middle East so that the accumulation of arms can be monitored.

The register will already be heaving with billion-dollar deals. Since August, 1990, when Kuwait was invaded by Iraq, the U.S. has announced arms sales to the Middle East worth $21.4 billion, of which nearly a third were agreed upon after May, 1991, when President George Bush proposed a Middle East arms-control initiative and called for restraint on "destabilizing" weapons shipments to the region. Saudi Arabia alone has bought American arms worth nearly $15 billion.

The Middle East is a region where war has always been a widely used means of achieving political ends and where all the big powers have alliances and interests. Even if all arms shipments were to be stopped tomorrow, the region would still be one of the most heavily armed in the world. In such a political cauldron, who can say what level of armaments is sufficient for each country? Military capability among the big players in the Middle East is only partly about defense. It is also about image, political identity, leadership, competitiveness—and fear. Syria is buying arms from North Korea, including ballistic missiles, using the financial aid given by the U.S. and Saudi Arabia. Iran is spending $2 billion a year on new weapons, mostly from Russia, China, and North Korea, in a blatant drive to become the pre-eminent power in the Gulf region. Fear of Iran's ambitions, fear of Saddam, and fear of the threat from proliferating ballistic-missile arsenals will determine how much money individual countries in the region spend on arms.

Responsible governments face a dilemma. National defense industries are desperate to offset the cuts in domestic military budgets with lucrative exports. So should governments continue to sell arms to safeguard jobs and local economies, or should they wholeheartedly embrace the concept of arms control in regions such as the Middle East by adopting a new policy of restraint?

Sam Cummings is the chief executive of Interarms, the biggest private arms company in the world, based in Manchester, England, and Alexandria, Virginia. He says, "There's an argument for arms control everywhere, but how do you do it? Countries have a right to defend themselves. Governments are responsible for 99 percent of arms sales, including covert ones, and none of them has come up with suggestions of how to control sales."

Al-Yamama will run and run. So, too, no doubt, will the flow of cheap arms from Russia and other former Soviet republics. In this context, the republics of the former Soviet Union and the countries of the West seem to share the same philosophy: "If we don't sell arms, someone else will."

Third World Militaries: New Suppliers, Deadlier Weapons

Amit Gupta

Amit Gupta, a junior fellow at the Center for the Study of Developing Societies, Delhi, is currently with the Program in South and West Asian Studies at the University of Illinois, Urbana-Champaign.

Until the 1980s, the global arms bazaar was dominated by the Western states and the Soviet Union, who were thus able to use arms transfers to further their political goals vis-à-vis a recipient country. In the 1980s, Third World countries such as Brazil, Israel, and the two Koreas emerged as major arms exporters. This rise of Third World arms producers has changed the arms bazaar from a sellers' market to a buyers' market, and recipient countries are now able to procure arms on commercially better terms and with less political dependency on their suppliers.

Yet these commercial and political changes are not what worry policy makers in Washington. Instead, concern is being voiced because of the range and lethality of weapons produced in the Third World. This weapons production capability, it is feared, will give Third World countries the ability to prosecute their ambitions more freely and aggressively. It will also make Western intervention more difficult as Third World states continue to acquire weapons of mass destruction and the means to deliver them. At the very least, it is believed, profit-hungry arms industries in the Third World will go in for the unrestricted transfer of weapons to other states, thereby increasing the level of regional conflict the world over.

THE ARMS MARKS IN THE 1980S

One reason Third World arms industries found a niche in the arms bazaar of the 1980s was their attractive sales packages—a combination of low prices, good customer service, and guaranteed availability. The net result of such policies was especially beneficial for two Third World countries: Israel and Brazil. Brazil was the tenth largest exporter of armaments in the world between 1986 and 1990, with sales of $1.189 billion. Israel was the twelfth largest with sales of $1.094 billion.[1]

A second reason lay in a set of opportunities that arose in the 1980s that allowed Third World countries to achieve substantial military exports. Specifically, the complexity of new Western weapons systems created a demand for simple rugged weaponry, and this demand was met by countries like Brazil. The Brazian arms industry specialized in producing weapons systems that were based on easily available components and low technology. Since most Third World countries did not expect to fight a technologically advanced opponent, they saw such low- and medium-tech systems as better satisfying their needs.

But this second reason also set limits for the Third World arms industries. Sales were primarily to other Third World countries rather than in the lucrative Western market. The only major South-North arms deal was the Brazilian sale of the Tucano turboprop trainer to the Royal Air Force in the late 1980s. Perhaps as a result, the prevailing hierarchy of arms producers and arms suppliers did not change despite the rising sales of Third World producers. During the period that the Brazilians and the Israelis sold a billion dollars each worth of armaments, the superpowers sold approximately $64 billion worth of weaponry.[2] Too, one must note that the Iran-Iraq war accounted for the bulk of arms sales by Third World countries. Indeed, one could make the case that if the Iran-Iraq war were set aside Third World arms sales would be miniscule.

Nevertheless, Third World arms producers hoped that the weapons programs they had embarked on in the 1980s would, in the 1990s, allow them the opportunity to compete with the Northern states for the advanced weapons market. Is this possible, in light of recent trends?

THE ARMS MARKET IN THE 1990S

Many analysts initially drew on the Gulf War experience to forecast the arms market of the 1990s. They saw that war as demonstrating the superiority of advanced-

Originally appeared in *Orbis*, Vol. 37, No. 1, Winter 1993, pp. 57-68. *Orbis: A Journal of World Affairs*, published by JAI Press, Inc., for the Foreign Policy Research Institute.

technology weapons; as showing the utility of anti-missile defenses; and as proving that crude ballistic missiles needed more lethal—nuclear, chemical, biological—warheads to be effective weapons. Given these assumptions, they believed the arms market would be marked by large sales of high-technology weapons systems and particularly by ballistic missiles with a capacity for mass destruction.

But a number of factors run counter to such a scenario. The high cost of weapons systems has created major problems for arms producers in the developed world. Individual countries, barring the United States and now Japan, are finding it increasingly difficult and expensive to design and produce weapons systems by themselves. Sweden and France are the only two West European countries left with national programs for producing supersonic combat aircraft. The ability of such states to off-set domestic costs with exports is diminishing, as competition among arms producers is increasing while the global market for weapons shrinks.

The market is further complicated by changes in the former Soviet Union. As the Russians reduce their armed forces, they will have a large surplus of weapons to sell. With changes in the global environment, markets hitherto closed to the Russians may open up and Moscow should be able to offer its large surplus of arms at bargain basement rates. Witness the attempt to sell the MiG-29 to Switzerland or the sale of the Su-27 to China. More recently, Ukraine has offered to sell China an aircraft carrier and has reportedly put nineteen Tu-16O strategic bombers on the market as well.[3]

Lastly, consider the Third World arms industries themselves. During the 1980s, there was a general upgrade in the quality of weapons produced by Third World countries—especially in countries that had extensive military-scientific bases, such as Brazil, Israel, and India. Thus twenty-six countries had on-going missile programs and at least four were developing combat aircraft (Israel, India, Taiwan, and South Africa). Other systems put into production included ships, tanks, and guided missiles (India, Israel, and Brazil). Brazil and India also initiated programs for the construction of nuclear-powered submarines. Coupled with the development of such systems was the growing capability of Third World countries to produce weapons of mass destruction. Libya and Iraq produced chemical weapons; North Korea and Pakistan embarked on nuclear programs.

But most of these countries will be hurt by their industries, heavy dependence on exports. Brazil, for example, has a very small internal market for its weapons systems and consequently its arms industry depends on exports for its survival. This is further complicated by a dependence on only a few countries for export orders. Brazilian firms have been particularly hurt by the inability of Iraq to pay for the systems that it purchased in the 1980s. Embraer, Brazil's leading aeronautics manufacturer, has been forced to declare bankruptcy and is being sold off to private firms. ENGESA and Bernadini Brothers invested heavily in developing the Osorio tank for Saudi Arabia, but Riyadh decided against purchasing it. Chile, another country dependent on arms exports to sustain its arms industry, was also hurt by the closure of the Iraqi market.[4] Thus the international arms market will witness an even more intense rivalry in the 1990s than it did in the 1980s.

Coupled with these trends is the entry of new producers. Iran, for example, has started showing its indigenously produced armaments in international exhibitions. Taiwan and Indonesia are also trying to enter the arms market as exporters. Significantly, all these countries provide the same sort of low-technology equipment; none has bridged the gap to provide high-technology weaponry such as supersonic fighters. Until they do, the goal of all Third World countries will be to seek the low-technology end of the market.

MISSILE PROLIFERATION

The threat posed by the proliferation of nuclear and chemical weapons would seem to have risen substantially by the increased availability of capable delivery systems. Ballistic missiles in the Third World, it is thought, may provide these states the capability to launch nuclear and chemical strikes against traditional rivals and to fend off Western interventionist forces. Thus, the West has placed an emphasis on pressuring Third World producer states to restrict the sales of such systems. Equally important has been the Missile Technology Control Regime (MTCR) of 1987, which prohibits exports of missiles or missile components by the cooperating countries. These countries were originally the Western powers but now include Russia, with China agreeing to follow similar constraints. In this context, recent U.S. insistence that Israel become an ICR signatory is a significant breakthrough.

One restraint on missile sales may come from the potential for mutual vulnerability. India, for example, is seen as a potential salesman of ballistic missiles, but its most likely market is the Middle East, and it would not be in India's interest to sell such weapons there because in every India-Pakistan war the Middle Eastern states, in the interests of Islamic solidarity, have supplied weapons to Pakistan. Israel, another state that has the technology and needs the money from such sales, faces a similar situation in the Middle East and an equally constraining situation outside its region. Israel has supplied technological assistance to the South African missile program in the past, but the continuation of such assistance may be in doubt given the changes in the South African political scene. And it would be difficult for Israel to sell weapons elsewhere within the international system, except to states facing a similar security dilemma, like Taiwan.

THE ROLE OF TECHNOLOGY

By the start of the 1990s, the attempt by Third World countries to advance a technological level had met with mixed success. On the production side, most were able to expand their range of systems and to upgrade the quality of these systems. Thus the Israelis and the Brazilians produced tanks, the Chileans and South Africans produced aircraft, and India began to build a new range of naval vessels. Further, in specific areas of weapons technology, particularly the development of a series of missiles, the research efforts of countries like India, Israel, and Iraq bore fruit. Certain Third World states were also able to make advances in the production of electronic subsystems—Israel and Singapore being the most prominent examples.

But when it came to developing state-of-the-art conventional weapons, the track record was far less successful. A number of programs were either terminated or pushed to the point of becoming uneconomical because of high development costs, technology restrictions, and external pressures. The most complete program to develop a supersonic fighter was Israel's Lavi fighter, but this was scrapped in 1987 owing to escalating costs and pressure from American aerospace firms, which saw the plane cutting into their market. India's Light Combat Aircraft program has been plagued by developmental delays and by a restricted production quota (400) that may lead to an astronomical price tag for the entire program.[5]

In sum, the rise in technological level that was expected to emerge from the weapons programs of the 1980s did not take place. Third World states will therefore tend to compete for the low-tech end of the global market as far as major weapons systems are concerned, the one notable exception being perhaps missile technology. Given these facts where are the Third World arms industries headed?

TRENDS: PREDOMINANCE OF LOW-TECH

First, the Gulf War will not spell the doom of low- and middle-tech systems. Most Third World countries do not have the resources to invest in expensive high-tech systems, and they do not face technologically advanced opponents in their immediate environment.

The conventional military build-ups of most Third World countries in the 1980s were due to the availability of subsidized weaponry from a superpower. Thus Afghanistan, India, Syria, and Vietnam were the largest recipients of Soviet military aid, while Israel, Egypt, and Pakistan benefitted from ties with the United States. India became the second largest importer of armaments in the 1980s (Iraq was the largest), primarily because the Soviet Union provided its most modern weapons systems on highly favorable terms.

With the cold war gone, such subsidies are going to be increasingly hard to come by and the potential of most Third World countries to buy such large amounts of weapons is going to decline. Consider that one estimate puts the cost of a Pakistani military satellite capability against India in the range of $4.2 billion.[6] Yet the total annual Pakistani defense budget is $3.19 billion.[7] No wonder current U.S. arms sales efforts are centered on the Middle East: it is the one region where states can afford to pay for such systems. The bulk of the Third World can acquire such systems only with Western loans or subsidies.

Also telling against the dominance of high-tech arms is the fact that Third World states do not expect to face a superpower as an adversary. They expect to fight their traditional rivals, who are at a similar technological level. Saddam Hussein's preparations, for instance, were aimed at combatting Israel. Similarly, India's principal military concerns, despite the growth of its naval power and the development of an intermediate-range ballistic missile, remain its South Asian neighbors and the still disputed Sino-Indian border. Third World countries will likely make token purchases of advanced weapons systems to be the showcase of their inventory, but this will not lead to a substantial increase in their capabilities.

Thus though high-tech arms sales will be dominated by Western companies, this domination will not lead to the complete exclusion of Third World arms industries. A major export market for less capable systems remains and will remain. It is instructive in this regard to remember that the overwhelming majority of orders placed with U.S. companies in 1990 were from Saudi Arabia.

TRENDS: SUB-NATIONALISM

A second area of opportunity for Third World arms industries lies in the rising tide of sub-nationalism and ethnic conflict that is sweeping the world. From Quebec to Tibet, ethnic groups are once again seeking to break away from the states in which they are presently located. Sub-nationalism creates opportunity for arms sales to insurgent groups or newly emerged states, and this may be an important market for Third World producers. The weapons such groups require are not high-tech systems; indeed, most groups would lack the military training to use such systems. Instead, these groups require the rugged middle- to low-tech weaponry that the Third World produces. Such armaments could include fixed and rotary wing aircraft for close support, but the bulk of such sales will be of weapons that can be supplied covertly to insurgent groups and are useful for waging guerrilla warfare. Assault rifles, anti-tank weapons, surface-to-air missiles, and anti-personnel weapons are likely to be in demand. Israel, for example, sold the Tamil Tigers Eagle pistols, Galil rifles, Uzi submachine guns, light machine guns, and shoulder carried field missiles.[8] Similarly, the Croatian national guard has received arms from Hungary, Romania, South Africa, and Singapore.[9] In fact, Singapore has sold the Croatian national guard a weapons package of SAR-80 assault rifles, Ultimax 100 Mk III light machine guns, and Crossbow light anti-tank weapons. The Croatians have also obtained 7.62mm rifles from Argentina and grenade launchers from South Africa's ARMSCOR.[10]

Ethnic conflicts also create a demand for counterinsurgency weapons from the beleaguered state. Third World arms industries that specialize in light arms (Israel), anti-personnel munitions (Chile, which makes cluster bombs), and counterinsurgency aircraft (Brazil) could take advantage of the situation. Sri Lanka, for example, raised its military expenditures from $25 million in 1982 to $583 million in 1988, in order to combat the Tamil secessionists. (By 1991, the military budget had slimmed down to $450 million.[11])

The opportunity to make sales in such situations will be dependent on the extent to which the supplier state is itself vulnerable to similar pressures. An India or an Iraq, which itself faces secessionist pressures, would increase its own vulnerability by making such arms sales. A hostile state could respond by providing weapons to insurgent groups in the supplier country. Mutual vulnerability, therefore, will condition such arms sales.

TRENDS: NORTH-SOUTH COLLABORATION

The third major trend will be increased collaboration between the arms industries of the North and the South. Western arms producers started transferring technology to Third World industries in the 1980s in order to penetrate these markets. Countries in the Asia-Pacific region, for example, demanded some form of technology transfer and co-production in the deals they cut with Western aerospace companies. Indonesia's IPIN aircraft company received significant technology transfers under the NBO 105 helicopter program and through its partnership with the Bell Helicopters. More recently, the Franco-German consortium, Eurocopter, had to agree to the joint development of the P120L helicopter with China and Singapore.

Further North-South collaboration is likely to take place in the development and production of new weapons systems. Examples include programs like the joint development of the Super Sabre by Grumman and the Chinese aircraft industry, and the co-development of the AMX fighter by Brazil and Italy. The Russians are also going in for joint development with both Western and Third World countries. The Yakovlev design bureau, for instance, is targeting both India and China for co-development and co-production of the Short Take Off and Vertical Landing Yak-141. Such collaboration is also likely to be seen in the research and development (R&D) of weapons systems. One means by which Western companies could hold down spiralling production costs is by transferring part of the R&D process for new weapons systems to the Third World industries. Both France and Sweden sought to interest India in tying its Light Combat Aircraft project to their own.

A number of Third World industries also have top-flight skilled labor that can be hired for a fraction of the cost of comparable labor in the West. Such skilled labor can be used for establishing computer-aided-design and computer-aided-manufacture programs. The German aeronautical company, VFW, for instance, has taken the first step in this direction by asking India's Aeronautical Development Agency to do a preliminary study for co-development of a 100-seater commuter aircraft that can be sold in both civilian and military markets.[12]

But the demand for North-South collaboration is not restricted to a top-down process, where the technologically advanced Northern states are seeking partners to decrease costs and gain access to markets. In a growing trend, Southern states seek Northern partners to gain entry to the markets of developed states. For example, Israel has sought to create joint companies with American firms so as to get a slice of the U.S. defense budget. Singapore is also seeking joint ventures so as to gain greater access to Northern markets.

Systems being phased out of production may also get a new lease on life by transferring assembly lines to Third World countries. In the mid-1980s, Northrop offered India the production line of the Northrop F-5 fighter/trainer, with the suggestion that Hindustan Aeronautics Limited might later be provided with the blueprints of the more modern F-20 Tigershark fighter. The French, similarly, want to transfer the Alpha Jet production line, which is being shut down, to South East Asia or India. The French Air Force would buy aircraft from this line to make up for attrition.[13]

Controversy over weapons might be muted by North-South collaboration. A forerunner of that trend could be the funding of the Israeli Arrow anti-missile program—72 percent of total program costs—by the American SDI program.[14]

North-South transfers need not go through government channels. One critical example may be the transfer of scientific personnel. The media have given attention to the possibility that Third World countries seeking to manufacture nuclear weapons could use the services of former Soviet scientists who are available on the international market. But the former Soviet Union is just one of a growing number of sources for Third World and East European countries seeking scientific personnel who might give them a nuclear capability. South African, Israeli, Brazilian, Pakistani, Indian, and possibly Korean scientists could also be asked to do the job. Moreover, as Western defense industries continue to face harder times, even Western scientists have come on the market. Argentina's Condor missile program, for instance, was to be developed by a team of freelance German scientists. Trying to control the spread of the relevant knowledge will thus be next to impossible, and alternative measures will have to be sought.

TRENDS: SOUTH-SOUTH COLLABORATION

Another feature of the arms trade in the 1990s will be increased South-South collaboration in the field of weapons production. In the 1980s, attempts at South-South collaboration were proposed to lessen development costs, to avoid restrictions on technology transfers, and to allow countries to develop weapons of mass destruction and the means to deliver them. Thus South Africa hired Israeli scientists who had worked on the Lavi—which incorporated a large amount of American technology—to work on its own fighter aircraft program. Israeli assistance was also sought by the South Africans for the development of ballistic missiles. Collaboration on both ballistic missile and nuclear development emerged between the Brazilians and Iraqis. Iran built up its domestic arms industry with the help of Argentina, Brazil, Taiwan, and Pakistan. And Iranian advances in missile technology came from Chinese and North Korean assistance, yielding the Iranian variant of the Chinese M-11 missile.[15]

Such collaboration is likely to increase in the 1990s, for the transfer of complete systems will be difficult to achieve given the current international mood. Rising non-proliferation concerns in the West and attempts to give teeth to regimes like the MTCR will make it tougher for countries such as North Korea and China to export such systems—especially if future trade, economic, and technology agreements are linked to the observance of non-proliferation regimes. For countries desiring ballistic and guided missiles, therefore, the easiest route to acquisition will be through technology and personnel transfers from other Southern states.

In addition, Third World arms industries are now facing the same problem which arms industries in the West face—the skyrocketing costs of development require the co-development of systems in order to reduce costs and enlarge markets. The ASEAN countries, therefore, are considering how to coordinate production from each member country's facilities and how to go in for joint procurement. Collaboration should also grow in the area of conventional weapons production, as exemplified by the Pakistani-Chinese co-development of the K-8 trainer aircraft.

There will also be a market for spare parts, as a result of the break-up of the Soviet Union, which has created a major shortage in the South of spare parts for Soviet weapons systems. This has led India to go in for the rapid indigenization of spare-part production, and exporting spare parts throughout the South could provide a means for retaining aging Soviet weapons systems in the armed forces of many countries.

OUTCOMES

Given these constraints and opportunities what impact are the Third World countries going to have on the international arms market? First, the stratification of the market that took place in the 1980s—with the North selling high-tech systems and the South providing low- and medium-tech ones—is likely to continue. Most of the Third World's advanced weapons programs have run into major developmental delays or have been scrapped outright. Southern producers' capacity to emerge as challengers to Northern producers has been severely hampered.

The results of this stratification can be seen in the small percentage of arms sold by the Third World in the latter half of the 1980s. According to the Stockholm International Peace Research Institute, the top 15 arms exporters to the Third World in the period 1986–1990 sold a total of $101 billion worth of weapons. Third World suppliers accounted for approximately $11 billion. Thus controlling the spread of weapons around the world still lies in the hands of the Western powers—a group to which Russia now belongs.

Despite restrictions on technology, Third World arms industries have increased their products' level of lethality.

Secondly, the move towards North-South collaboration, which began in other areas of high technology such as the development of software, is now being replicated in the global arms industry. Escalating development costs are pushing towards such collaborative efforts and this will have a major impact on the restriction of technology. As Third World countries get involved in such R&D processes, Western efforts to restrict technology transfers will be negated.

Thirdly, market forces will weed out the more vulnerable arms industries. As more and more countries enter the arms market, drawn by the success stories of the 1980s, a larger number of Third World states will be providing similar types of weaponry. To take just the example of field artillery, Israel, South Africa, Yugoslavia, Chile, Argentina, and Brazil are vying in this market. In this situation, countries with a large domestic clientele (such as China, India, and Israel) will be best able to deal with the difficult export market.

Fourthly, South-South military cooperation will have interesting implications for inter-state relations. Cooperation within regions, as in ASEAN, could work to increase regional integration as the integration of defense industries breaks down barriers imposed by national security concerns. Cooperation across regions on the other hand could lead to de facto alliances between states, thereby complicating the security environment. Now that India and Israel have established diplomatic relations, for example, defense cooperation between the two states could lead to a reshaping of threat perceptions in both South Asia and the Middle East.

Lastly, despite restrictions on technology and the delay or failure of advanced weapons programs, Third World arms industries have increased their products' level of lethality. Over twenty countries have ongoing ballistic missile programs, increasing the range, the magnitude, and the level of the destruction they can inflict on their enemies. Similarly, while these industries may not be able to produce state-of-the-art systems, they do have the capability to produce an entire range of weapons—ships, tanks, aircraft, and missiles. This increases the level of destruction at the regional level and potentially leads to the bridging of what were otherwise discrete regions. Thus the Indian acquisition of ballistic missiles has implications not only for South Asia but also for South West Asia and South East Asia. Similarly, the Saudi acquisition of the CSS-2 intermediate-range ballistic missile from China has implications for South Asian security.

POLICY IMPLICATIONS

What policy implications are suggested by the future capabilities of Third World arms industries?

One must recognize first that Third World arms industries are not going to change current patterns in the conventional arms trade. The Western countries still monopolize the sale of advanced weapons systems and the Third World lacks the capability to alter this state of affairs in the near future. The Third World can supply weapons to ethnic groups around the world, but this does not shift the arms transfer pattern or create significant instability within the international system. Such brush-fire wars have occurred frequently since the end of the Second World War and they have had international implications only when large-scale external support (not just arms sales) led to the broadening of the conflicts.

The real issue is the transfer of weapons of mass destruction and the means to deliver them. These weapons are not a threat because "crazy Third World dictators" have plans to hold California to nuclear ransom. Nor are they a threat because Third World countries are targeting downtown New York, Moscow, or Paris. Third World states have very small nuclear inventories or for that matter ballistic missile forces. For them to try such offensive actions would be suicidal. Would even Iraq, with 25–50 nuclear weapons, have been a threat to the continental United States?

One real threat is that, if Third World countries possess weapons of mass destruction, then invading them, or intervening in their regional conflicts, becomes an increasingly costly process. If countries like Israel, Iraq, Pakistan, India, North Korea, and Taiwan have the power to send large numbers of invading troops back in body bags—which weapons of mass destruction do give them—then it could serve as a deterrent against invasion. On the other hand, if these countries cannot produce such weapons, intervening in their affairs becomes much easier. Thus the real threat is not that Third World military industrialization is going to hurt the West's defensive capability, but it will blunt the offensive capability of the West. The Pentagon in fact, in its recently leaked report on threats in the post-cold war era, expects to face such threats in future regional conflicts.[16]

The answer to such threats does not lie, however, in trying to check Third World arms production capabilities. Technical solutions to what is essentially a political problem are not going to suffice. Political solutions on the other hand reduce or contain conflicts which give rise to the pressures for Western intervention. One move that needs to be pursued is creating regional arms control arrangements, which would lead to confidence building and a reduction in regional force levels. Most Third World states face a significant military burden and such moves could help redeploy it for economic development purposes.

It is also important to remember that some of these Third World countries are regional powers and that they should be included in plans for global security arrangements. Regional powers can be used for peacekeeping and could also form a more acceptable basis for intervention than Western armed forces. While such a role may still be difficult in the Middle East, it can be carried out in the Indian Ocean as well as in South East Asia. In fact, there is large-scale coordination between the different ASEAN states and, increasingly, Australia. Such regional security arrangements would obviate the need for a Western interventionist capability and provide Third World states with the security guarantees they desire.

Another useful step would be to broaden existing international regimes to incorporate Third World countries in them. One step in this direction may be to expand the Nuclear Non-Proliferation Treaty to include a new category—nuclear states. These would be states that have acquired the capability to produce nuclear weapons but do not have a visible nuclear force. Such states could be asked to help restrict technology transfers and the transfer of personnel.

In conclusion, therefore, the growth of Third World arms industries is not going to alter fundamentally the balance of military power or significantly alter trade patterns in the international arms market. What it will do is increase the lethality of regional conflicts and make external intervention in regional affairs an increasingly costly process. It has to be recognized that the military capability accorded by these industries cannot be taken back without expensive future conflicts, so the best solution is to work to create a new international system in which these states can be accommodated rather than contained.

NOTES

1. Stockholm International Peace Research Institute, *SIPRI Yearbook 1991: World Armaments and Disarmament* (Oxford: Oxford University Press, 1991), p. 198.
2. Ibid., p. 198.

3. Christopher K. Hummel, "Ukrainian Arms Makers Are Left On Their Own," *RFE/RL Research Report*, August 14, 1992, p. 36.

4. Adrian English, "Industry After Eldorado," *Jane's Defence Weekly*, June 15, 1991, p. 1037.

5. For a discussion of India's Light Combat Aircraft program, see Amit Gupta, "The Indian Arms Industry: A Lumbering Giant?" *Asian Survey*, September 1990, pp. 851–53.

6. Cited in Vipin Gupta, "Sensing the Threat—Remote Monitoring Technologies," in Stephen P. Cohen, ed., *Nuclear Proliferation in South Asia: The Prospects of Arms Control* (Boulder, Colo.: Westview, 1991), p. 260.

7. *The Military Balance*, 1991–92 (London: IISS, 1991).

8. Thalif Deen, "Sri Lanka Mauls Tamil Tigers in 'Mother of All Battles,' " *Jane's Defence Weekly*, August 17, 1991, p. 272.

9. Paul Beaver, "Croatia's Arms Revealed," *Jane's Defence Weekly*, October 5, 1991, p. 599; and "Armour to Small Arms," *Janes Defence Weekly*, February 22, 1992, p. 292.

10. Paul Beaver, "Croatian Armed Forces Open New Front," *Jane's Defence Weekly*, June 27, 1992, p. 1133.

11. *Jane's Defence Weekly*, August 17, 1991, p. 272.

12. Author's interview with Dr. Kota Harinarayana, Director, Aeronautical Development Agency, Bangalore, India, July 15, 1991.

13. "Asians Could Build Alpha Jet," *Jane's Defence Weekly*, March 7, 1992, p. 385.

14. "Defence Still Top Priority," *Jane's Defence Weekly*, February 15, 1992, p. 234.

15. Tony Banks and James Bruce, "Iran Builds Its Strength," *Jane's Defence Weekly*, February 1, 1992, p. 158–59.

16. *The New York Times*, February 17, 1992.

A PROLIFERATION PRIMER

DAVID ALBRIGHT

David Albright is president of the Institute for Science and International Security in Washington, D.C., and a Bulletin *contributing editor.*

Some might argue that the devastation of Iraqi society was a fair trade for keeping a nuclear weapon out of a ruthless murderer's hands—especially if it deterred other murderers. Iraq's nuclear potential has often been exaggerated, sometimes to justify military action, and at other times to bolster U.N. inspection efforts, but the Gulf War did unmask a determined, well-funded nuclear-weapons program that had largely escaped detection. If the war had not led to the program's destruction, Iraq might soon have had its first nuclear weapon.

It's obvious that peaceful means of blocking nuclear proliferation—the Nuclear Non-Proliferation Treaty (NPT), nuclear supplier controls, and the International Atomic Energy Agency (IAEA) safeguards system—failed to detect the Iraqi nuclear program or to stop it. But "bombing to stop the Bomb" is not the way to end proliferation.

If the nonproliferation system is going to work, existing approaches will need to be improved and expanded. Governments and international organizations will need to improve their ability to detect the existence and status of nuclear-weapons efforts in threshold countries and among terrorist groups.

Finding small nuclear facilities is difficult, and the record is mixed. Many secret programs have been discovered, but several important programs have escaped detection.

Detecting small, dedicated nuclear facilities is difficult, and the record is mixed. Although many secret programs have been detected and thwarted, several important programs have eluded detection. In some cases, the failure stemmed from inadequate monitoring; in others, from a lack of political commitment.

Better national and international monitoring is needed for the verification of existing agreements, particularly of the NPT. In some cases, clandestine nuclear-weapons efforts may not violate international agreements. Yet their early detection is in the interests of global security. Monitoring is becoming more complicated as the breakup of the former Soviet Union aggravates the problem of containing its stocks of weapons, materials, and technology.

Successful and early detection of future weapons efforts will require more resources, increased sharing of intelligence information, and the maintenance of a high political commitment to stemming proliferation. These efforts would be significantly easier if there were greater transparency about all nuclear programs—including their inventories of plutonium and highly enriched uranium, and their capability to make these materials.

Monitoring

There are two independent approaches to detecting secret nuclear activities. The first is the IAEA safeguards system, which now monitors nuclear material at some 900 declared nuclear facilities in more than 50 countries. This verification system entails a combination of on-site inspections, materials accounting, and containment and surveillance. In the non-nuclear weapons states, this system is intended to expose any use of civilian facilities for weapons purposes or the diversion of its nuclear material. And any facility in a non-nuclear weapon state that is not safeguarded is spotlighted as a suspected nuclear weapons site.

The second approach involves a melange of top-secret methods used by intelligence agencies. Techniques include communication intercepts, export monitoring, human intelligence, high-resolution photography, and detailed analyses of publicly available information.

In 1970, when the NPT was first brought into force, these two approaches were viewed as adequate. The telltale sign of a nuclear-armed country was an easily detectable full-scale nuclear test. With little civilian plutonium or highly enriched uranium in circulation, IAEA safeguards of the civilian nuclear industry were considered straightforward.

But now the situation is much more complex. The cases of Pakistan and South Africa show that it is not necessary to conduct a full-scale nuclear test to be a nuclear-armed power. And the Gulf War revealed the inadequacies of traditional IAEA safeguards and intelligence gathering.

Iraq is considered an intelligence failure because large-scale nuclear weapons activities were not discovered by the IAEA or Western intelligence agencies. The reasons for this failure, however, involve more than a deficiency in either safeguards or intelligence-collection methods.

Western governments did not aggressively pursue leads about Iraqi nuclear efforts or seriously impede Iraq's nuclear program during the 1980s. Most Western governments supported Iraq over Iran in their bloody war. Many European countries—Iraq's major source of critical equipment and technology—strongly resisted tightening controls on exports to Iraq and to other developing countries. Although export controls were being strengthened by the late 1980s, the new controls were too late to stop Iraq.

Despite a failure to detect the full scope of Iraq's program, intelligence agencies knew enough before the Iraqi invasion of Kuwait to have justified some sort of intervention. But Western governments were unwilling to risk the kind of political confrontation that they had with North Korea in the late 1980s and early 1990s. Tight export controls and more thorough international intelligence-sharing would undoubtedly have revealed more precise and complete information about Iraq's weapons program.

Post-war inspections

Fearing a repetition of past failures, after the Gulf War the U.N. Security Council decided to coordinate intelligence efforts with on-site inspections. This coordinated inspection effort, conducted under U.N. Resolution 687, has laid bare—and nearly destroyed—Iraq's nuclear program, despite Iraq's frequent refusals to cooperate and its attempts to disguise or hide major portions of its program.

Intelligence agencies have shared their carefully guarded information with the IAEA and the U.N. Security Council. These agencies have provided the IAEA and the United Nations with invaluable information from defectors, export transaction records, and analyses of high- and low-altitude imagery.

The IAEA action team has gone beyond the IAEA's normal safeguards approach, conducting on-site, no-notice inspections of undeclared facilities based on intelligence information. As a result of these inspections, governments have received detailed information about the Iraqi program.

The IAEA inspectors have seized tens of thousands of pages of documents, and analyzed and sealed hundreds of nuclear-related components and pieces of manufacturing equipment. Analyses of these items have been invaluable in gauging the scope and status of Iraq's nuclear program.

The action team also picked its own inspectors—another departure from IAEA routine. This freedom allowed the choice of experts from member states with expertise in all facets of nuclear weapons production. One team even included lock-pickers, to allow the team quick access to a secret design center in Baghdad.

Inspectors regularly interview experts from the Iraqi nuclear programs. Although the Iraqi experts are often uncooperative, particularly about their procurement networks, they have provided detailed information and insights into their programs.

To carry out Security Council-mandated long-term monitoring, the IAEA has begun implementing techniques to detect any resumption of the Iraqi nuclear program. One system will monitor Iraqi waterways for chemical and radioactive effluent that might be emitted by secret nuclear facilities. During the fifteenth inspection in November 1992, inspectors collected enough data to establish a baseline against which they will compare future measurements.

Another procedure that is being implemented is periodic monitoring of Iraqi dual-use equipment. Although the IAEA has traditionally verified quantities of nuclear materials, it has no mandate to verify the location or use of dual-use equipment. As another way to detect signs of suspicious activity, the IAEA has asked the Nuclear Suppliers Group to give the team data on their exports to Iraq.

Although U.N. resolutions since the Gulf War established an inspection regime in Iraq that has made it possible to learn a good deal about that country's nuclear program, it is unlikely that the nuclear inspection arrangements instituted in Iraq would be accepted elsewhere. Nevertheless, the Iraqi experience has led to a better understanding of the level of monitoring and inspection needed to detect and prevent nuclear weapons activities. This episode has also led to a better understanding of the paths that other nuclear aspirants have followed. The most difficult part of building a nuclear weapon lies in acquiring fissile material—either separated plutonium or highly enriched uranium.

Plutonium

The indigenous production of plutonium requires a major industrial infrastructure, including at least a 20–40 megawatt (thermal) reactor. A supply of uranium must be developed, as well as the ability to convert the uranium into fuel. Inside the reactor, the uranium fuel is irradiated, and plutonium is produced by neutron capture in uranium 238. The irradiated fuel is then sent to a heavily shielded chemical processing facility where the plutonium is separated from the uranium, transuranic elements, and fission products. All of these processes generate large quantities of nuclear and chemical waste that must be safely stored.

Although the technology is readily available, the successful construction and operation of a group of facilities to produce plutonium is demanding; it requires specialized materials and thousands of workers to build and operate the varied facilities.

One of the most difficult and most visible steps is acquiring or building a reactor large enough to produce significant amounts of plutonium. Even with outside assistance, it is likely to take several years to finish the reactor.

Another difficult step is acquiring a separation capability. The principle separation technology is called the PUREX (plutonium-uranium extraction) method, which involves dismantling and chopping up the irradiated fuel, dissolving it in hot nitric acid, and then partitioning the plutonium and the uranium with a technique known as "solvent extraction." Tributyl phosphate diluted in kerosene is commonly used as the solvent in the PUREX process.

Major "signatures" of clandestine plutonium production are: the reactor's cooling towers, a large labor force, the importation of specialized equipment or materials, the high heat output of an operating reactor, the extensive radiation shielding needed for even a modest plutonium separation facility, and the large amount of nuclear emissions and waste being generated.

North Korea. The case of North Korea illustrates that a small (5 megawatt-electric) reactor, large enough to produce enough plutonium for one bomb a year, can be detected before it begins operating. North Korea is believed to have started building a small reactor at Yongbyon in 1980; it began operations in 1986. The reactor, based on 1950s Magnox reactor technology, has a graphite moderator and gas cooling that North Korea developed indigenously.

By 1984, the United States had learned of the existence of this secret reactor. The methods used to discover it are not publicly known, but they would undoubtedly have included a range of techniques, including satellite surveillance. The United States subsequently discovered that North Korea was building larger reactors of the same type.

In the late 1980s, the world learned that a large, secret reprocessing plant was being built near the small reactor at Yongbyon. Although there was some controversy over whether this heavily shielded facility was a full-scale reprocessing plant, in 1992 North Korea told the IAEA that it was, although the North called it a "Radiochemical Laboratory." Some who did not believe that the Yongbyon facility was a reprocessing plant thought that the North was building an underground plant elsewhere, and that the building at Yongbyon was a decoy. North Korea denies that it ever built a smaller, pilot-scale plant, and no evidence for such a facility has emerged.

During the IAEA's inspections in spring 1992, North Korea admitted that it had separated gram quantities of plutonium in March 1990 at the Yongbyon plant. The North said the plutonium came from failed fuel elements taken out of its 5-megawatt electric reactor.

Based on friendly intelligence, in 1992 the IAEA asked to visit a facility in the capital, Pyongyang. The North subsequently admitted that it had separated minute quantities of plutonium in 1975 in Pyongyang in hot cells provided by the Soviet Union as part of the supply of a research reactor. This plutonium is believed to have been produced in the Soviet-supplied research reactor. The facility is considered too small to be a pilot plant.

Based on analyses of plutonium and waste samples, the IAEA has concluded that the North has separated more plutonium than it has declared. By early March 1993, the IAEA had been unable to estimate the total amount of plutonium that might have been separated, and the North had refused to admit to any other separation activities. In reaction to international pressure, on March 12 North Korea announced that it intended to withdraw from the NPT.

Israel. During the late 1950s and early 1960s, France is reported to have secretly supplied Israel with a nuclear reactor and an underground plutonium separation plant. U.S. intelligence learned of the reactor's existence during its construction. Questions remain about its historical power rating.

U.S. intelligence agencies apparently strongly suspected that there was a reprocessing facility at Dimona in the 1960s. But more complete details were not revealed until 1986, when Mordechai Vanunu, a former nuclear technician at the separation plant, told his story to the London *Sunday Times*.

The total amount of plutonium produced at Dimona can only be estimated. Intelligence estimates are certainly more exact, although they are not publicly available. According to *World Inventory of Plutonium and Highly Enriched Uranium 1992*, Israel is estimated to have produced about 240 to 415 kilograms of weapon-grade plutonium through 1991.[1]

India. India has the most transparent unsafeguarded plutonium production program of the developing nations. The centerpiece of the program includes two heavy-water reactors and a plutonium separation plant at the Bhabha Atomic Research Center near Bombay. Although the Indian government regards information about the amount of plutonium it has separated as classified, *World Inventory of Plutonium* estimates that India had accumulated almost 300 kilograms of separated weapon-grade plutonium by the end of 1991.

Iraq. After the Gulf War, IAEA inspectors uncovered a plutonium separation program based on the use of a safeguarded fuel fabrication plant, a research reactor, and hot cells at the Tuwaitha nuclear research center. IAEA safeguards had failed to detect the separation of a tiny amount—about 5 grams—of plutonium.

Despite months of searching, the IAEA has not found a dedicated Iraqi plutonium separation program rumored to include an underground reactor. The rumors still persist, and periodically IAEA inspectors visit suspect sites. Given the scope of the Iraqi program and the information uncovered so far, it seems logical to assume that Iraq at least thought about building a secret reactor and separation plant.

Enriching uranium

There are a number of ways to enrich uranium, although building enrichment plants requires extensive design and installation of large amounts of costly equipment. The two major commercial methods are gaseous diffusion and gas centrifugation. Other methods include aerodynamic techniques, the chemical approach, electromagnetic separation, and—still under development—laser separation. All approaches require a supply of uranium, which must be acquired either through indigenous production or foreign purchase.

Enrichment technology is not widely available, although early electromagnetic methods have been declassified. Europe's Urenco centrifuge technology has become more available over the years.

■ **Gaseous diffusion.** This technique exploits the fact that in gaseous form, heavier molecules travel more slowly than lighter molecules. As a result, the latter will strike a permeable wall more frequently, and the escaping gas will contain more of the lighter component. In a gaseous diffusion plant, uranium hexafluoride emerging from the end of a diffusion stage will be slightly enriched in the isotope uranium 235. Enriching it to weapon grade (90 percent or more) typically requires several thousand stages.

This method is highly energy intensive and it requires large facilities, making detection of a fully operating facility at least theoretically straightforward. A British gaseous diffusion plant at Capenhurst, with a capacity of about 500,000 separative work units (a standard measure), was about 500 meters long and required several large cooling towers to dissipate residual heat.

Diffusion barriers and pumps must be made of materials that can withstand the corrosive effects of uranium hexafluoride; the technology for de-

SECRET PRODUCTION PLANTS

	Technology	Plant	"Significant" activity began	Plant revealed	How revealed	Revealed before operating?
Argentina	Gaseous diffusion	Pilcaniyeu	1978	1983	Announced	no
	Plutonium separation	Ezeiza	1978	1978	Announced	yes
Brazil	Centrifuge	IPEN	1978	early 1980s	Intelligence	no
	Centrifuge	Aramar	early 1980s	mid-1980s	Announced	yes
Iraq	Calutrons	Tuwaitha	early 1980s?	1991	Defector/inspection	no
	Calutrons	Tarmiya	mid-1980s	1991	Defector/inspection	no
	Centrifuge	Tuwaitha	early 1980s	mid-1980s	Iraqi declaration	no
	Centrifuge	Rashidiya	late 1980s	1992	Defector/inspection	no
	Centrifuge	Al Furat	late 1980s	1991	Iraqi declaration	yes
	Plutonium separation	Tuwaitha	late 1970s	1991	Inspection/declaration	no
India	Plutonium separation	Trombay	1950s	1950s	Announced	yes
	Centrifuge	Trombay	1980s	1980s	Announced	yes
	Centrifuge	Mysore	early 1980s?	mid-1980s	Intelligence	yes
Israel	Reactor	Dimona	mid-1950s	late 1950s	U.S. intelligence	yes
	Plutonium separation	Dimona	mid-1950s	1960s?	U.S. intelligence	?
North Korea	Reactor	Yongbyon	1980	1984	Intelligence	yes
	Plutonium separation	Pyongyang	before 1975	1992	IAEA inspection	no
	Plutonium separation	Yongbyon	1980s	late 1980s	Intelligence	yes
Pakistan	Centrifuge	Kahuta	mid-1970s	late 1970s	Intelligence	yes
South Africa	Aerodynamic separation	Valindaba	1970	1970	Announced	yes

veloping such material and equipment is not generally available.

Argentina. Argentine nuclear officials surprised the world in 1983 when they announced that Argentina had been building a secret gaseous diffusion plant in the town of Pilcaniyeu in a remote section of Argentina. Officials said that the plant had already produced a small amount of enriched uranium.

The announcement revealed the limits of remote intelligence gathering. An official involved in building the plant said that Argentina had thrown off Western intelligence agencies by encouraging them to look for a nonexistent plutonium production reactor. Argentina was already known to be building an unsafeguarded reprocessing plant.

A U.S. official said that remote surveillance had made the United States suspicious of the construction at Pilcaniyeu, but the building's purpose was unknown. About six months before the 1983 announcement, some U.S. officials wanted to ask the Argentine government about it, but their superiors considered such an action inappropriate.

The enrichment plant was built using primarily indigenous capabilities in order to reduce the chance of outside discovery. According to Adm. Carlos Castro Madero, then head of the Argentine atomic energy commission, Argentina decided on gaseous diffusion because it had the industrial infrastructure to build the key components itself.

The Pilcaniyeu plant remains unfinished, beset with delays produced by budget cutbacks and technical difficulties. Despite the delays, the plant has produced an unknown quantity of low-enriched uranium.

Iraq. During the early 1980s, Iraq conducted a secret feasibility study on gaseous diffusion, including some laboratory work on barrier material. By 1987, the effort had failed and it was abandoned in favor of other approaches. The Iraqis found the technology too technically demanding and were unable to obtain outside assistance.

■ **Gas centrifuge.** In this method, the heavier molecules in a rotating gas move toward the inside wall of the rotating tube. An induced countercurrent in the gas increases the separation of uranium 235 from 238. A gas centrifuge plant can be somewhat smaller than a gaseous diffusion plant. It uses less than a tenth of the electricity consumption of a gaseous diffusion plant.

Once operating, a centrifuge plant has few unique signatures, so it is difficult to detect. One method of detection involves looking for a high-frequency electromagnetic signal radiated by motors running the centrifuges. Depending on the plant's design, however, this signal might be too weak to find, unless the detectors are nearby.

Because the centrifuges spin at supersonic speed, precision engineering and metallurgy are critical for success. Most developing countries require outside assistance, and Western monitoring of a trail of suspicious or illegal exports has often led to the detection of secret centrifuge programs.

The items intended for a centrifuge program can be readily identified: special materials such as maraging steel or advanced fibers; high-quality computer numerically controlled machines; and other specialized items, including special oils and magnets; and large quantities of aluminum piping.

Although the Urenco centrifuge (developed by a European consortium) has a remarkably simple design, operation requires mastery of complicated details. If these are not resolved properly, the centrifuge will be damaged. (A small, light-weight spinning centrifuge can contain the kinetic energy equivalent of a 10-ton truck traveling at 50 kilometers an hour.)

Export monitoring may reveal the existence of a centrifuge program, but it will rarely provide conclusive information about the locations of centrifuge research, development, and production facilities. Nevertheless, facilities in Brazil and Pakistan were identified before significant quantities of enriched uranium were produced.

Pakistan. Pakistan was the first country that used stolen European centrifuge designs and large procurement networks to acquire a gas centrifuge plant and associated facilities. It kept its program, begun in the mid-1970s, secret for a few years. This secrecy, coupled with weak Western export controls, enabled Pakistan to get a head start on accumulating large quantities of material, equipment, and components before Western governments took steps to stop its program.

Since the mid-1970s, Pakistani procurement agents managed to use circuitous buying patterns to stay ahead of slowly tightening Western export regulations, enabling them to acquire additional critical items. Pakistan has willingly broken export laws in the United States and in Europe, leading to some well publicized arrests of Pakistani procurement agents.

During the late 1980s, Pakistani scientists published a series of technical articles about certain aspects of manufacturing Urenco-type centrifuges that imply that Pakistan's program has been successful.

Pakistan's Kahuta enrichment plant is believed to have produced weapon-grade uranium. According to *World Inventory of Plutonium*, Pakistan is estimated to have produced about 120–220 kilograms of weapon-grade uranium by the end of 1991.

Iraq. The Iraqi centrifuge program was known to Western intelligence before the Gulf War, primarily because of Iraqi procurement efforts. After the Gulf War, many details emerged about what had been procured, where Iraq planned to produce its centrifuges, and when it expected to have an operational centrifuge plant.

At the time of the war the centrifuge program was at an early stage, using clandestinely acquired European designs, materials, manufacturing equipment, and components to conduct single-machine tests. There is no evidence of a secret cascade of machines, although a few centrifuges might have been connected together. Iraq intended to build cascades by the mid-1990s.

A disturbing aspect of the Iraqi program is that it appears to have purchased an early centrifuge design, and then independently bought the services of experts to improve the design. A German centrifuge expert who was involved in helping Iraq in 1988 and 1989 believes that Iraq probably acquired the design on the international "gray market." He believes that the likely source was Pakistan, although he thinks that Iraq probably acquired the design through a third party.

Armed with the design and foreign

technical advisers, Iraq was buying sophisticated manufacturing equipment in Europe, including numerically controlled machine tools that were then programmed to produce centrifuge components automatically and precisely. The use of these machines would have significantly lessened the need for skilled technicians.

Although Iraq's centrifuge program is believed to have been destroyed by the war and subsequent IAEA actions, important questions about the program remain. The inspectors have not learned the full extent of knowledge and experience acquired by Iraqi centrifuge experts. Important portions of Iraq's foreign procurement network are only partially understood. Answering these remaining questions would settle once and for all whether Iraq has hidden significant parts of its centrifuge program.

Brazil. Since 1978, Brazil has been pursuing centrifuges with limited success. Its program became known a few years after it started, and its successes have generally been announced or leaked to the Brazilian press.

■ **Calutrons.** In a large device called a "calutron," a strong magnetic field causes heavy and light uranium ions to follow trajectories with slightly different curvatures. Enriched uranium is collected and recovered in chemical processing buildings. The feed material is uranium tetrachloride.

Calutron facilities are expensive to build and operate, requiring a large labor force and massive amounts of electricity, making them relatively vulnerable, at least in theory, to outside detection. The chemical processing areas are one of the largest areas of a calutron facility. Here uranium is recovered from calutron parts and graphite collectors by scrubbing them with nitric acid, soaking them in acid baths, and burning or dissolving away disposable components.

The United States used calutrons to make the highly enriched uranium for the atomic bomb that destroyed Hiroshima. Because of its high costs, the United States abandoned the technology in favor of gaseous diffusion. But before the calutron buildings were finally closed in 1946, they processed a total of about one metric ton of weapon-grade uranium, using as feed the low-enriched uranium produced in the incomplete gaseous diffusion plant.

Calutron technology is considered easier to master than the other methods. In addition, most of the necessary technology has been declassified, although the art of making and operating calutrons is not widely available. Indicators of a calutron program include high power consumption, large heat discharges, a large staff for construction and operation, large chemical processing facilities, sophisticated high-energy power supplies, and many large high-vacuum pumps.

Iraq. The existence of Iraq's calutron program shocked the world. The West was caught by surprise when calutron research, development, and production facilities were found during the inspection process.

The Iraqis had made substantial progress toward the production of significant amounts of weapon-grade uranium at a site near Baghdad called Tarmiya. But they were encountering serious difficulties in finishing the plant; they would have needed a few more years to reach full-scale production of roughly enough weapon-grade uranium for one or two bombs every two years.

Iraq appears to have believed that it could keep its main production facility at Tarmiya hidden even after full-scale production began. It buried its major power lines and installed extensive filtration systems in the chemical processing buildings to reduce radioactive releases. Nevertheless, U.S. officials believe that the calutrons would have been detected once they were operating. The site was considered suspicious because it was remote and so large.

The calutron program was largely destroyed by the Gulf War and subsequent IAEA actions. Because this program is not easy to hide, the IAEA believes Iraq is unlikely to resurrect it.

■ **Aerodynamic separation.** This method separates uranium through the centrifugal effects of a fast flow of uranium hexafluoride gas in very small, curved-wall chambers. The method is even more energy intensive than gaseous diffusion.

Only South Africa and Germany have developed this technology. Brazil acquired a small, safeguarded aerodynamic plant from Germany, but it is abandoning the facility. The technology is not widely available, and there is little practical experience in monitoring its spread to other countries.

South Africa. The source of weapon-grade uranium for South Africa's nuclear weapons program was the aerodynamic process deployed at the Y-Plant at Valindaba. The plant was commissioned in 1974, began producing highly enriched uranium in 1978, and closed in early 1990.

Because South Africa has become a party to the NPT, it has had to declare its inventory of highly enriched uranium to the IAEA and agree to place all of its nuclear activities under IAEA safeguards. The IAEA has attempted to verify the accuracy of the declared inventory, particularly since the recent announcement by the South African government that it had built—and destroyed—six gun-type nuclear weapons.

Verifying the completeness and accuracy of South Africa's declaration is important, because South Africa is the first de facto nuclear weapon state that has placed its program under international inspection. This case will set important precedents for other countries, such as Argentina and Brazil, who have also agreed to apply safeguards on all their nuclear materials.

To help the IAEA, South Africa has provided the agency with extensive historical production information. But the information is insufficient to eliminate all discrepancies between the declaration and the IAEA estimate. A major problem is that a record of tails (waste) assays and amounts were either not kept or were recorded inaccurately. *World Inventory of Plutonium* estimates that the Y-Plant produced a total of from 200 to 525 kilograms of weapon-grade uranium.

■ **Chemical enrichment.** This method relies on the slight tendency of uranium 235 and 238 to concentrate in different molecules when uranium compounds are continuously brought into contact. Catalysts are used to speed the chemical exchange.

Both France and Japan have built pilot plants. The French Chemex method involves combining two immiscible uranium-bearing liquids in a tall column—an effect similar to shaking a bottle of oil and water. The

Japanese Asahi process involves an aqueous liquid and a finely powdered resin through which the liquid is slowly percolated.

Chemical methods require more electricity than centrifuges, but considerably less than gaseous diffusion. Other indicators of such a program include large quantities of acid-resistant piping, pumps, and vessels, specialized resins and catalysts, and a large inventory of natural uranium. In addition, the Chemex method is characterized by tall buildings.

Iraq. Iraq declared its chemical enrichment activities in 1991. Iraqi officials stated that they were pursuing laboratory-scale work similar to the French and Japanese methods. Iraq obtained encouraging results in these experiments and was planning a pilot plant.

No evidence has been found that Iraq planned to produce weapon grade uranium through chemical enrichment. Documents seized by inspectors, however, show that Iraq was studying the production of 6 and 8 percent enriched uranium through combining the French and Japanese methods and batch recycling. Because these enrichment levels are higher than needed for power reactors, Iraq is believed to have planned to take low-enriched uranium from a chemical enrichment plant and feed it into calutrons, dramatically boosting their output of weapon-grade uranium.

Illicit acquisitions

The need for facilities to produce fissile materials can be bypassed if a country can buy or steal fissile material—or even a complete nuclear device. Although these items are accounted for and heavily protected, this route to nuclear weapons has an obvious attraction to certain countries, as well as to criminal or terrorist groups.

With the breakup of the former Soviet Union, concern has grown that nuclear weapons or material could be stolen and sold on an international black market. Although Russia and the former Soviet republics maintain that no weapons or fissile materials are missing, low-enriched uranium, milligram-quantity samples of plutonium, and radioactive sources have appeared for sale in Western Europe.

Another concern is the growing supply of civilian plutonium now in international commerce. *World Inventory of Plutonium* estimates that if current plans are realized, about 190,000 kilograms of plutonium will be separated during the 1990s. The separated plutonium will be shipped to fuel fabrication plants, turned into fuel, and then sent to power reactors for irradiation. Many of these shipments will cross international boundaries.

Lacking access to separated fissile material, a country might try to obtain nuclear waste containing small quantities of fissile material. Once it had such material, the country could build the necessary recovery facilities, bypassing several difficult production steps. Depending on the type of waste, hundreds or thousands of waste containers might be necessary to obtain enough material for a nuclear weapon.

There could be few indications of a successful theft or purchase of either fissile material or a weapon. Accounting at facilities that handle large quantities of fissile material may not be precise enough to detect the diversion of a few kilograms—or a few nuclear weapons. Western officials also worry that the former Soviet states might not admit a successful theft or diversion in order to avoid political embarrassment.

The only indications of such a diversion might be the emergence of a weaponization program. Additional indicators that a country has illicitly acquired a nuclear device or managed to build one out of purloined fissile material include the modification of aircraft for nuclear delivery, changes in command-and-control systems, and unusual security at suspected storage sites.

Iraq and the Italian smuggling ring. According to evidence offered during a 1984 prosecution, a ring of Italian smugglers offered to sell senior Iraqi military personnel 34 kilograms of plutonium that it purportedly possessed. After members of the ring and Iraqi military officials exchanged cables and had several meetings in Rome and Baghdad, the deal collapsed because the smugglers were unable to produce samples. The offer was undoubtedly a hoax, possibly intended to lure the Iraqis into buying conventional weapons.

The former Soviet Union. There have been recurring rumors about international uranium smuggling or black-marketeering in Europe of material stolen from the former Soviet Union or Eastern Europe. There have been reports of attempts to sell small quantities of depleted, natural, and low-enriched uranium for grossly inflated sums of money.[2] On March 5, 1992, two Russian men arrested in Augsburg, Germany, were carrying slightly over one kilogram of 2.8 percent uranium. They allegedly wanted to sell the material for over $1 million. Its actual value was estimated at about $350.

Similarly, minute quantities of plutonium have been found in Europe. In one case, according to the IAEA, a sealed plutonium source was seized by Italian customs officials at the Rome airport from a passenger who set off a metal detector. The sealed source was marked with the emblem Techsnabexport (USSR). Consultations with Russian authorities revealed that the sealed source—a standard calibration source sold by Techsnabexport—contained less than one milligram of plutonium.

Iran. There have been several reports claiming that Iran acquired two nuclear weapons from the former Soviet Union. U.S. and Russian officials have been unable to confirm these stories and several U.S. officials regard the information as unreliable.

Pakistan. China is reported to have supplied Pakistan with enough weapon-grade uranium for two nuclear weapons. The reporter who originally described this transaction was given the information by a Western intelligence official.

Weaponization

The acquisition of fissile material is only one part of making a nuclear weapon. There are several additional steps.

A nuclear weapons team must be assembled and managed in secret. The team must be able to master several technical areas, including theoretical calculations; high-explosive lens and main-charge development; high-speed testing capabilities; fissile material metallurgy; neutron initiator development and testing; arming, fuzing, and firing systems; and environmental testing.

If a full-scale nuclear test is not practical, the team must rigorously calculate and test the reliability and predictability of the device. One way to do that is through the use of a proven design—acquired elsewhere. But it is also possible to conduct additional research and non-nuclear testing.

Many of these activities would be difficult or impossible to detect outside the program. But two indicators of a weaponization program are extensive high-explosive testing and the production or evidence of neutron initiator materials such as polonium 210 or tritium. Export monitoring might reveal a secret program if it showed that a country was trying to acquire special testing and diagnostic equipment, certain types of machining and inspection equipment, and high-speed electronic components.

Pakistan. U.S. officials have said on many occasions since the early 1980s that Pakistan got a proven weapon design from China. Little is known about this particular design, although it is likely to have utilized a nearly solid sphere of fissile material with a tiny hollow core for the neutron initiator surrounded by a tamper and high explosives.

Pakistan has said that it has all the components needed to assemble at least one nuclear weapon. This implies that Pakistan made weapon-grade uranium metal components for the core.

Pakistan has also conducted a large number of non-nuclear high-explosive tests. One U.S. official said that some of the tests were done in a horizontal shaft in a remote area of Pakistan.

Iraq. Before the Gulf War, Iraq had a broad program evaluating all the major areas of design, testing, and construction of a uranium core implosion weapon. Most of its research activities were conducted at the Al Tuwaitha nuclear research center. It was building a number of specialized facilities at Al Atheer where, it is now believed, weapons components were to have been built and tested.

Little of this program was known before the Gulf War. Al Atheer was only lightly bombed during the war while nearby missile development sites were heavily damaged. Many of the details about the weaponization program were revealed by some progress reports IAEA inspectors seized after the war. The inspectors say the program was at an early stage and a practical design had not been achieved. A number of problems remained to be solved, including the neutron-initiator design and high-explosives development. Iraq was, however, making polonium 210 for neutron-initiator research at its safeguarded Soviet-supplied research reactor. Target material made from bismuth was irradiated for about 15 days, then processed to recover the polonium. IAEA safeguards do not monitor for polonium. If safeguards had been thorough enough to detect polonium 210 production, Iraq's program might have been forced to use more difficult neutron-initiator designs. This could have delayed its weapons program significantly.

Clandestine programs have tended not to depend on safeguarded facilities, confirming the value of IAEA safeguards as a deterrent. Iraq and North Korea, however, have shown that safeguarded facilities can play an important role in the early stages of a plutonium separation program or in the production of radioactive materials for neutron initiators.

Most secret programs have not depended on illicitly acquiring separated plutonium, highly enriched uranium, or nuclear devices. Instead, they have aimed at developing an indigenous capability to make nuclear weapons. This could change if the former Soviet Union remains unstable, or if large amounts of separated plutonium enter international commerce.

The best results have been obtained when intelligence information is combined with on-site inspections of suspected sites.

India. India has been capable of building nuclear weapons since at least 1974, when it tested a plutonium-core fission bomb in the Rajastan desert. Little is known about India's weaponization program, although most of it is believed to have been conducted at the Bhabha Atomic Research Center.

There is some controversy over whether India has built plutonium cores or "pits." Senior Indian atomic energy officials have said that India has not made pits, but Pakistan claims to have done so with weapon-grade uranium, increasing suspicions that India may have built pits in response.

Nonproliferation prescription

A surprising number of secret, small-scale programs and facilities have been detected before enough fissile material was produced or nuclear weapons successfully built. The best results have been obtained when intelligence information is combined with on-site inspection of suspected sites.

Indigenous plutonium production and separation activities have generally offered enough clues to detect the accumulation of enough material for a bomb. Remote measurements of the heat output of a reactor can provide an indication of the amount of plutonium it has produced. But such techniques are of limited accuracy. There are no remote, reliable technical indicators of the total amount of plutonium separated at a small reprocessing facility.

Unsafeguarded enrichment programs have proven harder to detect. As expected, indigenously developed enrichment programs are more difficult to identify, particularly in their research, development, and construction phases. There are few, if any, external indicators of the amount of highly enriched uranium a plant has produced.

Weaponization activities, which can be done at small, scattered sites, are often poorly understood and difficult to detect. Deployment of nuclear weapons, accompanied by high security and specialized military procedures, might be easier to recognize.

Aggressive export monitoring, with the cooperation of the business community, can be particularly useful in detecting secret activities. Scrutiny of exports has revealed centrifuge and weaponization activities that might otherwise have been difficult to detect. Almost all countries have sought foreign assistance to bypass indigenous development or shorten the time to obtain an essential capability. Weapons programs in the developing world have depended on the import of equipment, materials, or components. These countries' programs are particularly vulnerable to disruption through export controls.

Stringent export controls have slowed nuclear weapons efforts, and bought time for political approaches to work. By denying modern computerized manufacturing equipment, for example, export controls can force clandestine programs to rely on less sophisticated machine tools. These machine tools usually produce items more slowly and require more skillful operators, who are often in short supply in developing nations.

But export controls are not a panacea. A determined country with adequate resources can mount an effort to defeat or bypass export controls. Because technology is spreading worldwide, export monitoring may eventually become less effective.

Continued cooperation between intelligence agencies and international inspection organizations should make it harder for countries to hide their programs in the future. A successful nonproliferation regime will depend on governments maintaining a high level of political commitment, aimed in part at compiling and sharing complete and precise information about secret weapons activities. This type of nuclear intelligence gathering can involve multiple agencies and governments, some of which might be embarrassed by the exposure of a piece of information. Without sufficient commitment, governments may find it easy to overlook or ignore vital information. Lack of precise information can compromise the effectiveness of export controls and undermine economic and diplomatic initiatives.

Additional resources are needed if secret nuclear programs are to be detected. Governments need to implement more aggressive export monitoring and control and to share their findings with other governments. They also need to conduct more research on sophisticated detection techniques. Two areas that need more development are thermal monitoring of small heat sources and ways to detect underground facilities.

The IAEA needs to continue to develop more intrusive inspections. It has requested unofficial "visits" to undeclared sites and has resurrected its right to conduct "special inspections" of undeclared facilities in NPT states with safeguards agreements. These efforts need to be bolstered, including the development of procedures to inspect both declared and undeclared sites quickly and effectively.

The IAEA should safeguard more nuclear materials. It has taken a step in this direction by inviting member countries to submit more information on nuclear materials, such as uranium concentrate, or "yellowcake." But the IAEA needs to apply safeguards to yellowcake, and to nuclear materials such as tritium and polonium 210, that are key to the development of neutron initiators.

The IAEA needs to expand its inspection of dual-use equipment beyond Iraq. It has already invited a number of member states to provide information on exports and imports of nuclear and dual-use equipment for a new registry.

Beyond these incremental improvements, a new climate of openness and transparency is required. It should be harder for countries to hide nuclear programs in the first place.

Since the beginning of the nuclear era, access to information about nuclear programs has been a matter of great sensitivity in both nuclear weapon programs and in nuclear commerce. But the main reasons for secrecy among the nuclear powers are disappearing; in fact, they are becoming counterproductive. Deep reductions in the U.S. and Russian nuclear arsenals are now proceeding. Under the reduction plans, hundreds of tons of fissile material are scheduled to be removed from the arsenals. Openness would help to build confidence that these materials are not misused. Excessive secrecy no longer serves commercial interests—in fact, it has fed public mistrust.

A first step toward a more transparent international system would be for all nations to declare their stocks and production sites of plutonium and highly enriched uranium. Fifty years after the beginning of the nuclear era, the world can no longer accept that the data about these dangerous materials are not available.

---

1. David Albright, Frans Berkhout, and William Walker, *World Inventory of Plutonium and Highly Enriched Uranium 1992* (Oxford: Oxford University Press, 1993).
2. Ann MacLachlan and Karoly Ravasz, "Rumors Persist About U, Pu Smuggling But So Far Amounts are Insignificant," *Nuclear Fuel* (March 16, 1992).

TACTICAL MISSILES: ANYONE CAN PLAY

AZRIEL LORBER

Azriel Lorber is principal assistant to the director general of Israel's Ministry of Science and Technology.

As often happens in the sluggish world of arms control, by the time the industrialized nations enacted the Missile Technology Control Regime (MTCR) in 1987 the genie was already out of the bottle. The MTCR may have helped curb the spread of long-range missiles that might threaten the United States and other industrialized nations. But it was too little and too late to prevent the proliferation of tactical ballistic missiles and the technology to make them. In the developing world, these missiles—those with ranges of 100 to 1,000 kilometers—present the real threat to security.

The acquisition and production of tactical ballistic missile systems is now limited only by the resources a country has to invest in them. A country interested in acquiring these missiles

Short-range missiles—in Third World hands—pose a serious threat to regional security.

DEFENSE DEPARTMENT

The Soviet-made Scud is in common use.

From *The Bulletin of the Atomic Scientists,* March 1992, pp. 38-40.

will not necessarily look for the latest technology, but will be guided instead by a practical approach: what is needed and what is available to obtain a minimum missile capability. Some potential users believe they need missiles not to use as efficient military weapons but as tools of terror and mass destruction. Therefore, they may be satisfied with weapons that are merely sufficient and not particularly sophisticated.

This kind of ballistic missile technology is readily available—and the MTCR is practically powerless to stop its spread. Further measures must be taken to stop missile-wielding aggressors.

A ballistic missile consists of three groups of subsystems: propulsion, guidance and control, and the warhead. The main distinction between a ballistic missile and an unguided artillery rocket is the guidance and control system—the most expensive and technologically most advanced subsystem in a ballistic missile. Another distinction is that guided missiles are usually multistaged, enabling them to attain considerably longer ranges. The figure on page 39 shows, schematically, a two-stage ballistic missile and the major technologies involved in its design.

■ **Propulsion.** Some current rockets and missiles—Scuds, for example, as well as the U.S. Lance—use liquid fuels. But with these exceptions, solid fuels are currently used almost exclusively. Solid fuels are generally less energetic than liquid ones but much simpler to handle in the field.

There are two major types of solid fuels. "Double-base" fuels are chemically similar to various propellants (powders) used in gun ammunition of all calibers—and the raw materials and most production procedures are basically the same. Obviously, rocket fuel production requires much bigger batches of material, which calls for somewhat different logistics. But the difference is a matter of scale rather than technological sophistication. It is more complicated to extrude the propellant for a large rocket and to perform the necessary quality control tests than to do so for a batch of bullets, but the chemistry and mechanics are essentially the same.

The second type of solid rocket fuel, "composite," is more energetic and thus more efficient than a double-base propellant. It has several other advantages, particularly for larger rocket motors, but it is also commonly used in a variety of small rocket motors, including unguided anti-tank rockets. And there are variants to the basic types, such as "composite modified double base." But anything other than double-base fuels may be considered frills for a Third World country.

Thus, a country with an established small-arms industry knows how to make rocket fuel. Producing it is a matter of increasing or diverting the suitable workforce and investing in facilities. It should be added that similar plants are used in the chemical industry and are easy to acquire.

The body of the rocket itself may pose some technical problems—but rockets flew before the advent of advanced, extremely strong, lightweight materials. Accepting lower performance standards enormously simplifies production problems. And if all this sounds too easy, one must remember that both Iraq and Iran, not the most advanced countries technologically, did exactly this during their protracted and costly war.

■ **Warheads.** Conventional warheads that can be fitted to a rocket include the unitary high explosive, which is old hat by now; various bomblet warheads, technologies for which are in the public domain; and fuel-air explosives, also well covered in the open literature. Most chemical warfare agents can be produced by any competent chemical concern, and a widespread embargo on raw materials or production plants will only make them somewhat more expensive or of lower quality.

Unfortunately, the "back to basics" approach may apply to nuclear weapons as well. The atomic secret is no secret at all—it is only a question of making a large investment and exercising patience. We hear occasionally about the attempted smuggling of sophisticated subassemblies for nuclear weapons, but a less efficient nuclear device can be detonated without fancy electronic hardware. The only two nuclear weapons ever fired in anger were used in the age of vacuum-tube electronics. A considerable range of scenarios can be devised around using, or threatening to use, such a device against civilian populations as an act of war or terrorism. In either case, somewhat inefficient devices will serve just as well.

■ **Guidance and control.** The difficulties of realizing this part of a missile system are real but often exaggerated. The theory of missile guidance and control is fully in the public domain. Besides books and magazine articles, university courses including laboratories and workshops are now available to all comers. The hardware—which consists of an inertial reference unit based on an array of gyros and accelerometers; a computer; a control mechanism to change the missile's flight path; and power packs for the electronics and controls—is almost as easy to come by.

Inertial reference units are used in all aircraft autopilots, including commercial ones; in navigation; and in weapons systems in most modern fighter and trainer aircraft. Practically all anti-ship and anti-tank missiles currently produced contain some form of gyro. Any country that can produce modern aircraft can embark on missile guidance. *Jane's All the World's Aircraft* lists 14 Third World countries that have access to inertial reference units or components thereof.

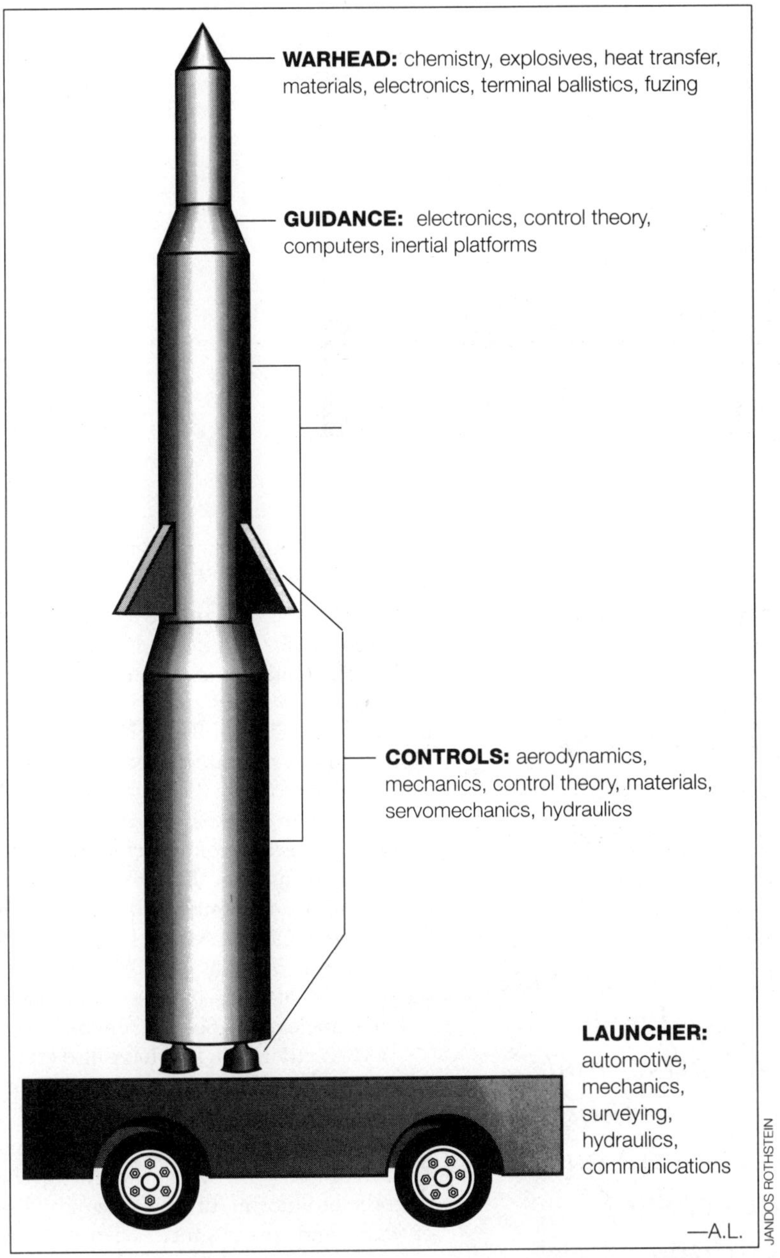

The technologies needed for simple missiles are readily available.

Missiles for use as weapons of terror need not be sophisticated.

A recent development in navigation technology may obviate the need for complicated, expensive inertial navigation systems. Anyone with a hand-held receiver (which costs about $3,500) can gain access to the Global Positioning System satellite network and determine his position within a few meters [see September 1991 *Bulletin*, page 3]. This technology, which is a modern version of the old celestial navigation art, can be adapted for use in missile guidance.

The control mechanism and power pack can be adapted from other devices, purchased commercially or designed locally. A competent engineer with the right background can solve most of the technological requirements of these components. And the availability of the necessary computer and programming skills does not merit discussion in this day and age.

Of course, a ballistic missile system cannot be designed on the kitchen table and whipped together in a two-car garage. There is the question of financial and human resources. Assuming that finances are available, however, technical knowledge, which is essentially a tradable commodity, can be obtained. Legal barriers to such transactions are routinely circumvented when the price is right. And most of the technology involved in tactical ballistic missiles is "dual use"; that is, it has non-missile or even non-military applications as well.

Because a certain number of countries, particularly in the Third World, have acquired most of this missile technology, a kind of critical mass has been achieved. The very wide production base and constantly shifting political alliances have made for strange bedfellows. It has become easier for interested parties to obtain from each other the technology, the plant facilities, and even the necessary workforce to carry on a missile project. The collaborative Condor program involving Egypt, Iraq, and Argentina is one example.

The cancellation of the Condor project last April was touted as one of the successes of the MTCR, and indeed the political and economic incentives employed by the regime may have been effective in that case. But these pressures are unlikely to work in the cases of Iran and North Korea—and they did not stop Iraq's missile and nuclear programs.

The breakup of the Soviet Union poses another problem—that weapons may fall even more easily into the wrong hands. The same may eventually apply to China.

Another threatening development on the horizon is the cruise missile. Various developments in the field of navigation and homing, and the slow but inexorable spread of unmanned air vehicles, may bring about the spread of cruise missiles, either built from scratch or adapted from existing systems. In this case, too, it appears that the MTCR can perform only a delaying action.

Yet the effort to strengthen and enforce the MTCR should continue—to slow, if not stop, improvements in weapons and to provide time for defensive technologies to catch up. Besides enforcing the MTCR, democratic nations should band together and develop, as quickly as possible, super Patriots or Arrows or any other defensive systems to dissuade potential aggressors and blackmailers. The world was in a sense fortunate that Saddam Hussein got too greedy before he was equipped to enforce his grab for territory and control. But we cannot count twice on that kind of luck.

The IAEA: Neutralizing Iraq's Nuclear Weapons Potential

Maurizio Zifferero

Maurizio Zifferero, an expert on radiochemistry and hot atom chemistry, was director of Italy's Fuel Element Reprocessing Laboratory before joining the International Atomic Energy Agency (IAEA) in 1980. He has been deputy director-general of the IAEA and leader of its "action team" on Iraq since April 1991.

"By the end of September 1991, the main components of Iraq's multifaceted clandestine nuclear program were uncovered: a program that involved over 10,000 scientists and technicians working on projects with an estimated cost of several billion dollars."

As we now know, the Gulf War fought over Kuwait in 1991 may well have spared the Middle East—and the entire world—a much more devastating future confrontation involving a nuclear-armed Iraq. It has been two years since the UNSecurity Council adopted resolution 687, the cease-fire arrangement that mandated the destruction, removal or rendering harmless of Iraq's unconventional weapons capabilities (nuclear, chemical and biological weapons and ballistic missiles with ranges over 150 kilometers). To fulfill this mandate, the Vienna-based International Atomic Energy Agency (IAEA), with the assistance and cooperation of the UN Special Commission On Iraq (UNSCOM) and a number of UN member states, has developed a detailed and nearly complete picture of the vast and previously undiscovered scope of Iraq's nuclear weapon program. In the process, the IAEA and the global community have learned valuable lessons which will help detect similar threats in the future.

UN Security Council Resolution 687 charged two bodies, the IAEA and the newly formed UNSCOM, with mapping and neutralizing Iraq's weapons of mass destruction programs. The IAEA, with more than 35 years of accumulated expertise in nuclear inspections, was tasked with neutralizing the nuclear component of Baghdad's programs, with UNSCOM's assistance. UNSCOM was given specific responsibility for dismantling Iraq's bacteriological, chemical and ballistic missile programs.

The objective spelled out under the Security Council resolution has two phases: first, full investigation and the destruction, removal or rendering harmless of those items relevant to the Iraqi nuclear weapons program (as listed in paragraph 12 of resolution 687), and second, establishing and implementing a longer-term monitoring plan to prevent any revival of the program. The first phase has involved highly intrusive on-site inspections at more than 70 sites, coordination with UNSCOM on the selection of new sites to be inspected, and the collection of information from various governments about the equipment and technical advice supplied to Iraq. With support from UNSCOM and staff members from several countries, the IAEA has succeeded in identifying and destroying most of Iraq's nuclear weapons potential.

IAEA activities in Iraq have also established a sound basis for long-term monitoring of Iraq. This will involve routine procedures and techniques and a number of imaginative ones as well, including the periodic monitoring of Iraq's main bodies of water and unannounced visits of resident inspectors to plants, factories and research centers.

UN Mandate for Action

Immediately after resolution 687 was adopted on April 3, 1991, the IAEA set about its initial task, establishing an "action team" on April 15 under my direction. The team drew on the agency's own expertise and that of its laboratories, and on its network of international contacts, thus making use of experts with special additional skills. This blend, when combined with UNSCOM participation in field missions, has proved very successful despite the difficult environment in which the teams have been forced to operate. The combined efforts, and results, have been praised on several occasions by the Security Council and UN General Assembly member states.

The first on-site inspection by the IAEA action team took place from May 15 to 20, 1991. During the earliest stages of the inspection process in Iraq, several disquieting discoveries came to light. None was more sobering than the growing realization of the true dimensions of Iraq's secret nuclear weapons program. By the end of September 1991, the main components of Iraq's multifaceted clandestine nuclear program were uncovered: a program that involved over 10,000 scientists and technicians working on projects with an estimated cost of several billion dollars. Iraq, we have learned, may have been within three to five years of producing its first nuclear weapon when the Gulf War began, and was pursuing no less than three different paths toward acquiring the key materials for a nuclear weapon.

Unquestionably, there had been serious intelligence failures. In particular, until the passage of resolution 687, the agency had no intelligence unit of its own or any access to other intelligence information. All IAEA inspections had been directed only at declared facilities.

Petr Pavlicek/IAEA

The huge weaponization center at al Atheer (including the powder building, above) escaped almost unscathed in the Gulf War. The complex was destroyed under International Atomic Energy Agency (IAEA) supervision in April and May 1992. All Iraqi plants and equipment for production or use of fissionable material have been destroyed by the allied bombing or subsequently at the IAEA's behest.

Iraq's nuclear program appears to have begun in earnest after the 1981 Israeli bombing of the French-supplied *Osiraq* research reactor under construction at the al Tuwaitha complex south of Baghdad. The clandestine program, undertaken after that attack, escaped largely undetected by Western intelligence agencies and indeed by the IAEA's own safeguards system. Iraq's cover-up was successful even though the program depended for its progress and success on the supply of substantial technical know-how, materials and equipment from abroad. Iraqi success in keeping the program secret was achieved by conducting its large-scale activities almost solely at secret and undeclared sites not visited by the IAEA.

Few people guessed, despite some hindsight evidence pointing in that direction, that in its quest for nuclear weapons, Iraq had revived and updated a 1940s-vintage uranium enrichment method known as electromagnetic isotope separation (EMIS), which uses calutrons. Baghdad had also progressed much further in its centrifuge capabilities than was generally anticipated.

Iraq had two EMIS uranium enrichment industrial sites, at ash-Shaqat and al-Tarmiya. The al-Tarmiya site was under commissioning at the time it was hit in an allied bombing raid during the Gulf War; ash-Shaqat was under construction at that time. Both sites were extensively destroyed during the war. The plant at which Iraq was preparing to begin large-scale production of centrifuges was code named "al Furat" (Euphrates). Al-Furat and the multi-billion dollar weaponization center at al-Atheer destroyed under IAEA supervision in April 1992, escaped almost entirely unscathed in the war.

Why were these massive portions of Iraq's program not detected earlier? In addition to previously mentioned intelligence failures, Iraq's closed society and large financial resources played a part. Another key factor is that prior to the Gulf War, IAEA safeguards inspections were limited in Iraq—as they still are elsewhere—primarily to inspections and accounting for nuclear materials and activities at declared facilities. The IAEA inspected the highly-enriched uranium fuel elements from Iraq's reactors twice a year and checked to see that declared facilities were not used for unapproved purposes. These operations were limited, in part, by the desire of IAEA member states to control the financial cost of safeguards measures. Moreover, prior to the Gulf War, no information was ever provided to the agency about illegal activities taking place at undeclared facilities in Iraq. Such information could have been used to uncover Iraq's program before the war if Iraq had submitted to inspections, or would have focused attention on this issue if Iraq had denied access.

The nuclear materials that Iraq had obtained legally from abroad—totaling over 12 kilograms of fresh weapons-grade uranium and over 35 kilograms of irradiated, but potentially usable, nuclear weapons-grade uranium—remained under IAEA safeguards throughout the agency's pre-war relationship with Iraq. Iraq must have felt the temptation to divert this material to the weapons program because it would have saved Baghdad many millions of dollars and several years in its efforts to produce a nuclear weapon. All of the unirradiated materials have now been removed from Iraq and preparations are continuing to remove the remaining irradiated fuel elements.

Destroying Iraq's Nuclear Potential

In May 1991, aided by intelligence input from IAEA member states and bolstered by the full support of the Security Council, full-scope inspections on an unprecedented scale began in earnest. As of mid-March 1993, the IAEA has conducted 18 on-site nuclear inspections in Iraq. Altogether, 52 inspections have been carried out by a variety of teams under resolution 687, including investigations of nuclear, ballistic, chemical and biological programs. Despite early Iraqi efforts to camouflage its blatant disregard of its obligations under the nuclear Non-Proliferation Treaty (NPT) and continuing intransigence regarding the submission of procurement data, an internally consistent picture of the Iraqi program, both in scope and technical detail, has now emerged. The program comprised nine major research and development, production and support facilities, including uranium enrichment plants; a complex and highly successful procurement network; a number of sources of technical advice from abroad; unlimited access to services from the Iraqi State Industrial Establishment; and a large, well-trained technical work force. It is worth noting that this picture is further validated by the analyses of hundreds of secret Iraqi documents taken by the agency's inspectors, and by intelligence information.

Iraq's Three-Track Approach

It is now clear Iraq was pursuing three different routes to uranium enrichment: EMIS, the ultracentrifuge and chemical enrichment. In addition, scouting experiments on a laboratory scale had been started in 1989 to produce and separate gram quantities of plutonium from fuel irradiated in Iraq's research reactor. The EMIS option was the closest to fruition. The industrial-scale plant at al-Tarmiya was 12 to 18 months from full operation when the Gulf War began and had already produced half a kilogram of low-grade enriched uranium (insufficiently enriched for nuclear weapons). Construction of a second, identical facility at ash Shaqat was 85 percent complete when the war began. Both plants were severely damaged during the war but Iraq made a major effort to disguise the true nature of them before UN inspection teams arrived. For example, all the EMIS equipment was removed and a new concrete floor had been laid. Despite these efforts, through a combination of chemical and isotopic analyses of samples, defector-generated information and the assistance of experts who were familiar with EMIS technology, the IAEA identified the real purpose of both sites and has rendered them harmless.

Iraq's efforts to enrich uranium with more advanced, efficient, productive ultracentrifuges had not progressed as far as the EMIS program, but were more developed than the international community had generally suspected. Iraq had accumulated enough information to begin to obtain all the materials needed to begin production of centrifuges, and had conducted a series of single centrifuge tests. Baghdad has declared that it was planning to produce a test assembly of 100 centrifuges by 1993 and a 500-unit assembly by 1996, but IAEA teams have uncovered no evidence that Iraq had begun to produce any significant numbers of centrifuges. Moreover, Iraqi scientists had made comparatively smaller efforts in uranium enrichment by chemical processes and in the production and separation of plutonium, although they had been successful in preliminary laboratory-scale experiments.

Killing The Hydra

Currently, all the plants and associated equipment identified as having been related directly to the production and use of fissionable materials (hundreds of millions of dollars worth of facilities and materials) have been destroyed either by coalition bombing in the Gulf War, or subsequently at the behest of the IAEA inspection teams. All known stocks of uranium have been ferreted out or otherwise identified, and have been verified and removed or are under seal. In the process, the IAEA has identified and inventoried more than 900 machine tools, and the manufacturers of most equipment and special materials have been identified. The one important gap, however, involves establishing a complete picture of all aspects of the Iraqi procurement network. While Baghdad has recently indicated it is willing to abandon its long-held position of not providing procurement-related information, it remains to be seen if this is a serious offer.

Knowledge and Uncertainty

Iraqi officials do not know in any great detail the procurement information already in the hands of the IAEA because most of it has been obtained outside Iraq. This is also largely true of the IAEA's identification of foreign sources of technical advice. In addition, while members of the Iraqi technical staff have scattered to other jobs, obviously retaining their technical expertise and know-how, many of the key personnel have been identified because of Iraqi declarations and from documentation removed from Iraq by the sixth IAEA inspection team.

While the picture of the Iraqi program is reasonably consistent, a compelling question is whether it is a complete picture. Most experts believe so, although a few still harbor doubts. This is the question that will—and must—haunt intelligence agencies and inspectorates alike. While nothing can ever be completely guaranteed as certain in any enterprise of this nature, this enduring question is precisely why the IAEA is now embarked on the second phase of its work by putting in place an ongoing monitoring program for the longer term.

Some of the elements of this long-term monitoring program include an extensive water sampling network designed to pick up any telltale radioactive traces that would betray any large-scale nuclear-related activity, the identification and regular on-site monitoring of facilities and equipment that could be used in reconstituting the Iraqi nuclear program, and a continuing regime of short-notice inspections.

The IAEA was given information from the intelligence resources of a member state that indicated the existence of an underground plutonium production facility comprising a nuclear reactor and, possibly, an associated chemical separation (reprocessing) plant. No evidence has been found so far that such a facility exists. On the contrary, the analysis of environmental samples taken in Iraq show that facilities of this kind, if they exist at all, have not operated in the recent past.

Concerns about the existence of a centrifuge cascade have been expressed by some individuals, apparently based on personal feelings more than on evaluated intelligence. Experts in centrifuge enrichment who assisted the IAEA in the inspection process and in the overall assessment of the Iraqi centrifuge effort do not believe there is any evidence at all to support the idea that a centrifuge cascade exists in Iraq.

The agency is nevertheless pursuing its activities in Iraq bearing in mind these concerns and following up on any credible information. While these areas continue to receive close scrutiny, it is the general consensus among experts and team members—shared by the US government—that the IAEA effort has put the Iraqi program out of business, at least for the time being. Some smaller equipment may have been concealed by Baghdad, but the vital uranium production and enrichment facilities have been destroyed. And while critics may point to the fact that blueprints and computer codes may be hidden, and the resident experts and technicians are still there, it is equally true to say that Iraq's coherent, industrial-scale support infrastructure has been devastated and cannot be re-established as long as effective monitoring of the country is in place.

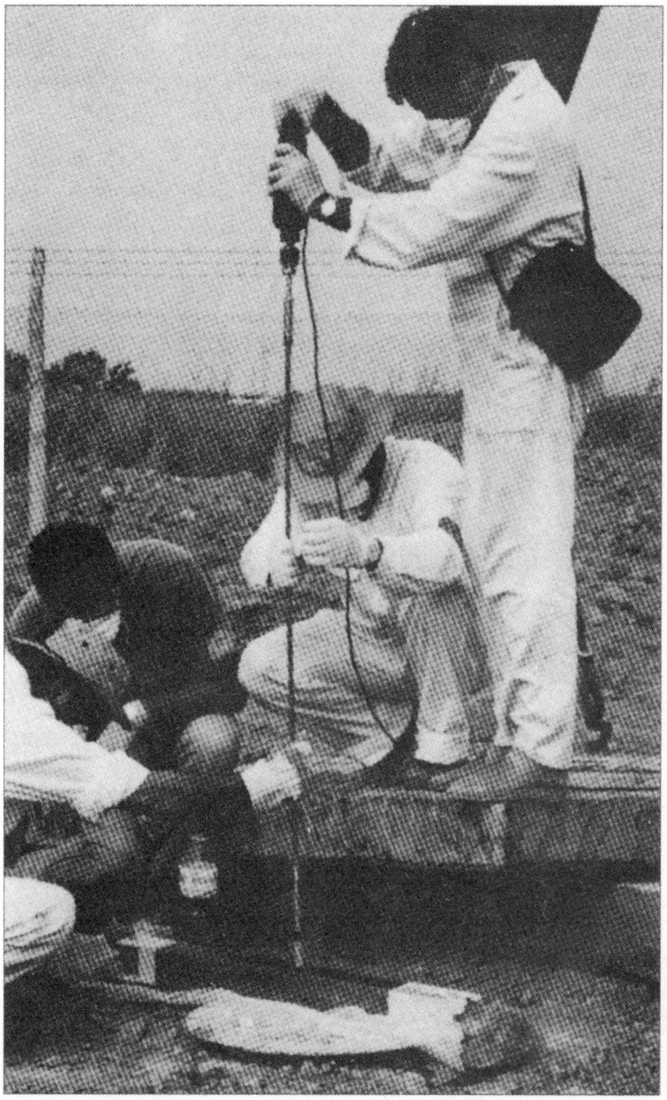

Vadim Mouchkin/IAEA

From the end of the Gulf War until mid-March 1993, the International Atomic Energy Agency (IAEA) conducted 18 on-site nuclear inspections in Iraq like this one, where inspectors are taking beryllium samples. UN inspectors were surprised at the size of the covert Iraqi programs in violation of IAEA and other agreements.

Lessons Learned

The lessons of Iraq for the IAEA safeguards regime have certainly not gone unheeded. The IAEA inspectorate, with substantial support from many governments, has embarked on an aggressive program to remedy the shortcomings revealed by the Iraq experience, and to augment traditional nuclear material accounting procedures by seeking universal reporting from NPT member states in a number of areas. These include nuclear and nuclear-relevant exports and imports for a data base; earlier information on nuclear facility designs; verification of equipment procurement data; environmental sampling; and, finally, a strengthened regime for initiating special inspections with the aid of additional information provided by external third-party sources—which was not received prior to the Iraqi case.

All of this information on procedures and progress is fully documented. The record of the IAEA's activities in Iraq since the war is contained in detailed inspection reports, thousands of photos, video tapes, sample analysis results, verbatim records of interviews with Iraqi technical staff, translations of hundreds of Iraqi secret documents confiscated during the inspections, and detailed correspondence with IAEA member governments and private companies regarding equipment procurement. This knowledge has been shared on a continuing basis as a matter of course with the Special Commission, and has been summarized regularly for the Security Council.

Are Criticisms Valid?

All of this progress, achieved often under the most difficult circumstances, contrasts sharply with the picture a few critics have sought to portray, generally quoting anonymous sources or evidence that, upon investigation is merely heresay.

One criticism is that IAEA inspectors should have more vigorously destroyed all machine tools and other "dual-use" items that might conceivably be connected to the Iraqi nuclear weapons effort. The IAEA has taken this criticism under careful consideration and has destroyed many items. The issue remains under review, but the IAEA must also avoid acting in a manner that might not only conflict with the carefully crafted mandate given to it by the Security Council, but might also undermine the critical, broadly based support of the Council and the United Nations as a whole for what is to be a long-term investigative and monitoring operation inside Iraq.

A few critics have also made much of Iraq's secret, undiscovered experimentation with plutonium separation. This was indeed a violation of Iraq's safeguards agreement with the IAEA and was roundly condemned. But what is involved is a minute amount of only about six grams of separated plutonium, and, more to the point, an item that was far less important in terms of proliferation significance than the best Iraqi uranium enrichment effort.

IAEA Needs Support

As for the proposition advanced by some critics that some governments know Iraq is still hiding major components of its nuclear weapons program, such an allegation strains credibility. The IAEA action team, which includes U.S. specialists, exchanges information with various member governments on a daily basis. It would be most peculiar if various member governments chose to keep such knowledge to themselves or share it only with a few outside specialists-turned-critics. Certainly some suspicions do remain, and it is for that reason firm evidence is being aggressively pursued—a process that will continue in parallel with the long-term monitoring effort now being mounted to prevent revival of Iraq's nuclear ambitions.

If anything has been learned from Iraq, it is the irreplaceable value of intelligence information from a variety of sources designed to increase the effectiveness of the IAEA. It must be underscored that while the IAEA *does* garner useful information from safeguards inspections, it is not, and should not strive to be, an intelligence organization.

Consequently, the IAEA requires, as something close to a *sine qua non* for its continued effectiveness, the full support of the international community if new threats of nuclear proliferation are to be averted in the future.

Atomic Shock Waves

Pyongyang's decision to withdraw from the Nuclear Non-Proliferation Treaty has put the UN in a bind. If the North gets away with it others could follow.

Nayan Chanda
in Hongkong and REVIEW *Correspondents*

North Korea's surprise decision on 12 March to withdraw from the Nuclear Non-Proliferation Treaty (NPT) has brought the spectre of conflict on the Korean peninsula into sharp focus.

By pulling out of the NPT less than two weeks before the expiry of a deadline to open its undeclared nuclear sites for inspection, North Korea all but confirmed the existence of a clandestine atomic bomb programme and rang alarm bells across Asia—particularly in South Korea and Japan. The unprecedented move has also challenged the UN's efforts to contain the spread of nuclear weapons. Its nuclear inspection arm, the International Atomic Energy Agency (IAEA), lacks the authority to investigate—far less indict—a country that does not want to belong to the NPT regime.

Some observers, however, believe North Korea's threat to leave the NPT may not be irrevocable. While submitting its intent to withdraw, Pyongyang has retained a number of options that could allow it to reverse its decision. "If [North Korea's] past performance is any guide, they would go up to the deadline and then come down," one Washington-based analyst said. "Once the US–South Korean joint Team Spirit [military] exercise ends on 19 March, we may well see the North Koreans reversing their position," he added.

In a letter to the UN Security Council on 12 March announcing its intention to leave the NPT, Pyongyang referred to the Team Spirit manoeuvres—carried out by 120,000 US and South Korean military personnel—as "a nuclear war rehearsal" that directly threatened North Korea. Pyongyang also accused Seoul and Washington of instigating the "unjust resolution" by the IAEA for "demanding us to open our military sites that have no relevance at all to nuclear activities."

The letter concluded that "this is an undisguised strong-arm act designed to disarm [North Korea] and strangle our socialist system, which jeopardises its supreme interests."

Since the IAEA's deadline for Pyongyang's compliance is 25 March, North Korea will have six days after the end of Team Spirit to reconsider its decision and step back from the brink. A senior US official is pessimistic that it will do so. "You can't really believe that a transitory thing like an [military] exercise could be a decisive factor for the NPT," he said, adding "the whole idea of inspection is deeply disturbing to them. It is a closed society."

Whatever the cost of compliance for North Korea, the price of its non-compliance could be heavy for the international community. As Leonard Spector, a nuclear non-proliferation expert at the Carnegie Endowment for International Peace says: "If the North Korean withdrawal stands it really destroys the sanctity [of the NPT], and it will give the message that defying the international community is not so unthinkable after all."

The North Korean move, which comes after the NPT regime gained in strength and stature following its inspection team's experience in post-Gulf War Iraq, could prove a major setback for the agency. "The IAEA is now between a rock and a hard place, or rather Iraq and a hard place. They can't afford to look weak because people will say that when you look weak [other countries with nuclear ambitions] take advantage," Spector says.

North Korea's action has also opened new opportunities, and dangers for China. With the international community relying heavily on Pyongyang's only major ally to persuade it not to leave the NPT, Peking has a chance to burnish its diplomatic credentials by delivering North Korea's compliance. However, a failure may force Peking to support international sanctions against Pyongyang, something China would not do lightly.

Ironically, perhaps, the present crisis stemmed from North Korea's recent cooperation with the IAEA. Although Pyongyang joined the NPT in 1985, it was not until April 1992

Reprinted by permission from *Far Eastern Economic Review,* March 25, 1993, pp. 10-11.

that it formally authorised the IAEA to undertake inspection of its three declared nuclear facilities. In the course of six inspections last year, North Korea admitted to the IAEA that it had reprocessed nuclear fuel from a research reactor to produce a "tiny" amount of plutonium—the raw fissionable material of atomic weapons—for research purposes.

Laboratory analysis of plutonium samples given to the IAEA, however, revealed there were three different "reprocessing campaigns," and not one as Pyongyang asserted. Spector explained that after plutonium has been extracted from used uranium fuel it breaks down into neptunium.

Existence of neptunium of three different ages in the sample was convincing enough evidence for the IAEA to order a special investigation of the sites where nuclear waste was dumped after reprocessing. Analysis of the waste would have given the IAEA a reprocessing history. "The North Koreans may not have realised what the samples could reveal," Spector noted.

A US specialist on North Korea says the site to which the IAEA is seeking access is a "nuclear cesspool." He told the REVIEW that "it is not that we have discovered any new facility. What we have seen is considerable physical changes to disguise the radioactive waste site."

The IAEA inspectors had expected to discreetly examine the waste sites without publicity, but their efforts were rebuffed. Further, recent US spy satellite imagery showed the North Koreans building walls and sentry posts around the sites. Pyongyang then officially denied IAEA access to the sites on the grounds that they were military bases.

North Korea watchers continue to speculate on what lies behind Pyongyang's dramatic move. Theories range from an internal power struggle to buying time so that nuclear weapons could be developed and give military authority to the heir-apparent Kim Jong Il. Analysts in Washington and Seoul also see Pyongyang's move as an attempt to test the resolve of newly elected presidents Bill Clinton and Kim Yong Sam.

Whatever North Korea's reasoning, it has presented the international community with some unprecedented problems. The most important of these is how to sanction a NPT member for violating its provisions after leaving the treaty. "If they are in the treaty and they have violated it you have a clear-cut case for going to the [UN] Security Council. But if they are outside the treaty and they are thumbing their nose at the international system there isn't much that you can do," Spector says.

An attempt to take the matter to the Security Council before 10 June, when North Korea's withdrawal from the NPT becomes effective, may have a slim legal basis. As Spector asks: "Are you going to impose sanctions against a country because it violated a treaty for a week and then withdrew from the treaty?"

One possibility would be for the issue to be brought to the Security Council after 10 June on the grounds that North Korea's nuclear weapons programme is a threat to international peace and security. But the move could be blocked on the grounds that such actions have not been taken against other nuclear proliferators like Israel, India and Pakistan who have not joined the NPT.

The only feasible course for the international community at this stage seems to be a threat to sanctions combined with quiet diplomatic persuasion. China's abstention at an IAEA board meeting is seen by some analysts as a signal to North Korea that if the issue were raised before the Security Council, it would abstain again. Equally, and more ominously, it could also mean exactly the opposite.

Levers for Plowshares: Using Aid to Encourage Military Reform

Nicole Ball

Nicole Ball, a visiting fellow at the Overseas Development Council (ODC), is the author of Pressing for Peace: Can Aid Induce Reform? *(ODC Policy Essay no. 6, 1992), from which this article is drawn.*

In a December 1991 *Washington Post* article, former World Bank President Barber Conable noted that "where military expenditures rise above, say, 5 percent of GNP (or, as in the case in some developing countries, more than expenditures on health and education combined), it is hard to see the good sense of lending to such nations and in doing so reduce the capital available to other borrowers."[1]

Was this just another case of a senior official now safely out of office prescribing policy in an area he had ignored during his tenure? On the contrary. Along with International Monetary Fund (IMF) Managing Director Michel Camdessus, Conable began speaking out on the imbalances between military spending and the resources available for economic and social development in 1989—months before the Berlin Wall crumbled, well before the demise of the Soviet Union and the end of the Cold War, and long before the Gulf War revealed that the major powers' arms transfer and nonproliferation policies were an emperor with no clothes.

The need for reductions in military spending in the developing world—as well as continued reductions in the developed world—is clear. During the Cold War, the developing world spent over five percent of its gross national product on the military, depriving economies of desperately needed resources. While millions of people were struggling in poverty, developing countries spent $167.7 billion on their military forces in 1989—the last year for which official figures are available—according to the U.S. Arms Control and Disarmament Agency (ACDA). Nearly a fifth of the world's developing countries spend more on their militaries than on education and health programs combined—sometimes by a significant margin. Nor is the issue only misallocation of economic resources. Iraq, which used external loans to free up funds for military purposes, provides a clear example of the threats to international security posed by large military budgets and an unrestrained arms trade. By the time the Cold War ended in 1990, some 40 million people had died as a result of wars in the developing world—wars which often blocked or rolled back any economic development in the area where they took place.

"Among the major international lenders, consensus on the importance of considering military spending in aid decisions is slowly building—stemming in significant part from the World Bank and International Monetary Fund efforts."

In short, as a 1991 report of the U.N. Development Programme put it:

> "If a government chooses to spend more on its army than on its people, it cannot be regarded as committed to human development, and this bias should certainly count against it in aid negotiations. High military expenditure should be a legitimate area of policy dialogue in all forums of development cooperation."[2]

The Game So Far

Among the major international lenders, consensus on the importance of considering military spending in aid decisions is slowly building—stemming in significant part from the World Bank and IMF efforts. This is key, as the greater the consensus and coordination among the lenders, the more effective they will be in influencing government policies among the borrowers.

At first glance, the World Bank and the IMF might seem unlikely leaders of an effort to introduce security-related considerations into the development dialogue. Their mandates are economic, prohibiting them from tying lending decisions to political criteria. Many developing countries point to this fact in strenuously opposing any link between these institutions' lending policies and the size of borrowers' military budgets. Yet where military spending poses a substantial drag on a country's economy and its ability to develop, it is a legitimate subject to place on the table. Already, the World Bank and the IMF routinely insist on economic steps that have important political implications, from cutting budget deficits to valuing currencies. And few institutions are as well equipped to examine the developmental impact of government priorities skewed in favor of the military sector as the World Bank and the IMF, with their capacities to delve deeply into the economies of member states. Moreover, these institutions wield enormous influence, both through the billions of dollars in annual financing each provides directly to borrowers and through the impact their policies have on individual lending countries.

With the end of the Cold War, Camdessus, Conable, and Conable's successor, Lewis Preston, have argued forcefully that changing international conditions create opportunities for transferring resources from the military to economic and social development in all countries. The World

From *Arms Control Today,* November 1992, pp. 11-17.

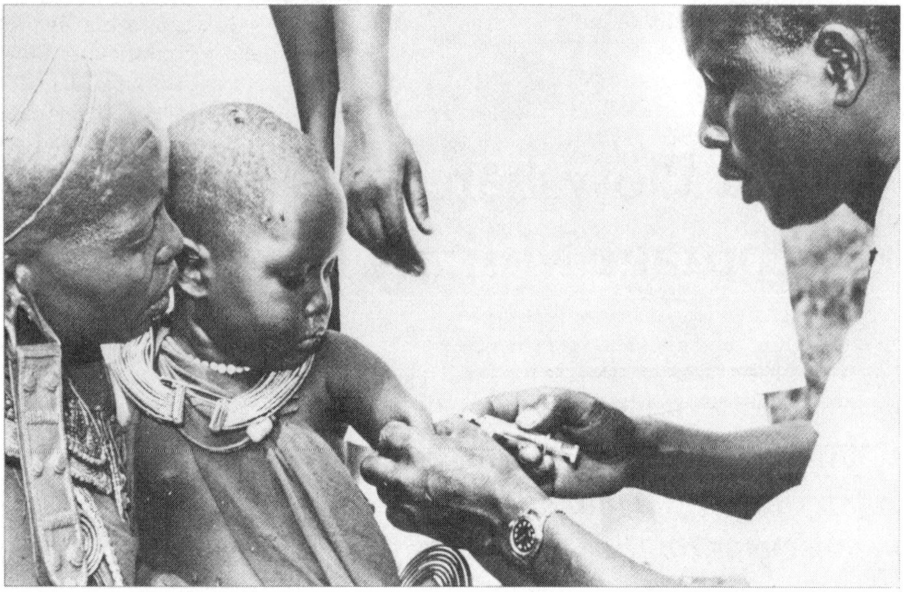

A Masai child in Kenya being immunized in a program sponsored by the U.S. Agency for International Development. Unlike Germany and Japan, the United States has so far failed to develop any policies for using its aid as a lever to discourage excessive military spending.

Agency for International Development

Bank-IMF activity began in earnest in 1989, with public statements questioning excessive military spending and justifying the idea that such issues should be considered in aid discussions. Both institutions, however, have made clear that they will not force countries to meet specific military-related conditions to qualify for funds. These statements were complemented by numerous in-house seminars, training sessions, and the like. The discussions reached a new pitch of intensity in 1991. In April, military spending was one of the "cutting edge" issues addressed at the World Bank's annual Conference on Development Economics, when former bank President Robert McNamara gave a major address calling for drastic military budget cutbacks worldwide, to be encouraged, in part, by links to aid. That fall, after the joint World Bank-IMF meeting in Bangkok, Preston said publicly that while "it is the sovereign right of nations to decide" how much to spend on their military, "if we found a situation where defense expenditure was 35 percent to 40 percent of the [government] budget, we might wonder if it was an appropriate use for [World Bank] funds." While Camdessus was more circumspect, he too made clear that the IMF would be putting military spending on the table in lending discussions.[3]

Both institutions have also raised military expenditure issues privately with a growing number of governments. In South Asia, for example, press reports indicate that both the World Bank and the IMF have pressed for cuts in military spending. In 1991, the last part of a World Bank aid package for Pakistan was reportedly held up, in part, because Islamabad was initially unwilling to discuss reductions in military spending as part of efforts to cut its deficit, and the IMF, by one report, called for a nine percent cut in military spending. Germany and Japan have exerted similar pressure on Pakistan, and while Islamabad has yet to announce any reductions in the absolute level of military spending, it has spoken of a freeze, while budgets for health, housing, education, and rural development have increased. India has also reportedly been subject to World Bank-IMF pressures for military cutbacks. By some reports, New Delhi is now reducing military spending in real terms, and in September 1991, the IMF approved nearly $3 billion in new loans to India. Another example is Uganda, where the military budget has consumed about a third of the national budget in recent years. Aid institutions urging lower military spending have received a sympathetic hearing from the Ugandan government, and in June 1992, Kampala announced a plan for deep cuts in the military.

The World Bank has also begun to respond to requests for demilitarization assistance, such as helping demobilized soldiers and their families find housing, training, and employment, and converting defense industries to civilian production. In 1991, for example, Argentina and the World Bank began negotiating a loan that would support the privatization of firms in the defense industry that produce primarily civilian goods.

While lenders have made it clear that they believe military spending in a sizable number of member countries is excessive, they are less certain as to how much is "too much." Conable has raised the five-percent-of-GNP standard and Preston the possibility of a 35-to-40-percent-of-state-spending guideline, while Camdessus has repeatedly pointed out how much certain nations could save if they reduced their military spending to the world average of roughly 4.5 percent of GNP. But officials in both institutions recognize that a broader analysis is needed. In a December 6, 1991 memorandum, senior management at the World Bank indicated that it would be appropriate to raise the issue of resource allocation to the military with countries where development-related outlays are "seriously inadequate" and military budgets are high—vague but potentially flexible guidelines.[4]

Equally important, the willingness of the multilateral lending institutions to address military spending has encouraged individual national donors to formulate their own policies. Germany and Japan are the donors that have gone furthest in formulating and implementing policies linking economic assistance with military factors. Neither country absolutely conditions aid on meeting any particular military criterion, and each uses more complex analyses than a flat percentage of GNP or of government expenditure.

Germany begins by examining a borrower's military spending as a share of GNP and of central government spending, arms imports as a share of total imports, arms production as a share of industrial output, military spending as a share of domestic savings, and soldiers as a share of total population. Any recipient of German aid that exceeds the regional average in any one of these areas is subject to a more in-depth study focusing on qualitative factors. These factors include possession of or efforts to obtain weapons of mass destruction, long-range delivery systems (both missiles and aircraft), and other technologically sophisticated weapons (fighter aircraft, electronic warfare equipment, and precision-guided munitions); the nature of the domestic arms industry; the role of the military in politics and domestic conflicts; and the domestic use of repression. The recipient's attitude toward international arms control negotiations and treaties and the effect of military spending on the economy are also factors in this assessment.

While the German Ministry of Foreign Affairs has accepted this approach (developed by the Ministry of Economic Cooperation), there have been some disagreements between the two over its implementation. After Syria's participation in the Gulf War, for example, the Foreign Ministry ensured that questions about Syria under these criteria would not hold up aid. Similarly, in the case of India, the Ministry of Economic Cooperation agreed with the World Bank and the IMF that military spending was too high (as were the budget deficit and restraints on free markets), and proposed cutting German aid to New Delhi by 25 percent. But after discussions in which Indian leaders pointed out the progress they were making in these areas, the Foreign Ministry convinced the Ministry of Economic Cooperation to reconsider.

In April 1991, Japan announced that three military-related criteria would be taken into account when determining aid allocations to developing countries: military spending, the development and production of weapons of mass destruction and ballistic missiles, and participation in the arms trade (as both importers and as exporters). These criteria were codified in Japan's Official Development Assistance Charter of June 30, 1992. Concrete examples of Japan's policy include Tokyo's October 30, 1991 announcement that it will not provide recognition or aid to North Korea unless it dismantles the plutonium reprocessing plant at Yongbyon, and its October 1992 threat to cut aid to China if Beijing proceeds with plans to purchase an aircraft carrier from Ukraine, a sale which seems to have fallen through for a variety of reasons.

In April 1992, the Japanese government urged its partners in the Development Assistance Committee of the Organization for Economic Cooperation and Development (OECD)—a group of Western developed nations—to "take into account the trend of military expenditures and arms trade of recipients in their provision of assistance, and request recipients to cut 'excessive military expenditures.'"[5] To identify countries whose military budgets are "excessive," the Japanese government proposed examining trends in military spending, both in absolute terms and as a share of GNP. Resources allocated to the military would then be compared with those available for development purposes, particularly social expenditure. Finally, the Japanese government suggested that these factors be weighed against determinants of military spending—such as external threats, internal security requirements, geographic location, length of borders, and collective security arrangements.

Unfortunately, the United States, with its billions of dollars in annual foreign aid, has so far been conspicuously absent in this dialogue. The U.S. president is required, under section 620(s) of the Foreign Assistance Act of 1961, to take into account the share of each recipient's national budget that goes to the military, and the amount of foreign exchange used for arms procurement. But no country has ever been denied aid on the basis of such a review. Indeed, for much of the Cold War, the United States, like the former Soviet Union, explicitly provided aid to friendly countries to allow them to spend *more* on their militaries. Virtually every country in the developing world has received some portion of the billions of dollars of military hardware, training, technology, and aid that the United States, the Soviet Union, their allies, and a few wealthy oil-producing countries provided on concessional terms during the Cold War. Even today, the United States continues to spend a substantial part of its foreign aid budget on military assistance, and is by far the world's largest arms

H. Arvidsson/United Nations

Iraq's "supergun" (above), and the Iraqi buildup it was part of, are archetypal examples of the dangers of unrestrained military spending. During the Cold War, nearly 40 million people died in dozens of wars in the developing world.

exporter. And like other arms exporters, the United States continues to subsidize many of its sales—a policy IMF head Camdessus has explicitly criticized. The links between development, military issues, aid, and arms exports cry out for attention from the new Clinton administration—particularly as the president-elect has indicated that he supports efforts to restrain the international arms trade.

The German and Japanese methodologies require the collection and evaluation of a considerable amount of information—though they rely on published tabulations from the Stockholm International Peace Research Institute, the International Institute for Strategic Studies, and ACDA for quantitative information. Some analysts have suggested that such information-intensive methodologies are too cumbersome to be of real use in the policy process, and have suggested relying on simple approaches, such as cutting aid to all countries spending more than a certain percent of their GNP on the military. To arrive at well-informed decisions about the complex relationship between a developing country's military sector and its economic situation, however, a relatively detailed analysis is required. The alternative of applying simple formulas across-the-board fails to take into account regional and local differences or special circumstances, and relies too heavily on quantifiable data that may be of very low quality.

What The Lenders Can Do

There are major differences between what multilateral lenders such as the World Bank and the IMF can do and what individual lending countries can do. The mandate of the World Bank and the IMF is to strengthen the economies of member governments, therefore the objective of enhancing security will always be secondary, at the very best. In contrast, individual countries providing aid can address overtly political issues, if they choose to do so, by using economic tools to alter government policies on weapons procurement and conflict resolution as well as on the level of military budgets. They may also have the capability (although not in their aid agencies) to evaluate the security needs of other governments, help restructure security forces, and provide them with professional training.

Thus, Japan can insist that North Korea dismantle the Yongbyon plutonium facility before providing aid, and the United States can tie the resumption of aid to Pakistan to specific nuclear nonproliferation steps from Islamabad. The World Bank, however, is likely to rely more on persuasion, support for reform-minded governments, and pressure to spend more in economic and social sectors—designed to squeeze the military budget indirectly.

All of the lenders, however, have a fairly broad menu of possible strategies open to them for bringing military issues into the development dialogue, from simple persuasion at one end of the spectrum to sanctions on the other. This is in sharp contrast to the public debate on the subject that has focused heavily on only one of these tools, known as "conditionality," which provides particular amounts of aid only if the recipient agrees to take certain actions (such as cutting the defense budget to a specific level) or not to take others (such as acquiring nuclear weapons). While conditionality may be effective in some cases, many of the other approaches are less confrontational and more flexible, and therefore may have a better chance of producing the desired results. The following are a few of the different, but often complementary, strategies lenders are developing.

Persuasion

Persuasion—designed to convince borrowing governments that changes in military policy are in their own best interests—has played a central role in recent efforts to bring military budgets and policies into the development dialogue.

Public expressions of concern by lenders about the competition between military spending and development have served to warn the recipients of international financing that the rules of the game are changing. Henceforth, military spending will be viewed as an economic as well as a strategic or political issue. Giving such notice, both publicly and privately, should be a precondition for applying more direct pressure for change.

Some governments would like to change their spending priorities, but face substantial obstacles in doing so because of the political power of the military, which often controls the defense budget process. External support, beginning with policy dialogue, can help such governments raise the issue with their armed forces. As Conable has commented, "Weak or uncertain civilian governments may publicly protest, as invasion of their sovereignty, admonitions that arms expenditures be reduced. I speak from experience when I say that such pressure may be privately welcomed by the new democracies."[6] Indeed, in some cases it may be desirable to reward countries that make steady progress in reducing military budgets, even if expenditure remains relatively high at the outset.

Policy dialogue is also important because the more borrowers feel that the reform programs are theirs and not imposed from outside, the more likely these programs are to succeed. Lenders should give high priority to identifying ways to avoid appearing to force one specific course of action on borrowers. Even governments that are already seeking external support for locally initiated reform programs can be sensitive on this point.

In the same vein, lenders should also accord high priority to working through multilateral forums in which military expenditure and other related issues can be raised in a nonconfrontational fashion. The Global Coalition for Africa—whose members include African governments, bilateral donors, and multilateral organizations—is addressing the possibility of reducing military expenditure as one element of improved governance. In Central America, consultations between regional governments and industrial countries under the San Jose accords (which involve the European Community and its members) or under the Partnership for Democracy and Development (which includes all OECD governments) could be broadened to include opportunities for lowering military spending.

Support

External support in various forms can facilitate borrower governments' efforts to implement military changes.

Financial support can help governments absorb extra costs associated with reform, such as compensating soldiers released from the armed forces or workers laid off from defense jobs. The World Bank negotiations with Argentina to help with privatization of defense firms producing civilian goods is a good example. Similarly, several major lenders to Nicaragua and Uganda are working with those governments to underwrite programs designed to integrate demobilized soldiers into the civilian economy. In a November 11, 1992 op-ed in *The New York Times*, Oscar Arias, former president of Costa Rica, pointed out that a Panamanian referendum on a package of constitutional amendments, which included banning military forces entirely, "might have stood a better chance" of passing if

Panamanians had been assured "that a positive vote would have met with a favorable response from creditor governments, lending institutions and investors."

Technical support can provide skilled manpower or equipment to carry out specific demilitarization tasks, from weapons destruction to monitoring to conversion. The Organization of American States, for example, provided demobilized Nicaraguan resistance fighters with construction materials and farm implements to assist their transition to civilian life, while bilateral donors have provided training to enhance their skills.

Pressure Without Conditions

As mentioned, the World Bank and the IMF have clearly stated that they will not apply specific military-related conditions to their lending. If policy dialogue is to be a credible tool for these two institutions, however, they must have some means of motivating borrowers to reexamine their military budgets.

One tool the World Bank has developed is to use structural adjustment lending to squeeze military budgets. The bank sets expenditure targets in economic and social sectors that cannot be met without a significant reallocation of resources, leaving governments little choice but to shift funds from other sectors the bank sees as unproductive, including the military. A similar strategy is available to the IMF when it sets targets for cutting fiscal deficits. For these institutions, this approach, combined with policy dialogue and targeted support for reforms, is among the most promising, as it directly addresses the link between wasteful military spending and domestic development without straying beyond these institutions' economic mandates.

Conditionality

Conditionality can take several forms and be applied with varying degrees of stringency. Most lenders are reluctant to identify specific military expenditure targets that borrowers *must* meet to obtain financing. Aid suspension and other forms of sanctions have been applied, however, particularly by the United States, in response to specific activities such as military *coups d'etat*, efforts to obtain nuclear weapons, and failure to negotiate in good faith. Thus, Washington sought to encourage the Israeli government to enter into significant negotiations with the Palestinians and several of its Arab neighbors by threatening to place conditions on the $10 billion in housing loan guarantees requested by Israel in 1991.

Agency for International Development

Nearly one-fifth of the world's developing countries spend more on their militaries than on education and health combined, diverting desperately needed resources. Above, schoolchildren in Bangladesh.

Although bilateral donors may link aid to particular actions to promote nonproliferation, conflict resolution, and regional arms control, few are likely to tie their aid absolutely to a specific level of military spending. As described above, while the lenders generally agree that lower military budgets are preferable, there is no agreement on how much is too much. Lenders are therefore more likely to press for sustained progress in cutting military spending than to insist that borrowers meet a particular target level.

Nevertheless, some military expenditure "threshold"—perhaps along the lines of Preston's reference to countries devoting more than 35–40 percent of their budgets to military spending—might eventually be established. If preceded and combined with intensive policy dialogue, support for desired changes, and diplomatic efforts to reduce security threats in particular regions, such an approach could ultimately be effective.

Explicit conditionality raises hackles in many countries in the developing world, as it suggests a loss of sovereignty over providing for their own defense (a function guaranteed to them by the U.N. Charter), and often involves little, if any, consultation with the borrower or flexibility on the part of the lender. Many borrower countries have argued that demanding reductions in military spending without reference to security needs is a dangerous exercise. In their view, only the country concerned has the capacity to define those needs and the resources needed to meet them. After the October 1991 joint World Bank–IMF meeting, for example, the "Group of 24" developing countries circulated a communique warning "against the involvement of the fund and the bank in issues beyond their strict economic and financial mandate."

Nevertheless, while there is clearly a need for lenders to work collaboratively with borrowers, lenders should not allow their desire to "persuade" rather than "force" to serve as an excuse for allowing the military *status quo* to go unchanged. The human, financial, and material losses that wars, excessive arms procurement, and high military budgets have inflicted in the developing world over the last four decades render the sovereignty argument increasingly invalid. It may at times be necessary to place conditions on economic cooperation to force a government to reconsider a policy that a majority of the international community—and perhaps of its own people—views as unacceptable.

"Carrots" Instead of "Sticks"

Lenders may choose not to impose specific conditions on their aid, but to give preference to governments whose performance is favorable. The Japanese government is particularly interested in rewarding good behavior, reserving denial of aid for rare occasions when governments fail to pursue certain policies. A reward-based strategy is grounded upon the premise that positive reinforcement is more likely to produce change than punishment.

While such an assessment may be valid for governments with a fairly firm commitment to reform, it is unclear how much leverage this sort of strategy provides over less committed countries. Furthermore, desirable as it may be to offer the carrot rather than the stick, reward strategies virtually always require official lenders to *shift* resources from one country to another. Japan, whose aid budget has been expanding more rapidly than most other countries, may find it easier to reallocate resources. A number of other OECD countries are facing cuts in aid budgets, as recessions push up fiscal deficits. And in the United States, congressional earmarking of substantial portions of aid resources imposes significant limits on the U.S. capacity to offer rewards substantial enough to make a difference.

Next Steps

The international lending community is making progress in bringing military issues into the development dialogue, but specific policies are still embryonic. The following are four suggestions for next steps.

1. Actively seek to support and promote military reform—including cutbacks in military spending—in the developing world.

All lenders should adopt policies that actively promote reform, rather than simply punishing bad behavior or passively rewarding good behavior. Specific conditionality may at times prove necessary, but the core of lenders' policies should be policy dialogue and financial and technical support designed to assist governments in restraining and reforming their military sectors. The objectives should include establishing greater transparency and accountability in the military sector; encouraging civilian control over the armed forces, paramilitary groups, and the police; supporting reductions in the size of military forces and domestic arms industries; and promoting new security arrangements that will enable governments to provide enhanced security at lower levels of expenditure.

One of the most important contributions that lenders can make is simply helping governments to integrate the military sector into normal development practices, such as assisting in strengthening government management and in increasing the efficiency of the money that is spent.

2. Build cooperation among national and multilateral lenders, borrowers, and relevant political institutions to create the conditions needed for enhanced security at lower levels of military spending.

For the purposes of devising strategies in this area, developing countries can be divided into two broad groups. The first group—which includes countries such as Egypt, Paraguay, and Uganda—spends demonstrably more on the military than is warranted by existing internal and external security threats, compared to development needs. These are the countries with which lenders feel most comfortable discussing military reform—particularly those among them that have already decided to undertake military cutbacks. Even in these cases, the international community may need to provide assistance in reaching arms control agreements or creating regional security mechanisms that will reduce the likelihood of renewed emphasis on the military in the future. Lenders should explore opportunities for using their lending to encourage such activities.

In the second group of countries, the security picture, either external or internal, will have to be changed before the economic burden of the military sector can be significantly reduced. In South Asia and the Koreas, for example, some reductions in military spending are possible now, but fundamental changes would require resolving outstanding political and armament issues. Here, political institutions must take the lead in pursuing the kinds of negotiated settlements, arms control pacts, and regional security arrangements that would make enhanced security at lower levels of military spending possible. Again, lenders should actively cooperate with these efforts, using their financial and technical resources to encourage the necessary changes in policies.

Although the bilateral donors and organizations such as the United Nations may be best suited to link official financing with arms control and conflict resolution, the World Bank and the IMF can clearly participate in certain activities, such as helping to devise and implement job creation and retraining programs for demobilized soldiers.

In addition, it would be worth exploring whether the multilateral development banks (the World Bank and the African, Asian, and inter-American regional development banks) could, under certain circumstances, link development assistance to the cessation of hostilities and the inauguration of serious negotiations between disputing parties. If it were agreed that a high level of military spending in a particular area or an ongoing conflict constituted a serious obstacle to development, and that only negotiations to resolve underlying security imbalances could free up resources urgently needed by economic and social sectors, multilateral development bank action might be justifiable on economic grounds.

3. Build agreement among the bilateral donors and U.N. agencies that countries receiving their financial support will generally conform to certain internationally agreed-upon security standards.

These standards should generally be norms of behavior that are already internationally accepted, such as international treaties and conventions. As a first step, they might include:

- adherence to international arms control treaties such as the nuclear Non-proliferation Treaty, the Biological Weapons Convention, the Environmental Modification Convention, and the just-completed Chemical Weapons Convention, or to internationally recognized alternative arrangements;
- respect for the territorial integrity of other countries, including support for the

principles of nonaggression and nonintervention;

- participation in dialogues designed to increase regional security and stability, where these exist;
- a willingness to negotiate in good faith as necessary to end longstanding conflicts, both internal and external;
- participation in the United Nations' standardized military expenditure reporting exercise and the U.N. arms register; and
- a willingness to subject the military sector to the same scrutiny and discipline as other public sector expenditure.

4. Match the donors' policies to those expected of developing countries, wherever possible.

To build credibility and avoid charges of discrimination and unwarranted interference in borrowers' affairs, lenders and developed nations in general should be willing to accept the same norms for themselves that they are applying to developing countries. The military cutbacks already underway in the industrial countries have given greater authority to calls from the international lending community for military reform in the developing world, but there is more that the developing countries should do. It will be difficult for the lenders of the developed world to demand that developing countries spend less than five percent of their GNP on the military, for example, if the lenders are spending substantially more than that themselves.

Military cutbacks should continue in many countries, as military spending in most of the developed world remains substantially higher than is justified, given the benign security environment most developed countries now face. To the extent possible, future international arms control agreements and supplier groups should be universal in membership and nondiscriminatory in scope, treating all states alike. When military intervention in the developing world is necessary, it should be multilateral, not unilateral, in nature, and given legitimacy in some broadly accepted way; for example by the United Nations or a regional organization.

One of the areas of greatest disparity between the objectives industrial countries are pursuing in the developing world and their own behavior is the arms trade, in which virtually all developed countries take part. The United States, Russia, France, and Britain export a substantial amount of arms to the developing world and are currently seeking to expand their share of the market in the face of declining domestic orders, sometimes using unrealistically low prices and subsidized financing. Clearly, countries that aggressively promote arms sales—including the United States—seriously undermine their ability to promote military reform. Eliminating arms sale subsidies, as IMF Managing Director Camdessus has urged, would offer concrete proof that the industrial countries do not expect all concessions to be made by the borrowing countries. More broadly, the largest arms exporters have a special responsibility to work toward genuine international limits on the arms trade.

Conclusion

The end of the Cold War has brought many positive changes in international relations, creating new opportunities for military reform in both the developed and developing worlds. But continuing problems from Yugoslavia to Cambodia make clear that conflicts have by no means been eradicated. The challenge of the 1990s is to ensure that emerging trends toward international cooperation in security and other fields, reduced military spending, and domestic political participation are maintained and strengthened.

The international lending community clearly has a role to play in this process. Lenders can help to change norms of behavior—from military secrecy to appropriate means of settling disputes within and among states. Where the objective is primarily to free resources for development, lenders, including the World Bank and the International Monetary Fund, can legitimately act on their own initiative. Where the objective is primarily to alter the security environment, as in constructing a regional security and arms control regime, political institutions will take the lead, but lenders will continue to have an important role to play in nurturing and supporting the process.

While far-reaching military reform in developing countries will occur only if governments in those countries accept the need for change, lenders have a role to play in building that acceptance. It is past time for the developing nations to take a hard look at their priorities and devise policies that will promote reduced tensions and increased development. For their part, the industrial countries can underline their commitment to the emerging norms they promote by applying them to their own behavior as well, and by using all the strategies outlined above to encourage beneficial changes. But it is ultimately the people and the governments of developing countries who must seize the current opportunities to create a more equitable and prosperous future for themselves.

NOTES

1. Barber B. Conable, Jr., "Growth—Not Guns," *The Washington Post*, December 24, 1991.
2. U.N. Development Programme, *Human Development Report 1991*, New York: Oxford University Press, 1991, p. 83.
3. Paul Blustein, "World Bank, IMF to Press Defense Cuts: Institutions Hint at Withholding Loans," *The Washington Post*, October 18, 1991.
4. Jonathan E. Sanford, *Multilateral Development Banks: Issues for Congress*, IB87218, Washington, DC: Congressional Research Service, March 13, 1992, p. 13.
5. Japan International Cooperation Agency, *Annual Report 1991*, Tokyo, 1992, p. 19; and statement by Nobuyuki Sugimoto, director of Multilateral Cooperation Division, Economic Cooperation Bureau, Ministry of Foreign Affairs of Japan, at the Informal Meeting on Participatory Development and Good Governance, Organization of Economic Cooperation and Development, April 9, 1992, p. 2. See also, "Japan's ODA Policies for a Peace Initiative," address by Takao Kawakami, director-general, Economics Cooperation Bureau, Ministry of Foreign Affairs, to the Tokyo Conference on Arms Reductions and Economic Development in the Post-Cold War Era, November 5, 1992.
6. Conable, "Growth—Not Guns," op. cit.

Can the Third World Afford Guns *and* Butter?

". . . Under conditions prevalent in many poor nations today, military spending does not always thwart growth."

Glenn Firebaugh

Dr. Firebaugh is professor of sociology, Pennsylvania State University, University Park

Military spending worldwide reached one trillion dollars in 1987. The Soviet Union and the U.S. were the biggest spenders by far, accounting for 60% of that total. Yet, in terms of "military burden"—the outlay as percentage of gross national product (GNP)—military spending in poor nations rivals that of rich ones. According to estimates of the U.S. Arms Control and Disarmament Agency, military burden averages approximately 5.1% in developing countries, as opposed to about 5.5% in the developed ones.

Until recently, it widely was assumed that military spending has lowered the standard of living throughout the Third World. What could be more obvious? Money spent on the military is money not invested in something else. In poor nations, where human needs are great and capital is scarce, large outlays of funds for the military seems unconscionable. Even in the U.S., where capital is more plentiful, the debate over military spending often is couched in zero-sum terms—Trident submarines vs. anti-drug programs or college loans. In poor nations, the contrast seems even more stark—tanks to feed the egos of those in power vs. wells to provide safe water for the masses.

Is there a guns-or-butter trade-off in the Third World? In theory, of course, there is. In the antiseptic world of most textbooks, capital and labor are completely mobile, political leaders are all-wise and altruistic, and class interests don't exist. In such a world, money not spent on the military would be put to better use.

However, in the real world of barriers to capital and labor movement, ineffective and corrupt governments, and class interests, it is patently naive to assume that money not spent on the military automatically is diverted to some more productive enterprise. So, the trade-off question only can be answered by examining the data. All else being equal, do Third World nations that invest heavily in the military tend to be worse off than those which do not?

Though some studies find the expected adverse effect of such expenditures, many conclude that military spending has little or no effect, and yet others conclude that it actually promotes economic growth in the Third World. This much seems clear: under conditions prevalent in many poor nations today, military spending does not *always* thwart growth.

Though there surely are more effective ways to do it, military spending could foster economic growth in the Third World by stimulating aggregate demand, spurring infrastructural development, promoting political security, elevating national loyalties and diminishing regional or tribal ones, and developing human capital. Of these, human capital development may be the most important. Military training in itself can cultivate the types of attitudes, aspirations, and values that some scholars see as the key to development. For many poor nations, military training does what an underfunded school system does not, since soldiers must have minimal literacy, learn to drive, and know basic mechanics. Frequently, a soldier's horizons are broadened as he moves from place to place and works with those from different regions and cultures. Especially in the poorest countries, where formal educational opportunities may be limited, the military might be viewed as an important educational institution.

Militarization also can play a key role in promoting or providing public goods—roads, airports, communication systems, and other infrastructural investments that are critical for economic growth. Moreover, a military force can promote another type of national good—public safety and confidence—by providing insurance against developmental disruptions (for example, internal political instability and invasions from external armies). In some instances, militarization can prompt societal integration and nation-building by bringing together ethnically and tribally diverse people under a single agenda. The importance of such integration scarcely can be overstated for many Third World countries, whose boundaries—as established by colonizing nations—divide tribal and linguistic groups.

Critics will respond that military spending is a very indirect and wasteful way to build bridges, create national solidarity, and teach people to drive. The critics are right—direct spending would be better, but entrenched elites in Third World nations often are little inclined to invest directly in welfare programs. It is only a slight exaggeration to say that, in some countries, the issue is not guns or butter, but guns or caviar. In that light, military spending—which has at least some developmental spinoffs—may be preferable to elite expenditures on imported luxury items.

GUNS OR SOLDIERS?

If this argument is correct, guns vs. butter is misleading. Fewer guns do not necessarily mean more butter. Guns vs. soldiers is the more telling comparison. Money spent on soldiers should have developmental payoff. Money spent on armaments—especially imported weapons—probably does not.

By spending on soldiers, Third World nations are doing more than investing in human capital for later growth. They also are providing immediate benefits—both direct and indirect—for part of the population. Direct benefits result because countries maintaining a large standing army must meet at least the basic needs of military personnel and their dependents. This is especially important in the Third World, where powerful groups might oppose more direct welfare programs for the poor. Indirect benefits result because armies are labor-intensive enterprises, precisely the sort of "industry" most suitable for labor-rich countries of the Third World. Hence, large standing armies might help to relieve congested labor markets, thereby contributing to the welfare of civilian workers as well.

To test the guns-or-soldiers hypothesis, Bradley Bullock, a sociologist at Randolph-Macon Woman's College, and I collected data on military spending and size of standing army for 66 Third World nations with market economies. We divided military spending by GNP to measure a country's military burden, and size of standing army by total population to measure "military participation ratio" (MPR). If the guns vs. soldiers argument is correct, MPR should have a positive effect on economic growth and living standards. Military burden, by contrast, should have an adverse effect, once size of the standing army is taken into account. In other words, military spending is beneficial only to the extent that it represents investment in people or infrastructure. Aside from that, it is a diversion of resources—as the guns-or-butter argument has it—so investment in armaments *per se* stunts economic growth in the Third World.

We assessed the effect of military burden and MPR on the following: economic growth rate, as measured by rate of change of average income; food availability, as measured by change in total calorie and protein supply, divided by population; change in infant mortality rate (deaths per 1,000 live births); and change in adult literacy.

Food availability, infant mortality, and adult literacy were included here because economic growth does not necessarily result in improved living standards for the masses (sometimes economic growth will benefit only—or primarily—the upper and middle classes). Food, infant mortality, and literacy often provide a better indication of standard of living for a typical person in a poor nation. We also included several "control variables" in the analysis to avoid mistaken inferences. In this instance, we did not want to attribute an effect to the military that is actually due to something else.

What did we find? More soldiers on average meant faster growth and better living standards—more food, lower infant mortality, and higher literacy rates. The positive "soldiers effect" appeared consistently in the data. The "guns effect"—spending on nonpersonnel military items—was erratic, but usually adverse.

The positive soldiers effect does not mean investment in armies is the best way to spur development or a foolproof way to develop. When wedded to adventurism, a large military machine can have disastrous effects for a country—witness Iraq.

The soldiers effect, however, does point to the importance of having institutions—such as the military—that systematically develop human capital. Because the military is one of the few such institutions in the Third World, it is not necessarily the case that poor nations would be better off if they would just quit "wasting so much money on their armies." In the perfect world of textbooks, armies would be dismantled and the money diverted to more productive enterprises. In the real world, the dismantling of armies might eliminate one of the few dependable sources of human capital development in poor nations and—as noted earlier—there is no guarantee the "peace dividend" would be spent productively.

Because of possible error in estimates of military spending, economic growth, literacy, etc., a single study never is taken as final proof. Nonetheless, these findings generally are congruent with those of prior studies and may help explain apparent discrepancies in them. Like the blind men and the elephant, studies of the economic effects of Third World militarization have been examining different parts of the animal. Those of militarization as military spending most often find adverse effects. Studies of militarization as investment in armies most often find positive ones. Though armies and arms tend to go together, their effects can be distinguished. Our overarching conclusion is that militarization promotes development in the Third World to the extent that it involves direct investment in people—armies, not arms. Otherwise, militarization carries no economic or welfare benefits.

Transitions

The trend toward democratization in the Third World has been fueled by a legitimacy crisis, demands for greater political participation, and the collapse of the Soviet Union, which effectively eliminated the socialist alternative of development. The democratization experience has varied throughout the Third World, and its success is by no means guaranteed. Nevertheless, democratic reform efforts offer fascinating and complex issues and problems for those interested in political development.

Few Third World countries have a democratic past. The colonial powers often failed to adequately prepare their possessions for democracy and independence. Even where there was an attempt to foster parliamentary government, the experiment frequently failed due to factors such as a lack of democratic tradition and factionalism. Leaders frequently resorted to centralization of power and authoritarianism to pursue development programs or simply retain their own power. In some cases, leaders experimented with socialist development schemes that emphasized ideology and the role of party elites. The promise of rapid, equitable development proved elusive, and the collapse of the Soviet Union discredited this strategy. Other countries had the misfortune to come under the rule of tyrannical leaders concerned with enriching themselves and who brutally repressed anyone with the temerity to challenge their rule. Although there are a few notable exceptions, Third World experiences with democracy have been very limited.

During the 1980s, much of Latin America underwent a redemocratization after a period of authoritarian rule. This trend toward democracy spread to some Asian countries, such as the Philippines and South Korea, and by 1990 democracy also began to be felt in sub-Saharan Africa and the Middle East.

The democratization process in the Third World has been sporadic and uneven and is likely to continue in this fashion. For example, in 1992 in Latin America, the fragile nature of democracy was exposed. In Venezuela there were two coup attempts and the former president was finally forced out of office and charged with corruption. A caretaker government was put in place pending new elections. Also in 1992 in Peru, the democratically elected president Alberto Fujimori dismissed the legislature and suspended the constitution, ending 11 years of democracy. Guatemala's president attempted a similar action, resulting in his removal from office. In Nicaragua a group of former Contras seized hostages to force the government of Violetta Chamorro to reduce Sandinista influence. Some Sandinistas responded by seizing their own hostages to force the release of the first group of hostages and the crisis briefly threatened to rekindle the civil war. These incidents highlight the tenuous hold that democracy has in some parts of the region.

Beginning in 1990, a wave of democratization swept over Africa and many leaders, some of whom had held power since independence, were seriously challenged or ousted. Kenneth Kaunda was defeated in Zambia's 1991 multiparty elections. President Hastings Kamuzy Banda of Malawi, who has ruled harshly since independence in 1964, has been forced to accept multipartyism. International pressure forced President Daniel arap Moi of Kenya to agree to multiparty elections in December 1992. Although Moi survived these elections, the political process has opened up for opposition groups. On the downside, however, ethnic violence has increased since Kenya's elections. President Mobutu Sese Seko of Zaire is besieged by challenges to his rule, but he continues to cling precariously to power. In the meantime, Zaire appears to be edging toward collapse. Constituent assemblies stripped leaders of power in a populist wave and forced elections in a number of other countries. The last vestiges of formal apartheid will be swept away in April 1994 when, if things go as scheduled, blacks will be allowed to vote in nationwide elections. South Africa's experience illustrates the complexity of the democratic transition process. Democratic reform has been complicated by deep factionalism, political violence, and controversy over future constitutional arrangements especially regarding federalism and civil-military relations. Economic issues will also contribute to the complexity of South Africa's democratic consolidation.

There have also been movements toward democratic reform in the Middle East, although, like other regions, the results have been varied. In Algeria, the military annulled the 1991 elections when the Islamic Salvation Front was on the brink of winning, bringing an end to Algeria's democratic experiment. This clearly illustrates the potential for the armed forces, frequently a major political player in developing countries, to assert its power. The promise of democratic reforms in Kuwait in the aftermath of the Gulf War remains unfulfilled. The pace and scope of reform have not been as sweeping as it has been elsewhere.

South Korea elected its first real civilian president in early 1993 and has embarked on an ambitious effort to further consolidate democracy by attacking entrenched interests. Internationally supervised elections in Cambodia were regarded as free and fair and produced a 90

Unit 5

percent turnout. Although democracy is fragile and the new government faces numerous challenges, the situation represents a dramatic improvement over the totalitarian horrors of the Khmer Rouge era.

While democratic transitions have begun throughout the world, there is no guarantee that these efforts will succeed. Indeed, challenges loom large as fledgling democracies seek to take hold. The lack of a democratic tradition, factionalism, resistance by powerful interests, and military intervention are among the obstacles to democratic transition and consolidation.

Looking Ahead: Challenge Questions

What is socialism? Why did socialist development fail in the Third World?

Why have many African governments faced political challenges? What are the roots of these challenges?

How did political reform in Algeria backfire?

What are the obstacles to successful democratic transition in South Africa?

What problems lie ahead for future South African leaders?

What are the main threats to Cambodia's fragile democracy?

How was South Korea's 1993 election different from past elections? What challenges face President Kim Young Sam?

What are the obstacles to Vietnam's economic progress?

What are the prospects for democratic consolidation in Central America? What problems do these countries face?

Why did Peru's President Fujimori suspend the constitution in 1992? What are the implications of this action?

The Collapse of Socialist Development in the Third World

Christopher Clapham

Christopher Clapham is Professor of Politics and International Relations at the University of Lancaster, UK.

For about 140 years, since the publication of Marx and Engels' *The Communist Manifesto,* it has been usual to think in terms of two broadly contrasted ways of organising political and economic arrangements, very loosely describable as capitalist on the one hand, and socialist on the other. For about half of that time, since the Soviet revolution of 1917, it has been possible to point to actual examples of societies plausibly claiming to be socialist as well as capitalist; and these alternatives could be regarded not merely as mechanisms for managing the production and distribution of a given stock of goods and services, but as means of substantially increasing the total stock over a long period–in other words, as alternative strategies of development.

For rather more than half of this period, since the rapid accession to independence of formerly colonial Asian and African states in the aftermath of the Second World War, this simple dichotomy has likewise provided the framework for rival strategies of development within what is now known as the Third World.

The dramatic developments in Eastern Europe have effectively destroyed the pretensions of socialism as a system of economic and political management in industrial societies, with obvious knock-on effects for the Third World. But the question may also be raised of whether the capitalist/socialist dichotomy has had its day in the Third World too, on the grounds that the idea of a socialist path to development has collapsed beyond the point of resuscitation.

A WORKING DEFINITION OF SOCIALISM

Having bluntly posed the question, a fair amount of preliminary work is needed before we can tackle it. We need, in particular, a workable definition of 'socialism', which will distinguish states or economies deemed to be socialist in a way precise enough to produce useful generalisations, without being so restrictive as to be almost inapplicable. Like many terms in common political use, 'socialism' has acquired both a high emotional content, and an almost infinite plasticity of meaning. It has extended from the abolition of the state on the one hand, to the creation of the most rigid and centralised structures of state control on the other. It appears sometimes as a blueprint for producing rapid industrialisation, at other times as a distributive mechanism which assumes that the major articulation of productive forces has already taken place. And it encompasses a wide variety of political arrangements, from preindustrial communalism, through personalist and populist regimes, to multiparty liberal democracies and states ruled by Leninist vanguard parties.

This combination of emotional commitment and definitional variety not only provides an arena within which numerous factions compete for an exclusive copyright in the term, but also presents considerable obstacles to an external observer. The definitional ground is constantly shifting. What is seen at one moment as a socialist system is seen at another (especially when it fails to deliver expected benefits) as no more than an inadequate or even fraudulent misappropriation of the term. It sometimes is hard to avoid the impression that socialism is for its adherents not a set of actual arrangements, so much as a Platonic ideal which it is essential to preserve in untarnished purity, and which consequently comes to exist only in the imagination of the devout.

In this paper, then, I define socialism as an ideology, and a structure of institutional practices derived from it, which treats the state as the key agency of direct economic planning and management, and which therefore attempts to allocate resources according to priorities established by the state, rather than through mechanisms provided by the market. This involves the abolition or severe restriction of private property own-

From *Third World Quarterly,* Vol. 13, No. 1, 1992, pp. 13-25. Permission for reprinting given by *Third World Quarterly.*

ership or accumulation; the nationalisation of major productive enterprises, which are then managed by the state through parastatal corporations or government ministries; the allocation of investment resources in accordance with central priorities, characteristically through a central plan; the management of distribution, through government agencies which purchase privately produced goods at monopoly state-controlled prices, as well as through state control of imports, transport and retailing; and the organisation of those forms of production not directly controlled by the state into cooperatives or collectives. This is, of course, a very broad definition, which has been realised to a varying extent in different cases, and which will require further refinement; but it seeks to base itself not on any idealised conception of socialism, but on what the term has actually meant in the great majority of cases where regimes which have seriously claimed to be socialist have sought to put their principles of political and economic management into practice.[1]

The classic cases of socialism in this sense have of course been Marxist-Leninist regimes, modelled to a greater or lesser extent on the example of the Soviet Union. Regardless of whether one accepts their exclusive claim to 'scientific socialism', these do at least provide a recognisable and coherent model of political and economic management which has been both defined as socialist by themselves, and generally recognised as such by others. I would not restrict the application of the term to Marxist-Leninist regimes, however, since many other Third World regimes have also sought to use the state as the dominant agency of economic management, in an attempt to bring about rapid economic development, and their own claims to be socialist cannot reasonably be denied.

Many of these fall into the category which Crawford Young has defined as 'populist socialist',[2] exemplified in Africa by states such as Ghana under Kwame Nkrumah, Guinée under Sekou Toure, or Tanzania under Julius Nyerere, and elsewhere by states which may include Ne Win's Burma and several of the radical Arab regimes. These have normally lacked the Leninist vanguard party which forms a critical feature of the 'scientific socialist' regimes, relying instead on a single party which has had (or at least claimed) a mass popular membership. They have also generally fallen short of Marxist-Leninist regimes in the extent to which they have sought to control agricultural production or retail distribution. But the central role of the state, often expressed through the nationalisation of major companies and an attempt to introduce comprehensive economic planning, nonetheless entitles them to consideration.

This is not, of course, the only way of defining socialism. An alternative conception looks not to the state but to self-regulating collectivities as the key instruments of socialist construction. In principle, at least, this leads to the building of socialism from the bottom upwards, rather than its imposition from the central state apparatus downwards, and averts many of the problems–of inefficient dirigisme, political repression, and the eventual emergence of an exploitative bourgeoisie of the public sector–which have characterised state socialist regimes. In many areas of the Third World, cooperatives or collectives have played a prominent role as agencies of lower-level economic management. But at least in the cases with which I am familiar, these have almost always come into existence as agencies of state policy, rather than as the autonomous expression of local initiative, as which they are publicly described. Characteristically, they have had the function of 'capturing' the peasantry within a state-controlled structure of agricultural production and marketing. Even where cooperatives originated from local initiative, this role within the state structure has accounted for the most important aspects of their operation–and notably the almost invariable assumption of control by individuals with access to the external political and economic resources provided by the state, the party, or the marketing board.

What has mattered, in short, has been not the local organisation of cooperatives or collectives, but the way in which they have been incorporated into wider processes of production and exchange–and thus, in practice, their relations with the state. I therefore do not see this view of socialism as forming, in practice, a viable alternative to the state-centred conception that I have adopted.

I also exclude from the definition of socialism regimes managed by the social democratic parties of Western Europe, such as the Parti Socialiste in France or the Labour Party in the United Kingdom. Though these may retain, for largely nostalgic reasons, an extensive repertoire of socialist rhetoric, they can only be regarded for our purposes as a means of managing advanced capitalism, through policies which do not seriously threaten a capitalist structure which is broadly accepted across the political spectrum. More generally, socialism must be seen–as its own proponents have seen it–as a *system* of political and economic management, which seeks to replace the market, with its emphasis on individual choice and tolerance (or encouragement) of private wealth, by an equally comprehensive structure based on collective (and hence in practice on state) action. A genuinely socialist system can only be instituted or (as current events in Eastern Europe remind us) dismantled, at the cost of considerable upheaval.

The concept of socialism thus becomes meaningless if it is extended to include any system of economic management in which the state plays an important role. There is no such thing as a pure *laissez faire* economy in the modern world. The state is always centrally concerned with setting the conditions under which the economy operates. In many of the most successful cases of Third World capitalist development, such as Japan or South Korea, the state has played an especially prominent role. Issues such as exchange rates, credit policy or labour law have been critically important to economic success or failure. More generally, it may plausibly be argued that rapid economic development under conditions of global late capitalism requires the active involvement of a powerful 'developmental state', in a way that was not necessary for early industrialising economies such as Great Britain or the USA.

This, however, is not an issue into which I propose to enter here. I simply make the distinction between the state as an essential adjunct to successful capitalism, and the state as the core agency of socialist management and development. In the first case, the state sets the conditions within which private economic organisations are encouraged to take advantage of the opportunities (including, characteristically, export opportunities) offered by the market. In the second, the state itself takes direct control of economic production and distribution. The evident problems of parasitic capitalism in a number of Third World states may help to blur the distinction in practice, but do not obscure the fundamental difference between market-oriented and state-oriented economic organisations which underlies it.

Finally, questioning the relevance of socialism to Third World development does not imply uncritical acceptance of a capitalist alternative, least of all as this has operated in many of the most dependent areas of the Third World. Capitalist experience in the Third World has been varied, ranging from South Korea and the South-east Asian NICs at one end of the spectrum to the most degenerate economies of central America, the Caribbean and much of sub-Saharan Africa at the other. The deficiencies of much of this experience, especially when it has taken the form of primary production for the world economy, are all too familiar, and it is no part of my purpose to dispute them. Much of the lure of socialist development strategies has derived precisely from an often justified appreciation of the inadequacy of the familiar capitalist models, and the need for an alternative which has often, therefore, been accepted by default. Underlying this, in turn, is the perfectly understandable human feeling that there *must* be light at the end of the tunnel–or a crock of gold at the end of a socialist rainbow. But human nature, in this respect, does not correspond to the requirements of social science; and the socialist experience is every bit as liable to examination as its capitalist counterpart.

THE SOCIALIST THIRD WORLD

A small but significant number of Third World states have pursued socialist development strategies over a long enough period to make such an examination possible. The most important of these states is without any doubt the People's Republic of China. Though its sheer size and historical uniqueness may well invalidate any simple comparison of the Chinese experience with the rest of the Third World, it does provide a striking case of a socialist state that has been able to avoid many of the obvious obstacles to socialist development in other parts of the world. It had at least the beginnings of an industrial economy prior to the revolution; it has not been sucked into primary production for the capitalist world economy; its vast size has allowed development for an internal market; the strength and stability of its domestic regime have spared it the external destabilisation from which several smaller states have suffered; while the period of just over forty years since the establishment of the PRC in 1949 should have been long enough to provide an assessment.

The Kim Il Sung regime in North Korea has been established for slightly longer than the PRC, while socialist regimes in South-east Asia date from the creation of North Vietnam in 1954; unlike the PRC or North Korea after 1953, however, the Indochinese experience has been drastically affected by warfare–first against local capitalist regimes with external military support, but subsequently, since 1975, by internecine conflict between varieties of indigenous socialism. Burma has also had substantial problems of domestic political control.

The only long-established Third World Marxist-Leninist state outside East and South-east Asia has been Cuba, where the revolutionary regime is now over 30 years old. Elsewhere, socialism in the Soviet mould has largely been a product of the extraordinary period of expansion between 1974 and 1979, which saw the victory of socialist movements throughout Indochina, in Afghanistan and Nicaragua, and in Ethiopia, Angola and Mozambique. Another upheaval of the same period, though leading to a rather different outcome, was the Islamic revolution in Iran. Elsewhere in the Third World, the attempt to put the state at the centre of economic management has largely taken the form of 'populist socialism'.

The experience of these regimes is variable, and must be subject to specialised studies of their success or failure. On the broadest assessment, however, it is difficult to present Third World socialist regimes as a successful response to the challenges of development. Their inadequacy has been most evident in East and South-east Asia, because there, almost alone in the Third World, it is possible to find long-established socialist regimes such as North Korea, Vietnam, or the PRC itself, in close proximity to the most dynamically successful examples of indigenous capitalism anywhere in the Third World. The extent to which these are genuinely comparable–the PRC with Japan and the Chinese diaspora, North with South Korea, Vietnam and Cambodia with Thailand and Malaysia–is obviously open to dispute; but on the face of it, any comparison must be sharply to the advantage of the capitalist alternative.

In Africa and Central America, by contrast, socialism has been adopted in deeply impoverished states, within regions where the local experience of metropole-dominated capitalism has been much less impressive, quite apart from the issue of external destabilisation which has notably affected socialist regimes in Central America and southern Africa. But at least for the African states with which I am most familiar, it is hard to discern ways in which socialist strategies have improved economic performance, and easy to find ways in which they have impaired it.

THE APPEAL OF SOCIALISM

If this crude assessment is admissible, at least for purposes of argument, it may be helpful to examine some of the general reasons why state-socialist development strategies have nonetheless proved so attractive throughout the Third World–and why the foundations of such strategies have been progressively undermined over the past decade. For this purpose, both the attractions and the problems of socialist development may be divided into three groups of arguments, corresponding in turn to the relationship of Third World socialism to the 'first' or capitalist world, the 'second' or socialist world, and the internal dynamics of the Third World itself.

At the level of the first world, the arguments for socialism have been essentially reactive. Socialism has been seen as the only available means by which the Third World states and peoples could escape from a capitalist economic structure which was wrong and exploitative in itself, and the means by which the imperialist states ensured the subordination of the Third World. If dependence was the corollary of incorporation into the capitalist world order, then socialism became the necessary precondition for authentic and autonomous development–as well as the only way the Third World could avoid the levels of internal inequality and exploitation characteristic of the capitalist path to development.

The level of the second world correspondingly looked to existing socialist states for a pattern of development which at least appeared to offer two enormously important benefits. The first of these was the promise of rapid and purposive economic expansion on a non-capitalist basis, much of the allure of which lay in the idea of planning: the idea that it was possible to lay down in advance the direction in which one wished to proceed, and then organise the future through a comprehensive process of institutional construction–single parties, collectives, state corporations, and so on. The second, especially attractive to the large number of Third World states with ethnically diverse populations, was the ideal of socialism as a means by which different nationalities could be integrated, within an overarching common ideology and organisational structure, into a single collectivity subject to a very high level of central control. Many of the perceived benefits of this model were directly available only to that comparatively small group of Third World states which opted for Marxism-Leninism in its most articulated form, including notably a Leninist vanguard party and the creation of a structure of command planning.

The appeal of the model as a whole, however, has been much more widely pervasive. Given that socialism in the Third World has, above all else, been a project for the creation and consolidation of state power, what the USSR and PRC offered was a living assurance that this goal could be achieved, even by countries at a fairly low level of economic development. There were few more effective advertisements for the socialist cause than the visits paid by many Third World leaders to Beijing during the later years of Chairman Mao, or to Kim Il Sung's North Korea. Confronted in Tiananmen Square or Pyongyang by massive gymnastic displays, they were presented with an intoxicating vision of a people moulded to their leaders' needs–and were correspondingly inspired to achieve similar results in the altogether less promising conditions of their own societies. The Chinese example appears even to have profoundly affected the policies of Nicolae Ceaucescu in Romania.

This in turn points to the attractiveness of socialism at the level of the Third World, since an ideology of economic and political development guided by the state held a special appeal to elites for whom the state was central, because it was what they controlled. The most important feature of socialism in the Third World has been its reliance, not on proletarian classes (which have generally been weak), but on classes dependent on state employment, whether these were the politicians who currently controlled the state, or alienated intellectuals (ill-prepared for employment in either industry or agriculture) who hoped to do so. Where these in turn managed to gain the mass backing required for a thoroughgoing social revolution, this almost invariably came from a peasantry desperate to free itself from a settler colonialist or landlord-dominated regime–only to discover, after the revolution, that it had exchanged the landlords for a much more highly organised and state-directed structure of surplus expropriation, through which the new rulers sought to raise the capital required for essentially urban-centred strategies of development. There was nothing about such strategies that made them incompatible with the Leninist model of development, which sprang from very similar origins. The Leninist model was perfectly adapted to the self-image of Third World revolutionary elites as a group of qualified and dedicated functionaries whose mission was to tell the backward and ignorant masses what to do. It provided them both with a moral and intellectual basis for what they sought to do, and with an assurance that it would work.

Despite these attractions, socialism as a doctrine is now in deep crisis. While specific reasons for that crisis can certainly be found in the individual circumstances of particular states, and in the knock-on effects of developments in eastern Europe, a more general explanation lies in the increasing strain to which all three pillars of the socialist project have been subjected in the past decade.

THE FIRST WORLD: THE IMPOSSIBILITY OF ESCAPE

At the level of the first world, the major problem facing any socialist development strategy has been the inability of any but a very small minority of Third World states to escape from the global structure of exchange, dominated by the major capitalist states, by which their own economies were formed. Under these circumstances, socialism could be little more than the reorganisation of domestic economic management. It could not touch the 'commanding heights' of the economy, because these lay well beyond the national boundaries of the state itself. In some cases, 'socialist' strategies may scarcely have been intended to weaken the links between Third World and capitalist economies anyhow, providing instead a handy rhetorical smokescreen behind which the newly dominant political elites could appropriate the benefits of international trade for their own enjoyment.

Even in those states where socialist strategies were more seriously adopted, only the PRC offered any plausible prospect of autonomous development. Cuba and Vietnam–because of their strategic location and importance to Soviet foreign policy–were provided with alternative external economic linkages through membership of the Council for Mutual Economic Assistance (CMEA). The 'observer' status with the CMEA enjoyed by a number of other socialist Third World states was of little more than symbolic significance.

The level of Third World states' incorporation into the capitalist world economy has not significantly changed, but its political and economic implications were intensified by the resurgence in the 1980s of triumphant capitalism. Symbolised in the West by the election of Margaret Thatcher in the UK in 1979, and Ronald Reagan in the USA in 1980, this was imposed on many Third World states through the structural adjustment and lending policies followed by institutions such as the IMF and the World Bank. Their impact was in turn intensified by the Third World debt crisis and the readiness of other donors and lenders to tie their own aid and investment programmes to the conditions stipulated by the major international financial institutions.

This was, however, more than a simple matter of external power. The intellectual climate of the 1980s, shared by international agencies and charitable foundations alike, was profoundly hostile to grand schemes for social engineering imposed by national governments. Salvation was sought instead in the wisdom or rationality of the individual producer or consumer. Nowhere was this more evident than in Third World agriculture, where state farm and large collective were almost universally regarded as inferior in their use of resources to the independent peasant family. The result was a much greater confidence on the part of first world elites in the universal applicability of capitalist or market principles which they had previously been content to restrict to their own societies.

THE SECOND WORLD: THE FAILURE OF THE EXAMPLE

The counterpart to the 1980s' triumph of capitalism was the dramatic erosion (or virtual destruction) in the second world of the very model which socialist Third World states sought to emulate. Nowhere was this more poignantly symbolised than in Fidel Castro's criticisms of Eastern European states for abandoning the ideas which they and Cuba had previously held in common. Only to a very limited extent, however, have events in Eastern Europe and even the USSR been a source of direct *economic* pressure on Third World regimes. The linkages between the two sets of economies were generally too slight for developments in one to have much impact on the other. The major effect, ironically, may be the diversion to Eastern Europe of capital and market opportunities which would otherwise have gone to the South.

Apart from the special cases of Cuba and Vietnam, the characteristic feature of socialist bloc aid to the Third World was its concentration on the political and military superstructure of the state, rather than the economic infrastructure which any Marxian analysis would necessarily treat as vastly more important. The USSR's abandonment of military commitments in the Third World has thus weakened its client regimes across the whole spectrum from the Caribbean through Africa to Southeast Asia. But when Soviet Gosplan advisers in the Ethiopian central planning office were recommending as long ago as 1985 policies which (under the rhetorical cover supplied by references to Lenin's New Economic Policy) were scarcely to be distinguished from those put forward by the World

Bank, it was already all too evident that the amount to be offered by a Soviet-style economic model was very slight indeed.[3]

A second and perhaps more important lesson of events in the socialist bloc was the collapse of the Stalinist model of national integration. One of the great appeals of scientific socialism to the Third World was, as already noted, as a doctrine which claimed to resolve ethnic differences within the framework of a common socialist ideology, which removed the political content of ethnicity by destroying the exploitation of one group by another. It might well have been supposed that even if socialism failed as a doctrine of economic development, it could at least help to create a sense of national identity which would be of lasting value to ethnically divided states.

The dramatic resurgence of national identities in the USSR, coupled with the disintegration of Yugoslavia and the all-too-evident inability of 40 years of socialist construction to create any lasting legitimacy for the German Democratic Republic, could only be deeply dispiriting to Third World leaders and intellectuals who had seen in socialism a solution to one of the most intractable problems facing their own societies.

THE THIRD WORLD: PROBLEMS OF SOCIALIST CONSTRUCTION

More important than changes in either the power or the example of the industrial states, however, have been the inherent problems of socialist construction within the Third World itself. It is easy, and in some measure plausible, to ascribe the failures of socialist construction to specific factors which permit the sympathetic observer to retain some faith in the socialist project itself. The inherited burden of dependence *has* severely limited the options open to socialist regimes. For at least some of them, destabilisation has been a major issue, which has obstructed development, diverted resources, and led to a countervailing dependence on the protection of the Soviet bloc. There was evidently a learning process, during which serious tactical mistakes were made by inexperienced rulers who were suddenly forced to confront the problems of government. Socialist states have had at least their fair share of droughts, floods, earthquakes and other natural calamities. But beyond all these, there have been real problems which followed, not from specific conjunctural factors, but from the nature of the project itself.

The first has been the frequent weakness of the very instrument (the state) which provided the essential motor for the entire strategy. This was partly a matter of technical or managerial experience and ability. The establishment of a socialist structure of government, frequently under the conditions of confusion and disruption brought about by revolution, violent decolonisation, or the victory of the insurgent forces in a long civil war, required the state to take on a vastly increased range of functions at precisely the moment when it was least equipped to do so. A state which previously had difficulty achieving the most basic tasks of economic maintenance and public order was then required to run the economy and dynamise the population. The individual enthusiasm and popular support which frequently accompanied the socialist takeover of power provided indispensable backing for the new regime, but brought little by way of technical expertise, while the managerial classes on whom so much depended were often alienated by the new regime.

Still more basic, however, was the political weakness of the state. The creation of an effective socialist regime called for a high level of popular acceptance and political organisation, through which the regime could extend its grasp throughout the national territory and induce people to manage their lives in ways very different from those that were previously expected. At the top, it required a group of dedicated political managers who were prepared to devote themselves to creating the new system, without conspicuously profiting (in terms of either self-enrichment or personalist autocracy) from the opportunities which the greatly increased power of the state gave them. At the bottom, it required people to change previous modes of living to those now induced by the state, to substitute collective or cooperative farming for individual family plots, or to abandon communal solidarities for an undivided loyalty to the new political order. Whatever the ideals from which the new regime started, it cannot be surprising if it led to a hierarchy of privilege on the one hand, and a dependent but alienated mass on the other.

The second characteristic problem was the diversion of resources away from economic production, and towards state maintenance and consolidation. The machinery of state power had to be created before anything could be done with it. The rapid expansion of the state apparatus that almost inevitably followed the establishment of a socialist regime often included a dramatic increase in the share of the national product appropriated for the armed forces and other instruments of control. This element was obviously much intensified when socialism was accompanied by external destabilisation and internal revolt—the two of which, of course, were usually closely linked. But the socialist structure of economic production and exchange also had to be policed—from ensuring that peasants delivered their produce at state-controlled prices, to preventing the abuse of power by high-level managers—to a degree that was generally not required for its capitalist equivalent.

The third problem was, commonly, a set of development priorities which were often highly unequal in their impact, and inefficient in their implementation.

'Socialist gigantism' (the building of one huge productive enterprise, rather than a mass of little ones) is the result not only of a demand for showpiece projects, but, more important, of the requirements of centralised management. It is much easier for the state to run a state farm of 10,000 hectares, than for it to control the activities of 5000 peasant families, each farming tiny two-hectare plots. The creation of massive operations of this kind was readily justified in terms of the 'efficiency' allowed by mechanisation and economies of scale, while ignoring the inefficiencies created by unemployment (a large farm or factory employs many fewer people than a lot of small ones, while costing much more in terms of foreign exchange) and the loss of personal supervision and commitment. More generally, socialist priorities tended to favour urban areas, through an emphasis on industry as the touchstone of economic modernisation, and the subsidy of urban food prices at the expense of rural producers. These are, of course, common problems of Third World development, going well beyond regimes which explicitly regard themselves as socialist. However, they reflect a level of urban centredness which has often been most marked under socialist economic strategies.

This led to the fourth and most critical problem affecting virtually all Third World socialist states, the crisis of agricultural production. While centralised direction may be an effective way of organising some aspects of the urban economy, it has almost always been disastrous in the countryside and hence especially disastrous in states where agriculture normally accounts for a high proportion of the national product. State farms have usually required a high level of subsidy, in exchange for inefficient production, and have at the same time appallingly exploited their labour force. Cooperative farms have likewise only been kept going through central subsidy on the one hand, or state power used to enforce collectivisation on the other. The establishment of centralised marketing structures served to squeeze a surplus from the peasantry, while offering virtually nothing in return. The problems of socialist agricultural mismanagement have been sufficiently emphasised, but it is worth reiterating that these were not merely technical problems of inadequate supervision or the lack of skilled manpower, but were inherent in the socialist project itself. Only the PRC has effectively combined a continuing commitment to socialism at a national political level with a market-oriented structure of agriculture production, and the length of time over which this combination can be maintained remains uncertain.

All this has created the fifth problem – alienation, and especially rural alienation, which may take the form of ethnic conflict or the reassertion of 'traditional' values such as religion, but which more basically springs (in classic Marxian fashion) from political exclusion and economic exploitation. It is remarkable to what extent rural insurgency, once regarded as the virtually exclusive province of left-wing liberation movements, came in the 1980s to be used against centralised (and usually Soviet-supported) socialist regimes. The encouragement of dissent by external opponents or domestic class enemies, so often emphasised by socialist regimes themselves, would rarely have got anywhere without a basis for it in the structures of domestic politics and economic mismanagement.

A final problem remains. Given that socialism in the Third World is overwhelmingly an ideology of state consolidation, what happens if this objective is actually achieved? Implicit in the socialist project is the assumption that the state is a machine which, properly organised and in the right hands, can be used to achieve the welfare of Third World peoples – their economic development, political unity and identity, and autonomy from external exploitation. The preliminary objective is one which some socialist Third World states have gone a long way towards achieving. Whatever reservations one may have about regimes like Kim Il Sung's North Korea, the PRC, Castro's Cuba, or even Mengistu's Ethiopia, there can be little doubt that they succeeded in building vastly more effective state structures than those that they inherited.

Effective states can likewise achieve at least some objectives that ineffective ones cannot. They can raise armies, build roads, reorganise rural life and vastly extend the scope of services such as education and health care. They can remove at least some forms of social inequality – though often at the cost of intensifying inequalities entrenched in the state itself. But organisation from the top down necessarily inhibits initiatives and developments which have to be created from the bottom up. The most immediately important of these for most Third World states is agricultural production, which in practice at least depends on the skills of the producers and the incentives given them to increase their levels of production.

More generally, economic development requires a capacity to change and adapt which centralised state systems are inherently ill-equipped to provide. Ultimately, and often very rapidly, these run up against the sclerosis induced by the interests of the state itself, and of those who manage it. Finally, the state is inherently ill-equipped to provide effective mechanisms for participation in its own management, a deficiency which a single party heavily geared to the exercise of state power is in no position to remedy. Statism thus almost automatically leads to political alienation, regardless of the state's own efforts to organise public participation, and this in turn negates its goals of political legitimacy and national integration. The goal of state consolidation may at best be a stage on the road to more solidly based development. Where the attempt to achieve this goal is itself counterproductive, it may not even be that.

CONCLUSION

Despite what may seem a fairly comprehensive dismissal of the applicability of a state socialist development model to the Third World, reports of its death may be exaggerated. For one thing, no academic can be unaware of shifts in intellectual fashion, and the way in which the simple certainties of one decade may seem obviously fallacious to the next. Whereas the late 1970s were a period of rapid expansion in the numbers of Soviet-style Third World regimes, the 1980s have been the decade of the market.

While we will have to wait to taste the authentic flavour of the 1990s, it is safe enough to predict that many of the already evident problems of Third World capitalism will still be with us, and may well prompt a reaction to a renewed emphasis on the role of the state. Inequality and injustice are unlikely to disappear, and though there is only a contingent relationship between a gut reaction against poverty and exploitation, and a belief in the role of the state as an all-encompassing agency of political reconstruction and economic management, this gut reaction has provided the impetus for much of socialist theory and practice in the past, and is likely to continue to do so in the future.

Whatever the problems of post-revolutionary China, Cuba, Ethiopia or even Iran, it is hard not to see such revolutions as necessary (in a sense, 'progressive') steps in sweeping away old regimes which were either grossly exploitative, or else too anachronistic and politically ineffective to survive. The systems which have replaced them have in turn proved vastly more capable of mobilising both popular energies and organisational effectiveness. But mobilising them at what cost, and to what end? Here, I must confess to a deep scepticism about the ability of state socialist development strategies to achieve anything beyond the very limited tasks can be implemented by top-down organisation.

Even these achievements can be won only at the expense of creating a bureaucratic structure which itself becomes a brake on development, and substitutes its own institutional interest for those of the population which it was supposed to serve.

If there is light at the end of the tunnel, I would look for it in the possibility that revolution might be seen as the precursor, not to socialism, but to an effective process of capitalist development. It may be the only way to destroy a level of dependence on external capitalism which obstructs the emergence of a domestic bourgeoisie, whose role derives from control not over the state, but over the domestic structure of production. It may increase national self-confidence and organisational capacity, promote the level of equality needed to release stunted human capabilities, and create a viable internal market based on satisfying popular demand, rather than the import-biased taste of an elite. In the process, it may remove the obstructions to development presented by an often corrupt and externally dependent oligarchy. The point remains to be proved, because revolution in the 20th century has been so closely associated with socialism that a revolutionary capitalism has come to seem a contradiction in terms. But the Marxian idea of bourgeois revolution may well now be due for revival.

NOTES

This article was originally written as an introductory paper for a workshop on socialism in the Third World at the European Consortium for Political Research, Bochum, Germany, April 1990. It is fair to point out that my own fieldwork on socialism in the Third World has been conducted in Ethiopia under the Mengistu regime, and is reported in C Clapham, *Transformation and Continuity in Revolutionary Ethiopia,* Cambridge: Cambridge University Press, 2nd edition, 1990.

1. See Gordon White, 'Revolutionary socialist development in the Third World: an overview', in G White *et al* (eds), *Revolutionary socialist development in the Third World,* Brighton: Wheatsheaf, 1983, p 1, for a similar definition by a more sympathetic observer.
2. See Crawford Young, *Ideology and development in Africa,* New Haven, CT: Yale University Press, 1982.
3. This document has been published in Paul B. Henze, *Ethiopia: Crisis of a Marxist Economy.* Santa Monica, CA: RAND Corporation, R-3677-USDP, 1988.

THE CRISIS OF LEGITIMACY IN AFRICA

A Time of Change and Despair

Abiola Irele

ABIOLA IRELE is professor of African, French, and comparative literature at the Ohio State University, Columbus. He is the author of *The African Experience in Literature and Ideology*.

A bleak picture emerges from today's Africa. One glaring aspect is the material deprivation suffered by most Africans: the situation has degenerated to outright destitution because of steep economic decline across the continent in the past decade or so. Nearly every national economy has collapsed or is on the verge of doing so.

The gravity of the situation has to be measured not just in terms of painful statistics but against the economic optimism that pervaded the majority of African states in the early sixties. Substantial economic development and rising living standards were achieved in the aftermath of independence, and a few cases sustained their gains well into the late seventies and early eighties. We are therefore witnessing a complete reversal of the rising expectations that came with the triumph of nationalism.

The gloomy economic reality of Africa today is compounded by chronic political instability. Africa's political scene has long been characterized by civil wars, dreary successions of military coups and various civic disorders. The two aspects of the African condition—the economic and the political—are inevitably tied. The linkage has been underlined in recent years by graphic television pictures of starving refugees fleeing the ravages of civil war in Ethiopia, Chad, Liberia, and other theaters of ethnic and political violence. Africa has become so closely associated with instability that the popular image of our part of the world seems to be of ongoing politically induced disruptions of life with the attendant insecurity and constant misery. That this is a simplification often promoted and reinforced by selective reporting in the Western media does not diminish its basis in reality. There are enough signs of accumulated distress to warrant the growing pessimism that has taken hold of African minds over the past decade and now dominates discussion of the continent's affairs among qualified observers.

It is against this background—a despair that has assumed the dimension of existential angst—that recent developments require a special form of attention. There has been a rolling movement of challenges to existing power structures across the continent. Major transformations have been effected in a number of countries (for example, Ethiopia, Benin, and Zambia) and there has been vigorous contestation in many others (such as Zaire and Kenya). In the West, outside of a narrow circle of specialists, not much attention has been paid to these developments; in fact, they have been largely ignored by the media. Recent events in Africa continue to be interpreted as signs of a condition of chaos, thereby confirming colonialist ideology, according to which Africans are inherently incapable of governing themselves.

The most distinctive feature of recent African developments is that localized manifestations of dissidence have metamorphosed into a determined and general reassessment of long-standing post-independence political and social arrangements. From this point of view, events in Africa parallel those in other parts of

From *Dissent,* Summer 1992, pp. 296-302. Reprinted by permission.

the world, notably the transformations in Eastern Europe (which helped stimulate current agitation in Africa). As in Eastern Europe there has been both a quantitative scope and a qualitative dimension that distinguish the current African events from previous convulsions. Principles of political participation and civic association are central. At long last the inherent crisis of political legitimacy that was masked both during the colonial period and after has ripened.

The Legacy of Imperialism

To understand this crisis, we must consider how Western imperialism profoundly modified the way questions of political legitimacy were posed by and for Africans. In the nineteenth century massive historical transformations touched nearly every corner of Africa. Forces were at play that, though often initially independent of the European incursions, became directly implicated in the imposition of European rule. Contradictions within African societies were not transcended but given new complications by the impact of colonialism.

A few examples will illustrate this point. Othman dan Fodio's *jihad,* undertaken at the very dawn of the century, imposed Fulani hegemony over the northern parts of what came to be known as Nigeria and precipitated the fall of the Yoruba empire centered at Oyo to the south. These were important factors enabling British penetration of the Niger-Benue basin, leading to the eventual emergence, after the First World War, of present-day Nigeria. Similarly, French conquests in Western and Central Africa were facilitated by a process of dissolution already at work within the traditional state formations in these areas. In the Sahel (in Western Africa) in particular, disaffection of Samori Toure's vassal states and populations (the background to Ahmadou Kourouma's recent novel, *Monnè, outrages et défis*) paved the way for both his defeat in 1898 and the ensuing incorporation of these populations into the French empire.

The history of Southern Africa provides perhaps the most striking instance of convergence between internal African developments and external pressures. The meteoric rise of Shaka and the unsettling effects of the Zulu empire he fashioned in the early nineteenth century provoked general upheaval throughout the region that has imprinted itself on the collective memory as the *mfecane,* or "the great dispersal." This disruption remains an essential backdrop to Cecil Rhodes's colonizing enterprise in Southern Africa and, in retrospect, may be seen as the first act in the historical drama enmeshing the indigenous populations of Southern Africa, the English, and the Boers—a drama still being played out in our own day.

These cases demonstrate that, even when allowance has been made for the superior arms of the Europeans, the aims of Western imperialism were often furthered by internal crises within African societies. To put the matter another way, the Europeans exploited dynamics within African societies to their own imperial advantage. Europeans appeared at a particular historical moment, when important readjustments were taking place in Africa, and they brought a new complexion to the process. They imposed their own order on an especially fluid internal situation. By the end of the nineteenth century, Europeans had refashioned the continent, giving it an entirely new configuration.

In an important sense, the Europeans simplified matters by integrating large populations of diverse ethnic and linguistic backgrounds into their colonial possessions. But they failed to resolve the problem of political legitimacy, which had been fundamental to antecedent history in Africa. The order imposed by the colonial powers was conceived on European terms, served their interests, and came at considerable cost to Africans. Apart from humiliation and servitude, this order proceeded from haphazard patterns of conquest and annexation and left a legacy of untidy borders.

Because of the conflictual nature of the colonial situation (graphically underlined by racial and cultural differences between rulers and ruled), the question of legitimacy was largely irrelevant for the imperial powers. The French simply suppressed traditional, precolonial institutions, and the British fashioned a myth of indirect rule. But on the essentials there was no fundamental difference: there was no question as to where ultimate authority lay, who was ruler and who was subordinate. This authoritarianism was codified in the colonial legal arsenal with an array of laws that prohibited assembly, restricted movement, proscribed "sedition," and so on. (After independence, these laws survived in nearly every African state and proved to be convenient repressive tools in the hands of the successor governments.)

It is understandable that African attitudes to colonial regimes were governed by what might be called affective disengagement. The African was not a citizen but a subject. Exceptions were made for certain categories (for example, for those born in the so-called four communes of Senegal and within the crown colony of Lagos, in Nigeria) but these merely confirmed the degraded status of everyone else. In such a situation, any wholehearted identification with the structures of power—I leave aside opportunistic collaboration—would have been unnatural. In any case, there was little incentive for active identification, for the colonial regimes provided very limited scope for personal advancement, except in the indirect or frankly devious ways so well shown in Ahmadou Hampaté Ba's novel *The Fortunes of Wangrin*.

Economic, Cultural and Moral Dimensions

The economics of colonial dependency played a vital role in shaping the crisis of legitimacy. In the early period of imperial rule, widespread recourse to forced labor made blatant the brutality of colonialism's economic imperatives. African populations were forcibly thrust into the imperial cash nexus and the consequent social dislocations unraveled the fabric of communal life everywhere. African productive capacities were systematically reorganized on behalf of the economic interests of the colonial powers, and this produced distortions in African economies that remain to this day. The premise of the colonial "pact," as this reorganization was frequently portrayed, was the deliberate narrowing of horizons open to Africans; Africa, in colonialism's scheme, only existed as a source of raw materials and primary labor.

The implications were not only political and economic but cultural and moral as well. Africans were sucked into a new world system—an expanding capitalist order—and into an immense vortex of social and cultural change demanding painful adjustments, not just by individuals but of whole collectivities. Colonialism involved nothing less than a comprehensive reconstitution of African societies: of the traditional modes of production and governance and of social organization, cultural expression, and fundamental norms. The consequence of transitions from agrarian to industrial modes of production was severe dislocation due to the exploitation of the continent's resources for the direct benefit of Europeans. Colonialism was a transformative trauma, signaling a moment of profound historical discontinuity for Africans. In all spheres of life a new paradigm was imposed. It rested largely on Western models of industrial and technological civilization driven by the capitalist mode of production. The nation-state was its political and territorial expression. In short, the colonial experience in Africa, as in other parts of the non-Western world, amounted to a wrenching and harsh confrontation with triumphant (Western) modernity.

Needless to say, the colonial imposition did not yield in Africa the type of societies that industrial transformation created in capitalist Europe; Africans stood no real chance of benefiting collectively from the material advantages such transformations offered, even though they had been incorporated into the cogwheels of its world system—and even though the discomforts were as real for Africans, if not more so, as for the European masses. Importantly, an outstanding element of the Western model was missing when it was applied to Africa in the context of colonialism: the liberal values that had been shaped by the Enlightenment. African nationalism, especially its Pan-African variants, was initially an intellectual response to this contradiction. But its motive force derived ultimately from sociological factors: nationalism in colonial Africa, in its mass aspect, was a reaction not only against foreign rule but also to particular pressures of historical change. There was deep-seated resentment against exclusion from the benefits of modern civilization—benefits visible in the living standards of Europeans living in Africa itself. Thus it was, ironically, the colonial conflation of the material trappings of European modernity with "standing" in the world that fueled African nationalism.

Paradoxes

The consequence was a paradox for African nationalism, both in its intellectual expression and in its popular manifestations. On one hand, there was a need for self-affirmation, which drew on cultural (precolonial) antecedents to give substance to claims to autonomy; on the other, there was an acknowledgement that those antecedents would be superseded in a new order that drew from the West and therefore risked undermining those same claims to autonomy. From this point of view, nationalism was an overtly political expression of a fundamental dilemma arising out of an ambivalent relation to a modernity associated with the historic encounter with the West. For, despite frequent use of the rhetoric of archaism, it was always clear to African nationalists that the African past to which they appealed was, in the final analysis, irretrievably lost. To be meaningful, nationalism required a prospective rather than a retrospective vision.

This accounts for the utopianism that was integral to nationalism in colonial Africa. It assumed a salvational and even messianic significance, one that shined through popular forms of reaction to colonial rule such as the Kibangi movement in the Congo. The same impulse pervaded the more reflective forms of the nationalist project, as is evident in Kwame Nkrumah's injunction to his followers, expressed in terms adapted from the Christian Bible: "Seek ye first the political kingdom, and all else shall be added unto ye." The meaning of this injunction was clarified in the Action Group's electioneering slogan on the eve of Nigerian independence in 1959: "Freedom for all and life more abundant." Commitment to modernization conceived as the recovery of historical initiative by Africans was thus made unambiguous. African nationalism was predicated on new beginnings on the continent, in immediate and specific relation to the exigencies of modern life.

In this way, the ideology of nationalism was firmly linked to the ideology of development. The various theories of African socialism propounded in the early years of independence, notably by Leopold Sédar Senghor, Julius Nyerere, and Kwame Nkrumah, sought to expand the utopian vision inherent in the nationalist project, to resolve the tension between its two poles of reference in the quest for a new society. They sought an accommodation between traditionalism, conceived as a counter discourse to imperialism, and the pragmatic requirements of the Western paradigm. Their emphasis on socialism as the preferred route to economic development proceeded logically out of disaffection with the historical nexus between capitalism and colonialism. But the appeal of socialism also lay in the instrumental value ascribed to it, the application of rationality to social life, which, it was thought, offered the means of accelerated development. Although Soviet achievement certainly impressed African ideologists at this time, what they proposed was an original form of socialism, uniquely African in its attention to the human rather than the instrumental import of its modalities. And the mobilizing force of the moral ideals associated with socialism counted as a strategic consideration.

While African socialism did not represent a general consensus, it was the most serious conceptual effort to cope with the urgent tasks facing Africa at independence, tasks that came to be subsumed under the term "nation-building." As the term suggests, the first priority was to consolidate the territorial basis inherited from colonial regimes. This meant welding disparate populations brought together in each new state by the vagaries of European conquest. This territorial imperative was a consequence of the original "modular" framework (to borrow Benedict Anderson's term) within which African nationalism had to operate in the colonial context. In the new states, primary affiliations conditioned by factors such as ethnicity and language had to be subordinated to the claims of the nation-state. The latter was envisaged essentially in legal terms. Although the theoretical separation between formal citizenship and original nationality (made familiar by the American model) did not enter into the thinking of African leaders at this point, something resembling it became established as the norm: political identity was deemed to stem from one's spatial situation within administrative and juridical boundaries rather than from rooted connections. Given the extreme diversity that characterized most African states, the problem was to infuse the political community defined in these spatial and legal terms with an "organic" quality.

The preoccupation—and even obsession—with territorial integrity and "national unity" arose from the fragility of the institutional framework of the newly independent states. Colonialism bequeathed not national entities but administrative structures, at best intimations of future national formations—from the point of view of history, modes of hypothesis rather than embodiments of fact. As such, the new structures were in direct competition for legitimacy with traditional precolonial systems. The formal and legal status of the latter were often ill-defined, even nonexistent. Still, traditional authorities exercised more than a vestigial pull on political and moral sensibilities. A strict application of the national principle to satisfy these sensibilities was impracticable, more so than in other parts of the world with similar problems. The justified fear of general chaos arising from any attempt to "unscramble" Africa—the crisis in the Belgian Congo (now Zaire) was an early, dire portent—induced an official rigidity concerning the inviolability of colonial boundaries. But this rigidity had to contend with national realities on the ground, realities so powerfully dramatized by the movement for Biafran secession and highlighted by Somali irredentism in the Ogaden.

But as these examples also demonstrate, ethnicity operated in a dynamic context of social interaction in which economic competition was exacerbated by the constraints of underdevelopment. National and ethnic loyalties were called into play more by economic and social factors than sheer atavistic impulses. It is in these circumstances that the Western model of the nation-state as the unit of political life assumed critical importance for African governments, which were also preoccupied by social development.

What needs to be stressed is that African leaders staked their claims to legitimacy on their ability to realize the promise of independence in concrete terms. In the early years of independence, efforts were undertaken to tie the immediate political objectives of national independence to the spread of the amenities of modern civilization. The political leaders and the emergent bourgeoisie of Africa assumed in real earnest the role of a modernizing elite. This was a brief but heroic period, when energies that had lain dormant were effectively released. In the process self-confidence returned to Africans. Kwame Nkrumah's Ghana played an exemplary role, for his grandiose ambitions for modernization corresponded to the inspirational needs of the moment. Without a doubt, this set the pace for what came to be seen everywhere in Africa as a political imperative.

As a result, the meager infrastructures bequeathed by colonialism to many African countries began to be expanded or overhauled: roads, ports, and railways were built or improved (the "Tanzam" line from Dar-es-Salaam to Lusaka, constructed with Chinese help in the face of Western opposition, took on a symbolic value in this regard). Industries were established, often with foreign investment, but sometimes with capital generated from internal sources. The endeavor to endow Africa with industrial capacity was complemented by an effort to institute a system of social services, with palpable and often dramatic results. For example, considerable expansion of education set in motion a process of social mobility, whose dynamics (admirably captured in the adventure of Amamu, Kofi Awoonor's fictional hero in *This Earth, My Brother*) produced a whole category of Africans with new aspirations and life orientations. These were Africans for whom, as Mariama Ba's novel *So Long a Letter* demonstrates, Western life-styles were taken for granted. In addition, the spread of modern medicine led to a sharp drop in infant mortality, drastically altering the demographic picture of Africa.

Although all these achievements were modest in comparison, say, to those of the Asian Pacific rim countries, they were real, and in some instances such as in Côte d'Ivoire, impressive. The country enjoyed an "economic miracle," with annual growth rates of over 10 percent throughout the sixties; its capital, Abidjan, became a model of urban development in Africa. Côte d'Ivoire thus became a measure of new possibilities, pointing to a real fulfillment of the hopes of formal independence.

Burdens and Ambiguities

Such successes vindicated the central proposition of nationalism—that Africans could really take charge of their destiny—but fostered great—revolutionary—expectations. This put tremendous burdens on states that had deliberately assumed the role of agents of development. Making matters more difficult were a variety of structural constraints, often ignored by Western critics and African radicals, which effectively blocked progress toward sustained growth—toward initiating Rostow's celebrated "take off."

We need not dwell here on the external constraints, besides noting that they ensured a post-independence perpetuation of the colonial pact and guaranteed the vested interests of African ruling classes in neocolonial arrangements. For our purposes, most salient are the internal impediments to the political legitimacy of African rulers and the links to development. Here we must focus on the one-party state, which has been rationalized as the political expression of the ideology of development, as the means of concentrating the political community's collective energy and will on the problems of nation-building. While this idea was argued with persuasive force, especially by Nyerere (whose views derived, it needs to be said, from admirable principles), it harbored obvious contradictions from the beginning. The party was summarily assimilated into the state as an embodiment of the people, thus substituting a part for the whole. Coercion became the inevitable practical corollary, as history has shown us in Africa and elsewhere. Yet there was a particular irony to the African development, for one government after another fell back upon the authoritarian methods of colonial rule to enforce an impossible unanimity on national objectives. The one-party state turned out to be the negation of the very principles—socioeconomic and political advance of the people—that it was supposed to enshrine. Consequently, it undermined the basis of the legitimacy craved by African rulers.

Furthermore, a one-party state could not be reconciled with the Pan-African ideal with which African nationalism had been closely associated in the colonial period. Obsession with national unity soon became a narrow territorialism that often served as a means by which dictators protected individual turfs. As state policy such unity limited broader scope, such as the continental vision of earlier ideological leaders. Colonial borders became effective barriers to the movement of people and the normal flow of trade and other transactions, with serious implications for the traditional economies from which the common people derived their livelihood. Also, there were grave ecological consequences, such as the rapid depletion of pastures through overgrazing in the case of the Masai. The breakup of the East African Community is instructive in this regard, as is the fact that the Economic Community of West African States (ECOWAS) has maintained only marginal interest for the populations of the subregion, in spite of countless protocols signed by leaders over the past twenty years.

The length to which the tunnel vision of national interests can go is depressing. It is demonstrated, for instance, by official promotion of xenophobia in order to justify the expulsion of "aliens" (that is, other Africans) from Ghana and Nigeria. The terrible suffering that resulted provides sad confirmation that Africans have become locked into a nation-state model that is not only inappropriate to their situation but patently dysfunctional.

This, then, is the underside of modernization as pursued in the era of African independence. It is the story of an inspiring idea that lost its way through mismanagement, corruption, and the arrogance of power. It has cast a shadow on African prospects and created the current mood of disillusionment so well reflected in the dystopias that now dominate African literature, especially fiction. The moral ambiguities explored in such works as Ayi Kwei Armah's *The Beautyful Ones Are Not Yet Born,* Ahmadou Kourouma's *The Suns of Independence,* and Nurrudin Farah's *Maps* proceed directly from the problematic relation between the immediacies of consciousness and the public context of individual life. The themes of legitimacy, national identity, and the quest for a new order, which provide the background for the narrative development in works like these, also ground explorations of the defining dilemmas of contemporary Africa.

Current agitation for democratization and human rights is a response to these dilemmas, the sign of a profound movement of the collective consciousness. It addresses the question of legitimacy not merely in terms of the competence and morality of today's leaders but in terms of the adequacy of present arrangements to the lives and aspirations of the African people. That fundamental institutional questions are being posed is attested to by the means of struggle, in particular the calling of a "National Conference" by the reform movement in Benin, and similar patterns that ensued in other francophone African countries. If agitation across Africa has not assumed the proportions of the *levée en masse* of Frantz Fanon's populist imagination, it conforms to his call for a reprise of the nationalist project in the context of post-independence Africa.

The full significance of these developments must be grasped in the broad perspective of Africa's history—of long decades of misery in which this continent's people were tossed about by internal and external forces always beyond their control. In the colonial period, the discourse of freedom elaborated by Europeans as a function of their own internal development—the source of contemporary modernity—was deployed by Africans against the unprincipled (European) violation of Africa. In the present "season of our discontent" we see Africans deploying it inward, proposing freedom as a condition of political legitimacy and as the principle enabling the implementation in Africa of the original project of modernity—the maximization of life chances for all humanity.

"Algeria stands divided against itself as two essentially authoritarian solutions—one military and the other theocratic—battle for supremacy while secular democrats agonize over the narrow space left to them."

Algeria: The Clash between Islam, Democracy, and the Military

ROBERT A. MORTIMER

ROBERT A. MORTIMER *is a professor of political science at Haverford University. Along with Naomi Chazan, John Ravenhill, and Donald Rothchild he is the coauthor of* Politics and Society in Contemporary Africa 2d ed. *(Boulder, Colo.: Lynne Rienner, 1992).*

The Algerian historian Mohamed Harbi once remarked that in most countries the state has its army, but in Algeria the army has its state—an observation that was once again confirmed last January when President Chadli Bendjedid was deposed by a coalition of military and civilian leaders that brought the army back to the forefront of Algerian politics.

The military has always been a powerful institution in Algeria. In 1962, 1965, and 1979 the army largely determined who would hold Algeria's top office; in 1988 and 1991 it restored civil order after serious confrontations between the government and civil society. With the support of civilian politicians such as Prime Minister Sid Ahmed Ghozali, the military established a High State Council last January to replace Bendjedid, but the maneuver barely masked the acute conflict between the state and a rising Islamist social movement.

By annulling the elections of December 26, 1991, which had brought the Islamic Salvation Front (FIS) to the brink of controlling parliament, the military-bureaucratic elite halted the political liberalization that Bendjedid had initiated in 1989. The great irony of Bendjedid's experiment was that it opened the door to a popular movement unwilling to commit itself to the principles on which democracy rests: electoral accountability and civil rights. The decision to oust Bendjedid cheated the Islamic Front of its victory, but failed to resolve any of the fundamental questions about where Algeria was headed. The subsequent crackdown on the front drove part of the Islamist movement underground and provoked a wave of terror that bloodied the country. The assassination in June of Mohamed Boudiaf, head of the High State Council—whether by the FIS or others—dramatized the severity of the crisis.

ISLAM AS POLITICS

Bendjedid's policy of political reform was in response to the riots of October 1988, which revealed the gulf that had opened between the regime and the post-independence generation.[1] Since 1962 Algeria's rulers had drawn their legitimacy from their role in the war between 1954 and 1962 for independence from France and the institutions forged during that period, notably the army and the National Liberation Front (FLN). During the 1980s that authority wore thin as the economy faltered and government corruption grew. In ending one-party rule by means of constitutional reforms in 1989, Bendjedid unleashed a potent social movement that spoke to widespread sociopolitical discontent. The Islamists offered a relatively simple explanation for the economic ills and social problems troubling Algerians: the government had strayed from the path of Islamic piety.

The emergence of an Islamist current in Algerian politics was to be expected, since Islam remained the major source of cultural identity during the colonial period. For many of the "moudjahidines" who took up arms against France, nationalism was defined by their Muslim heritage. When more secular forces took control of the state after independence, the Islamic cultural nationalists largely withdrew into the mosques, maintaining a stand that was bound to find political expression sooner or later.

As grievances accumulated in the 1980s the Islamists' audience expanded considerably. Many of the recruits were young men without jobs; others were shopkeepers resentful of the ruling party's socialist ideology. The latter were a source of funds for the movement, as were some foreign governments (such as Saudi Arabia), which permitted Islamist "brothers" to provide modest social services in poor, overcrowded

[1]For an analysis of the cause and the aftermath of the 1988 riots, see Robert A. Mortimer, "Algeria After the Explosion," *Current History*, April 1990.

neighborhoods. The movement's vague message of public morality appealed to many Algerians fed up after 25 years of FLN rule.

The Islamists thus were waiting in the wings when Bendjedid made his audacious move and opened up Algerian politics. Whether it should recognize the Islamist movement as a legal political party—something most Arab governments have not done—was a question that divided the ruling elite at the time. At odds with the left wing of the FLN over economic policy, Bendjedid may well have counted on enlisting the Islamists in a new coalition. Whatever his reasoning, the decision to recognize the Islamists transformed Algerian politics, because, as Algerian political scientist Abdelkader Djeghloul has pointed out, "the FIS. . .is not a party like the others."[2]

The front is a movement organized around the idea that the religious and political spheres are one and the same. It has successfully brandished the slogan, "to vote against the FIS is to vote against God." Its most prominent leader, Abassi Madani, said the front was not a political party but an all-embracing expression of the popular will, while his deputy, Ali Benhadj, declared that Algeria "was not a nation that thinks in terms of a majority and a minority." These and similar declarations sowed serious doubt about the long-term intentions of the Islamist party. Did it accept freedom of conscience and political pluralism? What would the fate of secular Algerians or of women's rights be if the front came to power? Questions like these were left unanswered in the 27 months between recognition of the FIS in September 1989 and the movement's sweeping electoral victory in December 1991.

The Islamic Salvation Front was an amalgam of several currents of Islamist thought. According to Ahmed Rouadjia's 1990 book, *Les frères et la mosquée*, it brought together four major groups—Jamaat at-tabliq (The society of the message); Ahl at-talia (The people of the vanguard); Jamaat al-jihad (The holy war society); and Dawa (The call, or propagation of the faith)—that embraced a "multitude of ideological and religious nuances." The founders organized a 35-member governing council that appointed as the front's spokesman Madani, a university professor imprisoned from 1982 to 1984 for his support of acts of political violence; he would be the person to lead the FIS toward its first electoral triumph.

Repudiation and Aftermath

As the FIS closed ranks to contest municipal and provincial elections in 1990, the FLN was coming apart at the seams. It was split into three major factions: socialists who had dominated state policy under President Houari Boumedienne; economic liberals who had found favor under Bendjedid; and Arabists who were close in many ways to the Islamists. Bendjedid's choice of Mouloud Hamrouche as prime minister in September 1989, which signaled the ascendancy of the liberal reformers, left both the socialist old guard and the Arabists unenthusiastic about the party's direction. The November 1989 party congress accentuated these rifts, leaving the FLN poorly equipped to take on the insurgent Islamic Front in the upcoming elections. Bendjedid toyed with the idea of a presidential alliance with the FIS, but the Islamists had no interest in the scheme.

A great many other parties were organized in the period leading up to the June 1990 elections, but most lacked any social base. Many made a tactical decision to boycott the balloting, which basically made the election a contest between the FIS and the FLN. Not only did this assure the FIS the Islamist vote, but it also left it the prime vehicle for the protest vote. These two constituencies gave it 54 percent of the ballots cast, which translated into control of some 850 cities and towns including Algiers and Oran, and over two-thirds of the 48 provincial assemblies. The victory exceeded all estimates of the opposition's strength, suggesting that the elite was seriously out of touch with the masses. Immediately after his party's striking win, Madani called for national parliamentary elections. After resisting briefly, Bendjedid announced late in July that elections for the National Assembly would be held the following year.

Voter repudiation of the ruling party, which had garnered only 28 percent at the polls in the local elections, was a clear call for change. Yet because of the boycott by many of the non-Islamist democratic parties and the relatively low turnout (65 percent), some doubted the FIS would do as well once other alternatives were presented; the 1990 elections did not test, for instance, the chances of a coalition of democratic parties opposed to both the FIS and the FLN. The government, the army, and the non-Islamic parties all believed it was still possible to stem the tide of the Islamist challenge.

The military high command, however, was stung during the Persian Gulf crisis of 1990–1991, when the FIS criticized the army for not training and dispatching "volunteers" to defend Iraq. The front's opportunistic rhetoric on the Gulf conflict reinforced the army's suspicions of the movement, fed by an awareness of Islamist influence among army recruits—a phenomenon the top brass sought to control through strict discipline. Although the military hesitated to intervene directly in the rivalry between the FIS and the FLN—and even removed some officers known for their strong anti-Islamist views—it did not look benignly on the idea of further electoral gains for the FIS.

By the same token, the army's distrust of the ruling party also grew, especially during the spring of 1991,

[2]Abdelkader Djeghloul, "Le multipartisme à l'algérienne," *Maghreb-Machrek* (Paris), January–March 1990, p. 199.

when the FLN, under Prime Minister Hamrouche, took advantage of its complete control of the sitting parliament (elected in 1987 when a single-party system was still in effect) to push through an outrageous redistricting bill. The plan increased the number of seats in the Popular National Assembly from 295 to 542, with most of the new seats going to small towns in southern Algeria—the only part of the country where the FLN had done well in the 1990 elections. A poll conducted in May indicated the tactic might work: it showed the FIS receiving 33 percent of the popular vote and sending 206 deputies to parliament, while giving the FLN 244 seats for only 24 percent of the vote.

All the other parties denounced this blatant exercise in gerrymandering. Prophetically, Hocine Ait Ahmed, leader of the Socialist Forces Front (FFS), declared that it would leave Algeria no choice but a police state or a fundamentalist state. The FIS termed the law "high treason" and demanded its abrogation. At the end of May it decided to go to the streets to overturn the law. When protesters occupied key transit points around Algiers, Bendjedid ordered them removed. After violence erupted, Bendjedid canceled the scheduled elections and declared martial law, as he had in 1988. The military restored calm but also insisted that the president fire Hamrouche, whom it held responsible for the breakdown in civil order. It proposed Sid Ahmed Ghozali, a prominent figure during the Boumedienne era, for the post.

The army thus moved back to the front line in Algerian politics. For the second time in less than three years it had intervened on behalf of the state in a clash with elements of civil society. Since the army had earlier withdrawn its bloc of representatives from the Central Committee of the FLN, it viewed this crisis as primarily the fault of the politicians who had pushed through the election law. Ghozali was handed the task of organizing "free and clean elections" not only for parliament but for the presidency as well—thus meeting one of the FIS's demands. This suggested that the military leadership included Bendjedid among the politicians at fault. At the same time, the army distrusted the militant element within the Islamic Front, and it began to arrest Islamist activists for their alleged role in sparking acts of violence; when tensions failed to subside, the army hardened its position by arresting Madani, Benhadj, and five other top leaders at the end of June. Having thus decapitated the FIS, the military leadership lifted martial law and allowed the electoral process to resume under Ghozali's direction.

THE DECEMBER 1991 ELECTIONS: DEFEAT IN VICTORY

The army assumed that more moderate elements would now take control of the Islamic Front. Bashir Faqih, for example, a leader from western Algeria, publicly charged Madani with disregarding the majority view of the front's governing council during the events of early June. El Hachemi Sahnouni, one of the party's founders, reportedly wanted to reorganize the front, leaving out its "stray sheep." Ahmed Marani, another member of the governing council, went on television to criticize Madani: "The FIS's success has gone to his head. He heeds only the flatterers who glorify him." Despite these divisions within the leadership, the Madani faction held onto control through Abdelkader Hachani, a member of the younger generation of Islamist leaders who was made head of a new "provisional executive bureau" of the FIS in July.

Throughout the fall of 1991 the FIS cultivated an air of uncertainty regarding its intention to participate in the rescheduled parliamentary elections. Many observers speculated that it had lost some of its electoral following after the disruptions and internal disputes of May and June, yet it organized a huge rally on November 1, the anniversary of the outbreak of the war for national independence, which demonstrated its continuing hold on many voters. Meanwhile, the Ghozali government prepared a new redistricting bill that set the number of seats in the new parliament at 430; members were to be elected in two rounds of voting. Only the FIS succeeded in running a candidate in every district; the ruling FLN had a candidate in all but one of the constituencies, and five other parties were represented in at least two-thirds of the districts around the country.

Although rumors circulated throughout the fall that the army would intervene if the Islamists won the election, the most common expectation was that no party would win a majority and some kind of coalition government would be formed. Just a few days before the December 26 balloting, Bendjedid announced that he was available to remain in office until the end of his term in December 1993, implying that he anticipated some form of "cohabitation" with a prime minister selected by a parliamentary coalition.

The election returns dispelled any such presumption. The FIS captured 188 seats by achieving absolute majorities in the first round—just 28 seats short of a parliamentary majority. The FLN won only 16 seats, while Ahmed's FFS took 25 and three independents were also elected; this made a total of 232 races that were decided in the first round. Moreover, the Islamic Front was fielding one of two candidates in 186 of the 198 districts scheduled for runoffs—in most cases, the candidate in the lead. Its victory in the second round, therefore, was virtually assured.

However, several irregularities were noted in the election, chief among them a surprisingly low level of participation. Only 7.8 million (59 percent) of Algeria's 13.2 million registered voters took part; thus, although the FIS received 47 percent of the ballots cast, this represented less than 25 percent of those registered to vote. In the aftermath of the election it was discovered that some 900,000 electors cards had never been distributed by municipal governments, generally in towns controlled by the FIS; distribution that had taken place often occurred at the mosques. Moreover, about 1 million additional voters went to the polls only to be told that their names were not on the voting lists. In all, some 2 million voters appear to have been disenfranchised by one mechanism or another. The results also showed that despite its overwhelming victory, the FIS had lost more than 1 million votes in comparison to its total in the 1990 elections. No doubt some of this loss came because husbands were not allowed to cast votes for their wives in 1991, as had been permitted the previous year.

Whatever doubts may have hung over the electoral process, the more fundamental issue was what would happen if the FIS took control of the government and the National Assembly. Large numbers of Algerians feared the imposition of a theocratic Islamic republic if the front came to power. Although Abdelkader Hachani sought to reassure secular Algerians that public liberties would be guaranteed, other Islamist activists spoke of banning non-Islamist parties and closing down anti-FIS newspapers. Various editors expressed their concern that Algeria was on the verge of returning to a monolithic order similar in form if not in content to the past single-party ideology. On January 9, 1992, women's groups demonstrated against FIS disregard for women's rights. These real divisions in Algerian society provided a rationale for the military-bureaucratic elite's intervention against the FIS.

The coup followed a complex scenario designed to perpetuate the role of the army as kingmaker rather than direct ruler. The first step was to have Bendjedid announce his resignation as a "sacrifice in the service of the higher interests of the nation." Before stepping down on January 11, Bendjedid signed a decree dissolving the National Assembly, thus preventing its president from serving as acting president of the republic, as would normally occur under the constitution. The decision on how to proceed in light of this double vacancy fell to the Constitutional Council, which decreed that the army and the prime minister held the primary responsibility for "assur[ing] the continuity of the state." Ghozali convened an advisory organ, the High Security Council, which made two important decisions: it annulled the results of the parliamentary elections, and announced it would name a new collective executive organ to assume the powers of the presidency. The point of all this fancy footwork was to avert a new presidential election—which the FIS could be expected to win, of course—and to set up a new institution in which the military would be represented but not in overt control of the government. Unsurprisingly, the FIS condemned the coup as a "plot against Algeria and the Islamic project"; some of the other parties (although neither the FLN nor the FFS) welcomed the intervention.

Boudiaf's Struggle

The second act began with a major surprise: the choice of Mohamed Boudiaf as head of the new High State Council. Boudiaf, one of the nine founding fathers of the FLN in 1954, left Algeria for exile in Morocco in 1964 after clashes with the government of Ahmed Ben Bella. Respected as a man of great personal and political integrity, Boudiaf was nonetheless little known to the post-independence generation. Only a few days before the coup, Boudiaf had declared in an interview from Morocco that it would be a good thing if the Islamic Front came to power and ended the FLN's long hold on the Algerian political system. He could, therefore, be viewed as a distinguished opponent of the old order and a potential voice for reconciliation. His selection was both imaginative and promising, but the inflamed situation that led to his return to his native land was far from favorable for political compromise.

The second key member of the ruling council was Major General Khaled Nezzar, leader of the Algerian military establishment. Nezzar, who had become defense minister in July 1990, was viewed as one of the architects of the modernization and professionalization of the Algerian military, an officer whose mission was to maintain the military's role as the power behind the scenes. But the crises of October 1988 and June 1991 had thrust the army to the forefront of politics. Seconded by other top military leaders, Nezzar had led the crackdown against the FIS in the summer of 1991. Clearly Nezzar was the military's strongman in the new five-man directorate.

The key to the new powerholders' strategy was Boudiaf's credibility. His great asset was his early break with the FLN; his great liability that he was virtually unknown to the generation that came of age after independence. He had no popular mandate to govern, and lacked any popular power base in Algeria. That his unsullied reputation might accord legitimacy to the new ruling body, as Prime Minister Ghozali and General Nezzar hoped, was a desperate gamble—all the more so because the army was now determined to dismantle the FIS.

Even before Boudiaf arrived in Algeria last January 16, security forces began to arrest prominent members of the Islamic Front, including some who had been elected in the December balloting. Soon Hachani was taken into custody for allegedly inciting soldiers to desert, and another prominent FIS spokesperson was detained for condemning the coup. At the same time, militant Islamists began a campaign of attacks on soldiers and policemen. As the frequency of these incidents increased, the authorities carried out more arrests. Some 5,000 people were arrested in the month following the cancellation of the election. Disorder spread rapidly across the country, and on February 9 the ruling council declared a state of emergency and called for the dissolution of the FIS.

For five months Boudiaf waged a lonely struggle for a fresh approach to Algeria's discontents. He opposed the theocratic pretensions of the Islamists: the mosques, he declared, must once again become "places of prayer and not of political propaganda." At the same time, he declared that he was "attuned to popular opinion which [was] seeking a radical change" in the way Algeria should be governed.

His personal agenda clearly focused on punishing malefactors and restoring public confidence in the integrity of government. Yet Boudiaf had an inherent credibility problem, because large numbers of Algerians had voted in December for "radical change" only to see their intentions thwarted. Moreover, the military's number one priority was stamping out the FIS, not corruption.

Striving heroically to chart out a third path between an Islamic republic and a militarized version of the old regime, Boudiaf discovered he had very little room to maneuver. He called for a change in the makeup of the Ghozali government, but when a new government was presented at the end of February, it looked very much like its predecessor (one newspaper headline read "Ghozali replaces Ghozali as head of government"). All the important ministries (defense, interior, economy, foreign affairs, energy) remained in the same hands. The most notable change was the recruitment of two ministers, who had ties to the Islamists. This modest gesture in the direction of a movement that had thousands of members currently under arrest did not have much impact; two weeks later an administrative court officially dissolved the FIS, saying it was responsible for the violence plaguing the country.

Boudiaf began to question the manner in which the army was conducting its campaign against the Islamists. He called for a sharper distinction between the treatment of armed terrorists and mere sympathizers, and closed some of the detention camps where Islamists were being held. Meanwhile, daily clashes between guerrillas and security forces took their toll.

On June 29 Boudiaf himself fell victim to the climate of violence when he was assassinated while delivering a speech in eastern Algeria. He was slain by a member of his own security guard, in circumstances that were hardly clarified by the government's preliminary report on the assassination. Although it was plausible that radical Islamists could have infiltrated the special services responsible for presidential security, an alternative hypothesis held that rogue elements in the military eliminated Boudiaf. The head of state had opponents in both camps, but his course of action was perhaps more threatening in the long run to those in power. Whichever side brought Boudiaf down, his murder left the country even more polarized than before.

Despite this exacerbation of the crisis, the military did not put General Nezzar forward to replace Boudiaf. Instead, ruling council member Ali Kafi was tapped, as once again the elite turned to a figure known for his role in the war for independence. Though unquestionably a patriot, Kafi did not have the independence from the old regime that Boudiaf had brought to the post. While perceived as a conciliator and critic of certain past abuses, Kafi appeared more of a figurehead.

Confidence in Kafi's capacity to lead the country in new directions was hardly enhanced when the ruling council named Belaid Abdesslam the new prime minister. Economic czar of the Boumedienne years, Abdesslam had been a steady critic of the market-oriented economic reforms of Bendjedid's administration. The military presumably saw in him a resolute leader, firm in his economic convictions and secular political beliefs; still, he represented a throwback to the past at a moment of national anguish about the future.

The day Abdesslam announced his cabinet, guerrillas staged attacks in three cities. A month later they exploded a bomb at the Algiers airport, killing 10 people and wounding more than 100. In the midst of all this bloodshed, a military tribunal sentenced Madani and Benhadj to 12 years in prison for their roles in the disorders of June 1991—events that appeared mild compared to the terrorism of 1992. Although the security forces made some headway against the violence late last year, Algeria had lost its way.

THE MYTH SHATTERED

Islam is a powerful ideology in the Arab world today because secular regimes have often failed to deliver economic and social justice. Algeria slipped in this direction in the 1980s, when the Islamists enjoyed in the mosques a political space that other opposition forces were denied. The FIS captured the protest vote because it was the most credible alternative to the old elite; nonetheless, 53 percent of the electorate voted for other alternatives in 1991. Because democracy in Algeria was still so untested, many Algerians feared the possibility of a theocratic party in power. Yet cutting the democratic experiment short provoked bitterness and recrimination, violence and repression.

At present there are currents in the army favorable to a complete takeover and others edging toward a dialogue with moderate Islamists. Politicians from Bendjedid to Kafi have recognized the need to find some middle path that can bridge the gap between secular and Islamist Algerians. The bloody polarization of 1992 inexorably narrowed this middle ground; moreover, the political crisis sapped the energies needed to cope with economic and social problems. Algeria stands divided against itself as two essentially authoritarian solutions—one military and the other theocratic—battle for supremacy while secular democrats agonize over the narrow space left to them.

FINDING COMMON GROUND

Even before the assassination of Chris Hani, head of the South African Communist Party and a charismatic leader of the African National Congress, South Africa's peace negotiations were proceeding delicately. Now, the killing has shaken the foundation beneath the discussions and tested the resolve of the country's political factions to stay on track to a peaceful settlement.

PATRICK LAURENCE

Patrick Laurence is a specialist writer on the Johannesburg Star, *South African correspondent of* The Economist, *and a contributor to* The Guardian *of London and* The Irish Times.

After faltering and then breaking down completely, South Africa's search for a negotiated settlement to its protracted conflict had resumed again when the news of Chris Hani's assassination shook the country. The resumption had generated cautious optimism. Heads which were kept below the parapet during the second half of last year were now peering anxiously over it as political leaders tried once again to find a formula for a peaceful compromise.

If the assassination doesn't derail the process, the resumed negotiations—a preparatory conference in February cleared the way for full-scale multi-party bargaining in April—appear to have a better chance of success than the aborted discussions at the Convention for a Democratic South Africa between December 1991 and May 1992.

The new talks are more inclusive. Parties present at the resumed talks which were absent from earlier negotiations include the vociferously militant Pan Africanist Congress (PAC), the right-wing Conservative Party (CP) and its off-shoot, the Afrikaner Volksunie (AVU).

Places at the negotiating table have also been found for traditional or tribal leaders, including, significantly, the Zulu monarch, King Goodwill Zwelethini, whose presence was repeatedly demanded by Mangosuthu Buthelezi's Inkatha Freedom Party (IFP) during last year's talks.

The renewed negotiations cover the entire political spectrum, with the exception of the neo-fascist Afrikaner Weerstandsbeweging (AWB) on the extreme right and the Azanian People's Organization (Azapo) at the opposite end of the continuum. Azapo, however, has decided in principle to come to the negotiating table and is waiting for an opportune moment to take its seat.

The greater inclusivity of the resumed negotiations means that if an agreement is reached it will have a better chance of forming the basis for a durable settlement. On the other hand, it will be harder to forge an agreement among such a disparate range of parties.

The most hopeful aspect of the present negotiations is the bilateral agreement hammered out in a series of high-powered and secret meetings between the de Klerk administration and the African National Congress (ANC).

The agreement—described as a pact or collusion by rival political forces—rests on four salient points:

(1) The final constitution for a non-racial and democratic South Africa should be drawn up by a popularly elected constituent assembly, consisting of 400 members and functioning within the boundaries of a set of constitutional principles agreed to at preceding multi-party negotiations. Target dates have been set for the election: September 1993 (ANC) and April 1994 (de Klerk).

(2) The constituent assembly will fulfill a dual function: serve as a constitution-making body and as a transitional Parliament pending finalization of the new constitution.

(3) After the elections, a Transitional Government of National Unity (TGNU) will be established, drawn from all that win between 5 and 10 percent of the vote (the ANC favors 5 and de Klerk 10 percent). Parties will be represented in the TGNU in proportion to their strength in the constituent assembly.

(4) The life of the TGNU could be extended for five years, meaning that if the final constitution is completed in, say, two years, its implementation could be delayed for another three.

Thus, under the ANC-de Klerk accord, South Africa

Reprinted by permission from *Africa Report*, May/June 1993, pp. 25-27.

will have a TGNU, in which the ANC and the National Party (NP) are likely to be dominant partners. It may last until the turn of the century and provide a link between the old and new orders and, it is hoped, guarantee the loyalty of the white-dominated civil service and security forces.

The ANC-de Klerk deal is seen by observers and many South Africans as a hopeful development. The belief is that it will serve as a cornerstone upon which the new South Africa will be constructed, that it will help buttress the center and, to quote Yeats, prevent things from falling apart and anarchy from being "loosed upon the world."

The deal, however, has been criticized from within both the ANC and the government. In the ANC, radical elements see it as a risky compromise, accepted to ensure, in the words of Winnie Mandela, "a short-cut route to Parliament by a handful of individuals." In the government and its handmaiden, the NP, malcontents see it as capitulation to the ANC and betrayal of Buthelezi's IFP. Already two of de Klerk's men, Jurie Mentz and Hennie Bekker, have defected to the Zulu-based IFP. They may be straws in the proverbial wind.

The deal has been criticized by parties on the outside. To them it reeks of "collusion." They suspect an ANC-de Klerk maneuver to impose their will on the negotiating process. The response of parties as divergent as the PAC and the IFP is to cry: "Hijack!"

Taking a broader view, two blocs can be identified at the negotiating table as the different parties haggle for advantage.

In the first, which includes the ANC, the government, and the PAC, believes that the new constitution must be drafted by an elected constitution-making body if it is to acquire the necessary legitimacy.

The second, led by the IFP, argues that an elected body will result in the majority party imposing its will and that its constitutional strategy will be to secure its own power rather than to establish democracy. The second bloc wants the new constitution to be drafted by the multi-party conference, aided by constitutional experts. It cites the 1979 Lancaster House conference —which drafted Zimbabwe's first post-independence constitution—as a precedent for its approach.

But another fundamental difference divides the negotiating parties, one which put the government closer to Buthelezi's bloc than to the ANC. It concerns regionalism.

With the exception of the PAC and Azapo, all the parties—including the ANC—favor regionalism, or, more specifically, the division of South Africa into some 10 regions with a high degree of autonomy over their own affairs.

The ANC, however, advocates a system under which the balance of power will rest unequivocally with the central government. It will have concurrent and overriding powers. Against that, the remaining parties favor a division of power in favor of regions rather than the center. Under their plans, regional governments will have original and inviolable powers.

Buthelezi's IFP favors a system in which the regions will retain all the powers which they do not specifically cede to the center. Buthelezi has already published a constitution for KwaZulu and Natal, an area where he hopes that the IFP will emerge as the majority party.

Under the proposed constitution, KwaNatal, as KwaZulu and Natal are known collectively, would be able to veto the deployment of federal troops or the imposition of federal taxes and decide, via a special constitutional court, which South African laws had jurisdiction in Natal.

Some observers contend that the IFP constitution provides for KwaNatal to be a largely independent state in a South African confederation rather than an autonomous region in a federation. Thus Etienne Mureinik, professor of law at the University of Witwatersrand, writes: "KwaNatal would require a separate and insular statehood, just as Hendrick Verwoerd might have hoped."

The ANC, as Thomazile Botha, head of its department of regional and local government, has made clear, fears that confederation is the first step to secession and disintegration of the South African polity. It will resist any move in that direction of confederation.

The dispute over the question of regional power tends to obscure another equally important divergence over the issue of who should determine the regional boundaries.

Buthelezi believes the existing regions should do so. He is supported by the CP, the AVU—both of which aim at establishing an Afrikaner state—and the governments of Bophuthatswana and Ciskei, putatively independent states established under the now discarded doctrine of territorial apartheid. The ANC reckons that it is a task that should be referred to the elected constituent assembly.

Thus the negotiating parties face two interconnected and fundamental questions. Should the new constitution be drafted by an elected constituent assembly or by the multi-party conference? Should the powers and borders of the regions be determined by the constitution-making body or by the existing regions (provinces and tribal "homelands")?

A possible middle course is under discussion. It will require great ingenuity for the negotiators to get it accepted.

The "third way" is for the multi-party conference to draw up a list of constitutional principles. These will serve as guidelines within which the constituent assembly will have to draft the constitution. Thus there will be input from both the multi-party conference and the constituent assembly.

Much will depend, however, on whether agreement can be reached on the constitutional principles.

The ANC is wary of attempts to define these principles in such detail that the constituent assembly will find that its work has been pre-empted. Joe Slovo, the shrewd national chairman of the South African Communist Party, fears that the constituent assembly could be left to decide

WISDOM AND PATIENCE WILL BE NEEDED BY THE NEGOTIATING PARTIES TO AVOID THE MANY SNARES.

minor issues such as the color and design of the flag and the wording of the preamble to the constitution.

On the other side, the Buthelezi bloc is determined to guard against what it fears will be the tyranny of the majority party. It will thus want to draw the boundaries as narrowly as possible, leaving the constituent assembly with little scope.

In theory the multi-party conference will seek to reach consensus. If it cannot reach complete consensus, however, it will decide on the basis of the doctrine of "sufficient consensus." The problem is that "sufficient consensus" is an ill-defined concept. It has been defined tautologically so far. The multi-party planning conference defines it as "enough agreement" from enough participants to enable the process to move forward.

If the parties cannot agree, who will decide whether or when there is sufficient consensus to proceed?

Does sufficient consensus mean, as some political analysts contend, concurrence between the ANC and the government? If so, is there not justification for these two central forces of collusion? Have they secretly decided to try to persuade as many of the parties to join them as possible and then to move forward anyway?

These tricky questions lie waiting to ensnare the negotiating parties. To avoid the traps will require the wisdom of Solomon and the patience of Job.

Meanwhile violence threatens to tear the country apart. Even as the negotiators talk, civilians die every day, as assassins strike, killing women and children, white as well as black. Murderous ANC fanatics, IFP zealots, and renegade security force members have been joined by fanatical gunmen from the PAC's armed wing, the Azanian People's Liberation Army. Killing is now part of the South African way of life.

Buthelezi, who wants elections to be held under a constitution drawn up by the multi-party conference, has declared that free and fair elections cannot be held in this prevailing climate. De Klerk has insisted that South Africa's first priority must be to end the violence.

But Slovo argues, "In moving rapidly, now, towards one person/one vote elections, we will show those forces who have unleashed the violence in our country that they cannot stop the movement toward democracy with an escalating body count. But if we falter now, we will encourage ongoing carnage."

The problem of going to the vote before the violence subsides is that it may result in the elections being decided by the party or alliance of parties which can create the biggest or most "no-go" areas. It would be a most inauspicious start for the "new South Africa."

BIRTH OF A NATION

A historic agreement to hold South Africa's first free elections next April promises no miracle solution for the country's profound economic and social woes

SCOTT MAC LEOD JOHANNESBURG

"I consider myself neither morally nor legally bound to obey laws made by a Parliament in which I am not represented."
—Nelson Mandela, 1962

THAT BRAVE REPUDIATION OF A REgime bent on perpetuating white hegemony in South Africa earned Mandela a lifetime's incarceration, while his jailers pressed on with their megalomaniac construct called grand apartheid. At the same time, his stance just as surely launched South Africa on the road to democracy. Last week the country took an irreversible step forward when black and white political leaders declared that every citizen will be able to vote to choose the government. With that historic agreement, Mandela and South Africa's 28 million blacks will be able to savor the success of their freedom struggle when the country holds its first-ever free elections on April 27, 1994.

The announcement came at the end of a tension-filled day in the fitful talks among 26 parties that began in December 1991. While dissenters will be able to raise the issue again, a majority nonetheless provisionally set the poll date to bolster the hopes of blacks impatient for more rapid change. Afterward, African National Congress Secretary-General Cyril Ramaphosa rushed to a previously scheduled gala dinner to receive a Man of the Year award jointly with government negotiator Roelf Meyer. To the cheers of 400 guests, who represented all the country's races, Ramaphosa declared, "We now stand at the gateway of the democracy that so many of us have worked so hard for and so many have died for."

For blacks, the long-awaited vote will formally end the humiliation, injustice and injury of the past four decades and complete the dismantling of apartheid, that pervasively dysfunctional experiment in political and social engineering. The balloting will allow the pariah state to regain a place in the community of nations. And the voters will almost certainly reward Mandela's stoic struggle by conferring on him the leadership of his country.

But the elections will not usher in a ready-formed New South Africa. Even as most South Africans delight in the prospect of free elections, they are beginning to sense that the immediate future holds much hardship and that the three years of turmoil following De Klerk's decision to dismantle apartheid and release Mandela is a taste of things to come. "The pattern has already been set," warns Zulu Chief Mangosuthu Buthelezi, leader of the Inkatha Freedom Party. "It is going to be turbulent, no matter who is at the helm."

Frustrating too, particularly when it comes to fulfilling the expectations of a populace impatient to see political power translated into a more equitable distribution of resources. "People have suffered so much that they now expect the opposite," says Harry Gwala, a senior member of Mandela's African National Congress in strife-torn Natal province. "But we can't perform miracles."

Indeed they cannot. South Africa may be rich in gold and diamonds. It may again qualify for international aid and may even succeed in luring back foreign investors kept out by sanctions or scared off by violence. But it will still take years of patient reconstruction to undo the damage of the apartheid era and break the cycle of violence. Nor will it be easy to find jobs for a fast-growing work force that cannot be absorbed by a capital-starved economy.

The country's main hope as the perils and pressures crowd in is that the remarkable spirit of cooperation and compromise that has developed in recent months can be preserved and built upon. Former enemies are already gathering in countless forums to address critical issues like the economy, education, jobs and housing. Says Anglo American Corp. labor negotiator Bobby Godsell: "We cannot achieve political and social stability without addressing the issue of poverty immediately." For the A.N.C., contact with business has made it warier of socialism's nostrums. "We have no intention of introducing a command economy," insists the A.N.C.'s chief economist, Tito Mboweni. "We want to improve productivity and the investment climate."

Despite the legacy of hatred, negotiations have progressed with a smoothness that few would have predicted when Mandela was released from prison in 1990. Although many important issues remain unresolved, the blueprint for the country's political future has been drawn, and in the coming weeks negotiators hope to complete the details. The next move should be the appointment as early as this month of a multiparty Transitional Executive Council that will have no executive authority but will oversee De Klerk's government policies to ensure their nonpartisan nature. When South Africans finally go to the polls, they will elect a bicameral legislature that will serve during a five-year transitional period and double as the constituent assembly responsible for drafting a postapartheid constitution. The party receiving the largest number of seats will choose the new President to succeed De Klerk—almost certainly Mandela.

But for that five-year transition period, Mandela will be required to form a government that includes leaders from all the major parties as a safeguard against an A.N.C. monopoly on power. Negotiators have also accepted National Party demands that in sensitive areas like security policy, Mandela could be overruled by one-third of the Cabinet's members.

The most serious sticking point remains De Klerk's demand for permanent power sharing, which the A.N.C. regards as an effort to deprive blacks of the chance for true majority rule. During the period of Mandela's national-unity government, De Klerk proposes that real power be invested in an Executive Committee made up of party leaders and that the presidency become a largely ceremonial job. He is also demanding up-front guarantees of power-sharing in the final constitution, although he rejects suggestions that he is trying to secure a permanent white veto.

Forcing Mandela and De Klerk to compromise is the recognition that time is running out for South Africa's once mighty economy. Apartheid cost the country millions in lost investment. Since 1990, some 500,000 jobs have been wiped out by recession, drought and violence. With South Africa heading toward its fourth straight year of zero growth, the repair task will be that much harder.

Most daunting of apartheid's legacies is the near total collapse of education for most of the 6 million school-age black children. Ever since the 1976 Soweto uprising, students have manned the barricades under the slogan "Liberation Now, Education Later," and the government has funneled much more money into white schools. The results have been horrendous: 40% of black students drop out, and last year only 44% of those remaining passed. An estimated 3 million young blacks make up a "lost generation" that is virtually unemployable.

At least Soweto and other townships have schools and additional basic services. They are the envy of the country's worst off: the estimated 7 million blacks—18% of the population of 38 million—living in urban shanty towns. Like Crossroads, the notorious squatter camp on the edge of Cape Town, these settlements are mostly populated by impoverished peasants from the countryside seeking jobs. The squatter camps are a breeding ground for black extremists who will make life difficult for a Mandela-led government unable to work economic miracles overnight.

Hopes are high that a political settlement will greatly reduce the potential for black-against-black violence. Since 1986, some 10,000 people have died in an A.N.C.-Inkatha power struggle that in parts of Natal has taken on civil-war proportions. Even assuming the rivalry cools among top leaders, blood feuds, local turf wars, scrambling for scarce jobs, general intolerance and even tribal antipathy could spark continued fighting.

The A.N.C. goes into the April elections as the anti-apartheid champion and the party of change. But it will be handicapped by its lack of experience in government, and both the National Party and Inkatha are certain to exploit the competence factor as well as employ scare tactics that draw attention to the A.N.C.'s links with the Communist Party of South Africa. Although De Klerk says he will be out to win the election, his basic goal is to get at least 34% of the vote. That way he can block any constitution the A.N.C. tries to ram through the constituent assembly. Wild cards in the electoral deck will be the 3 million colored, or mixed race, voters and the 1 million Asians. Although both groups suffered under apartheid, their conservative outlook is working in De Klerk's favor. Says Magda Bellwood, a Cape Town receptionist: "Better the devil you know than the devil you don't."

It should be heartening that despite years of anti-A.N.C. propaganda, the majority of whites seem ready to live with black rule. Although many talk of leaving, a 1992 survey showed that only 27% of English-speaking and 13% of Afrikaans-speaking whites contemplate emigration. Some, like Wilhelm Verwoerd, 29, grandson of Prime Minister Hendrik Verwoerd, the architect of apartheid and head of the government that locked up Nelson Mandela, have decided that what they cannot fight they should join. Last month Verwoerd stood on an A.N.C. platform in Parow, a conservative suburb of Cape Town, and confessed his political conversion to fellow Afrikaners. "I am much more than just the grandson of a symbol," he told them. "I am the symbol of a new generation who wants to stand up for democracy." Whatever their voting preferences, South Africans have good reason to say amen to that. ***—With reporting by Peter Hawthorne/Cape Town***

MANDELA AND DE KLERK SPEAK OUT

In exclusive interviews, South Africa's black and white leaders both profess optimism about a multiracial future

NELSON MANDELA

Q. *How important a milestone is the setting of the election date?*

A. This decision to have an election by April 27 introduces an element of irreversibility. It is a landmark.

Q. *Is it a safe assumption that you will be the next President of South Africa?*

A. (Chuckling) Some of the young men would not agree with you because they all want to be President. The opinion polls say that if elections were held today, the A.N.C. would probably win by an outright majority. It is then for the A.N.C. to decide who should be President. We have many dynamic people, and I would be prepared to serve under them.

Q. *Do you believe De Klerk's National Party will abide by the results of the election?*

A. I have no reason to doubt they are negotiating in good faith. But of course their concept of democracy is different from yours and mine. We have already encountered this problem in their concept of power sharing, which to them means the party that loses the elections should continue to govern. Now we have moved them away from that, and they are coming to accept our concept of a government of national unity which is based on majority rule. We are saying all political parties with a substantial following should be included in government, so we can face problems together.

Q. *But in the end, won't their bottom line be permanent power sharing?*

A. My view is that they are moving away from that bottom line.

Q. *Can you deliver on people's expectations, or is the damage of apartheid too deep?*

A. Forty years of apartheid have been like 40 years of war. Our economy and our social life have been completely devastated, in some respects beyond repair. That was the situation in Europe after the last World War. What the Western world did was to mobilize their resources and introduce Marshall Plan aid to ensure that the countries of Europe devastated by the war recovered. What we expect—and this is a matter which I'm going to raise with President Clinton—is that the Western world, led by the U.S., should ensure that massive measures of assistance are given to the people of South Africa so we can address their expectations.

Q. *What do you say to your supporters who don't want to share power with former practitioners of apartheid?*

A. Last week I met the executive committee of the African National Congress Youth League, which has been vocal in criticizing the government of national unity. Quite understandably, they say, "These are the people who have been oppressing us since 1948. We are on the verge of overthrowing apartheid and their government, and now you say we must work with these people." That is perfectly reasonable. But we discussed the matter at length, and at

BUT ELECTIONS WILL NOT USHER IN A READY-FORMED NEW SOUTH AFRICA

the end of that meeting they accepted that the strategy of a government of national unity is a correct one.

Q. *And what about those on the right who fear and might resist black majority rule?*

A. In the referendum last year, the right wing polled no less than 800,000 votes. In addition, they have got a substantial section of the civil service, the police force, the army, which support them. Now they have said if the A.N.C. wins the elections and establishes the government, they will take up arms. That is the threat facing us. It's a serious threat, but we aren't overly concerned. We have to reorganize the police force and make sure it is capable of defending democracy.

Q. *Can you think of any precedent for a minority that has held power for centuries and surrendered it peacefully?*

A. We are now making joint decisions with that minority. They said they would never talk with the A.N.C., and they fought almost every election on that basis. We have made them sit down and talk to us. We are now together planning the future South Africa. They have had to unban the A.N.C., to lift the state of emergency, to allow a climate of free political activity, which they had not allowed for more than 40 years. They have released political prisoners, allowed political exiles to return to the country, amended and even repealed repressive legislation, and agreed on the installation of a transitional executive council. And now they are agreeing with us on a date for an election in the country.

Q. *Why have they cooperated?*

A. I think they realized that not only were the overwhelming majority of South Africans prepared to fight for the right to run their lives, but the whole international community was against South Africa.

Q. *So, did sanctions work?*

A. Oh, there is no doubt.

Q. *Should sanctions now be lifted?*

A. We have come to the verge of calling them off. Our official policy was that until free and fair elections were held, we would maintain sanctions. But the problems facing our country—7 million people unemployed, rocketing crime, the violence and so on—has made us revise our time frame. If the transitional executive council is installed and if an election date is set, we would call off sanctions.

Q. *Three and a half years ago, you were still under arrest. Now you're engaged in the process of rebuilding the country. Did you ever think this was going to happen in your lifetime?*

A. There were definitely moments when I was not so certain this day would come. But as you know, I did send a message that was read by my daughter at a public meeting attended by Archbishop Tutu where I said, "I will return." So that perception was always there. But that doesn't mean there were not moments when I doubted whether this moment would come. But the strength of the struggle in the country and the support of the international community has always been powerful, and that kept our morale very high, and it made us feel that the forces of change were too powerful to be ignored by the government.

Q. *Many have commented about your lack of bitterness. How could you put the past behind you?*

A. Perhaps if I was idle and did not have a job to do, I would be as bitter as others. But because I have been given a job to do, I have not had time to think about the cruel experiences I've had. I'm not unique. Others have every reason to be more bitter than I. There are countless people who went to jail and aren't bitter at all, because they can see that their sacrifices were not in vain, and the ideas for which we lived and sacrificed are about to come to fruition. And that removes the bitterness from their hearts.

F.W. DE KLERK

Q *The announcement of the election suggests the tide of history is running against you and the National Party.*

A. No, not at all. We've been in the lead of this process all the time. What is happening is exactly what we envisaged should happen, as the result of our initiatives. We see a major role for ourselves in the future; we are not liquidating as a political force. The National Party opened its membership to all South Africans a few years ago, and we should no longer be regarded as a party representative of only white South Africans.

Q. *After next April you don't expect to be State President?*

A. Being State President isn't important. There is already a convergence of opinion that for a period of five years we need a government of national unity, with a form of power sharing among the parties who attain a reasonable percentage of the total vote. There is no doubt that we will be one of the major players.

Q. *Is it your bottom line that there must be entrenched power sharing at the Executive level in the final constitution?*

A. No. We asked for power sharing, and we will get it in the transitional period in a government of national unity. We believe it would be necessary to have a form of power sharing also in terms of a final constitution, but we have a totally open mind as to how that should be structured. I do not think a permanent form of enforced coalition can be written into a final constitution. But we need more than five years to ensure that the various components of our community will all feel secure and that they need not fear suppression or the misuse of power. We must ensure that there will never be domination again in South Africa. I'm not talking about minority vetoes but about preventing the misuse of power to the detriment of minorities.

Q. *So you're not demanding a minority veto?*

A. We never stood for a minority veto. To oversimplify it, what we think is that if you get 51% of the vote, you don't get 100% of the power: you get 51% of the power.

Q. *It sounds like you're trying to take the prize away from the winner.*

A. Well, in the U.S. they found ways and means of limiting the power of the Executive to such an extent that the presidency is quite circumscribed. What I am pleading for is that we must move away from the winner-take-all system that we inherited from Great Britain. It works in homogeneous societies, but it is not the right system for a big country with vast regional interests and many language and cultural groups. It is not a question of taking the prize away, but of ensuring that a government won't be able to do again what the National Party did with absolute power, merely because it had a majority.

Q. *Do you ever worry that you're the South African Gorbachev and that the winds you unleash will blow you aside?*

A. No, I don't think that is a true comparison. I'm not changing the very essence of a philosophy; I'm broadening democracy. It is not as if we are moving from the dark ages where there was no form of democracy suddenly into a new system. I'm not moving from communism to free-market enterprise. We have a basically sound economy. South Africans have been prepared for the final process of reconciling with each other, of becoming part of one entity and one nation, over a long period.

Q. *What reason is there to fear an A.N.C. government?*

A. I think its alliance with the South African Communist Party is one of the main stumbling blocks in the hearts and minds of the overwhelming majority of South Africans. As the A.N.C. now is, if they were to get absolute power, I think people would have to fear them because they have wild elements in their ranks.

Q. *Are you confident Mandela is up to being South Africa's leader?*

A. I really don't want to discuss my opponents and interlocutors. I'll be fighting an election against him. But I don't fight on an ad hominem basis. I have respect for him. He is highly intelligent. He has a strong personality. We get along well together as opponents, and we find it possible to put our differences aside to try to create the circumstances which can bring peace to our country. There's a mutual acceptance of each other's integrity.

Q. *Are whites afraid of the prospect of a black President?*

A. I won a referendum among whites with more than a two-thirds majority, and they had a very clear picture of the ultimate goal we had in mind. So I think the shock of the change away from the old to the new system has already been accommodated by most whites.

Q. *Do you expect international economic or political help now?*

A. The sooner the few remaining sanctions are lifted, the sooner we will be able to address the heartrending problems many of our people have. South Africa's future lies in Africa, and the developed world cannot sit by and see a continent go to pieces. South Africa can play an extremely constructive role as a partner with the international community in addressing the problems of Africa.

Q. *How will you deal with people's high expectations?*

A. I think it is one of the biggest challenges we face. I'm glad to see the A.N.C. leadership is beginning to realize this too and is publicly starting to admonish their crowds and cool down the expectations. But no one will be able to do it on his own. How we fight the election campaign is going to be very important: we must start to defuse unduly high expectations. I also think our economy is poised for a good recovery that could have a fairly substantial effect within a short period.

Q. *What role might you play in the new government?*

A. I think I'll be part of the top management of the country, playing a crucial and leading role in stabilizing our country, in the reconciliation process, in interacting with the international community.

Q. *Is the April election going to be the biggest fight of your political life?*

A. No. At the moment my party has lost a lot of support, but not because people have deserted us and have joined other parties. There's a lot of uncertainty, a lot of apprehension—the violence coupled with the fact that we haven't reached a final agreement so that people can draw conclusions about the future. Once we have those agreements, we will get a more clear-cut position of the political parties. Then I will attain very strong support from all sections of our community because there is a very strong belief that moderate leadership is essential for the future.

In Test with Democracy, African Leaders Lose Some, Win Some

Wave of democracy rocks incumbents, but some survive to reign another day.

Africa News Service

Since Africa's spreading democracy movements started gathering steam in 1990, over half the continent's 54 countries have begun the transition from autocratic political systems to multiparty governments.

Late last month, President Didier Ratsiraka of Madagascar became the fifth African leader in just over three years to go down to defeat at the polls. Five other heads of state have been forced from office by popular uprisings or coups, and several more strongmen have been compelled to adopt significant political reforms.

The dramatic changes have prompted a palpable sense of euphoria in many parts of the vast region, which is more than three times the size of the United States. In some countries, the reforms have been more cosmetic than real, and everywhere the challenge of creating governments that are truly accountable to their people is daunting. But the pressure for a new political order continues.

In Madagascar, the Indian Ocean island nation off Africa's southeastern coast, the winner by a margin of two-to-one was Albert Zafy. A 65-year-old medical professor, Zafy emerged as the leader of a broad-based democracy campaign in 1991 that drew as many as

Countries currently voting

half a million people to near-daily protests and forced Ratsiraka, who has been in office since 1975, to abandon one-party rule and agree to a competitive vote.

A transitional government that included both government and opposition members organized the presidential balloting. In the first round last November, Zafy emerged from a field of eight candidates with 45 percent of the votes. A new parliament, which will name the prime minister and key government officials, is to be elected in April.

In the West African nation of Senegal, the outcome of elections, while different, was not unexpected. Abdou Diouf, who has been president since 1981, won another term in voting on February 21. Preliminary results showed him defeating his long-time rival, Abdoulaye Wade, and six other candidates.

Senegal, whose first president was the internationally known poet Leopold Senghor, is one of the few African countries that has held regular multiparty elections throughout its post-independence history. Diouf's assumption of the presidency when Senghor retired is cited as a model of peaceful transition on an often turbulent continent.

Like Senghor, Diouf has made a name for himself beyond Senegal. He currently chairs both the Organization of African Unity and the Organization of the Islamic Conference, a worldwide grouping of Islamic nations.

But the Senegalese leader has been criticized for failing to resolve economic woes and internal divisions at home. The former French colony is deep in debt and heavily dependent on outside aid, due in part to plummeting world commodity prices since the mid-1980s. Last year alone, the country's leading export product, peanut oil, dropped in price by nearly 35 percent.

The most serious political crisis is a serious separatist rebellion in the southern region of Casamance. During the recent election, several dozen people were reported killed in attacks attributed to a Casamance rebel group, and thousands have been forced by the violence to flee their homes.

Diouf's margin in the last presidential vote, in 1988, was widely disputed, and protests over the results prompted the government to impose a state of emergency and arrest leading opposition figures.

This year's election has been criticized as well. Observers from the United States and France said the polling was generally fair, although hampered by shortages of voting equipment and personnel. But the seven opposition parties charge Diouf's party with widespread electoral fraud.

A new test for Diouf and his ruling Socialist Party lies just ahead. Parliamentary elections later this month will provide Wade's Democratic Party and several of the smaller opposition movements the opportunity to garner enough representation to pose a significant challenge to government policies in legislative deliberations.

First elected president for Niger. Another African nation in the process of choosing a new leader is Niger, where the final round of presidential voting is scheduled to take place on March 20. Eight candidates were on the ballot for round one on February 27.

Niger has spent most of its post-independence history as a one-party state with an authoritarian military leader at the helm. No previous president has been chosen in a contested vote. Widespread popular protests in 1991 forced the military leadership to yield to an interim administration that has been guiding the country toward the ballot box. Ali Saïbou, a military officer who has been head-of-state since 1987, is barred from running but remains in office as figurehead leader.

In last month's vote, a coalition of nine political parties—the Alliance of Forces for Change—won a combined majority in the one-chamber national assembly. However, the largest bloc of seats for a single party went to the former ruling party, the National Movement for a Developing Society, which won 28 out of a total of 83 places in the assembly.

Obstacles Along Election Road. None of the countries making the transition to multiparty government are finding the changeover to be uncomplicated, and some have encountered major pitfalls. Electoral plans have been delayed in a number of countries, including Angola, where civil war has resumed, Mozambique, where a United Nations observer team has been slow in arriving, and Togo, where an entrenched military regime has blocked democratic reforms from being implemented.

Nigeria, the continent's most populous nation, is currently in the process of beginning its presidential election process again, after an embarrassing false start in 1992.

Last month, the country took the first of a series of steps to nominate new presidential candidates. President Ibrahim Babangida, the military leader who has pledged to hand power to an elected civilian regime later this year, nullified last September's presidential primaries, saying the process was characterized by large-scale fraud, including vote buying. The two legally recognized political parties have been directed to choose their presidential nominees through a process that begins with wards and moves up through local and state organizations to the national level.

At state party congresses this week, one candidate from each of the country's 30 states and the federal capital territory, Abuja, will be chosen to stand for the nomination of the Social Democratic Party and the National Republican Convention, as the two parties are called. The presidential election is now scheduled to take place on June 11.

Another country that canceled a 1992 vote is the Central African Republic. With the assent of the opposition, Gen. André Kolingba, the head of state, "disallowed" the results of last October's elections because of widely reported irregularities. After a delay, new presidential and parliamentary balloting is set for April 18 and May 2.

Congo, too, will be holding new parliamentary elections soon, although a parliament and president were chosen last July and August. In November, President Pascal Lissouba dissolved the assembly after the prime minister lost a no-confidence vote. The ensuing political crisis, which brought the country to the brink of political instability and raised the specter of a return to military rule, was eased by the formation of a coalition government. But deep divisions remain, and final agreement on a new election is still to be announced.

Political contests unresolved. Two African rulers who won hotly contested votes late last year have had their victories challenged by distrustful opponents. Ghana's Jerry Rawlings and Kenya's Daniel arap Moi have been accused of using their positions as incumbents to manipulate the voting in their favor.

Opposition parties in Ghana boycotted legislative elections in December to protest the outcome of the November 3 presidential balloting. Rawlings, a former air force flight lieutenant, who won with 58 percent of the votes, has led Ghana since staging a widely popular military coup that ousted a corrupt civilian administration in 1981.

If unresolved, the election dispute could jeopardize the country's continued access to sizable assistance from the World Bank and International Monetary Fund and from a number of Western countries. Efforts to encourage a workable compromise between Rawlings and his leading opponents have begun, involving, among others, the Carter Center in Atlanta. An election observer team from the center was among those international monitors who found the November poll to be generally fair.

In Kenya, Moi's win was a bitter pill for political reformers. After forcing the president to back away from an insistence on continued one-party rule, his opponents failed to unify to defeat him at the polls. With the opposition splintered, Moi was able to cling to office by winning 36 percent of the votes. Opposition parties won 88 out of 188 elected parliamentary seats.

Observers from Commonwealth countries concluded that the elections "cannot be given an unqualified rating as free and fair," but they also called the voting "an important turning point in Kenya's history."

Since the election, Moi has been criticized for failing to take any conciliatory steps to heal the political divisions. Using his constitutional prerogative to appoint 12 members of parliament, he named 11 senior members of his ruling Kanu Party who had been defeated at the polls. And on the day after parliament, convened last month with its first opposition membership in over 25 years, Moi used another constitutional provision to suspend the proceedings and send legislators home.

The political situation is further clouded by court challenges to election results in 90 parliamentary districts, according to the Nairobi-based newsmagazine *Weekly Review.*

Despite the problems, the government has declared the elections a success and has begun campaigning to have international aid suspended in late 1991 restored.

An even more serious stand-off between a besieged ruler and his opponents resulted from last October's election in Cameroon. The incumbent president, Paul Biya, claimed victory with a reported 40 percent of the vote, compared to 36 percent for John Fru Ndi, his chief rival. Biya, who quickly organized elections after being forced into political concessions by popular pressure, won financial backing from France after the vote and was sworn in for a new five-year term. Fru Ndi, however, continues to dispute the results and to call for an election monitored by outside observers.

Learning the ropes. In many other countries, preparations for upcoming votes are actively underway. The East African nation of Burundi has scheduled parliamentary and presidential elections for June.

National elections are set to take place at about the same time in Lesotho, the tiny mountain kingdom surrounded by South Africa. The country's last election was aborted by then-president Leabua Jonathan 23 years ago with backing from South Africa after it became clear the opposition would win.

In neighboring Malawi, voters will have the chance to decide on whether to end one-party rule in a referendum scheduled for June 14. The country's "president for life," Hastings Kamuzu Banda, who has ruled with an iron grip since independence in 1964, agreed to a referendum on the issue after popular protests last year and a cutoff in international aid.

Although the government has rejected secret balloting, Banda has agreed to international observers and to the inclusion of opposition politicians on the commission that will oversee the vote. Meanwhile, Malawi authorities retain a tight reign on political opponents. In a continuation of the regime's traditional hard-line approach to dissent, police arrested two exiled politicians on their arrival in the country last month to participate in the referendum. And the country's leading opposition figure, Chakufwa Chihana, was sentenced in December to two years in prison for sedition.

Voters in Eritrea will cast ballots in April to decide on independence for the former Italian colony, annexed by Ethiopia in 1962. Across the continent, a referendum on independence for Western Sahara, which was occupied by Morocco in 1975, has been delayed by disagreement over the voters roll.

The most active voter preparation effort anywhere in Africa—and the one attracting the greatest outside funding—may be in South Africa. No date has been set, but the country is likely to hold its first one-person, one-vote poll sometime in early 1994.

South Africans don't have to look far for an example of successful elections. Neighboring Namibia, which until 1990 was controlled by South Africa, held its first national vote in late 1989 under United Nations supervision. Swapo, the independence movement that fought South African rule, chalked up a 57 percent majority, giving it control of the government, although a large and lively opposition has acted as a watchdog.

In regional and local elections three months ago, however, Swapo won a landslide. The party was victorious in ten out of 13 regional constituencies and in most of the 50 local councils. The rout of the official opposition was complete enough to threaten its future political viability.

"How can we maintain a healthy multiparty system if our party's platform wins such wide public acceptance that we trounce the opposition at the polls?" asked one bemused government official following release of the December results.

CAMBODIA

Difficult Birth

A successful UN-sponsored election gives way to rising tension as the ruling party alleges electoral irregularities and threatens not to accept the results.

Rodney Tasker and Nate Thayer in Phnom Penh

For a while it all seemed too good to be true. Cambodia's first truly democratic, multi-party election went so smoothly with an astonishing 90% turnout of registered voters that UN officials and Cambodians alike were congratulating themselves.

Then came the morning-after hard reality and doubts: would there be a peaceful transition to a new power equation, or would there be another round of violent political confrontation?

The immediate aftermath of the 23–28 May UN-sponsored election produced a depressing sense of *déjà vu*. Those controlling the government in Phnom Penh were clearly reluctant to relinquish power, and appeared ready to fight for their right to maintain the *status quo*. The Cambodian People's Party (CPP)—the political arm of the State of Cambodia (SOC) regime—rejected the running poll tally issued by the UN Transitional Authority in Cambodia (Untac) that had organised the election when the poll showed it lagging behind the pro-royalist Funcinpec party.

By 1 June, according to Untac figures, Funcinpec was leading with 42% of the vote compared to the CPP's 37% after 60% of the ballots had been counted. At an earlier stage of counting the ruling party had appeared to be pulling marginally ahead of its royalist rival. With 850,000 ballots counted out of the total of 4.2 million on the evening of 30 May the CPP had won 44% of the vote against Funcinpec's 38%.

The CPP sought to bolster its case for questioning the poll by claiming instances of widespread fraud. In particular, it alleged that ballot boxes were tampered with, the indelible ink on electors' fingers—intended to prevent double voting—was in fact washable and that so-called safe havens for counting the ballot were actually unsafe.

A government statement that interrupted programmes on the country's state run television station on the night of 31 May said: "Because of these complications, SOC/CPP is forced to conclude that it cannot recognise that the election process has guaranteed the fairness and justice of the results."

In a bid to prevent exactly the kind of question that the Phnom Penh regime has raised, the UN and major countries promptly expressed their approval of the election process. The day after the polls closed Untac chief Yasushi Akashi said "I have no hesitation in declaring that the conduct of the election was free and fair."

Akashi added that "the determination of the election as free and fair does place a strict obligation on all parties to abide by the people's choice whatever it may be."

The CPP's reaction to finding itself matched more closely than it expected by Funcinpec, did not surprise some foreign observers. They had never thought the former communist party would gracefully accept a dilution of the power it has enjoyed since 1979. But the post-election wrangles quickly threw the prospect of further development of the embryonic democratic process into doubt. As the counting progressed the mounting tensions between winners and losers were clearly starting to worry Cambodia's considerable army of potentially generous international well-wishers.

The tense situation also played into the hands of the Khmer Rouge—the third contender for power—which has long argued that the SOC would never turn over the government to a rival party. The radical guerilla faction, which had vainly called for an election boycott, vowed over its own radio station that "we will continue the struggle."

Many concerned observers have now turned their attention towards Prince Norodom Sihanouk. The prince heads the four-faction Supreme National Council set up under the UN Security Council–brokered November 1991 Paris peace accord to guide the country to national reconciliation, and is widely viewed as the key to future peace in Cambodia.

Sihanouk, who returned to Phnom Penh from Peking on the eve of the polls, appeared to be playing his familiar political games. He managed to both welcome the election as "a tremendous and historic success, while saying the Khmer Rouge had suffered "a historic defeat, and that they would not recover from such a blow."

The prince had earlier said he would include the Khmer Rouge in a national reconciliation quadripartite government but, while polling was still in progress,

Reprinted by permission from *Far Eastern Economic Review,* June 10, 1993, pp. 18-22.

he backtracked, noting that this decision would be up to whatever government emerged from the election.

"We are now seeing a very bad case, of nerves," a senior Western diplomat in Phnom Penh said. The diplomat was commenting on the CPP's claim there had been irregularities in polling procedures. As a further sign that it could not digest defeat the party issued a call for new elections in at least four provinces where it had fared badly but had expected to win.

"We will try to calm these nerves," the diplomat said. He added that top officials from the five permanent UN Security Council members and other key players in Cambodia—notably Japan, Indonesia and Australia—planned to meet in Phnom Penh shortly after the final election count to endorse the polls and plan future assistance to the new government.

But the failure of Untac to abide by the mandate of the November 1991 Paris peace accords and disarm the various factions' military forces means the SOC and its political wing, while facing the prospect of losing the election, is in full control of more than 200,000 armed troops, security service and police personnel. Funcinpec, by contrast, has virtually no military forces. In the Cambodian context of power politics, that could spell disaster—not least because the UN has no mandate to force a transfer of power.

Diplomatic sources said they had feared that problems would arise if—as now seems likely—the election result forced the CPP into a power-sharing, coalition arrangement with Funcinpec. Another major problem, the sources said, was that the Paris accords did not adequately address the prospect of a political vacuum in the immediate aftermath of the election. As a result of the failure to clarify this question, the chances are that the SOC/CPP administration may have to remain in place at least until late August while an elected constituent assembly draws up a new constitution and prepares to form a government.

If the CPP had gained a massive majority it would have been able to retain power almost on its own, and then carry out its pre-election pledge to prosecute a full-scale anti-insurgency campaign against the Khmer Rouge—with the full backing of the international community.

For now, the immediate problem is to assuage the CPP, and to convince it that the election result means it will have to surrender at least some of its levers of power. But a statement issued by government spokesman Khieu Kanarith at a news conference on 1 June, suggested that the party might stiffen its attitude in the election aftermath. Khieu warned that the situation might get out of control and added: "we have asked the army to take every step possible to prevent [this]." Such a pious hope seemed as unlikely to be heeded as his call for people to remain calm and quiet.

Untac and intelligence sources in the Cambodian capital say the only faction which runs the risk of getting seriously out of control is the CPP and its military forces. The REVIEW has learned from diplomatic and intelligence sources that the CPP has already drawn up a list of opposition figures—mainly Funcinpec officials—and targeted them for arrest.

The Phnom Penh regime has also mobilised the army and other elements of the security apparatus to prepare for what essentially amounts to a coup against Untac and the election results. The sources say that the CPP nearly gave the go ahead for the army to intervene and carry out the mass arrest of SOC's political opponents when early results from the polls began to show the CPP losing ground. The threat of such action remains, the sources said.

If there is a smooth transition of power, however, then the international community is set to give massive amounts of economic and military assistance—but only to a government that seems able to exclude the Khmer Rouge from power sharing.

If the CPP were to contest the election results, the result might well be to force Funcinpec, the Khmer Rouge and Sihanouk back into an alliance in exile. At the very least such a move by the CPP would infuse new life into the Khmer Rouge by giving it back its old allies. It would certainly give the Khmer Rouge a new support base and a chance to renew civil war.

If this can be done there is a chance that the SOC can be induced to get on with the difficult task of organising a transition. In the meantime it is clear that neither Funcinpec nor the CPP will be able to muster a two-thirds majority and that the major parties will be forced to join a coalition.

This becomes even more obvious from the poor showing of the 18 smaller parties that participated in the election. Early results suggested that only three of the smaller opposition parties were likely to hold seats in the 12O-seat assembly. Son Sann's Buddhist Liberal Democratic Party (BLDP) seemed likely to pick up five seats at most, while two other parties appeared likely to gain one seat each. The BLDP lost support in the final days of the election campaign despite heavy covert financial backing from the US, China and Singapore.

Despite the dim prospects of a successful meeting of minds between the two main parties, some Phnom Penh-based diplomats still hope that parties have learned something from the election process. "One must hope that all of Cambodia's political leaders have seen a message in this void and that, instead of problems, we want to find solutions", US Chief of Mission Charles Twining told the REVIEW.

"Solutions are going to include not only how to find a consensus on the terms of a new constitution, or a possible role for Prince Sihanouk, but also integration of the armed forces, police and civil service. These are things that Cambodians are going to need solutions to very quickly." But the chances of the CPP, led mainly by former cadres of the Khmer Rouge suddenly giving way to the forces of democracy appear remote.

Diplomats and Cambodian officials say that the role of Prince Sihanouk will be crucial in the coming weeks. He remains the sole Cambodian figure who garners the respect and allegiance of all the parties and is expected to play [a] key role in brokering some power-sharing between the factions.

Diplomats also believe that creating an effective national administration will require that Sihanouk be given real power even before the constitution is promulgated. Another urgent need is to form a national army, police and security service that is loyal to a new government rather than to any single faction. If this can be done diplomats hope that Sihanouk's currently titular role as head of the SNC might be transformed into that of a head of state with real power.

But with no provisions for implementing the poll result in the 1991 Paris accords, and with the Khmer Rouge waiting in the wings, the chances that stability is in sight appear dim. At best the elections may turn out to have been one small step on the long road to an eventual political settlement.

Quiet Satisfaction

Rodney Tasker in Thmar Puok, Battambang province

On the eve of the Cambodian election, Capt. Jeff Jaso sat down and wrote farewell letters to his family in the US. "We were prepared for an all-out offensive [by the Khmer Rouge] the next day," he said on the fifth day of voting in the six-day election.

"But nothing came," he added with a smile. Instead, at mid-morning on 23 May—as hundreds of Cambodians filed peacefully to the local polling stations—the young US army officer found himself "giggling—we couldn't believe it."

Jaso is the official UN military observer in the dusty, barren district of Thmar Puok, near northwestern Cambodia's border with Thailand. During the polls, this lawless "liberated zone" served as a vivid microcosm of the Khmer Rouge's failure to stop an election it had vowed to disrupt. The fact that some 85% of the district's 40,000 registered voters went to the polls, including members of the Khmer Rouge, attests to that.

It is unclear exactly how many Khmer Rouge fighters operate in the area, but the faction controls many of the villages outside Thmar Puok town. The town itself is administered by the Khmer People's National Liberation Front (KPNLF), one of the country's four main political factions, backed up by its own troops. There are also hundreds of troops from Anki, the military arm of the royalist Funcinpec party, in the area to help the KPNLF keep a wary eye on the Khmer Rouge.

In the weeks before the election, the Khmer Rouge raised the profile of their armed presence in the district. They demonstrated with anti-election slogans and, according to UN civilian police, threatened to kill people if they voted.

Why did the Khmer Rouge's disruptive strategy fail? That is a question which puzzles UN officials in Thmar Puok, including Maj. Oscar Smith, commander of the Dutch Marines who enforce the UN's writ in the district. "It would have just needed one more blow [by the Khmer Rouge], and all the election officials would have left this area," he said. Many poll officials did indeed flee when the Khmer Rouge earlier stepped up attacks on UN personnel. Six Dutch Marines were wounded in Khmer Rouge pre-election attacks, four in an ambush in which a Japanese civilian policeman was killed, and one when the Khmer Rouge lobbed four hand grenades into the Dutch camp.

But on 24 May, the second day of polling, Khmer Rouge commander Ta Saroeun and two of his aides came to see Smith to say the Khmer Rouge did not intend to disrupt the election. "That's because they knew they could not stop it," Smith said. He added that the local Khmer Rouge forces had also been warned by the KPNLF not to interfere in a poll in which one of its leaders, Gen. Dien Del, was running.

After the Khmer Rouge failure became apparent, KPNLF troops trucked in people from known Khmer Rouge-controlled zones to vote. Australian UN policeman Peter Baldwin said on at least one occasion, uniformed Khmer Rouge fighters put down their weapons outside polling stations before going in to vote. Most independent observers had little doubt that Khmer Rouge soldiers and their families who voted supported Funcinpec, which has said it would include the guerilla faction in a national reconciliation coalition government if it gained a majority.

Ngeth Sophan, the unofficial KPNLF administrator in Thmar Puok, may have been caught up in the understandable euphoria that accompanied the surprisingly smooth election when he commented: "We know the Khmer Rouge are not very strong. They cannot take over this area."

Other observers are less sanguine. They feel instinctively that the Khmer Rouge will remain a major force in the area after the election, whatever the ideology and composition of Cambodia's next government.

CAMBODIA

Survival Tactics

Khmer Rouge plans its post-poll strategy

Nate Thayer in Phnom Penh

In the aftermath of UN-sponsored elections, Khmer Rouge chief Pol Pot and his small collective leadership are hunkered down at a jungle base near the Thai border. In this remote camp, they are trying to come to terms with the hardest blow administered to the secretive faction since the Vietnamese invasion broke their grip on Cambodia 14 years ago.

The Khmer Rouge radio has yet to broadcast any reaction to the elections, while its missions abroad—which are usually sent daily updates of the leadership's political thinking—have received no instructions in the wake of the election. But interviews with Khmer Rouge leaders and internal documents suggest that the group is planning to maintain control over part of Cambodia's countryside and that it will press to be included in a government of national reconciliation.

While that may be the strategy, Khmer Rouge sources and other analysts agree that, for the time being, the group is isolated and vulnerable. Moreover, top Khmer Rouge leaders seem to be obsessed with a belief that the major powers and the other Cambodian parties are plotting to deliver a final blow designed to destroy or marginalise the faction.

They may well be right. A debate continues among the key foreign powers and Cambodian parties over whether the

Khmer Rouge should be offered a place within a new government, or whether a campaign should be launched to try to destroy it.

Many foreign analysts believe the Khmer Rouge has been significantly weakened since the Paris peace accords were signed in 1991, and see it as being incapable of raising an army strong enough to relaunch another civil war. UN Transitional Authority in Cambodia (Untac) analysts estimate the Khmer Rouge now fields fewer than 15,000 troops, compared to more than 30,000 before the peace accord.

However, despite this dramatic reduction in numbers, the Khmer Rouge organisation remains essentially intact throughout Cambodia. The faction is estimated to control more than 20% of the countryside, including areas rich in rice, gems and timber. These economically self-sufficient zones are competently administered, and have secure supply lines to willing Thai commercial partners that keep the group's finances buoyant.

Nor is there any evidence the Khmer Rouge treats the population of its zones any more harshly than the other factions treat those in areas under their control.

Nevertheless, while the Khmer Rouge may feel generally secure in its jungle fastness—regardless of what government is formed in Phnom Penh—analysts say the election process has undermined popular support and eroded morale. That could make it difficult for the leadership to spur its fighters back to war.

Even by its own terms, the election represents the group's worst case scenario. One effect of the poll has been to destroy the carefully nurtured group of domestic and international "united front" allies that kept the faction alive after it was driven out of Phnom Penh in 1979.

In a major policy speech to Khmer Rouge cadres in 1988, Pol Pot stressed the need for a "policy of great national solidarity and of garnering international strength" as the key to keeping the movement alive.

Without internal popular support, he warned, "we [would be] unable to maintain a grip on the people, we would not have any state jobs to do in the villages and the sub-districts, and by the same token we would not have any job to do in the parliament. Then who would protect our people and who would protect our ranks? If this was the way things were, then our ranks would . . . collapse and disintegrate."

This is essentially the position the Khmer Rouge now find itself in. In pulling out of the peace process the group mistakenly assumed that other major players, notably Prince Norodom Sihanouk and its two former guerilla allies—the pro-royalist Funcinpec and Son Sann's Buddhist Liberal Democratic Party (BDDP)—would follow suit in the face of government-sponsored electoral violence. Together, the Khmer Rouge hoped, they could form a strong coalition that would negate the elections and form a Sihanouk-led government in which all three factions were included.

But the return of Sihanouk from exile in Peking just days before the election, and Funcinpec's strong showing in the polls has left the Khmer Rouge with little leverage. The group's former alliances, which were and are essential to its survival, are evaporating. The faction no longer receives any material or political support from Peking, which has already announced that it will respect the election results.

Other countries, notably the US and those Western nations which supported the Khmer Rouge-dominated guerilla coalition during the Vietnamese occupation, are now trying to create a stable government in Phnom Penh that can defend itself against a Khmer Rouge threat. Funcinpec relied on the military strength of the Khmer Rouge during the war against the Vietnamese, but now finds its links with the faction a political liability.

In a February 1992 speech, Pol Pot outlined the dangers of such a scenario: "Democratic Kampuchea [the Khmer Rouge] cannot be strong all on it's own . . . An alliance [may be formed] between the West, the [Vietnamese], the contemptible puppets [the Hun Sen government], and two of the three parties [Funcinpec and BLDP]."

Pol Pot concluded that: "If this were the situation, then the Chinese, the Asean would have to accept it . . . That is why we need friends among the three parties until the day we die, and we need [foreign] friends until the day we die."

The faction has made clear what it wants. In a radio broadcast on 17 May, which was repeated on 29 May, the Khmer Rouge announced that it "fully, unconditionally and unswervingly" supported the creation of "a four-party provisional government of national reconciliation with Prince Sihanouk as head of state and prime minister."

The group also called for a "national reconciliation army made up of the Cambodian armed forces of the four factions . . . with Sihanouk as supreme commander."

The Khmer Rouge clings to the belief that during the coming months the election results will not lead to the formation of a stable government and Sihanouk will have to intervene. If this belief proves wrong, the movement could face permanent isolation. At worst, the Khmer Rouge might find itself the target of an internationally supported military campaign aimed at destroying—or at least marginalising—it.

A key factor in the situation is the attitude of Sihanouk himself. Sources say Sihanouk still believes that the Khmer Rouge must be included in a new government in order to avoid a return to conflict. They add that he has requested patience from Khmer Rouge and has sent messages to the faction since the elections. Sihanouk is said to be waiting until he is given real influence in the coming weeks to put together proposals that will mollify the faction's fears.

Perhaps it was in preparation for this moment that Pol Pot, in a message sent to supporters in March and obtained by the Review, offered some rare self-criticism. He acknowledged that during the Khmer Rouge's disastrous years in power during the 1970s, "we were immature and incapable of running a whole country."

However, in what must be seen [as] a warning, Pol Pot continued: "In 1979, we were on our death bed . . . Why didn't we die? Because even though we made a lot of mistakes, and had many enemies who hated us, we still had the capacity to gather forces . . . Our army was completely defeated and dismantled, but was rebuilt from the countryside. The necessity for us is the countryside, not communism."

This theme was reiterated in a Khmer Rouge statement dated 17 May: "Between the path for survival and the path for death, we choose the path for survival."

Despite the success represented by a high election Nateturnout, the Paris peace accords' aim of forging national reconciliation has yet to be achieved. Cambodia still faces the danger of partition, with the Khmer Rouge controlling enough of the countryside to sustain itself indefinitely.

The Next Great Leap

Vietnam's impoverished economy is poised to enter a period of rapid growth if multilateral aid resumes. But can it cope with all that kindness?

Murray Hiebert in Hanoi and Susumu Awanohara in Washington

After spending more than two years in Vietnam looking for business opportunities, the Hanoi representative of a giant South Korean firm is in no doubt about what the country requires. "For foreign investment to take off, you need better roads and ports, more reliable electricity and telecommunications," he says. "On this, Vietnam is still very poor."

The development of Vietnam's infrastructure cannot be done by foreign companies, according to the Korean businessman, who declines to be named. "This needs huge amounts of capital, which only the international financial institutions can provide," he says.

Those institutions stand ready to answer his call. Since the late 1980s, the IMF, World Bank and Asian Development Bank (ADB) have been sending teams to Vietnam to prepare their plans for the day that multilateral project lending, stalled since 1979, can resume.

Vietnam's long wait may end soon. During a series of IMF meetings starting on 28 April, board members will discuss whether to resume aid to Vietnam. Some of the most powerful members of the fund—France, Japan, Germany—have said they intend to push for the recommencement of aid. But the most powerful of all, the US, has not officially changed its opposition to such a move. America has still not exorcised the ghost of the Vietnam War and it now has a president, Bill Clinton, who was alleged during last year's election campaign to have avoided being drafted into the war. Despite this, there have been signs that the US administration is changing its stance not only on the question of aid to Vietnam, but also on the trade embargo that has been in force against the north since 1964 and against the whole country since 1975.

But Washington may now harden its position at the IMF, following newspaper reports about the discovery of secret Vietnamese documents purportedly showing that Hanoi may have lied to the US in the 1970s about how many American prisoners it was holding.

Even if the US blocks multilateral aid at this latest meeting, as it has for the past four years, it still looks as if 1993 will be the year when Vietnam is allowed fully to rejoin the world economy. Clinton may well decide not to renew the trade embargo in September. And the UN Development Programme (UNDP) and the World Bank are preparing to sponsor a meeting of aid donors to Vietnam, due to take place in Geneva in the last quarter of the year.

But the IMF meeting is seen as the crucial first step. "Access to IMF resources would serve as a catalyst for the flow of capital from other sources," observes Erich Spitaeller, the IMF's resident representative in Hanoi. "It would help reassure investors that the country was embarked on the right economic path."

It is hard to underestimate the effects on Vietnam of a resumption of multilateral aid and an expansion of trade. Decades of war and Soviet-style central planning beggared the economy. The US ban on Vietnamese trade and aid, designed to pressure Hanoi into accounting for American servicemen missing in action, hobbled the country's attempts to escape from poverty.

Since 1986, however, Vietnam's leaders have embarked on a series of radical reforms, which, as in China, are designed to modernise the economy while preserving the dominance of the Communist Party. Farm output is growing, privately owned factories are springing up and foreign investment is flowing in.

Yet Vietnam's infrastructure, social as well as physical, is in tatters. Without better roads and plentiful supplies of electricity, private investors will find it hard to tap the country's highly educated workforce and its oil wealth. So aid and more trade could provide a shot of adrenalin.

The country's leaders regard foreign aid as indispensable to meet their economic goals. Premier Vo Van Kiet told the National Assembly last December that the government wants to double living standards by 2000. This, he said, would require investment of US$4 billion a year in order to achieve annual GDP growth of 9.5%, while the population is growing at a rate of 2.2% a year. Half that money is expected to come from inside the country and half from outside—much of it in the form of government assistance.

But not everybody regards aid as essential. After all, observers note, Vietnam's economy managed to grow 8.3% last year, a sharp increase from 4.7% in 1991. Annual inflation has fallen from 680% in 1986 to 18% last year. The currency has stabilised and official reserves are growing. Even Vietnam's trade deficit virtually disappeared in 1992. Not bad for a country that one year earlier had suffered the sudden disappearance of US$1 billion of annual Soviet non-military aid, as well as the continued US trade embargo.

Even a few foreign-aid officials and Vietnamese technocrats wonder whether the country needs huge amounts of additional financial assistance from overseas. In the first 11 months of last year, Hanoi received US$300 million in aid from UN agencies and other donors. Then in November, Japan pledged ¥ 45.5 billion (US$390 million), partly to pay off the Japanese portion of Vietnam's arrears on US$4.6 billion of convertible-currency

Reprinted by permission from *Far Eastern Economic Review,* April 22, 1993, pp. 68-71.

On the Right Track

Although Vietnam's economic growth is rising, inflation and the fiscal deficit have dropped. The currency has strengthened and trade is almost in balance

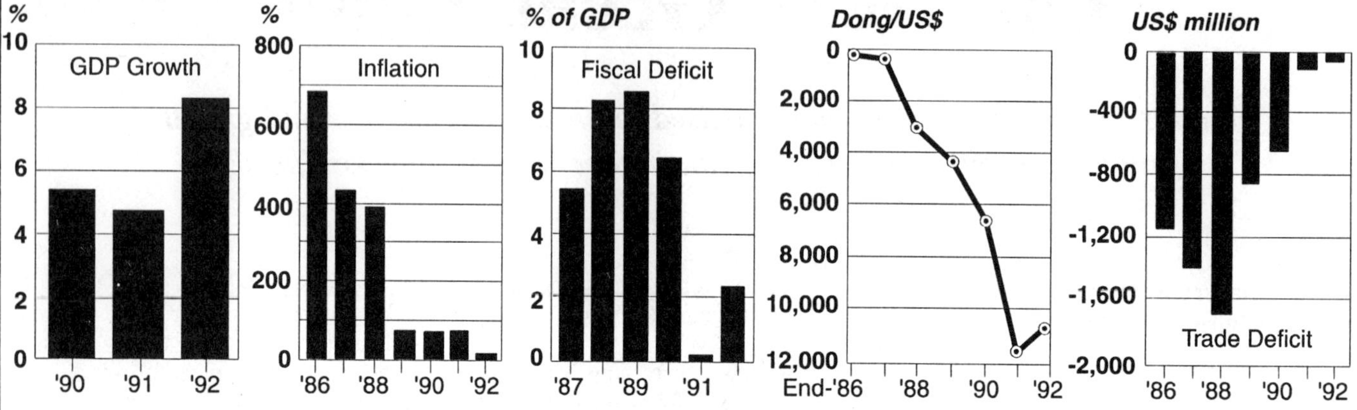

Sources: IMF, Institute for Research on Market and Prices, Smith New Court, State Bank of Vietnam, Ministry of Trade

Ringo Chung

debt. If aid from multilateral institutions were to start up, the total inflow would probably rise to more than US$1 billion a year.

Such sums would keep aid officials busy for years. "The World Bank is always looking for new clients and trying to push money on them," argues an American working for an international financial institution in Washington. "But Vietnam can push domestic reform further without multilateral aid. It might even be good for Vietnam not to have access to aid," he says.

But most local officials and foreign observers disagree. "Vietnam is on the verge of a great leap forward," argues a British official with an international aid agency, "but it hasn't leapt forward yet. It is still a poor country and has accumulated arrears. It needs assistance. The question really is the pace at which aid can be absorbed."

One businessman who concurs is John Brinsden, the representative in Ho Chi Minh City of Britain's Standard Chartered Bank. "The first US$3 billion in infrastructure development will encourage more foreign investors," he says. "We'll see a snowball effect once they know a bridge won't collapse or that they'll have a hospital for their expatriate staff."

Hanoi lacks the resources needed to upgrade the country's infrastructure to the level required by investors. Although the telecommunications network is being modernised with earnings from long-distance calls, Hanoi needs grant aid or soft loans to tackle most of its other infrastructure bottlenecks.

Transport is a key area. Vietnam requires at least US$3 billion merely to prevent a further deterioration of its roads, ports, rail network and inland waterways. Another US$4 billion would be needed to upgrade these facilities to cope with the level of traffic anticipated by 2000, says Dao Xuan Lam, director of the Transport Engineering Design Institute, which has studied the country's transport needs.

An inventory of Vietnam's infrastructure makes dismal reading:

► **Roads.** Only 10% of Vietnam's 105,000 kilometres of roads is paved. Roads around major cities have not been maintained and Highway One, the country's north-south artery, has only a single lane in each direction. About 830 of the country's communes cannot be reached by road.

► **Bridges.** At least one-third of Vietnam's bridges need major repairs or should be replaced, Lam's study says.

► **Ports.** The cargo-handling equipment in the country's two major ports—Saigon in the south and Haiphong in the north—is run down. Haiphong has difficulty receiving large vessels because the country lacks dredgers to clear silt from the harbour.

► **Electricity.** Energy poses another difficulty, particularly in Ho Chi Minh City, where electricity demand is growing 10% a year. The city suffered brownouts four days a week between March and June of last year. Hanoi loses a quarter of its electricity because power lines have not been maintained.

► **Social welfare.** The government can no longer afford to finance the country's social programmes. Morale has plummeted among poorly paid teachers, and large numbers of children have dropped out of school. Hospitals do not have enough drugs and equipment.

Lack of resources is not the only reason why the physical fabric of Vietnam's economy is so badly frayed. In the first flush of optimism following the unification of the country in 1975, much of the aid supplied was squandered on "white elephant projects. A paper mill in Bai Bang in the north, supplied in the early 1980s with Swedish aid, ran out of raw materials, and had to import them from abroad.

The Soviet Government helped build the Xuan Hoa industrial city, 30 kilometres from Hanoi, but failed to attract much investment. These days, officials describe the city as "dying." The 3.2-km Thanh Long bridge near Hanoi is hardly used because it is located on the west side of the city and most people want to head east.

Vietnam is having a hard time learning from its mistakes. A current project to build a 1,500-km electricity line costing US$500 million raises disturbing questions about whether Vietnam is equipped to handle new aid. Construction of the line, from Hoa Binh power station near Hanoi to Ho Chi Minh City, was begun early last year, even before a feasibility study had been completed to see how long the north would have an energy surplus to send to the south. The project has been plagued by corruption and strong domestic opposition.

"It's a misconception of this one-party state to think you're dealing with a monolith," says a foreign economist. "In this period of transition, there are many centres of power and influence."

To avoid similar problems with credits from the international financial institutions, World Bank and ADB consultants have been working with Hanoi's State Planning Commission to prepare a list of key projects so that the banks can "hit the ground running once we're allowed to operate." The first phase of multilateral assistance will be spent on upgrading the existing infrastructure. Nobody knows what the money will be spent on after that.

"All we have is a lot of separate, isolated proposals and wishes," says a Vietnamese government economist. "We haven't prepared a master plan indicating which projects are most important to the overall economy."

One problem is that the country lacks technocrats and managers to set priorities and formulate and execute projects. "We're desperately short of capital, but in my opinion our biggest difficulty is the lack of economic know-how," says Nguyen Thanh Bang of the National Institute for Scientific and Technological Forecasting.

During the decades of war, most resources were ploughed into training military officers, and when peace finally came, most bureaucrats went to the former Soviet Union to learn socialist economics. It is only in the past few years that international agencies have been educating officials about how free markets work.

Foreign specialists give high marks to Vietnamese technocrats for their willingness to learn. "I have not found any other country where participants come from such senior levels, where they are so highly motivated and attend [classes] so regularly," says Vinyu Vichit-Vadakan, a private consultant from Thailand who trains Vietnamese officials for the World Bank. Even ministers have attended entire courses.

The list of economic achievements is already considerable. Agrarian reforms have enabled Vietnam to become a big rice exporter. Financial reforms have stabilised prices and the currency. The economy has received US$1.2 billion in foreign investment and boasts one of the most liberal investment codes in the developing world. "If you look at all of the economies making the transition from planning to the market, Vietnam stands out as one of the most successful," says a World Bank official.

But the country still has a long way to go. Hanoi has to grasp the nettle of its loss-making state enterprises. More reforms are required before Vietnamese have confidence in the banking system. And capitalist laws need to be introduced and enforced to persuade local businessmen that the authorities will not at some point confiscate their enterprises.

"The bureaucracy is still half way between a command economy and the free market system," says a European economist with an international institution in Hanoi. The question is: can foreign aid carry it the rest of the way?

Plugging The Gap

Vietnam's communist leaders have seen what China's economy has achieved in the past decade and want to emulate it—their GDP growth target is 9.5% a year until 2000. One World Bank official feels this target is "a bit ambitious, but not off the wall."

For their part, economists at the World Bank and IMF believe a more conservative 8% expansion rate would be more likely for Vietnam over this period, according to unpublished documents obtained by the REVIEW. Both institutions assume there will be a resumption of multilateral aid this year and that the US trade embargo will eventually be lifted. But although they agree on the likely pace of the economy, they differ on the amount of aid that will be needed in order to grow by 8% a year.

The bank reckons the so-called resource gap (the amount of money required from aid donors to reach a given economic growth rate) will rise from US$275 million this year to US$869 million in 1997. The fund is projecting a resource gap of US$61 million in 1993, growing to US$529 million four years later. But the fund expects a much larger inflow than the World Bank to come from official grants—as opposed to concessional bilateral and multilateral aid which comprises the resource gap.

Both agencies are forecasting a similar increase in foreign direct investment over this period—from US$270 million this year to US$640 million in 1997—while disagreeing in their forecasts for trade. Both foresee that Vietnam's trade deficit will increase over the next few years. But the bank expects it to grow to US$1.3 billion by 1997, while the IMF is looking for a trade deficit of US$515 million by then.

These differences are more than a question of arithmetic. Sources close to the IMF say that the World Bank's projected resource gap grows too rapidly for Vietnam's good. Too large a capital inflow could revive inflation and create bottlenecks in the economy, they say.

A number of things could upset the institutions' forecasts. Vietnam's oil exports, which reached about US$780 million last year, 40% more than the 1991 level, could grow even faster than people expect. A consortium of Western oil companies has recently won the right to develop the highly promising Big Bear field off the coast of southern Vietnam.

Tax revenue and domestic investment may pick up, if only because they are so low in the first place. Taxes comprise only 15% of GDP and Vietnamese are hoarding US$1 billion in gold and hard currency, waiting for the introduction of capitalist laws in the country before investing, says a government economist.

Whatever the outcome, Vietnam is unlikely to join the ranks of Asia's tigers for a good while yet. Fuzzy official estimates put the country's living standard at US$200 a head, half that of China and a third of Indonesia's.

Even so, some foreign firms have faith in the country. The German car maker BMW said on 7 April that it will set up a sales network in Vietnam and in 1994 will start assembling its cars there.

■ **Susumu Awanohara and Murray Hiebert**

Ready to Help

Agencies prepare their menus of projects

If the Clinton administration allows the IMF to normalise its relations with Hanoi, a host of new aid and credit options would open up to help launch Vietnam's economy onto its next stage of development. Economists expect that an IMF-funded economic restructuring programme will be followed by loans from the World Bank and the Asian Development Bank (ADB) as well as from major bilateral and commercial creditors.

Once the IMF board agrees to restore Hanoi's eligibility for lending from the fund—it was suspended in 1985 after Hanoi fell into arrears with the institution the previous year—Vietnam would be allowed to settle its US$140 million debt to the IMF. France's Banque Francaise du Commerce Exterieur has already prepared a bridging loan for Hanoi, while France, Japan, Sweden and Australia have pledged to help Vietnam settle this debt.

After these arrears are repaid, Hanoi would become eligible for new credits from the IMF at near-market interest rates. At the same time, the IMF is likely to begin working with Vietnamese officials and the World Bank to develop a structural adjustment programme that would include long-term credits. The fund may provide US$50–100 million a year in loans.

Vietnam's normalisation of relations with the IMF will also be followed by meetings to reschedule the country's outstanding hard-currency debts, which totalled US$4.6 billion at thc end of last year. Most foreign creditors have been unwilling to provide new credits to Vietnam until the old debt is rescheduled, though a few countries such as Japan have broken ranks and resumed lending.

Washington's green light would also open the door for the resumption of concessional loans from the World Bank and the ADB. The World Bank, which can be expected to supply US$300–350 million a year in soft loans, has been studying aid priorities in the fields of energy, transport, irrigation, telecommunications and water supply.

The ADB is engaged in similar preparations and will probably lend Vietnam about US$200–250 million a year. In northern Vietnam, it is planning to lend money to repair the dyke protecting Hanoi from flooding and to modernise the capital's electricity grid, says Richard Vokes, the ADB's economist on Vietnam.

In southern Vietnam, the ADB plans to help upgrade the Saigon port, rehabilitate Ho Chi Minh City's water supplies and refurbish Highway One, the country's main north-south road. The bank is also preparing a project to help train teachers and improve school buildings.

Among bilateral donors, Japan will be the biggest, providing US$300–400 million a year, followed by France with US$60 million and Sweden with US$50 million. The US is said to be studying the possibility of providing US$25 million a year, mainly in technical help through the US Agency for International Development, though agency officials decline to confirm this.

■ **Murray Hiebert and Susumu Awanohara**

Out of the ditch

For the first time, all six countries of Central America are living more or less peacefully under elected governments that are pursuing free-market policies. One doubt: can they keep it up?

EVER since Central America was liberated from three centuries of Spanish colonial rule in 1821, the isthmus has had a tormented history of military dictatorships and occasional democratic experiments. It was dismissed by the rest of the world as small, backward and therefore inconsequential. All that [...] Reagan decided to [...] the imminent com[...] Salvador. He then [...] as the actual comm[...] gua. The world su[...] Central America's [...]

The images of [...] stark: tortured vi[...]

thrown into ravines in El Salvador; villagers slaughtered in Guatemala; "contra" rebels massed in Honduras on the Nicaraguan border; arbitrary arrests, land confiscations and press censorship by Nicaragua's Sandinists; and, in Panama, brutality and drug-trafficking under General Manuel [...] Of the six Spanish-speaking coun-[...]

Salvador is starting to consolidate it; and Guatemala nearly has it. Every Central American president has been freely elected (although the guerrillas have not voted in El Salvador and Guatemala). Governments are on good terms with the International Monetary Fund, the World Bank and the Inter-American Development Bank, and apply policies approved by these bodies with considerable success. Their inflation rates are all relatively low. All six countries are members of the GATT.

For the first time, the presidents and ministers of the six countries these days meet their equivalents in summit sessions, EC-style, every six months. They know each other as well as EC ministers do. Guatemala, El Salvador and Honduras will launch a free-trade area next year.

Outsiders can fairly be sceptical. This quiet revolution is only a few years old. Central America is notorious for corruption, violence, instability and a low level of government and business expertise. Democracy has been tried before and failed. So has economic integration. Having climbed out of the ditch, the region, or parts of it at least, could fall back in again. Yet what has been done is remarkable, and deserves more attention than the world has given it. Let good news, for a change, be news.

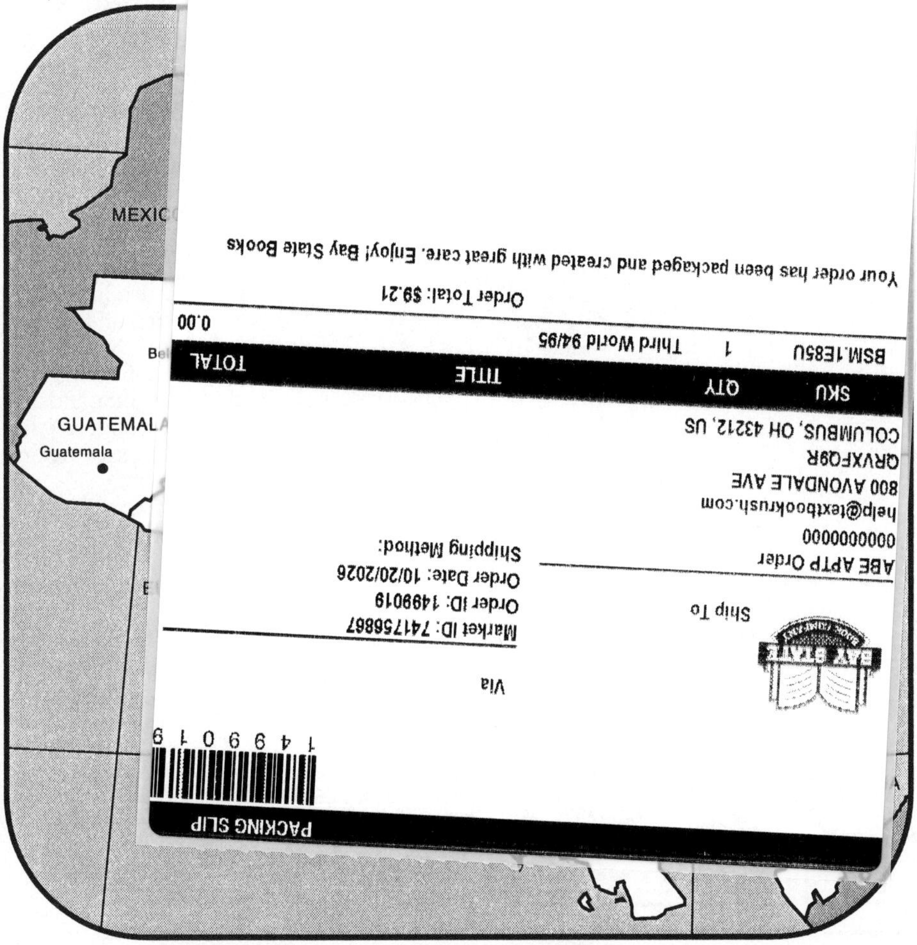

Too close to the Sandinists

One country of the six has had plentiful media attention: Nicaragua, whose Sandinist regime was shoved by the United States into allowing free elections in 1990, and then, to its bewildered rage, lost them. Alas, this is one country where good news is already turning sour again.

It will probably be decades before Nicaragua is at peace with itself. Under the Somoza dynasty (1933-1979), it was polarised between haters and lovers of the Somozas. After 1979 it was split between old-fashioned democrats and the Sandinists. Under Mrs Violeta Chamorro, who won the presidency in 1990, national reconciliation has come nearer. She is a symbol of Nicaragua's history: widow of a murdered anti-Somoza hero, and publisher of the anti-Sandinist newspaper, *La Prensa*. One son and daughter are Sandinists, another son and daughter are anti-Sandinists.

In a conciliatory gesture after her election—too conciliatory by half, some think—Dona Violeta (as she is universally known) abandoned the anti-Sandinists who had helped her win. She allowed the Sandinist General Humberto Ortega to stay on as head of the armed forces, and the Sandinist René Vivas to keep his job as police chief. Lenin Cerna, head of the former secret police, is now chief of military intelligence. But General Ortega has co-operated, cutting the army from 80,000 men to 19,000.

The word is: avoid confrontation. When the interior minister, Carlos Hurtado, tried to make his overwhelmingly Sandinist-run ministry non-political, and to make the police more professional, he received no support from Dona Violeta and resigned. The Ortegas' power seems to be growing. Daniel boasts of "governing from below" and warns of a "social uprising" when he wants to get his way. Humberto is alleged to stir up demobilised and land-hungry soldiers and contras. Dona Violeta and her right-hand man (and son-in-law), Antonio Lacayo, do not seem to realise how they have weakened themselves by alienating their allies among anti-Sandinist businessmen and farmers, and by talking mostly to the Ortegas.

Mr Lacayo's strategy worked for two years. In the first, he achieved internal peace, apart from some Sandinist strikes, land-grabs and disorders. In the second, stratospheric inflation was sharply lowered; by now it has been almost eliminated. Privatisation began (160 state enterprises will be sold this year). A 1990 fiscal deficit of 14% of GDP became in 1991 a slight surplus, which will probably be repeated this year. Western aid rolled in at $600m a year. A mission to the World Bank to seek aid was accompanied by a helpful Daniel Ortega.

This is Mr Lacayo's third year, when investment, domestic and foreign, was expected to help the economy start to grow again. It has not happened. The reason lies in what Nicaraguans call the *pinata*. When a child has a birthday party, the parents fill a bag with sweets and hang it up. The child thwacks it, the sweets spill out and the party-goers grab them. Between Dona Violeta's election and her inauguration, the outgoing Sandinists offered their pals a *pinata*.

Sandinist hangers-on who had not already grabbed a home were given one or allowed to buy one for a derisory sum. Government cars were handed out to lesser flunkeys. The presidential offices were cleared out, except for a couple of rocking chairs painted in violet. There was next to nothing in the central bank, where officials reckon some $6 billion in aid is unaccounted for. The Sandinists are still sitting in their new homes and cars. Unsurprisingly, potential investors are sitting on their hands.

Slow and unsure in El Salvador

Peace and democracy were slow to reach El Salvador. The first break came in 1980, when Napoleon Duarte, the Christian Democratic leader, agreed to share power with the army while elections were prepared. An election for a constituent assembly was held in 1982. Duarte won a presidential election two years later. Death squads did their worst, but their toll was cut. Civilian government took root. It was consolidated when Freddy Cristiani, of Arena, the opposition Nationalist Renewal Alliance, won the presidential election in 1989.

With the help of the UN, Mr Cristiani made peace with the guerrillas last December, after 11 years of civil war and the loss of some 60,000 lives. The hard part is making peace work. Everything is behind schedule or tricky. The government was meant to "suppress" its notorious treasury police and the para-military national guard. Instead it gave them new names and new jobs.

The guerrillas cried foul, but did little better themselves. American sources say their list of weapons to be handed over is a third of what they have. Nor did the guerrillas assemble in agreed areas to be assimilated into civilian life. They grabbed scores of farms after the peace pact was signed. Even so, the government insists that the peace process is working. "Not a shot has been fired this year," claims the president's spokesman.

El Salvador is still in deep trouble: world prices for coffee and cotton are in a slump, and the country's biggest source of foreign exchange, around $800m a year, is remittances from Salvadorans living in the United States. Many are there illegally, and have been facing deportation. They have just been given an extension of a year, to Mr Cristiani's great relief. But they will have to come back to El Salvador eventually.

The economy is nonetheless improving, and will be boosted this year by the peace agreement. Mr Cristiani is privatising banks that Mr Duarte nationalised: three have been sold and the remaining two will go this year. State-run monopolies for the export of coffee and cotton have been dismantled. By the end of 1991, inflation had fallen to about 10% from 19% a year earlier. The target this year is 8%. Foreign exchange reserves have risen to about $400m.

More foreign aid is pouring in, thanks to the work of the development minister, Mrs Mirna Lievano, whose persuasion (yes, and perhaps her striking good looks) so impressed donors at a recent meeting in Washington that they agreed to part with $800m over five years.

Nobody cries for Noriega

Panama is enjoying both democracy and peace for the first time since 1968, when Colonel Omar Torrijos seized power. It owes them, paradoxically, to a bloody but short, sharp and effective piece of violence. In Operation Just Cause, which ended in January 1990, the United States carried off the local strongman, General Manuel Noriega, to Florida to be tried for drug-trafficking, and installed in his place the easy-going and unfashionably tubby Guillermo Endara, who had been robbed by Mr Noriega of victory in the 1989 presidential election.

President Endara has chosen to be easy-going because he wants the country to relearn the democratic experience. Even when his own young and unpredictable wife, Anna Mae, publicly criticises aspects of the government, he declares, like any politically correct *norteamericano* husband, that she has every right as a citizen to do so. When Panama's gutter press insults him, he turns the other cheek. His rival, Mr Ricardo Arias Calderon, who leads the Christian Democratic Party, says Mr Endara has restored the nepotism of the pre-Torrijos era. Some Panamanians agree with him. The president's standing in one opinion poll has fallen from 32% in 1990 to 12%.

Mr Arias Calderon was part of the

Better, mostly

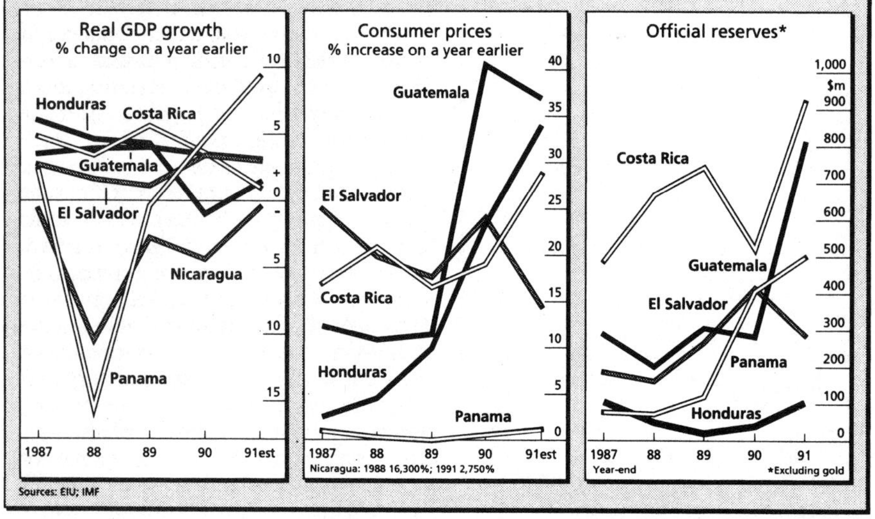

Sources: EIU; IMF

Endara coalition at the start, and, as interior minister, created a new police force. But the mixture was oil and water. Mr Endara and his planning minister, Guillermo (Billy) Ford, are by nature political fixers. Mr Arias Calderon has an amiably episcopal manner, talks in paragraphs and likes to quote from papal encyclicals. The relationship became strained, then snapped. Mr Arias Calderon, who would like to be the next president, now controls a slight majority in the legislative assembly. Usually he co-operates with the government.

Mr Endara lets things slip. He has done little about an impending social explosion in impoverished Balboa, Panama's second city. Privatisation is slow. Nothing has been done to develop land and the railway alongside the Panama Canal that the Americans handed over. But the economy, brought to its knees in the Noriega era, is recovering. GDP grew by 9.3% in 1991. The fiscal deficit was cut from 11% of GDP in 1990 to 3.4% in 1991, and the budget is now said to be roughly in balance. The near-bankrupt social-security administration has been reorganised. Inflation is higher than it used to be, but at only 2.6% that is no great worry. Arrears owed to the World Bank and IMF have been cleared. Import tariffs are coming down from 60% to 40% for manufactures and from 90% to 50% for farm products.

The controller-general, Ruben Carles, a gravel-voiced retired banker previously at Chase Manhattan, brandishes computer print-outs to prove his point as he holds down government spending. He is known as "the man with the iron fist". Mr Carles has introduced a new and irritating concept to Panama: tendering for public contracts.

Still unsettled is Panama's $1.3-billion commercial-bank debt. Mr Carles says it will have to wait. But Panama badly needs foreign investment. To reassure foreigners, some influential Panamanians want to ask the United States to leave some soldiers protecting the canal after it hands over in 2000. The country might do better by electing Mr Arias Calderon as president in 1994.

Guatemala's generals get the bullet

Democracy in Guatemala has by now survived, and grown stronger, for six years. The first elected president, Vinicio Cerezo, a Christian Democrat, lasted a full presidential term partly by not facing up to the armed forces and the death squads. His successor, Jorge Serrano, has fired two defence ministers (both generals), the air force chief and the commander of the Guatemala City garrison. A colonel in charge of the police, who had been accused of permitting torture, was replaced by a civilian lawyer. About 1,000 policemen have been fired for alleged corruption. The government wants to send a judge to every municipality.

The vice-president, Gustavo Espina, proudly told *The Economist* that "since we have been in office not one trade-union leader, and only one university professor, has been murdered". But an observer appointed by the UN Commission for Human Rights describes the military police and army-backed civil self-defence patrols as "an element of uncontrolled violence". A human-rights campaign is under way.

Guatemala has an ugly tradition of right-wingers who think they see reds under the bed, shoot first and ask no questions. The president reckons he controls 75% of the army (Mr Cerezo did not think he controlled it at all). The out-of-control 25% may have planted the dozen or so bombs that were found in the capital in May. The left-wing guerrillas, who amount to no more than 1,500 fighters, are no real military threat. But their existence discourages tourism and investment. Sporadic peace talks have yet to bear fruit.

For all these troubles, here is another country whose economy is improving. Inflation is down from an annual rate of 60% in December 1990 to 10% in 1991, and may drop to 8% this year. GDP grew by 3.5% in 1991, and may grow by 4.2% this year. The public-sector deficit fell from 3.8% of GDP in 1990 to 1.7% last year. A law to increase tax collections has passed Congress. Foreign-exchange reserves have risen from $275m in January 1991 to $850m, more than six months of imports, and tariffs are being cut.

Refloating USS Honduras

As in Guatemala, democracy in Honduras has lasted six years. Military rule ended officially in 1980, when Roberto Suazo, an amiable country doctor, won the presidency. But he had to cede power to the commander of the armed forces, who was accused of allowing death squads a loose rein. The army—and the United States—exerted considerable influence over the next president, Jose Azcona de Hoyo, during the Honduras-based contras' war against the Sandinists in Nicaragua, and the country came to be known as *USS Honduras*.

Within these constraints, Mr Azcona still ran Honduras in a democratic manner. But it was only in 1989, when a young, American-educated reformist, Rafael Callejas, won the presidency, that Honduras began to look like an independent country. The security forces are still being accused of murdering land-hungry peasants and labour activists—although on only three occasions since 1991. Mr Callejas has shaken up the economy, and Honduras, though still impoverished, is no longer living hand-to-mouth on international aid.

Inflation roared temporarily up in 1990, under an economic stabilisation plan. At the cost of a period of stagnation in GDP, prices were then reined in. They have been rising at around 1% a month for the past six months. Foreign-exchange reserves have gone from $21m when Mr Callejas took office to $180m. Arrears at the IMF and World Bank have been paid off, with a little help from Honduras's friends. Tax collection has improved, and the fiscal deficit has declined from 8.5% of GDP in 1990 to 3.8% last year. Import tariffs have been cut to a range of 4-35%. Honduras has a long way to go, but it is on the move.

Constitutional Costa Rica

Costa Rica, by Central American standards, is a most peculiar place. It has had a constitutional government since 1920, apart from a blip in 1948. It has had no army since 1948. Its health service and old-age pensions, though below most first-world levels, are far superior to anything else available in the region. There is a doctor for every 1,000 people. About 27% of the budget goes on health and 17% on education. The rate of illiteracy is 7%.

Such virtues have their cost. The fiscal deficit in 1982 was around 15% of GDP. That had to be cut, and it has been: to less than 4% of GDP in 1988, and, after a surge under President Oscar Arias, now to 2%. Inflation remains high—by first-world standards—but at least it is well down from the 100% a year or so of the early 1980s. President Rafael Calderon is cutting import tariffs to a maximum of 20% in 1993. The currency is floating. A debt-reduction package has been agreed with commercial banks and official creditors. Costa Rica is in good shape.

Can they stay on track?

Since survival is the politician's first art, the rigour that has proved so successful in Central America will always be under threat. More vigorous tax collection, tight monetary control, elimination of subsidies and purges of unnecessary state employees are not vote-winners. But, for now at least, the region's leaders can afford to be brave. Inflation seems today to be the key to public support, and it is down throughout the isthmus to respectable levels. Exchange rates are stable. Economic growth is still too low, but it will surely come, with the aid of foreign investment, once governments have established reasonable records of economic competence and political stability.

Investors will see an added attraction if part of Central America can become a free-trade area and talk about still closer union. It would help too if the governments of the region were to pursue offers of free trade with Mexico and Venezuela.

Where will it all lead? The target must be sound public finance coupled with a stable business climate that encourages sustained, non-inflationary growth. The trouble, as in many third-world countries, will be staying on track while that is achieved. As even the World Bank puts it, Central America has a "tremendous deficit in social services" and urgently needs a "safety net for the poor". That advice is easy for rich countries to accept, not for poor ones. Will the poorest of Central America's citizens wait patiently until the benefits of growth reach them too?

In early 1992, President Fujimori announced a "self-coup" that startled international observers. "By the end of the year, having weathered a counter-coup attempt by the military. . .and having boosted his new political vehicle to a majority position in constituent assembly elections. . . , Fujimori was riding high. To an even greater degree than previously, however, he was also riding roughshod over his political enemies."

Peru's Fujimori: A Caudillo Derails Democracy

CYNTHIA MCCLINTOCK

CYNTHIA MCCLINTOCK *is a professor of political science at George Washington University. She is the author of* Peasant Cooperatives and Political Change in Peru *(Princeton, N.J.: Princeton University Press, 1981) and with Abraham Lowenthal, co-editor of* The Peruvian Experiment Reconsidered *(Princeton, N.J.: Princeton University Press, 1983). She is presently completing a book comparing the origins of revolutionary movements in Peru and El Salvador.*

On April 5, 1992, Peru's 11-year-old democracy was shattered by President Alberto Fujimori. Fujimori, who had been duly elected 20 months earlier, suspended the 1979 constitution, arrested several opposition leaders, padlocked congress, and dismantled the judiciary. The *autogolpe* (coup by the president's own hand) was supported by the majority of military officials and business elites, and most important, by the Peruvian people. Fujimori emerged a new caudillo, destroying the conventional wisdom that institutions, whether civilian or military, had become more important than individual leaders in Peru and elsewhere in Latin America.

While the vast majority of intellectuals and political leaders condemned the coup, Fujimori's move was supported by most citizens; the president's approval rating stood at 60 percent or higher throughout the year. Most Peruvians seemed to believe that the democratic regime as it had been fashioned had failed. Since 1980, when the first presidential elections in 17 years were held, living standards had plummeted and political violence had surged. International concern with the Peruvian people's plight had been minimal at best (primarily because the nation's two presidents during the 1980s failed to reach international agreements about servicing the foreign debt, to shift toward freer markets, or to advance significantly in the drug war). Suffering drastically more severe poverty and more pervasive political terror than at the onset of the 1980 constitutional regime, Peruvians believed that, after 11 years, it was time for a change.

Yet, while Peruvians wanted an improvement in their lives, they were not clear about the political means to that end. Democracy was not being rejected in principle. President Fujimori based the legitimacy of his "Government of Emergency and National Reconstruction" in part on a promise to build a "true democracy," and emphasized popular support for his measures: "In Peru it is the people who are sovereign." And indeed, a majority of Peruvians expressed the view that the Fujimori government was "democratic."

By August, it appeared dubious that Fujimori was suffciently improving conditions to retain power. The economy remained in desperate straits. Preliminary estimates for 1992 suggested a decline of about 3 percent in gross domestic product. Wages, salaries, and employment—which had fallen to rock-bottom levels after the 1990 economic reform labeled "Fujishock"—had not recovered. Especially after unprecedentedly large and bloody terrorist attacks in Lima in July, the Shining Path (Sendero Luminoso) guerrilla movement appeared to be inexorably approaching its goal of taking over the state. An effective anti-drug effort seemed as illusory as ever.

But, on September 12, 1992, Abimael Guzmán Reynoso, the founder and leader of the Shining Path, was captured in his Lima hideout by the National Directorate Against Terrorism (DINCOTE). Not only was Guzmán captured, but many other key Sendero leaders were as well. Although President Fujimori had not even been notified of the pending capture of the Shining Path leader, he claimed credit for an impeccable police operation that transformed Peru's political equations overnight.

By the end of the year, having weathered a counter-coup attempt by the military on November 13 and having boosted his new political vehicle to a majority position in constituent assembly elections on November 22, Fujimori was riding high. To an even greater degree than previously, however, he was also riding roughshod over his political enemies. While the president seemed likely to continue to govern, a more militant domestic political opposition also seemed likely.

AN ERODING DEMOCRACY

Political analysts talk of "new democracies" as if they are more vulnerable than older democracies. But, by the early 1990s, Peru's democratic institutions were actually weaker than they had been a decade before. The primary reasons for their erosion were twofold: the economic plummet and human-rights abuses by guerrillas and security forces.

Peru's economic decline over the last decade is unparalleled in South America. By 1989, the real minimum wage was a mere 23 percent of its value in 1980, in contrast to a 75 percent figure for the region as a whole. The decline in Peru's real minimum wage was the steepest by 13 percentage points among the 19 Latin American nations for which figures were reported. Moreover, after the "Fujishock," wages plunged further to barely half 1989 levels. By mid-1991, "critical poverty" (specified as a per capita income of $15.50 per month in a nation where the cost-of-living is as high as it is in the United States) afflicted about half the population. The Fujimori government failed to implement a social emergency program that might have assured at least some subsistence for the country's citizens.

The economic disaster eroded Peruvian democracy in various ways. Without resources, the state was no longer providing the services that are a customary source of legitimacy. Dismally paid state employees (including soldiers, police, and judges) were demoralized, and more likely to be tempted by bribes and extortion schemes. Also, since workers were more fearful of losing their jobs, they were less active in labor unions, traditionally a major means of political participation. Increasingly compelled to work numerous jobs and/or offer services informally, Peruvians had little or no time for civic organization.

The Shining Path's expansion also eroded the democratic state. A key guerrilla strategy was to target leaders who opposed them or represented an alternative. Between 1988 and August 1992, more than 400 political authorities were killed by terrorists; accordingly, local authorities were increasingly absent from rural areas, or beholden to the guerrillas. In 1991 and 1992, the Shining Path more frequently targeted civic leaders, such as priests and leaders of community food programs. One of the group's most egregious crimes was the killing on February 15, 1992, of community activist María Elena Moyano during a celebration for the "glass-of-milk" program in Villa El Salvador, a shantytown that was traditionally a stronghold of the democratic political left; terrorists dynamited her body to pieces in front of her children. Said a community organizer: "We were practically defeated by fear."

By the early 1990s, more than half of Peru's citizens were living in "emergency zones." In most of these zones, military officials were the maximum authority, and human-rights abuses were flagrant. The number of individuals disappeared or extrajudicially executed by Peruvian security forces was estimated at 328 in 1990 and 399 in 1991—making Peru's human-rights record the worst in the Western Hemisphere. As travel by journalists and human-rights monitors to conflicted areas became ever more perilous and as victims' relatives became more fearful of reporting violations, the actual number of disappearances and extrajudicial executions was probably greater than the official figures showed.[1]

Peru's major political parties were debilitated, having failed to lead effectively or build solid networks of supporters. The parties that had governed during the 1980s—Popular Action (AP) in alliance with the Popular Christian party (PPC) between 1980 and 1985 and the American Popular Revolutionary Alliance (APRA) from 1985 to 1990—were perceived to have performed badly and were widely discredited. For much of 1990 and 1991, APRA and its former president, Alan García Pérez, were mired in charges of corruption. The only other major parties that had been active throughout the 1980s that were still competing in the 1990 election were leftist; these parties had constituted the United Left, but by 1990 this coalition had ruptured. Of course, the left was also weakened by the demise of the Soviet bloc and increasing ideological uncertainty.

Nor was Fujimori's party, Cambio '90 (Change '90), well organized or coherent.[2] Formed for the 1990 elections as Fujimori's political vehicle, its members were politically inexperienced. The party brought together primarily small-business groups and Peru's evangelical Protestant community (disillusioned by Fujimori's government, some evangelical Protestant legislators abandoned the party in 1991).

The judiciary reflected the problems undermining Peru's democracy. During the early 1990s, the conviction rate for cases of terrorism was less than 10 percent; judges released about 200 suspected rebels in the first 20 months of Fujimori's government. Sometimes judges were persuaded to free terrorist suspects by bribes; sometimes, by threats. Often the criminal code was inadequate; it was not a crime, for example, to be a member of the Shining Path. While Fujimori introduced a major counterinsurgency package to the legislature in November 1991, it did not address judicial reform. Nor did any other political party promote such reform. For its part, during 1990 and 1991 the United States provided less than $1 million annually for the administration of justice in Peru.

THE ROUTE TO THE AUTOGOLPE

In retrospect, the risk of a presidentially inflicted coup was evident soon after Fujimori's inauguration. His arrogance toward political leaders, including his own key advisers, his vitriolic slander of civilian institutions, and the keenness with which he eyed the military—especially promotions and dismissals—were all harbingers of his intentions. But, political analysts considered a coup unlikely because they assumed that the United States was informing President Fujimori that the international reaction to a coup would be extremely negative, and that this message had been duly received by Fujimori. In the event, however, if a clear message had been sent by the United States embassy, it certainly had been not heard in the presidential palace.

Although most analysts agreed with Fujimori's diagnosis that Peruvian democracy was seriously troubled, few thought that these problems could be cured by a Fujimori dictatorship. Rather, it was believed that Fujimori liked power—absolute power. Indeed, in Peru's popular newsmagazines, Fujimori had been satirized as a would-be Japanese emperor for months. In an interpretation echoed by most analysts, one senator who had worked closely with Fujimori commented that "Fujimori is. . .an authoritarian personality. I know for certain that he never had any liking, nor respect, nor desire to govern the country democratically. From the beginning he tried to create the conditions that would permit the concentration of power. . . ." [3]

During his first 15 months, President Fujimori enjoyed tremendous policymaking power. While Peru's 1979 constitution concentrated great power in the executive, the two previous presidents under this constitution (AP's Fernando Belaúnde Terry, who served between 1980 and 1985, and APRA's Alan García Pérez, who held office between 1985 and 1990) were constrained at least somewhat by their political parties, whose members filled most cabinet offices and held near-majorities or majorities in the legislature. By contrast, members of Fujimori's Cambio '90 wielded little power over the president. After his first six months in office, almost all of Fujimori's cabinet members were political independents appointed by Fujimori himself and indebted directly to him, or to him as well as international actors, for their power.

Despite Cambio '90's minority position in the legislature (holding slightly less than one-fourth the seats in each of the two legislative houses), Fujimori implemented policies without significant legislative obstruction. The president moved rapidly to re-insert Peru into the international financial community and liberalize the economy: state expenditures were slashed, state revenue increased, tariff barriers cut, and foreign investment laws eased. With respect to counterinsurgency, Fujimori emphasized the establishment of civilian self-defense patrols (*rondas*); while debated in the legislature, this policy was a major success, according to Fujimori himself. As part of the anti-drug effort, in May 1991 Fujimori signed a crucial agreement with the United States that was much more to the right than where Fujimori had stood on the issue during his campaign—but he did not submit the agreement to the legislature for approval. Fujimori's bypassing of the legislature was criticized, but no effort was launched to compel legislative review of the agreement.

Fujimori was able to govern autocratically despite his minority position in the legislature for various reasons. First, the parties were seriously weakened. Also, especially in the area of economic policy, Fujimori's free-market initiatives enjoyed considerable support in the legislature (about one-third of whose members had been in novelist Mario Vargas Llosa's pro-free-market coalition in the 1990 election). Also important were provisions in the 1979 constitution that allowed the executive to wield vast unilateral power over economic policy, and to issue decrees in any policy area if authority were delegated to it by the legislature. In previous administrations this authority was frequently delegated, especially at the start of the new presidency, and Fujimori too was given this political honeymoon.

However, as 1991 ended tensions between the executive and the legislature increased. In November, just as legislative power granted to Fujimori was about to expire, Fujimori issued an avalanche of some 126 decree laws—almost the same number as García had issued in his first three years—on a host of important issues, many of which he had not been given authority to legislate. In a special session two months later, the legislature modified or repealed 28 of these, most of which dealt with counterinsurgency. The decrees were draconian; one, for example, would have banned the publication of any information deemed secret by the government and imposed sentences of five to ten years in prison for offenders. The provisions prompted Peru's leading newsweeklies to run front-page images of Fujimori as Hitler and dressed half as a soldier and half as a civilian.

The increasing acrimony between the executive and the legislature was apparent on other issues as well. Disagreement over the 1992 budget was intense. In particular, the legislature sought greater fiscal support for the agricultural sector, which it declared to be in an emergency. The Chamber of Deputies censured the minister of agriculture—the first time that a minister had been asked to resign under the 1979 constitution. Smugly pointing out that the constitution did not stipulate a timeframe for the minister's resignation, Fujimori kept him on. Fujimori threatened to dissolve congress and call new elections if his ministers were censured. Fujimori insulted legislators, and they responded by suggesting he might be impeached on grounds of moral incapacity.

Fujimori feared the future emergence of greater legislative opposition. After many months of legal battles against charges of illicit enrichment, former President García was finally exonerated by the supreme court (many of whose members were García appointees). Reelected secretary general of APRA, García hoped to unify and galvanize the political opposition to Fujimori, and presumably win the presidency again in 1995. Although it was unlikely that García could achieve these goals, Fujimori evidently did not want to risk the possibility.

Still, the political context was far from obstructionist. Consider, for example, that whereas the legislature under Fujimori censured one minister in 20 months, the legislature during Belaúnde's first term in the 1960s had censured more than 50. Although the legislature modified or repealed 22 percent of Fujimori's November decrees, it passed 78 percent of them. Overall, legislators wanted to negotiate with Fujimori—but Fujimori did not want to negotiate with them. As one key adviser to Fujimori told a journalist: "[Fujimori] could not stomach [the other] option, which would be to invite the chairman of the Senate along to the palace for a meal every time he wanted a law through congress."[4]

One event that may have hastened the coup was an accusation of corruption against members of Fujimori's family by the president's own wife, Susana. Mrs. Fujimori charged that used clothing donated by Japan for Peru's needy was being sold for profit by members of the president's family. After the coup Fujimori suspended the body that would have investigated his wife's charges. Was the leader who threw so many stones—the constant accusations that Peru's democracy was corrupt—living in a glass house?

International Ambivalence

On the evening of April 5, when President Fujimori announced his self-styled Government of Emergency and National Reconstruction and the military command indicated its support, United States Assistant Secretary of State for Latin America Bernard Aronson had just arrived in Lima, expecting to speak with Fujimori the next day. Astounded by the coup, Aronson canceled his meeting with the president and left Peru. The United States immediately suspended most nonhumanitarian aid to the country, as did Canada and Spain; most Latin American nations condemned the coup.

International hostility apparently persuaded Fujimori to soften his stand. The night of the coup, security forces had seized internationally respected opposition journalist Gustavo Gorriti as well as several APRA leaders, and had tried unsuccessfully to capture García. Military officials forced their way into the offices of most of Peru's main newspapers, newsmagazines, and television and radio stations. Within a few days, however, Fujimori ceased his most egregiously repressive actions.

At the same time, international opposition abated as Peruvian support for Fujimori's measures became clear. Apparently agreeing with Fujimori that the pre-April 5 regime was inefficient, frivolous, and corrupt (in part because Fujimori had been repeating these accusations for months), more than 75 percent of the people approved Fujimori's administration and his actions against the legislature and the judiciary. (At the same time, however, 75 percent expressed a preference for democracy rather than dictatorship, and more than 80 percent said municipal elections should be held as scheduled in 1992 and presidential elections as scheduled in 1995; apparently, Peruvians believed Fujimori's statements that his new regime would be transitional.) Aware that sanctions had failed to restore democracy in Haiti, and the complex issues posed by the facts that Fujimori had been elected, that he continued to enjoy popular support, and that Peru's democratic institutions had not been performing effectively, international diplomats hesitated to impose similar sanctions on Peru.

The key pending question was Peru's restoration into the good graces of the International Monetary Fund and the international banks. This goal was paramount for Fujimori, and the threat to suspend support for Peru's re-insertion was the primary lever wielded by international actors in their attempts to nudge Fujimori back toward democracy. However, the international community knew that Fujimori had cards to play as well; if re-insertion was denied, Fujimori could reverse free-market policies and terminate Peru's servicing of its debt arrears (payments of about $750 million annually). Moreover, a possible beneficiary of increased problems for the Fujimori government, at least in the short run, was the Shining Path.

An additional factor important to increasing international toleration of Fujimori's coup was the friendship between Fujimori and the Japanese government. As the first Latin American president of Japanese origins, Fujimori was perceived by the Japanese as a spectacularly successful native son. After his inauguration, Fujimori traveled to Japan several times. The Japanese government donated about $400 million to his government in 1992 and would have been reluctant to prevent Peru's readmission into the international financial community on political grounds.

An incident on April 24 at first appeared likely to further alienate the United States and Peru, but ultimately seemed to have little impact: a United States Air Force Hercules C-130 plane was downed by two Peruvian fighter jets; one American airman died. Peruvian authorities claimed that the plane was hundreds of miles off course from a routine counterdrug surveillance mission, and that its crew had failed to respond to repeated Peruvian warnings; Peru later sent the Pentagon a bill for its incurred costs.

From mid-April to mid-May, negotiations between key international actors and the Fujimori government were intense. Assistant Secretary of State Aronson returned to Peru to speak with Fujimori, and two OAS missions led by Uruguayan Foreign Minister Héctor Gros Espiell also met with him. In these meetings, Fujimori proposed a July 5 plebiscite on his rule, after which his cabinet would draft constitutional reforms; he rejected holding elections for a constituent assembly. International actors and the political opposition favored scheduling elections. Moreover, the opposition argued that, in its view, the 1979 constitution remained in effect; since Fujimori's actions had violated the constitution, the first vice president, former Cambio '90 leader Máximo San Román, was Peru's legal president. To advance their arguments, Peru's traditional parties and unions successfully organized a large rally in downtown Lima on May 15.

On May 18, at an OAS meeting in the Bahamas where foreign ministers were deciding further policy toward Peru, Fujimori surprisingly appeared. Speaking to the meeting, Fujimori promised elections for a constituent assembly within five months. Fujimori's shift towards the position of his international and domestic opposition was a crucial compromise. While after the OAS meeting the official attitude of the United States remained "wait-and-see," most Peruvian analysts (and apparently Fujimori himself) believed that the international spotlight would no longer be focused on Peru and that, unless the elections were entirely fraudulent, Peru's re-insertion into the international financial community would proceed. In the months that followed, as Fujimori delayed municipal elections and skewed electoral procedures to his advantage with hardly a comment from the international community, the Peruvian view appeared to have been correct.

THE COUP'S AFTERMATH

During the course of 1992, Fujimori managed to maintain several accomplishments that Peruvians had welcomed during his first 20 months. Paramount among these was the low rate of inflation, estimated at 55 percent for 1992 (in contrast to over 7,000 percent in 1990). The government also scored major blows against a secondary guerrilla group, the Túpac Amaru Revolutionary Movement, including the capture of its leader, Victor Polay Campos, in June.

Otherwise there were few apparent bright spots. Except for the relatively low inflation rate, the economy was faring poorly. As mentioned earlier, GDP declined during 1992, and the rate of decline was greater after April 5. An exchange rate undervaluing the United States dollar impeded the development of new export industries. Peru was spending about $60 million to $90 million per month to service its arrears on a roughly $20-billion foreign debt, and new international resources were not being disbursed. President Fujimori continued to eschew the establishment of a social emergency program to cushion the blows of the "Fujishock" against the poor. Poverty levels remained among the worst in the region.

During June and July, the Shining Path escalated its attacks, especially in Lima. On June 5, a car bomb devastated television channel two, and on July 16 another car bomb exploded in one of Lima's well-to-do suburbs, killing 21 people, injuring 250, and damaging 6 hotels, 10 banks, 20 shops, and 400 homes. Nationwide, the guerrillas' July offensive included 293 attacks that left 179 persons dead. The Shining Path was perceived to be gaining, not losing, in the wake of the April 5 coup. When Guzmán was finally captured, he was preparing "Operation Conquer Lima."

While the Peruvian government won some battles in the "war against drugs," overall the war was still being won by the drug producers and traffickers. Some corrupt officials were removed, airstrips in drug-producing areas were controlled during daylight hours, and arrests and cocaine seizures in 1992 were slightly higher than in 1991. But the percentage of Peruvian territory planted in coca or other drugs and controlled by drug traffickers and/or guerrillas, continued to expand. Only one-half of 1 percent of Peru's raw cocaine is seized before its export to Colombia, and less than 1 percent of all drug flights to Colombia are intercepted. Under current conditions it is impossible to discern a path toward victory in the war against drugs in Peru.

Peruvians were gradually becoming skeptical that Fujimori's coup would improve their lives. Whereas roughly 75 percent of Peruvians approved the coup just after the event, in May the number approving fell to 56 percent and by June the figure was 41 percent.

THE CAPTURE OF GUZMÁN

On September 12, 1992, the Peruvian government scored its first major triumph against the Shining Path. At a minimum, the capture of Guzmán and other key leaders would require the organization to regroup and choose new chiefs, and thus provide the government important breathing space. Quite possibly the threat that had been posed to the Peruvian state by Sendero was over.

While Fujimori claimed credit for the capture, there was no objective basis for his claim. Indeed, Fujimori had suggested that the key to counterinsurgency would be a hard-line military approach. But it was the anti-terrorist police, not the military, that captured Guzmán. The elite DINCOTE unit, established under President García and led by General Antonio Vidal, had almost captured Guzmán twice before (once during the final months of the García administration).

DINCOTE's raid was admirably professional. Apparently having followed a Shining Path leader recently released from jail, the police found the Lima hideout. DINCOTE maintained surveillance of the house with undercover agents disguised as city employees, street peddlers, and guests at a backyard barbecue in a police officer's nearby home. A police couple, posing as smooching lovers, parked across the street from Guzmán's hideout. They spotted a woman stepping out of the house to buy Winston cigarettes, Guzmán's brand; when the door was reopened for her, 35 heavily armed agents burst in. "Bingo—we got him!" exclaimed a jubilant detective. "My turn to lose," Guzmán reportedly said.

The effectiveness of the DINCOTE operation contrasted with the apparent carelessness of Guzmán and his lieutenants, which gave the government a tremendous victory over Sendero. Most analysts believed that, if Guzmán had been captured dead (reportedly the mode preferred by the Peruvian military), or if he had been able to commit suicide, he would have retained his mythical aura and become a martyr to the movement. Alive and videotaped, however, Guzmán revealed himself a man—indeed, a paunchy middle-aged man with a ragged beard and thick glasses. Peruvians viewed the ideologue who was called "Puka Inti" ("Red Sun") and the "Fourth Sword of Communism" meekly zipping up his pants. The image of invincibility that Sendero had cultivated for 12 years was punctured.

Almost as important as the capture of Guzmán was the arrest of many other Sendero leaders and militants. In Guzmán's hideout police captured two other members of the top echelon of the Shining Path's central committee; presumably using information found in the house, police rounded up about 200 suspected Senderistas within a few days, and within a few weeks more than 1,000. Approximately 80 computers and 200 diskettes were seized, facilitating the capture of more top leaders, both in Lima and in provincial cities. By the end of the year, about 12 of 19 central committee members were behind bars. The only member of Guzmán's innermost circle still at large was reportedly Oscar Ramírez Duran (Comrade Feliciano), who was believed to be in the mountains above Arequipa.

However, while the information from hideouts enabled a more selective pattern of arrests in some areas, the number of disappearances and extrajudicial executions was similar to the 1990 and 1991 totals. Moreover, Fujimori's criticism of human-rights groups became more vitriolic. The National Intelligence Service (SIN) compiled a list of alleged Shining Path sympathizers that included several respected human-rights activists whom virtually everyone outside of the Peruvian government believed to be innocent.

On October 7, in a military trial closed to the public, a hooded navy judge sentenced Guzmán to life imprisonment. Guzmán's lawyer complained that he was not able to call any defense witnesses and that he was allowed to meet only twice with his client, for a total of 20 minutes. Fujimori's legal innovations in the trials of suspected terrorists—anonymous judges, military trials, and life sentences—did not trouble most Peruvians when the suspect was Guzmán, but the application of the same procedures to individuals arrested for tenuous reasons in shantytowns or rural villages was worrisome.

Still, violence continued. In the first 100-odd days after the capture of Guzmán, the number of terrorist attacks resembled that in the previous 100-odd days, and the number of deaths was only about 25 percent less. Before the November 22 elections, Sendero bombs again rocked Lima, taking the lives of several civilians. Yet, Sendero's attempt at an armed strike a few days prior to the elections and its call for an electoral boycott were largely defied. A dramatically smaller number of Peruvians now considers the Shining Path an omniscient, omnipresent, invincible movement.

The Attempted Counter-Coup

Rumors of a counter-coup circulated for many of the days following April 5, and were especially intense after the escalation of Shining Path attacks in July and August. At this time, the army chief of staff, General José Valdivia, was so frequently mentioned as the key coup-plotter that he published full-page advertisements in Lima newspapers stating his loyalty to Fujimori.

Various motives for a counter-coup were apparent. First, especially among officers who feared that Fujimori's regime would isolate Peru internationally, there was a desire to return to constitutional government. Second, neither officers nor soldiers saw as much improvement in their economic lot after the coup as they thought they had been promised.

Perhaps most important, however, was that large numbers of officers resented the flagrant politicization of promotions and the purges within the military. Whereas there had been some politicization of appointments and dismissals since 1980, it drastically increased under Fujimori. The president's national security adviser, Vladimiro Montesinos, was directly involved in virtually all promotions and dismissals. The fact that a man of Montesinos's background—he was a cashiered army intelligence captain who had provided legal defense to drug traffickers during the 1980s—was manipulating appointments at the apex of the military hierarchy was galling to many officers.

On November 13, retired General Jaime Salinas Sedó hoped to lead a group of about 100 officers in an attempt to overthrow Fujimori. Salinas, who had been at the top of his army class and had been forced into retirement for political reasons under Fujimori in July

1992, wanted to return Peru to constitutional government. Apparently, he timed the plot in an effort to preclude legitimization of the Fujimori government by the constituent assembly elections. However, Fujimori learned about Salinas's plan (which apparently was to enter the presidential palace unbeknownst to the president and seize him), and Fujimori escaped to the Japanese embassy before the conspirators arrived at the palace.

Fujimori subsequently charged that Salinas and his colleagues planned to assassinate him. These charges were denied by the coup-plotters. However, the government arrested about a dozen high-ranking military officers, and also accused numerous civilian leaders of complicity in the plot, spurring several to seek political asylum. The intense political questions raised by the coup attempt dominated many Peruvians' thoughts despite the fact that the constituent assembly elections were only about 10 days away.

THE NOVEMBER 22 CONSTITUENT ASSEMBLY ELECTIONS

President Fujimori hoped that the elections for the Democratic Constituent Congress (CCD) would legitimize his government and constrain the opposition much like the 1980 plebiscite on a new constitution did in General Augusto Pinochet's Chile. Moreover, he wanted as large a majority in the assembly as possible for his own political party, Nueva Mayoría/Cambio '90 (New Majority/Change '90) in order to aid him in dominating the institution. To this end there were a number of electoral manipulations; yet, the elections gained the stamp of approval of a 210-member OAS delegation. Presumably, Fujimori feels assured that he will be able to manipulate future elections without international reverberations.

Upon Fujimori's return from speaking to the OAS meeting in the Bahamas and promising the constituent assembly elections, he was greeted with considerable skepticism by Peru's traditional parties. Not only had Fujimori already demonstrated his disdain for democratic institutions with his April 5 coup, but various steps before his OAS appearance had suggested that he would try to manipulate the elections. Shortly after the coup, Fujimori had dismissed the head of the National Elections Tribunal, and his replacement, César Polack, was considered spineless. Fujimori had also indicated that members of the constituent assembly would be ineligible to run for elective office for at least one term—a condition obviously deterring participation by leading figures of the traditional parties and thereby clearing the field for Fujimori.

As discussions between Fujimori and the opposition parties began, confidence was further eroded by several new announcements by the president. First, he postponed the constituent assembly elections for more than a month after the original deadline promised at the OAS meeting. The Fujimori government seemed to be delaying the establishment of specific guidelines for the elections. Most important for the opposition, Fujimori also postponed municipal elections (which according to the 1979 constitution were to be held in November 1992). The opposition believed that Fujimori wanted to delay these elections as long as possible so his political coalition could field a sufficient number of candidates for the 1,900-odd races at provincial and district levels.

Only in late July and August did the Fujimori government begin to establish the framework for the Democratic Constituent Congress. Fujimori announced that the congress would be a one-chamber body with 80 members elected nationally, whose term would last until July 28, 1995 (when, according to the 1979 constitution, Fujimori's presidency should end). The congress would write a new constitution, which would be submitted to a national referendum, and also pass laws and exercise oversight of the executive. By contrast, the political opposition contended that, after the assembly revised the constitution, new elections should be held for a legislature. The Fujimori government did not precisely stipulate the constituent assembly or legislative functions of the CCD, or how these functions would be meshed.

Fujimori's machinations presented a complex dilemma to the traditional political parties. If the parties participated, their decision would be interpreted as acceptance of the procedures, thus legitimizing the elections. On the other hand, if they did not participate and Fujimori achieved international approval for the elections, they would be politically marginalized. On top of this complex issue was the fact that opinion polls showed the major traditional political parties with minimal popular support.

While either participating in the elections or boycotting them appeared a rational decision for Peru's parties, the fact that some parties participated while others boycotted may have been the worst possible outcome for them. Divided on the election, the parties could not make a clear statement of opposition to the international community; nor could they achieve the higher electoral tallies that would have been likely if better-known opposition leaders had participated. The boycotting parties could not even agree on whether opponents to Fujimori should abstain (potentially subjecting themselves to a fine in the $15 range), spoil their ballots, or vote for collegial parties.

The parties tended to hedge their bets: a better-known party would abstain, and a lesser-known stand-in or faction would participate. Accordingly, APRA abstained, but a faction, the Democratic Coordination ran; Belaúnde's AP abstained, while its erstwhile coalition partner, the PPC, participated; Mario Vargas Llosa's Liberty Movement abstained while the splinter group Renewal took part; the largest leftist group, the

Mariáteguista Unified party, abstained but smaller leftist entities formed a new front, the Democratic Movement of the Left.

Perhaps the division among the political parties was one of Fujimori's goals. Often, he seemed to be trying to provoke political actors, or keep them off-balance for purposes only he knew. For example, on at least one occasion during the campaign, Fujimori stated that, if the assembly did not behave, he would boot it out again. (Hearing Fujimori's threats, former president Belaúnde dubbed the CCD "the Alka-Seltzer Congress" since Fujimori could dissolve it whenever he felt like it.) At the last minute, Fujimori proposed that a referendum on the introduction of the death penalty be held simultaneously with the constituent assembly elections; the proposal prompted a threat of withdrawal by the PPC and criticism by the Organization of American States, and Fujimori withdrew the initiative.

Fujimori's machinations continued during the campaign. His new political coalition, Nueva Mayoría/Cambio '90, distributed considerable benefits to potential voters, some from public funds. In a reversal of the traditional interpretation of electoral law, new parties and parties that had received less than 5 percent of the vote in the preceding election were required to collect 100,000 signatures in order to qualify to compete. Most of the parties that ultimately participated spent much of the pre-electoral period collecting these signatures. Delays by the National Elections Tribunal in validating the signatures and recognizing parties meant that the actual campaign period was brief—only about two weeks. This was insufficient, given that most of the competing parties were unknown to the voters and had scant resources for media advertising (and that much of the news during this period turned out to focus upon the attempted countercoup).[5]

Questions were also raised about voting-day conditions. In some observers' views, adequate numbers of voting-table officials were not fielded. Also, as "an alliance," rather than a party, Nueva Mayoría/Cambio '90 received a separate spot at the bottom of the ballot, standing out much more clearly than the other parties, which were clustered together.

The OAS did not loudly object to the Fujimori government's maneuvers. Perhaps influenced by officials in United States President George Bush's administration who favored Peru's return to international good graces, or by representatives of other Latin American nations who feared intensive international analysis of their own elections, or by top OAS leaders who believed a Fujimori government was Peru's best option, the OAS's focus was on the absence of fraud on election day.

Installed on December 30, 1992, the CCD's immediate mission is to revise the 1979 constitution. Presumably, the CCD will grant greater powers to the executive. Two possible revisions appeared especially controversial: introducing the death penalty for crimes of terrorism and allowing the immediate reelection of the president, which would enable Fujimori to run in 1995.

PROSPECTS FOR DEMOCRACY

By the end of 1992, having overcome a number of international and domestic obstacles, Fujimori appeared to be consolidating his power. However, especially given Fujimori's lack of an institutional base, his current support in the business and popular sectors could dissipate quickly if the Peruvian economy does not improve. Also, the more arrogant the Fujimori government acts toward its political enemies, the more likely that a strong domestic and international political opposition will be forged. With the inauguration of President Bill Clinton, the United States could decide not to support Peru's reentry into the international financial community—a decision that could doom Fujimori.

In any case, a new era began for Peru in 1992. It will be shaped by the widespread perception that democracy as fashioned in the 1979 constitution failed, and by the intense political polarization between Fujimori and political leaders of the 1980s. Given this, it will be harder than ever to build democracy in Peru.

---

[1]Francisco Soberón Garrido, executive committee member of Peru's National Human Rights Coordinating Committee, in Washington, D.C., February 7, 1991. In his talk, Soberón estimated the number of 1990 disappearances in one province to have been almost as high as the official figure for the nation as a whole.

[2]For background on the party, the 1990 election, and the new government's first six months, see David P. Werlich, "Fujimori and the 'Disaster' in Peru," *Current History*, vol. 90, no. 553 (February 1991).

[3]Enrique Bernales, interviewed in *Ideéle*, vol. 4, no. 37 (May 1992), p. 12. As a senator Bernales dealt extensively with Fujimori, but was not considered a vehement opponent of his.

[4]"Political and Economic Trend Report," *The Peru Report*, vol. 6, no. 3 (May 1992), p. 3. Some analysts, including journalist Gustavo Gorriti and scholar-political leader Henry Pease García, believe that Fujimori actually provoked executive-legislative tensions in order to justify the coup.

[5]Nueva Mayoría/Cambio 90 is estimated to have outspent all but one other party (one of whose candidates was a media magnate who may not have spent funds for media time) by a factor of at least three to one. Altogether, 9 of the 18 competing parties spent only 12 percent of what Fujimori's group spent. *Caretas*, November 26, 1992, p. 13.

Population, Poverty, and Environment

Population, poverty, and the environment are inextricably linked. Third World population continues to grow at an annual rate of between 2.5–3.5 percent, with some countries experiencing even higher growth rates. The Earth's population is currently growing at the rate of approximately one billion people every 11 years. Most of this increase is taking place in the Third World where poverty is widespread. The combination of higher population and poverty rates inevitably results in increased exploitation of resources and environmental degradation.

The United Nations estimates that if population growth rates continue, the Earth's population may double before it stabilizes sometime in the next century. Even if, by some miracle, population growth were immediately reduced to the level found in industrialized countries, Third World population would continue to grow well into the next century. Because such a large proportion of the population is young and will be starting families of their own, it will be some time before population growth slows substantially. There has been some progress in reducing fertility rates (that is, the average number of children per family) through family planning programs, but much remains to be done.

There are differences of opinion about the best way to

Unit 6

slow population growth. Some analysts regard development as the best contraceptive, while others view lower population growth as a prerequisite for development. These differences in perspective have politicized the population issue between those who favor family planning and wider availability of birth control and others who believe that development itself will slow population growth, as it did in the industrialized countries. Debate over this issue was related to the abortion controversy in the United States and resulted in static funding for family planning programs throughout the 1980s.

Estimates vary, but as many as one billion people may live in absolute poverty, as measured by a combination of economic, and social indicators. As population increases, it makes it more difficult to meet the basic human needs of Third World citizens. Alleviating poverty is a daunting challenge and will require massive efforts on a number of fronts. Economic development, regarded by many as a panacea, has not only failed to eliminate poverty, it has exacerbated it in some ways. Ill-conceived economic development plans have diverted resources from more productive uses. Where economic growth has occurred, the benefits are often inequitably distributed and widen the gap between rich and poor in Third World countries. Rural to urban migration has caused an enormous influx of people to the cities, lured there by the illusion of opportunity and the attraction of urban life. In reality, opportunity is limited. Nevertheless, most opt for marginal lives in the cities rather than returning to the countryside. Additional resources are diverted to the urban areas in an attempt to meet demands for services. Meanwhile, food production is affected, with those remaining in rural areas often choosing to farm for subsistence because of artificially low prices or turning to cash crops for export.

Population and poverty also contribute to environmental degradation. Larger populations of poor people place greater strains on scarce and fragile resources. Deforestation for agriculture and to provide fuel has reduced forested areas and contributed to erosion, desertification, and global warming. Intensified agriculture, particularly for cash crops, has depleted soils, necessitating increased fertilization that is both costly and produces runoff that contributes to water pollution. Rapidly expanding urban populations overwhelm meager sanitation facilities, resulting in additional water pollution and increased incidence of water-borne diseases. In arid regions like the Middle East, added demand for scarce water resources has depleted aquifers, perhaps irreversibly.

The drive for economic development also contributes to pollution and generates toxic waste. The toxic waste problem is often compounded by the shifting of production facilities to Third World countries to take advantage of cheaper labor and looser environmental regulations. In some cases, unscrupulous entrepreneurs have collaborated in the export of toxic waste from the industrialized countries to the Third World.

In June 1992 the UN Conference on Environment and Development (UNCED) was held in Rio de Janeiro, Brazil. In her address to the opening session of the conference, Norway's prime minister Gro Harlem Brundtland noted that population, poverty, and the environment could not be separated. Nevertheless, the documents that came out of Rio did not explicitly address this connection. Moreover, the divisions between North and South on environmental issues became more pronounced. The conference highlighted the fundamental differences between the industrialized world and developing countries over the causes of and solutions to global environmental problems. This politicization along North-South lines only serves to postpone constructive steps to preserve the Earth's environment.

Looking Ahead: Challenge Questions

Why is population growing so rapidly? What are the consequences of continued population growth?

What are the implications of the differing views on how to slow population growth?

What is the demographic transition theory?

How are population growth, poverty, and the environment connected? What can be done to address these problems?

What accounts for the dramatic growth in Third World urban areas? What are the implications of this growth?

How can family planning programs be strengthened in Third World countries?

What are the differences in perspective between industrialized and developing countries on global environmental issues?

How might industrialized countries contribute to pollution in Third World countries?

Why have World Bank projects been criticized from an environmental standpoint? How is the bank addressing this criticism?

What is a nongovernmental organization? What roles are these organizations playing in the Third World?

World Population

Progress in slowing the increase in people on the earth is critical to finding solutions for global problems in the 21st century

George D. Moffett III

Staff writer of The Christian Science Monitor

NEW YORK

In a world of complexity and change, at least three facts stand out with stark simplicity:

■ The number of people living on the earth is growing more rapidly than ever before in human history and will continue to do so for at least four more decades, according to United Nations estimates.

■ Unless fertility rates—that is, the average number of children per family—fall significantly by the end of the decade, the world's population could expand to more than three times its current 5.4 billion before stabilizing a century or more from now.

■ Without major technological breakthroughs and changes in patterns of consumption, even the most optimistic population-growth projections are likely to be accompanied by increases in poverty, hunger, and environmental degradation.

"Whether we look at population, the environment, or development, the next 10 years will be critical for our future," says Nafis Sadik, executive director of the United Nations Population Fund. "The decisions we make or don't take will widen or narrow our options for a century to come. They could decide the fate of the earth as a home for human beings."

The raw data on population growth tell a compelling story. Every day the human family grows by a quarter of a million people. Every four days the equivalent of a new Detroit or Dallas is added to the earth. Every eight months a new Germany. Every decade, at just under 1 billion new inhabitants, the equivalent of a new Africa and South America combined. Demographers say the decade that it will take to reach the next billion is an instant in time compared with thousands of years needed to reach the first, in the early 1800s.

Beyond the sheer scope of population growth, the future will be profoundly influenced by its distribution:

■ Population growth is occurring in regions of the world least able to respond to the demand for food, housing, education, and employment opportunities that it will create. Ninety-five percent of world population growth will occur in the developing world. Africa, where birthrates are highest, is now growing 13 times faster than Europe, where population may actually decline in the years ahead.

■ Population growth will be concentrated in the most vulnerable areas of the developing world: cities. In 1950, only one third-world city had a population of 5 million. By the year 2000, there will be 46, all taxed to or beyond the limit to provide needed services and maintain political stability. A historic turning point will be reached in 1997 when a majority of the world's population will live in urban areas, according to the UN Population Division.

The runaway population growth that began in the 1940s and peaked during the 1960s is a historical aberration. Largely the product of improvements in public health and sanitation, it will taper off during the last half of the next century. Exactly where it levels off could determine whether upward trends in economic growth and longevity will be reversed.

Demographers have been heartened by steady declines in fertility that have occurred since the late 1960s in response to economic development and the rapid spread of family-planning programs around the world.

But lower fertility is not an immediate panacea. With so many people in their reproductive years—one-half will be under 25 in the year 2000—the world's population will actually grow for the next several decades by larger numbers than ever before.

According to UN estimates, if fertility is reduced during the 1990s to replacement level—that is, to the two children a couple need to replace themselves—there is a good chance population growth will begin to level off by mid-century at just twice today's total. If fertility rates remain high, the population could expand far beyond the earth's capacity to provide for it.

"There's no question that population growth is eventually going to come to a halt," says Stanford University demographer Paul Erlich. "The question is whether it's going to end because we manage to humanely lower birthrates or because we exceed the earth's carrying capacity."

The fact that most of today's 5 billion people have escaped famine is credited partly to the "green revolution" of the 1960s. The dramatic increases in world food production that resulted from breakthroughs in plant technology, irrigation, and farm management are a hint, say some economists, of the limitless possibilities offered by technology and human ingenuity to keep up with the needs of an expanding world population.

But as the growth in human numbers rolls relentlessly past the finite productivity of the green revolution, the future seems less promising. Since the mid-1980s, increases in food production in some regions have fallen behind population growth. In the poorer nations of Latin America, harvest deficits have been widening for a decade. In sub-Saharan Africa, which was once self-sufficient in agriculture, food production is growing at only half the rate of population, leaving an estimated one-third of the continent undernourished.

"Population growth is clearly outpacing agricultural potential in Africa," says Stephen Vosti, a research fellow at the International Food Policy Research Institute in Washington. "It is a Malthusian train crash waiting to happen," he adds, referring to the predictions of Thomas Malthus, the 19th-century British economist who warned that population growth would someday outpace food supplies.

Population growth has also contributed to the worsening poverty that now affects hundreds of millions of people living in Africa, Asia, and Latin America.

Many economists and demographers warn that population growth combined with inefficient agriculture, inappropriate government policies, and outdated technologies has brought the world to critical thresholds of sustainability. Demographers point to the contribution of relentless population growth to deforestation, overgrazing, and the degradation of the very agricultural lands needed to sustain such growth.

Finding solutions to the global problems that will dominate the agenda of the 21st century will be nearly impossible without progress on the population front.

"There's no possible solution to the global problems of poverty and environmental degradation that does not include action to reduce projected population-growth rates, says former World Bank president Robert McNamara.

Environmental problems, such as global warming and depletion of the ozone layer, are not caused by population growth but by the extravagant use of resources in the rich industrialized countries, where 75 percent of all energy is consumed. But if even the most optimistic population projections materialize, the sheer weight of human numbers will soon make the third world a major burden on the global as well as local environment.

"For the most part, global pollution is a consequence of the use of resources and the waste of developing countries. But the simplest projections into the future tell you that's not going to be the case 10 years from now, even if per-capita consumption rates stay the same," says George Zeidenstein, president of the Population Council, a private research group in New York. "We're at a transitional moment."

Alternative Futures: Population Projections to 2150

Ahead lie four decades of the fastest growth in human numbers in all history. The three outlooks shown here only diverge significantly after 2050, when the world's population will be about double today's.

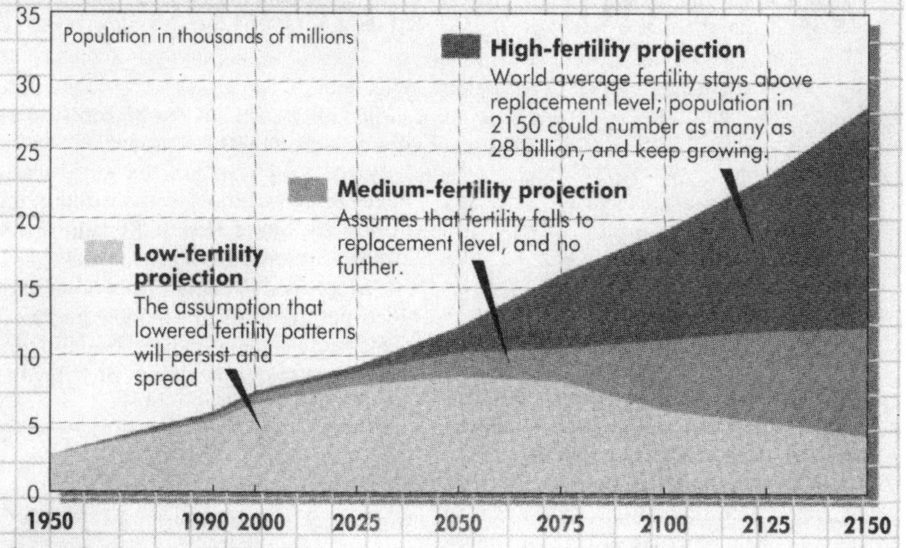

Source: United Nations Population Fund

The Future Is Urban: Urban and Rural Growth Projections to 2025

Between 1950 and 1990, the world's urban population more than tripled to 2,390 million. In the 1990s the world's urban population will grow at the rate of 10 Paris-sized cities a year. (This chart is based on medium-fertility projection.)

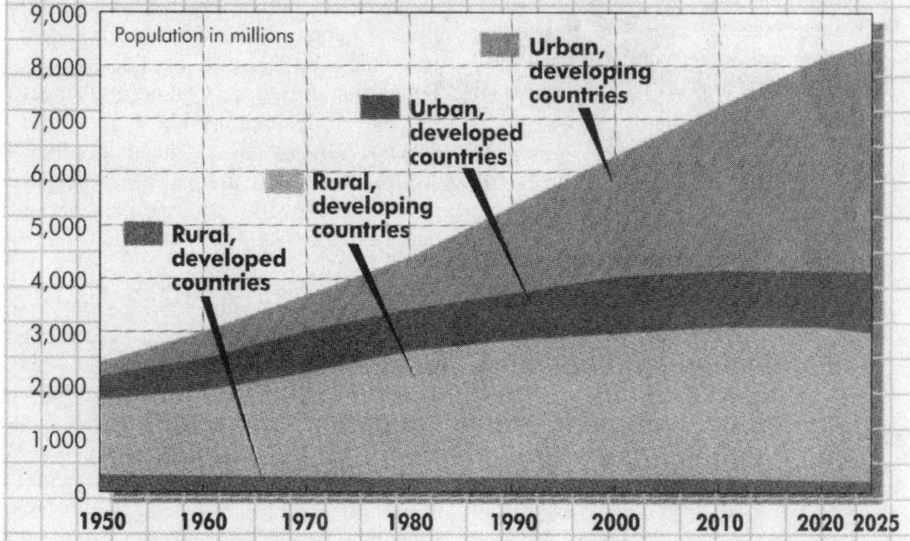

Too Many People? Not in the View of Some Economists

WASHINGTON

Can the planet Earth, regions of which are already sagging under the weight of its 5 billion passengers, sustain 5 billion or 10 billion more?

By the conventional wisdom, the answer is a resounding no. A majority of demographers and environmentalists say the earth's soils, forests, and water resources are already being depleted at a dangerous rate. If population doubles or triples, they warn, the human load could produce an ecological nightmare.

But a sturdy group of demographic contrarians takes exception, scoffing at the notion that population growth will mortgage the world's future.

"Why should we worry?" asks Ben Wattenberg, a scholar at the American Enterprise Institute in Washington. "We've gone from 1 [billion] to 5 billion while living standards have gone up exponentially. There's no evidence that population growth diminishes or dilutes development."

The optimism of academics like Mr. Wattenberg is rooted in an array of hopeful statistics on rising incomes, food production, and literacy rates that seem to belie the notion that population growth breeds declining living standards and ecological overload. If population growth creates problems, they say, then history has proved time and again that it also calls forth the human ingenuity needed to solve them. Case in point: the green revolution.

"The track record of these kinds of extrapolative predictions is simply historically dismal," says Larry Summers, chief economist of the World Bank in Washington, referring to the forecasts of doomsayers. "1990 is as close to 1930 as it is to 2050. No one in 1930 predicted the green revolution, antibiotics, North Sea oil, or the environmental movement."

Demographers acknowledge that they have failed to anticipate such developments. But they say they also failed to anticipate global warming, ozone depletion, and deforestation, all attributed in part to population growth.

"It makes you wonder what else is going on out there that we don't know about yet," says Paul Erlich, author of the 1968 bestseller "The Population Bomb" (Ballantine).

The main locus of disagreement between mainstream demographers and some economists is whether the world will be able to feed billions more people.

The economists say that by using technology and management skills already available, farmers in Bangladesh can become as productive as farmers in Kansas.

Demographers say sweeping political and social changes will be required to make such technical possibilities a reality. They also note the thorn on the rose of the green revolution, that even as output is being increased, soils are being eroded, ground water polluted, and forest lands destroyed.

"In some areas agricultural production is stripping the resource base and the bank is going to run out soon," says agronomist Stephen Vosti.

One middle view is expressed by an agronomist, an official of the Rome-based Food and Agriculture Organization, a United Nations agency. "Expanding onto the limited remaining agricultural lands available and utilizing incremental improvements in technology, farmers in most parts of the world may be able to keep pace with population growth," he says.

But sub-Saharan Africa will lose the population race, producing a sustained crisis, he says. "We are talking about famines, severely aggravated by the collapse of civil order."

Where the more optimistic economists accent aggregate trends, demographers tend to focus on distribution. Statistics on per-capita increases in food production, for example, provide cold comfort to the billion or more people worldwide who now live on the edge of starvation, they say.

"We're seeing increased polarization of the world in terms of living standards, with a small fraction of the world living in affluence and most of the world living in poverty," says Robert Repetto of the World Resources Institute in Washington.

"More food is being raised now, but it does not feed hungry people more. It feeds more hungry people," adds Donella Meadows, a coauthor of "Beyond the Limits" (Chelsea Green).

Optimists say that the population bomb has been defused because fertility rates have plummeted in most parts of the world within one generation. They say improving economic conditions will make reductions to and even below replacement-level fertility faster and easier.

"Defense budgets are coming down, market economies are taking root, and democracy is spreading," says Wattenberg. "That's an enormous boon to economic development, and that's the key to lowering fertility rates."

"The fact remains, we're adding 100 million people to the world each year," responds Jane DeLung, president of the Population Resource Center in Princeton, N.J. "Technology has reduced the specter of mass famine, but it may not reduce the sheer impact of projected population growth if you're talking about quality of life."

—George D. Moffett III

The Demographic Dimension

Now 5.4 billion, world population will probably double before it stabilizes

Raúl Urzúa

Raúl Urzúa is co-ordinator of UNESCO's population programmes and director of its Division of Population and Human Settlements. A sociologist, he is a former director of the Roberto Bellarmino Centre for Sociocultural Research at Santiago and professor of sociology at the Catholic University of Chile. His many published works include Desarrollo Regional, Migraciones y Concentración Urbana en América Latina *("Regional development, migrations and urban concentration in Latin America", 1985) and* La opción preferencial por los pobres: de la teoria a la práctica *("The preferential choice for the poor: from theory to practice", 1987).*

Under the guidance of its first Director-General, Julian Huxley, the 1948 General Conference of UNESCO highlighted three major groups of problems facing the postwar world—nationalism, obstacles on the path of technological advance and population growth. The gravity of "the problem of world population" led Huxley to the view, expressed in "The Report of the Director-General on the Activities of the Organization in 1948", that "somehow or other, population must be balanced against resources, or civilization will perish".

In the same report, Huxley noted with alarm that world population had already reached 2 billion and that the 3 billion mark would certainly be topped early in the twenty-first century. This turned out to be a very optimistic forecast. The world today has a population of 5.4 billion and recent United Nations projections indicate that by 2025 it will have reached 8.5 billion, almost three times the figure forecast by Huxley, and that demographic growth will not be halted until the twenty-second century, when world population will stabilize at around 11.6 billion.

The very magnitude of these figures puts population growth into the category of what the National Research Council of the United States recently described as "self-evident problems, such as crime, sickness, illiteracy, hunger and poverty, which must be resolved by means of appropriate social policies". Since then, better knowledge of the relationships that exist between demographic, economic, social, political and cultural factors has undermined some of our old certainties without providing others to replace them.

Few today would venture to suggest that a slowing of the rate of demographic growth would of itself be enough to ensure a rapid improvement in the standard of living of the world's most impoverished classes. Nor would those who are not unduly alarmed by present demographic changes go so far as to deny that lower population growth rates and a more even distribution of populations would make it easier to combat underdevelopment and poverty and environmental problems arising from excessive population pressure. What, then, are the most effective forms of action we can take to correct present demographic trends?

Possible scenarios

The World Population Conference, held in Bucharest in 1974, was the scene of a clash between two contradictory theories as to how to reduce population growth. The first of these, which received the backing of a majority of the developing countries, has been summed up in the catchphrase "development is the best contraceptive". According to its supporters, an improvement in the standard of living, coupled with educational advances, would inevitably lead to a better acceptance of, and demand for, means of birth control.

The opposing viewpoint, described as "neo-Malthusian" by its

Courtesy of *The UNESCO Courier*, January 1992, pp. 14-17.

detractors, despite the fact that it diverged considerably from the theories of Malthus, was based on the principle that a reduction in the rate of population growth, achieved by means of a reduction in fertility, was a prerequisite and not a consequence of development. Supporters of this theory therefore advised the organization of huge campaigns for the spread of information and the distribution of contraceptives.

The World Population Plan of Action, approved at the Bucharest Conference, adopted a less dogmatic tone and succeeded in taking some of the initial virulence out of the debate. Nevertheless, ten years later, at the International Conference on Population, held in Mexico, in August 1984, to assess the working and results of the Plan, this debate re-emerged, but in a very different political and ideological context. Dressed up in neo-liberal guise, the "development first" argument received the support of the United States, whereas, this time, the developing countries were calling for vigorous family-planning programmes.

The defenders of the neo-liberal standpoint maintained that a development model based on free, individual initiative, with the market as the principal regulator of the economy, was the only mechanism capable of ensuring lasting development and of creating the necessary conditions under which couples would, in their own interest, come to modify their perception of the family and themselves choose to have fewer children better spaced out. This transformation of the scale of values and of family preferences would generate a demand for contraceptives which the market could itself meet with only marginal assistance from the State.

The principle of non-intervention by the State applied also to the question of internal migrations—any interference by the public authorities would be likely not only to infringe individual liberties, but also to distort the workings of the market in goods and services and this in the end would aggravate the very social and community problems such interference was designed to resolve.

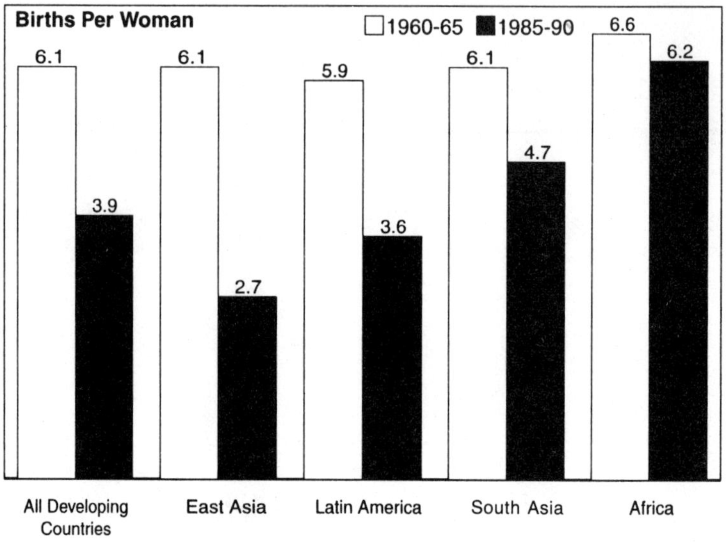

Fertility trends in the developing world, by region(Source: United Nations, 1990).

Although to do so was in contradiction with the principles they stood by, for political reasons, the governments and many of the theoreticians supporting this view treated international migration as a separate case, as though in this field the laws of supply and demand did not apply.

The argument of those who favoured family-planning programmes seemed to find some justification in the rapidity of the demographic transition in Latin America and in certain Asian countries, which appeared to contradict the notion that a reduction in birth rates is conditional on structural change and to entail acceptance of the view that the fall in the birth rate is due, at least in part, to an evolution in the understanding of and the aspirations, attitudes and values relating to procreation.

On this basis, some have sought to draw the conclusion that a vigorous family-planning programme could act as a brake on fertility without the need to introduce major social and economic reforms. At this stage in the debate, such a conclusion seems premature. Comparative historical studies that have been made on the demographic transition have shown that whilst too much emphasis may perhaps have been placed on structural factors as the prerequisite of a reduction in the birth rate, their importance cannot be entirely denied.

Learning from experience

Social and demographic indicators concerning all countries were recently published in "The State of World Population, 1991", the annual report of the United Nations Population Fund. They reveal that:

- the highest rates of population growth are to be found in the poorest countries;
- there are, however, some exceptions; in some countries the population growth rate is lower than might have been expected in view of the level of the per capita Gross National Product;
- the reverse is true in other countries where, although the economic indicators, comparatively speaking, are not so low, population growth rates are high;
- whether or not there is an official population policy, the percentage of women making use of family-planning services is, almost without exception, higher in the more developed countries.

Given these facts, it might well be asked whether there is any means by which population growth rates can be significantly reduced. United Nations projections according to which

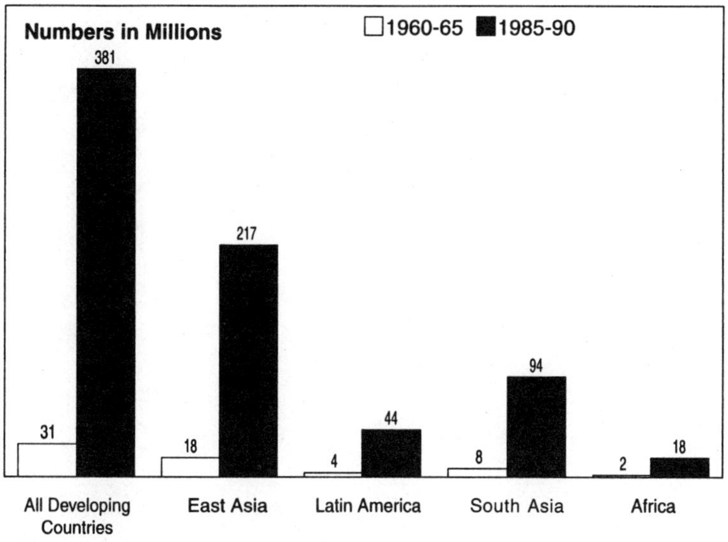

Trends in the number of contraceptive users, by region (Source: United Nations, 1990).

world population will stabilize around the middle of the twenty-second century, at about 11.6 billion, are based on the supposition that there will be a diminution in the overall fertility rate in the developing countries, which will reduce from 3.8 to 3.3 births per woman by the year 2000. For this to occur, the percentage [of] regular use of contraceptives in these countries would have to rise from the present 51 per cent to 59 per cent. In absolute figures, this would mean that, within a period of nine years, 186 million women would have to be persuaded to make regular use of contraceptives.

Experience over recent years indicates that it is extremely difficult to achieve a rise of these proportions in the regular use of family-planning methods. With the exception of Latin America (excluding central America), the Caribbean, east and south-east Asia, the other regions, which are those that contribute most to world population growth, would have to achieve a reduction of at least 1.1 in the average number of births per woman; in Africa south of the Sahara the average would have to be reduced by more than half (from 6.8 births per woman to 3.3).

Although they have been prime recipients of international aid over recent years, the poorest countries still have high fertility rates. Judging by results, the efforts made to stem the rising demographic tide through campaigns for the distribution of contraceptives, coupled with information, education, communication and family-planning programmes, have clearly not been very effective. This relative failure casts considerable doubt on the theory that dissociated demographic evolution from economic progress and leads us to ask what other options are open to us.

In theory, there are three such options. The first is to establish an obligatory maximum limit to the number of children per family. This, however, would be contrary to paragraph 29 of the World Population Plan of Action, which recommended that all countries "respect and ensure, regardless of their overall demographic goals, the right of persons to determine, in a free, informed and responsible manner, the number and spacing of their children".

The second option is to rely on "the magic of the market economy" in the hope that it will quickly rescue the poorest countries from the abyss of underdevelopment, change family attitudes concerning numbers of children and encourage the public and private sectors to respond more effectively to the demand for contraceptives. It is questionable whether such faith in the market economy is justified, at least as far as the poorest countries are concerned—their market mechanisms are weak and they are in competition with the industrialized countries which firmly protect their internal markets and erect trade barriers against the importation of products from the developing countries.

The third option, put forward primarily by economists and social science experts of the developing countries, is also supported by the regional institutions of the United Nations as well as by a number of eminent specialists of the developed countries. It proposes that the newly-developing international division of labour be so oriented as to favour more equitable trading between the developed and the developing countries whilst enabling national economies to give priority to the elimination of extreme poverty and to raise the level of well-being of the general public.

This third option, sometimes referred to as "equitable development", involves raising governments' social policies—education, public health, housing and employment—from their present secondary role and placing them on at least an equal footing with strictly economic policies aimed first and foremost at growth. Among these policies, demographic policies concerning population growth rates and distribution should be given priority if population pressures are not to become an obstacle to the fight against poverty.

Action along these lines seems to offer the best chance of achieving the goal of preventing the pressures of population growth and distribution fuelling even more alarming trends than those forecast by the United Nations. This will only be possible if the developed countries, which hold the reins of world economic power, are prepared to accept that demographic and environmental problems will not be resolved so long as long-term objectives are sacrificed to the benefit of short-term interests. Furthermore, the experience of recent decades demonstrates that, in the struggle for justice and against poverty and social inequality, a necessary prerequisite is a major effort to establish, consolidate and extend democracy.

Whether we like it or not, the probability is that the world population will double before it becomes stabilized. Resolution of the problems that this entails and preventing them from growing to unforeseeable proportions is not a question of means but of political will. The current upheaval of the world political scene provides an opportunity, perhaps unique, to give a new momentum to efforts by the international community to increase the well-being of ordinary people everywhere.

Poverty, population, pollution

One person in five lives in absolute poverty

Nafis Sadik

Nafis Sadik is Executive Director of the United Nations Population Fund (UNFPA), the world's largest source of multilateral assistance to population programmes. On her appointment in 1987, she became the first woman to head a major voluntary-funded UN programme. A physician of Pakistani nationality, she is the author of many articles in the field of family planning and health, and has edited a book Population: The UNFPA Experience *(New York University Press, 1984).*

The elimination of poverty is first and foremost a moral imperative; but it is also essential for the protection of the global environment and for the health of the global economy. On all these grounds, we can no longer tolerate a situation in which one in five human beings—a total of 1 billion people—lives in absolute poverty.

Protection of the environment is a requirement for ending poverty—a ruined and plundered resource base could not support our current and future numbers—and slower, more balanced population growth is both a precondition for, and an outcome of, finding solutions to the twin problems of the environment and poverty.

In the past, economic development was seen as the solution to poverty, and demographic transition as the eventual solution to population growth. Some damage to the environment was accepted as a necessary, but only marginally important, cost of development. These assumptions are no longer justified.

In many cases development has not only failed to eliminate poverty but has actually increased it, with deadly effects on population growth and environmental damage. For when development efforts are ineffective, they disrupt existing social and economic systems without providing compensating benefits. Even when development is effective it vastly increases human sources of pollution and environmental destruction. The industrial technology in use in most of the world was developed without thought for its environmental effects.

An unwanted side-effect of incomplete development has been to encourage rapid population growth. Mortality has fallen and life expectancy has risen, but there has been much less effect on birth rates. Increasing income and improving child survival leads in the first place to larger families. Only when development programmes include a family-planning element does family size fall significantly.

Another unintended side-effect of incomplete development has been massive and sustained urban growth. Classic development theory relies on the city as the engine of economic growth and therefore encourages urbanization. However, no one foresaw rates of urban growth of between 4 and 7 per cent such as are being seen now in many developing countries where urban growth has spiralled beyond control.

The crisis is produced as much by numbers and concentrations as by technologies and structures. This is a peculiarly difficult dilemma. If development is simply the replication of world experience to date, it condemns the environment, and therefore itself.

The keys to modern development

Education, health care and balanced population growth, with special attention to the status of women, are the keys to modern development. They also form a basis for the elimination of poverty and protection of the environment.

Developing countries' own resources of food and raw materials—and above all their human resources—are sufficient for balanced development, if they are exploited in a thoughtful way rather than for short-term gain. The aim of all who are committed to development must be to work towards the marriage of public policy with private interest and a full sense of community combined with respect for human rights and dignity.

There are many reasons why so many people are and remain so poor. One is the sheer scale of the problem; the poor are the fastest-growing segment of the population in any country and in the world as a whole. Another reason is that the

Courtesy of *The UNESCO Courier,* January 1992, 18-21.

poor are trapped in a vicious cycle where poverty, lack of education, lack of earning power, poor nutrition and poor health feed on each other. However the main reason for continuing, large-scale poverty is quite simple—the lack of a concerted will, nationally or internationally, to do something about it. Many promises have been made, but few have been kept. Many development theorists have pointed out that poverty can kill us all, but they have not been heeded. Ending poverty has simply not rated a high priority in most countries, whether industrialized or developing.

The poor themselves certainly have the will and the motivation to defeat their poverty. Anyone who has ever set foot in a slum, a poor village or a shanty-town knows what ingenuity, skill and effort go into the daily struggle to survive. We in government and the development business must learn not to get in the way. This is not the same as abdicating responsibility; consider how many ready-made anti-poverty programmes have come to grief because the poor were not involved in their design and execution; consider how many more have failed because they ran foul of some contradictory policy.

Consider in particular how women have been excluded and how their contribution to the national and local economy and society has been undermined by schemes with the word "development" in their titles. The pattern is so consistent across continents and levels of development that it is difficult not to conclude that the intention was to exclude women from the new society and to keep them safely at home with the children.

Community involvement

Experience shows that the successful grass-roots development programmes are those which respond to national needs through local action and involve both men and women, rich and poor. For national policy to succeed, effective and appropriate services must be delivered locally and at the family level. Even more important, families and communities must be involved in the policy-making and management process.

There is considerable scepticism today about the ability of governments to deliver development services to the poor and even more about governments' ability to involve communities in decision-making, although in most countries this has scarcely been given a fair trial. Where governments are committed—

as, for example, in Sri Lanka, or in Costa Rica—the experience has certainly been that services such as education, health care, family planning, agricultural extension and even housing can be delivered with community co-operation. Recent reports say that the State of Kerala, in India, has achieved universal literacy—largely through a combination of official and community action.

The other aspect of service delivery is, of course, self-help. The poor are almost completely self-reliant, because they have no one else to rely on. Considering what they achieve with so few resources, it should come as no surprise that they can do a great deal when resources are more plentiful. With small amounts of outside help and organization, shanty communities in Sri Lanka have made themselves the model for a national self-help housing programme. The Grameen Bank in Bangladesh is a famous example of success in extending credit to the poor.

Can successful community-based experience be transferred to productive areas of the economy, for example to industry or agricultural policy? A growing number of economists and other analysts of the development process now think so. If, for example, the supply of water for irrigation is controlled and paid for by user groups, the result is that less water is used and it is used more effectively.

The mix depends upon the country and the community. Flexibility is the key to a successful approach. Above all, understanding that improving services to the poor is an important development goal must be inculcated at all levels. The banking industry in Indonesia was very sceptical about making loans to women's groups, but it has been shown that with outside funding women's groups will both repay on time and make profitable investments. Commercial banks are now much more enthusiastic about such business.

If the global importance of small-scale development is to be recognized, the big organizations—intergovernmental groups, multilateral agencies, international policy-making institutions—must give it their seal of approval. It is very difficult for the very big to see the very small, but it is important for them to learn. There are too many examples of massive, internationally-funded development projects that have ended in expensive, environmentally dangerous and socially catastrophic failure.

A role for the United Nations

The United Nations system is being given more work to do in the post-

-cold war era. The system has already proved its value as a neutral forum for discussion of different approaches to development. It has proved its value as a channel for development assistance which is not tied to one ideology or approach. Greater resources are now needed so that the system can work towards a new international consensus on the shape of development.

Even more important, perhaps, than resources for the future effectiveness of the United Nations system will be a clearer sense of direction. The United Nations is an inter-governmental system and, in the end, governments decide how effective they want it to be. It is quite clear that the various parts of the system need better co-ordination. It is equally clear that our agencies and their mandates, their political direction and their management, are fragmented and need to be reviewed and revised so as to meet the needs of the next century. After three development decades, the best we can say—and it is a considerable boast—is that we have survived. We are supporting the largest number of humans ever to have inhabited the planet at one time. We have escaped nuclear war and we seem to have reassessed the risks of nuclear meltdown. The United Nations has not collapsed, blown apart or withered away. Some of our institutions are stronger than before and some of them have learned how to work effectively. There is international consensus on the need for action to protect the environment, even if there is disagreement as to what that action should be. There is a very strong and practical consensus on the need for slower, more balanced population growth worldwide.

There seems to be an even chance that the female half of the population will get its share of development investment in the future and be allowed to make a full contribution to development work. The international community may come to understand that enabling the poor to escape poverty may be the key to survival for the rest of us.

The Urban Explosion in the Third World

Around one and a half billion people in the developing countries today live in cities, a figure which is expected to double in the next 20 years; in the 1950s, by contrast, fewer than 300 million people in the Third World were city-dwellers. Such rapid urbanisation, on such a massive scale, has never been encountered before. It brings with it the danger of disequilibria and strain, for the demands to be met are huge and the policies, infrastructure and services to cope with them are not yet in place[1]

Nicole Massignon

Nicole Massignon is in charge of technical assistance, urban development and agriculture in the OECD Development Co-operation Directorate.

A comparison of the pace of urban and population growth in the developed world and in the developing countries brings home the unprecedented nature of the process of urbanisation under way in the Third World. The developed countries are largely urbanised, with nearly three-quarters of their population now living in towns and cities. But the urban growth rate there is low (0.8% in 1990), and falling: the number of city-dwellers—some 800 million in 1990—is not expected to hit the billion mark before 2005.

In the developing countries urban growth has been sudden, swift and massive, under the double impact of population growth and a drift from the land. Forty years ago a little fewer than 300 million people (17% of the population), or roughly one in five, lived in or near a city. Recent United Nations estimates[2] suggest this figure will reach 1.4 billion (34%), or one person in three. The latest forecast is for 2 billion (40% of the population) by the turn of the century and 4 billion (57%) in 2025. By 2015 in the Third World there will be more people living in towns than in the country. Within three generations the lifestyles of most people on the planet will have been radically transformed.

These figures, of course, contain a degree of uncertainty. In 1992 the United Nations—the principal source of demographic and urban statistics for the world as a whole—revised their 1990 projections, producing substantial differences for a small number of towns. For Mexico City, for example, the numbers were revised downwards after the most recent census, in 1990. These revisions don't change the wider trends, of course.

There are evidently wide variations between and within regions (Table). Latin America is already heavily urbanised (72% of the population); it is Asia and Africa, where the proportion of city-dwellers is still a little over 30%, that are feeling the full onslaught of the change. By the end of the century, nearly 600 million more inhabitants will have poured into Third World cities. And it is in Africa, particularly East Africa, that urban growth is most rapid. An increase of 120 million in the number of African city-dwellers between 1990 and 2000 is predicted (the equivalent of urban growth in the entire developed world between 1975 and 1990). In Asia, the urban population will have soared to 1.4 billion by the year 2000. In cities like Calcutta, Bombay and New Delhi, it is shooting up by some 200,000 to 400,000 every year.

When the century draws to a close, there will be 21 cities with over 10 million inhabitants—17 of them in developing countries. São Paulo already has nearly 20 million inhabitants, Mexico City more than 15 million (less than an earlier estimate of more than 20 million in 1990), and Lagos, a medium-sized city (300,000) in the 1950s, had swollen to 8 million by 1990. Lagos, indeed, is expected to grow to accommodate 13 million people by the end of the century, many more than Paris (9.5 million by 2000). The forecasts for 2010 involve staggering sums, thanks to a high

Reprinted from *The OECD Observer*, June/July 1993, pp. 18-22.

Table

URBAN POPULATION GROWTH, 1990–2000

	1990		2000		1990–2000
	Urban Population *millions*	Urban Population/Total Population %	Urban Population *millions*	Urban Population/Total Population %	Growth *millions*
World	**2,282.4**	**43**	**2,962.1**	**48**	**679.7**
Developing Countries	**1,401.4**	**34**	**1,993.7**	**40**	**592.3**
Africa	**205.5**	**32**	**322.1**	**38**	**116.6**
Algeria	12.9	52	19.5	60	6.6
Ivory Coast	4.9	40	8.0	47	3.1
Egypt	23.0	44	30.0	46	7.0
Kenya	5.7	24	11.1	32	5.4
Nigeria	38.2	35	63.9	43	25.7
Zaire	10.5	28	15.8	31	5.3
Latin America	**315.5**	**72**	**400.6**	**77**	**71.1**
Bolivia	3.7	51	5.2	58	1.5
Brazil	112.1	75	140.8	82	28.7
Mexico	61.3	73	79.7	78	18.4
Peru	15.0	70	19.6	75	4.6
Asia	**974.3**	**31**	**1,370.0**	**37**	**395.7**
Bangladesh	18.7	16	33.1	23	14.4
China	302.2	26	451.7	35	149.5
India	216.1	26	290.9	29	74.8
Indonesia	53.1	29	79.5	37	26.4
Pakistan	37.8	32	58.6	38	20.8
Philippines	26.7	43	37.2	49	10.5
Thailand	12.1	22	17.7	29	5.6
Developed Countries	**880.9**	**73**	**968.4**	**76**	**87.5**
Australia	14.6	85	16.8	86	2.2
United States	188.1	75	213.3	78	25.2
Europe	373.4	73	401.4	77	28.0
Japan	95.3	77	101.1	79	5.8

Source: *World Urbanisation Prospects 1992,* United Nations, New York, 1993

growth rate and the numbers in question (Figure). By contrast, the large cities of the West (London, New York, Paris) are not expected to grow much.

Urban and Rural Development

Any reversal, even slowing down, of the move to the cities simply won't occur for years, for three reasons: first, the rapid population growth expected—city-dwellers are young and of childbearing age (the estimates put over half the anticipated increase down to this factor); second, the transformation of rural areas, where modernisation is forcing more and more farmers and farm-workers off the land to look for jobs in the cities; third, the increased likelihood of finding work in cities.

Cities have always been a driving force in economic development. According to the World Bank,[3] they already account for an average of 50% of GDP in the Third World, a proportion that may rise to two-thirds by the end of the century. Cities are major centres of production for industry, services and trade and so generate resources and jobs. They have a two-edged effect on national budgets, bringing in tax revenue on the one hand and increasing the demands on revenue on the other. Conversely, urban activities rely heavily on macro-economic and sectoral policy decisions. Taxation, trade, structural adjustment, the location of industry—all have repercussions for urban areas. So the framing of macro-economic policies should give consideration to their implications for cities and, indirectly, for rural areas.

In the long run, urbanisation ought to curb population growth, the birth-rate falling as standards of living and education rise and family planning targetted on a more limited area. But in most developing countries the requisite conditions do not yet exist.

It is now accepted that urban and rural development, far from conflicting, are mutually re-inforcing and

Figure
POPULATION GROWTH IN SELECTED CITIES, 1950-2010
millions of inhabitants

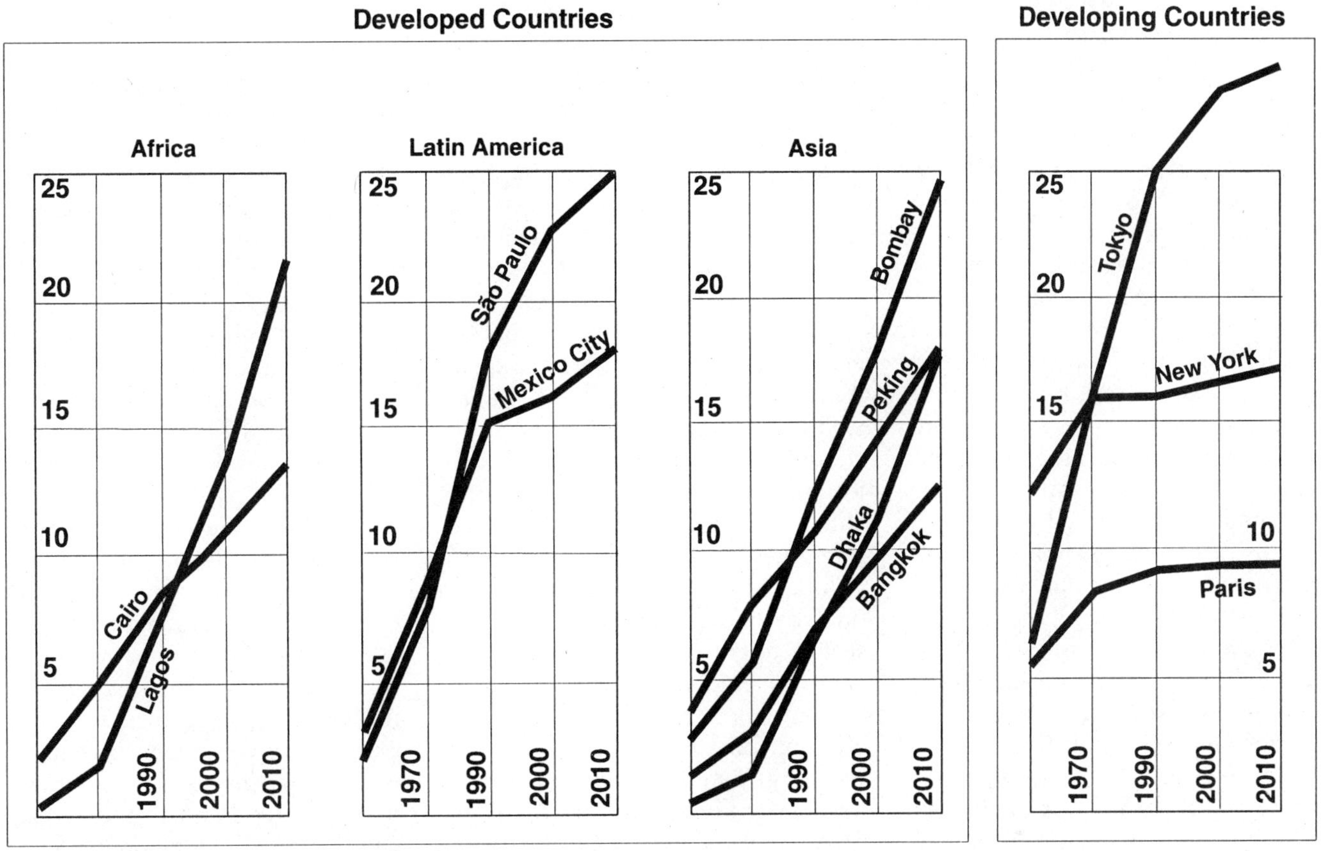

Source: *World Urbanization Prospects 1992*, United Nations, New York, 1993

ought to be pursued simultaneously. The idea that the various problems of urbanisation can be solved through strategies designed to improve life in rural areas has to be abandoned. If the rural labour force does not turn to urban activities, it will, to be able to grow crops, have no choice but to destroy forests or move onto land that is environmentally sensitive or ill-suited to farming. That process is already well under way in a large and steadily increasing number of countries.

A city cannot be separated from its hinterland. So an all-inclusive national approach is required. Cities have to support agriculture by providing the inputs, equipment, services and, above all, markets for farm produce; indeed, many smaller towns offer this very function. And for rural workers who cannot find employment, leaving the land offers the best hope of finding a job. They may be able to find work in the cities, particularly in the informal sector which sometimes accounts for two-thirds of all jobs.[4]

But if this interaction between town and country is to benefit both, cities have to continue to offer the right conditions for productive resources to be built up. Deficient infrastructure, inappropriate laws and regulations and the weakness of municipal institutions in many developing countries mean that urban productivity cannot be raised, restricting growth in both urban and rural areas alike.

Cities and Poverty

If urbanisation can thus take some of the pressure off the rural environment in developing countries, it is nonetheless putting ever-increasing pressure on the urban environment. Galloping urbanisation, with its attendant congestion and pollution, and coupled with a lack of resources, has disastrous effects on living conditions: squalid and overcrowded housing, scarcity of clean water, no proper sewage or drainage systems, no services (schools, dispensaries), and no provision of law and order whatsoever. 'Street children' (and there are 2 million of them in Latin America) often fall prey to organised crime, drugs and prostitution. Poor neighbourhoods are often located in areas where the risks of soil erosion, water pollution and natural disasters are higher than elsewhere.

Measures to alleviate poverty and protect the environment therefore have to be linked with the provision of better living conditions in the towns. Poverty, once more prevalent in rural areas, is now becoming a primarily urban problem. The number of people living in shanty towns on the outskirts of Third-World cities is growing much faster than the population housed in modern residential areas. In the 1980s, in cities such as Addis Ababa, Bombay and Cairo, between 60 and 80% of the population were reported to live in slums and informal settlements.

The World Bank states bluntly that poverty in urban areas could become one of the most explosive political problems of the 21st century.[5] And indeed, cities carry a lot of political weight because they have a high concentration of resources and institutions, and their inhabitants are better educated, better trained and consequently have more political, economic and cultural clout. Cities also draw young people in search of a better life. In most Third-World cities, over half the population is under 25. In sub-Saharan Africa, as much as a quarter of the population is aged between 15 and 25. And although young people can be a stimulus for entrepreneurship and initiative, they can also erupt into unrest and violence if they lose hope and feel alienated and marginalised.

Facing Up to Difficulties

These various factors should encourage lenders and investors to work out an effective policy to help Third-World cities. But it has to be said that (with the exception of the World Bank) they have so far been reluctant to do so. Why? Is it the enormity and complexity of the task? Difficulty in perceiving what is required for balanced and sustainable urban development? Are there no clear models or policies for reference, even though cities in the developed countries also have their difficulties?[6] Are they unwilling to relinquish an approach that has hitherto given preference to rural development? Are the necessary structures and skilled staff not available?

In November 1992 the OECD Development Assistance Committee (DAC), taking up the challenge, held a meeting with the World Bank, the United Nations Centre for Human Settlements (Habitat) and the United Nations Development Programme (UNDP), jointly defining aid for urban development as encompassing all policies, programmes and projects that are designed to improve the management, infrastructure and the quality of life in areas identified by the country concerned as urban and that also have a population of 20,000 or more. The joint definition also stresses the importance of quality (of policies, management, life) as well as quantity (of investment). It should also lead to progress in collecting statistics, which currently suffer both from problems of definition and from incompleteness.

Today there is a broad consensus on what aid policies for the urban sector ought to involve. The aid agencies emphasise that urban development ought to be economically efficient, socially just and environmentally friendly.[7] A more comprehensive, co-ordinated approach to urban development should replace the narrow, sector-specific stance adopted hitherto. In the past, urban aid consisted basically of providing modern infrastructure. In the future, it will also have to take macro-economic factors into account, as well as education, health (not least family planning), welfare, job-creation and improving the environment for all city-dwellers, including those living on the outskirts. The new approach will also have to be flexible and pragmatic to accommodate innovation and adjustment.

Mobilising Involvement

For decades to come, urban growth will call for huge investment if the shortcomings in infrastructure and services are to be put right—$100–150 billion a year, according to the World Bank. Aid will have to be the catalyst here, and technical assistance high on the list in finding solutions in each country. The task is so huge that it will require the combined efforts of central government, local authorities, public and private enterprise, trade and user associations and NGOs.

Although central government does have a crucial role to play in the balanced and sustainable development of cities, lenders and investors have in the past focused too narrowly on that particular institution and overlooked three others, equally important: local authorities; the private sector and public/private sector partnerships; and individual inhabitants.

First, local authorities must be given more freedom of action and more say in developing the cities they run—in particular, more power to raise revenue and thus improve services. In return, they must be more readily accountable to both central government and to their citizens, while at the same time improving the services they provide and making their management more transparent. Allowing them to overspend will overburden the central-government budget. Lenders and investors should therefore plan on giving adequate technical assistance to allow the upgrading of technical and management skills. 'Decentralised co-operation', involving twinning or co-operation agreements between towns and cities in developed and developing countries, could be encouraged—they would make for an exchange, particularly of experience. Partnerships between local authorities and NGOs working in development could also be fostered.

Second, it is crucial to give free rein to the initiative potential of private enterprise and the informal sector for the provision of urban services. It would be a mistake to underestimate the perverse effects of regulation. Red tape complicates land-use, and zoning rules, over-fussy building standards, and long and complicated industrial planning procedures discourage investors by pushing up costs. Aid organisations could encourage initiatives which require satisfactory and reliable service delivery so that investing firms can operate efficiently, which call for the reform of laws, rules and administrative practices so that they help rather than hinder productive activities, harness market forces and competition, and which pay due attention to the requirement of the informal sector.

Third, experience has shown that allowing people to participate directly in urban-development projects makes for more efficiency and may even determine success. The providers of services should therefore forge closer links with their clients (NGOs, local action groups, neighbourhood and consumer associations) from the outset of a project and throughout its duration. Lenders and investors should support initiatives that encourage the flowering of a community spirit in the urban areas they are working in. The attitude of the relevant municipal services, and the way a project dovetails into municipal, even national, structures are also decisive. 'Neighbourhood development projects' seem to be among the best ways of building effective partnerships. With projects on a larger scale, it may be advisable to base the approach on consultation rather than participation, or to link action by local office-holders with work done by other institutions (central government, city councils and technical services).

The DAC also emphasises the importance of acknowledging gender in framing urban development projects and programmes: staff in both donor and recipient countries have to be trained to deal with it. Men and women do have different requirements (particularly in infrastructure, services and housing) because they play different roles in society and at home. On average, one-third of all households in developing countries are run by women (compared with 10–15% in OECD countries), and in the cities the proportion is probably higher still. So women should have more say, perhaps more decision-making power, than men in matters of housing design, spatial planning and urban services, particularly transport. Law-and-order issues, too, are of vital importance to women.

Aid for urban development has suffered in the past not only from the weakness of the national institutions involved but also from the structural weaknesses of aid agencies when it comes to organising tasks of such complexity, which transcend traditional ministerial and policy-area divisions.[8] A number of bilateral and multilateral agencies still have no department or unit working expressly on the urban sector; instead, urban projects are shunted between the services in charge of infrastructure and social affairs. Aid agencies do not always have access to the partners most closely involved with the city, the local authorities in particular. Another drawback is that few agency personnel have been trained to work in an urban environment.

The lack of co-ordination between central units, technical units and the projects themselves, as well as among aid agencies, is sorely felt, too. Some agencies acknowledge that several projects have been undertaken in the same city without those in charge knowing about the others, simply because each was run by a unit of the agency concerned that dealt with a different area of policy. The main problem in the field appears to be the difficulty of linking infrastructure projects with social projects, and of co-ordinating the various policy-area components of each.

Whatever the differences between situations and resources, officials in both the developed and the developing countries must face up to the complexities of urban management. More and more city-dwellers are falling into poverty. The kind of urban development that has been so popular until now threatens the environment. Discussion and exchange of experience among officials and experts from North and South could help address these problems.

Notes

1. **Development Co-operation: 1993 Report,** OECD Publications, Paris, forthcoming end 1993, will include a chapter on this subject.
2. *World Urbanization Prospects 1992,* United Nations, New York, 1993.
3. *Urban Policy and Economic Development: An Agenda for the 1990s,* World Bank, Washington DC, April 1991.
4. Raundi Halvorson-Quevedo, 'The Growing Potential of Micro-Enterprises', **THE OECD OBSERVER,** No. 173, December 1991/January 1992; see also Friedrich Kahnert, *Improving Urban Employment and Labour Productivity,* World Bank Discussion Paper, No. 10, May 1987.
5. *Op cit.*
6. Christopher Brooks, 'Rethinking the City', **The OECD Observer,** No. 178, October/November 1992 (conference held at the OECD in November 1992 on the economic, social and environmental problems of cities); Rémy Prud'homme, 'City Limits', **The OECD Observer,** No. 181, April/May 1993.
7. *Urban Policy and Economic Development, op. cit.;* see also *Cities, People and Poverty—Urban Development Co-operation for the 1990s,* UNDP Strategy Paper, UNDP, New York, 1991; Nigel Harris (ed.), *Cities in the 1990s: The Challenge for Developing Countries,* Overseas Development Administration, Development Planning Unit, UCL Press, London, 1992; and *Coopération française pour le développement urbain, Ministère de la Coopération et du Développement and Caisse centrale de coopération économique,* Paris, October 1990.
8. Isabelle Milbert, *Coopération et développement urbain—Politiques des agences d'aide bilatérales et mutilatérales,* Swiss Development Co-operation (SDC), Geneva, second edition, November 1992.

OECD Bibliography

- **Development Co-operation: 1993 Report,** forthcoming 1993
- Rémy Prud'homme, 'City Limits', **The OECD Observer,** No. 181, April/May 1993
- Christopher Brooks, 'Rethinking the City', **The OECD Observer,** No. 178, October/November 1992
- **Development Co-operation: 1991 Report,** 1991
- Raundi Halvorson-Quevedo, 'The Growing Potential of Micro-Enterprises', **The OECD Observer,** No. 173, December 1991/January 1992
- Carl Wahren, 'The Imperative of Population Control', **The OECD Observer,** No. 167, December 1990/January 1991.

Family Planning: The Unfinished Revolution

RODOLFO A. BULATAO

Rodolfo A. Bulatao, a Philippine citizen, is a Senior Demographer with the Population Policy and Advisory Staff of the Bank's Population and Human Resources Department. He holds a PhD from the University of Chicago.

Voluntary family planning programs in the developing world help reduce population growth and contribute to better maternal and child health and to poverty alleviation. Despite the notable success of family planning programs in a number of regions, population growth remains high in many areas. The challenge lies in the better design and implementation of programs—whether new or ongoing—to ensure wider reach.

Family planning makes a difference. In 1960, Ethiopia's population was 10 percent smaller than that of the Republic of Korea. Over the next three decades, Ethiopia recorded almost two-and-a-half times as many deaths as Korea, but by 1990, Ethiopia's population was 20 percent larger. At least as significant, by 1990 each Korean of working age (15-64 years) had 0.44 dependents to support, whereas each Ethiopian of working age had 1.04—more than twice as many—dependents to support. Ethiopia had 26 million people in the dependent ages, compared with only 13 million in Korea.

Partly responsible for the contrasting demographic trends was an effective family planning program that Korea started in the early 1960s. Contraceptive prevalence (the proportion of married women 15-49 using contraception) climbed from under 10 percent to over 70 percent—a level comparable to that in developed countries—and fertility fell correspondingly. Almost within a generation, Korean parents went from having six children to having barely enough, and lately not quite enough, to replace themselves in the population. This substantial secular decline in fertility, which paralleled but was faster than earlier changes in developed countries, is often referred to as the fertility transition.

In countries spread over every region of the world, family planning is seen as a means of reducing high rates of population growth and of helping to improve the living conditions of individuals and families. Family planning has contributed to lower fertility, and at the same time to better child survival, lower maternal mortality, and reduced burdens for parents. The spread of family planning has now reached a tipping point: half of all couples in developing countries—about 365 million—are using contraception.

Family planning programs have especially benefited the poor. They typically have larger families, and commercial contraceptives are often priced beyond their reach. Contraceptive pills and condoms cost more than 5 percent of per capita GNP in the majority of sub-Saharan African countries, as well as in at least a few countries in every other region. This makes it difficult for poor women to avoid pregnancy. That they want to do so is suggested by the substantial unmet need for contraception, which ranges from 10 percent to as high as 70 percent of women of reproductive age.

Program experience

Family planning programs started slowly in the early 1950s, expanded rapidly in the 1970s and 1980s, and now exist in almost one hundred developing countries around the world (see table). These programs basically provide contraceptive services and counseling on the use of a variety of contraceptive methods. Communication campaigns to reach potential users, which explain the benefits of smaller families and ease concerns about contraceptive technology, are an essential part. Some programs also provide, or are linked with, a variety of other services, such as maternal and child health services and income generation activities.

Family planning programs, in country after country, have encountered similar obstacles: initial skepticism that a social program can change highly personal behavior; shortages of resources, particularly skilled management staff; ideological opposition, sometimes religious and sometimes political, as the program becomes more visible; jurisdictional quarrels between health providers and family planners, or between ministries and nongovernmental organizations, or among various donors eager to put their mark on a program; stalls in performance if programs focus narrowly on particular client groups; and an increasing concern with costs, as the number served grows and donors turn their attention elsewhere.

At the same time, the fundamental viability of a family planning program in any culture and at any level of socioeconomic development has been increasingly established, as shown by the experience in selected countries in two regions—East and Southeast Asia and sub-Saharan Africa. The experience of these countries demonstrates the elements of program successes, as well as the obstacles that frequently prevail.

East and Southeast Asia. This region had some of the earliest family planning programs and showed rapid increases in contra-

From *Finance & Development*, December 1992, pp. 5-8. *Finance & Development*, a quarterly publication of the International Monetary Fund and the World Bank.

Room for improvement
Strength of family planning program, 1989

Strong	Moderate		Weak		Very weak or none
Bangladesh	Chile	Korea, PDR	Afghanistan	Madagascar	Cambodia
Botswana	Colombia	Lebanon	Algeria	Mali	Chad
China	Costa Rica	Malaysia	Angola	Mauritania	Gabon
El Salvador	Cuba	Morocco	Argentina	Mozambique	Iraq
India	Dominican Republic	Nepal	Benin	Niger	Côte d'Ivoire
Indonesia	Ecuador	Pakistan	Bhutan	Nigeria	Kuwait
Korea, Republic of	Egypt	Panama	Bolivia	Papua New Guinea	Lao PDR
Mauritius	Ghana	Peru	Brazil	Paraguay	Liberia
Mexico	Guatemala	Philippines	Burkina Faso	Rwanda	Libya
Sri Lanka	Guyana	South Africa	Burundi	Senegal	Malawi
Taiwan Province of China	Honduras	Singapore	Cameroon	Sierra Leone	Myanmar
Thailand	Iran	Venezuela	Central African Republic	Syria	Namibia
Trinidad & Tobago	Jamaica	Zambia	Congo	Tanzania	Oman
Tunisia	Kenya	Zimbabwe	Ethiopia	Togo	Saudi Arabia
Viet Nam			Guinea	Turkey	Somalia
			Guinea-Bissau	Uganda	Sudan
			Haiti	Uruguay	United Arab Emirates
			Jordan	Yemen	
			Lesotho	Zaire	

Source: W. Parker Mauldin and John Ross, The Population Council.

ceptive use. The chart shows dates when national family programs started in selected countries and subsequent trends in contraceptive use. Contraceptive prevalence increased steadily by around 3 percentage points annually in Indonesia, Korea, and Thailand. Prevalence increased much more slowly in the Philippines, by only 1.7 points annually on average (see chart).

Initial conditions in these East and Southeast Asian countries were not particularly favorable to fertility transition. Socioeconomic conditions when programs were established—income, infant mortality, female education, and urbanization—were roughly comparable to conditions in the average low-income economy today. The cultural barriers to reducing fertility included, for instance, Confucian traditions in Korea that stress the centrality of the family. The extended household was common, and the patrilineal family structure allowed parents to influence their children's reproductive decisions. Political opposition to family planning also appeared, often based on religion.

But some desire for smaller families did exist, and increased over time. Near the start of fertility transition in Indonesia, Korea, and Thailand, women reported their ideal families to be around four children. Over the next two decades, this number fell by one child every 12 years in each country. As ideal family size declined, socioeconomic conditions—especially income and infant mortality—were improving rapidly.

Family planning programs in these countries succeeded by taking advantage of opportunities to mobilize political support, meeting the existing demand for contraception, and developing innovative ways to deliver services. Political stability and strong governments created conditions in which such social programs could be run effectively, although political upheaval sometimes provided some initial impetus. In Korea, the program started in the context of a massive reconstruction effort begun by a new administration a decade after the end of the Korean War. Widespread existing demand for contraception was demonstrated by pilot projects, such as the Jakarta pilot project in Indonesia, and by private voluntary organizations, such as the Planned Parenthood Federation of Korea—which was instrumental in laying the groundwork for the government program.

The contribution of programs to the rise in contraceptive use was substantial in all the countries. For instance, 40 percent of the fertility decline in Korea in 1963–73 was contributed by program-supplied contraceptives, as opposed to other proximate determinants (for example, abortion) or other sources of contraceptives.

Fertility transition is far from complete in the region, however. A number of countries, such as the Philippines and Viet Nam, remain mired in slow fertility transitions. Even in the more successful countries significant numbers of people still do not have adequate access to contraception. In Indonesia, the Outer Islands are well behind Java and Bali. Provincial total fertility rates range from 2.4 in Bali to as high as 5.3 in South East Sulawesi and Irian Jaya.

Sub-Saharan Africa. Family planning programs have made much less headway in sub-Saharan Africa. Even in this region, however, some countries show unmistakable signs that fertility transition is underway, and

A remarkable increase in contraceptive use[1]
Selected Asian and African countries

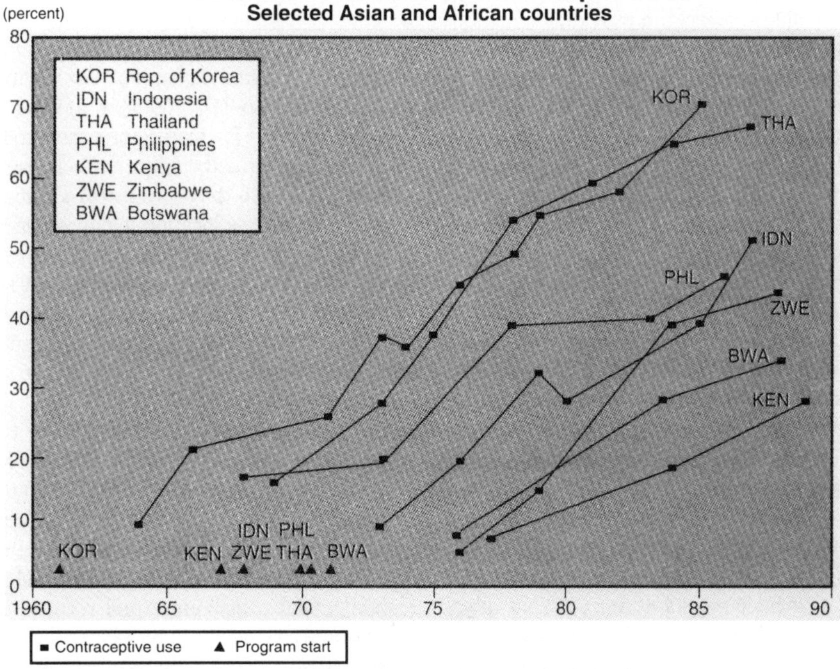

[1] Percent of married women between the ages of 15-49 or spouse using family planning methods.
Source: The World Bank.

in other countries, small-scale successes in particular communities demonstrate the potential for family planning programs.

Programs in Botswana, Kenya, and Zimbabwe started in the late 1960s or early 1970s, but prevalence did not exceed 10 percent until the 1980s. When fertility transition started, contraceptive prevalence increased at widely divergent rates: 1.7 points a year in Kenya, 2.1 points a year in Botswana, and 3.1 percentage points a year in Zimbabwe.

Both socioeconomic and cultural influences have been used to explain the delay in the start of transition, but neither provide an adequate explanation. Socioeconomic conditions when programs started were slightly behind conditions in Korea and Thailand, but better than conditions in Indonesia. Relative to Asian countries, these countries experienced relatively slower income growth but comparable improvements in social indicators—infant mortality, female education, and urbanization.

The cultural barriers to family planning in these countries, and elsewhere in sub-Saharan Africa, parallel in important ways those in Asia. For both regions, children are seen as assets to the older generation, providing assistance and security—strong motives for the extended family to encourage high fertility. As in Asia, these motives have not proven to be absolute barriers to fertility transition.

What was distinctive about Botswana, Kenya, and Zimbabwe was the nature of existing demand for contraception, which was largely to space births rather than to reduce the total number. Programs attempted to address this demand by emphasizing the benefits of child spacing and providing temporary methods, often birth control pills. However, delivery systems have been quite different. Botswana, with presumably stronger demand because of socioeconomic factors, as well as a public health system that covers the country fairly evenly, has relied on health posts and health centers to provide contraceptives. Zimbabwe has placed primary emphasis on community-based distribution to the rural population. Kenya has also emphasized outreach, but has relied to a much greater extent than Zimbabwe on private voluntary organizations to complement public services.

In contrast, Ghana, Rwanda, and Zaïre have not started fertility transition. They differ from the other three countries not in initial socioeconomic conditions—they actually had slightly higher GNP per capita at the time their programs started—but in socioeconomic trends since then. They have had negative economic growth and relatively small improvements in social indicators. Nevertheless, family planning programs have had some effect in small areas.

In the city of Kananga, Zaïre, the Institut Medical Chrétien du Kasai reoriented its two family planning clinics to make their services more accessible; provided apprenticeships for nurses from a dozen other clinics and helped improve their procedures; and marketed subsidized contraceptives through 30 pharmacies and shops. Visits to the Institut's clinics increased 15-fold, and the prevalence of modern methods went from 4 to 8 percent in 18 months.

In Ghana, the midwives association provided its members with training in family planning, supervision, and assistance with supplies. After one to two years, the first 130 midwives trained reported an average of 100 new family planning clients each, 80 percent of them using contraceptives for the first time.

In the Ruhengeri region of Rwanda, Abakangurambaga (wakers of the people), who provide information on development topics to small groups of households, were used to provide family planning information and referrals to clinics. In the commune where they were most active, a survey showed the prevalence of modern methods rising to 29 from 5 percent in 16 months.

Each of these approaches suggests a different way family planning can be effectively delivered in a relatively unfavorable socioeconomic setting.

Program challenges

By the year 2000, the number of contraceptive users in developing countries will have to be 40 percent higher if fertility declines are to match projections. New programs will be needed where family planning has received little attention so far, and new approaches must be invented for mature programs to enable them to expand their clients. Social development will also have to proceed apace: women need more education to appreciate the benefits of smaller families, and they need firmer assurance that their children will survive. Both new and ongoing programs will have to emphasize some basic approaches that research and experience have shown can contribute to wider contraceptive use.

Improving quality of services. Programs need to focus on providing quality services that attract clients. A good program provides access to a range of appropriate contraceptive methods and facilitates their continued use; provides adequate counseling, respects client sensibilities, and responds to client concerns; and is run by technically competent providers according to proper medical standards.

These elements of quality are not always present. About half of almost 100 national programs rated in 1989 were judged to provide inadequate access to each of five contraceptive methods. When methods are available, counseling may be unsatisfactory: large numbers of birth control pill users in such countries as Brazil and Egypt have been shown to be using them incorrectly. Client sensibilities are often offended by long waiting times and rude and impatient staff.

Quality services, on the other hand, attract clients. Providing an additional contraceptive method, for instance, appears to add an additional layer of contraceptive users. Reducing waiting times allows a clinic to serve more users. A clinic in Ecuador reduced waiting times with additional staff and experienced a more than proportional increase in clients served. At the same time, quality services can be more efficient. The Matlab project in Bangladesh stressed quality, offering more reversible methods than the government program, recruiting workers with higher credibility who were more intensively supervised, giving clients better counseling about side effects, adding more intensive follow-up through home visits, and providing added maternal and child health services. Because it attracted more users, the cost per birth averted through contraception was two thirds that of a comparison area with less intensive services.

Ensuring accountability and strategic management. Programs must be managed strategically. A program manager must be responsive to its environment, taking advantage of cultural tendencies and social factors and negotiating its way through the political and other obstacles that arise. Programs typically develop in three ways: from seeking clients among those already disposed to contracept to focusing on the large disadvantaged majority among whom the small-family norm must be cultivated; from heavy reliance on donors and volunteers to reliance on a network of agencies and eventually on the public at large; from services provided passively in a few sites to active outreach and eventually to services carefully differentiated by market segment. Programs need to recognize the challenges posed by this evolution.

Management responsibilities are varied, from mobilizing public support for a program to managing staff. Most critical are ensuring reliable logistics and providing adequate field supervision. The logistical systems for handling contraceptives are often weak. Supply shortages contribute to contraceptive discontinuation and user dissatisfaction, damage morale among staff, and contribute to a poor program image. Supervision of the field staff who actually distribute the contraceptives and provide counseling is critical, because it strengthens their motivation and helps them apply their skills to program tasks.

Encouraging the private sector. Programs need greater involvement of the private sector. In family planning, this sector is quite varied, including nongovernmental organizations, private practitioners, and commercial outlets for contraceptives. The sector can provide additional resources and is sometimes more flexible and efficient than public services.

Private services may be useful in introducing family planning generally, or in introducing specific services. They may reach specific populations, not only through their own clinics but also through networks of private practitioners and commercial distributors for the marketing of subsidized contraceptives. Involving the private sector often requires reform of laws or regulations that limit them, such as import duties on contraceptive supplies and prescription requirements that unnecessarily restrict contraceptive availability.

Designing effective promotion campaigns. The creative promotion of programs—both government and private—is essential to their success. Like any new product, contraceptives have to be brought to the attention of potential users, made attractive, and shown to be safe. This effort is essentially educational, aimed at producing satisfied and effective users willing to encourage others.

Interpersonal channels and the mass media can be effective tools. Both must be used with all the skills and techniques of modern public relations and advertising, so that family planning messages are able to compete in the noisy marketplace.

Obtaining official assistance. Government and donor support must be constant. By the standards of large-scale social interventions, family planning programs are not expensive. In 1990, programs cost about $4 billion–$5 billion. Donor assistance in population was about 1.2 percent of official development assistance, barely 2 percent more (in constant dollars) than it was in 1985. If individuals themselves had to pay for family planning, the cost could have been beyond the means of many. Commercial prices for contraceptives are such that, for over 60 percent of sub-Saharan countries, a supply of contraceptive pills would cost more than 5 percent of average annual income.

Political commitment is also essential to allow programs to recruit essential staff, obtain the cooperation of other agencies, and free programs from webs of regulation that could otherwise severely hamper their operation.

For an in-depth study of the evidence, see "Effective Family Planning Programs" to be published as a "Best Practice" paper by the World Bank.

EARTH SUMMIT '92—II

North vs. South On Pollution

PRAFUL BIDWAI

Praful Bidwai is a senior editor with The Times of India.

The United Nations Conference on Environment and Development (UNCED) in Rio de Janeiro shows all signs of becoming an arena of North-South confrontation over the division of environmental resources; responsibility for global warming and depletion of the ozone layer; distribution of the burden entailed by the necessary remedies; and the financing of cleanup measures. The April conference of the Group of 77 (developing countries) in Kuala Lumpur, Malaysia, on this issue and the response to it from the Group of Seven finance ministers during their meeting in Washington put the North-South divergence in a harsh light.

The financial aspect of this divergence is the starkest. The North would like the South to take measures that will cost $125 billion a year, which must come through funding over and above official development assistance from international bodies and individual states. That assistance totals only about $50 billion a year, equivalent to 0.3 percent of the North's gross domestic product. The South would like a new institutional arrangement that is more democratic, broad-based and better funded than that provided by existing multilateral agencies such as the World Bank, which are heavily weighted in favor of the North. However, the North rejects a new mechanism and insists that the present arrangement, in the form of the Global Environmental Facility, is adequate and could be strengthened. The facility—operated by the World Bank for two U.N. agencies—was launched two years ago with a mere $1.2 billion. Its actual disbursals have been marginal.

Within a broader perspective, North-South differences run much deeper. The most basic of the South's environmental problems are the erosion and degradation of an already inadequate natural resources base. The North's biggest problems—waste, emission and pollution—arise from overconsumption and intrusion into the global environmental space. The disproportion in the per capita consumption of resources between the North and the South is on the order of 3 to 1 or even 15 to 1, depending on the measures chosen; in the extreme case, the North may consume thirty times more than the South. The South rightly argues that the bulk of the truly global problems confronting humanity are in fact Northern in origin and are caused by the North's gargantuan overconsumption. Again, while the South consumes products of nature, including relatively unprocessed ones such as wood, to meet survival needs (e.g., 70 to 90 percent of wood used is burned for fuel), the North uses them as a part of luxury consumption (four-fifths as lumber in construction or manufacturing).

The most serious feature of this inequity is the phenomenon of global warming, which is attributable to emissions of carbon dioxide (mainly from fossil-fuel burning), methane (from cattle and agriculture) and chlorofluorocarbons, or CFCs (from refrigeration, air conditioning, paints, aerosols and electronics). The North accounts for up to 90 percent of the carbon dioxide that has so far accumulated in the earth's atmosphere. Going by the index called "natural debt of a nation," developed by environmental scientist Kirk Smith, the disparities are indeed huge. If U.S. per capita annual emissions (5.2 tons) were to be frozen and India's (0.22 tons) were to grow at recent rates, India would not reach one ton a year until 2024—a level surpassed by the United States well before 1900. As the Center for Science and Environment in New Delhi has shown in a remarkable study, the true impact of greenhouse gas emissions is clearly revealed when a country's gross emissions are discounted by its share of the global "sink" (the earth's natural capacity to absorb greenhouse gases). If the sink is divided in relation to the population on the premise that all human beings have an equal right to the earth's atmosphere, the North's net emissions account for up to 91 percent of the total. If Northern emissions could be traded with the South at $15 per ton of carbon equivalent and damages were to be paid at $25 per ton, the top fifteen polluters would have to pay $110 billion to the South; the United States alone would have to pay $45 billion a year.

And yet the North is asking the South to restrict its consumption as part of a "global" effort. The worst example of this inequity is the Montreal Protocol on Substances That Deplete the Ozone Layer (1987), an international treaty that restricts the consumption of CFCs on pain of trade penalties for noncompliance. This is an exercise in dealing with symptoms, not causes, and of treating unequals as equals. Since no responsibility is attached to different countries for their varying contributions to the CFC burden, no rights and obligations follow. So the South, with its current emission of 12 percent of CFCs, is asked to make the same commitment, albeit over a longer period of time, as the North, which produces 88 percent of the total. The underlying assumption is that it would be a disaster if every Chinese or Indian (not American or Japanese) had a refrigerator, but that it is not necessary for the rest of the world to find substitutes for CFCs.

And yet it is the Montreal protocol that is being offered by Northern governments as the preferred model for global environmental regulation—in waste dumping, tropical forestry, climate control and conservation of genetic resources—of which last the South accounts for 90 percent of the world total. The South has so far resisted pressures on the last three, but it is far from clear how long the region can hold out, given its parlous financial state, rapidly deteriorating trade position (today a barrel of oil costs ten times more, and steel three times more, in biomass than it did twenty years ago), global recession, competitive demand from the Eastern European economies, the declining effectiveness of U.N. development-related agencies and the growing meanness of the North.

At Kuala Lumpur, G-77 made an impassioned proposal for effective, equitable partnership, an environment tax and a new model of global environment management. Southern nongovernment organizations have also called for participatory democracy with global equity based on the right to survival, the right to information, equal rights to the atmosphere and global resources, and appropriate compensation for community biological knowledge. However, they have failed to move either Northern governments or the bulk of nongovernment organizations and Green parties in the North. While the former remain helplessly tied to industrial interests and lobbies, the latter tend to be oblivious of Southern (and truly global) concerns, narrowly focused on domestic issues and limited by an inability to change Western consumption patterns. If UNCED becomes a forum for an equal dialogue between the more environmentally concerned people of the North and South, it could perform an invaluable role. But the Rio conference may show that the world still has a long way to go before environmental equity and justice emerge in a sustainable way on a truly global scale.

Stop Dumping On the South

The Lure of Loose Laws

FINANCIAL EXPRESS

Pravin Kumar

Industrialized countries, where tight laws and urbanization make it difficult to dispose of hazardous wastes, are using the vast open spaces in developing countries as dumping grounds. In 1987, an Italian entrepreneur shipped 10,000 barrels of chemical waste from the Italian port of Leghorn to the Nigerian port of Koko, from where it was dumped into the bush. When the perilous nature of the waste came to light, Nigeria asked the Italian government to take it away. It was loaded on the *Karin B*, which sailed from country to country without being able to unload the cargo. Finally, the *Karin B* returned the waste to Leghorn.

Last year, *World Watch* magazine reported that Western companies had dumped more than 24 million tons of hazardous waste in Africa alone during 1988. The report says, "Perhaps the ultimate form of hazardous export is the relocation of whole manufacturing plants to parts of the world where manufacturing standards are lax."

To cope with their rivals, especially Japanese companies, U.S. firms are moving high technology to industrializing countries. In the automobile industry, for instance, by 1988, captive imports—cars produced offshore but sold under U.S. nameplates—accounted for 20 percent of all U.S. auto imports. Many of these imports came from four industrializing countries—South Korea, Taiwan, Mexico, and Brazil.

One attraction for foreign companies is the low wages in developing countries. Another attraction is that most developing countries have little or no environmental or worker-safety regulation.

In Mexico, for example, companies such as IBM, General Motors, Sony, and Hitachi have set up plants that manufacture a wide range of products, from automobile parts to high-technology electronic components. The $3 billion now earned by these industries in foreign exchange is second only to Mexico's earnings from gas and oil. These plants (known as *maquiladoras*) have created severe environmental problems on both sides of the U.S.-Mexico border. Workers live in squatters' colonies without heat or electricity. At least 10 million gallons of raw sewage from the factories are discharged into the Tijuana river daily, polluting San Diego's beaches. Most of the $192-million cost of the sewage-treatment plants is being paid by the U.S. government, the state of California, and the city of San Diego. Hence, the lower

From the independent "Financial Express" of New Delhi.

Africa Should Care

JEUNE AFRIQUE économie

Suddenly, environmental problems have become something that Africa must face up to, not only in their local implications, such as deforestation, desertification, soil erosion, and water shortages, but also in their global dimensions. Many African leaders are angered that developing countries may become subject to standards that could be burdensome constraints on what is already a difficult path to development.

In the short term, development is an absolute priority. Nothing is more urgent than eradicating hunger, malnutrition, and the lack of health care and education. But in the long term, if drastic remedial and preventive measures are not taken by all countries to protect an already badly battered environment, the survival of the human race will be at stake a few generations from now.

The Earth's environment affects Africa as much as any other part of the world. The most urgent task is fighting global warming, which threatens the world's economic and social system. This phenomenon will lead to changes in climate and rainfall patterns, altering the geography of agriculture. It will also lead to a rise in the sea level and could swallow up whole areas of the Maldives and major deltas such as that of the Nile.

This is a challenge to all mankind and requires a vast international effort. Developing countries will have to shoulder their share of the burden. Their influence on the world climate is rapidly increasing, because of their demographic and industrial growth. In these countries, development will swell energy demand, and virtually the only source will be fossil fuels.

It is important that new, "clean" technologies being developed in the industrialized world be made available free of charge to the developing countries and that they be helped to put them to use. The urgency of international cooperation in the environment is something that Africa cannot afford to ignore.

—Bertrand Schneider, "Jeune Afrique Économie" (business-oriented monthly), Paris.

From *World Press Review,* June 1992, pp. 12-13. Reprinted by permission.

manufacturing cost is offset by the higher taxes paid by the taxpayers of the industrialized country toward cleaning up the pollution.

Industrialized countries have double standards for environmental and worker safety—one for themselves and one for developing countries. The latter group generally does not have the well-funded environmental groups of Europe and the U.S. This situation is exploited by First World corporations. Under Mexican laws, toxic materials imported into the country or produced during manufacture must be re-exported to the country of origin or recycled in Mexico. But according to the Texas Water Commission, only 60 percent of the waste materials ever leave Mexico; the rest—most of it toxic—is disposed of illegally in Mexico's sewers and landfills.

Workers in poor countries have lower education and skills than their First World counterparts. They labor in small, crowded factories with old, unsafe machinery. The factories are located in areas inaccessible to health inspectors. This could hardly be said of Union Carbide's Bhopal, India, plant, but the workers there were unaware that the plant was potentially lethal. Even government officials claim that they were ignorant of the dangerous nature of the chemicals being produced in the plant.

PCBs (polychlorinated biphenyls) were banned in the U.S. in 1977 on account of their toxicity, but pregnant Mexican women employed at the Mallory Capacitors plant in Matamoros, Mexico, were required to work with PCBs. Twenty retarded children born to these mothers showed the same kind of retardation seen in children of pregnant women exposed to PCBs in Taiwan and Japan.

There is a growing realization that all technologies are hazardous, some more than others. Even the seemingly environmentally friendly electronics industry produces hazardous waste, including solvents used for cleaning and drying. While new products will bring in new hazards, old products and processes in new locales also will bring in new hazards. The rapid restructuring of world industrial production will reduce hazards in places that have learned to cope with them and shift hazards to places that lack the knowledge and resources to control them.

Fortunately, there is some awareness of the problem. The United Nations World Health Organization and the International Labor Organization now provide some guidance on occupational health and safety to developing countries. But their activities are directed to large employers, whereas the bulk of work sites in developing countries are small. The UN Environment Program and the World Bank now provide location advice and environmental-impact assessments when the host country is not able to do so. While clearing foreign-investment and technology proposals, such bodies should be fully involved.

A greener bank

The World Bank's new World Development Report argues that wise environmental policies may often make poor countries less poor

ENVIRONMENTALISTS love to hate the World Bank. Over the years it has lent money for projects that have encouraged deforestation, moved settlers to lands that could not sustainably support them and financed dams, roads and power plants. If pressed, it has usually argued that development must come before the environment.

This year's *World Development Report**, published earlier than usual to be ready for the Earth Summit in Rio de Janeiro next month, defends a different proposition. Not only is sound environmental policy essential for durable development, but many of the policies that improve environmental quality will also strengthen development.

Green lobbyists may decline to be wooed by the report. It was written not by the Bank's environment department but, like all its predecessors, by a team of economists specially assembled for the task. None was an environmental economist by training. The result was inevitably tension between the team and the Bank's in-house environmentalists, which culminated in the leaking of an intentionally provocative memo by Lawrence Summers, the Bank's chief economist (and so boss of the report's team).

Such friction aside, two aspects of the report will jar with deep greens. One is its insistence on the need to consider the costs and benefits of taking action, and the relative costs of different policy measures. This may be the way real-world policy-makers think (or ought to think), but many environmentalists seem to shudder at the thought of trade-offs between environmental and other objectives, or the weighing of costs and benefits.

Second, the report is mainly concerned with the kinds of environmental damage that harm human health or wealth in the poor countries, such as dirty water, dirty air and soil erosion. The report devotes far more space to these environmental problems, rarely on the agenda of northern greens, than to issues that many rich-country environmentalists believe are more pressing: conserving biological diversity and preventing climate change.

Dirt and development

The cure for poverty is economic growth. This is a fact that makes environmentalists wince—because poor countries often argue that economic growth and protection of the environment are incompatible.

Not so, says the report. Or rather, not so as long as growth is regarded as a means to achieve development in the broad sense of improving the well-being of people. If economic growth fails to take proper account of environmental costs, it will not durably improve well-being.

But how are development and the environment to go hand in hand? To start with, environmental quality is itself part of the improvement in welfare that development must bring. For example, 1 billion people in developing countries have no access to clean water; 1.7 billion lack access to sanitation. The result is a huge toll of disease and death.

Next, environmental damage can undermine economic productivity. Some estimates suggest that the productivity of a tenth of all irrigated land has been severely affected by increased concentrations of salts, a direct result of bad irrigation practices. Dirty air can also affect future productivity: estimates for Bangkok, which has awful traffic congestion, suggest that children lose an average of four or more points of IQ by the age of seven because of high levels of lead in their bodies.

Moreover, it is often the poorest people who suffer most from the consequences of environmental degradation. The rich can afford decent drinking water; the poor cannot. The rich cook on electricity; poor people cook on wood or charcoal stoves, whose fumes can cause the same sort of lung damage as smoking several packets of cigarettes a day. "Sound environmental policies", the report concludes, "are thus likely to be powerfully redistributive."

Just as protecting the environment is often a way to improve the lives of the poor, poverty is often a main cause of environmental damage. Poor people, living on the edge of subsistence, are much less able to invest in environmental protection. Studies in India found implicit discount rates among poor farmers of 30-40%—implying that they were willing to make an investment in, say, preventing soil erosion or planting trees only if it would treble its value in three years.

Bank policy has changed to take these high discount rates into account. For instance, the Bank now tackles erosion by encouraging farmers to plant hedges of tough grass, which are cheap and fast-growing, rather than build walls; and it encourages the planting of trees that can be coppiced for fodder and kindling while they grow.

Win-win

The cure for poverty is development. Development may also cure some kinds of pollution. Since 1970 emissions of particulates (soot and dust) have fallen 60% in the industrial countries; emissions of oxides of sulphur (a component of acid rain) have fallen 38%. Lead emissions have dropped by 85% in North America and by 50% in most European cities. The frequency of oil spills has declined. Forested areas and protected habitats have been extended in many countries.

Plenty of environmental problems remain in developed countries, and some have got much worse. The output of nitrogen oxides (a component of city smog), of municipal and toxic wastes and of carbon dioxide has increased. The survival of many plant and animal species is threatened. But the moral is clear: given the right technologies, developing countries can decouple some kinds of pollution from economic growth.

Indeed, the policies that will help to bring about such decoupling may also be good for the economy. Many policies are

*World Development Report 1992, "Development and the Environment." Published by Oxford University Press. Frances Cairncross, our environment editor, was seconded to the team that produced the report

justified on economic grounds alone, but have the incidental effect of improving environmental quality. Some of these "win-win policies" have no net financial cost to governments, but they deliver gains to both economic efficiency and the environment. Others cost money, but bring economic gains that would justify them even without their benefits to the environment. The benefits of a third group of policies and investments outweigh their costs only when their environmental effects are included.

Policies against pollution

For policy makers, the most valuable parts of the report may be its road maps of how to get there. Again and again, the emphasis is on proper pricing policies. Frequently, governments in developing countries deprive themselves of desperately needed revenue and set the wrong incentives by underpricing resources.

One extraordinary example is the provision of clean water. For years, development specialists have assumed that clean water should be provided cheaply by the government to the poor. The effective price charged for water, a recent Bank study reveals, is only about 35% of the average cost of supplying it. The upshot has been that supplies have often failed to keep up with fast-growing populations; and even when they have, they have been unreliable. In Latin America, for example, the level of leakage and of pipe breaks are respectively four times and 20 times higher than is normal in industrial countries.

As a result, the very poor frequently have to fall back on privately provided drinking water. In Latin American cities, water bought from vendors costs between four and 100 times as much as piped water. In Lima, a poor family uses only one-sixth as much water as a middle-class household, but its water bill is three times bigger.

Inadequate water supplies carry other economic costs. In many countries, families build storage tanks or dig wells to improve supply. To boil drinking water for ten minutes (as Peru's health ministry recommended during the recent cholera outbreak) would have cost more than a quarter of household income in a squatter settlement. The first ten weeks of that cholera outbreak lost Peru an estimated $1 billion in revenue from agricultural exports and tourism—more than three times the country's investment in water and sanitation for all of the 1980s.

In the case of water, sensible pricing policies would provide more revenue to install and maintain supplies. They would also encourage farmers to use irrigation water less wastefully, and thus release supplies for thirsty cities. But water is not the only resource that developing countries sell too cheaply for the good of their economies and their environments. The same is true of electricity.

Electricity prices in developing countries are typically about half those in the OCED industrial countries. The results match those for water: delivery is irregular, with consequent economic losses for industry, and waste is prevalent. In Bangladesh 31% of electricity is lost during transmission and distribution, compared with 8% in the United States. And developing countries use about 20% more electricity than they would do if consumers paid the true cost of supply.

Timber is another resource that is ludicrously underpriced. Although commercial logging is rarely the main cause of deforestation, it opens the way for the settlers who clear land. Forestry departments are chronically short of skilled manpower and equipment to police their territory. Yet the rates charged to loggers often cover only a tiny part of the costs of replacing the timber removed with wood grown in plantations.

Removing subsidies and setting proper prices will not be enough, of course, to reduce every sort of environmental damage. For that, governments need to introduce specific policies of various sorts. Some will be market-based, such as the hazardous-waste charges being considered in Bangkok; others will be regulatory, such as controls on land use. In every case, it will be important that standards are realistic and enforceable. Developing countries are all too apt to adopt the standards of OECD countries and then enforce them selectively. This breeds corruption and cynicism.

Institutions in developing countries are often too weak to meet the demands environmental policy places upon them. Often government departments lack skilled people and money. Donors, the Bank's report notes, often prefer to finance individual projects, which tie up scarce staff, rather than pay to set up and strengthen environmental administrations, which may in the end be more effective.

How much will all this cost? The report reckons that $75 billion a year, or 1.4% of developing-country GDP, would buy a wide range of measures, many of which would have non-environmental benefits (such as better education for girls, "the most important long-term environmental policy in the developing world"). Costs will vary among countries and rise over time. But an annual figure of 2-3% of GDP by 2000 should be "appropriate and sufficient".

That seems high in absolute terms, but is small in relation to the additional incomes that good economic management can bring. Last year's report reckoned that countries with good policies achieved growth rates 2.5% higher than those with average or poor policies: by 2000, in other words, good policies could make output more than 20% higher than it would be otherwise.

Who pays?

Ministers from developing countries who read the report on their way to the Earth Summit will hope to squeeze some of the added cost of domestic environmental policies from donor nations. They will note the report's recommendation that aid should go to new kinds of projects with environmental, rather than purely economic, gains. They will also be interested in the report's approach to biological diversity and greenhouse warming, the two issues that most interest the developed countries.

In both cases, the report argues that rich countries should be willing to pay poor ones for taking measures that go beyond their national interests. In the case of conservation, the World Bank estimates that it would cost $2.5 billion a year to extend protected areas by 50% over the next decade. Compare that with the $2 billion spent annually by the United States alone on its national parks.

In the case of global warming, the report's attitude is distinctly downbeat. The damage from climate change appears likely to be "relatively modest"; in the case of the United States, the cost of adapting to a doubling of atmospheric carbon dioxide might be 1% of GDP. By contrast, the costs of reducing the output of greenhouse gases might be between 3% and 7% of world GDP, and possibly much more in the case of developing countries. The implication is clear. Compared with cleaner water or the prevention of soil erosion, curbing global warming is a poor investment.

The Growing Influence of NGOs in the Developing World

Because of the intricate links among developing countries, NGOs there do not always serve distinctly environmental purposes. This is in sharp contrast to developed countries, where the environmental NGO is a separate entity, more often than not.

Robert Livernash

ROBERT LIVERNASH is senior editor of the *World Resources Report*, which is published every other year by the World Resources Institute in collaboration with the United Nations Environment Programme and the United Nations Development Programme. This article is adapted from a chapter in *World Resources 1992-93*, published by Oxford University Press.

An extraordinarily diverse and growing body of private organizations around the world now provide assistance in a variety of areas, such as small-scale development, tropical forest conservation, and sustainable agriculture. In industrialized countries, many of these nongovernmental organizations (NGOs) are small and operate at the community level, while others—particularly those with a broad mandate—have grown large and prosperous. In the developing world, on the other hand, most NGOs are community-based and relatively small. Their chances of failure often far outweigh their chances of success. For many NGOs in developing countries, survival depends on the courage and persistence of a few individuals. Members of these NGOs frequently must contend with hostility from governments and, in a few cases, may be risking their lives.

Nevertheless, NGOs are growing both in number and influence, especially in "southern," or developing, countries. The reasons for this growth are complex. NGOs often form at the local level in response to specific needs or incentives, such as the need to improve water supplies or new opportunities to get bank credit.[1] NGOs also may form at the national level to fulfill such needs as environmental protection, often with the support of "northern" NGOs from industrialized countries. In some cases, ineffective or nonexistent government programs create a vacuum that private organizations can fill; in other cases, resource-poor governments use private organizations as an efficient way to extend their reach.

Because of the intricate links among developmental and environmental activities in developing countries, NGOs there do not always serve distinctly environmental purposes. This is in sharp contrast to developed countries, where the environmental NGO is a separate entity, more often than not. Furthermore, as the links among environment, development, and population become clearer, organizations devoted to a single issue have begun to see the

From *Environment*, June 1992, pp. 12-20, 41-43. Reprinted with permission of the Helen Dwight Reid Educational Foundation. Published by Heldref Publications, 1319 Eighteenth St., NW, Washington, DC 20036-1802.

> ## WHAT IS AN NGO?
>
> The term *nongovernmental organization* (NGO) encompasses all organizations that are neither governmental nor for-profit. What is left is a residual category of organizations, many of which have little in common. NGOs can be large or small, secular or religious, and either donors or recipients of grants. Some NGOs are designed only to serve their own members, while others serve those who need help. Some NGOs are concerned only with local issues, but others work at the national, regional, or international levels.
>
> Organizations that could fit under this giant umbrella definition include savings clubs, squatter associations, communal labor-sharing groups, rural peoples' leagues, village water associations, irrigation user groups, women's associations, tribal unions, environmental advocacy groups, consumer and farmer cooperatives, human rights groups, policy analysis centers, labor unions, community service clubs, local development associations, tenants' associations, private colleges or hospitals, private relief organizations, and political actions groups.[1]
>
> ---
>
> 1. L. D. Brown and D. C. Korten, "Understanding Voluntary Organizations: Guidelines for Donors" (Washington, D.C.: World Bank, Country Economics Department, September 1989), 3.

advantages of working with other groups. NGOs promoting development, for example, may join with NGOs advancing entrepreneurship, environmental protection, or human rights. The rapidly growing number of national and international NGO networks and coalitions fuels this trend toward cooperation, which, in turn, is helped by rapid advances in communications technology.

Most NGOs share a common vision to reduce poverty, advance human development, and manage natural resources in a sustainable fashion. They believe that local participation and control is important to the success of sustainable development. They put less emphasis on growth in production and more emphasis on involving local people in solving problems (see box on this page).

Why are NGOs important? In developing countries, NGOs can solve some pieces of the development puzzle by taking an unconventional approach; by listening carefully to what people want and working to enlist their participation and support; or by trying to foster development and husband natural resources. NGOs can be a truly independent voice, either by serving as a focal point of opposition to government programs or by serving as the models for new government programs. In the developed north and, to some extent, in the south, NGOs can place strong pressures on governments to create and implement new policies. They also can work in partnership with governments, though such alliances carry the risk of dependence on government funds.

The character and number of NGOs in a country depend to a significant extent on the approach taken by the government. In industrialized countries, the governments have learned to live with NGOs as both opponents and proponents of government programs. However, many developing country governments are uncomfortable with NGOs as opponents. NGOs cannot, however, compete with governments, nor can they pass laws, and they do not have the resources to manage national programs.

Although there is no single classification system for NGOs, at different levels of development, a few common types emerge:

- Grassroots NGOs work in rural and urban communities in the developing world. Most of these NGOs are membership oriented.
- Service NGOs support the development of grassroots groups. Some service NGOs result from the development of local groups into regional or national federations; others are nonmember groups that serve at the regional and national levels.
- Some regional, national, and international NGOs work in specific areas, such as development, human rights, environment, disaster relief, and family planning. Such organizations may have a particular emphasis, such as field work, legal defense, or policy research.
- Many NGOs form national, regional, and international networks and coalitions.

Only about 30 percent of all development NGOs in the south are more than 15 years old, and only 50 percent are more than 10. Almost all environmental NGOs and most NGO networks and umbrella groups were started in the 1980s.[2]

Origins and Differences

The history of the intervention of independent organizations in the affairs of developing countries differs greatly from region to region and among countries. Asia is generally considered to have the largest number of NGOs and the most active involvement of NGOs in policymaking. NGOs in Latin America are often critical of government policies. NGOs in Africa are relatively fragile and generally do not play the same advocacy roles that many NGOs fill in Asia and Latin America.

International NGOs have had a strong impact on the development of national NGOs in the developing world, especially in Africa and some parts of Asia. Indigenous NGOs in Africa are still relatively dependent on international NGOs for financial support. For a variety of reasons—political, economic, and cultural—NGOs still are scarce in many parts of the world, including China, the Middle East, North Africa, northeastern India, and parts of sub-Saharan Africa.[3]

Northern NGOs in the South

Many of the early independent organizations in Europe and North America had similar purposes, such as establishing missions or providing relief to victims of war or famine. During and after World War II, religious and secular organizations—such as Catholic Relief Services and

CARE—were started to provide refugees and displaced persons in Europe with clothing, food, and medical supplies. Later on, they focused on developing nations.[4] For example, in the United Kingdom, the Oxford Committee for Famine Relief was started in 1942 to aid starving civilians in Nazi-occupied Greece.[5] The end of World War II did not bring an end to the need for emergency relief organizations, however. The partitioning of India in 1947 and famines in Asia and Africa in the 1950s were among a long series of events that drew NGOs to the developing world.[6]

In the 1960s, many NGOs began to see their mission as a mix of relief and development work. Churches started to promote development projects that were unrelated to usual church activities. In 1958, the World Council of Churches proposed that the industrial countries transfer 1 percent of their national income to the developing countries for development assistance. The Vatican, in the mid 1960s, strengthened its commitment to eliminating poverty in the Third World. Protestant churches later were urged by the World Council of Churches to send 2 percent of their resources to developing countries.[7] The Freedom from Hunger Campaign, which was sponsored by the UN Food and Agriculture Organization and began in 1960, as well as numerous programs that sent volunteers overseas, such as the U.S. Peace Corps, provided additional impetus for development work overseas.[8]

NGOs formed in the 1960s and 1970s began to focus on the root causes of poverty in developing countries.[9] The U.S. Congress created the Inter-American Foundation (IAF) in 1969, followed by the African Development Foundation in 1980. By mid 1991, IAF had provided 3,111 small grants to NGOs in Latin America and the Caribbean.[10]

In the early 1970s, the World Bank began to focus on the need to improve income distribution, to develop affordable technologies for the poor, to promote rural development, and to address people's basic educational, health, and family-planning needs. Other official donors followed the World Bank's lead.[11] Many NGOs, however, continued to criticize the World Bank for emphasizing large development projects that did not directly benefit poor people. In the 1980s, this criticism led to increasing interaction between the World Bank and some NGOs.

As new reports began to surface in the 1980s about global environmental concerns, such as deforestation, many U.S. environmental groups extended their coverage to include environmental issues overseas. Although the Worldwide Fund for Nature and its U.S. affiliate, the World Wildlife Fund (WWF), for example, originally supported overseas scientific missions, they eventually began to support the work of local scientists. In the early 1980s, WWF began to develop relationships with organizations such as Fundación Natura in Ecuador, and, by the late 1980s, WWF was actively supporting projects in developing countries.[12]

Interest in women's poverty and their economic contributions rose dramatically in the mid 1970s. A conference in Mexico City in 1975 marked the beginning of the International Women's Year, and the United Nations declared its Decade for Women in 1976. The Decade for Women inspired the formation of many new formal and informal women's organizations, such as the United Nations Development Fund for Women, which increased its work with NGOs between 1978 and 1984.[13]

By 1989, NGOs from the north were distributing an estimated $6.4 billion to developing countries—about 12 percent of all public and private development aid.[14] In fact, industrial NGOs collectively distribute more money in net transfers than does the World Bank.[15] Roughly one-third of the development aid from northern NGOs now comes from government sources. Since the 1960s, the governments of developed nations have established partnerships with NGOs for the distribution and management of government aid.[16] By 1988, $1.8 billion (in 1986 dollars), or 35 percent, of the annual budget of all NGOs came from government sources. Government donations account for much of the increase in NGOs' funds in the past few decades.[17] United Nations agencies have increasingly promoted community development projects by supporting indigenous NGOs and cooperation between governments and NGOs (see box on next page).

NGOs in Asia

The British occupation, competition among European missionary groups, the nationalist movement, and a constitutional right to free speech have all contributed to the proliferation of voluntary groups in India.[18] Tax incentives and a long history of donations to religious organizations also have supported the growth of independent organizations in India, which now has probably hundreds of thousands of local NGOs, including an estimated 12,000 that focus on development.[19] Foreign funding has been a sensitive political issue. For instance, a law passed in 1976 requires NGOs to obtain government approval before accepting foreign donations.[20]

Bangladesh also has fostered some especially notable independent organizations, such as the Bangladesh Rural Advancement Committee.[21] More than 10,000 national NGOs operate in Bangladesh, and about 250 receive funds from foreign sources.[22]

Indonesia's independent organizations were helped by a strong tradition of community group efforts.[23] However, the Indonesian government has maintained fairly close control over independent organizations.

In the Philippines, the current constitution recognizes the role of NGOs in the process of development, and President Corazon Aquino has encouraged their growth. NGOs have multiplied in the Philippines, usually acting as advocates and lobbyists for specific causes. NGOs have formed numerous networks and coalitions, including sectoral and issue-based coalitions, such as the Congress for People's Agrarian Reform and the Green Forum, which is working to promote sustainable development.[24]

NGOs AND THE UNITED NATIONS SYSTEM

In the past, nongovernmental organizations (NGOs) have used UN conferences as forums for holding alternative conferences. At the 1972 Stockholm Conference on the Human Environment, for example, a parallel conference of NGOs—under the leadership of economist Barbara Ward and anthropologist Margaret Mead—was particularly influential and garnered major press attention.[1] The pattern of launching parallel conferences has continued at other UN conferences.

The focus of NGO activity at the 1992 United Nations Conference on Environment and Development (UNCED) in Rio de Janeiro this month will be the '92 Global Forum, a series of simultaneous, independent events that will be held in the Flamengo Park area, in a downtown Rio convention center, and in about 50 auditoriums in Rio and nearby neighborhoods. Some 335 substantive meetings are scheduled for the forum, which is cosponsored by the Brazilian NGO Forum and by the International Facilitating Committee, which includes representatives from international NGOs. The forum events include an International NGO Forum, which will hold daily discussions on UNCED issues; a two and one-half-day Inter-Sectoral Dialogue, which will assess the differences and commonalities among different groups; a Parliamentary Earth Summit, which will focus on the human and social dimensions of environment and development; a number of events that will focus on the world's indigenous peoples; a series of meetings and workshops on women's issues at the Women's Center of Activities in Flamengo Park; a number of events focusing on children and young people; and an International Forum of Arts, Culture, and Environment. Many of the NGOs participating in the forum have been accredited by the UNCED Secretariat to participate in preparatory meetings and attend the official conference.

By 28 March, forum organizers had received commitments from 5,436 representatives of 1,845 NGOs from 110 countries. About 41 percent of the organizations are based in Latin America, 22 percent in North America, and 20 percent in Europe. UN officials increasingly are encouraging participation by NGOs; UNCED may break new ground in this direction.

The United Nations has devised a system of formal relationships with NGOs. For example, about 460 NGOs, including some environmental NGOs, have consultative status with the Economic and Social Council (ECOSOC).[2] Consultative status allows NGOs to attend meetings of ECOSOC, to submit written statements, to testify before ECOSOC, and, in some cases to propose agenda items.

As preparations for UNCED got under way, it appeared likely that participation in the preparatory process would be opened to a relatively broad range of relevant NGOs, not just to those with consultative status.[3] NGOs in many countries have been actively seeking a voice in their countries' preparations for UNCED. For example, NGOs in Brazil are trying to build the broadest possible coalition of NGOs for the conference.[4] The Centre for Our Common Future in Geneva organized a worldwide series of "ECO-92" public forums in preparation for UNCED.[5] The conference also will take full advantage of computerized information. A global electronic network will allow worldwide electronic access to UNCED information via computers and modems.[6]

Many UN agencies have relatively long traditions of cooperating with NGOs. The United Nations High Commissioner for Refugees and the United Nations Fund for Population Assistance have both relied on NGOs for project implementation. Between 1969 and 1986, the population fund spent about 10 percent of its budget on activities implemented by NGOs. UNICEF (United Nations Children's Fund) also works extensively with NGOs. Community rotary clubs, for example, work with UNICEF on the global immunization campaign.[7]

The United Nations Environment Programme (UNEP) and the United Nations Development Programme (UNDP) are increasing their cooperation with NGOs. UNDP's Partners in Development Programme, which operated in 60 countries in 1990, offers small grants ($25,000 per country) to NGOs and grassroots organizations to support projects. In Rwanda, for example, an NGO received $13,500 to purchase animals for livestock projects and for management training.[8] In addition, UNDP's Sustainable Development Network identifies and links all governmental, nongovernmental, grassroots, and entrepreneurial organizations that could contribute to sustainable and environmentally sound development. The program operates in all 152 UNDP countries.[9]

In 1988, UNEP spent $8.6 million to support NGOs and other intergovernmental organizations. UNEP also is a key funder of NGOs in the regional assemblies on women and the environment.[10] UNEP allows NGOs to attend all UNEP meetings and works actively with them to plan and implement projects.[11]

---

1. A. Kilgore and C. Roosevelt, "The Non-Governmental Organizations and the United Nations System," in D. Williams, ed., *The Specialized Agencies and the United Nations: The System in Crisis* (New York: St. Martin's Press, 1987), 266.

2. United Nations Department of Public Information, *Non-Governmental Organizations Association with the Department of Public Information* (New York: United Nations, 1990).

3. United Nations Preparatory Committee for the United Nations Conference on Environment and Development, "Arrangements for the Effective Contributions of Relevant Non-Governmental Organizations in the Preparatory Process," press release (New York: United Nations, 13 August 1990), 1–2.

4. World Resources Institute, "Brazilian Groups Organize for 1992," *NGO Networker* (Washington, D.C.), Summer 1990, 3.

5. World Resources Institute, "Public Forums—ECO-92—To Be Held," *NGO Networker* (Washington, D.C.), Summer 1990, 3.

6. United Nations Preparatory Committee for the United Nations Conference on Environment and Development, "The UNCED Information System," press release (New York: United Nations, 13 August 1990), 2.

7. Organization for Economic Cooperation and Development, *Voluntary Aid for Development: The Role of Non-Governmental Organizations* (Paris: OECD, 1988), 95–96.

8. United Nations Development Programme "UNDP/NGO Partners in Development Programme," press release (New York: UNDP, 15 May 1990), 1–4.

9. United Nations Development Programme, "Sustainable Development Network" (Communication from the administrator, UNDP, New York, 27 February 1990), 1.

10. J. Martin-Brown, special adviser to the executive director, United Nations Environment Programme, Washington, D.C., personal communication with the author, 6 June 1990.

11. Y. J. Ahmad, senior advisor to the executive director, United Nations Environment Programme, Nairobi, personal communication with the author, 14 November 1990.

NGOs in Latin America

Until the mid 1960s, the work of the Catholic church and other NGOs in Latin America focused chiefly on charitable relief and welfare efforts, especially transfers of food from industrialized nations.[25] However, NGOS diversified in the late 1960s and 1970s, and new groups began working in such areas as small-scale local development. Many organizations were created in reaction to the authoritarian military regimes that held power throughout Latin America during this period; NGO activity was highly politicized particularly during the 1970s.[26] Following the Vatican II council of bishops from 1962 to 1965 and a 1968 conference of bishops in Medellin, Colombia, the Catholic church committed itself more actively to social justice. This move led to a massive organizational effort at the grassroots level, with priests and nuns forming NGOs to work with poor people in rural and urban areas.[27] Many secular antipoverty organizations, such as neighborhood associations, also have been started.[28]

The democratization of many Latin American governments during the 1980s bolstered the creation of new NGOs, such as rural and neighborhood associations, as well as those that support ethnic groups, women, and the environment. Although NGOs often criticize government policies, NGO–government relationships are gradually improving in many countries, and cooperative projects are now relatively common.[29]

A recent survey of 1,000 NGOs in Brazil found that 47 percent were independent, 37 percent had church affiliations, and the rest were linked to other institutions, such as universities. Thirty-five percent of the organizations were started in the 1970s, and 55 percent began in the 1980s. However, the greatest weakness of NGOs in Brazil appears to be their reliance on foreign support.[30]

NGOs in Africa

Though less numerous than those in Asia and Latin America, NGOs are nevertheless important in Africa. During the colonial period, churches and missionary societies were the principal providers of health and formal educational services, especially in rural areas. Later, ethnic welfare groups, professional associations, and separatist churches formed, often to contest the authority of their foreign rulers.[31]

Community self-reliance has a strong tradition in many African countries, including Zimbabwe, Senegal, Kenya, and Burkina Faso.[32] Since becoming independent, many countries have received assistance from local NGOs in environment and development work and the delivery of basic care services, such as potable water and medical supplies. Much of this activity has been in response to the difficulties African governments have experienced in fighting and providing relief from poverty.[33] International NGOs also maintain an active and sometimes dominant—some would argue too dominant—presence in Africa by providing food relief and health services.[34]

Strengths and Weaknesses

At the grassroots level, NGOs can provide their members with greater financial and negotiating leverage than they would have as individuals. NGOs also provide a public voice for members' views. For example, dairy farmers in Durazno, Uruguay, traditionally transported milk into the city on small wooden carts and spent the morning making deliveries. Those farmers who could not go into the city would sell their milk to a middleman at his price. With the help of an IAF grant, the dairy farmers formed a cooperative and built a milk-processing plant to pasteurize and package milk in Durazno. The plant has helped provide the farmers with a stable income and easier access to credit.[35]

Many local NGOs, however, are small and have limited interest in increasing their activities or influencing government strategies for alleviating poverty. Furthermore, these NGOs may have relatively weak managerial skills and little technical expertise. The survival and growth of local groups also may depend on public policies, such as laws that govern the formation and operation of grassroots organizations.[36]

Local NGOs often confront obstacles beyond their control. For example, farmers who successfully start growing vegetables may be unable to get a truck to market their produce, or squatters who have gained physical control over a piece of land may be unable to get municipal services without legal title to the land. To cope with such problems, local NGOs may wish to ally with larger service NGOs.[37]

Studies of successful service NGOs have found that they are relatively effective at reaching the poor, mobilizing local resources, delivering services, and solving similar problems. But service NGOs have been more effective at reaching poor people who have some assets and less effective at reaching very poor people who have few or no assets.[38] A study of 30 successful Latin American service NGOs found that they generally benefited the "middle poor," or those people in the third and fourth quintiles of the income spectrum, but that many very poor households were indirect beneficiaries.[39]

Effective service NGOs rely on the active participation of their beneficiaries. An important component of participation is a commitment by beneficiaries to invest their own resources in the project. For example, the Asociacion de los Nuevos Alquimistas (ANAI) is a professionally led service organization in Costa Rica that has tried to promote low-resource agriculture.[40] ANAI's nursery program requires beneficiaries to contribute land, materials, and labor to receive seeds and technical assistance.[41]

Successful service NGOs often try innovative methods to solve problems.[42] For example, the NGO Gram Vikas has worked with technology centers and state banks in India to build more than 20,000 family and village biogas plants that convert organic wastes into energy. Gram Vikas's costs are a fraction of government costs for similar plants.[43]

Many service NGOs fail, however, in that they do not

help poor people, are not innovative, and are as rigid as government departments. In addition, some service NGOs have been criticized for having limited technical capacity for complex projects, for an inability to replicate successful projects, for a limited ability to sustain themselves after initial outside help is withdrawn, and for relatively weak managerial and organizational skills.[44]

Service NGOs often do not benefit very poor people, and, in many cases, grassroots participation, especially by women, may be limited. As one study points out, "the provision of credit, irrigation, or market outlets to small farmers is easier than the provision of land, farming skills, and confidence to the landless."[45] A study of 75 NGO projects found that what was often called grassroots participation was, in practice, a form of decentralized decisionmaking still dominated by NGO staff and local elites.[46]

Many projects may be conceived with little thought given to the next step. Long-term planning is difficult for many NGOs in developing countries because of their dependence on limited project grants from industrialized partners.[47]

The documentation of NGO projects is often "irregular, subjective, and geared more to fundraising than to institutional learning," according to one report.[48] Donors in industrialized countries who are sensitive to the need to let Third World NGOs run their own programs are reluctant to insist on independent monitoring and evaluation. Once a project is completed, few funding NGOs pay much attention to its impact or to whether it provided any lasting benefits.

Key Organizational Factors

NGOs can multiply an initial success by expanding beyond the community level or by creating similar organizations that work in other communities under central leadership. Such successes are not common, however. Many factors—for example, isolation or a lack of energy and motivation—may restrain the growth potential of small projects. At the grassroots level, a few projects that were carefully matched to a regional culture have grown rapidly. In the Yatenga region of Burkina Faso, for instance, the term *naam* traditionally referred to a temporary sharing of tasks by young people for common activities, such as feasts. The *naam* NGOs initially organized women and young people—but eventually entire villages—to undertake community projects, including building small dams, landscaping to control erosion, maintaining communal forests, and making fuel-efficient ovens. About 100 *naam* NGOs were operating in 1973, and, by 1987, the number had grown to more than 2,500.[49]

Another notable example of a grassroots NGO that now operates on a large scale is the Bangladesh Rural Advancement Committee (BRAC), which grew from a small relief organization set up in 1972 to one of the largest NGOs in the world, with a staff of more than 2,000 people.[50] BRAC focuses on the poorest 50 percent of village populations and organizes groups of 20 to 30 people with similar backgrounds to analyze and seek solutions to their own problems. BRAC also helps landless laborers to organize to lease land, women's groups to undertake rice paddy processing, and fishermen to buy boats with BRAC credit. Initial BRAC groups are expected to form other groups in the village, and local leaders can visit BRAC training centers to learn organizational methods.[51]

The Role of Women

Though examples abound of women organizing to advance their interests, many NGOs have not integrated women into their programs. Institutional legacies, cultural constraints, and competition for scarce financial resources have all contributed to the exclusion of women.[52] Relief agencies formed in the 1940s and 1950s and NGOs formed in the past few decades have tended to view women solely in their domestic roles. In Latin America, the Catholic church played a major role in the development of grassroots efforts to fight poverty, but the church's efforts did not take into account a changed role for women. Moreover, although many NGOs have tried to work within the framework of local cultures, those cultures are often highly patriarchal and view the role of women primarily in domestic terms.[53] Thus, NGO projects often do not sufficiently involve women in planning and decisionmaking processes, may increase the workload of women without improving their productivity, and may not address women's real economic roles or enhance their potential leadership management skills.[54]

Consequently, many new NGOs have been started exclusively for women. For example, the Kenya Water for Health Organization, a consortium of NGOs established to respond to women's self-help efforts for water and sanitation improvements, organized a cooperative program in the Kwale district south of Mombasa to train women to build and maintain simple water systems. Cooperation between project staff and the community was developed by five female extension workers who facilitated village-level decisionmaking. The pilot project was so successful that it was established throughout the entire district.[55]

Like most local organizations, women's NGOs tend to have limited financial resources, limited organizational and technical expertise, and limited access to the networks that allocate resources. They may also lack institutional clout, which is reflected in the small size of their projects and the difficulties they encounter raising funds.[56]

Despite these impediments, women's NGOs have been effective in encouraging women's participation in decisionmaking, teaching technical and managerial skills, allowing poor women to develop skills and confidence without male competition, providing access to resources, raising women's awareness of gender issues, and building their self-confidence.[57]

Government-NGO Relations

The relations between governments and NGOs are complex and vary considerably from country to country. In many cases, NGOs have had considerable impacts on governments, either by offering models for new government programs, proposing reforms of existing policies, or critiquing proposed government policies. In some cases, NGOs have opposed government policies, even to the point of organizing demonstrations or using more confrontational tactics. The relationship between governments and NGOs can be a strong determinant of NGO activity in a country.

Government-NGO relations hinge on several factors, including the fitness of the government, the type of political system, and the type and location of particular NGO projects. The best relations occur where "a confident and capable government with populist policies meets an NGO that wishes to pursue mainstream development programs in a nation's heartland;" on the other hand, the worst relations occur "where a weak and defensive government with a limited power base meets an NGO that seeks to promote community mobilization in a contested border area."[58]

The purpose of NGO projects also influences the governments' response. Governments in developing countries often regard as desirable noncontroversial projects, such as child immunization or clean water programs, but may not warmly welcome NGOs working in such areas as basic human rights advocacy.[59]

Invariably, tension exists between a government's interest in controlling activities and the NGO's interest in maintaining organizational autonomy. For example, a government may seek to manage the NGO sector by passing laws requiring NGOs to register and report regularly on their activities or by coopting NGO activity through the creation of "quangos" (quasi-NGOs, or publicly sponsored NGOs that are organizational affiliates of a government ministry). Government funding of NGO programs—or government controls on funding by external donors—can also reduce the autonomy of NGOs.[60]

Gaining Influence

NGOs can influence public policy. In Peru, for example, Instituto Tecnologico Agrario Proterra's land-titling activities in the Lurin Valley influenced the government to pass new agrarian reform laws to distribute lands.[61] NGOs also can build coalitions to create or implement new policies. In the Philippines, the International Institute for Rural Reconstruction worked with UNICEF (United Nations Children's Fund), school teachers, and government officials to create a program that would train students in biologically intensive gardening. The program helped increase the capacity of poor families to feed themselves from small plots and served as a model for other school programs.[62]

Many NGOs also are using the legal system successfully. In Malaysia, Friends of the Earth and the Consumers Association of Penang won a suit against a Japanese company that was mining rare-earth elements and polluting the waterways.[63] NGOs also can be effective in demonstrating innovations on which improved policies could be based. For example, Fundación Natura in Ecuador paved the way for a $10-million debt-for-nature program to pay for high-priority parks and reserves.[64]

Cooperation and Confrontation

Many governments have increasingly welcomed the participation of environmental and developmental NGOs. With the creation of new democratic governments in Latin America, for example, many new collaborative initiatives have been launched between NGOs and the new governments to seek novel approaches to development.[65] In many countries, NGOs have begun to act as subcontractors for government programs and to collaborate with government ministries.

NGOs with established programs can be an effective outlet for government support. For example, a program coordinated by the Kenya Water for Health Organization to develop, test, and produce ceramic *jiko* stoves proved so effective that the Ministry of Energy became involved in organizing the training of artisans and the construction of demonstration centers.[66] In another case, a program of informal education and training for urban children, developed by the Undugu Society in Nairobi, has been so successful that it now receives government financial support, and the curriculum for its basic education school has been formally recognized by the government.[67] NGOs also can help stretch thin government resources by organizing their members or clientele to receive extension services in a group setting, by training government field workers, and by integrating their programs with government programs.[68]

In some cases, governments are themselves forming NGOs. As part of its effort to create parks and reserves, the Costa Rican government created the Netrópica Foundation and the National Parks Foundation. These NGOs buy lands and transfer them to the government, pay the salaries of park rangers, and channel donations for specific projects, such as saving the dry tropical forest in Guanacaste National Park.[69] More often than not, however, government-launched NGOs have lacked the resources to be effective and have failed to win allegiance from other NGOs.[70]

When no other options exist to effect change, some NGOs have used the risky strategy of confronting the government to call attention to their concerns. Confrontation tactics can have dramatic results, but groups who use such tactics must be prepared to risk repression, imprisonment, and even the death of members. Furthermore, confrontations can continue for years, with victories and defeats shared by both sides, before an outcome is reached. For example, from 1987 to 1989, more than 125 members of a Malaysian nomadic rain forest tribe, the Penan, were arrested for blockading logging roads into their homeland. The tribe started the Penan Association to organize Penan communities.[71]

Emerging Trends

NGOs are evolving in three main directions. First, many southern NGOs are seeking greater autonomy from those in the north. Second, NGOs are increasing their efforts to make connections both by forming networks and associations of NGOs and by using new communication technologies to stay abreast of issues and keep in touch with NGOs in other countries. Third, NGOs in developing countries are performing new roles, such as legal defense and policy research.

Evolving North-South Relations

Many southern NGOs believe that their dependence on northern NGOs for funds has caused them to lose their autonomy, compromise their priorities, and reduce their institutional identity.[72] Because southern NGOs have raised their numbers, skills, and management capabilities, they are increasingly eager to set agendas on their own terms.

Southern NGOs are pressing their northern partners to agree that the principal responsibility for development in the south lies ultimately with the southern countries and their indigenous NGOs and that financial aid from industrialized nations should not be the controlling criterion that defines the relationship between northern and southern NGOs. Although northern NGOs may claim superior technical expertise, southern NGOs maintain that they have more practical and relevant development experience in their own countries.[73]

Some donors are responding to southern NGOs' efforts to assert more authority over projects by supporting southern NGOs directly. Other donors are choosing to support northern NGOs that develop collaborative relationships with southern NGOs or give technical assistance to southern NGOs on their own terms.[74]

The Indonesia-Canada Twinning Project, which links two Canadian NGOs with three NGOs in Indonesia, is one example of the way northern NGOs are transferring technical knowledge to southern NGOs. In the project, Canadian specialists will help Indonesians use available technology to monitor water pollution in the Surabaya River in East Java and will assess how existing legislation can protect the river's environmental quality.[75]

Networks and Associations

A notable trend in developing countries is the creation of NGO networks that share information and coordinate activities. For example, the Indonesian Environmental Forum (WALHI) is an umbrella organization of more than 400 smaller environmental NGOs. WALHI organizes conservation education programs, runs environmental training programs, provides technical assistance on issues such as fundraising, and lobbies government officials. WALHI recently led several environmental groups in bringing Indonesia's first lawsuit against a corporation for violating environmental laws.[76]

Some networks have a global focus. The U.S.-based Pesticide Action Network (PAN) is an international coalition of 300 NGOs in 50 countries working for sustainable pest control methods. PAN is an important source of information on pesticides for grassroots NGOs in the developing world.[77]

Associations can play an important role in disseminating information. The Coalition for Agrarian Reform and Rural Development in Asia, for example, disseminates research findings to its members and the development community.[78] Other environmental and developmental networks have been formed at the international, regional, and national levels.

Networks also can be used to bring together groups with overlapping interests. The Coordinating Body of the Indigenous Organizations of the Amazon Basin, an umbrella organization for five NGOs representing 1.2 million indigenous inhabitants of the Amazon River basin, held a meeting with environmental NGOs in May 1990 in an effort to forge an alliance.[79]

Efforts to merge the environmental and developmental perspectives of NGOs are increasing. NGOs and NGO networks with a primary focus on environmental issues and a secondary focus on developmental issues include Environment and Development in the Third World, Environment Liaison Centre International, the Haribon Foundation, the Regional Network of Energy Experts in Zimbabwe, the Kenya Water for Health Organization, and WALHI.[80]

Global Networking

Radios, televisions, fax machines, and personal computers can each instantly transmit information throughout an increasingly dense global network. In Latin America, for example, radio stations blanket virtually the entire continent, more than 60 million television sets have been bought there since the early 1950s, and the number of television stations there is mushrooming.[81] Computers and telephone-linked networks also are spreading rapidly. Scores of larger NGOs have access to telephone-linked computer systems. Also, NGOs are forming nonprofit computer user networks, such as Nicarao in Central America and Alternex in Brazil, which are linked to U.S. computer networks. Sending information over such networks costs about one-fourth of a fax transmission and about one-fortieth of a telex.[82] EcoNet, a U.S.-based computer network, links thousands of environmentalists, peace activists, and NGOs throughout the world.[83]

Policy Research and Legal Defense

A small but growing number of southern NGOs at the regional and national levels are taking on new roles in such areas as policy research and legal defense. The Haribon Foundation in the Philippines has a legal program modeled after U.S. legal defense groups, such as the Environmental Defense Fund.[84] Other national organizations are focusing on technical services and policy research. The African Center for Technology Studies in Nairobi is a think tank that works on public policy issues concerning the environment and other matters.[85]

Importance of NGOs

NGOs in the developing world are growing quickly in numbers and sophistication. To a large extent, their potential remains unfulfilled, however, because of funding limitations, their own institutional weaknesses, and the uneasiness of many governments about the role of NGOs. Nevertheless, NGOs are becoming increasingly important players in environmental and developmental policymaking in the developing world.

Grassroots organizations can make numerous contributions to sustainable development. They can mobilize local people and resources to support projects over the long run; enable all the people of a society to improve their quality of life; increase their own effectiveness and potentially influence national policymaking, either through growth or building alliances; link all the elements of sustainable development, incluing ecology, economics, politics, and culture; and enable individuals to cope with change.[86]

Service NGOs and national NGOs also play a significant role. The two can help resolve the economic and cultural differences among local organizations, government agencies, and industrialized nations' institutions; use their money and expertise to help grassroots NGOs; bridge the gap between local and technical knowledge in the effort to find long-term solutions that are widely accepted by target groups; find new approaches to solving problems and disseminate this knowledge to other organizations; and provide connections to local organizations by joining networks or building links to international organizations.[87]

International NGOs can offer national and local NGOs new ideas and alert them to ongoing international policymaking. These NGOs can serve as international lobbyists to attack the policies of governments, corporations, and multilateral institutions. Indeed, NGOs in the developing world are increasingly insistent that lobbying should be the primary role of northern NGOs.[88] International NGOs also can show how otherwise disconnected communities share similar problems and can increase awareness of global issues, such as deforestation, loss of biodiversity, and global warming.

NGOs are not perfect. Most NGOs could be better managed, more accountable, and more professional. Most NGOs could pay more attention to designing projects that are durable. More NGOs should pay attention to the needs and roles of women and the very poor. Northern NGOs could do more to treat their southern counterparts as equal partners.

Political leaders who tolerate or encourage NGOs—both as critics and collaborators—will be serving their own best interests in the long term. In the many newly emerged democratic countries, NGOs should seek to create a dialogue with governments to strengthen the elements of political culture that are favorable to NGO growth. Although NGOs cannot compete with or replace governments, they can help significantly to reduce poverty on a lasting basis and to build new understanding about the links between environment and development.

NOTES

1. S. Annis, "Can Small-Scale Development Be a Large-Scale Policy? The Case of Latin America," *World Development* 15, supplement (Autumn 1987):130–31. For further information on the roles of NGOs see W. V. C. Reid, "Sustainable Development: Lessons from Success," *Environment*, May 1989, 6; W. B. Wood, G. J. Demko, and P. Mofson, "Ecopolitics in the Global Greenhouse," *Environment*, September 1989, 12; and J. G. Speth, "Coming to Terms: Toward a North-South Compact for the Environment," *Environment*, June 1990, 16.
2. D. Richards, director, Environment, Enterprise, and Social Progress, Brattleboro, Vt., personal communication with the author, 11 November 1990.
3. A. B. Durning, "People Power and Development," *Foreign Policy* 76 (Fall 1989):71.
4. T. H. Fox, "NGOs from the United States," *World Development* 15, supplement (Autumn 1987):11–12.
5. Organization for Economic Cooperation and Development, *Voluntary Aid for Development: The Role of Non-Governmental Organizations* (Paris: OECD, 1988), 18.
6. Ibid., 19.
7. Ibid., 20.
8. Ibid., 20–23.
9. Fox, note 4 above.
10. Inter-American Foundation, *Annual Report 1989* (Rosslyn, Va.: IAF, 1990), 1.
11. M. Buvinić and S. W. Yudelman, *Women, Poverty, and Progress in the Third World*, headline series, no. 289 (New York: Foreign Policy Association, Summer 1989), 35–36.
12. D. Wood, vice president for Latin America, World Wildlife Fund, Washington, D.C., personal communication with the author, 6 July 1990.
13. Buvinić and Yudelman, pages 36–39, note 11 above.
14. J. Clark, *Democratizing Development: The Role of Voluntary Organizations* (West Hartford, Conn.: Kumarian Press, 1991), 39.
15. Ibid. World Bank lending is less after debt payment service because past loans are deducted.
16. OECD, page 25, note 5 above.
17. Clark, page 40, note 14 above.
18. K. D. McCarthy, "The Voluntary Sector Overseas: Notes from the Field," Center for the Study of Philanthropy working paper (New York: Graduate School of the City University of New York, undated), 9.
19. Durning, page 69, note 3 above.
20. McCarthy, page 10, note 18 above.
21. Clark, pages 83–86, note 14 above.
22. J. Pfohl and J. Yudelman, *Asian Linkages: NGO Collaboration in the 1990s* (New York: Private Agencies Collaborating Together, 1989), 40.
23. McCarthy, page 5, note 18 above.
24. J. Smith, U.S. Coordinator, Philippine Development Forum, Washington, D.C., personal communication with the author, 24 June 1991.
25. D. C. Korten, "NGOs and Development: An Overview" (Paper prepared for the World Bank and the Institute for Development Research, Boston, Mass., 1989), 5.
26. Ibid.
27. S. W. Yudelman, senior fellow, International Center for Research on Women, Washington, D.C., personal communication with the author, 11 October 1990.
28. Durning, page 70, note 3 above.
29. Korten, page 6, note 25 above.
30. McCarthy, page 25, note 18 above.
31. M. Bratton, "The Politics of Government-NGO Relations in Africa," *World Development* 17, no. 4 (1989):570–71.
32. Durning, page 71, note 3 above.
33. Korten, page 6, note 25 above.
34. Ibid., 6–7.
35. P. Breslin, *Development and Dignity* (Rosslyn, Va.: Inter-American Foundation, 1987), 40–41; and A. O. Hirschman, *Getting Ahead Collectively: Grassroots Experiences in Latin America* (New York: Pergamon Press, 1984), 18–21.
36. Annis, pages 132–33, note 1 above.
37. Ibid., 131.
38. Clark, page 47, note 14 above.
39. T. F. Carroll, "Tending the Grassroots: Performance of Intermediary Non-Government Organizations" (Unpublished manuscript, Inter-American Foundation, Rosslyn, Va., 1990), IV-1.
40. Ibid., III-5.
41. Ibid., V-3
42. L. D. Brown and D. C. Korten, "Understanding Voluntary Organizations: Guidelines for Donors" (Washington, D.C.: World Bank, Country Economics Department, September 1989), 3.
43. Institute for Development Research and World Resources Institute, "NGO

Contributions to Environment and Sustainable Development Policy Formulation" (Draft proposal, Washington, D.C., and Boston, Mass., 14 June 1990), 3–4.

44. Brown and Korten, pages 16–17, note 42 above.

45. Clark, page 47, note 14 above.

46. J. Tendler, *Turning Private Voluntary Organizations into Development Agencies: Questions for Evaluation*, program evaluation discussion paper no. 12 (Washington, D.C.: U.S. AID, 1982), 11–14.

47. R. Sharp, director, Southern Networks Programme, International Institute for Environment and Development, London, personal communication with the author, 4 January 1991.

48. Clark, pages 60–61, note 14 above.

49. OECD, pages 47–48, note 5 above.

50. Ibid., 62; and Clark, page 83, note 14 above.

51. OECD, page 62, note 5 above.

52. S. W. Yudelman, "The Integration of Women into Development Projects: Observations on the NGO Experience in General and in Latin America in Particular," *World Development* 15, supplement (Autumn 1987):180.

53. Ibid., 180–82.

54. Ibid., 183.

55. I. Dankelman and J. Davidson, *Women and Environment in the Third World* (London: Earthscan Publications, and the International Union for the Conservation of Nature and Natural Resources, 1988), 37.

56. Buvinić and Yudelman, pages 44–46, note 11 above.

57. Dankelman and Davidson, pages 4–5, note 55 above.

58. Bratton, page 585, note 31 above.

59. Ibid., 576.

60. R. Tandon, "NGO-Government Relations: A Source of Life or Kiss of Death?" (Paper prepared for the Society for Participatory Research, New Delhi, undated), 17.

61. D. B. Bendahmane, "New Perspectives on Evaluation," *Grassroots Development* 14, no. 1 (1990):36.

62. J. M. Flavier, president, International Institute of Rural Reconstruction, Silvang, Cavite, Philippines, personal communication with the author, 10 January 1990.

63. Clark, page 97, note 14 above.

64. L. Fernandez, "Private Conservation Groups on the Line in Latin America and the Caribbean," *World Wildlife Fund Letter*, no. 1 (1989):4.

65. S. L. Timpson, director, and J. Jacqz, senior advisor, Human Development Division, United Nations Development Programme, New York, personal communication with the author, 1 November 1990.

66. G. Arum, "KENGO's Experience in Environment and Development" (Paper prepared for the World Resources Institute, Washingon, D.C., November 1990), 3–4.

67. D. Munyakho, "Kenya: The Parking Boys of Nairobi," in D. De Silva, ed., *Against All Odds: Breaking the Poverty Trap* (Cabin John, Md.: Seven Locks Press, 1989), 80.

68. Bratton, page 582, note 31 above.

69. Y. Rovinski, "Costa Rica: The Private Arm of Public Interest," *Panos*, no. 6 (May 1988):4.

70. Bratton, page 579, note 31 above.

71. "With the Penan at the Last Blockade," *Earth Island Journal* 4, no. 2 (1989):28.

72. A. Gordon Drabek, "Development Alternatives: The Challenge for NGOs—An Overview of the Issues," *World Development* 15, supplement (Autumn 1987):xi.

73. K. Kajese, "An Agenda of Future Tasks for International and Indigenous NGOs: Views from the South," *World Development* 15, supplement (Autumn 1987):79–81.

74. Yudelman, note 27 above.

75. U.S. Agency for International Development, *Toward an Environmental and Natural Resources Strategy for ANE Countries in the 1990s* (Washington, D.C.: U.S. AID, 1990), 77.

76. Ibid., 74–75.

77. *Global Pesticide Monitor* 1, no. 2 (May 1990):2.

78. L. D. Brown, "Bridging Organizations and Sustainable Development," working paper no. 8 (Boston, Mass.: Institute for Development Research, 1990), 5.

79. B. Cabarle, "Indians, Environmentalists and the Fate of the Amazon" (Paper prepared for the World Resources Institute, Washington, D.C., 1990).

80. Timpson, note 65 above.

81. S. Annis, "Giving Voice to the Poor," *Foreign Policy*, no. 84 (Fall 1991):93–106.

82. J. Garrison, "Computers Link NGOs Worldwide," *Grassroots Development* (Fall 1989).

83. Annis, page 137, note 81 above.

84. N. Johnson, associate, Program in Environmental Planning and Management, World Resources Institute, personal communication with the author, August 1991.

85. Institute for Development Research and World Resources Institute, page 18, note 43 above.

86. Ibid., 2.

87. Brown, pages 2–3, note 78 above.

88. Clark, page 126, note 14 above.

Women and Development

There is a growing recognition of the important role that women play in the development process. Women are crucial to the success of family planning programs, bear much of the responsibility for food production, and account for an increasing share of wage labor in developing countries. Despite their important contributions, women continue to face formidable social, economic, and political barriers.

Women's lives in the Third World are invariably difficult. Often female children are valued less than male offspring, resulting in higher infant and child mortality rates. In extreme cases, this undervaluing leads to female infanticide. Those females who do survive face lives characterized by poor nutrition and health, multiple pregnancies, hard physical labor, discrimination, and perhaps violence.

Clearly, women are central to any successful population policy. Evidence shows that educated women have fewer and healthier children. This connection between education and population growth indicates that greater emphasis should be placed on educating women. In reality,

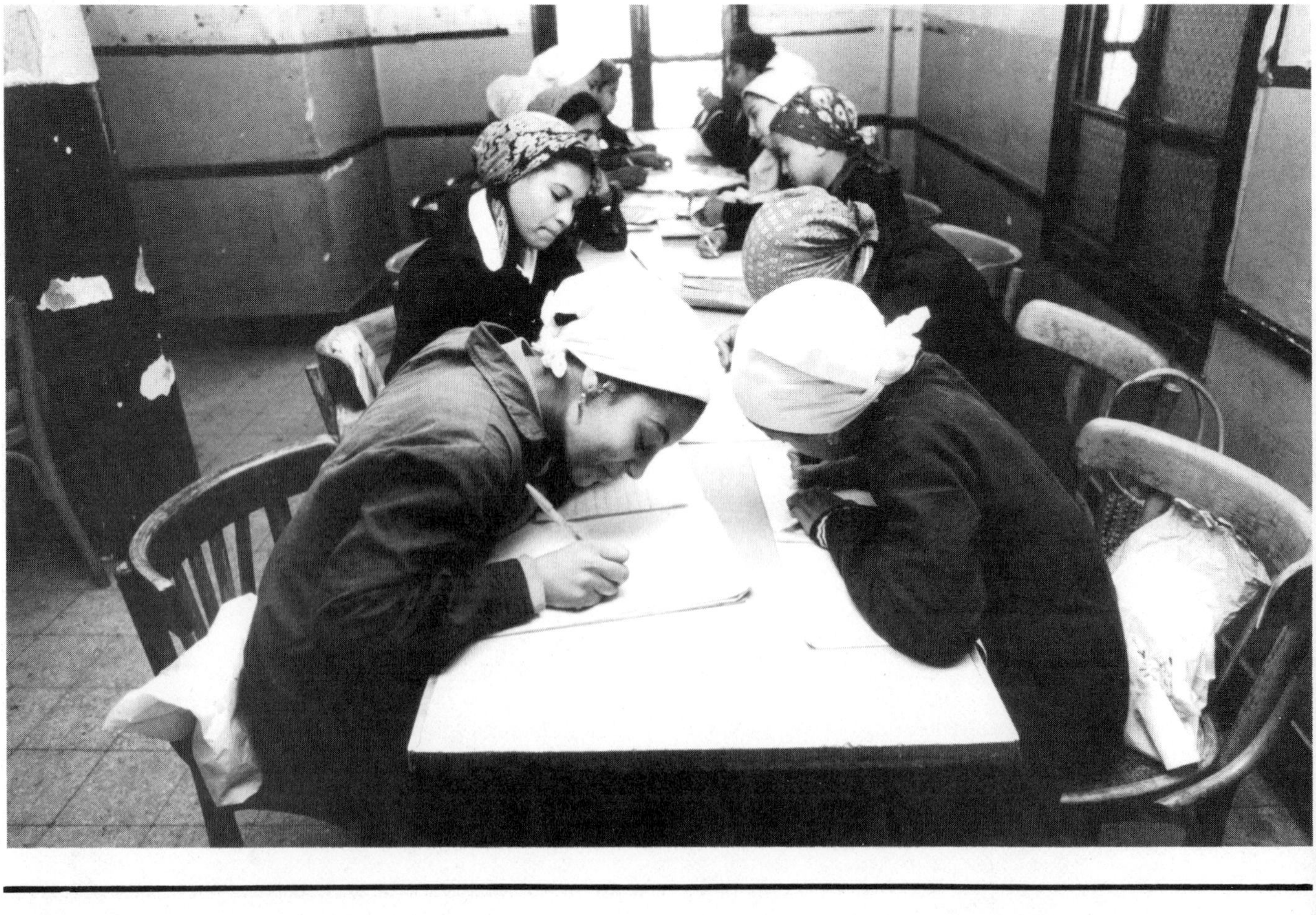

Unit 7

female school enrollments are lower than that of males for several reasons—state priorities, insufficient family resources to educate both boys and girls, female socialization, and cultural factors. Although education is probably the largest single contributor to enhancing the status of women and thereby promoting development, access to education is still limited for many women. Higher status also has benefits in terms of improved health, better wages, and greater influence in decision-making.

Women make up a huge portion of the agricultural work force. They are heavily involved in food production from planting to cultivation, harvesting, and marketing. Despite their agricultural contribution, women frequently do not have adequate access to advances in agricultural technology nor the benefits of extension and training programs. They are also discriminated against in land ownership. As a result, important opportunities to improve food production are lost when women are not given access to technology, training, and land tenure commensurate with their agricultural role.

As industrialization takes place, larger numbers of women are entering the wage economy primarily as production and clerical workers. Expanding opportunities for women to assume these positions contributes to family income and higher status. The informal sector, where jobs are smaller-scale, more traditional, and labor-intensive, has also attracted more women because these jobs are often the only source of employment due to family responsibilities or discrimination.

Development does not always provide benefits to women, however. Advances in technology may further erode the status of women, relegating them to less valuable work or even eliminating their jobs. The industrialization that has accompanied the globalization of production has meant more employment opportunities, but often these are low-tech, low-wage jobs. The lower labor costs in the Third World that attract manufacturing facilities may come at the expense of women. Increasingly women are recruited to fill these production jobs because wage differentials allow employers to pay women less.

The consequences of the structural adjustment programs that many Third World countries have had to adopt have fallen disproportionately on women. As employment opportunities have declined because of austerity measures, women have lost jobs in the formal sector and faced increased competition from males in the informal sector. Less spending on health care and education also affects women who already receive less of these benefits. Currency devaluations further erode the purchasing power of women.

Although women play a very important role in development, their status in Third World countries does not reflect their contribution. Enhancing this status would go a long way toward overcoming population and food production problems and would help boost economic growth. The key to enhancing this status is to assure women greater influence on social, economic, and political issues particularly in the areas that affect them most directly. Accomplishing this goal will require the collective action of women from the grass roots to the national and international levels as well as overcoming gender stereotypes and discrimination.

Looking Ahead: Challenge Questions

What types of cultural, political, and economic barriers do Third World women face?

What are the connections between educating women and development? How can educational opportunities for women be improved?

What are the obstacles to increasing women's participation in the wage economy?

How does female empowerment contribute to limiting population growth?

What are the myths that contribute to gender bias? How does discrimination contribute to female poverty?

What constraints do female farmers face? How can these constraints be overcome?

What is the status of health care for Third World women? How can this be improved?

The Burden of Womanhood

Too often in the Third World, a female's life is hardly worth living

John Ward Anderson and Molly Moore

Washington Post Foreign Service

GANDHI NAGAR, India

When Rani returned home from the hospital cradling her newborn daughter, the men in the family slipped out of her mud hut while she and her mother-in-law mashed poisonous oleander seeds into a dollop of oil and forced it down the infant's throat. As soon as darkness fell, Rani crept into a nearby field and buried her baby girl in a shallow, unmarked grave next to a small stream.

"I never felt any sorrow," Rani, a farm laborer with a weather-beaten face, said through an interpreter. "There was a lot of bitterness in my heart toward the baby because the gods should have given me a son."

Each year hundreds and perhaps thousands of newborn girls in India are murdered by their mothers simply because they are female. Some women believe that sacrificing a daughter guarantees a son in the next pregnancy. In other cases, the family cannot afford the dowry that would eventually be demanded for a girl's marriage.

And for many mothers, sentencing a daughter to death is better than condemning her to life as a woman in the Third World, with cradle-to-grave discrimination, poverty, sickness and drudgery.

"In a culture that idolizes sons and dreads the birth of a daughter, to be born female comes perilously close to being born less than human," the Indian government conceded in a recent report by its Department of Women and Child Development.

While women in the United States and Europe—after decades of struggling for equal rights—often measure sex discrimination by pay scales and seats in corporate board rooms, women in the Third World gauge discrimination by mortality rates and poverty levels.

"Women are the most exploited among the oppressed," says Karuna Chanana Ahmed, a New Delhi anthropologist who has studied the role of women in developing countries. "I don't think it's even possible to eradicate discrimination, it's so deeply ingrained."

PHOTOS BY JOHN WARD ANDERSON—THE WASHINGTON POST

Rani, 31, with Asha, 2, says she killed another daughter 3½ years ago. "I wanted to kill this child also . . . . Now I have killed, I still haven't had any sons."

From *The Washington Post National Weekly Edition*, March 22-28, 1993, pp. 6-7.

This is the first in a series that will examine the lives of women in developing countries around the globe where culture, religion and the law often deprive women of basic human rights and sometimes relegate them to almost subhuman status. From South America to South Asia, women are often subjected to a lifetime of discrimination with little or no hope of relief.

As children, they are fed less, denied education and refused hospitalization. As teenagers, many are forced into marriage,sometimes bought and sold like animals for prostitution and slave labor. As wives and mothers, they are often treated little better than farmhands and baby machines. Should they outlive their husbands, they frequently are denied inheritance, banished from their homes and forced to live as beggars on the streets.

The scores of women interviewed for this series—from destitute villagers in Brazil and Bangladesh, to young professionals in Cairo, to factory workers in China—blamed centuries-old cultural and religious traditions for institutionalizing and giving legitimacy to gender discrimination.

Although, the forms of discrimination vary tremendously among regions, ethnic groups and age levels in the developing world, Shahla Zia, an attorney and women's activist in Islamabad, Pakistan, says there is a theme: "Overall, there is a social and cultural attitude where women are inferior—and discrimination tends to start at birth."

In many countries, a woman's greatest challenge is an elemental one: simply surviving through a normal life cycle. In South Asia and China, the perils begin at birth, with the threat of infanticide.

Like many rural Indian women, Rani, now 31, believed that killing her daughter 3 1/2 years ago would guarantee that her next baby would be a boy. Instead, she had another daughter.

"I wanted to kill this child also," she says, brushing strands of hair from the face of the 2-year-old girl she named Asha, or Hope. "But my husband got scared because all these social workers came and said, 'Give us the child.' " Ultimately, Rani was allowed to keep her. She pauses. "Now I have killed, and I still haven't had any sons."

Amravati, who lives in a village near Rani in the Indian state of Tamil Nadu, says she killed two of her own day-old daughters by pouring scalding chicken soup down their throats, one of the most widely practiced methods of infanticide in southern India. She showed where she buried their bodies—under piles of cow dung in the tiny courtyard of her home.

"My mother-in-law and father-in-law are bedridden," says Amravati, who has two living daughters. "I have no land and no salary, and my husband met with an accident and can't work. Of course it was the right decision. I need a boy. Even though I have to buy clothes and food for a son, he will grow on his own and take care of himself. I don't have to buy him jewelry or give him a 10,000-rupee [$350] dowry."

Sociologists and government officials began documenting sporadic examples of female infanticide in India about 10 years ago. The practice of killing newborn girls is largely a rural phenomenon in India; although its extent has not been documented, one indication came in a recent survey by the Community Services Guild of Madras, a city in Tamil Nadu. Of the 1,250 women questioned, the survey concluded that more than half had killed baby daughters.

In urban areas, easier access to modern medical technology enables women to act before birth. Through amniocentesis, women can learn the sex of a fetus and undergo sex-selective abortions. At one clinic in Bombay, of 8,000 abortions performed after amniocentesis, 7,999 were of female fetuses, according to a recent report by the Indian government. To be sure, female infanticide and sex-selective abortion are not unique to India. Social workers in other South Asian states believe that some communities also condone the practice. In China, one province has had so many cases of female infanticide that a half-million bachelors cannot find wives because they outnumber women their age by 10 to 1, according to the official New China News Agency.

The root problems, according to village women, sociologists and other experts, are cultural and economic. In India, a young woman is regarded as a temporary member of her natural family and a drain on its wealth. Her parents are considered caretakers whose main responsibility is to deliver a chaste daughter, along with a sizable dowry, to her husband's family.

"They say bringing up a girl is like watering a neighbor's plant," says R. Venkatachalam, director of the Community Services Guild of Madras. "From birth to death, the expenditure is there." The dowry, he says, often wipes out a family's life savings but is necessary to arrange a proper marriage and maintain the honor of the bride's family.

After giving birth to a daughter, village women "immediately start thinking, 'Do we have the money to support her through life?' and if they don't, they kill her," according to Vasanthai, 20, the mother of an 18-month-old girl and a resident of the village where Rani lives. "You definitely do it after two or three daughters. Why would you want more?"

Few activists or government officials in India see female infanticide as a law-and-order issue, viewing it instead as a social problem that should be eradicated through better education, family planning and job programs. Police officials say few cases are reported and witnesses seldom cooperate.

"There are more pressing issues," says a top police official in Madras. "Very few cases come to our attention. Very few people care."

7. WOMEN AND DEVELOPMENT

Surviving childbirth is itself an achievement in South Asia for both mother and baby. One of every 18 women dies of a pregnancy-related cause, and more than one of every 10 babies dies during delivery.

For female children, the survival odds are even worse. Almost one in every five girls born in Nepal and Bangladesh dies before age 5. In India, about one-fourth of the 12 million girls born each year die by age 15.

The high death rates are not coincidental. Across the developing world, female children are fed less, pulled out of school earlier, forced into hard labor sooner and given less medical care than boys. According to numerous studies, girls are handicapped not only by the perception that they are temporary members of a family, but also by the belief that males are the chief breadwinners and therefore more deserving of scarce resources.

Boys are generally breast-fed longer. In many cultures, women and girls eat leftovers after the men and boys have finished their meals. According to a joint report by the United Nations Children's Fund and the government of Pakistan, some tribal groups do not feed high-protein foods such as eggs and meat to girls because of the fear it will lead to early puberty.

Women are often hospitalized only when they have reached a critical stage of illness, which is one reason so many mothers die in childbirth. Female children, on the other hand, often are not hospitalized at all. A 1990 study of patient records at Islamabad Children's Hospital in Pakistan found that 71 percent of the babies admitted under age 2 were boys. For all age groups, twice as many boys as girls were admitted to the hospital's surgery, pediatric intensive care and diarrhea units.

Mary Okumu, an official with the African Medical and Research Foundation in Nairobi, says that when a worker in drought-ravaged northern Kenya asked why only boys were lined up at a clinic, the worker was told that in times of drought, many families let their daughters die.

"Nobody will even take them to a clinic," Okumu says. "They prefer the boy to survive."

For most girls, however, the biggest barrier—and the one that locks generations of women into a cycle of discrimination—is lack of education.

Across the developing world, girls are withdrawn from school years before boys so they can remain at home and lug water, work the fields, raise younger siblings and help with other domestic chores. By the time girls are 10 or 12 years old, they may put in as much as an eight-hour work day, studies show. One survey found that a young girl in rural India spends 30 percent of her waking hours doing household work, 29 percent gathering fuel and 20 percent fetching water.

Statistics from Pakistan demonstrate the low priority given to female education: Only one-third of the country's schools—which are sexually segregated—are for women, and one-third of those have no building. Almost 90 percent of the women over age 25 are illiterate. In the predominantly rural state of Baluchistan, less than 2 percent of women can read and write.

In Islamic countries such as Pakistan and Bangladesh, religious concern about interaction with males adds further restrictions to females' mobility. Frequently, girls are taken out of school when they reach puberty to limit their contact with males—though there exists a strong impetus for early marriages. In Bangladesh, according to the United Nations, 73 percent of girls are married by age 15, and 21 percent have had at least one child.

Across South Asia, arranged marriages are the norm and can sometimes be the most demeaning rite of passage a woman endures. Two types are common—bride wealth, in which the bride's family essentially gives her to the highest bidder, and dowry, in which the bride's family pays exorbitant amounts to the husband's family.

In India, many men resort to killing their wives—often by setting them afire—if they are unhappy with the dowry. According to the country's Ministry of Human Resource Development, there were 5,157 dowry murders in 1991—one every hour and 42 minutes.

After being bartered off to a new family, with little education, limited access to health care and no knowledge of birth control, young brides soon become young mothers. A woman's adulthood is often spent in a near constant state of pregnancy, hoping for sons.

According to a 1988 report by India's Department of Women and Child Development: "The Indian woman on an average has eight to nine pregnancies, resulting in a little over six live births, of which four or five survive. She is estimated to spend 80 percent of her reproductive years in pregnancy and lactation." Because of poor nutrition and a hard workload, she puts on about nine pounds during pregnancy, compared with 22 pounds for a typical pregnant woman in a developed country.

A recent study of the small Himalayan village of Bemru by the New Delhi-based Center for Science and the Environment found that "birth in most cases takes place in the cattle shed," where villagers believe that holy cows protect the mother and newborn from evil spirits. Childbirth is considered unclean, and the mother and their newborn are treated as "untouchables" for about two weeks after delivery.

"It does not matter if the woman is young, old or pregnant, she has no rest, Sunday or otherwise," the study said, noting that women in the village did 59 percent of the work, often laboring 14 hours a day and lugging loads 1 1/2 times their body weight. "After two or three . . . pregnancies, their stamina gives up, they get weaker, and by the late thirties are spent out, old and tired, and soon die."

Studies show that in developing countries, women in remote areas can spend more than two hours a day carrying water for cooking, drinking, cleaning and bathing, and in some rural areas they spend the equivalent of more than 200 days a year gathering firewood. That presents an additional hazard: The International Labor Organization found that women using wood fuels in India inhaled carcinogenic pollutants that are the equivalent of smoking 20 packs of cigarettes a day.

Because of laws relegating them to a secondary status, women have few outlets for relaxation or recreation. In many Islamic countries, they are not allowed to drive cars, and their appearance in public is so restricted that they are banned from such recreational and athletic activities as swimming and gymnastics.

In Kenya and Tanzania, laws prohibit women from owning houses. In Pakistan, a daughter legally is entitled to half the inheritance a son gets when their parents die. In some criminal cases, testimony by women is legally given half the weight of a man's testimony, and compensation for the wrongful death of a woman is half that for the wrongful death of a man.

After a lifetime of brutal physical labor, multiple births, discrimination and sheer tedium, what should be a woman's golden years often hold the worst indignities. In India, a woman's identity is so intertwined and subservient to her husband's that if she outlives him, her years as a widow are spent as a virtual nonentity. In previous generations, many women were tied to their husband's funeral pyres and burned to death, a practice called *suttee* that now rarely occurs.

Today, some widows voluntarily shave their heads and withdraw from society, but more often a spartan lifestyle is forced upon them by families and a society that place no value on old, single women. Widowhood carries such a stigma that remarriage is extremely rare, even for women who are widowed as teenagers.

In some areas of the country, women are forced to marry their dead husband's brother to ensure that any property remains in the family. Often they cannot wear jewelry or a *bindi*—the beauty spot women put on their foreheads—or they must shave their heads and wear a white sari. Frequently, they cannot eat fish or meat, garlic or onions.

"The life of a widow is miserable," says Aparna Basu, general secretary of the All India Women's Conference, citing a recent study showing that more than half the women in India age 60 and older are widows, and their mortality rate is three times higher than that of married women of the same age.

In South Asia, women have few property or inheritance rights, and a husband's belongings usually go to sons and occasionally daughters. A widow must rely on the largess of her children, who often cast their mothers on the streets.

Thousands of destitute Indian widows make the pilgrimage to Vrindaban, a town on the outskirts of Agra where they hope to achieve salvation by praying to the god Krishna. About 1,500 widows show up each day at the Shri Bhagwan prayer house, where in exchange for singing "Hare Rama, Hare Krishna" for eight hours, they are given a handful of rice and beans and 1.5 rupees, or about 5 cents.

Some widows claim that when they stop singing, they are poked with sticks by monitors, and social workers allege that younger widows have been sexually assaulted by temple custodians and priests.

On a street there, an elderly woman with a *tilak* on her forehead—white chalk lines signifying that she is a devout Hindu widow—waves a begging cup at passing strangers.

"I have nobody," says Paddo Chowdhury, 65, who became a widow at 18 and has been in Vrindaban for 30 years. "I sit here, shed my tears and get enough food one way or another."

Educating Girls

Many social and economic conditions restrict educational opportunities for girls in the developing world. How can these hurdles be overcome?

Rosemary Bellew, Laura Raney, and K. Subbarao
Population and Human Resource Department, The World Bank

The economic and social benefits of educating girls are substantial; the latter are on the whole probably greater than those for boys. Yet, paradoxically, both parents and society invest less in educating girls than in educating boys in most developing countries. This article outlines the nature of this "female education paradox," reviews the constraints to female education, and identifies promising approaches to increasing educational opportunities for girls.

The female education paradox

A wealth of research in the past 20 years has established that improving female education is crucial for development. Not only are the private economic returns to education, represented by the proportional increase in wages, substantial and generally as high for women as for men, but, more important, the benefits to society are striking. Research has convincingly shown that women's education contributes to smaller families. Educated parents have healthier children, and while the father's education has some influence on the children's health, the mother's education has far more. Analysis based on cross-country regressions shows that, controlling for all other factors, women's primary and secondary

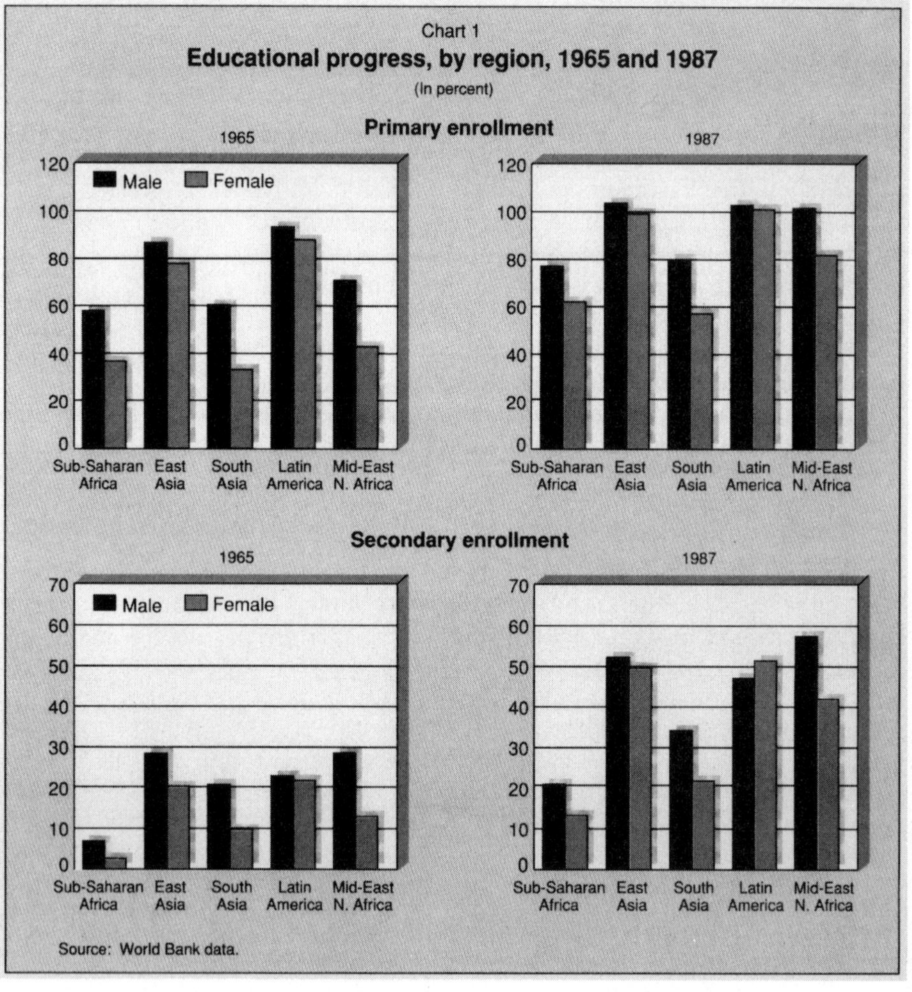

Chart 1
Educational progress, by region, 1965 and 1987
(In percent)

schooling contributes to fewer and healthier children. Moreover, the participation of educated women in the labor market and the ensuing incremental income growth is an important means of alleviating poverty. Recognizing these benefits, in his recent address to the Board of Governors at the 1991 Annual Meetings, Lewis Preston, President of the World Bank, underscored that investments in human resources, especially education for girls, "must have the highest priority."

During 1965–87, there was considerable progress in overall primary and secondary enrollments across the developing world. Female enrollment rates rose faster in secondary schools than in primary schools but their levels relative to those of boys remained low. Regional differences are also pronounced

This article draws on two complementary works produced in the World Bank's Population and Human Resources Department: "Letting Girls Learn: Promising Approaches in Primary and Secondary Education," by Barbara Herz, K. Subbarao, Masooma Habib, and Laura Raney (Bank Discussion Paper No. 133, September 1991); and "Women's Education in Developing Countries: A Review of Barriers, Benefits and Policy," edited by Elizabeth King and Anne Hill, PHREE Background Paper 91/41, September 1991, and forthcoming as a book from The Johns Hopkins University Press.

From *Finance & Development*, March 1992, pp. 54-56. *Finance & Development*, a quarterly publication of the International Monetary Fund and the World Bank.

(see Chart 1). A large gender gap is evident in the Middle East, Sub-Saharan Africa, and South Asia. In Latin America, however, gender gap is nil or negligible except in Bolivia, Guatemala, and Haiti.

These regional averages tell only a part of the story. Data for individual countries show that even where enrollment rates rise, gender parity does not necessarily improve. Some countries have achieved gender parity in primary school at an average enrollment rate of about 60 percent, but there are many which did not do so even at an average enrollment rate of 80 percent. Disparities are even greater at the secondary level.

Research also shows that achieving a high per capita income does not necessarily guarantee gender parity, even if it brings about an expansion in enrollment (see Chart 2). At low levels of per capita income, female enrollment rates and parity vary the most. Some low-income countries achieved high enrollment rates for all children; some wealthier countries—particularly the oil exporters in the Middle East—did so mainly for boys. Even higher levels of public expenditure on education do not necessarily translate into greater gender parity in enrollments. Countries spending 3–4 percent of gross national income on education include best performers with high enrollment rates and high gender parity (e.g., Sri Lanka and the Republic of Korea) and worst performers with low enrollment rates and low gender parity (e.g., Liberia and Mali).

Constraints to female education

Why? The answer is that even where education is effectively free, the parents usually decide which of their children will go to school and for how long. Many parents in developing countries, especially poor parents with large families, feel that they cannot afford to send all their children to school, especially girls. Girls are often seen as household help. Parents bear not only the direct costs such as school fees, books, and clothing but, more important, also the opportunity costs, because they lose their children's time for household chores. In societies that allow children to be used as wage labor, parents also risk forfeiting wages of both boys and girls by sending them to school. However, careful time allocation studies have shown that in very poor agrarian economies, the economic contribution to the families—measured by the total time spent on paid and unpaid work as a whole—is typically much greater for girls than for boys. To this extent, parental decisions are more likely to be adverse to girls' schooling than to boys' schooling. Cultural traditions and concern for the safety of their daughters are also likely to affect a decision to send girls to school. In addition, the limited economic opportunities that especially affect girls' future earning capabilities hinder parental investment in girls' education.

Parents also see themselves bearing the costs of educating girls, but in many societies they see benefits accruing largely to the individual and her children. Girls "marry out," thus carrying the benefits of education with them, whereas sons are expected to sustain parents as they age. To parents, though not to society, investing in girls' education may seem less attractive than in boys' education. A vicious cycle ensues: Girls are kept home to help the family subsist day to day. Uneducated, they cannot compete with boys for wages when they grow up. Women end up earning less, making boys a better educational investment in the parents' eyes. This exacts a development cost in terms of lost opportunities to slow population growth and to raise incomes, productivity, and quality of life.

Chart 2
How a rise in per capita income affects female enrollment in LDCs 1987

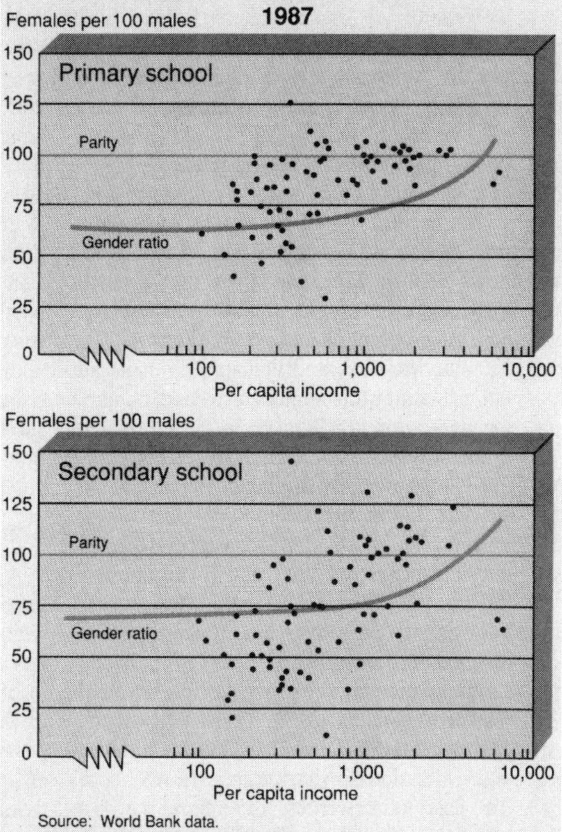

Source: World Bank data.
Note: Income in dollars is plotted on a log-linear scale to allow a closer look at countries with lower per capita incomes.

Promising approaches

How does one break this cycle? Since society gains from girls' education, there is a strong case for special publicly financed measures to promote such education. Education policy is the most direct means of reducing the costs of girls' schooling and thus persuading more parents to educate their daughters.

Over the past two decades, a few developing countries have begun to adapt their educational systems to meet parental concerns better. They have designed incentives to attract both boys and girls to schools. But such societal commitment is not widely evident in the developing world.

Where actions have been taken to encourage girls' education, two broad sets of policies have been tried. One set motivates parents and compensates them for the costs of girls' schooling (e.g., through information campaigns and financial and other incentives). Another set increases access to education and improves the quality of schooling (e.g., by improving curricula and facilities).

Reducing costs. In combination with other measures, reducing the direct and indirect costs to parents of schooling has worked well in a number of countries to encourage them to send their children to school. In Korea, for example, compulsory education was combined with the waiving of fees, provision of free textbooks and school meals, and reduced uniform costs. Sri Lanka has offered free textbooks for all students, school feeding programs at the lower primary level, alternative school structures, and scholarships for students from needy families to supplement a policy of compulsory education. Evidence from Peru indicates that when free textbooks were supplied to primary schools, controlling for all other factors, girls were 1.3 times more likely to enroll, whereas no effect was recorded for boys' enrollment.

But special financial incentives may be required to persuade parents to educate girls. Because the net social gains from female education are most likely to exceed the private gains to the parents who pay, such incentives involving subsidies are economically justifiable. Scholarships at primary and secondary levels have proven to be very effective in raising girls' enrollment in Bangladesh and Guatemala. The scholarship program in Bangladesh has succeeded in almost doubling female secondary school enrollment—from 27.3 percent of eligible girls before the project, to 43.5 percent after its completion. The program has had other benefits as well: increased female attendance in primary schools, higher labor force participation, later age of marriage, and lower fertility rates.

Reducing the opportunity costs of the time girls spend attending school or preparing lessons can also improve girls' enrollment. For instance, flexible scheduling of school hours and the school calendar, to take into account girls' participation in household activities, has been introduced with favorable results in China and India. Provision of child care or permission to bring siblings to school is yet another option tried in some countries. Labor saving technology, improved and more accessible supplies of water and fuel wood, as well as better public transport can also obviate or facilitate girls' chores and make parents more willing to let them attend school.

Information campaigns, involving community leaders, appear to be an inexpensive and promising way to raise girls' primary enrollments. In Morocco, meetings are held in areas receiving new primary schools to sensitize community representatives and parents to the importance of girls' education.

Meeting parental concerns. Distance to school is an important parental concern and, therefore, a deterrent, more for girls than for boys. Parents are more reluctant to send girls than boys to distant schools. In Egypt, the location of a school within 1 kilometer of a community resulted in an enrollment rate of 94 percent for boys and 74 percent for girls; when the distance was 2 kilometers (km), boys' enrollment fell only slightly to 90 percent, while girls' enrollment plummeted to 64 percent. A project in Pakistan uses school mapping techniques to locate new schools in currently underserved areas. In the Sindh province, girls' primary schools will be located within 1.5 km. of a community compared with 2.5 km. for boys' schools.

A critical minimum of infrastructure, including separate sanitation facilities for girls, is also necessary. In certain areas, boundary walls around girls' or mixed schools may be culturally appropriate and help alleviate parental concerns for their daughters' safety. Experience also suggests that single-sex schools rather than coeducational schools may help to increase female enrollment and may improve girls' achievement and self-perception. Research from several countries shows that girls tend to perform better in a variety of subjects ranging from language to mathematics if they attend girls' schools, especially at the secondary level.

Current Bank-assisted projects in Bangladesh, Mali, and Pakistan provide for the revision of school texts to remove the portrayal of gender discrimination. Bangladesh, for example, is ensuring that positive role models are depicted in textbooks and that teacher training includes an awareness of gender issues to reflect the need to enhance the self-image of girls. In Nigeria and the Gambia, girls are actively encouraged to enroll in science, mathematics, and technical courses through the development of clubs and special incentives.

Evidence also suggests that the presence of female teachers encourages girls' enrollment. In rural areas, however, where there is a shortage of female teachers, innovative recruitment and teacher training schemes may be needed. Successful experimental programs in Yemen and Nepal have included a comprehensive mix of local recruitment and posting, tutoring, stipends, and transportation.

What broad lessons can be learned from this project experience? First, a "package approach" comprising a minimum combination of actions appears most promising. In very poor agrarian countries, girls typically face a broad range of constraints arising from the direct and opportunity costs to parents of their education. Education projects in such countries must have a range of components to address both the direct and opportunity costs of girls' education to parents. Some of the past and on-going Bank-assisted projects in The Gambia, Morocco, and Pakistan do make an effort to adopt this approach. Second, no matter what approach is taken to raise girls' enrollment, efforts should be made to simultaneously improve the quality and effectiveness of schools. Third, the community must be involved in all these efforts, especially when financial incentives are offered to parents. Fourth, incentives to overcome direct costs may involve subsidies, but these should be justified on economic and social grounds and carefully monitored to prevent misdirection of resources. Finally, in Bank-assisted projects, greater resources should go into monitoring and evaluation so that more is learnt about the cost effectiveness of alternative approaches in a given sociocultural setting.

Bank support for female education

Over 1972–80, there were 105 Bank-assisted primary and secondary education projects. Of these, about 20 percent identified the presence of gender issues, but only 10 percent included significant actions to improve female enrollment. The situation improved over 1981–91, with about half the Bank's education projects acknowledging gender issues and nearly a quarter including actions to encourage female enrollment.

More important than the quantitative change, however, has been the qualitative change in the nature of these projects. By and large, early Bank projects had a single aim: They typically concentrated on expanding school places. The results were disappointing. However, one early project in Bangladesh, which addressed parental attitudes reflecting both household-level and school-level constraints, had much more favorable results. This project combined a variety of components, such as improved school facilities, female teachers, reduced costs (free textbooks), and special incentives (e.g., scholarships). As a result, female enrollment improved 9 percent annually in project areas compared with only 2 percent in the country as a whole.

Many current Bank-assisted projects contain multiple components. For example, one project in Pakistan is providing boundary walls for girls' and mixed primary schools, free textbooks to rural primary school girls, scholarships for rural secondary schools, pilot programs to introduce flexible school hours and abolish uniform requirements, and amended age requirements and local posting for female teachers. Under a new project in Morocco, middle schools will be located close to targeted communities and have canteens to provide meals for students, with financial assistance available for students who cannot pay for their own meals. A program of low-cost textbooks is planned, and in the schools with boarding facilities, one half of boarding scholarships will be for girls. These and other current projects demonstrate the evolution of thinking in Bank projects and suggest the potential of the "package approach."

Conclusions

A substantial body of research has established that the economic and social returns to women's primary and secondary schooling are impressive. Yet, a significant gender gap in primary and secondary schooling persists in many countries. Given the economics of poverty and the traditions prevailing in much of the world, from the parents' perspective—though not from the society's—male education may understandably appear to be a better investment and female education a luxury they can ill afford. To create a more compelling case for parents' sending their daughters to school, policymakers should recognize the costs and benefits from the parents' perspective and incorporate suitable incentives in the project design. Though country-level project experience is too recent to draw firm conclusions, it certainly suggests the need for future projects to take an integrated view of the various constraints. Multiple economic and social spin-offs from female education in terms of lower poverty, reduced fertility, and mortality justify selective targeted subsidization of school inputs and scholarships for girls in education projects in poor countries.

Women in the Workplace in Developing Countries

Although more women are now entering formal job markets, they face major social and economic hurdles, posing challenges for policymakers

In spite of the increasing public attention to the importance of women in the economies of the developing world, progress toward increasing their participation in the job market has been less than satisfactory. Women work. In most cases, they work longer hours than men. Studies have shown, for example, that in Africa, Asia, and the Pacific, women average 12-13 hours more a week than men. Moreover, an increasing number of women now function as heads of households in the developing world, as ill-health, death, migration, and other disruptive factors have separated males from their families or made them unable to take on the task of running the household. But much of the work done by women is not captured by formal employment statistics, since it is in the household or in family run agricultural or other subsistence activities.

Recent international estimates, prepared by the Statistical Office of the United Nations Secretariat from International Labour Office data (see box), indicate that the proportion of economically active women rose between 1970 and 1990 in most parts of the world except Sub-Saharan Africa. But gaps between women and men's economic participation in the developing world remain wide, reflecting, among other things, fewer educational opportunities and lingering social restrictions.

Roughly 830 million women are economically active today. About 70 percent of them live in developing countries. The accompanying tables and charts reflect the state of women in the workplace in the developing world today.

More than three quarters of the world's women live in the developing world

Regional shares (In percent)

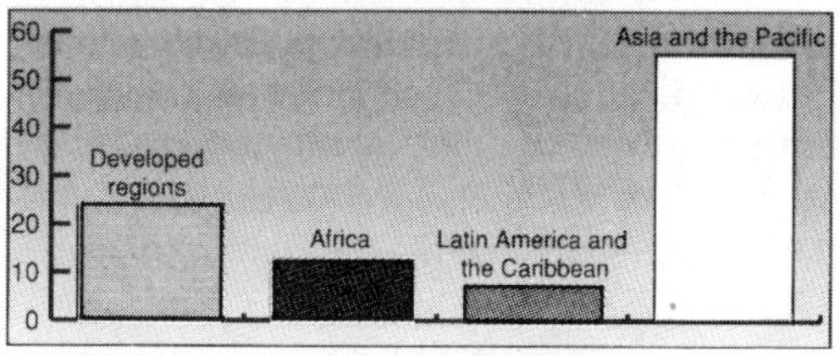

Seventy percent of economically active women live in developing countries, half of them in Asia

Regional shares (In percent)

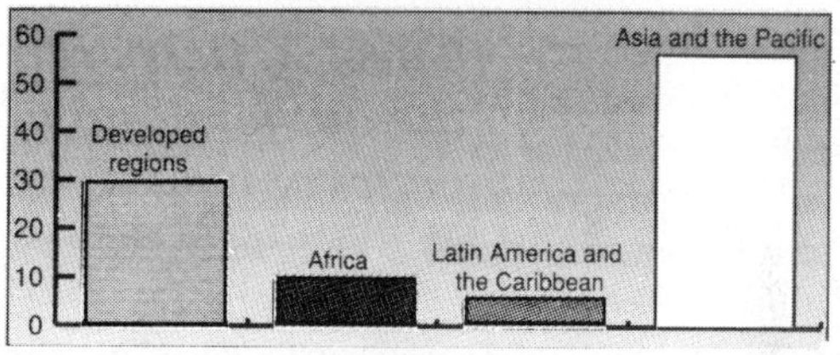

But three out of four women over 25 years in Asia and Africa are illiterate

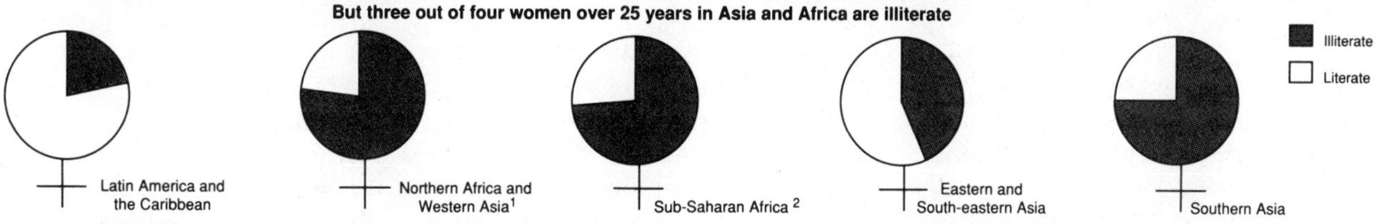

Note: Based on total population of women aged 25 years and over in each region.

1/ Includes Somalia and Mauritania; excludes Cyprus, Israel and Turkey.

2/ Includes Sudan; excludes South Africa.

Young women in rural areas face high barriers of illiteracy

Illiterate women aged 15-24, 1980 (In percent)

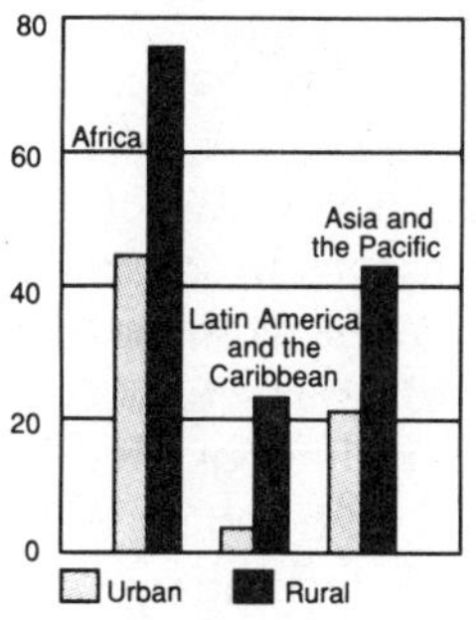

Note: Averages based on a limited number of countries in each region for census years around 1980.

Much fewer girls than boys are enrolled in secondary schools

Girls enrolled per 100 boys, 1985

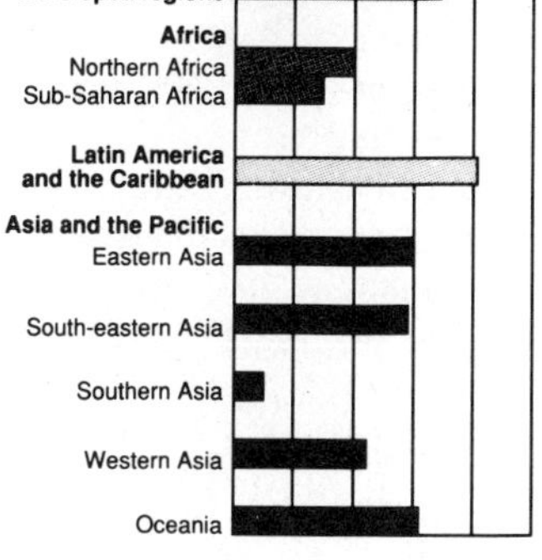

As a result, fewer women are economically active than men

Average percentage aged 15 and over

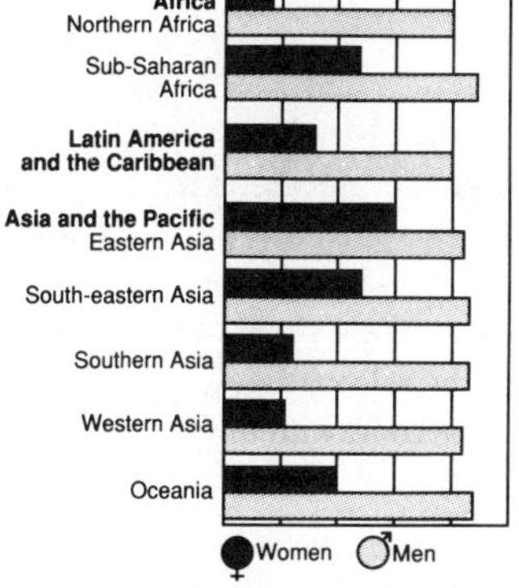

From *Finance & Development,* June 1992, p. 44. *Finance & Development,* a quarterly publication of the International Monetary Fund and the World Bank.

Female Empowerment Leads to Fewer Births

Cameron Barr

Staff writer to The Christian Science Monitor

DHAKA, BANGLADESH

Batashi, a woman in her 30s wearing gold jewelry and a bright blue sari, stands in front of her tidy cement and packed-mud home in a village called Nabogram. She and millions of women like her in the developing world are helping to answer a question that is central to the effort to slow global population growth: Is it enough to hand a poor woman a contraceptive?

Batashi's village, about two hours outside Dhaka, Bangladesh, is perched on earthen ridges that divide rice paddies and keep people above the flood plain during the rainy season. Most people work tiny plots of land they don't own. But Batashi's economic situation is better than average because of small loans and other assistance she has received from a private development agency called BRAC, the Bangladesh Rural Advancement Committee.

She now owns three cows, tethered in a nearby shed, that produce 10 kilograms (22 pounds) of milk every day. She also owns three bicycle rickshaws, one pulled by her husband and the other two rented to men who earn their living by pulling them.

Do the cows and the rickshaws have any bearing on Batashi's decision to use family-planning services? "Yes, family planning is easier for me," she says. Economic opportunity "gives me freedom and . . . gives me power." Batashi has two sons and a daughter. "This is enough," she says, "because I want these three to be educated persons. I don't want my children to be rickshaw pullers."

Batashi's case illustrates why many population analysts now believe that "parallel efforts" and "holistic approaches" to overpopulation—that is, combining the delivery of family-planning services with programs that improve women's standing in society—are critical to slowing birth-rates.

"What's clear," says Sharon Camp, senior vice president of the Population Crisis Committee in Washington, "is that if you can do good family planning and secure improvements in the status of women—legal, economic, social, and political—those things interact so powerfully that you can get declines in birth-rates at breathtaking speeds. That's probably the solution to the world's population problem."

Even so, family-planning bureaucracies in many developing countries have been slow to expand beyond the traditional approach to family planning—providing contraceptives and advice on using them.

"From a program standpoint, the woman is a target to achieve demographic ends," says Saroj Pachauri, a program officer at the Ford Foundation in New Delhi. "It's not her concerns that are paramount."

Population experts have long understood the importance of "female empowerment"—a catchall term that covers women-centered health care, improvements in social and legal status, access to education and jobs, and a fairer distribution of responsibility for children between mothers and fathers.

But during the past 10 years, a growing body of evidence has verified the correlation between empowerment and reducing family size.

One of the best examples in the world is nearby in the southern Indian state of Kerala, where the fertility rate—on average, 2.3 children per woman—is one of the lowest in the developing world. One reason is a female literacy rate of 66 percent, several times the average in India's northern states, according to a United Nations report.

The other reason is the status of women. According to tradition, women inherit land in Kerala, and families pay a "bride price" to the parents of the bride, symbols, the UN Population Fund says, that women are considered an asset and not a liability.

Education changes outlook

There is plenty of evidence to show that eight or more years of education for women, because it encourages later marriages and broadens a woman's outlook, results in fewer births. "With education and economic opportunities, women begin to define themselves as citizens, not just family members," says Judith

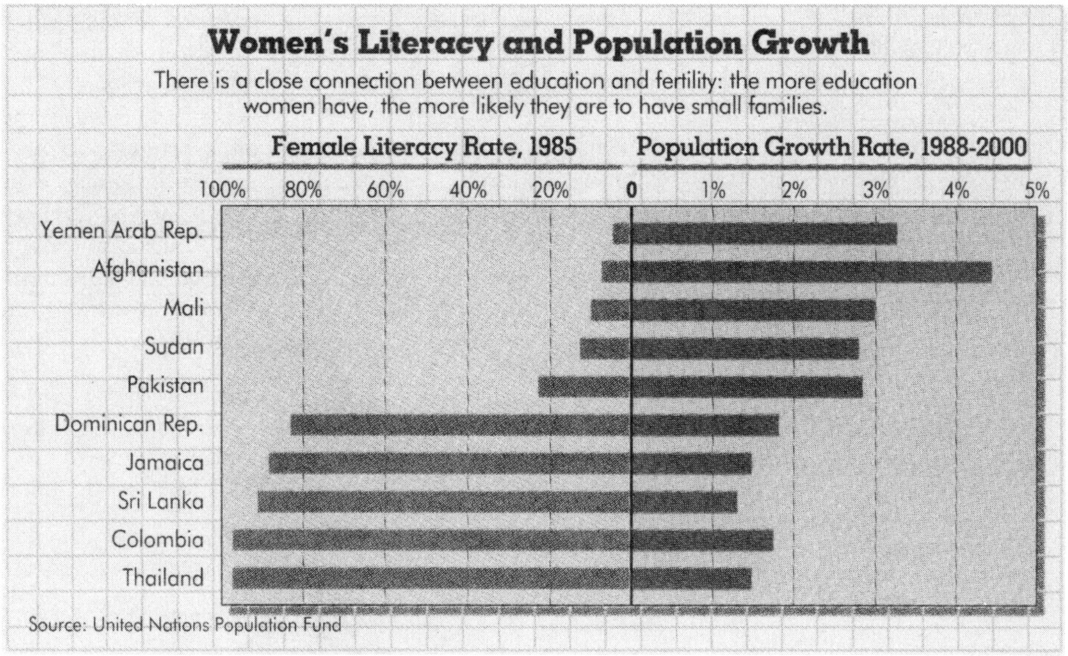

Bruce, a senior associate at the Population Council, a private research group in New York. "Interacting in a wider set of relationships means having access to more objective information [on the costs and benefits of having more children]. It means more equality in the marital relationship."

Research also links increased family planning with economic opportunity. One study looked at a group of 1,600 women members of the Grameen Bank, a Bangladeshi institution that provides small loans to promote small businesses. Fifty-nine percent of the bank members were using some sort of family planning, compared with 43 percent of women in a control group.

Economic insecurity, on the other hand, can have a reverse effect, driving up birthrates since children, especially sons, are considered essential to old-age security.

According to recent research, 60 percent of women in India over age 60 are widows. But some of India's many castes prohibit widows from returning to the village of their birth or joining the lineage of their married daughters.

"Unless she has adult or married sons, she is left virtually on her own," says Marty Chen of the Harvard Institute for International Development, in Cambridge, Mass., and author of the research.

In a village near Batashi's, a woman named Behula says she had three girls before she bore a boy.

"When my three daughters marry, my house will be completely empty," she says. "If I have a boy, he will be present in front of my eyes [and] in the end he will see me in my old age."

"To me it seems so obvious that we really don't have to explain it because women are [the] ones who make the choice," says Amina Islam, a program officer at the UN Population Fund in Khaka. "If you improve their status, they will be in a [better] position to make decisions about their fertility."

Sitting in the government family-planning office for Manikganj District, where Batashi's village is located and where BRAC has been active, two low-level male bureaucrats corroborate the point.

"It is very easy to talk about family planning with a working woman," says one, Motalib Hussain, the district family-planning supervisor. "It is very easy for us because she has already developed herself. [But] it is very difficult to talk about family planning with housewives."

At the higher levels of Bangladesh's family-planning bureaucracy, however, there is less regard for the impact that education and economic opportunity can have on fertility. "We are proud of our success," says A. K. M. Rafiquzzaman, director-general of Bangladesh's Family-Planning Directorate, sitting in an office air-conditioned against Dhaka's 100-degree heat.

"Bangladesh has disproved the theory," he asserts, that economic development and literacy are prerequisites to a contraceptive-prevalence rate of 40 percent.

'Can't wait for development'

"The main problem," writes Alia Ahmed in her 1991 book, "Women and Fertility in Bangladesh," "is that one cannot wait for socioeconomic development to solve the problem of overpopulation when development itself is being stifled by the high rate of population growth."

But most experts insist that there are limits to relying exclusively on a "supply side" approach to family planning, providing contraceptive services to interested couples.

To produce deep cuts where they count most—in fertility rates—the "demand side" of the equation must be addressed as well by providing the education and economic opportunities that create a desire for smaller families and thus a wider demand for family-planning services.

"It's one thing to reduce fertility rates from five or six children per woman to three or four using traditional family-planning services," says Ronald Ridker, a senior economist at the World Bank in Washington. "But unless there is substantial social and economic progress, including improvements in the status of women, it will be impossible to get from three or four [per mother] to a replacement level of 2.1.

"We can't wait for social and economic progress to occur to accomplish these things," adds Dr. Ridker. "We have to intervene selectively in the development process to ensure that the conditions that change attitudes toward family size are fostered."

Women's Work

Why "development" isn't always good news for the second sex

Jodi L. Jacobson

Jodi L. Jacobson is a senior researcher at the Worldwatch Institute in Washington. The research for this article was done for the Worldwatch study, Gender Bias: Roadblock to Sustainable Development.

The women of Sikandernagar, a village in the Indian state of Andhra Pradesh, work three shifts per day. Waking at 4 a.m., they light fires, milk buffaloes, sweep floors, fetch water, and feed their families. From 8 a.m. until 5 p.m. they weed crops for a meager wage. In the evening they forage for branches, twigs, and leaves to fuel their cooking fires, wild vegetables to nourish their children, and grass to feed the buffalo. Finally, they return home to cook dinner and do evening chores. These women spend twice as many hours per week working to support their families as do the men in their village. But they do not own the land on which they labor, and every year, for all their effort, they find themselves poorer and less able to provide what their families need to survive.

As the 20th century draws to a close, some 3 billion people—more than half the earth's population—live in the subsistence economies of the developing world. Most of these subsistence producers find themselves trapped in the same downward spiral as the women of Sikandernagar. Because they have cash incomes insufficient to meet their most basic needs, they must rely heavily on their own labor to secure whatever food, fuel, and water they can from the surrounding environment.

Women perform the lion's share of work in subsistence economies, toiling longer hours and often contributing more to real family income than their male relatives, but their work is not given monetary value and they are viewed as unproductive by many government statisticians, economists, development experts—even their husbands. A huge proportion of the world's real production, therefore, remains officially undervalued, and the essential contributions women make to the welfare of families and nations remain unrecognized. So, while the growing scarcity of resources within subsistence economies increases the burden on women and erodes their productivity, little is being done to reverse the cycle.

Ironically, by failing to address the pervasive gender bias that discounts the contributions of women, many development policies and programs intended to alleviate impoverishment actually are making the problem worse. There are development groups in both the private and public sector that focus on the role of women, but the flaws inherent in current development practices cannot be fixed by relatively minor allocations of funds to women. Fundamental changes are needed in mainstream policies and approaches.

18-HOUR DAYS

Gender bias is especially pernicious in less-developed nations, where most of women's activity takes place in the non-wage economy. Women's work is essential to survival, but because little or no money changes hands, it is not counted as economically productive. United Nations data indicate that on average, women work longer hours than men in every country except Australia, Canada, and the United States. Hours worked producing subsistence goods are rarely offset by a reduction of duties at home. Moreover, gender disparities in total hours worked are greatest among the poor: in developing countries, women work an average of 12 to 18 hours per day, producing food, managing and harvesting resources, and working at a variety of paid and unpaid activities, compared to 8 to 12 hours for men.

Since the cultivation or collection of food directly for the family is not considered a "business," the women who engage in such work usually are not granted access to land, credit, or other resources. While men are more likely both to have access to resources and to

From *Foreign Service Journal,* January 1993, pp. 26-29, 31. Adapted from *World•Watch.* Reprinted by permission.

earn cash wages for their work, they are less likely than women to spend it on family maintenance–food, clothes, health care, and the like. Such patterns are disturbingly prevalent across countries and cultures.

Gender bias is thus a fundamental cause of poverty, because in its various forms it prevents hundreds of millions of women from obtaining the education, training, health services, child care, and legal status needed to escape from poverty. It is what prevents women from transforming their increasingly unstable subsistence economy into one that is not forced to cannibalize its own declining assets.

Gender bias is also the single most important cause of high birth rates. Where women have little access to productive resources, and little control over family income, they depend on children for social status and economic security. A necessary step in reducing births voluntarily, then, is to increase women's productivity and their control over resources.

REINFORCING GENDER BIAS

Conventional approaches to development not only fail to accomplish this goal, but by ignoring the obstacles faced by women they actually formalize and reinforce gender bias in several devastating ways.

First, many current development strategies do not benefit men and women equally. Although women are the main producers and procurers of household food supplies in subsistence economies, conventional agricultural development and strategies to promote cash crops have actually shifted resources *away* from female farmers. Environmental policies likewise discount the value of resources used in subsistence economies and thus work against environmental sustainability. Women, depending on croplands, forests, and other natural resources for food and fuel have a greater interest in guarding the long-term productivity of these resources, whereas men are more often concerned with converting these resources into immediate cash. Development programs that vest control over natural resources solely in the hands of men, or profit-making enterprises in general, are in effect explicitly supporting short-term consumption at the expense of long-term sustainability.

Second, women rarely are involved in designing or carrying out development programs. Consequently, these programs do not address women's needs or utilize their practical knowledge. For example, in rural Africa, 60 to 80 percent of all domestic fuel supplies are gathered from forests by women and girls. Yet, countless programs to reverse deforestation have failed because their planners did not consult village women who are the primary harvesters of forest products in their communities.

Third, conventional economic policies often contribute to increasing poverty within subsistence economies, which in turn increases the relative burden on women. In Sikandernagar, for example, the green revolution and other agricultural development schemes promised economic advancement but brought subsistence producers only greater impoverishment by further reducing their access to cropland and forest resources. With government and private interests controlling much of the once commonly owned land where subsistence families collected fuel and fodder, women were forced to go farther afield to meet their families' needs. At the same time, the replacement of human labor by tractors increased competition for, and lowered the wages of, the much smaller number of jobs available. So women who do work for wages now work longer for less money.

A FAMILY OF MYTHS

Implicit in the theory and practice of conventional economic development are three assumptions that are influenced by gender differences and that reinforce the biases. One assumption is that within a society, economic growth is gender-blind, and both men and women will benefit equally from it. The second is that the traditional Western model of a "household," in which a father, mother, and children share common interests and work toward common goals, is applicable to all societies. The third is that within households, the burdens and benefits of poverty and wealth will be distributed equally regardless of gender. Unfortunately, none of these assumptions holds true.

Economic growth is not gender blind. As economies develop, existing gender gaps in the distribution of wealth and in access to resources usually persist, and in many cases grow worse.

First, economic growth is not gender blind. As economies develop, existing gender gaps in the distribution of wealth and in access to resources usually persist, and in many cases grow worse. From the 1950s through the early 1980s, for example, worldwide standards of living as measured by widely used basic indicators, including life expectancy, per capita income, and primary school enrollment, rose dramatically. Yet women never achieved parity with men, even in the so-called developed countries. According to the Human Development Index, a measure created by the United Nations Development Program to gauge the degree to which people have available to them the resources needed to attain a decent standard of living, women lagged behind men in every country for which data were available. Gender differences were least pronounced in Finland, where measures of women's level of access as a share of men's reached 94 percent. They were most pronounced in South Korea and Kenya, where the index of women's access to resources did not even reach 70 percent of that for men.

Not only do women not automatically benefit from economic growth; they may even fall further behind. Unless specific steps are taken to redress inequity, gender gaps often increase over time, especially where access to resources is already highly skewed. This has happened with literacy. In 1985, 40 percent of the adult population worldwide was unable to read, compared to about 54 percent in 1970, clearly a significant improvement. The gender gap in literacy actually widened during these 15 years, however, as the number of women unable to read rose by 54 million (to 597 million), while that of men increased by only 4 million (to 352 million).

Second, individuals within poor families do not necessarily have common interests or work toward common goals. Development programs have been built on the premise that what is good for men is good for the family, but in many areas, this is patently not the case, because women effectively provide the largest share of the family's basic needs, and the incomes of men often are siphoned off by the purchase of alcohol, tobacco, or other consumer products. While a woman labors to produce food for her family, her husband may focus his energies on developing a business or pursuing cash interests that may not benefit his wife and children.

In much of sub-Saharan Africa, for example, both men and women plant crops, but they do so with different goals. Husbands and wives maintain separate managerial and financial control over the production, storage, and sale of their respective crops. Men grow cash crops, the income from the sale of which they retain, even though their wives still do the weeding and hoeing. Women, by contrast, use their land primarily for subsistence crops. They also are the ones expected to provide shelter, clothing, school fees, and medical care for themselves and their children. Given adequate acreage, high yields, or both, women do plant and market surplus crops to earn cash, but when land is scarce, or the soil poor, they put more time into other income-producing activities, or sell their labor for needed cash.

An increase in the income of a male within a household may not mean an increase in total consumption by family members. In Africa, according to a 1992 World Bank report, children's nutrition may actually deteriorate even while men in the household acquire wristwatches, radios, and bicycles. The connection between malnutrition and the diversion of income by males to personal consumption also has been found to be a problem in Belize, Guatemala, Mexico, and throughout the Indian subcontinent. In Guatemala, for example, the children of women earning independent incomes had better diets than those of women who were not earning their own money and had little control over how their husbands' earnings were spent.

Finally, resources within poor households often are skewed toward the males. When household income rises, men and boys throughout the developing world fare far better than do women and girls. In parts of India, for example, male children consistently receive more and better food and health care than their sisters. Consequently, far more girls than boys die in the critical period between infancy and age five. And with the exception of girls aged 10 to 14, who are clearly economically productive, Indian females die from preventable causes at far higher rates than males through age 35. This pattern is contrary to that found wherever females have equal access to food and health care. Evidence of similar patterns of discrimination in the allocation of household resources has been found in Bangladesh, Nepal, Pakistan, throughout the Middle East and North Africa, and in parts of sub-Saharan Africa.

Globally, much of the discrimination against females in families and societies stems from another form of gender gap: the huge disparity that prevails between the actual economic and social benefits derived from women's work, and the social perception of women as unproductive.

Studies in every region of the Third World confirm that it is the mother's ability to grow or purchase food rather than the father's food production or cash income—and the degree of control she maintains over her production and income—that determines the relative nutrition of children. However, women's work that does not produce cash directly is heavily discounted. The low valuation of women's work is reinforced by women's lack of control over physical resources. In most subsistence economies, for example, females have few legal rights regarding land tenure, marital relations, income, or social security.

But ignoring the full value of women's economic contributions cripples efforts to achieve broad development goals. Lack of investment results in lower female productivity. Coupled with persistent occupational and wage discrimination, this prevents women from achieving parity with men in terms of jobs and income, and leads to further devaluation of their work. The omnipresence of this bias is a sign that virtually every country is operating below its economic potential.

CONSERVING THE LAND

In the not-so-distant past, subsistence farmers and forest dwellers were models of ecologically sustainable living, their numbers not threatening available resources. Today, however, as the subsistence producers' circumstances grow more and more tenuous, pressures on forests and croplands grow increasingly acute. Yet in an era when "sustainable development" has become a global rallying cry, most governments and international development agencies pay scant attention to this dilemma.

To provide for their families, women depend heavily on community-owned croplands, grasslands, and forests. Research shows women to be more effective at protecting and regenerating the environment than is either the state or private landowners. The reasons are obvious: community resources are as indispensable to land-poor women in subsistence economies as these women are to the maintenance of the resources.

Given access to appropriate land, traditional farmers employ "managed" fallowing, crop rotation, intercropping, mulching, and a variety of other soil conservation and enrichment techniques. Women farmers, who have a great deal of unacknowledged skill in these areas, also play a leading role in maintaining crop diversity.

Women in subsistence economies also are active managers of forest resources, and traditionally play the leading role in their conservation. Forests are a major source of fuel for home consumption as well as of plant fibers, medicinal plants and herbs, seeds, oils, resins, and a host of other materials used to produce goods or income for families.

Unfortunately, the widespread depletion and degradation of resources leads to equally widespread impoverishment of subsistence families. Women's access to farm lands and the goods they yield is fast diminishing. The results are already evident in the declining food security among subsistence households. Under strategies to promote cash crops in southern Ghana, for example, commonly owned village land traditionally available to women to grow food for their families is being "privatized" and shifted increasingly into the hands of male farmers who are not responsible for domestic food supplies. Left with smaller holdings, on poorer soil, Ghanaian women can no longer practice crop rotation and must farm the same plots year after year. As a result, soil becomes eroded and less fertile. Food production declines, and malnutrition deepens.

MISDIRECTED DEVELOPMENT

On balance, conventional agricultural development strategies have marginalized women farmers. Instead of increasing the productivity of food crops and domestic food production, which are controlled by women, governments and international agencies have promoted cash crops, which are generally controlled by men.

Four major–and interrelated–trends, all set in motion or perpetuated by the agricultural strategies of low-income countries since the 1950s, have been particularly damaging to the ability of rural women to produce or procure adequate supplies of food. All four are a product of the increasing emphasis on cash crops.

First, large amounts of land once jointly owned and controlled by villagers, and accessible to women, have shifted into the hands of government agencies and private landowners. Second, the distribution of resources on which cash crop agriculture is heavily dependent, including land, fertilizers, pesticides, irrigation, and hybrid seeds, has reflected persistent gender bias. Third, the mechanization of agriculture has reduced or replaced the labor traditionally done by men but increased that done by women without increasing their income. And, finally, the labor available to subsistence households in many countries has become increasingly scarce, largely as a result of the shift of male workers away from subsistence production into cash crops and urban-based industries.

The shifting of land out of the hands of those who are most responsible for producing food for domestic consumption has been hastened by development strategies that make false assumptions about who benefits from gross economic gains. Governments throughout the less-developed world since the end of the colonial era have privatized land in favor of male land-holders. As a result, the amount and quality of land available to women food producers in large parts of the developing world is declining. Legal and cultural obstacles prevent women from obtaining title to land and, therefore, from participating in cash crop schemes.

A woman's production is undercut when she spends more time working on her husband's land, and less tending the crops she needs to feed her family or sell in the market. . . . She is drawn into a cycle of more labor for lower gains.

Agricultural development schemes encourage expansion of cash crop operations by offering market incentives, improved agricultural technologies, credit, seeds, and the like, with access to these resources independent mainly on the use of land as collateral. But without ownership and control over land, women are further disadvantaged because they cannot compete in cash crop schemes and have fewer resources with which to produce food crops.

In Africa, men have responded to cash crop farming incentives by reserving the better land–and their own labor–for their crops. This has two damaging effects: it raises women's workloads, and it increases environmental degradation by forcing women to produce food crops on already exhausted fields. A woman's production is undercut when she spends more time working on her husband's land, and less tending the crops she needs to fee her family or sell in the market. Her personal income–an important source of community respect and economic independence–declines, and her labor is increasingly spent on activities for which she receives no remuneration. She is drawn into a cycle of more labor for lower gains, which only deepens her impoverishment and dependence.

Green revolution technologies also are skewed in favor of men. In India, investments in agriculture consistently bypass women even though most of the rural female population is engaged in agriculture. An International Labor Organization study of how rural women spend their time indicates that up to 90 percent of rural women in central India participate in agriculture. Nevertheless, the distribution of irrigation outlets favored large landholders at the expense of the small family farms on which women work and produce food for domestic consumption. And the credit needed to enhance productivity remains out of reach of women, again largely because they lack ownership of land as collateral.

Improving the status of women, and thereby the prospects for humanity, will require a complete reorientation of development efforts toward establishing an environment in which women and men can prosper together.

The focus of agricultural research and development, too, has often favored cash crops over food crops, to the detriment of women and of family nutrition. This has not only led to diminished production but increased the perception that cash crops are more "valuable."

THE LOSS OF JOBS

Mechanization has replaced millions of agricultural jobs, throwing large numbers of men out of their traditional occupations. Meanwhile, the privatization of commons lands has made large numbers of land-poor and landless female subsistence producers even more reliant on wage income. An increased number of both men and women were forced to compete for traditional jobs. For example, in many regions of India, the increased competition for agricultural work has further driven down wages and led to increasing pauperization among subsistence producers, and especially among women.

As wages fall and productivity declines, more and more men from the land-poor and landless households of the developing world migrate to towns and cities in search of work. Subsistence households may or may not benefit from male migration, however, depending on whether or not husbands or sons send back to their families the money they earn. Indeed, studies show that female-headed households are among the poorest in large part because the money sent back by male relatives tends to dwindle over time.

The growing number of female-headed households is one indication of how widespread these conditions are. Some estimates indicate that women are the sole breadwinners in one-fourth to one-third of the world's households. And at least one-fourth of all other households rely on female earnings for more than 50 percent of total income.

PROSPERING TOGETHER

Improving the status of women, and thereby the prospects for humanity, will require a complete reorientation of development efforts toward establishing an environment in which women and men can prosper together. This means creating mainstream development programs that increase women's control over income and household resources, improve their productivity, establish their legal and social rights, and increase the social and economic choices they are able to make.

The first step toward achieving these goals–a step that is consistently overlooked–is to ask women themselves what needs should be accorded top priority. Some answers were provided in a forum on international health held in June 1991. Among the key needs identified by participants from Africa, Asia, and Latin America were investments in the development and dissemination of appropriate technology to reduce women's work burden, and access for women to credit and training programs.

The second step is to act immediately to increase the productivity of subsistence producers, whether in rural or urban areas. Immediate gains can be realized by increasing women's access to land, credit, and the tools and appropriate technologies with which they can increase their own and their families' welfare. Enforcement of laws guaranteeing gender equity in the distribution of land resources, for example, needs to be assigned high priority. Given the intimate connections between women's lack of access to land, their increasing work burden, and their dependence on children as a force of labor, land distribution and allocation policies should be at the top of the agenda for groups concerned about the environment, human rights, hunger, and population issues.

The third step is to change the definitions and assumptions made by conventional development policies, in order to collect information that creates a realistic picture of subsistence economies. A redefinition of the concepts of "productivity," "value," and "work" is needed in many places to include activities that are indeed productive–such as those that yield family income in goods rather than in cash or that support people without degrading the environment–which would dramatically alter the base of relevant information sought by those who are truly interested in improving human prospects. This recognition, in essence, is a necessary precondition to environmentally sound economic systems.

The collection of this type of data on a small scale already has helped policymakers to recognize the different effects on men and women of conventional gender-blind development practices. But for many areas of the economy in which women play important but officially ignored roles, there are still too little data available to truly inform public policy. Such data need to be incorporated into all relevant areas of economics, health, and environment.

Research and development in the sciences and in appropriate technologies need to be far more gender sensitive, not only to benefit women but to benefit from them, especially in areas of crop production and biodiversity. Focusing research on the needs of women in subsistence economies could dramatically boost food crop and forest production within a decade.

But these objectives cannot be met unless women enjoy the same degree of independence and freedom of choice as men. Governments and international agencies also need to be pushed to recognize the effects of their policies on how such resources as money, food, and opportunities for learning are allocated within the household. Development should encourage more cooperation between the sexes with the goal of ending poverty, reducing fertility, and securing the environment.

These ends can most easily be achieved by directing resources into the education of young girls and the training of women, and by establishing policies that increase women's access to credit and opportunities to establish businesses, earn income, and create jobs.

Experience suggests that these reforms will not be easily accomplished. Gender bias dies hard. Much of the information regarding women's roles in agriculture and forestry, for example, has been available to governments and development planners for two decades and has yet to provoke real changes in policy. Yet it is in the interest of every person, from the poor farmers of Sikandernagar to the chiefs of industry, and from grassroots activists to heads of state, to combat gender bias. Nothing could be more important to human development than the reform of policies that suppress the productive potential of half the earth's people.

Extending Help to Women Farmers in LDCs

What works and why

Katrine A. Saito

Katrine Saito, a British subject, is a Senior Economist in the Bank's Women in Development Division. She joined the Bank staff in 1974 after having attended the Universities of Wales and Edinburgh.

Throughout the developing world, women have long played a pivotal role in agriculture, both as laborers and decisionmakers. Besides being the main ones responsible for food production—in Sub-Saharan Africa, women account for at least 70 percent of the food staple production—they figure prominently in other agricultural activities, including food processing and marketing, cash cropping, and animal husbandry. Moreover, as more men migrate to cities and other countries for work, increasing numbers of women are becoming heads of households, managing farms on a day-to-day basis.

If these women are to carry out their extensive and multifaceted roles in agriculture and respond to market incentives more efficiently, they need effective agricultural extension services. Yet the evidence clearly shows that, despite a growing awareness of the need to reach women farmers, these services—considered to be a prerequisite for widespread and sustained agricultural development—are generally geared toward male farmers. This is sometimes by design, but more often by default. Bias is evident in the delivery of extension, which is generally provided by male agents to male farmers on the fallacious assumption that the message will "trickle across" to women. Bias is also evident in the message itself, which tends to ignore the unique workload, responsibilities, and constraints facing women farmers.

Troubled by this highly inefficient use of resources, not to mention suboptimal levels of agricultural production, many policymakers and donors—such as the World Bank, which has invested about $2 billion in agricultural extension in 79 countries since the mid-1960s—have begun to work with countries on innovative approaches. Pilot programs now underway are providing useful guidance on how best to fully integrate women into the agricultural extension system and the most likely problems to emerge in different socioeconomic environments. This is a relatively new field and much remains to be learned. Even so, it is possible to craft guidelines for (1) better identifying the information and technology needs of women, thereby helping to develop more appropriate messages for them; and (2) improving the cost-effectiveness of the delivery of these messages. While the recommendations are relevant for most extension systems in use by governments, parastatals, and private agencies, particular attention is paid to the "training and visit" system of agricultural extension, favored by the World Bank (see "The World Bank and the training and visit system," by Joslin Landell-Mills, *Finance & Development*, June 1983).

Why women farmers need help

After nearly two decades of studies, it is clear that regional differences aside, women provide most of the labor and make many key decisions in agriculture. In Malawi, for example, women perform 50 to 70 percent of all agricultural work and account for 69 percent of all farmers. But women face special constraints in carrying out agricultural activities, making it more difficult for them to operate effectively in factor markets, if they can obtain access at all. As a result, most women have less access to—and higher effective costs for—information, technology, inputs, and credit than men. The end result is depressed productivity.

Land. Typically, women must farm more fragmented, smaller plots than men, and they are less likely to have secure tenure. This acts as a strong disincentive to investing in new techniques. In many parts of the world, land title is in the name of the male head of household, and women are allocated land that is far from their villages and far from other plots they cultivate—posing problems of childcare and transportation.

Technology. Lack of suitable farm and household technology also impairs women's efficiency, restricts their time, and saps their energy for participating in extension. In Zambia, weeding can be performed six times faster with animal traction, but few women can afford this technology, and in many cases, cultural traditions discourage its use by women.

Credit. In most of the developing world, women are bypassed by formal credit systems, because of lack of collateral (usually land title), lower levels of numeracy and literacy, lack of information, burdensome bureaucratic procedures, distance and cost of travel to credit institutions, and cultural attitudes. Available credit is also often limited to the production cycle (most women work in processing) and to cash crops for export (which women are less likely to grow). Without credit, women are less likely to be able to afford the inputs recommended by extension agents, if they come into contact with them at all.

This article is based on World Bank Discussion Paper No. 103 (1990), "Agricultural Extension for Women Farmers in Sub-Saharan Africa," by Katrine Saito and C. Jean Weidemann, and on contributions by Nancy Axinn and Nadine Horenstein.

From *Finance & Development*, September 1991, pp. 29-31. *Finance & Development*, a quarterly publication of the International Monetary Fund and the World Bank.

Mobility and time. Women tend to be less mobile and enjoy less uncommitted time than men, making it more difficult for them to participate in training courses outside their villages and inhibiting their ability to respond to opportunities. A study from Burkina Faso, for example, shows that women contribute as much time per day to food and cash crop production as men—in addition to food processing and fetching water and fuelwood—with men averaging twice as much time resting. Similarly, surveys from Pakistan reveal that agricultural and household activities typically take up to 12–15 hours of a woman's day, significantly more than the time spent by men on productive work. In addition, women must contend with less cash for transportation and less likelihood of owning transport. In some countries, sociocultural and religious barriers also limit their mobility.

Cultural norms. In most countries, cultural norms affect interactions between agents and farmers—often, male extension officers may not meet with female farmers—and between male and female farmers. In many parts of South Asia, for example, the strict observance of "purdah" (separation of sexes) results in women remaining in the "inside" labor force. From within the compound, women undertake various agricultural tasks, particularly processing, but cultural conditions make it difficult for male agents to give them advice.

Education. Throughout the developing world, women tend to be less educated than men, severely compromising access to agricultural extension and the ability to comprehend and use technical information. Because of their lower level of education—in most of Africa, the adult male literacy rate is almost twice that of women, and in Bangladesh and India, more than 80 percent of rural women are illiterate compared with 60 percent of rural men—women are less able to respond to written extension messages and, in some cases, cannot be chosen as contact farmers.

Improving the message

Given these gender-related constraints, it is clear that accurate information at the local level—what women farmers do, how they do it, and why they do it—is essential if the research and extension services are to produce and deliver technical advice that is both needed by the farmers and appropriate to their circumstances. Information is needed on the following topics:

- the division of labor between men and women by crops, livestock, and farming operations (this may involve "men's" versus "women's" crops—traditionally, cash versus subsistence crops—or complementary roles for the same crop). In the production of irrigated rice in The Gambia, Senegal, and Burkina Faso, for example, women specialize in transplanting, weeding, winnowing, harvesting, and threshing, while men prepare the fields and maintain the irrigation system. In South Asia, caste and class differences tend to be the dominant influences, with women of lower caste generally having more limited access to the factors of production (including water and public land), as well as to extension services and credit;
- who owns or controls factors of production, crops, or income derived from the sale of produce—women are most likely to invest time and resources in production when they retain control of the harvested crop;
- the types of women farmers—farm managers in their own right, farm partners with their husbands, or laborers. In parts of South Asia, even women in "landless" households need extension services ("landless" in this context frequently means having a small patch of land that, when intensively cultivated, can contribute significantly to the family's survival); and
- geographical variations and local conditions that define production possibilities and constraints. In South Asia, women farmers in the hill and mountain regions of northern India, northern Pakistan, Nepal, and Bhutan need advice that differs sharply from that needed in the tropical plains.

To date, diverse collection methods have proved effective in planning services for female farmers, including seasonal calendars (providing a sense of the farm "enterprise" as well as times of peak labor by gender), seasonal labor profiles, and household record-keeping. Lengthy costly surveys should be avoided. Indeed, one of the most successful approaches uses the quick, inexpensive, informal survey technique of Rapid Rural Appraisal (which involves local populations in the early discussions and design of projects), combined with a two- to three-day field visit. Another useful technique, requiring only a few hours, is to question carefully selected groups of women farmers, preferably without the inhibiting presence of their husbands and other male authority figures.

All of this information must then be fed into research systems that have the ability to generate new knowledge and techniques to improve productivity and sustain rural families. Linkages with both national and international research institutions must be strengthened, and their research agenda broadened to include crops and livestock produced by women (particularly vegetables and small animals), tasks normally performed by women (such as weeding, food processing, preservation, and storage), and technologies and farming systems suitable to the circumstances of women farmers (such as home gardens or alley cropping). Tools and machines also need to be developed—when possible, produced locally—that are suitable for women (i.e., multifunctional and of appropriate size and strength), and most important, distributed widely.

Transmitting the message

Once the relevant message—which is highly location specific—is formulated, the challenge lies in transmitting it to women farmers. There are many ways to do this without transgressing cultural mores. The answer is to find a method suitable for the local traditional culture, financial and human resources, and institutional arrangements.

Using women extension agents. Whether the gender of the agent matters varies greatly depending on the sociocultural context. Even so, evidence suggests that communication with women farmers is definitely enhanced when female agents are used. But how can the number of women agents be quickly increased? How can they be integrated into the extension system? How can male colleagues be convinced to accept them? How should conflicting family responsibilities be dealt with? And how can adequate logistical support (including transportation) be ensured?

One answer is to sharply boost the number of women in agricultural schools, as these schools will be the main source of trained extension agents—in Africa, only 13 percent of the students are female. To accomplish this, more girls should be enrolled in secondary schools, and agricultural schools should institute targeted growth rates for female enrollment, or economic incentives, such as temporary tuition subsidies. Boarding facilities for female students should be made available (as at Nepal's Institute of Agriculture and Animal Science), and parents of secondary school girls should be informed of opportunities in agriculture. Admission policies of intermediate agricultural institutions should be reviewed to ensure that female enrollment is encouraged (for example, until 1980, none of the agricultural schools in the Republic of Yemen were open to girls), and the curriculum offered should be the same for both sexes.

Then, to retain women in the extension system, efforts should be made to assure equal treatment with men and accommodate those who are married. This means equal access to staff housing, equipment, and transportation. Moreover, the practice, common in many countries, of expelling women extension agents once they marry or become pregnant, must be stopped. One way of coping with a reluctance of women to accept rural posts if their children attend urban schools is to select new female agents from the local government area where they will serve.

But the training and recruitment process takes time, and in the shorter term, one solution is to redeploy female agents already teaching rural women subjects related to agriculture. In many African countries, home economists constitute a large female professional cadre—Nigeria, for example, has some 4,500, and even Sierra Leone, a much smaller country, has over 200. They are particularly common in former British colonies, where they are known as domestic or home scientists, and some are also trained nutritionists and community development workers. In recent years, a number of countries have begun to experiment with this approach. In Nigeria, home economists with agricultural training have been integrated into the extension service and are working very effectively in the highly successful nationwide Women in Agriculture program.

Given that male agents will remain the norm for many years, efforts must also be made to help men overcome attitudes that can undermine programs—one recent study of five African countries found that most male agents perceived women as wives of farmers, rather than farmers in their own right. Training and supervision is one way. Using women extension agents as the initial contact—to introduce groups of women farmers to male agents—is another. This strategy has worked particularly well in northwestern Cameroon, and a similar approach has been suggested in Bangladesh, where male block supervisors form teams with their female counterparts.

Using women contact farmers and women's groups. Using farmers' groups, rather than individuals, as the recipients of extension has been found to be a particularly cost-effective way of reaching farmers, especially women. In many developing countries, there is a long tradition of women forming groups to exchange labor, mobilize savings and credit, provide self-help, and carry out social and ceremonial functions. Such groups offer a channel through which resources and information from government and donors can flow. Indeed, the advantages are numerous: they provide economies of scale through maximizing the farmer-to-agent ratio; they save travel time and increase the time spent on the actual task for the extension agent; they facilitate adoption of new techniques through peer learning (groups can be especially effective in reinforcing knowledge among illiterate women, who can then rely on collective memory); they allow members to pool resources for production or collateral to obtain credit and other inputs; they serve as an effective means for sharing expensive equipment and provide a vehicle for effective large-scale distribution of inputs; and they help lessen the sociocultural difficulties of male/female interaction. In Chile, for example, existing village groups have been carefully selected and successfully used for extension delivery; family groups were found ineffective since women had difficulty speaking up.

Recruiting more women as contact farmers—or links with extension agents—can also be helpful, but at present, the selection criteria—such as the requirement for land ownership in South Asia—often discourage the participation of women. In Kenya, however, the problem has been effectively tackled by encouraging local chiefs, ministers, and political leaders to support such involvement by women at local gatherings and in the media; emphasizing the selection of women farmers during training sessions; and encouraging extension agents to select contact farmers on the basis of merit, rather than patronage.

Improving access to training. A crucial link in the extension chain is making sure that the client is able to receive the message. Faced with dual responsibilities at home and on the farm, women often cannot attend courses at residential farm training centers, even if transportation is provided. It is important, therefore, that training be brought to them. One way is through mobile training courses, but the mass media hold the greatest potential.

Radio has a long history as a communication tool, particularly in agriculture. Its low cost and wide reach make it a relatively simple, effective technology, especially among illiterate farmers and those in purdah. The key, however, is making sure that the broadcasts fit into the women farmers' work schedules and that the vernacular is used. Pakistan, for example, has made a practice of agricultural broadcasting in local languages. Radio messages should also slightly precede the messages from extension agents. Evidence from Ghana has shown that female farmers question extension agents about subjects already discussed on the radio.

Television is less widely used, because of production and equipment costs. But with its rapid spread across parts of South Asia, it must be regarded as the media of the future—even in places where there is not yet electricity, video machines have been found (in South Asia, generators are used). Videotapes offer a low-cost way of reaching large numbers of women farmers, many of whom can choose to watch at a convenient time. They are increasingly popular in Yemen, where Muslim women can view programs in seclusion. They are also used in Latin America for training, and in India to strengthen farmer-to-farmer sharing of technical information.

Women's health: Tragedy of gender

Around the world, women play a key role in the health of their children, husbands and families. However, the care they give, the work they do and the burdens they carry are often at the expense of their own health.

An estimated 500,000 women—99 per cent of whom are in developing countries—die each year from pregnancy-related causes, according to a recent WHO report on reproductive health. The report also notes that some 300 million couples who do not want any more children have no access to family planning services.

Women generally live longer than men, but throughout their lives they face many challenges to the quality of their health and well-being.

Some health experts believe that girls are born with certain natural strengths which make them more resistant than boys to infections and malnutrition. But these are often cancelled out by social, economic, political and cultural disadvantages. In many societies, females suffer discrimination from birth to old age because of attitudes and values that are upheld and perpetuated by men and women alike. As children, girls are likely to be less well fed than boys, less likely to receive medical attention and to be allowed to finish their education.

The legacy of such childhood is short stature, low body weight and anaemia, which are major contributors to maternal death.

"Women suffer ill-health and die because they are neglected as children; married as adolescents; are poor and illiterate, underfed and overworked, subjected to harmful traditional practices, denied equal social, legal and economic status and excluded from decision-making", Dr. Nakajima said.

Health care strategies for women should be designed to cover a broad spectrum of their health problems and should encompass the whole life-cycle, including reproductive health care, family planning, disease control, mental health, nutrition, and occupational health, concluded some 400 participants attending special technical discussions on women's health at the forty-fifth World Health Assembly (4–14 May, Geneva).

Another serious cause of concern are reproductive tract infections, including sexually transmitted diseases, which are often hidden in what WHO describes as a"culture of silence". Some 250 million new cases of sexually transmitted diseases occur each year.

Since 1987, WHO has promoted the Safe Motherhood Initiative, which seeks to reduce maternal deaths by at least half by the year 2000. It aims to: improve the socioeconomic and political status of women; provide appropriate family planning services for all; ensure high equality prenatal and delivery care for all women; and provide skilled obstetric care for high-risk and emergency cases.

WHO, together with UNICEF, has also waged a decade-long campaign to protect and promote the health of both mothers and babies by encouraging breast-feeding, which is more nutritious, more hygienic, and cheaper than bottle-feeding. Breast-feeding is also said to immunize against common infections, protect mothers against pregnancy and reduce the risk of breast and ovarian cancer. The most recent joint initiative, launched in 1991, designates hospitals which promote breast-feeding as "baby-friendly".

Index

Credits/ Acknowledgments

Cover design by Charles Vitelli

1. Understanding the Third World
Facing overview—United Nations photo by Ray Witlin.

2. Trade, Aid, and Debt
Facing overview—United Nations photo.

3. Conflict and Instability
Facing overview—United Nations photo.

4. Weapons Profileration and Arms Control
Facing overview—United Nations photo.

5. Transition
Facing overview—United Nations photo by Allan Tannenbaum. 169—The Dushkin Publishing Group, Inc.

6. Population, Poverty, and Environment
Facing overview—United Nations photo by John Isaac. 183—John Van Pelt in *The Christian Science Monitor,* © 1992 TCSPS. 190—United Nations photo by John Isaac. 191—United Nations photo.

7. Women and Development
Facing overview—United Nations photo by John Isaac. 228—John Van Pelt in *The Christian Science Monitor,* © 1992 TCSPS.

PHOTOCOPY THIS PAGE!!!*

ANNUAL EDITIONS ARTICLE REVIEW FORM

■ NAME: ______________________ DATE: ______________________

■ TITLE AND NUMBER OF ARTICLE: ______________________

■ BRIEFLY STATE THE MAIN IDEA OF THIS ARTICLE: ______________________

■ LIST THREE IMPORTANT FACTS THAT THE AUTHOR USES TO SUPPORT THE MAIN IDEA:

■ WHAT INFORMATION OR IDEAS DISCUSSED IN THIS ARTICLE ARE ALSO DISCUSSED IN YOUR TEXTBOOK OR OTHER READING YOU HAVE DONE? LIST THE TEXTBOOK CHAPTERS AND PAGE NUMBERS:

■ LIST ANY EXAMPLES OF BIAS OR FAULTY REASONING THAT YOU FOUND IN THE ARTICLE:

■ LIST ANY NEW TERMS/CONCEPTS THAT WERE DISCUSSED IN THE ARTICLE AND WRITE A SHORT DEFINITION:

*Your instructor may require you to use this Annual Editions Article Review Form in any number of ways: for articles that are assigned, for extra credit, as a tool to assist in developing assigned papers, or simply for your own reference. Even if it is not required, we encourage you to photocopy and use this page; you'll find that reflecting on the articles will greatly enhance the information from your text.

We Want Your Advice

Annual Editions revisions depend on two major opinion sources: one is our Advisory Board, listed in the front of this volume, which works with us in scanning the thousands of articles published in the public press each year; the other is you—the person actually using the book. Please help us and the users of the next edition by completing the prepaid article rating form on this page and returning it to us. Thank you.

ANNUAL EDITIONS: THIRD WORLD 94/95

Article Rating Form

Here is an opportunity for you to have direct input into the next revision of this volume. We would like you to rate each of the 57 articles listed below, using the following scale:

1. Excellent: should definitely be retained
2. Above average: should probably be retained
3. Below average: should probably be deleted
4. Poor: should definitely be deleted

Your ratings will play a vital part in the next revision. So please mail this prepaid form to us just as soon as you complete it.
Thanks for your help!

Rating	Article
	1. The Third World and the New World Order in the 1990s
	2. The South Looks North: The Third World in the New World Order
	3. The Economist's Blind Eye
	4. Let's Abolish the Third World
	5. The Developing Countries and the World Trading System
	6. Benefits and Beggars
	7. In Mexico, NAFTA Isn't Just About Trade
	8. Rethinking Development: A Market-Friendly Strategy for the Poor *and* A Response to 'Rethinking Development'
	9. Still in the Missionary Position
	10. The Third World: Living With Debt?
	11. African Debt: Borrowed Time
	12. The Disaster That Didn't Happen
	13. Why Is Africa Eating Asia's Dust?
	14. Ethnic Conflicts Worldwide
	15. We Must Hear the Third World
	16. Islam Resumes Its March
	17. The Islamic Threat
	18. India: The Crisis of Secularism
	19. Trouble in the South
	20. Asia's Bosnia
	21. Sudan's Human and Political Crisis
	22. The Familiar Face of Battle
	23. The Gulf Between the Rulers and the Ruled
	24. The World's Top Arms Merchant
	25. Third World Militaries: New Suppliers, Deadlier Weapons
	26. A Proliferation Primer
	27. Tactical Missiles: Anyone Can Play
	28. The IAEA: Neutralizing Iraq's Nuclear Weapons Potential
	29. Atomic Shock Waves
	30. Levers for Plowshares: Using Aid to Encourage Military Reform
	31. Can the Third World Afford Guns *and* Butter?
	32. The Collapse of Socialist Development in the Third World
	33. The Crisis of Legitimacy in Africa
	34. Algeria: The Clash Between Islam, Democracy, and the Military
	35. Finding Common Ground
	36. Birth of a Nation
	37. In Test With Democracy, African Leaders Lose Some, Win Some
	38. Difficult Birth
	39. The Next Great Leap
	40. Out of the Ditch
	41. Peru's Fujimori: A Caudillo Derails Democracy
	42. World Population
	43. The Demographic Dimension
	44. Poverty, Population, Pollution
	45. The Urban Explosion in the Third World
	46. Family Planning: The Unfinished Revolution
	47. North vs. South on Pollution
	48. Stop Dumping on the South
	49. A Greener Bank
	50. The Growing Influence of NGOs in the Developing World
	51. The Burden of Womanhood
	52. Educating Girls
	53. Women in the Workplace in Developing Countries
	54. Female Empowerment Leads to Fewer Births
	55. Women's Work
	56. Extending Help to Women Farmers in LDCs
	57. Women's Health: Tragedy of Gender

(Continued on next page)

ABOUT YOU

Name______________________________ Date__________
Are you a teacher? ☐ Or student? ☐
Your School Name ______________________________
Department ______________________________
Address ______________________________
City ____________________ State ________ Zip ________
School Telephone # ______________________________

YOUR COMMENTS ARE IMPORTANT TO US!

Please fill in the following information:

For which course did you use this book? ______________________________
Did you use a text with this Annual Edition? ☐ yes ☐ no
The title of the text? ______________________________
What are your general reactions to the Annual Editions concept?

Have you read any particular articles recently that you think should be included in the next edition?

Are there any articles you feel should be replaced in the next edition? Why?

Are there other areas that you feel would utilize an Annual Edition?

May we contact you for editorial input?

May we quote you from above?

No Postage Necessary if Mailed in the United States

ANNUAL EDITIONS: THIRD WORLD 94/95

BUSINESS REPLY MAIL

First Class Permit No. 84 Guilford, CT

Postage will be paid by addressee

The Dushkin Publishing Group, Inc.
Sluice Dock
Guilford, Connecticut 06437